BIBLICAL RESEARCH INSTITUTE
STUDIES IN ADVENTIST ECCLESIOLOGY-2

MESSAGE MISSION
AND UNITY OF THE CHURCH

ÁNGEL MANUEL RODRÍGUEZ, EDITOR

Biblical Research Institute
Silver Spring, MD 20904

2013

Copyright © 2013, by the Biblical Research Institute
General Conference of Seventh-day Adventists
Silver Spring, MD 20904

Scripture quotations credited to ESV are from *The Holy Bible, English Standard Version*, copyright © 2001 by Crossway Bibles, a division of Good News Publishers. Used by permission. All rights reserved.

Texts credited to KJV are from the *King James Version* of the Bible.

Scripture texts credited to NAB are from the *New American Bible*, copyright © 1970 by the Confraternity of Christian Doctrine, Washington DC and are used by permission of copyright owner. All rights reserved.

Texts or quotations credited to NASB are from the *NEW AMERICAN STANDARD BIBLE®*, Copyright © 1960, 1962, 1963, 1968, 1971, 1972, 1973, 1975, 1977, 1995 by The Lockman Foundation. Used by permission.

Texts or quotations credited to NIV are from the *HOLY BIBLE, NEW INTERNATIONAL VERSION*. Copyright © 1973, 1978, 1984 International Bible Society. Used by permission of Zondervan bible Publishers.

Texts credited to NKJV are from the *New King James Version*. Copyright © 1979, 1980, 1982 by Thomas Nelson, Inc. Used by permission. All rights reserved.

Texts or quotations credited to NRSV are from the *New Revised Standard Version of the Bible*, copyright © 1989 by the National Council of the Churches of Christ in the USA. Used by permission. All rights reserved.

Texts or quotations credited to RSV are from the *Revised Standard Version of the Bible*, copyright © 1952 [2nd edition, 1971] by the Division of Christian Education of the National Council of the Churches of Christ in the United States of America. Used by permission. All rights reserved.

Printed in the U.S.A. by the
Review and Herald Publishing Association
Hagerstown, MD 21740

ISBN 978-0-925675-21-7

Editor

Ángel Manuel Rodríguez

BRI Staff

Marlene Bacchus
Elias Brasil de Souza
Kwabena Donkor
Brenda Flemmer

Ekkehardt Mueller
Gerhard Pfandl
Artur Stele
Clinton Wahlen

BRICOM Members 2010–2015

Niels-Erik Andreasen
Radisa Antic
Delbert Baker
Daniel K. Bediako
Merlin Burt
Lael O. Caesar
Gordon E. Christo
Gerard Damsteegt
Jo Ann Davidson
Richard M. Davidson
Ganoune Diop
Denis Fortin
Roy Gane
Michael Hasel
Elie Henry
Myron A. Iseminger
Sung-Ik Kim
Gregory A. King
Miroslav M. Kiš
Gerald Klingbeil
Bill Knott
Robert E. Lemon

Barna Magyarosi
John K. McVay
Jiří Moskala
G. T. Ng
Brempong Owusu-Antwi
Jon K. Paulien
Leslie Pollard
John Reeve
Teresa Reeve
Richard Rice
Richard Sabuin
Benjamin D. Schoun
Ella S. Simmons
Reinaldo Siqueira
Tom Shepherd
Michael Sokupa
David Tasker
Alberto Timm
Efrain Velazquez
Ted N. C. Wilson
Randall W. Younker
Eugene Zaitsev

E. Edward Zinke

Contents

Preface	xi
Abbreviations	xiii

Chapter 1
The People of God in the Old Testament — *Gerhard Pfandl* — 1

Chapter 2
The Universality of the Church in the New Testament — *Ekkehardt Mueller* — 19

Chapter 3
Biblical Metaphors for the Church: Building Blocks for Ecclesiology — *John McVay* — 41

Chapter 4
Mission in the Old Testament — *Jiří Moskala* — 61

Chapter 5
Mission in the New Testament — *Clinton Wahlen* — 81

Chapter 6
Missiological Perspectives in the Book of Daniel — *Sung Ik Kim* — 105

Chapter 7
Mission in the Book of Revelation — *Ekkehardt Mueller* — 129

Chapter 8
Understanding Apostasy in the Christian Church — *John W. Reeve* — 155

Chapter 9
The Sixteenth Century Protestant Reformation and Adventist Ecclesiology — *Darius Jankiewieck* — 191

Chapter 10
  Seventh-day Adventist Ecclesiology, 1844-2012
    A Brief Historical Overview   219
      —Alberto R. Timm

Chapter 11
  Oneness of the Church in Message and Mission:
    Its Ground   243
      —Ángel Manuel Rodríguez

Chapter 12
  The Message and the Mission of the Remnant:
    A Methodological Approach   261
      —Fernando Canale

Chapter 13
  The Role of the Fundamental Beliefs in the Church   287
      —Kwabena Donkor

Chapter 14
  The Holy Spirit and the Church   303
      —Denis Fortin

Chapter 15
  The Role of the Church in the Interpretation of Scripture   323
      —Richard Davidson

Chapter 16
  The Role of Ellen G. White in the Life of the Adventist Church   345
      —Alberto R. Timm

Chapter 17
  Adventist Mission Among World Religions:
    Some Theological Foundations   361
      —Ganoune Diop

Chapter 18
  Israel and the Church: Continuity and Discontinuity—I   375
      —Richard Davidson

Chapter 19
  Israel and the Church: Continuity and Discontinuity—II   401
      —Richard Davidson

Chapter 20
  World Religions and Salvation: An Adventist View   429
      —Ángel Manuel Rodríguez

Chapter 21
   Adventist Mission Today: A Personal Reflection   443
   —William G. Johnsson

Appendix: Roadmap for Mission   455

Selected Scripture Index   461

Subject Index   467

Preface

This is the second volume on the topic of ecclesiology (the doctrine of the church) produce by the Biblical Research Institute under the guidance of the Biblical Research Institute Committee. The first volume, entitled *Toward an Adventist Theology of the Remnant*, has been well received by the world church and is being translated into several languages. Since the introduction to this three-volume project is found in that volume, it is not necessary to repeat it here. The topic of ecclesiology continues to be a significant one for the church at the beginning of the twenty-first century. The church faces new challenges and in most cases what is needed is a clear understanding of the nature, role, and authority of the church. This ecclesiological project provides the occasion for a fruitful dialogue by emphasizing the global nature of the church, its message, mission, and authority.

In this volume the main emphasis is on the unity, message, and mission of the church but the nature of the church is also addressed in a few articles exploring the notion of the people of God in the Old Testament (Pfandl), the universal church in the New Testament (Mueller), and a careful study of the most important metaphors for the church in the New Testament (McVay). The study of the mission of the church begins with an exploration of mission in the Old and New Testaments (Moskala; Whalen). Due to the fact that the apocalyptic books of the Bible are particularly important for the Adventist church, it was thought that it would be useful to study their missiology (Kim; Mueller).

In order to understand the mission and nature of the Adventist church it is also important to place it within the history of Christian ecclesiology, beginning with the post-apostolic church (Reeve). The ecclesiology of the Reformers is also discussed and its possible contribution to Adventist ecclesiology is explored (Jakiewieck). Included is also a very useful discussion of the history of Adventist ecclesiology itself (Timm) and the ecclesiological role of Ellen G. White (Timm). These studies provide a valuable background for the more narrow study of the unity, message, and mission of the Adventist church.

The discussion on the unity of the church examines the theological and practical elements that contribute to the global unity of the church (Rodríguez). The message and unity of the church is also discussed from the perspective of the history of biblical interpretation in the Christian church providing a fresh way of looking at the topic (Canale). We also include studies on the nature and role of the Adventist Statement of Fundamental Beliefs (Donkor), the church's function in the interpretation of the Bible as a global community (Davidson), and the close relationship between the Spirit and the church (Fortin).

The book concludes with four chapters on mission and world religions. This is a very relevant topic today because world religions have become, in the Western world, part of the context where we try to fulfill our mission. Besides, they remain the most challenging aspect of our mission to the world. In this volume we examine the need to proclaim our message in an effective way in the context of world religions (Diop). We also discuss the challenges we face in a discussion of Israel and the church (Davidson). This section concludes with a study of salvation and world religions (Rodríguez) and a personal reflection on Adventist mission (Johnsson).

We thank the members of the Biblical Research Institute Committee for the time they spent reading the first drafts of the papers and for their invaluable suggestions and comments that made the papers stronger in their content. We also thank the writers for the many hours they employed in research and writing and for their willingness to listen to the counsel and suggestions coming from all of those involved in the project. Our appreciation goes to the leadership of the General Conference who provided the funds needed to accomplish our task. We would also like to honor the superior work done by Marlene Bacchus, our Desktop Publishing Specialist, whose critical eye helped us to produce a better product, and Brenda Flemmer, the Administrative Assistant, who was always willing to use her expertise for the benefit of this project. But above all, we thank our Savior and Lord Jesus Christ who gave to all us the strength and wisdom needed to bring this volume to fruition

We offer these studies to the world church hoping and praying that they would contribute to build up the faith and commitment of our global family of believers to the unity, message, and mission of the church. We praise the one who prayed for us saying: "My prayer is not for them alone. I pray also for those who will believe in me through their message, that tall of them may be one, Father, just as you are in me and I am in you. May they also be in us so that the world may believe that you have sent me" (John 17:20–21; NIV). Amen!

Arthur Stele
Director
Biblical Research Institute

Abbreviations

ABD	*Anchor Bible Dictionary*
AdvBibComm	*Seventh-day Adventist Bible Commentary*
AH	*Adventist Herald*
ANEP	*Ancient Near East in Pictures Relating to the Old Testament*
ANET	*Ancient Near Eastern Texts Relating to the Old Testament*
ANF	*Ante-Nicene Fathers*
AOS	*American Oriental Studies*
AUSS	*Andrews University Seminary Studies*
BASP	*Bulletin of the American Society of Papyrologists*
BBR	*Bulletin for Biblical Research*
BDAG	Bauer, W., F. W. Danker, W. F. Arndt, and F. W. Gingrich *Greek-English Lexicon of the New Testament and Other Early Christian Literature.* 2000
BSac	*Bibliotheca sacra*
BT	*Bible Today*
BThB	*Biblical Theology Bulletin*
CBQ	*Catholic Biblical Quarterly*
CDCWM	*Concise Dictionary of the Christian World Mission*
CTM	*Currents in Theology and Mission*
DJG	*Dictionary of Jesus and the Gospels*
DLNT	*Dictionary of the Later New Testament and Its Developments*
DMT	*Dictionary of Mission Theology*
DPL	*Dictionary of Paul and His Letters*
EDBT	*Evangelical Dictionary of Biblical Theology*
EDNT	*Exegetical Dictionary of the New Testament*
EDT	*Evangelical Dictionary of Theology*
EDWM	*Evangelical Dictionary of World Missions*
EvT	*Evangelische Theologie*
Et	*Eternity*
HAL	L. Koehler, W. Baumgartner, and J. Stamm. *Hebrew and Aramaic Lexicon of the Old Testament.* 2001.
IDB	*Interpreter's Dictionary of the Bible*
IDBSup	*Interpreter's Dictionary of the Bible Supplementary*

	Volume
IJFM	International Journal of Frontier Mission
Interp	Interpretation
IRM	International Review of Missions
ISBE	International Standard Encyclopedia of the Bible
JAAS	Journal of Asia Adventist Seminary
JAMS	Journal of Adventist Missiological Studies
JAOS	Journal of the American Oriental Society
JATS	Journal of the Adventist Theological Society
JBL	Journal of Biblical Literature
JCS	Journal of Cuneiform Studies
JES	Journal of Ecumenical Studies
JETS	Journal of the Evangelical Theological Society
JNES	Journal of Near Eastern Studies
JSNT	Journal for the Study of the New Testament
JSOT	Journal for the Study of the Old Testament
MC	Midnight Cry
MSt	Mission Studies
NASB	New American Standard Bible
NDBT	New Dictionary of Biblical Theology
NDCT	New Dictionary of Christian Theology
NIBD	New Interpreter's Dictionary of the Bible
NIDOTTE	New International Dictionary of OT Theology and Exegesis
NIDNTT	New International Dictionary of NT Theology and Exegesis
NIV	New International Version
NovT	Novu testamentum
NPNF	Nicene and Post-Nicene Fathers
NRSV	New Revised Standard Version
NTS	New Testament Studies
RE	Review and Expositor
RH	Review and Herald
RSV	Revised Standard Version
ScrB	Scripture Bulletin
SJOT	Scandinavian Journal of the Old Testament
ST	Studia theologica
Targ.	Targum
TDNT	Theological Dictionary of the NT
TDOT	Theological Dictionary of the OT
TRE	Theologische Realenzyklopädie
TS	Theological Studies
TT	Theology Today
VT	Vetus testamentum

ZEB	*Zondervan Enciclopedia of the Bible.* Merril C. Tenney and Moses Silva, eds.
ZPEB	*Zondervan Pictorial Encyclopedia of the Bible.* Merril C. Tenney, ed.
ZNW	*Zeitschrift für die neutestamentliche Wissenschaft und die Kunde de ältere Kirche*

par.	parallel
parr.	parallels
v.	verse
vv.	verses

cf.	*confer* (Latin for compare)
e.g.,	for example
i.e.	*id est* (in other words)

CHAPTER 1

THE PEOPLE OF GOD IN THE OLD TESTAMENT

Gerhard Pfandl

The term, "people of God,"—either ʿ*am Elohîm* (Judg 20:2; Ps 47:9) or ʿ*am YHWH* (Num 11:29; 2 Kgs 9:6)—indicates the unique relationship that exists between Yahweh and His people.[1] Frequently, God speaks of "my people" (2 Kgs 20:5; Isa 3:15) to emphasize those who, in a special sense, belong to Him. But, who exactly are "the people of God?" We seek to answer this question by tracing the identity, characteristics, and purpose of "the people of God" throughout the Old Testament.

The Antediluvian Period

Our search begins with the creation narrative, where God's people consisted only of Adam and Eve. A pure expression of God's love and goodness, they existed for communion and service, to Him and the rest of creation. Their primary relationship was with God. This was the fundamental experience from which all others were derived. The couple's singularity was a result of their common commitment to the Creator—the very source of their lives. He was the nucleus of their very existence. This system collapsed when they rejected God as the center of their lives and sought their own well-being, independent of Him. And God was left without a people on this Earth.

The reconstitution of God's people takes place through divine initiative, offering humanity a way out of their predicament—a return to God through the Seed of the woman (Gen 3:16). What defines the people of

---

[1] E. Lipinski, "עם ʿam" *TDOT*, 11: 172.

God now is His work of redemption on their behalf and their willingness to be reconciled to Him through the Seed of the women, identified in the New Testament as Christ (e.g., Gal 3:16). From this moment, God's people are defined by their hope, an anticipation of the Redeemer's return and complete reliance on His forgiving grace. By faith, they await the moment when the serpent will be crushed under the feet of the Seed of the woman (Gen 3:16). They leave the Garden as God's people in a pilgrimage of faith and hope, centered on the worship of God, the Creator and Redeemer.

Since then, in every generation, God has had a people unified in their worship and submission to His caring will in a sinful environment. Indeed, He has never left Himself without witnesses in this world (cf. Acts 14:17).[2] The line of faith preserved in Genesis 5, which began with Adam and Eve, included their descendants and culminates with Noah. We know very little about the individuals listed in this genealogy. There is, however, an interesting parenthetical statement: "Enoch walked with God and he was not, for God took him" (Gen 5:24).[3] The communion that one of God's people had with the Lord was so deep that one day God took him to Heaven. One could suggest that in this exemplar is illustrated the ultimate destiny of God's people in the Old Testament—permanent union with God.

At the end of this line of faith, we find another person who stands out. "Noah was a just man, perfect in his generations. Noah walked with God" (Gen 6:9). Here is a representative of God's people, actively involved in God's salvific mission for the human race. The emphasis is on his close fellowship with God. He, like Enoch, *walked with God*. *Walking with God* was an expression of fellowship and intimacy, a way of life (cf. Deut 30:15-16). *Walking with God*[4] refers to an intense awareness of His presence that determines one's actions. It presupposes that God is at the center of the existence of His people during their pilgrimage on earth, guiding and protecting them.

Noah, in spite of his lapse in judgment (Gen 9:21), is described as a "just [or righteous] man, perfect in his generation." The word "just" (*tsaddiq*), refers to a person who relates conscientiously and responsibly with

---

[2] Ellen G. White, *Testimonies for the Church* (Mountain View, CA: Pacific Press, 1948), 8:214.

[3] In the LXX, the phrase, "Enoch walked with God," is replaced with "Enoch was well-pleasing to God," making the statement less anthropomorphic. In Jewish tradition, Enoch was the recipient of special revelations about the spirit world and the ages to come (1 Enoch 17-36; 83-90 in *The Old Testament Pseudepigrapha*, ed. James Charlesworth, [Garden City, NY: Doubleday, 1983], 1:23-29, 61-69).

[4] The hitpael stem of *hālak*, used in this text, has the sense of walking "back and forth" (*HAL*, 1:248), indicating intimacy. The phrase is also applied to Levi in Malachi 2:6.

God and others, thus fulfilling the proper requirements of a relationship. In terms of social interaction, it refers to uprightness, honesty, and virtue in one's dealings with others.[5] The word "perfect" or "blameless" (*tamim*) is frequently used to describe sacrificial animals. In reference to people, it indicates moral integrity or honesty.[6] The two terms together describe a life of true faith and sincere consecration to God who is acknowledged as Creator and Redeemer.

The experience of Enoch and Noah implies that not all were part of God's people. As humans increased, two classes of people emerged: those who called upon the name of the Lord (Gen 4:26), who recognized Him as the true God and worshiped Him and those who did not. "There was an open profession of loyalty to God on the part of one [group], as there was of contempt and disobedience on the part of the other."[7] The people of God during that time were a community of faith gathered around the Creator and Redeemer who worshiped Him and lived in expectation. In time, the two groups intermarried (Gen 6:2) and the community of faith was corrupted. Consequently, God brought upon the world the judgment of the Flood.[8]

After the Flood, the genealogy in Genesis 11 continues the line of faith, ending with the birth of Terah's sons Abram, Nahor, and Haran (Gen 11:27). As humans increased upon the earth, apostasy and division soon took hold and they began to build a tower. Yet, there were still people "who humbled themselves before God and cried unto Him, 'O God,' they pleaded, 'interpose between Thy cause, and the plans and methods of men.' "[9] They remained loyal to God, completely relying on His plans for them. In response, God confused their language and the building project

---

[5] *HAL*, 3:1002.

[6] Ibid., 4:1748–1750.

[7] Ellen G. White, *Patriarchs and Prophets* (Mountain View, CA: Pacific Press, 1958), 80. She also indicates that the descendants of Cain spread out in the valleys, and the children of Seth withdrew to the mountains to escape the negative influence of their contemporaries (81).

[8] This was the view of some Church Fathers, such as Augustine, of the Reformers, and is still today the view of most conservative interpreters. See Kenneth A. Mathews, *Genesis 1—11:26* (Nashville, TN: Broadman and Holman, 2002), 329; Donn W. Letherman, "Who Were the 'Sons of God' and the 'Daughters of Men'?" *Interpreting Scripture*, ed. Gerhard Pfandl (Silver Spring, MD: Biblical Research Institute, 2010), 135–137. Jewish interpreters following *Targum Neofiti* translate the b^eney $ha'elohîm$ in Genesis 6:2 as "the sons of judges" (Martin McNamara, *Targum Neofiti 1: Genesis* [Collegeville, MN: The Liturgical Press, 1992], 71). U. Cassuto, however, believes the "sons of God" are angels (*From Adam to Noah* [Jerusalem: Magness Press, 1961], 292). This is also the view of many modern scholars; see Gordon J. Wenham, *Genesis 1–15* (Waco, TX: Word Books, 1987), 140.

[9] White, *Testimonies*, 8:214.

came to a halt.[10] Furthermore, "the LORD scattered them abroad over the face of all the earth" (Gen 11:9).

The Patriarchal Period

During the patriarchal period,[11] God promised His people an identity and a future. In fulfillment of Noah's prophecy—"Blessed be the LORD, the God of Shem, and may Canaan be his servant" (Gen 9:26)—God called Abram, a descendant of Shem (Gen 10), and made a covenant with him. The corruption of the nations made it necessary for the Lord to choose one person: Abram, whom He renamed Abraham. The promise of salvation will be preserved through him and his descendants who will become a great nation (Gen 12:2).

Apart from a few familial facts (Gen 11:26-32), we know nothing about Abram until he is called by God to become the father of a nation—the true people of God. Abraham's story focuses on God's initiative and sovereignty. God's people exist because of God's grace. There was no human initiative; God chose Abraham. God provided him with a son. God initiated the covenant with him. Thus, the people of God "only exist as a people because of an act of God."[12] They are not only the biological descendants of Abraham, but they also include those who joined God's people (e.g., Eliezer, Gen 15:2; and Hagar the Egyptian, Gen 16:1).

In Genesis 12:1-3, Abraham is asked to break his family ties, to leave his "father's household" in Haran (Gen 11:31), and go to an unknown land that God would reveal to him. God's call included a threefold promise: the land, the blessing, and the Son. The people of God were still defined by what God would do for them and by the gift of hope. As a result God

---

[10] If all the descendants of the post-diluvian world were descendants of Noah, they must all have spoken the same language. Genesis 11:2 says "they found a plain in the land of Shinar." The reference to known Babylonian cities in Shinar (Gen 1:10; 11:2) and the equation of Shinar with Babylon in Daniel 1:2 make it fairly certain that Shinar is Babylon.

[11] Assuming a 430-year stay of the Israelites in Egypt (Exod 12:40), the Patriarchal Period, according to biblical chronology, would extend from about 2100 B.C., the time of Abraham, to about 1450 B.C., the time of the Exodus from Egypt. Modern scholarship denies the existence of the Patriarchal Period. These stories, it is claimed, "reflect the self-understanding of the community at the end of the period of settlement, about 1000 B.C.E" (P. Kyle McCarter, "The Patriarchal Age: Abraham, Isaac and Jacob," *Ancient Israel*, ed. Herschel Shanks [Washington, DC: Biblical Archaeological Society, 1999], 17). However, the biblical information has been supplemented by discoveries of modern archaeology. Customs of the Patriarchal Age are paralleled in the cuneiform tablets discovered at Nuzi, Mari, and other places. See C. F. Pfeiffer, "Patriarchs," *ZEB*, 4:695-697 and K. A. Kitchen, *On the Reliability of the Old Testament* (Grand Rapids, MI: William B. Eerdmans, 2003), 316-352.

[12] J. Goldingay, *Theological Diversity and the Authority of the Old Testament* (Grand Rapids, MI: Eerdmans, 1987), 62.

would make Abraham "a great nation" (11:30), make "his name" great, and make him a blessing to the nations. In Hebrew, this is in the form of an imperative: "Be a blessing." In Genesis 12:3 Abraham is told "all the families of the earth shall be blessed" in him. This blessing is the gospel of salvation (cf. Gen 3:15). From his seed, the "seed of the woman," the Messiah, would come.[13]

Once Abraham entered the Promised Land, the Lord appeared to him and promised it to his descendants (Gen 12:7). After Abraham's separation from Lot, God appeared to him again and repeated the promise of the land in greater detail. The land is defined as "all the land which you see" and it is given to Abraham as well as to his descendants forever (Gen 13:14-15). The people of God will inherit the land as a divine gift to them.

In Genesis 15, God makes a covenant with Abraham. The covenant-ratification ceremony (vv. 9-10, 17-18) was similar to ancient forms of a contractual agreement.[14] This covenant is referred to in Jeremiah 34:18-20, and contained the implied promise/curse, "May God make me like one of these divided animals, if I do not fulfill the terms of this covenant." Since it is God who walks between the animal pieces, "it is suggested that here God is invoking the curse on himself, if he fails to fulfill the promise."[15] God's promise of salvation is certain and secure. The his-

---

[13] The word "seed" in Genesis 3:15 is used as a collective noun. The seed of the woman refers to the believers and the seed of the serpent to the unbelievers. Both times, "seed" is used figuratively. Eve stands for all believers, whereas Satan represents the unbelievers. However, the parallel is not quite exact. We must remember that Christ is first of all the *literal* offspring of Eve, whereas unbelievers are the seed of Satan only in a spiritual sense. Hebrew thinking does not separate the individual from the group to which he belongs. Therefore, an individual and a group can be referred to by the same word (e.g., "seed") in the same context. Furthermore, the literal and figurative meaning of a word can be superimposed upon one another. Thus, "her seed" can refer at the same time to Eve's collective offspring (believers) and to one particular offspring (Christ). And in the same passage, "your seed" can refer figuratively to the followers of Satan (unbelievers). Since "seed" can be used for groups and individuals marked by a common moral quality, the two "seeds" can stand for two "races" or "communities" each marked by distinct moral qualities. At the historical beginning and end of each group stands an individual representing the whole group. On the side of the believers, Eve stands at the beginning and Christ at the end; on the side of the unbelievers, Satan stands at the beginning and at the end. (see Afolarin Olutunde Ojewole, *The Seed in Genesis 3:15 An Exegetical and Intertextual Study* [Berrien Springs, MI: Adventist Theological Society, 2002], 428-430).

[14] John H. Walton, V. H. Matthews, and M. W. Chavalas, *The IVP Bible Background Commentary: Old Testament* (Downers Grove, IL: InterVarsity, 2000), 48. See also Kenneth A. Mathews, *Genesis 11:27-50:26* (Nashville, TN: Broadman and Holman, 2005), 172; John H. Sailhamer, "Genesis," *The Expositors Bible Commentary*, ed. Frank E. Gaebelein (Grand Rapid, MI: Zondervan, 1990), 2:130. See also Gerhard F. Hasel, "The Meaning of the Animal Rite in Gen 15," *JSOT* 19 (1981): 61-78; C. L. Rogers, "The Covenant with Abraham and Its Historical Setting," *BSac* 127 (1970): 241-256.

[15] Wenham, *Genesis 1-15*, 332.

tory will reveal a God willing to take upon Himself the curse that was ours as a consequence of our sin (Gal 3:13).

The sign of the covenant between God and Abraham was circumcision (Gen 17:10–11). This does not mean that God established the rite of circumcision. In biblical times, it was practiced among the Western Semites as well as in Egypt,[16] long before the time of Abraham. God invested a common cultural practice with new religious meaning and designated it as the sign of the covenant.[17] This signified the permanency of the people's commitment to their Redeemer.

The promise of the Son was partially realized through the miraculous birth of Isaac (Gen 21:1–2). This promise was to remain alive until the coming of the *Seed of the woman*, through whom God was to provide a sacrifice that would bring reconciliation and redemption to the human race (Gen 22). God's people in the Old Testament were looking forward to this most important and unique salvific event. Meanwhile God's people, represented by Abraham and his descendants, were expected to believe in the promises of God and remain faithful to the covenant stipulations. The community of faith emerging from Abraham's household was to be different from the societies around them. Their lifestyle and their values were to be of a different order.

God's dealings with Abraham did not mean that salvation was limited to him and his family. On the contrary and as already indicated, through him, God was dealing with mankind on the universal level, expressing the hope that people from other nations would be counted among God's people as well (Gen 12:3; Ps 22:27; 87; Isa 2:1–4). This is true even in the prophetic judgment speeches against the nations, for often there is a hint of restoration for the nations after the judgment (Jer 48:47; 49:6, 39; Ezek 16:53). Nevertheless, God did have a special people called by His name (Deut 28:10), a kingdom of priests, a holy nation (Exod 19:6), the people of Yahweh (Deut 27:9). The Old Testament is, by and large, the history of God's special people—Israel and the mission entrusted to them (Exod 19:5).

With the call of Abraham, God set in motion His Messianic plan. The key purpose of the covenant, He told Abraham, was that "in you all the families of the earth shall be blessed" (Gen 12:3; 18:18; 22:18; 26:4; and 28:14). Abraham's posterity inherited the sacred trust of being God's chosen representatives on the earth (Deut 7:6–8). Their loyalty to the cov-

---

[16] "Depiction of Syrian warriors circumcised in the West Semitic manner unearthed in Syria and Egypt date from early in the 3rd millennium B.C.E." (Robert G. Hall, "Circumcision," *ABD*, 1:1025).

[17] Leslie C. Allen, "Circumcision," *NIDOTTE*, 4:474–476. See also R. de Vaux, *Ancient Israel* (New York: McGraw-Hill, 1965), 1:46–48.

enant would bring great blessings (Deut 28:1–14). Other nations would see Israel's unprecedented success and would seek to serve their God.[18]

As the nations of antiquity should behold Israel's unprecedented progress, their attention and interest would be aroused. "Even the heathen would recognize the superiority of those who served and worshiped the living God."[19] Desiring the same blessings for themselves, they would make inquiry as to how they too might acquire these obvious material advantages. Israel would reply, "Accept our God as your God, love and serve Him as we do, and He will do the same for you." "The blessings thus assured Israel" were, "on the same conditions and in the same degree, assured to every nation and to every individual under the broad heavens."[20] (see Acts 10:34–35; 15:7–9; Rom 10:12–13; etc.). All nations of earth were to share in the blessings so generously bestowed upon Israel.[21]

God was to be glorified in Israel (Isa 49:3) and its people were to be His witnesses (Isa 43:10; 44:8), so that salvation could come to the Gentiles through the witnessing of Israel.[22] God's plan was that "as the numbers of Israel increased they were to enlarge their borders, until their kingdom should embrace the world."[23] It has been correctly suggested that "the 'nations' and 'Gentiles' were envisioned as equal recipients of that same Good News from the very beginning of time along with Israel herself."[24] And throughout the Old Testament, we find individuals who were reckoned as part of God's people. Among them, we find Melchizedek, a resident of Canaan. He was king of Salem and also a priest of "God Most High" (El Elyon; Gen 14:18). Abraham obviously believed Melchizedek worshipped the same God he did. While he appears in the narrative suddenly and just as quickly is gone, he seems to be one of perhaps many others who worshiped Yahweh in various places.

The Mosaic Period

While in Egypt, the tribes of Israel—God's people—were oppressed and enslaved. God was going to show Himself to be the Redeemer of Israel (Exod 4:31). The manifestation of God's redemptive power was such that Pharaoh and his people had to acknowledge that Yahweh is God over

---

[18] On mission in the Old Testament, see J. Moskala, "Mission in the Old Testament," in this volume.

[19] Ellen G. White, *Christ's Object Lessons* (Washington, DC: Review and Herald, 1941), 289.

[20] *Patriarchs and Prophets*, 500.

[21] *AdvBibComm*, 4:28.

[22] See Walter C. Kaiser Jr., *Mission in the Old Testament* (Grand Rapids, MI: Baker Books, 2000), 61.

[23] Ellen G. White, *Christ's Object Lessons*, 290.

[24] Kaiser, *Mission*, 40.

Egypt just as He is over His own people. Israel left Egypt with much plunder (Exod 12:36), traveling to Mount Sinai (Exod 19:1). Their experience at the foot of this mountain would dramatically change their lives.

The Sinai Experience

While still in Egypt, God promised the Israelites, "I will take you as My people, and I will be your God" (Exod 6:7). When they arrived at Mount Sinai He told them what it meant to be His people: "Now therefore, if you will indeed obey My voice and keep My covenant, then you shall be a special treasure[25] to Me above all people; for all the earth is Mine" (19:5). The term "special treasure" suggests something exceptional. They were to become God's crown jewel, so to speak, His "masterwork, the one-of-a-kind piece."[26] The announcement of the special covenant relationship between God and Israel (Exod 19:4–5) opens with a conditional clause, "if you will indeed obey My voice and keep My covenant," requiring Israel's faithfulness to the covenant.

Unfortunately, not long afterwards, the Israelites broke the covenant (Exod 32) by worshipping a golden calf. It was then that God renewed their covenant: "Behold, I make a covenant" (34:10). Yet this was not an entirely new covenant, "Rather than describing it as new, we should consider it essentially as continuation, enlargement, and particularization of God's earlier covenants, containing in essence the same design, purpose, and goal for Israel's and mankind's redemption as contained in the earlier covenants."[27] Thus the "Sinai covenant" was not a covenant of works, but of grace, because it was based on God's gracious redemption of Israel from Egypt. Obedience to the covenant stipulations was not a way to gain salvation, but a response of love for the redemption accomplished for them by the Lord (cf. Exod 20:2). It was also a way of life required by the covenant relation that revealed something about the lawgiver.[28]

More importantly, this covenant included laws regulating worship. God was dwelling in the midst of the people, as their travel companion. From His dwelling place, He dealt with sin through the sacrificial system

---

[25] The LXX reads "peculiar people." The Hebrew *segullah* has been linked to the Akkadian *sikiltu*, which refers to a personal collection or hoard (M. Greenberg, "Hebrew segullah: Akkadian sikiltu," *JAOS* 71 [1951]: 172–174).

[26] John I. Durham, *Exodus* (Waco, TX: Word, 1987), 262.

[27] Gerhard F. Hasel, *Covenant in Blood* (Mountain View, CA: Pacific, 1982), 63.

[28] P. R. Williamson, "Covenant," *NDBT*, 424, comments: "Just as ancient law-codes generally made a statement about the king who promulgated them, so the covenant obligations revealed at Sinai disclosed something of the nature and character of Yahweh."

and priestly services. God's people were defined as those who had access to the tabernacle of God to worship and praise Him and to find atonement for their sins through the sacrificial system and the work of mediation of the high priest. God's permanent presence among them provided a center that unified them as one people (Exod 25:8). From that center, they were instructed in the way of the Lord, concerning their redemption and interactions with one another. The covenant stipulations were used to shape them as one people in the common hope of the coming Messiah.

One Nation Under God

Sinai stands midway between Israel's flight from Egypt and their settlement in Canaan. The Israelites came to Sinai as liberated slaves; they left as a theocracy. At Sinai, God provided the institutions and laws that molded the freed slaves into an orderly, functioning society. They became an independent people in their own right, a political entity in its own history. Israel's new status as "God's people" (Num 11:29; 16:41) came with a commitment to certain social objectives embodied in God's law—justice, honesty, equality, and love (Exod 23:6–10; 22:21; Lev 19:18). "Being the people of God at this stage was a moral and social task to be worked out."[29] It required "detailed obedience in the ethical, social and cultic spheres."[30] The Decalogue was at the center of what God gave to Moses for the people on Mount Sinai (Exod 201:17).

Compared to the rest of the ancient Mesopotamian nations, Israel was peculiar, especially in regards to religion. While Egypt and others were steeped in polytheism, Israel worshiped one God. The heart of the Decalogue, the basis of the covenant between Yahweh and Israel, "is in the first commandment which prohibits the worship of other gods, the host of heaven, and idols."[31] When Yahweh entered into a covenant with Israel, the Israelites accepted the faith in one God and promised to reject polytheism forever. Israel, established as a theocracy, is called Yahweh's "kingdom of priests and a holy nation" (Exod 19:6), over which He will reign as king forever (Exod 15:18). Their human leaders only served under God's direction.

---

[29] Christopher J. H. Wright, "The People of God and the State in the Old Testament," *Themelios* 16.1 (1990):5.

[30] Goldingay, *Theological Diversity*, 66.

[31] Yehezkel Kaufmann, *The Religion of Israel* (Chicago, IL: University of Chicago Press, 1960), 233.

Jethro, Zippora, and Balaam

In the time of Moses, we find among God's people Jethro and Balaam—worshipers of the true God. When Moses fled from Egypt, he found refuge with the Midian priest Jethro (Exod 3:1), whose daughter Zippora he eventually married. Although Scripture does not call him a priest of Yahweh, upon visiting Moses and the Israelites in the desert and hearing of God's work on behalf of Israel, Jethro acknowledged the superiority of God over all other gods. As witness to his faith in Yahweh, he offered a sacrifice to Him (Exod 18:11–12).[32] Since the Midianites[33] were descendants of Abraham by Keturah (Gen 25:2), it is possible that some Midian tribes continued worshiping Yahweh until the time of Moses.

Balaam was a non-Israelite prophet from the city of Pethor near the river Euphrates (Num 22:5). He was called by the Moabite king Balak to curse Israel, but was stopped by Yahweh. The account leaves no doubt that that he knew Yahweh and attempted, at first, to remain obedient to him. But greed got the better of him and he lost his way (Num 22–24). Some scholars see him as a good prophet who lost his way; others believe that he was a pagan sorcerer "for whom the God of Israel was just another deity he might manipulate."[34] Interestingly, Balaam refers to God with the personal name, "Yahweh" (Num 22:8). Here we have a non-Israelite who knew Yahweh before he knew Israel.[35] Balaam certainly had the gift of prophecy when he uttered his oracles (24:4, 16).[36] This suggests that there were people outside Israel with knowledge of the Lord and who worshiped and served Him.

---

[32] Ellen White, speaking of Moses, wrote, "The Lord directed his course, and he found a home with Jethro, the priest and prince of Midian, who was also a worshiper of God (*Patriarchs and Prophets,* 247).

[33] According to some scholars, the Midinaites were the earliest, identifiable Arabic-speaking social group (George E. Mendenhall, "Midian,"*ABD,* 4:815. See also Michael G. Vanzant, "Midian, Midianites," *NIDB,* 4:79).

[34] Ronal B. Allen, "Numbers," *The Expositor's Bible Commentary,* ed. F. Gaebelein, (Grand Rapids, MI: Zondervan, 1990), 2:888.

[35] Hence Ellen White says, "Balaam was once a good man and a prophet of God; but he had apostatized, and had given himself up to covetousness" (*Patriarchs and Prophets,* 439).

[36] Extra-biblical evidence for Balaam was found at Tell Deir Alla in Transjordan. The excavated text describes a divine vision received by Balaam: "Lo, the gods came to him at night and [spoke to] him" (Alfred J. Hoerth, *Archaeology and the Old Testament* [Grand Rapids, MI: Baker Books, 1998], 204. See also John H. Walton, ed., *Zondervan Illustrated Bible Background Commentary* [Grand Rapids, MI: Zondervan, 2009], 1:380–381).

The Period of the Judges

The book of Judges dramatically illustrates the effects of apostasy among God's people. "Israel served the LORD all the days of Joshua, and all the days of the elders who outlived Joshua" (Josh 24:31). But once that generation passed away, Israel descended into apostasy, disorganization, tribal discord, and repeated defeat at the hands of their enemies. By displacing God from the center of their lives, God's people became fragmented. Nevertheless, when they cried out to the Lord in their oppression, He "raised up judges who delivered them" (Judg 2:16). The book of Judges shows God constantly coming to the aid of His people and His willingness to forgive them.

While the judges operated under the guidance of the Holy Spirit (6:34; 11:29; 14:6, 19), their lives often exhibited a lack of spirituality. Ehud assassinated Eglon, King of Moab (Judg 3:17–21); Gideon settled his family feud in the course of his victory over the Midianites (8:18–21); and Samson's uncontrolled sexual urge, involving foreign women, eventually proved his undoing (16:15–22). "The judges were men who lived in an age of low standards, and this fact is reflected in the narrative, giving a graphic representation of the conditions in a period of apostasy, when the Mosaic covenant, with its high standards, was in partial abeyance."[37]

The days of the judges were the Dark Ages in the history of God's people. It seemed as though Israel could not exist as Yahweh's people in Canaan. Surrounded by the Canaanite religion,[38] which appealed to the human sensual nature,[39] Israel experienced a pronounced moral and religious decline. This was due, in part, to the decline in the standard of individual leaders and the lack of a centralized authority (Judg 17:6; 18:1; 19:1). God was still their king, but they did not listen to Him. The cultural influences around them were a significant threat to their commitment to the Lord. But even in the midst of the chaos of apostasy, God still had a faithful remnant—His true people. We even find a non-Israelite woman accepting Yahweh as her God: Ruth (Ruth 1:16–17). She became the wife of Boaz of Bethlehem and the great-grandmother of King David. God's

---

[37] A. E. Cundall, "Judges, Book of," *ZEB*, 3:844.

[38] For an extended treatment of the Religion of Canaan, see William F. Albright, *Yahweh and the God's of Canaan* (Winona Lake, IN: Eisenbrauns, 1968) and Dennis Pardee, *Ritual and Cult at Ugarit* (Atlanta: Society of Biblical Literature, 2002). A good summary can also be found in John Day, "Canaan, Religion," *ABD*, 1:831–836.

[39] In contrast to the biblical material, the texts from Ugarit do not emphasize the sensual nature of the Canaanite cult. What we find in Scripture seems to reflect the popular expression of the Canaanite religion.

people, during the period of the Judges, had nearly lost their religious and national identity. What defined them and kept them united as one people—their God—was replaced by self-preservation, at almost any cost. The result of this apostasy was spiritual and moral degradation. Yet, the Lord did not abandon them. Instead, He struggled with them, attempting to guide them to a deeper understanding of who He was and the power of His salvation.

The Institutional State–The Monarchy

From the 11th century on, Israel's territory as a nation was established by God Himself (Gen 15:18; Exod 6:8; Ps 135:11–12). Jerusalem was its capital, with God's temple in the center, amidst His people (1 Kgs 6:13; 8:11). Though theocratic in nature, it was, at the same time, an earthly kingdom ruled by men. This duality is evident in 1 Samuel where the introduction of a monarchy is depicted as rebellion against God (1 Sam 8:5–7). Yet, we read that God specifically chose Saul, David, and Solomon as kings of Israel and blessed them (1 Sam 9:16–17; 16:12–13; 2 Sam 7:12–13). This tension between what God wanted (a theocracy) and what God allowed (a monarchy) surfaced throughout Israel's history. The prophets frequently clashed with the institutional authority in the name of the Lord (1 Kgs 13:1–5; 18:18; 2 Kgs 9:6–7; 21:10–12; Jer 21:4–5), underscoring the tense relationship between the sovereignty of the human king and that of the divine king. The monarchy, therefore, stood "in a position of ambiguous legitimacy before God, neither totally rejected nor unconditionally sanctioned."[40]

At its best, the Davidic kings were servants of God reigning over Israel on Yahweh's behalf (1 Chr 29:22–23). However, for long periods of time in the history of Israel, the Lord's rule was divorced from politics and justice and was limited to piety and worship. In the time of the monarchy, social developments led to a class system with inequalities, unfairness, and excesses (cf. 1 Sam 8:10–18; 1 Kgs 21).[41] The prophets spent more time rebuking the people of Israel and their kings and calling them to repentance (e.g., Isa 1; Jer 2; Ezek 2; Hos 4; Amos 5, etc.). This illustrates the perennial tension between the Lord as the leader of His people and the human instruments He uses to accomplish His purposes. When the kings submitted to the Lord and placed the worship of Him at the center of their role as leaders, the people prospered.

---

[40] Wright, "People," 6.
[41] Goldingay, *Theological Diversity*, 71.

Israel and Worship

An important part of Israel's life was individual, family, and corporate worship in the temple of the Lord. The individual lament Psalms presuppose individual or family worship settings, and the yearly festivals were celebrated by all the people together (Lev 23:27–30; 2 Chr 30:5). "In Israel's worship, ritual form, orthodox belief, awed reverence, and joyful hope appear together as essential features of Israel's relationship with God, without any sense of tension (e.g., Ps 22; 147:11; 1 Chr 15:25–28; 2 Chr 30:13–27; Ezra 3)."[42] However, whenever Israel's worship became formalistic, an outward ritual without the inner spirit, a pious performance without works of righteousness in their daily lives, the prophets rose up against it (e.g., Isa 1:12–17; Amos 5:21). As a result, we find tension between prophets and priests (e.g., Jer 1:17–18; Ezek 22:26; Hos 5:1), similar to the tension between prophets and kings. True worship defined the identity of the people of God in a very visible way. Divorcing it from its ethical, moral, and social significance resulted in apostasy and the corruption of the system itself.

The Gentiles as "the People of God"

While the term, "people of God," is used in the Old Testament primarily for the nation of Israel, we find in the writings of the prophets clearer references to a future in which those outside of Israel will have a part in the privileges of those called by His name. Looking forward to the Messianic Age, Isaiah sees a time when Israel shall "be one of three with Egypt and Assyria . . . whom the LORD of hosts shall bless, saying, 'Blessed is Egypt My people, and Assyria the work of My hands, and Israel My inheritance.'" (Isa 19:24–25). Similarly, through Zechariah God teaches that at that time "many nations shall be joined to the LORD in that day, and they shall become My people" (Zech 2:11). Other texts, while not mentioning the phrase "My people," refer to the salvation of heathen people and their sharing in the worship of the true God (Isa 2:2; Jer 16:19; Isa 25:6–7; 45:20–25; 55:4–7; 56:4–7; Amos 9:7–12). Interestingly, the Old Testament inclusion of Gentiles among God's people is done by embracing the faith of Israel. "Thus, even before New Testament times the concept of 'the people of God' is seen as embracing both Israel and those outside of that nation."[43]

---

[42] Idem, "Images of Israel: The People of God in the Writings," *Studies in Old Testament Theology*, ed. Robert L. Hubbard, Jr., Robert K. Johnston, and Robert P. Meye (Dallas, TX: Word Publishing, 1992), 206.

[43] Robert L. Saucy, "Israel and the Church: A Case for Discontinuity," *Continuity and Discontinuity*,

The Failure of the People of God

God's plan for Israel was not fully realized in the Old Testament. Not only did His people fail in their missionary outreach, they failed in protecting their religion from pagan influences.[44] The tenor of the prophetic writings, therefore, is primarily negative in its tone—condemning the religious, legal, and social institutions of Israel (Hos 4:1; Amos 5:12; Isa 1:10; Jer 2:13). References to God's grace are often cited to heighten the contrast between God's faithfulness and Israel's irresponsibility: "Out of Egypt I called my son," but "they sacrificed to the Baals" (Hos 11:1–2; Amos 2:11–12; Isa 5:4).

Throughout prophetic literature, we find calls for repentance (Hos 6:1; Isa 1:16–17). Jeremiah and Ezekiel frequently reproached the people for worshiping other gods (Jer 7:9; 11:10; 35:15; Ezek 8:10–16). Israel and Judah could have avoided the Assyrian and Babylonian exiles if they had listened to the admonitions of the prophets (Isa 1:19–20; (Jer 4:1). But they refused to listen. Consequently, the judgment of God on the Southern kingdom came more than a century after the Northern kingdom had come to an end (2 Kgs 17:5–11).

The Exilic Period

In 586 B.C., Nebuchadnezzar destroyed Jerusalem and deported all "but the poor of the land" (2 Kgs 25:12). The number of Israelites from the Northern and Southern kingdoms living in exile in Assyria/Babylon was considerable—possibly several hundred thousand.[45] Those who remained in the land after the destruction of Jerusalem were soon decimated further by the flight of "all the people, small and great" (2 Kgs 25:26), to Egypt. God's people lost their land and were scattered all over the earth, reduced to a remnant.

In Jeremiah 24, the Lord showed the prophet two baskets of figs. One basket had very good figs and the other had very bad figs. The Lord then identified those carried away captive to Babylon with the good figs (v. 5) whom he was going to return to Judah (v. 6). The bad figs represented those who remained in the land. The exile reduced those carried away to a remnant that had to learn to live like their forefathers as strangers in a

---

ed. John S. Feinberg (Westchester, IL: Crossway Books, 1988), 240.

[44] On the influence of Canaanite religion on Israel's faith, see Albright, *Religion*, 208–264.

[45] Modern scholarship puts these figures much lower. See Edwin M. Yamauchi, "Ezra-Nehemiah," *The Expositor's Bible Commentary*, ed. F. Gaebelein (Grand Rapids, MI: Regency Reference Library, 1988), 4:567–568.

strange land. The remnant concept was not new in Israel.[46] Joseph was sent to Egypt to preserve a remnant (Gen 45:7); and Elijah and the seven thousand who did not bend their knees to Baal (1 Kgs 19:18) were also a remnant in Israel. In regard to the Israelites during the Assyrian and Babylonian exiles, it has been stated:

> At this point in their history, then, the people of God constitute a persecuted remnant, with the state as an ambient, hostile power within which they have to survive and somehow continue to live as the people of God. The danger at such times was twofold: to lose their identity by compromise and assimilation into their new environment, and thus cease to be distinctive; or to stand out as so intractably different that they brought destructive fires of persecution on themselves that might finally consume them.[47]

Daniel and his friends certainly stood out and brought persecution on themselves, but they were not consumed. The historical chapters of the book of Daniel illustrates how God vindicated and delivered the faithful remnant in the midst of pagan nations. In each chapter, trials and temptations are followed by blessings for those obedient to God.[48] God's people were the object of attacks by forces of evil working through corrupted social, political, and religious institutions. In that battle, the Lord was with them—sustaining and preserving His remnant people.

However, after seventy years of exile, many Jews were almost indistinguishable from their Babylonian neighbors. They spoke their language (Aramaic), wore similar clothes, and felt thoroughly at home in Babylon. Therefore, when the call came to return to Zion, only a remnant of the exiles responded. For this remnant, the hope of a return to the land of their fathers was a beacon of light during the exile. They cried, "If I forget you, O Jerusalem, Let my right hand forget its skill" (Ps 137:5). And through the prophet Jeremiah, God promised to bring them back and re-establish them in the land (Jer 29:10–14; 30:3; 31:16, 23, etc.). This promise was

---

[46] See G. F. Hasel, *The Remnant* (Berrien Springs, MI: Andrews University Press, 1974), 135–159.

[47] Wright, "People," 8.

[48] For example, in chapter one, the four young Hebrews are tested concerning their commitment to the law of God. They are found faithful and are promoted to the palace of the king. In chapter two, Daniel and his friends survive the threat of death (v. 13), they prove themselves superior to those who know not God, and are elevated to positions of leadership. In chapter three, Daniel's friends are tested again, this time more severely. Again they are found to be faithful to the commandments of God. They experience Yahweh's deliverance from their time of trouble, and, instead of being burned alive, they prosper as the result of further promotion by the king (v. 30).

God's divine gift to His people, showing that they had not been discarded by their Lord.

These promises must have caught the attention of all the exiles. In the end however, only about 42,000 (Ezra 2:64)—a remnant (Haggai 1:12, 14; 2:2)—returned to Judah.[49] One could say that "the exceptional feature of Jewish history is the reluctance of so many of the exiles to go back. They remained in Mesopotamia but, paradoxically, continued to care for the Holy City generation after generation, for centuries and millennia."[50] In time, Mesopotamia became a center of Jewish learning[51] that produced the standard Talmud,[52] the Babylonian Talmud, still in use today.

The Post-Exilic Period

The Assyrian and Babylonian exiles did not mean the Israelites and Jews were cast off as God's elect; rather the judgment was designed to elicit a positive response from them. And those who returned from the exile did respond positively, restoring the worship of Yahweh (Ezra 3:3), building the temple (Ezra 3:8), banishing idolatry, and sincerely committing to the covenant law. They became, first, a community with a distinct ethnic and religious identity (Ezra 4:1-3). With the temple services restored and the worship of the true God at the center of their lives, they established a common identity and a unifying core. Although the Jews remained a society organized by tribe and family, it was not closed to non-Jews, as the story of Esther demonstrates (Esther 8:17; Ezra 6:21).

Secondly, they were a waiting community. As the Old Testament comes to a close, we find a community of faith looking forward to the fulfillment of God's glorious promise of salvation for His people. That hope was stimulated and strengthened not only through the word of classical prophets but also, and perhaps more specifically, through the apocalyptic prophecies of Daniel that emphasized God's final victory over the forces that oppose His work of redemption in His temple on behalf of His people.

Thirdly, they were an obedient community. The restoration after the

---

[49] Though Cyrus' edict allowed all Israelites and Jews in Assyria/Babylon to return to their homeland (Ezra 1:3-4), many remained in Babylon as indicated by the large number still living in the East in Esther's day "for the slayers," says L. J. Wood, " must have outnumbered the 75 000 who were slain." (Leon J. Wood, *A Survey of Israel's History* [Grand Rapids, MI: Zondervan, 1970], 408).

[50] Elias Bickerman, *From Ezra to the Last of the Maccabees* (New York: Schocken Books, 1962), 6.

[51] The cities of Sura in the south and Pumbedita in northern Babylon were for eight centuries home of important Jewish academies. Founded in the 3rd century A.D., these academies produced the Babylonian Talmud.

[52] The Talmud was created in the period between the 100 B.C. and 500 AD. See Leo Trepp, *Judaism* (Belmont, CA: Wadsworth Publishing, 1982), 218.

exile precluded a restoration of statehood. They were still under the control of a foreign power (Medo-Persia) and would remain so until the establishment of the Maccabean kingdom in the second century B.C. They organized their existence around the worship of the Lord and obedience to the Torah. There was, among the Jews, a sincere effort to obey the covenant stipulations. They acknowledged that the experience of the exile was the result of their rebellion and now were determined to conform their lives to the covenant law. During the intertestamental period, these concerns would be developed in different ways, resulting in the Judaism of the first century A.D.

Conclusion

The history of God's people in the Old Testament was characterized by conflict, partial loyalty to the Lord, and apostasy. But within them, there was always a remnant that placed God at the center of their very existence. His person and self-revelation unified them as one people. This magnificent God, who resided in His temple, was their exclusive object of worship. They worshiped Him as their Creator and Redeemer, constantly relying on Him for forgiveness. This was a community totally aware of the presence of God among them and of their dependence on Him. To them, the Lord had promised the land and the coming of the Savior, thus giving them a deep sense of hope.

From His people, God expected love and gratitude expressed through submission to the covenant law. This obedience was grounded on nothing else but His redeeming power given to Israel as an undeserved gift of divine love. In guiding and providing for His people, God used leaders from their community (e.g., patriarchs, judges, kings, priests, teachers). They were to strengthen the commitment of the people to Him as Redeemer and covenant Lord and maintain unity. When the leaders failed, God was always able to preserve a remnant from among His people. Through them, He was able to accomplish His purpose for the human family.

From the very beginning of the history of salvation, it was God's intention to reach out to the human race at a universal level. His election of one people in particular was not exclusivist, but aimed at having a human instrumentality through which He would be able to bless all the nations of the earth. This blessing was to reach them through the fulfillment of the promise of the Son. At the close of the Old Testament, God's people were looking forward to the realization of the promise, united in the worship of the true God, and committed to His covenant law.

CHAPTER 2

THE UNIVERSALITY OF THE CHURCH IN THE NEW TESTAMENT

Ekkehardt Mueller

In this chapter we will be dealing with one major ecclesiological issue, namely the New Testament understanding of the church as local and universal and how these two expressions of the church relate to each other. We will examine biblical materials, but pay particular attention to the use of the term *ekklēsia*, "church, congregation," in the New Testament. Attention will also be given to other terminology and images of the church that will assist us in establishing clear biblical distinctions between the local and the global church and their mutual interaction.

The Local Church and the Universal Church

In secular Greek, the term *ekklēsia* originally designated a gathering of people—for example, the assembly of citizens as a political entity. In the Septuagint, the word is most often employed as a translation of the Hebrew word *qāhāl*,[1] "gathering," "congregation," or "assembly." In the New Testament, it usually describes a group of those who believe in Jesus Christ, accepting Him and His teachings.[2] They "are joined to the organization originated by Him,"[3] and are His disciples and followers called to

---

[1] See, H. J. Fabry, F. L. Hossfeld, and E. M. Kindl, "קהל *qāhāl*," *TDOT*, 12: 561.

[2] Cf. Erwin Fahlbusch, "Church: Subject, Tasks, and Problems of Ecclesiology," *Encyclopedia of Christianity*, ed. E. Fahlbusch et al. (Grand Rapids, MI: Eerdmans, 1999), 1:477–478 and Jürgen Roloff, "Church: Historical Aspects," *Encyclopedia of Christianity*, 1:481.

[3] Siegfried H. Horn, *Seventh-day Adventist Bible Dictionary* (Washington, DC: Review and Herald,

minister to one another and to proclaim to the world as He commanded them (Matt 28:20).[4] *Ekklēsia* is used for "(1) a church meeting (1 Cor 11:18), (2) the total number of Christians living in one place (1 Cor 4:17), (3) the church universal (Matt 16:18)."[5] It is the community of the Holy Spirit and the people of God. Whereas "universal church" refers to the church in general, not limited by geography or time, the local church is defined as a local congregation in a city or village that may be limited in time.

The Church in the Gospels and in Acts

The Synoptic Gospels

The term *ekklēsia* is found in the Gospel of Matthew and quite frequently in Acts. Although it is disputed whether or not Jesus talked about His *ekklēsia* (Matt 16:18; 18:17–twice),[6] the evidence in the Synoptic Gospels shows that:

> Jesus intended to create a visible community . . . He came to give birth to a fellowship of men and women under the Kingship of God, a religious community of which He was the leader . . . As the destined Messiah Jesus gathered a remnant community to Himself . . . A Messiah without a community was unthinkable to the Jewish mind. The concepts of disciples, a remnant, and messiahship were constitutive of a new community, a people of God, which is the Messiah's possession.[7]

Although Jesus was talking about the church as His specific people, its

---

1979), 210.

[4] Cf. G. Gloege, "Gemeinde. Begrifflich," *Die Religion in Geschichte und Gegenwart*, ed. Kurt Galling (Tübingen: J. C. B. Mohr, 1958), 2:1325–1329.

[5] Horn, *Dictionary*, 210.

[6] Cf. Leonhard Goppelt, *Theology of the New Testament, Volume 1: The Ministry of Jesus in Its Theological Significance* (Grand Rapids, MI: Eerdmans, 1981), 213. See also the discussion in Donald Guthrie, *New Testament Theology* (Downers Grove, IL: InterVarsity, 1981), 711–712; George Eldon Ladd, *A Theology of the New Testament* (Grand Rapids, MI: Eerdmans, 1974), 109–111, 342; and K. L. Schmidt, "*Ekklēsia*," in *TDNT*, 3:518–526.

[7] Raoul Dederen, "The Church," *Handbook of Seventh-day Adventist Theology*, ed. Raoul Dederen (Hagerstown, MD: Review and Herald, 2000), 540. Cf. Raoul Dederen, "Wollte Jesus eine Gemeinde gründen?," *Die Gemeinde und ihr Auftrag*, ed. J. Mager (Lüneburg: Saatkorn-Verlag, 1994), 36–40, 43–47. For more detailed discussion of Jesus and the remnant in the gospels, see Clinton Wahlen, "The Remnant in the Gospels," *Studies in Adventist Ecclesiology 1: Toward a Theology of the Remnant*, ed. Ángel Manuel Rodríguez (Silver Spring, MD: Biblical Research Institute, 2009), 61–76.

organizational aspects were not totally absent. It prepared the way for the church, as we later find in Acts and in other New Testament epistles.

The concept of Jesus' church is not limited to the term *ekklēsia*. Jesus' call to individuals to become His followers (Matt 4:19; 8:22; 19:21; Mark 2:14; 10:21; Luke 5:27; 9:59; 18:22), the election of the Twelve out of a larger group of His disciples, and their designation as apostles and missionaries (Mark 3:13-19; Luke 6:13-16; Matt 10:1-20)[8] indicate that the Synoptic Gospels are well aware of the fact that Jesus was gathering a special people—His church, a remnant community.[9] To this evidence we could also add Jesus' particular teachings: the Sermon on the Mount addressed to His disciples (Matt 5-7); His teachings about His flock (Luke 12:32, Matt 26:31); and His family (Matt 12:46-50; Mark 3:31-35; Luke 8:19-21).

The Gospel of John

The Gospel of John agrees with the Synoptics. According to John 1:43 and 21:22, Jesus called people to follow Him. In John 15:1-8, Jesus compares Himself to a vine and His community to its branches, challenging them to remain in Him. There is an extended section on Jesus as the good shepherd (John 10:1-18). At the end of the Fourth Gospel, Jesus charges Peter to tend His lambs and His sheep (John 21:15-17). It is clear that there is a Messianic community, Christ's church.

In John 10:16, Jesus makes an interesting statement: "I have other sheep, which are not of this fold; I must bring them also, and they will hear My voice; and they will become one flock with one shepherd."[10] This indicates He has other sheep outside the immediate Jewish circle and that, in the future, they will also believe in Him. These Gentile believers will not form a Gentile church separate from a church consisting of Jewish believers. "They are to become united in one flock. And they all stand under the leadership of one shepherd. The unity is not a natural unity but one brought about by the activity of the Shepherd in 'bringing' them."[11] It is almost obvious that this "flock will be universal in character."[12] In John 10:16 as well as in Jesus' teachings about His church in Matthew 16, we

---

[8] See also the mission of the Seventy (Luke 10:1-17).

[9] See Clinton Wahlen, "Remnant in the Gospels," 69-75.

[10] All Bible text quoted are from the NASB unless otherwise indicated.

[11] Leon Morris, *The Gospel According to John* (Grand Rapids, MI: Eerdmans, 1992), 512; cf. Rudolf Schnackenburg, *The Gospel According to St. John* (New York: Crossroad, 1990), 2:299.

[12] R. V. G. Tasker, *John* (Grand Rapids, MI: Eerdmans, 1992), 130.

have a future dimension and, at the same time, a universal dimension.[13] Jesus knows His church will continue to grow and expand. It will be one church, a universal entity.

Acts of the Apostles

In Acts, a number of terms are used to describe the church: "brothers" (1:15), "believers" (2:44), those "who call on Your name" (9:14), "flock" (20:28–29), etc. But the word *ekklēsia* is found twenty-three times and requires attention. It is used twice in the plural, the rest in the singular. In Acts 7:38, *ekklēsia* occurs in an Old Testament quotation. Three times *ekklēsia* is a political entity, the secular assembly of citizens without theological significance (19:32, 39, 40).[14] In all the other places, it refers to the community of believers. In Acts, *ekklēsia* is usually used to describe the local church: the church in Jerusalem (8:1; 11:22; 15:4), the church in Antioch (13:1), the church in Caesarea (18:22), the church in Ephesus (20:17), or the churches in Syria and Cilicia (15:41). Paul and Barnabas appointed elders in every church (14:23). Acts indicates that at Pentecost the church was empowered by the Holy Spirit and sent out on its mission.[15] Whereas Jerusalem was originally the seat of the Messianic community, additional churches were soon established throughout the world. A tremendous growth took place, requiring the establishment of some type of organization. In addition to the apostles, the Seven were chosen and elders were elected to serve local congregations.

However, the question must be asked whether or not Acts, with its strong emphasis on local congregations, also knows about a universal church. Before responding, we must affirm that the churches mentioned in Acts are in line with Jesus' expectations of His future church. Acts uses twice the expression "the whole church," but in Acts 5:11 the expression seems to refer to the church in Jerusalem. In Acts 15:22, although in the context of the Jerusalem Council, the term may again refer to the church in Jerusalem.[16] This would explain, to some extent, why the apostles and elders in the very same verse, as well as in verse 4, are mentioned separately. The council consisted of delegates from various churches and members of the Jerusalem church.

A broader view of the church is presented in Acts 9:31: "So the church

---

[13] Cf. Millard J. Erickson, *Christian Theology* (Grand Rapids, MI: Baker, 1998), 1044.

[14] See Schmidt, "*Ekklēsia*," 505.

[15] See Clinton Wahlen, "Mission in the New Testament," in this volume.

[16] Cf. F. F. Bruce, *The Book of the Acts* (Grand Rapids, MI: Eerdmans, 1988), 297.

throughout all Judea and Galilee and Samaria enjoyed peace, being built up; and going on in the fear of the Lord and in the comfort of the Holy Spirit, it continued to increase." Though Luke does not yet speak about the universal church, an important step is taken in that direction. The churches in a certain geographical area are the *church*. "The local connection is not the decisive point. This is shown by the further references to the *ekklēsia* in Judaea, Galilee and Samaria. . . . It is not that the *ekklēsia* divides up into *ekklēsiai*. Nor does the sum of the *ekklēsiai* produce the *ekklēsia*. The one *ekklēsia* is present in the places mentioned . . ."[17]

A rich text, and the last one in Acts to contain the term *ekklēsia*, is Acts 20:28. It is part of Paul's farewell speech addressed to the elders of Ephesus: "Be on guard for yourselves and for all the flock, among which the Holy Spirit has made you overseers, to shepherd the church of God which He purchased with His own blood." The verse is unique as it contains the phrase "the church of God," not found elsewhere in Acts. Also, the term "flock" is introduced here and found again only in Acts 20:28-29. In addition, it is stated that this church of God was purchased by His blood. It seems appropriate to understand this text as referring to the church in general, rather than to a local congregation. Jesus has purchased His church and He calls it His "flock."[18]

> The church is described as a *flock*, a familiar Old Testament metaphor for God's people (Ps. 100:3; Is. 40:11; Je. 13:17; Ezk. 34) which was taken up by Jesus (Lk. 12:32; 15:3-7; 19:10; Jn. 10:1-30). The picture is applied to the church and its leaders . . . .The church belongs to God because he himself bought it . . . . The thought is of the act of redemption by which the church became God's special property, and is based on the picture of God redeeming Israel in Isaiah 43:21 (*cf.* Ps. 74:2, which significantly follows a verse in which Israel is likened to a flock).[19]

Whereas Jesus emphasized the universality of His church, Acts specifically mentions local congregations without denying the larger picture.

The Universal Church in the Pauline Literature

Paul sees the church as a local entity as well as a universal group of believers. Yet, his emphasis differs from letter to letter. We will first exam-

---

[17] Schmidt, "*Ekklēsia*," 505.

[18] The same noun for "flock"—*poimnion* instead of *poimnē*—is used here and in Luke 12:32.

[19] I. Howard Marshall, *Acts* (Grand Rapids, MI: Eerdmans, 1991), 333-334.

ine the letters that focus on the local church, then at letters emphasizing its universal nature.

Emphasis on the Local Church

Romans

In Romans, *ekklēsia* is found only five times, all in the final chapter. The church is either a local church (16:1) or a house church (16:5, 23), which is also local. In Romans 16:4, all Gentile churches give thanks and in 16:16 all the churches of Christ greet the Christians in Rome. But the concept of the church is also expressed by using terms and phrases such as the saints (1:7; 15:25; 16:2), those being called (8:30), and those who were chosen (8:33). In Romans 9–11, Paul discusses the election and unbelief of Israel and their relation to Christians. He mentions a remnant (9:27), uses the example of an olive tree in which wild branches (Gentile Christians) are being grafted, and states that "all Israel will be saved" (11:26). The latter statements as well as the reference to "one body" in Romans 12:4–5, seem to refer to the universal dimension of the church.

1 Corinthians

1 Corinthians frequently mentions the church. The term *ekklēsia* is found twenty-two times, six times as a plural. In most cases, the term refers to the local church in Corinth (e.g., 1:2; 16:19), but we also find references to other Christian churches (4:17; 7:17), such as the churches of Galatia (16:1) and Asia (16:19). These churches are "the churches of the saints" (14:33) and the "churches of God" (11:16).[20] Are we able to detect a universal element? There are at least three texts in which *ekklēsia* may cross local boundaries and express a universal concept: 1 Corinthians 10:32, which references Jews, Greeks, and the church of God; 1 Corinthians 12:28, discussing functions and spiritual gifts in the church in the context of the metaphor of the body;[21] and 1 Corinthians 15:9, where Paul admits his persecution of God's church. This suggests that, "according to Paul, the designation *ekklēsia* was applicable to three different groups: 1) In 1 Corinthians 10:32, it meant the people of God in its entirety; 2) In 1 Corinthians 1:2, it meant the particular local community; 3) In 1 Corinthians 11:18, it meant the worshipping assembly of the community."[22] In the case of 1 Corinthians 15:9, we could say that "this is one of the rare

---

[20] The phrase, "church of God," in the singular occurs another four times (1 Cor 1:2; 10:32; 11:22; 15:9).

[21] Cf. Leon Morris, *1 Corinthians* (Grand Rapids, MI: Eerdmans, 1993), 174.

[22] Leonhard Goppelt, *Theology of the New Testament 2: The Variety and Unity of the Apostolic Witness to Christ* (Grand Rapids, MI: Eerdmans, 1982), 144.

instances in Paul's earlier letters where he uses *hē ekklēsia* ['the church'] with the qualifier *tou theou* ['of God'] to refer to the church in a more universal sense rather than to a local body (cf. Gal. 1:13 and the plural in v. 22)."[23] Thus, 1 Corinthians seems to contain a universal element, although the local church is also stressed.[24]

2 Corinthians

Second Corinthians employs *ekklēsia* nine times, once referring to God's church as it was in Corinth (1:1) and eight times to other churches or all churches (8:1, 18-19, 23-24; 11:8, 28; 12:13). All of these references describe local churches as probably does the term "saints." The letter is addressed "to the church of God which is at Corinth with all the saints who are throughout Achaia" (1:1). A glimpse at the universal church may be found in 2 Corinthians 6:16 where Paul states, "We are the temple of the living God."[25] In 1 Corinthians, the image of the temple had already been applied to the Corinthian church (3:16) and in 6:19 to the individual Christian. The difference in 2 Corinthians is that here Paul includes himself by using "we" instead of "you" and thus enlarges the image of the temple of God by possibly including the entire Christian community.[26]

Galatians

Galatians mentions both the churches of Galatia (1:2) and the churches of Judea (1:22). Furthermore, Paul refers to his persecution of the "church" (1:13). The latter text must be understood in a universal sense. His reference to the church of God, which he wanted to destroy, is "a reference to the universal Church as the messianic people of God in its entirety, which is, however, to be met with in various local 'churches of God' (1 Cor 11:16; 1 Thess 2:14; 2 Thess 1:4) representing the one universal Church."[27] Additionally, the phrase "household/family of the faith," which is contrasted with "all people" (Gal 6:10),[28] and the phrase

---

[23] Gordon D. Fee, *The First Epistle to the Corinthians* (Grand Rapids, MI: Eerdmans, 1991), 734.

[24] Schmidt, "*Ekklēsia*," 506, points out that the saying addressed to the church in Corinth also applies to the church as a whole because "each community, however small, represents the total community, the Church."

[25] Cf. Ralph P. Martin, *2 Corinthians* (Waco, TX: Word, 1986), 202.

[26] Cf. Colin Kruse, *2 Corinthians* (Grand Rapids, MI: Eerdmans, 1991), 138.

[27] Ronald Y. K. Fung, *The Epistle to the Galatians* (Grand Rapids, MI: Eerdmans, 1990), 55; cf. Richard N. Longenecker, *Galatians* (Dallas, TX: Word, 1990), 28.

[28] Cf., Fung, *Galatians*, 298-299; Longenecker, *Galatians*, 283: "The expression *hē pistis* ('the faith') is used here as a locution for the Christian movement (cf. 1:23; see also 3:23, 25)."

"Israel of God" (Gal 6:16)[29] seem to have universal connotations.[30]

Philippians and 1 and 2 Thessalonians

Philippians contains two occurrences of *ekklēsia*, one referring to the local church (4:15) and the other to the universal church (3:6). Church members are again called "saints" (1:1; 4:21–22). In Thessalonians, the phrase "the church of the Thessalonians in God the/our Father and the Lord Jesus Christ" (1 Thess 1:1; 2 Thess 1:1) is found twice. Also mentioned are "the churches of God in Christ Jesus that are in Judea" (1 Thess 2:14) and "the churches of God" (2 Thess 1:4). The church consists of "brothers" (1 Thess 5:1, 4, 12; 2 Thess 2:1; 3:1) and "believers" (1 Thess 1:7; 2:10; 2 Thess 1:10). The universal church is not directly mentioned in the Thessalonian literature.

The Pastoral Epistles (1 Timothy, 2 Timothy, and Titus) and Philemon

The Pastoral Epistles deal with specific situations and problems facing Timothy and Titus. The term *ekklēsia* is missing in 2 Timothy. References to the troublemakers in the church (2 Tim 2:17–18; 3:1–9; 4:14–15) point to a local flavor. However, the image of the church as a household containing different types of vessels (2 Tim 2:30–21) and the references to God's firm foundation and His awareness of those who are His (2 Tim 2:19) may be more universal in nature.[31] The Letter to Titus does not employ *ekklēsia* either, but is interested in church order, namely the appointment of elders in different cities (Titus 1:5–9) and the question of how to deal with false teachers (Titus 1:10–16; 3:8–11). Titus 2:14 seems to broaden the perspective when Paul talks about Jesus "who gave himself for us to redeem us from every lawless deed, and to purify for himself a people for His own possession, zealous for good deeds."[32]

1 Timothy deals also with church order, the appointment of bishops and deacons (3:1–13), false teachers promoting ascetic practices in the church of Ephesus (1:3–11; 4:1–5; 6:20–21), and proper conduct within the Christian community (1 Tim 5–6). Here, the term *ekklēsia* is used three times (3:5, 15; 5:16). We hear about "the household of God, which is the church of the living God, the pillar and support of the truth" (3:15).

---

[29] See the discussions by Fung, *Galatians*, 310–311, who understands the phrase as "the new Israel, the new people of God–both Jews and Gentiles being included . . . "; and Longenecker, *Galatians*, 298–299.

[30] For the ecclesiological use of the metaphor of a family, see the article by John McVay in this volume.

[31] Cf. Donald Guthrie, *The Pastoral Epistles* (Grand Rapids, MI: Eerdmans, 1990), 162–163.

[32] Cf., Guthrie, *Pastoral Epistles*, 213.

This is the only reference where "church" could be understood in broader terms. However, the absence of an article before *ekklēsia* may suggest "that the local community is again primarily in mind, yet conceived of as part of the larger whole."[33] Paul's letter to Philemon speaks of a local, house church only (Phil 1:2).

These Pauline letters strongly emphasize the local church. However, in a number of them, we also find the picture of the universal church. Paul maintains that while there are local Christian congregations, there is the church in certain regions, and the universal church which we already encountered with Jesus. We now turn to the Pauline letters that emphasize the universal church.

Emphasis on the Universal Church

Ephesians

Paul's Letter to the Ephesians is the most prominent epistle stressing the universal church.[34] It was sent to the church in Ephesus and intended to be a circular or encyclical letter for the Christian churches in general, or at least the churches in Asia Minor.[35] This explains the special nature of its ecclesiology and universal scope. Paul writes about Jesus, salvation, and the church. At the end of Ephesians 1, he summarizes the life of Jesus from incarnation to glorification and closes with Jesus as the head of His church (1:20-23). The second half of the second chapter illustrates the essence of the church—emphasizing its corporate and universal aspects (2:11-30). Jesus abolished the barrier between Jews and Gentiles and made the church a holy temple. In chapter 3, Paul shows that the knowledge of God is now being made known through the church (3:10-11). And chapter 4 calls for unity. Although believers have received different spiritual gifts, they are to work towards the unity of the body of Christ (4:1-16). The relationship between husband and wife mirrors the relationship between Christ and His church (5:21-33).

"The Letter to the Ephesians represents the church as the goal of the

---

[33] Ibid., 99. That the local community is the focus of 1 Timothy 3:15 is supported by Ralph Earle, "1, 2 Timothy," *The Expositor's Bible Commentary*, ed. Frank E. Gaebelein (Grand Rapids, MI: Zondervan, 1978), 11:369, although he states that "the general church of Jesus Christ may also be in view;" Gottfried. Holtz, *Die Pastoralbriefe* (Berlin: Evangelische Verlagsanstalt, 1980), 88; and William D. Mounce, *Pastoral Epistles* (Nashville, TN: Thomas Nelson, 2000), 220-221.

[34] In almost all extant manuscripts and in all versions, the Greek title of the first prison letter of the New Testament is "To the Ephesians." Some old manuscripts lack "in Ephesus" in Ephesians 1:1 and just address the saints; e.g., Codex Vaticanus, Codex Sinaiticus, and p^{46}.

[35] For a detailed discussion, see Donald Guthrie, *New Testament Introduction* (Downers Grove, IL: InterVarsity, 1970), 508-514.

Christ event in a way that is unique in the New Testament."[36] Here, we find an explicitly Pauline doctrine of the church. In fact, in this letter, "Christology and ecclesiology are reciprocally related."[37] Ephesians presents a "christological ecclesiology."[38] The term *ekklēsia* occurs nine times in this short letter and it always refers to the universal church. The wisdom of God is "made known through the church to the rulers and the authorities in the heavenly places" (3:10; 3:21). The church is subject to Christ (5:24). He loves it and gave Himself for it (5:29, 25) to make it holy and blameless (5:27). But in the final analysis, the relationship between Christ and the church remains a mystery (5:32).

The church is the body of Christ, with Jesus as its head (1:22-23; 4:12). It is also a new person or new humanity (2:15; 4:13), a holy temple and building (2:21), God's household (2:19), and Christ's bride (5:23-32). The church has apostolic and prophetic roots with Christ as its foundation and cornerstone (2:20). Church members and the saints (1:1) are fellow citizens (2:19). Christ has brought Jews and Gentiles together (2:11-16; 3:4-6) to establish a unified church (4:3-6). Through baptism, people are incorporated into the church (4:5). Having received spiritual gifts and offices, the church is "a growing and dynamic organism"[39] (4:7-16). Its members have been saved (Eph 1) and are called to live up to their high purpose (Eph 4 and 5), demonstrating that Christ is their Lord in their household relations (Eph 5 and 6). In Ephesians, the church is not a local entity but the universal church.[40]

The term "unity" is found twice in the book (4:3, 13), but the concept is not limited to these verses. The numeral "one" is used in several places to express unity. The second chapter describes how Jesus formed His church by making two groups, Jews and Gentiles, into one (2:14-15, 16), allowing them access to God in one Spirit (2:18). In Ephesians 4:4-6, "one" is repeated seven times to stress the unity of the church: one body, one Spirit, one hope, one Lord, one faith, one baptism, one God and Father. In Ephesians 5:31, Christ's relationship with the church is compared

---

[36] Georg Strecker, *Theology of the New Testament* (New York: Walter de Gruyter, 2000), 569.

[37] Cf. Schmidt, "*Ekklēsia*," 509.

[38] Ibid., 511.

[39] Harold W. Hoehner, *Ephesians: An Exegetical Commentary* (Grand Rapids, MI: Baker, 2002), 111.

[40] Cf. Erickson, *Theology*, 1044; D. A. Carson, D. J. Moo, and L. Morris, *An Introduction to the New Testament* (Grand Rapids, MI: Zondervan, 1992), 315. See also Andrew Lincoln, *Ephesians* (Dallas, TX: Word, 1990), xcii-xcv; and Andrew T. Lincoln and A. J. M. Wedderburn, *The Theology of the Later Pauline Letters* (Cambridge: University Press, 1993), 91-126, 132-133, 137-141, 151-156, 158-161; Strecker, *Theology*, 568-575.

to marriage. As a couple becomes one flesh, so do the church and Jesus symbolically.[41] Ephesians presents the church as the one universal church united in the Father, the Son, and the Holy Spirit, i.e. the Triune God.

Colossians

The letter of Colossians is addressed "to the saints and faithful brethren in Christ who are at Colossae" (1:2) and was to be read in Laodicea (4:16). It deals with problems in the church of Colossae, especially syncretism containing Jewish and pagan ideas as well as ascetic tendencies. Colossians employs the term *ekklēsia* four times, two of which refer to a local church (4:15-16). In Colossians 1:18 and 24 the references are to the universal church which is the body of Christ and He is its head.[42] In Colossians, both the universal church and the individual congregation are on the mind of the apostle.[43] The metaphor of the body "emphasizes particularly its universal aspect."[44]

Hebrews

The Letter to the Hebrews uses *ekklēsia* twice. The first usage is found in a quotation from the Old Testament (2:12), but the second text is unique: "But you have come to Mount Zion and to the city of the living God, the heavenly Jerusalem, and to myriads of angels, to the general assembly and church of the firstborn who are enrolled in heaven, and to

---

[41] See *AdvBibComm*, 6:995; and Leander E. Keck and Victor Paul Furnish, *The Pauline Letters* (Nashville, TN: Abingdon, 1989), 128-133.

[42] Cf. G. B. Caird, *New Testament Theology* (Oxford: Clarendon Press, 1995), 215, who states: "*ekklēsia* is twice used of the universal Church without any immediate local reference." Cf. also Ladd, *Theology*, 537. On the church as the body of Christ, see Colossians 1:18, 24; 2:19; 3:15. The metaphor of the church as the body of Christ was also found in 1 Corinthians 12. However, there is a difference between this concept in 1 Corinthians and the same concept in Ephesians and Colossians. In all texts, the church is compared to a body, whereas in Ephesians and Colossians the head represents Christ, in 1 Corinthians the head represents individual members of the body. They are described as eyes and ears. 1 Corinthians 12:21: "And the eye cannot say to the hand, 'I have no need of you'; or again the head to the feet, 'I have no need of you.'" Cf. Ladd, *Theology*, 546.

[43] Ladd writes: "Paul uses the metaphor of the body to express the oneness of the church with her Lord.... Paul obviously goes beyond the ordinary analogy of the physical body and its head, for the body is pictured as deriving its nourishment and unity from the head (Col. 2:19); and the body is to grow up in every way into him who is the head (Eph. 4:15). This emphasizes ... the complete dependence of the church upon Christ for all its life and growth. This also means that the church is the instrument of Christ in the world.... This metaphor emphasizes also the unity of the church, especially since *ekklēsia* in Ephesians and Colossians refers to the universal church rather than the local congregation" (Ladd, *Theology*, 545-546).

[44] Guthrie, *New Testament Theology*, 745. On the metaphor of the church as a body, see the article by John McVay in this volume.

God, the Judge of all, and to the spirits of the righteous made perfect" (12:23). Both texts describe a congregation. "The term is thus used in v. 23a in the nontechnical sense of 'a gathering' or 'an assembly' of the redeemed people of God."[45] This ekklēsia cannot be understood as a local church on earth.

We also find references to "the people of God" (4:9; 11:25), "the house of Israel" and "My people" (8:10), and "His people" (10:30). The last two references are from Old Testament quotations. All of them should be understood in the context of the new covenant. In that case, *the people of God* "is a comprehensive term, suitable for the universal community, which embraces both Jews and Gentiles."[46]

For Paul, the church is the community of believers in a certain place and the universal church of Jesus Christ; His body, bride, people, and temple.

The Church in Other New Testament Documents

James, 1 and 2 Peter, Jude

James uses *ekklēsia* once, in the context of instructions for church elders related to praying for and anointing the sick (James 5:14). "The reference is not to a single congregation, but to the community as a whole, since this is a catholic epistle."[47] In James 2:2 the Christian assembly is called synagogue.[48]

Peter's letters, as well as Jude's epistle, do not employ the term *ekklēsia*. In 1 Peter the church consists of the "elect" who are "strangers" in the world (1 Pet 1:1). In chapter 2, Christ is the foundation of the spiritual house and believers, as "living stones," forming "a spiritual house for a holy priesthood" (1 Pet 2:4–5).[49] In 1 Peter 2:9 the church is "a chosen race, a royal priesthood, a holy nation, a people belonging to God." Along with these privileges comes the responsibility to proclaim "the wonderful deeds of him who called you out of darkness into his marvelous light."

---

[45] William L. Lane, *Hebrews 9–13* (Dallas, TX: Word, 1991), 468. For further information, see 467–471.

[46] Donald Guthrie, *Hebrews: An Introduction and Commentary* (Downers Grove, IL: InterVarsity, 1983), 115; cf. 176, where he explains the phrase "the house of Israel" and proposes that it is "an expression ideally inclusive of the whole people of God."

[47] Schmidt, "*Ekklēsia*," 513.

[48] Cf. Douglas J. Moo, *James* (Grand Rapids, MI: Eerdmans, 1993), 89–90; Ralph P. Martin, *James* (Waco, TX: Word, 1988), 61.

[49] John H. Elliott, *A Home for the Homeless: Sociological Exegesis of 1 Peter; Its Situation and Strategy* (Philadelphia, PA: Fortress, 1981), 148–150, 220–233, 282–288.

Gentiles who believe in Jesus have now become the people of God (1 Pet 2:10). The church is "the brotherhood" and the "brotherhood throughout the world" (1 Pet 2:17; 5:9)—a family. The existence of elders points to a degree of organization within the early church (1 Pet 5:13).

1 Peter belongs to the general epistles. These letters are not addressed to one particular church, but instead are sent to many churches. 1 Peter is for believers throughout Pontus, Galatia, Cappadocia, Asia, and Bithynia. The terminology used in 1 Peter, such as "people of God" and "flock," have a universal character in other New Testament writings and seem to have the same meaning here. It has been suggested that "'the flock' of God is universal in scope."[50] Obviously, the famous text about the priesthood of all believers in 1 Peter 2:9 must also be understood universally. Israel's privileges, recorded in Exodus 19:6, are now applied to all Gentile Christians. Finally, the "brotherhood throughout the world" (1 Pet 5:9)[51] points to the universal church of God.

Johannine Letters and Revelation

The term *ekklēsia* is found only in 3 John 1:6, 9, and 10. In all cases, it refers to the local congregation. The second letter is addressed "to the chosen lady and to her children whom I love in truth" (2 John 1:1). This lady receives greetings from her "chosen sister" (2 John 1:13). Some understand her to be an individual, whereas others prefer to speak about a church—a local church.[52]

Revelation places strong emphasis on the victory of the church.[53] The term *ekklēsia* is found 20 times and is used in both singular and plural. In each case *ekklēsia* stands for groups of believers. The Apocalypse contains a letter frame (chapters 1-3 and chapter 22b) in which all the references to *ekklēsia* are found (nineteen out of twenty are found in Revelation 1-3, and one in its conclusion).[54] The plural is only used in Revelation 1, while the singular predominates chapters 2 and 3, addressing the respective local church. However, at the end of each message, the formula "He who has an ear, let him hear what the Spirit says to the churches" connects the churches with one another.

In these passages, we hear about local congregations indicating

---

[50] J. Ramsey Michaels, *1 Peter* (Waco, TX: Word 1988), 286.

[51] Cf. Ibid., 301.

[52] Cf. D. A. Carson, D. J. Moo, and L. Morris, *An Introduction*, 451; John Drane, *Introducing the New Testament* (Minneapolis, MN: Fortress Press, 2001), 451.

[53] Cf. Ekkehardt Mueller, "Introduction to the Ecclesiology of Revelation," *JATS* 12 (2001): 199-215.

[54] Revelation 1:4, 11, 20; 2:1, 7- 8, 11-12 ,17-18, 23, 29; 3:1, 6 -7, 13-14, 22; 22:16.

that Revelation often regards the church as a local entity. However, the number seven and the mix of the singular and plural forms of *ekklēsia* in each message may point to the completeness and interdependence of the churches, telling us that there are not only local congregations but also a universal church. In this case, the seven churches would represent the universal church in different eras of church history. This is more evident in the apocalyptic part of Revelation (Rev 4–22a). In spite of their shortcomings, the seven churches are still God's church. The majority of them may have to face temporal judgment, but they are not yet totally separated from Him. Thus, the term *ekklēsia* in Revelation always points to some sort of relationship with God. It also always refers to the *ekklesia militans*, the church involved in battle, which toward the end of the book is depicted as the triumphant church.

In the main body of the Apocalypse, the term *ekklēsia* is replaced by symbols such as the woman clothed with the sun (Rev 12), the holy city (Rev 11:2), and the 144,000 (Rev 7:4–8; 14:1–5). These entities underline the universal nature of the church. Other terms related to the church or representing the church are the lampstands (1:20); fellow servants, brothers, servants (7:3; 12:10; 19:2, 5; 22:3, 6); priests and a kingdom (1:6; 5:10; 20:6); those who overcome (2–3; 15:2; 21:7); the remnant (2:24; 12:17); those in white clothes (3:4–5; 6:11; 7:9, 13); the saints (5:8; 8:3–4); those who are called, chosen, and are faithful (17:14); the great multitude (7:9–17); My/His people (18:4; 21:3); and the bride (21:9; 22:17). Revelation also presents a counterpart to the church: Babylon, the great harlot, also named the great city (Rev 16:9; 17:1, 18; 18:16). Babylon persecutes and kills true followers of God, but it will be judged. Finally, only the bride of the Lamb, the holy city, New Jerusalem will remain. Babylon and the true church are universal entities.

Revelation also recognizes the remnant, especially the end-time remnant. The conflict between the Satanic trinity and the end-time remnant is described in Revelation 12–14, where Satan wages war against this remnant. He also uses the sea beast and the beast coming out of the earth in his attempt to annihilate them. The picture is quite bleak. It seems as if none of the true believers could survive. Yet, they are depicted with Jesus on Mt. Zion. Revelation 15–22 reports the consequences of conflict between God's remnant church and the Satanic trinity/Babylon.[55]

Thus, in Revelation there are local churches and there is a universal church. Jesus walks among the churches. He is very close to them and cares for them, sending them messages of rebuke, recognition, and com-

---

[55] Cf. Ekkehardt Mueller, "The End Time Remnant in Revelation," *JATS* 11 (2000): 188–204.

fort. He loves the church. God's church has certain characteristics and tasks, encounters internal and external difficulties, and receives divine appeals and promises. The church in Revelation is the church militant and triumphant. It is visible and yet also partially invisible. It is the local church, but especially a universal entity. There is a strong emphasis on the end-time church.

The church is a community of believers. It stands in close relationship to God and Christ. Although in many places in the New Testament the local church is emphasized, the idea of a universal church was never lost. It is found in many Pauline epistles, but especially in Ephesians. It again emerges in some of the general or catholic letters of the New Testament. Both the local aspects as well as the universal are strongly emphasized in the last book of the Bible. The local church and the universal church should find its proper place in any biblical ecclesiology.

The Relationship Between the Local and Universal Churches

Suggested Models of Church Government

New Testament teachings on the local and universal church have several implications for us today, one of which is church government. There are four basic types of church government: episcopal, presbyterian, congregational, and non-governmental.[56] The most highly developed system of episcopal government is found in the Roman Catholic Church. Its strict hierarchical structure leaves little or no room for the priesthood of all believers. On the other side of the spectrum, we find congregationalism and non-government, in which individualism on a personal or local level prevails. From an Adventist perspective, Raoul Dederen presents a much more balanced view:

> The Scriptures do not warrant the existence of an episcopal system, structuring the church along monarchial, if not imperial, lines. Nor do they call for a pattern in which each church or congregation is the complete church, independent of every other, rejecting any authoritative organizational structure over the local congregation. It appears rather that the biblical data set forth a basic representative form of church government in which much is made of the priesthood of all believers and of the gifts of grace bestowed by the Spirit, while recognizing the authority of repre-

---

[56] Cf. Dederen, "Autorität der Gemeinde: Ihr Urspung, Wesen und Wirken,"*Die Gemeinde und ihr Auftrag*, ed. J. Mager (Lüneburg: Saatkorn-Verlag, 1994), 59; *Idem*, "Church," 553–554; Erickson, *Theology*, 1080–1097; L. Morris, "Church Government," *EDT*, 238–241.

sentative bodies.[57]

This brings us to the question of the local church and the fullness of the church.

The Fullness of God's Church

Even if we can agree that there exists both local churches and one universal church, that local churches are the church of God in a certain time and locality, and that the universal church is more than the sum of local churches, the question still remains: Is the local church the fullness of the church? As we already demonstrated, in the latter New Testament writings there is a stronger emphasis on the universality of the church than in the earlier. The climax is found in the Book of Revelation. One may wonder whether if from 60 A.D. to the end of the first century, the climate among local churches had grown worse and a stronger emphasis on the universal church had become necessary. At least in Corinth and Rome, factions of Gentile Christians were found within the church who may have boasted and looked down upon the Jewish Christians.

Although the local church exerts authority when it comes to church membership and other matters,[58] the New Testament is concerned that the different churches work together and that there is unity within the universal church. Just as an individual Christian cannot live in self-chosen isolation, so a Christian church is part of the sisterhood of churches. Living one's own life separate from others is, to say the least, unhealthy. Christian churches in a certain area form the church of that area and are also part of the larger body of Christ.[59] With regard to our question, the local church is the church of Christ in a specific time and place, and as such it is complete. On the other hand, a number of considerations suggest that the local church is not the full expression of the church. There are elements and ministries that transcend the boundaries of the local congregation.

First, the church as the body of Christ is not complete if the church of God is only located in one place. The existence of a universal church—the body of Christ with Jesus as its head—implies that separation of churches from each other cannot be God's will, unless the issue is apostasy. The Corinthians were reprimanded because of their independence: "Was it from you that the word of God *first* went forth? Or has it come to you only?"(1 Cor 14:36). On the contrary, the New Testament stresses unity.

---

[57] Ibid., 554.

[58] Cf. Dederen, "Church," 560.

[59] Cf. *idem.*, "Autorität der Gemeinde," 59.

Therefore, in the New Testament, churches exchanged greetings (Rom 16:16); shared documents sent by the apostles (Col 4:16); were hospitable to traveling brothers (1 Pet 4:9; John 1:5–10); and supported persecuted Christians who were not members of their respective local church (Acts 28:13–15).[60] It was particularly important for the local churches to help each other during times of persecution. Aquila and Priscilla moved from Rome to Corinth (Rom 16:3; Acts 18:2) and were involved with the Christian church in both places.

Second, the New Testament teaches that God has given to His church different spiritual gifts and functions (1 Cor 12). Yet, not all gifts are found in one local church. Some gifts surpass the local level. This is true in the case of administrative gifts such as the gift of apostleship. It is also true for the gift of prophecy. In Acts 11:28, several prophets came from Jerusalem to Antioch. One of them, Agabus, predicted a great famine. This prophecy was fulfilled some time later. Agabus not only served his own local church, but also another church. Paul and Barnabas appointed elders (Acts 14:23). Timothy and Titus did the same (Titus 1:5). Their sphere of influence surpassed the local level, but the local church was helped through their ministry and did not reject them. There was a ministry not limited to the local church.

Third, certain issues of theology and Christian lifestyle cannot be solved at a local level. Such a situation is portrayed in Acts 15. Judaizers had come from Jerusalem and had caused problems in Antioch, confusing some church members. Paul and Barnabas were sent as delegates of the church of Antioch to a council in Jerusalem (Acts 15:2). Larger issues and questions related to doctrinal matters were best discussed at a level more encompassing than that of an individual church.[61] "Major assemblies that address matters pertaining to the church in general and that concern the preservation of unity, therefore exercising authority on a broader and more extended scale than a local congregation, are unquestionably warranted by Scripture."[62]

Fourth, in the New Testament, local churches received directives from outside their specific area. The actions of the Jerusalem Council were not just recommendations; they were meant to be binding.[63] In Acts 16:4 Luke reports, "Now while they were passing through the cities, they

---

[60] Cf. Ibid., 60.

[61] Cf. *Seventh-day Adventists Believe: An Exposition of the Fundamental Beliefs of the Seventh-day Adventist Church* (Silver Spring, MD: Ministerial Association of the General Conference, 2005), 174–175.

[62] Dederen, "Church," 561.

[63] Ibid., "Autorität der Gemeinde," 63.

were delivering the decrees which had been decided upon by the apostles and elders who were in Jerusalem, for them to observe." The letters of the New Testament contain many exhortations and admonitions expected to be taken seriously by local churches. The rejection of the gospel or the alteration of the gospel received from the apostles was so serious that those being involved were *anathema* (Gal 1:8–9; cf. Heb 6:4–6). Paul states: "And so I direct in all the churches" (1 Cor 7:17).

Fifth, the Great Commission (Matt 28:18–20) cannot be only fulfilled by a local church. Resources and personnel of local churches must be pulled together in order to proclaim the gospel on a worldwide scale. In 1 Corinthians 9:1–14, Paul claims the right as an apostle and missionary to be financially supported by local churches. This seems to be a reference to tithing. The Philippians supported him, although, at that time, he was not in Philippi (Phil 4:10–19). The Colossians sent Epaphras to him as a coworker (Col 1:7; 4:12). The Great Commission requires more than what a local congregation can accomplish alone. Only the universal church is equipped to undertake such a comprehensive task assigned to the church by the Lord. This also applies to the proclamation of the Three Angels' Messages of Revelation 14:6–12. The challenge to reach every person with God's final message is enormous.[64]

Sixth, there are, in addition to mission outreach, other ecclesiological tasks that surpass the capacity of a local congregation. Take, for example, the collection for church members in Jerusalem (1 Cor 16:1–4; 2 Cor 8–9). Local congregations supported their fellow believers. They saved money, collected from the congregations, and a delegation took it to Jerusalem. Today, worldwide humanitarian work challenges the church to help as Jesus had helped (cf. Acts 10:38). Humanitarian work applies to church needs across the world as well as those of non-church members. By participating in large-scale projects around the world, the local church supplies experts, support staff, and financial means.

Seventh, the formation of the canon of the New Testament can probably be attributed to the fact that there was—aside from other factors—a concept of the universal church among local congregations. Churches did not just keep letters sent to them by an apostle. They shared them with other churches that apparently copied them. This also illustrates the incompleteness of local churches. If they had to only rely on their own

---

[64] Dederen, "Church," 563, writes: "The New Testament insists on the universality or catholicity of the church.... The church is meant to embrace all nations (Matt 28:19; cf. Rev 14:6). It is not bound to a particular time or place, but encompasses believers of all generations, nations, and cultures.... The church teaches universally and from first to last all the teachings Christ has commanded (Matt 28:20).... The universal nature of the church has clear missionary implications."

correspondence, some churches would not have received any part of the New Testament and others only a limited number.

One's view on the relationship between the local and universal churches is determined, to a large degree, by the form of church government one chooses. Obviously, not all forms of church government are equal and not all reflect the data found in the New Testament equally. A strictly hierarchical and episcopal approach as well as a congregational or a non-government one, would clash with some ecclesiological elements present in Scripture. Admitting that the local church is God's church in its time and place does not mean that the local church completely represents the fullness of the church.

Implications for an Adventist Ecclesiology

Seventh-day Adventists and the Universal Church

Although the Seventh-day Adventist church is a worldwide church with many local churches, Adventists do not claim to be Christ's universal church. The universal church is broader than any denomination. It is visible and invisible insofar as it consists of those who believe in Jesus and follow him.[65] This particular theological issue is heightened if we take into consideration apostasy among Christians, addressed poignantly in the Book of Revelation. The pure church of Revelation 12 is contrasted with the "harlot" of Revelation 17, Babylon the great city, which in turn is contrasted with the bride of the Lamb, the holy city or the New Jerusalem of Revelation 21 and 22. In the first century, the universal church may have been quite visible, it is much more difficult and complex to see it, for instance, during the Medieval Ages.

Therefore, Adventists do not limit the concept of God's true church to their own denomination, nor do they automatically extend it to other Christian churches. God's true church consists of those individuals who truly believe in him. God knows them. Adventists, on the other hand, claim that they are God's special visible end-time remnant of Revelation 12:17 and chapters 12–14. This remnant has a local as well as a universal character (Rev 2:24 and 12:17).

Although today a worldwide church cannot be easily equated with the universal church, it seems to us that the New Testament principles gov-

---

[65] Dederen, "Church," 546, states correctly: "The church, according to the New Testament, is not an invisible entity, nor a mental image.... At the same time the church can be described as having an invisible dimension..." See also Angel Manuel Rodriguez, ed., *Toward a Theology of the Remnant: An Adventist Ecclesiological Perspective* (Silver Spring, MD: Biblical Research Institute, 2009), where this question is also addressed.

erning the relationship between local churches and the universal church can and must be applied to the worldwide Adventist church and its local congregations. The New Testament also reminds us that the Christian churches in a certain area are the Christian church of that area. By analogy local Adventist churches throughout the world are an expression of the worldwide Seventh-day Adventist Church.

Recognizing the Importance of the Local Church

We should value the local congregation. It is at the local level that the most engagement with the world occurs. It is in the local church that the real growth takes place and lives are transformed. Decisions must be made by involving the local church, and not by bypassing it.

However, if the church administration becomes the *real* church, the priesthood of all believers is forgotten and the administration assumes functions not their own. Some people tend to focus so much on the local church that whatever transcends it is neglected, forgotten, or rejected. A specific local congregation teds to become, so to speak, the center of the world. The result would be congregationalism. In such cases, personal freedom and self-actualization have become the highest good, ruling out everything else. Congregationalism is always a potential threat to the unity and mission of the world church.

Individualism and the Worldwide Church

We should acknowledge and accept the worldwide nature of the church. The Western world's individualism can sometimes make it difficult for church members or local churches to work together with the worldwide church. In such cases, it can be difficult to submit to the decisions of a worldwide church council, especially if one's opinions differ from those of the global church.[66] The willingness to work together with church leaders at all levels within the church is important in the New Testament (Heb 13:17; 1 Cor 16:16; 1 Thess 5:12). Scripture challenges us to give up self-sufficiency, practice humility, and foster unity. Although the local church is God's church, it is not fully complete in itself. It finds its fullness in union with the world church. But all is to be done in love and respect, serving one another as the Spirit enables each. The words of Peter are very appropriate today:

> Therefore, I exhort the elders among you, as your fellow elder and witness of the sufferings of Christ, and a partaker also of the

---

[66] Cf., for instance, the question of the ordination of women to the ministry.

glory that is to be revealed, shepherd the flock of God among you, exercising oversight not under compulsion, but voluntarily, according to the will of God; and not for sordid gain, but with eagerness; nor yet as lording it over those allotted to your charge, but proving to be examples to the flock. And when the Chief Shepherd appears, you will receive the unfading crown of glory. You younger men, likewise, be subject to your elders; and all of you, clothe yourselves with humility toward one another, for God is opposed to the proud, but gives grace to the humble (1 Pet 5:1–5).

Conclusion

The New Testament contains a considerable amount of data on the subject of the church. We were interested in one topic, namely what the New Testament teaches about the local and the universal church and how they relate to each other. We have found that different terms are used to refer to the church. A crucial one is *ekklēsia*. It describes the local congregation in the singular and plural, the church/churches in an area, and the universal church, the body of Christ. Both expressions of the church, the local and the universal, are needed. Although the local is not in all respects the complete church, we enjoy fellowship with Christ and with brothers and sisters on the local level, in different churches worldwide. The right balance between the local and the universal, between the local and the worldwide church, belongs to the very essence of the church.

CHAPTER 3

BIBLICAL METAPHORS FOR THE CHURCH: BUILDING BLOCKS FOR ECCLESIOLOGY

John McVay

When I teach courses or workshops on the church, I often ask participants to write down their own definitions of "church." The ones they produce are usually impressive in their variety. Some write definitions like this: "The church is the remnant church of Bible prophecy with unshakeable foundations." Others might write, "The church is a place where I connect with friends and find fellowship."

What metaphors lie behind such descriptions? And how can such understandings be enriched through careful, prayerful appropriation of the Bible's own metaphors for the church? The purpose of this essay is twofold: 1) To survey biblical metaphors for the church and explore ways to analyze and understand them; 2) To reflect on how the biblical metaphors for the church could—and should—impact our thinking.

Introducing Metaphors for the Church

In his classic treatment, *Images of the Church in the New Testament*, Paul S. Minear catalogued ninety-six images of the church in the New Testament.[1] Minear sifted out thirty-two "minor images" (e.g., the salt of the earth; a letter from Christ) and grouped remaining images under the rubrics "People of God," "The New Creation," "The Fellowship in Faith,"

---

[1] Paul S. Minear, *Images of the Church in the New Testament* (Philadelphia, PA: Westminster, 1960).

and "The Body of Christ." While Minear's taxonomy is helpful, a different organization is adopted here. I have emphasized those metaphors that are present both in the earlier and the later letters of Paul, the apostle's sustained interest suggesting they are worthy of close attention. I propose to treat five clusters of biblical metaphors for the church:

1. Corporal: The Church as Body
2. Architectural: The Church as Building/Temple
3. Agricultural: The Church as Plant/Field/Vineyard/Vine
4. Martial: The Church as Army
5. Familial and Marital: The Church as Family and as Bride

In each case, I shall discuss the background (usually Old Testament), survey the uses of the cluster in the New Testament, examine selected passages more closely in view of the method described below, and emphasize the contributions the cluster makes to a well-rounded and vibrant understanding of the church.

Analyzing Metaphors for the Church

Exegetes and theologians have sometimes operated with a dated set of presuppositions concerning metaphor—presuppositions that denigrate the use of metaphor.[2] In the place of these, a distilled set of concepts about metaphor provide a truer perspective. The first of these ideas is that *metaphor is not mere adornment of language*. Metaphor is not "a sort of happy trick with words" or "a grace or ornament *added* to the power of language." Instead, metaphor is "the omnipresent principle of language," since language itself is metaphoric and metaphor simply illustrates the workings of human language and thought as a whole.[3]

Second, *the meaning of metaphor cannot be adequately or fully paraphrased*. In this sense, metaphor—and especially poetic metaphor—is "irreducible." "The richer and more suggestive a metaphor is, the more impossible it is to spell out explicitly all the similarities that underlie it."[4] We should not be surprised that our explanations of biblical metaphors

---

[2] See the elaboration of this point in Ian Paul, "Metaphor and Exegesis," *After Pentecost: Language and Biblical Interpretation*, ed. Craig G. Bartholomew, Colin Greene, and Karl Möller (Grand Rapids, MI: Zondervan, 2001), 389–390.

[3] I. A. Richards, *The Philosophy of Rhetoric* (London: Oxford University Press, 1936), 90, 92.

[4] William P. Alston, *Philosophy of Language* (Englewood Cliffs, NJ: Prentice Hall, 1964), 100–101. See also Edmund P. Clowney, "Interpreting the Biblical Models of the Church: A Hermeneutical Deepening of Ecclesiology," *Biblical Interpretation and the Church: Text and Context*, ed. D. A. Carson (Exeter: Paternoster, 1984), 71.

are not as convincing or durable as the metaphors themselves.

Third, *the communicative impact of metaphor should be appreciated* (rather than depreciated). Too often, in biblical studies and theology, statements regarded as "literally true" are set over against those thought to be "only metaphorically true." However, "to say that a statement is metaphorical is a comment on its manner of expression and not necessarily on the truth of that which is expressed." If we were to warn someone, "Watch out! That's a live wire!", we would not be inclined to add, "Of course, that is only metaphorically true." It is both true and expressed with metaphor.[5]

The fourth idea is closely related: *Complex and "mixed" metaphors are, similarly, to be acknowledged and studied rather than overlooked and devalued.* From a classical perspective, occurrences of metaphor should demonstrate harmony and congruity of metaphorical elements as well as visual clarity. From such a perspective, some uses of metaphor within the Bible do not measure up and, as a result, are devalued or dismissed. A more enlightened view demonstrates a willingness to explore biblical metaphor and appreciate its complexity.

With these four ideas clearly in mind, we may turn to some definitions and terms that will aid in disciplined analysis of biblical metaphors for the church.[6] How can we identify an occurrence of metaphor? Soskice provides a helpful, working definition: "Metaphor is that figure of speech whereby we speak about one thing in terms which are seen to be suggestive of another."[7]

Once we have identified such a case where, say, "the church" is spoken about in terms of a "temple," how can we identify the components of metaphor and ponder their interaction? Richards' terms, "tenor" and "vehicle," have proved enduring ones to identify respectively "the underlying idea or principal subject which the vehicle or figure means" and the basic figure which is used to carry the "tenor."[8] Richards illustrates these

---

[5] Janet M. Soskice, *Metaphor and Religious Language* (Oxford: Clarendon, 1985), 70. See also George B. Caird, *The Language and Imagery of the Bible* (London: Duckworth, 1980), 131–132.

[6] The Wikipedia articles on "Metaphor" and "Conceptual Metaphor" provide a helpful review of wider concepts of metaphor: Wikipedia contributors, "Metaphor" and "Conceptual Metaphor," *Wikipedia, The Free Encyclopedia*, http://en.wikipedia.org/w/index.php?title=Metaphor&oldid=47789471 and http://en.wikipedia.org/w/index.php?title=Conceptual_metaphor&oldid=46813884 (accessed March 19, 2006).

[7] Soskice, *Metaphor*, 15.

[8] Richards, *Rhetoric*, 95–96. It may be helpful to compare Cuddon's summary of Richards' terms: "By 'tenor' he meant the purport or general drift of thought regarding the subject of a metaphor; by 'vehicle', the image which embodies the tenor" (J. A. Cuddon, *A Dictionary of Literary Terms and Literary Theory* [Cambridge: Blackwell, 1991], 959).

terms by referring to Shakespeare's phrase from *Othello*, "Steep'd me in poverty to the very lips," where he identifies the "tenor" as poverty and the "vehicle" as "the sea or vat in which Othello is to be steeped."[9]

In addition to being able to identify the "tenor" and "vehicle" of an instance of metaphor, two additional concepts help us evaluate the mechanics of metaphor. First, *how full is the metaphor?* Full metaphors explicitly reveal the following (using the temple metaphor of Eph 2:19–22 as an example): 1) The tenor or object of the comparison (e.g., you, the church); 2) The vehicle or image of the comparison (e.g., temple); 3) The "ground" of the comparison (e.g., God dwells in you as a deity is thought to inhabit a temple). However, metaphors may be abbreviated, with one or two of these elements being implicit.[10]

Second, *to what extent is the metaphor guarded?* Metaphors are "frequently guarded, so as to take advantage of their values without courting their dangers." Such guarding occurs when "the metaphor is hedged about with protective rules and auxiliary explanations" and so "becomes less rich in meaning, but safer."[11] Among the ways an author can guard a metaphor is to express it fully, spelling out the tenor, vehicle, and ground of the comparison.

To understand a metaphor, though, we need to do more than ponder its mechanics, the pieces of the metaphor. We also need to consider how those components interact to create meaning. How do the tenor and vehicle interact? And what meaning(s) does this interaction yield? Here, another term is helpful, that of "associated commonplaces."[12] Imagine reading the metaphor, "Men are wolves." We would know that the writer is speaking about "men" in terms of "wolves." What "associated commonplaces" might the writer and hearers share about wolves? We could construct quite a list including that wolves run in packs, are voracious hunters, are wily and sly, etc. The more we know about the "associated commonplaces" attached to the vehicle, "wolves," the more likely we are to understand the metaphor and to be able to analyze the context to know which of these "associated commonplaces" may be active there.

A similar need confronts us as we interpret the Bible. We need to carefully consider the meaning of the metaphors within their literary and

---

[9] Richards, *Rhetoric*, 104–105.

[10] I am adapting the concepts of Jan de Waard, "Biblical Metaphors and Their Translation," *BT* 25 (1974): 109–111.

[11] Monroe C. Beardsley, "Metaphor," *Encyclopedia of Philosophy*, ed. P. Edwards (New York: Macmillan, 1967), 286.

[12] I borrow the term "associated commonplaces" from Max Black, *Models and Metaphors: Studies in Language and Philosophy* (Ithaca, NY: Cornell University Press, 1962), 40.

cultural contexts. "A given metaphor is capable of very diverse uses; the setting becomes as decisive for its meaning as the image taken by itself."[13] Metaphors for the church "need to be understood in their formative settings, in their social and religious contexts of origin."[14] Ellen White's exhortation applies here:

> Let us in imagination go back to that scene, and, as we sit with the disciples on the mountainside, enter into the thoughts and feelings that filled their hearts. Understanding what the words of Jesus meant to those who heard them, we may discern in them a new vividness and beauty, and may also gather for ourselves their deeper lessons.[15]

With the above concepts in view, a set of evaluative questions may be offered to guide the study of biblical metaphors for the church:

1. *Identification.* Is a specific biblical statement about the church an example of metaphor?

2. *Mechanics.* Assuming the statement constitutes a metaphor, what is its "tenor" and "vehicle"? How full is it? In what ways is the metaphor guarded?

3. *Interaction of Components.* What "associated commonplaces" might have occurred to the author and his audience? How many of these ideas does the context indicate are active? How do these "associated commonplaces" contribute to the understanding of the church?

4. *Function.* How does the metaphor function in this context? Why does the author employ it?[16]

Five Clusters of Metaphors for the Church

Corporal: The Church as Body

Of the clusters of metaphors employed to describe the church, the use of the human body is especially important.[17] Paul seems to draw on

---

[13] Minear, *Images*, 30.

[14] John Driver, *Images of the Church in Mission* (Scottdale, PA: Herald, 1997), 17.

[15] Ellen G. White, *Thoughts from the Mount of Blessings* (Washington, DC: Review and Herald, 1955), 1.

[16] This basic outline of metaphor analysis may be compared with benefit to the more detailed pattern offered by Peter W. Macky, *The Centrality of Metaphors to Biblical Thought: A Method for Interpreting the Bible* (Lewiston, NY: Mellen, 1990), with special attention to pp. 278–297.

[17] An Adventist who has explored this metaphor is Raul Quiroga, "El cuerpo como metáfora de la unidad doctrinal por los dones," *La iglesia, cuerpo de Cristo y plenitud de Dios*, ed. Mario Veloso

the frequent, Greco-Roman use of the body metaphor for the society or the state that harks back to the Aesop fable, "The Belly and the Feet:"

> The belly and the feet were arguing about their importance, and when the feet kept saying that they were so much stronger that they even carried the stomach around, the stomach replied, "But, my good friends, if I didn't take in food, you wouldn't be able to carry anything."[18]

1 Corinthians 10:17; 11:29. In the earlier epistles, Paul employs THE CHURCH IS A BODY[19] to describe the church in 1 Corinthians (10:17; 11:29; 12:12–27) and Romans (12:4–5). The first two uses in 1 Corinthians (10:17; 11:29) are in the context of a discussion of the Lord's Supper. Issuing a warning against partaking of the "cup" and "table" of demons (1 Cor 10:1–22, esp. vv. 14–22), Paul writes, "Is not the cup of thanksgiving for which we give thanks a participation in the blood of Christ? And is not the bread that we break a participation in the body (*sōma*) of Christ? Because there is one loaf, we, who are many, are one body (*sōma*), for we all partake of the one loaf" (vv. 16–17).[20] The uses of the body metaphor in 1 Corinthians 10:17 and 11:29 disclose a profound unity among believers, one rooted in God's action in Christ. Participation in the body of Christ through the "one loaf" and Christ's presence at the Lord's Supper joins believers together as "one body."[21]

1 Corinthians 12:12–27 and Romans 12:4–5. The uses of the body metaphor in 1 Corinthians 12:12–27 and Romans 12:4–5 are quite similar. In both cases, the body metaphor is offered in the context of affirming the smooth function and appropriate valuation of spiritual gifts. Romans

---

(Argentina: Editorial Universidad Adventista del Plata, 2006), 151–172; he only examines the connection between the metaphor and the gifts of the Spirit.

[18] The translation is from Lloyd W. Daly, *Aesop without Morals: The Famous Fables, and a Life of Aesop* (New York: Thomas Yoseloff, 1961), 148. For more detailed discussion, see John K. McVay, "The Human Body as Social and Political Metaphor in Stoic Literature and Early Christian Writers," *BASP* 37 (2000): 135–147.

[19] I adopt the standard of Lakoff and Johnson in capitalizing a summary statement of metaphors as a way of identifying them clearly. George Lakoff and Mark Johnson, *Metaphors We Live By* (Chicago, IL: University of Chicago Press, 1980).

[20] All Bible texts are quoted from the NIV unless otherwise noted.

[21] The use of *sōma* in 1 Corinthians 11:29 is debated. Is it eucharistic (failing to distinguish sacramental from common food), christological ("he fails to distinguish the Lord's body in the bread which he eats"), or ecclesial in the sense of failing "to discern and to give due weight to the church, assembled at the Supper as the body of Christ"? C. K. Barrett, *A Commentary on the First Epistle to the Corinthians* (London: Adam & Charles Black, 1971), 274.

12:4–5 serves nicely as a summary: "Just as each of us has one body with many members, and these members do not all have the same function, so in Christ we who are many form one body, and each member belongs to all the others." The accent here is on the need for healthy relationships among church members where due respect is given to the diversity of gifts in the context of treasuring every member, especially those who are "weaker," "less honorable," or "unpresentable" (1 Cor 12:22–23).

At this point, it is helpful to introduce an additional term used in the study of metaphor: sub-metaphors. Sub-metaphors are related to the overall metaphor as parts to the whole. So, in 1 Corinthians 12:12–27, the various "members" (*melē*) or body parts may be identified as sub-metaphors of the wider body metaphor: foot, hand, ear, eye, nose ("the sense of smell," v. 17), head, weaker parts, less honorable parts, unpresentable parts, presentable parts. While these are not supplied with direct referents, there is an implied, general identity with various gifts listed in verses 28–31.

Much like Aesop's fable, the function of the metaphor is to highlight the interdependence of church members who have been arranged in the ecclesial body just as God intended (1 Cor 12:18). Ideally, when this interdependence is realized and actualized there will be "no division in the body." Instead, the various parts will "have equal concern for each other. If one part suffers, every part suffers with it; if one part is honored, every part rejoices with it" (1 Cor 12:25–26).

Ephesians 4:1–16. Ephesians 4:1–16 represents the most detailed use of the body metaphor in the later writings of Paul. As in Romans 12, the passage focuses on the role of the "gifts" (*domata*, v. 8) as they relate to the theme of unity. It is instructive to compare the use of the body metaphor in Ephesians 4 with the earlier one in 1 Corinthians 12. In both passages, the body metaphor is employed in relation to a discussion of spiritual gifts. In 1 Corinthians 12, while God arranges the gifts in the body (vv. 18, 24, 28), it is the Spirit who gives the gifts (vv. 4–11). In Ephesians, the gifts are given by the triumphant Christ (Eph 4:8, 11).

As compared to 1 Corinthians 12, Ephesians 4 provides referents for a shorter list of body parts. Christ is the "head" (*kephalē*, v. 15; in 1 Cor 12 the head is not a particularly significant body part), ministers of the word (v. 11) are "ligaments" (*haphē* (s.), v. 16),[22] and other church members are "parts" (*meroi*, v. 16). In Ephesians 4, Paul is anxious to assert that ministers of the Word "are to be highly valued as gifts from the exalted Christ."[23]

---

[22] I follow the technical sense of the term defended in *BDAG* 155, J. Armitage Robinson, *St. Paul's Epistle to the Ephesians* (London: Macmillan, 1904), 186; Gerhard Schneider, "*Haphē* joint, ligament," *EDNT*, 1:181.

[23] Andrew T. Lincoln, *Paradise Now and Not Yet: Studies in the Role of the Heavenly Dimension in*

He also innovates by introducing the concept of the growth of the body, a thought that permeates verses 11–16.

An additional and important function of the body metaphor in Ephesians 4 is nicely highlighted by citing the closely related passage, Colossians 2:18–19:

> Do not let anyone who delights in false humility and the worship of angels disqualify you for the prize. Such a person goes into great detail about what he has seen, and his unspiritual mind puffs him up with idle notions. He has lost connection with the Head [*kephalē*], from whom the whole body [*sōma*], supported and held together by its ligaments and sinews [*haphōn kai sundesmōn*], grows as God causes it to grow.

Paul worries that some may not be "holding fast" to Christ as Head (Col 2:19) and that others may, in refusing the resources He offers, miss that growth and maturity, which finds its source, direction, and goal in Christ, the Head (Eph 4:11–16).

To survey the uses of the body metaphor is to be reminded that biblical metaphors for the church are not static images. "... 'the body of Christ' is not a single expression with an unchanging meaning. Paul's thought remains extremely flexible and elastic."[24] Close attention to the use in a specific context is essential to both the interpretation and appropriation of the metaphor.

The metaphor THE CHURCH IS A BODY/THE BODY OF CHRIST reminds us that healthy relationships among members and cohesion to Christ are essential for the church. While the missional significance of the metaphor is more assumed than detailed, "the thrust of these passages is one of activity. Christ directs, controls, and energizes the members ... so that they may serve his purpose in the world. Thus part of the church's reason for being is that *it may minister to the world as Christ's agent.*"[25]

Agricultural: The Church as Plant/Field/Vineyard/Vine

In the Old Testament, the grapevine and the vineyard symbolize Israel, pictured by the Psalmist as "a vine from Egypt" that God transplanted and nurtured in the Promised Land before judging Israel as vineyard by

---

Paul's Thought with Special Reference to His Eschatology (Grand Rapids, MI: Baker, 1991), 162.

[24] Minear, *Images*, 173–174.

[25] Ralph P. Martin, *The Family and the Fellowship: New Testament Images of the Church* (Grand Rapids, MI: Eerdmans, 1980), 123.

breaking down its walls (Ps 80). Isaiah crafts an extended parable, explicitly using the metaphor ISRAEL IS A VINEYARD ("The vineyard of the LORD Almighty is the house of Israel, and the men of Judah are the garden of his delight," Isa 5:7) and emphasizing God's care for the vineyard (vv. 1–2) and the divine judgment following a failed harvest (vv. 3–7).[26] Other plants, too, can be used to represent Israel, including an oak tree (Isa 61:3), a palm, or cedar (Ps 92:12), and an olive tree (Jer 11:16–17).

Matthew 21:33–46; Mark 12:1–12; Luke 20:9–19. There is considerable consistency as this cluster of metaphors is carried into the New Testament where it conveys both the sense of God's care and the potential of his judgment. This is the case in the Parable of the Wicked Tenants (Matt 21:33–46; Mark 12:1–12; Luke 20:9–19) and Jesus' discussion of the vine and its branches (John 15:1–8). In the parable, which seems to trace salvation history in an allegorical fashion, the metaphor is implicit and obvious: THE PEOPLE OF GOD ARE THE VINEYARD OF GOD.[27]

John 15:1–8. In John 15:1–8, Jesus becomes "the true vine" and disciples are branches that hold the promise of bearing much fruit but are under the threat of being "thrown away" and "burned" (v. 6). As fruit-bearing branches must "remain in the vine" (v. 4), so disciples who flourish and bear much fruit must remain organically connected to Christ and accept the nourishing resources he offers (vv. 5–6, 8).

1 Corinthians 3:6–9. Paul uses the agricultural metaphor BELIEVERS ARE GOD'S FIELD implicitly in 1 Corinthians 3:6–9a and explicitly in v. 9b. Here, though, the focus is on the workers (Paul and Apollos), their differing roles and essential equality, rather than the field itself.

Romans 11:17–24. The privilege/judgment theme is obvious in Paul's allegorical use of the olive tree imagery in Romans 11:17–24 to illustrate salvation history to Gentile addressees. They, as wild olive shoots grafted into the tree and sharing in "the nourishing sap from the olive root" (v. 17), should not "be arrogant" toward Jews who have been "cut off," "but be afraid. For if God did not spare the natural branches, he will not spare you either" (v. 21). Here, Paul employs THE PEOPLE OF GOD ARE AN OLIVE TREE in a way that accents the continuity of the people of God.

Agricultural metaphors, when used to elucidate the identity of believers in the New Testament, function to highlight the privileged connection believers have to Christ and the resources they receive from him. In line with earlier uses in the Old Testament, the metaphors also function to

---

[26] See also Jeremiah 2:21; 6:9; Ezekiel 15:1–8; 17:1–24; 19:10–14; Hosea 10:1–2, 13.

[27] Cf. the parables of the Laborers in the Vineyard (Matt 20:1–16), the Two Sons (Matt 21:28–32), and the Fig Tree (Luke 13:6–9) where the metaphor is less obvious, but may be present.

describe the attendant responsibility of Christians to offer a "harvest of righteousness and peace" (Heb 12:11) and warn of judgment for misuse of such exalted privileges. The offer of nourishment and growth to the church/believers is twinned with a warning against refusing it.

Architectural: The Church as Building/Temple

While the metaphor THE PEOPLE OF GOD ARE THE TEMPLE OF GOD is not explicit in the Old Testament, God as Creator is portrayed as a builder: "My own hand laid the foundations of the earth" (Isa 48:13; cf. Job 26:10; 38:4–7; Ps 102:25; 104:3; Prov 8:27–31; Isa 40:12; Jer 31:27; Amos 9:6). In giving detailed instructions for construction of the tabernacle, God is cast as the paradigmatic Builder (Exod 35:4–40:38, esp. 39:32). Importantly, God "builds" Jerusalem (Ps 147:2) and the remnant of Judah (Jer 31:4, 28).[28] Moreover, acts of justice and attitudes of humble worship are to be preferred to cultic acts of festival and sacrifice (Ps 40:6–8; Isa 1:10–20; 66:2b–4; Jer 6:20; Hos 6:6; Amos 5:21–27; Micah 6:6–8). To spiritualize the cultus of worship in this way was to take a significant step toward identifying the people of God as the locus of true worship.

Matthew credits Jesus with the pronouncement, "On this rock I will build my church" (16:18), identifying the church as a building rising on a solid foundation. Other New Testament authors use architectural terms to describe individual believers or the Christian community (Matt 7:24–27 [cf. Luke 6:47–49]; 1 Cor 3:9b–17; 6:19;[29] 2 Cor 6:14–7:1; Gal 2:9; Eph 2:19–22; Col 1:21–23; 2:6–7; 1 Tim 3:5, 15; 2 Tim 2:19; Heb 3:1–6; 10:21; 1 Pet 2:4–8; 4:17; Rev 3:12). Of these passages, four offer developed building/temple metaphors for the church: 1 Corinthians 3:9b–17; 2 Corinthians 6:14–7:1; Ephesians 2:19–22; 1 Peter 2:4–8.

1 Corinthians 3:9b–17. In this passage, Paul treats the issue of "jealousy and quarreling" among Christians in Corinth. Complaining that they align with himself or Apollos (vv. 1–9a), he modulates from an agricultural metaphor to an architectural one: "You are God's field, God's building" (*oikodomē*, v. 9b). With the architectural metaphor, Paul wishes to distinguish his role from those of Apollos and "other builders" on the foundation he laid as "expert builder" or "skilled chief builder" (*architektōn*, v. 10). He warns them to take care in their building, mentioning a variety of building materials suggestive of temple construction, and describing the eschatological test that awaits (vv. 10b–15). If the builder's work sur-

---

[28] Leland Ryken, James C. Wilhoit, and Tremper III Longman, ed., *Dictionary of Biblical Imagery* (Downers Grove, IL: InterVarsity, 1998), 128–129.

[29] 1 Corinthians 6:19 is the only passage that applies *naos* ("temple") to the individual believer.

vives, he will be rewarded; if not, he will "suffer loss." Addressing Christian believers directly, Paul explicitly employs the metaphor CHRISTIAN BELIEVERS ARE GOD'S TEMPLE:

> Don't you know that you yourselves are God's temple and that God's Spirit lives in you? If anyone destroys God's temple, God will destroy him; for God's temple is sacred, and you are that temple (vv. 16–17).

Associated commonplaces active in the context include: A temple belongs to its god and is of value to that deity, and damage to a temple is an affront to the deity.

2 Corinthians 6:14–7:1. Paul again uses temple imagery to query his addressees in 2 Corinthians 6:14–7:1, a passage in which he advocates separation from "idols" and the "unclean thing." As a culminating question he asks, "What agreement is there between the temple of God and idols?" He follows with a strong, declarative statement: "For we are the temple (*naos*) of the living God" (v. 16). The tenor of the temple metaphor in the passage may be described as "the distinct sanctity of Christians" and the associated commonplace, "a temple is inhabited by the deity," is clearly active ("I will live with them," v. 16). Here, Paul employs the temple metaphor in an exclusive manner to stress the need for separation between believers and unbelievers.

Ephesians 2:19–22. The exclusive use in 2 Corinthians 6:14–7:1 contrasts with the inclusive one in Ephesians 2:19–22 where the temple metaphor is the final in a string of telescoped metaphors and functions as a poignant metaphor for the inclusion of Gentiles as full partners in the Christian community.[30]

Sub-metaphors of builder (implied; God who is also the occupant of the structure), foundation (*themelios*; apostles and prophets), cornerstone (*akrogōniaios*; Christ), and building materials (*humeis sunoikodomeisthe*; both Jewish and Gentile believers) are used. A number of associated commonplaces are active including structural integrity (a building or temple made of different materials coheres), the process of building (temples are built), and habitation (here, the temple is "a dwelling in which God lives by his Spirit").

1 Peter 2:4–8. Here, believers as "living stones" are built upon "the living Stone," Jesus, who is the "chosen and precious cornerstone"

---

[30] By "telescoped metaphors," I mean a string of metaphors in which "the vehicle of one metaphor becomes the tenor of another" (so Cuddon, *Dictionary*, 958).

(*akrogōniaios*). Believers are also portrayed as priests who offer "spiritual sacrifices" in this temple (v. 5). A number of associated commonplaces are active including that a temple is the site for ministry of consecrated priests superintending sanctioned rituals. In the setting of a Christian community that is wrestling with problems of alienation and "homelessness," the house/temple metaphor functions to vividly portray the relationship between the addressees and Christ.

In the context of the Temple in Jerusalem as well as the ubiquitous Greco-Roman structures, New Testament authors employ the temple metaphor to enable believers to visualize the sanctity of the church, God's role in founding and growing the church, the defining nature of the work of Christ and the Spirit, and the solidarity of believers within the church. The architecture domain would seem to imply a static image. However, the metaphor is used in conjunction with biological imagery and the process of building is often accentuated. Rather than a static image, "we are impelled to visualize a story of the process of construction rather than a completed edifice."[31] The church is granted the wondrous privilege of humbly acknowledging in its life and story "the temple of the living God" (2 Cor 6:16).

Martial: The Church as Army

The identity of believers as combatants in an extended war between good and evil is an extension of Old Testament understandings of God as the divine warrior engaging in combat against his foes. This Old Testament theme, reflected in passages such as Isaiah 59, is "democratized" in the New Testament where it is now Christian addressees who wear the divine armor and do battle.[32] Seventh-day Adventists, for whom the Great Controversy serves as meta-narrative, should attend carefully to the corresponding biblical metaphor, THE CHURCH IS AN ARMY.

Revelation. The New Testament frequently reinforces the identity of believers as combatants in the cosmic war against evil.[33] This is especially true of the Apocalypse. In the face of satanic opposition (e.g., 2:10), the risen Christ offers repeated promises to believers who endure and "con-

---

[31] Minear, *Images*, 97.

[32] So Thomas R. Yoder Neufeld, *Put on the Armour of God: The Divine Warrior from Isaiah to Ephesians* (Sheffield, England: Sheffield Academic Press, 1997). I critique Neufeld's arguments in John K. McVay, "'Our Struggle': *Ecclesia Militans* in Ephesians 6:10–20," *AUSS* 43 (2005): 91–100.

[33] Gregory A. Boyd can argue that "almost everything that Jesus and the early church were about is decisively colored by the central conviction that the world is caught in the crossfire of a cosmic battle between the Lord and his angelic army and Satan and his demonic army" (*God at War: The Bible & Spiritual Conflict* [Downers Grove, IL: InterVarsity, 1997], 172). In the Gospels, one thinks especially of Matthew 6:9–13; 16:18–19 as reflecting concepts of the cosmic battle.

quer" ("to the one who conquers," *tō nikōnti* [and variants]; 2:7, 11, 17, 26–28; 3:5, 12, 21). The struggle is intense with the church (as the woman) bearing the brunt of the dragon's wrath, a foe who "makes war" on the end-time "remnant" (KJV) who "obey God's commandments and hold to the testimony of Jesus" (12:17). Casualties are to be expected (6:9–11; 14:13), as is victory (12:11) and celebration before the throne of God for those who have come out of "the great ordeal" (7:14, NRSV; 7:9–17; 14:1–5). Repeatedly, believers as combatants in this struggle are exhorted to exercise endurance and faith (13:10; 14:12) and to stay awake and clothed (16:15). Fighting behind enemy lines, they await the conquest of the Lamb (17:14), the victory of the rider on the white horse who leads "the armies of heaven" (19:11–16).

The cosmic battle and the role of believers in it are clearly reflected in the writings of Paul as well. When one thinks of military metaphor in Paul's writings, one passage looms large: Ephesians 6:10–20. However, earlier passages offer similar imagery, including Romans 13:11–14, 1 Thessalonians 5:8, and 2 Corinthians 10:3–6.[34]

Romans 13:11–14. Paul's urgent appeal mirrors exhortations to soldiers as dawn breaks on the day of battle: "The hour has come for you to wake up from your slumber, because our salvation is nearer now than when we first believed. The night is nearly over; the day is almost here" (vv. 11–12). The metaphor, THE CHURCH IS AN ARMY, becomes quite explicit with the command to "put on the armor of light" (*endusōmetha de ta hopla tou phōtos*, v. 12), with believers cast in the role of soldiers arming for battle. That a spiritual battle is in view is confirmed by the parallel exhortation to "clothe yourselves with the Lord Jesus Christ" (*endusasthe*, v. 14).

1 Thessalonians 5:8. Here, Paul offers a similar exhortation in a parallel framework. He exhorts his addressees to "not fall asleep as others do, but let us keep awake and be sober" (v. 6). Then, repeating the exhortation to sobriety, he enjoins: "But since we belong to the day, let us be self-controlled, putting on faith and love as a breastplate, and the hope of salvation as a helmet" (v. 8). Again, the metaphor, THE CHURCH IS AN ARMY, becomes quite explicit as Paul pictures believers as well-disciplined troops suiting up to do battle in the full light of day.

2 Corinthians 10:3–6. Paul employs the military metaphor differently at the outset of the stormy, final section of 2 Corinthians (chapters 10–

---

[34] For more thorough surveys of military language and imagery in Paul's letters, see David J. Williams, *Paul's Metaphors: Their Context and Character* (Peabody, MA: Hendrickson, 1999), 211–144; and Anthony Byatt, *New Testament Metaphors: Illustrations in Word and Phrase* (Edinburgh: Pentland, 1995), 192–204.

13), where he offers strident defense of his and his colleagues' ministry (2 Cor 10:3–6). Paul and his co-workers are now the combatants and emphasis is placed on the nature of their battle as a spiritual clash of worldviews, the quality of the weaponry they wield, and the complete victory to be expected. Paul issues a warning that the addressees, in agreeing with his opponents, not be found on the wrong side of a lopsided battle—the losing one.[35]

Ephesians 6:10–20. Paul works out the identity of the church in relationship to the theme of the extended, cosmic war between good and evil. Intriguingly, the presence of the metaphor THE CHURCH IS AN ARMY is often missed in the passage as, especially in popular Christian literature, the subject is assumed to be the individual Christian. That the passage comes at the end of an epistle that focuses on the church suggests the primary reference to be to a Christian community, a conclusion confirmed by the earlier mention of the church in relationship to the powers (3:10) and Paul's exhortation to pray "for all the saints" (v. 18).[36]

In the passage, with its vivid military imagery, the addressees are invited to outfit themselves with the armor of the divine warrior (6:10–11) as a way of ensuring victory in their struggle against the cosmic powers (6:12). A reprise of the exhortation to dress for battle offers the command in a more detailed way. Readers are to cloth themselves with a soldier's weaponry, donning it in the order in which a soldier might prepare himself for battle (6:13–17). This elaborate military imagery is completed by a call to prayer both for "all the saints" and for Paul (6:18–20).

In describing the church in terms of military conflict, Paul assumes some risk. However, as "an ambassador in chains" (v. 20), he shapes the rhetoric from below, as a victim of Rome's military might. The wider context, with its emphasis on unity, edifying speech, and tenderheartedness, also guards the meaning of the metaphor (see especially, 4:25–5:2). This guarding is carried into the immediate context by identifying armaments as "truth," "righteousness," "faith," "salvation," "Spirit," and "Word of God." The metaphor is guarded explicitly in the invitation for the addressees to have their "feet fitted with the readiness that comes from the gospel of peace" (v. 15). Moreover, as verses 18–20 make clear, the author expects

---

[35] See also Romans 16:20; 1 Corinthians 15:24–28; 2 Corinthians 6:7; Colossians 2:15; 1 Timothy 6:12; and 2 Timothy 2:1–4. It may be argued that "the idea of sinister world powers and their subjugation by Christ is built into the very fabric of Paul's thought, and some mention of them is found in every epistle except Philemon" (George B. Caird, *Principalities and Powers: A Study in Pauline Theology* [Oxford: Clarendon, 1956], viii.).

[36] For an extended defense of a corporate over against an individualist reading of the passage, see McVay, "'Our Struggle.'"

his addressees to press the battle through prayer and bold proclamation of "the mystery of the gospel." As someone has put it so aptly, the church is to "wage peace."[37]

Given this careful guarding, principal concepts that are underscored include (associated commonplaces are listed in parentheses): 1) Active, zealous engagement in the church's mission (soldiers are to be fully committed to battle). Holding one's ground as the two phalanxes came crashing together was the great challenge of ancient battle. Paul's vigorous call to arms reflects this often-sustained, close order combat in which soldiers were "bunched together, giving and receiving hundreds of blows at close range;"[38] 2) Believers must be alert to unseen dimensions (soldiers are to the look to the patron gods and goddesses for protection and aid); 3) They have the assurance of divine provision for their success (the gods have promised the success they have granted in the past). Paul draws on the Old Testament tradition of battle exhortations (e.g., Deut 20:1–9), mimicking these in form and theology in his opening command, which offers divine aid in battle: "Finally, be strong in the Lord and in his mighty power;"[39] 4) They are called to Christian community and collaboration (soldiers are to support one another and encourage one another to fight courageously).

The metaphor THE CHURCH IS AN ARMY has tended to be overlooked in favor of the body, building/temple, and bride metaphors in Ephesians and the wider New Testament. Such an approach will never do in spelling out a Seventh-day Adventist ecclesiology, in which THE CHURCH IS AN ARMY should play a central role. The military metaphor as developed in Ephesians 6:10–20 and elsewhere depicts the church's battle against evil

---

[37] Richard Rice critiques contemporary uses of the metaphor THE CHURCH IS AN ARMY. The adoption of such a metaphor can lead to tragic consequences. If it inspires physical combat, evangelism becomes equated with conquering the enemy or taking captives, the only measure of mission becomes whether or not it succeeds (since an "army church" may become "impatient with tactics that do not lead to victory") or members are depersonalized (Richard Rice, *Believing, Behaving, Belonging: Finding New Love for the Church* [Roseville, CA: Association of Adventist Forums, 2002], 98–100, 122–124, 147, 160, 172–173, 199–200, 205). I have no quarrel with these criticisms of a military metaphor for the church. I would point out, though, that these criticisms do not describe the use, or even overuse, but the misuse of the biblical metaphor THE CHURCH IS AN ARMY. Prayerful appropriation of the biblical metaphor provides a corrective to such misuse and inspiration in a moving call to the church to wage peace.

[38] Victor D. Hanson, *The Western Way of War: Infantry Battle in Classical Greece* (New York: Alfred A. Knopf, 1989), 152.

[39] For a discussion of how Ephesians 6:10–20 reflects the thought and genre of Old Testament battle exhortations, see John K. McVay, "Ephesians 6:10–20 and Battle Exhortations in Jewish Literature," *The Cosmic Battle for Planet Earth: Essays in Honor of Norman R. Gulley*, ed. Ron du Preez and Jiří Moskala (Berrien Springs, MI: Andrews University, 2003), 147–169.

as combat that requires sustained and energetic engagement of the foe. Believers are not merely sentinels, who stand stoically at watch, but combatants (albeit in the interest of a peace-filled gospel). The calls to arms issued in the New Testament are especially interested in the *esprit de corps* of believers. Christians are not seen as lone warriors battling in splendid isolation, but are fellow soldiers, battling against the church's common foes. The metaphor THE CHURCH IS AN ARMY highlights, in a way other metaphors do not, the church's engagement against the forces of evil and the real struggle and suffering that such conflict entails, all the while assuring believers of the adequacy of God's provision and the victory that awaits. The metaphor is a precious resource for understanding the church, especially as we engage in the final battles of the great controversy.

Familial and Marital: The Church as Family and Bride

God, in the role of Creator, is thought of in the Old Testament as the Father of Israel (e.g., Deut 32:6) who loves (Jer 31:1-9), protects (Ps 89:23-26), and disciplines (2 Sam 7:14) the nation, adopting them as His own (Exod 4:23; 6:6-8; Lev 26:12; Deut 32:10; Jer 3:19; Hos 11:1). As a result, "the people of Israel are with systematic regularity described as children, daughters and sons of God."[40] While it may be asked to what degree the metaphor of God as a father has slipped into the background, the fact that God is also described on occasion as a mother suggests the metaphor remains active.[41] God gives birth to Israel (Deut 32:18; Isa 42:14, 66:5-13; Num 11:10-15, by implication) and declares, "As a mother comforts her child, so will I comfort you" (Isa 66:13).[42]

This pattern of thought is carried forward in the New Testament where God is the Father (*patēr*, frequently, and, transliterated from Aramaic, *abba*, Matt 23:9; Mark 14:36; Rom 8:15; Gal 4:6), Jesus is Brother (Rom 8:29; Heb 2:11-12), and believers are thought of as related to one another as siblings. Early Christians met in homes and early congregations often mirrored the extended family of the patron or patroness of the group. It should be no surprise, then, that this cluster of metaphors is a pervasive one for early Christians and significantly reflected and shaped the life and mission of the early Christian church.[43]

---

[40] Eva Maria Lassen, "Family as Metaphor: Family Images at the Time of the Old Testament and Early Judaism," *SJOT* 6 (1992): 251.

[41] When a fresh metaphor is created, it is generally highly poetic and in the "foreground." With use, it can fade into the "background" and be described as "dead" or, better, "retired."

[42] Lassen, "Family as Metaphor," 253-254. I am indebted to Lassen's article for much of the thought and wording of this paragraph.

[43] The presence of the "household codes" in the New Testament provides evidence of the point:

The metaphor THE CHURCH IS THE FAMILY OF GOD becomes, for Paul, a profound, theological declaration. God is the Father (*patēr*) of every family (*patria*) in heaven and on earth (Eph 3:14–15; cf. Acts 17:24–29). It is through the atoning work of Christ that those once alienated from God and each other become members of God's family (*oikeios*, Eph 2:19; cf. Gal 6:10; 1 Tim 3:15; 1 Pet 4:17). The intimacy of the family is reflected around the table of the Lord where the hard-won unity of the ecclesial family is celebrated (1 Cor 10:16–17).

The New Testament presents us with a developed and specialized use of the family metaphor in THE CHURCH IS THE BRIDE/WIFE OF CHRIST. The development of this metaphor from its Old Testament origins is neatly summarized by Ortlund: "What begins as Pentateuchal whispers [Gen 1 & 2; Exod 34:11–16; Lev 17:7; 20:4–6; Num 15:38–40; Deut 31:16] rises later to prophetic cries [Hosea; Isa 1:21; 50:1; 54:4–6; 57:3; 62:5; Micah 1:7; Jer 2–3; 13:20–27; Ezek 16; 23] and is eventually echoed in apostolic teaching [Matt 9:14–15 (cf. Mark 2:18–20; Luke 5:33–35); 22:1–2; 25:1; John 3:28–30; 1 Cor 6:15–17; 2 Cor 11:1–3; Eph 5:21–33; Rev 14:4; 19:6–9a; 21:1–3, 9–10]."[44] The New Testament metaphor rests solidly on the Old Testament one, THE PEOPLE OF GOD ARE THE BRIDE/WIFE OF YAHWEH, a metaphor that is generally employed to spotlight the apostasy-as-adultery of God's people, Israel.

2 Corinthians 11:1–4. Paul views the Corinthian congregations as the betrothed bride of Christ. He views himself as the agent, friend, or best man of the bridegroom, Christ. In drawing them to faith, he has arranged the betrothal, the legal equivalent of marriage.[45] And he looks toward the Second Coming of Christ as the moment when he will be privileged to present the Corinthian believers to Christ as his bride: "I am jealous for you with a godly jealousy. I promised you to one husband, to Christ, so that I might present you as a pure virgin to him" (v. 2). Meanwhile, in the time between the betrothal and the marriage-presentation, he worries that they may succumb to other paramours and "be led astray from your sincere and pure devotion to Christ" (v. 3). The metaphor provides a vivid, eschatological setting for the Corinthians' current conduct. This stress on

---

Ephesians 5:21–6:9; Colossians 3:18–4:1; 1 Peter 2:18–3:7 4; Titus 2:2–10; 1 Timothy 2:9–15; 6:1–2.

[44] R. C. Ortlund, *Whoredom: God's Unfaithful Wife in Biblical Theology* (Grand Rapids, MI: Eerdmans, 1996), 8. I have inserted in the quotation the references that Ortlund designates in his wider discussion.

[45] As such, the sub-metaphor of betrothal "stresses the seriousness and permanency of the Corinthians' past encounter with God's elective love" (Richard Batey, *New Testament Nuptial Imagery* [Leiden: Brill, 1971], 13).

the risk of apostasy-as-adultery resonates with the dominant emphasis of Old Testament uses of the metaphor.

Ephesians 5:21–33. In this passage, Paul employs the metaphor more idealistically, as part of an extended exhortation to husbands in the household code. He recasts the metaphor THE CHURCH IS THE BRIDE/WIFE OF CHRIST with a decidedly Christological focus.[46] A number of elements and roles of wedding ceremony, representing sub-metaphors, are consolidated in Christ.[47] In addition to His central role as groom, Christ Himself is the bride price (since He "gave himself up for her"), who administers the bridal bath ("... to make her holy, cleansing her by the washing with water through the word," v. 26), and who presents the bride (to Himself!; v. 27). All of these represent contraventions of ancient wedding practice, but the resulting stress on the metaphor serves only to emphasize the importance of Christ for the church. While the passage underscores the past and present attentions of the bridegroom toward the bride, it retains an important element of eschatological expectation in the future "presentation" (v. 27). At that time, the full result of the bridegroom's work will be manifested in the splendor of the bride.[48]

The familial and marital cluster of metaphors has much to contribute to the doctrine of the church. No other cluster can vie with it in offering such an accessible and intimate portrait of relationships among fellow believers and the relationship between the church and its Lord. With such accessibility and intimacy, it harbors important warnings about the present and offers immense hope for the future in its portrait of Jesus Christ as the bridegroom returning to lay claim to his bride. Martin summarizes well the promise set forth in these metaphors:

> The church at its best reflects all that is noblest and most worthwhile in human family life: attitudes of caring and mutual regard; understanding of needs, whether physical or of the spirit; and

---

[46] Paul's formulation seems especially dependent upon Ezekiel 16:3b–14 in adopting the three basic events described there—the rescue, cleansing, and endowment of the foundling bride.

[47] I reflect the happy phrase of Daniel von Allmen who describes a "concentration christologique" in the passage (Daniel von Allmen, *La Famille de Dieu: La Symbolique Familiale dans le Paulinisme* [Fribourg: Editions Universitaires, 1981], 301.

[48] Many scholars support an eschatological reading of the "presentation" in Ephesians 5:27, including Markus Barth, *Ephesians* (Garden City, NY: Doubleday, 1974), 2:628, 69, 278; Batey, *New Testament Nuptial Imagery*, 29; and James D. G. Dunn, *Baptism in the Holy Spirit: A Re-Examination of the New Testament Teaching on the Gift of the Spirit in Relation to Pentecostalism Today* (London: SCM, 1970), 162. Dunn writes: "In Eph 5:27 it is clearly an eschatological 'presentation' of the church to Christ that is in view...;" Harold W. Hoehner, *Ephesians: An Exegetical Commentary* (Grand Rapids, MI: Baker Academic, 2002), 761.

above all the sense of 'belonging' to a social unity in which we find acceptance without pretence or make-believe.[49]

To the extent that we fulfill that promise in today's church, we revive the pattern of early Christians[50] and early Christian mission in which the family environment of the house church proved attractive to non-Christians.[51]

Metaphors for the Church and Seventh-day Adventist Ecclesiology

Lakoff and Johnson, in their masterful book, *Metaphors We Live By*, make the point that metaphors both "highlight" and "hide."[52] By speaking of one thing in terms of another, a metaphor brings a set of features to light. However, in accenting a specific set of realities, a metaphor downplays or hides other aspects. An architectural metaphor for the church may highlight church organization and durability. However, that same architectural metaphor may hide other, important aspects of the church, especially the dynamism and growth that might be made evident in, say, an agricultural metaphor. Paul, at least, seems to recognize this feature of metaphorical language, pushing the limits of the language by mixing the metaphors. So, for example, he describes the church as building/temple as "growing," employing a verb that is more naturally used of biological growth (*auxanō*, Eph 2:21).[53]

I do not believe that we should adopt a master metaphor for the church at the loss of the others. God has chosen to divulge, in Scripture, a rich variety of metaphors to provide a well-rounded understanding of the church. Since any given metaphor highlights some aspects of the church and hides others, we need to employ the variety of metaphors given to us to offer an accurate and inspiring view of the church.[54] The challenge is to continue to

---

[49] Martin, *Family and the Fellowship*, 124.

[50] Lucian, an early critic of Christians, writes: "Their first lawgiver persuaded them that they are all brothers of one another," Lucian, *Peregr.* 13, as cited in Joseph H. Hellerman, *The Ancient Church as Family* (Minneapolis, MN: Fortress, 2001), 221.

[51] See Roger W. Gehring, *House Church and Mission: The Importance of Household Structures in Early Christianity* (Peabody, MA: Hendrickson, 2004), 89–95.

[52] Chapter 3, "Metaphorical Systematicity: Highlighting and Hiding," 10–13 in Lakoff and Johnson, *Metaphors We Live By*.

[53] Following Joachim Gnilka, *Der Epheserbrief* (Freiburg: Herder, 1982), 158. See the helpful discussion of mixed metaphors in Ephesians in Gerald Klingbeil, "Metaphors and Pragmatics: An Introduction to the Hermeneutics of Metaphors in the Epistle to the Ephesians," *BBR* 16.2 (2006): 273–293.

[54] Reflecting on Minear's lengthy list of images for the church, Martin writes: "Each term has something special to contribute to our understanding, and we need the wide variety of these many terms ... to portray the fullness of the church" (*The Family and the Fellowship*, 112).

seek deeper understanding and truer appropriation of the biblical metaphors for the church, a task the church has often failed to accomplish.

John Driver describes what happened when Christians, more attune to contemporary realities than biblical images of the church, "recast" them "to serve as vehicles of the church's distorted self-understanding."[55] In the "Constantinian shift" of the fourth century, still worse occurred with the church increasingly drawing its models from the Roman empire. Each successive era of church history, it could be argued, has seen the church adopt the models and metaphor of its time, rather than remaining true to the biblical metaphors for the church. So, the church has, in turn, reflected feudal models, imperial expansion, colonial imagery, democracy, or a corporate business model. The church has repeatedly either adopted images from secular culture or "given" biblical images "unbiblical twists to carry its deformed self-understanding."[56] So what is to be done? "If the church is to recover the integrity of its life and mission, it must have adequate images to capture and inspire its imagination . . . Biblical images must be read and interpreted afresh . . ."[57]

As one reflects on the plethora of metaphors/images for the church, it becomes obvious that these metaphors are emphasizing—in different ways and with different accents—three relationships or sets of relationships that are vital to the church: 1) The relationship to God, Christ, and/or the Spirit; 2) The relationships among fellow believers; 3) The church's relationship to the world and the powers. A checkup of practical ecclesiology—how well the church is living out its identity—would query the health of each of these. Each of the metaphors invites us to consider carefully one or, usually, more of these relationships: Are we relating to God or Christ (as Head, Builder, Bridegroom, etc.) in the way we should? Are our relationships with fellow believers (as other body parts, building components, etc) healthy and appropriate, based on an attitude of humility and respect? Are we combating the evil influence of the powers and maintaining an appropriate engagement with and distance from the world?

We must pray for the God-given ability to interpret clearly and contextually the biblical metaphors for the church. We must pray for the courage to appropriate them obediently and convincingly, allowing them to transform our church today. And we must see in these poignant metaphors a call to sterling loyalty toward God, compassion and grace toward one another, and vigorous engagement with the world.

---

[55] Driver, *Images of the Church in Mission*, 17–18.
[56] Ibid., 17–21.
[57] Ibid., 21.

CHAPTER 4

MISSION IN THE OLD TESTAMENT

Jiří Moskala

The first and greatest missionary in the Old Testament is God. From the very beginning, He has been engaged in a personal relationship with His creation.[1] He spoke with Adam and Eve (Gen 3:8), searched for them (Gen 3:9), became the Savior of humanity (Gen 3:15, 21), and tried to win sinners back before the Flood (Gen 6:3). It has been correctly stated that "if there is a missionary in the Old Testament, it is God Himself who will, as his eschatological deed *par excellence*, bring the nations to Jerusalem to worship him there together with his covenant" people.[2] His field is the whole world and He has a universal mission:[3] "Turn to me and be saved, all you ends of the earth; for I am God, and there is no other" (Isa 45:22).[4] God's mission could be defined as doing everything possible to communi-

---

[1] On God as a missionary, see John R. W. Stott, *Christian Mission in the Modern World* (Downers Grove, IL: Inter-Varsity, 1975); Jon L. Dybdahl, "Missionary God—Missionary Church," *Re-Visioning Adventist Mission in Europe*, ed. Erich W. Baumgartner (Berrien Springs, MI: Andrews University Press, 1998), 8–14; Andreas J. Koestenberger and Peter T. O'Brien, *Salvation to the Ends of the Earth: A Biblical Theology of Mission* (Downers Grove, IL: InterVarsity, 2001), 21; Craig Ott, Stephen J. Strauss with Timothy C. Tennent, *Encountering Theology of Mission: Biblical Foundations, Historical Developments, and Contemporary Issues* (Grand Rapids, MI: Baker, 2010), 3–24; Timothy C. Tennent, *Invitation to World Missions: A Trinitarian Missiology for the Twenty-first Century* (Grand Rapids, MI: Kregel, 2010), 55; Christopher J. H. Wright, *The Mission of God: Unlocking the Bible's Grand Narrative* (Downers Grove: IL: IVP Academic, 2006), 22–23; and Georg Vicedom, *The Mission of God: An Introduction to the Theology of Mission* (Saint Louis, MO: Concordia, 1965), 5.

[2] David J. Bosch, *Transforming Mission: Paradigm Shifts in Theology of Mission* (Maryknoll, NY: Orbis, 1991), 19.

[3] Latin expression *missio Dei* means literally "the sending of God" or "the mission of God." This phrase was originally coined by German missiologist Karl Hartestein. See Tennent, *Encountering*, 55; Lalsangkima Pachuau, "Missio Dei," *DMT*, 233.

[4] All Bible texts are quoted from the NIV unless otherwise noted.

cate salvation to the world.[5] In this chapter we will discuss the presence, nature, extent, and human involvement in God's mission as recorded in the Old Testament.

Mission in the Old Testament

Some scholars have concluded that it is an oxymoron to speak about mission in the Old Testament. Eckhard J. Schnabel, for example, challenges Old Testament scholars, theologians, and missiologists by claiming that there is no commission in the Old Testament to go and "evangelize" the world. Abraham, Israel, and others were only passive witnesses for God, "a light to the world," but not actual participants in mission per se. He argues that there was no active plan to proclaim God's message to the whole world during the times of Israel's monarchy or intertestamental Judaism; they simply did not engage in mission.[6]

In response to this claim, one must first of all acknowledge that the Old Testament, at its core, is a storybook with a salvation metanarrative. It is not a handbook on mission or its philosophy nor a blueprint for a programmatic missiological activity. Further, the biblical language and imagery employed, in regard to mission, differs from what is used today. In Hebrew Scripture, one should not be surprised to find stories that contain specific hints and observations and even explicit statements uncovering the mission of God's people as opposed to a direct command to mission. The metanarrative of the Old Testament clearly unfolds God's universal plan for the world and His people's part in the realization of that plan. This may not be always clearly perceived, but it is there. Sometimes, "the main problem is that missiologists tend to look at the Old Testament with the same lenses used when looking at the New Tes-

---

[5] John A. McIntosh, "Missio Dei," *EDWM*, 631–632. God's mission, however, goes beyond this salvific goal because His mission is cosmic in scope. God wants to restore the original beauty, harmony, and meaning of life. Thus, as part of His soteriological mission, God also has the ecological goal of restoring everything to its original condition (Gen 1–2; Rev 21:1–5). In the beginning, God gave three Creation mandates to humans: love (multiply); govern (rule, work, and care for God's creation); and worship the Creator (see Gen 1:28–2:3). This was their Creation mission, their mission before sin. When sin occurred, it was necessary to face the rebellion and consequences of sin. God made provision for salvation (Gen 2:9; 3:15, 21; Rev 13:8) and called people to accept and then to proclaim His salvation. Mission in the Old Testament was centered on the theocracy. God's rulership was established in Israel's society, and everything flowed from it.

[6] Eckhard J. Schnabel, *Early Christian Mission* (Downers Grove, IL: InterVarsity, 2004), 1:73. See also Ferdinand Hahn, *Mission in the New Testament* (Naperville, IL: Allenson, 1965), 20. Bosch claims "there is, in the Old Testament, no indication of the believers of the old covenant being sent by God to cross geographical, religious, and social frontiers in order to win others to faith in Yahweh" (Bosch, *Transforming Mission*, 17). These claims are partially true, but the writers tend to ignore some specific biblical data.

tament, trying to find New Testament themes and patterns in the Old."[7]

Foundational Concepts

God's Mission and Human Participation

In His wisdom, God decided to use humans to accomplish His objective (Gen 12:1-3; Exod 19:4-6). It has been stated that "the mission of God is to bless all nations on earth . . . Israel in the Old Testament was not chosen *over against* the rest of the nations, but *for the sake of* the rest of the nations."[8] Thus God's universal activity is actually the "basis for the missionary message of the Old Testament."[9] God has a mission, and the Israelites were to participate in His mission.[10] Thus, mission was not a human performance, but the engagement of Israel in God's work. We can, therefore, define mission[11] as a privilege. Israel participated, as a people and as individuals, in God's salvific plan by being a blessing to others and a light to all families of the earth. Mission was more than "sending" someone somewhere.[12] Mission was understood to be theocentric because it was the result of an encounter with God. The effectiveness of this ministry was, to a large extent, determined by genuine commitment and faith in God that revealed His goodness and His loving and righteous character (Exod 34:6-7; Ezek 36:22-28).[13]

Mission, Creation, and Election

God's mission culminates in the eschatological time, but begins at

---

[7] Cristian Dumitrescu, "Mission Theology in the Old Testament: A New Paradigm," *JAMS* 4.1 (2008): 45.

[8] Christopher J. H. Wright, *Knowing the Holy Spirit through the Old Testament* (Downers Grove, IL: InterVarsity, 2006), 99-100.

[9] Johannes Blauw, *The Missionary Nature of the Church: A Survey of the Biblical Theology of Mission* (Grand Rapids, MI: Eerdmans, 1974), 17.

[10] See Jürgen Moltmann, *The Church in the Power of the Spirit: A Contribution to Messianic Ecclesiology* (New York: Harper and Row, 1977), 64. John Stott correctly states that the mission of the church arises from the mission of God: "We cannot talk about mission and evangelism without first talking about God. For mission and evangelism are not the novel ideas of modern men, but part of the eternal purpose of God" (John R. W. Stott, ed., *Making Christ Known: Historic Mission Documents from Lausanne Movement 1974-1989* [Grand Rapids, MI: Eerdmans, 1997], 9; see also, 29-30).

[11] The concept of "mission" includes a sense of identity, an awareness of its purpose and service.

[12] The Hebrew word *šālaḥ* ("send") occurs 846 times in the Old Testament (see Abraham Eve-Shoshan, *A New Concordance of the Old Testament* [Jerusalem: 1993], 1148-1152). For concrete examples of God sending some people out, see Isaiah 6:8, 66:19; and Malachi 4:5. Other vocabulary to consider is "go," "do," "proclaim," "tell," "announce," "call," "raise up," "prophecy," etc.

[13] The rest of this article provides justification for our brief description and definition of mission.

Creation. Mission theology is rooted in creation theology. Since God created humankind, every person belongs to Him and, consequently, everyone is the object of His love. One can experience re-creation while looking forward to the new creation, because God is the Creator and Giver of life.[14]

God's election is inseparable from mission. In the Old Testament, God's people are never without a mission; there is no election without a commission. Biblical theology is a mission-oriented theology.[15] The Hebrew Scripture does not know anything about an election of individuals or people for salvation,[16] but knows about election for mission (Exod 3:7–10; 7:1–2; 19:5–6; Deut 7:6–8; Jer 1:5). The mission and the message of the Old Testament people may be separated for analysis, but they belong firmly together. The mission includes the proclamation of the message.

A Twofold Mission

The mission of the Old Testament people was twofold: 1) It had an inward focus aimed at the children of Israel and succeeding generations. Parents were to repeat the stories of deliverance to their children (Exod 12:24–27; Deut 6:4–9; Isa 38:19): "One generation will commend your works to another; they will tell of your mighty acts. They will speak of the glorious splendor of your majesty, and I will meditate on your wonderful works" (Ps 145:4–5; cf. Exod 10:2); 2) It also had an outward focus aimed at the other nations, the Gentile world.[17] As we will demonstrate, the mis-

---

[14] K. Koyama, "New World–New Creation: Mission in Power and Faith," *MSt* 10 (1993): 59–77; P. J. Robinson, "Integrity of Creation and Christian Mission," *Mis* 19 (1991): 144–153. See also Sidney H. Rooy, "Creation/Nature," *DMT*, who states that "creation affirms the essential unity of humankind, made in the image of God. This fundamental unity is the basis and first level of contact for all mission between people. Thus, we relate to people in mission first of all on the basis of their humanity, not their sinfulness" (77).

[15] For mission theology based on biblical material, consult Walter C. Kaiser, Jr., *Mission in the Old Testament: Israel as a Light to the Nations* (Grand Rapids, MI: Baker, 2000); Jon L. Dybdahl, "Doing Theology in Mission: Part I," *Ministry*, November 2005, 19–22; Idem, "Doing Theology in Mission: Part II," *Ministry*, January 2006, 19–23; Russell L. Staples, *Community of Faith: The Seventh-day Adventist Church in the Contemporary World* (Hagerstown, MD: Review and Herald, 1999); Gerald Anderson, *Theology of the Christian Mission* (New York: McGraw-Hill, 1961); David Filbeck, *Yes, God of the Gentiles Too: The Missionary Message of the Old Testament* (Wheaton, IL: Billy Graham Center, Wheaton College, 1994); and Roger E. Hedlund, *The Mission of the Church in the World: A Biblical Theology* (Grand Rapids, MI: Baker, 1991).

[16] God did not make a decree in past eternity to save some people and to condemn others to eternal damnation, regardless of their will, attitude, life, and response to His love (Gen 12:3; Isa 45:22; Ezek 18:23, 32; 33:11; compare with 1 Tim 2:3–4; 4:10; Titus 2:11). See also Romans 8:28–39 and Ephesians 1:1–10. Salvation is only in Christ Jesus and eternal condemnation is for those who refuse to believe in Jesus as their personal Savior (John 1:12; 3:16–17, 36; 16:9; Acts 4:12).

[17] See Kaiser, *Mission*, 9.

sion of the people of God in the Old Testament was to be directed toward others who did not belong to the covenant people.[18] God was interested in all the nations and His message transcended Israel's borders.

Universal Mission

One can speak about the mission of the people of God in the Old Testament only after the appearance of sin, when two different ways of life were chosen (see the two lines of genealogies, Cain and Seth, in Gen 4 and 5). The followers of God were to carry the message of salvation to others (Isa 66:19; Ps 67:2; 96:3). This mission was universal in scope and was gradually disclosed. Unfortunately, God's people did not always succeed in their mission.

Mission before Abraham

Because of sin, Adam and Eve failed in their mission to lead all of their family to God.[19] The power of evil was a destructive force and it degraded people to such an extent that God had to intervene with the Flood (Gen 6:5-6, 11-13). The first hint of intentional missiological activities in the Bible can be found in Genesis 4:26b when Seth "began to proclaim/preach the name of the Lord." The NIV provides an alternative translation, "At that time men began to proclaim the name of the Lord." Comparison between Genesis 4:26b and Exodus 33:19 and 34:5 demonstrates that "to call on the name of the Lord" does not only mean to worship Him

---

[18] There is a growing number of scholars who take the Old Testament as a basis for biblical mission; see, among others, Robert Martin-Achard, "Israel's Mission to the Nations," *IRM* 51.4 (Oct 1962): 482-484; Johan H. Bavinck, *An Introduction to the Science of Missions* (Grand Rapids, MI: Baker, 1960); Johannes Verkuyl, *Contemporary Missiology* (Grand Rapids, MI: Eerdmans, 1978); Francis M. Debose, *God Who Sends: A Fresh Quest for Biblical Mission* (Nashville, TN: Broadman, 1983); Ferris L. McDaniel, "Mission in the Old Testament," *Mission in the New Testament: An Evangelical Approach*, ed. William J. Larkin, Jr., and Joel F. Williams (Maryknoll, NY: Orbis, 1998), 12-13; and Walter C. Kaiser, Jr., "Israel's Missionary Call," *Perspectives on the World Christian Movement: A Reader*, ed. Ralph D. Winter and Steven C. Hawthorne, 3rd ed. (Pasadena, CA: William Carey Library, 2000), 11. Kaiser uses three basic texts—Genesis 12:1-3; Exodus 19:4-6; and Psalm 67—to make it clear that God sent Israel with the mission to the Gentiles. See also Harold Henry, *The Missionary Message of the Old Testament* (London: Kingsgate, 1944), 15; David J. Bosch, "Reflection on Biblical Models of Mission," *Towards the 21st Century in Christian Mission*, ed. James M. Phillips and Robert T. Coote (Grand Rapids, MI: Eerdmans, 1993), 175-176; Bryant Hicks, "Old Testament Foundations for Mission," *Missiology: An Introduction to the Foundations, History, and Strategies of the World Mission*, ed. John Mark Terry, Ebbie Smith, and Justice Anderson (Nashville, TN: Broadman & Holman, 1998), 53-62; and Verkuyl, *Missiology*, 96.

[19] Allusion to this function can be seen in Gen 1:28. This implicit role for Adam and Eve derives also from the fact that they were directly created by God Himself. It follows that they should keep the creation order and lead humanity in respect, admiration, and obedience to God in order to maintain a right relationship with Him. See Arthur F. Glasser, "Biblical Theology of Mission," *EDWM*, 127.

but "to proclaim the name of the Lord" before an audience. It seems that this practice was originally family-oriented and gradually came to include all of humanity.[20] Seth's descendants continued the proclamation as is suggested by the phrase "Enoch walked with God" (Gen 5:24; cf. Gen 6:9; Micah 6:8; Jude 14–15).[21] But as they mixed with the descendants of Cain's line, they began to fail, and God's faithful people almost disappeared (Gen 6:1–8).[22]

Genesis 1–11 is universal in scope.[23] Before the Flood, when iniquity was rapidly growing, the Spirit of God was calling people to repentance. (Gen 6:3, 5). In addition, God called Noah to be His messenger, a preacher of righteousness to the antediluvian world (2 Pet 2:5; cf. Amos 3:7), and to urge all peoples to make the right decision for God. Since the biblical flood was worldwide,[24] Noah's mission had to be worldwide too. After the flood, the Tower of Babel ended what was intended to be a good beginning (Gen 11:1–9). God, for the third time, had to start all over again, but this time He elected Abraham (Gen 12:1; 15:7).

Mission and Abraham

The universality of the mission was explicitly mentioned for the first time in regard to Abraham. The Great Commission of the Old Testament declares: "And all peoples on earth will be blessed through you" (Gen 12:3).[25] The Lord mentioned it three times to Abraham (Gen 12:3; 18:18; 22:18). He was to be a blessing to the "all families on earth." God's blessing contained the key imperative phrase: "I will bless you.... Be a blessing!...

---

[20] For details, see my article "The Concept and Notion of the Church in the Pentateuch," *"For You Have Strengthened Me:" Biblical and Theological Studies in Honor of Gerhard Pfandl in Celebration of His Sixty-Fifth Birthday*, ed. Martin Proebstle, Gerald A. Klingbeil, and Martin G. Klingbeil (St. Peter am Hart, Austria: Seminar Schloss Bogenhofen, 2007), 13–14.

[21] The expression "walked with God" replaces the word "lived" in similar descriptions for other individuals, thus pointing to the quality of the relationship between Enoch and God— he did not merely "live." This phrase may hint to Enoch's witnessing activities (see Jude 1:14–16).

[22] Sven Fockner, "Reopening the Discussion: Another Contextual Look at the Sons of God," *JSOT* 32 (2008): 435–456.

[23] Claus Westermann, *Beginning and End in the Bible* (Philadelphia, PA: Fortress, 1972), 21.

[24] Richard M. Davidson, "Biblical Evidence for the Universality of the Genesis Flood," *Creation, Catastrophe, and Calvary: Why a Global Flood Is Vital to the Doctrine of Atonement*, ed. John Templeton Baldwin (Hagerstown, MD: Review and Herald, 2000), 79–92; idem, "The Flood," *EDBT*, 261–263; Gordon J. Wenham, *Genesis 1–15* (Waco, TX: Word, 1987), 155–166.

[25] The New King James Version renders this text in the following way: "And in you all the families of the earth shall be blessed" (Gen 12:3). The proper translation depends on the understanding of the Hebrew preposition b^e ("in," "by," "through," "on," etc.) and its syntactical function (taken here as an instrumental *bet*).

and all peoples on earth will be blessed through you" (Gen 12:2-3).[26] God commanded Abraham to be a blessing to others because He had blessed him. The Lord's blessing cannot and should not be taken selfishly. Abraham needed to live for others.[27] Genesis 12:2-3 was God's programmatic statement for Abraham and for those who would follow the same faith. Genesis 12:2-3 provides "the formative theology" for "a divine program to glorify himself by bringing salvation to all on planet earth."[28] Abraham became the special messenger—a missionary—to the entire world[29] with a mission which would only later be carried on by Israel and that would find its fulfillment on an even greater scale in the *Ebed Yahweh*, the Servant of the Lord (Isa 42:1-9; 49:1-7; 50:4-9; 52:13-53:12; 61:1-3). He was to be the Salvation (not only that He would declare, bring, or proclaim it) of the whole world (Isa 49:6)![30]

In many places where Abraham lived and traveled, he built altars and called on the name of the Lord (Gen 12:7-8; 13:4, 18; 22:9-13). This way, he was a witness for his unique God. However, Abraham's first "missionary" journey to Egypt failed because of his disbelief (Gen 12:10-20). Later, he fulfilled his prophetic role in regard to the king of Sodom (Gen 14:17-24). His faith grew through his defeats (Gen 16 and 20), struggles, and victories (Gen 18:16-33; 22:1-19). At the end God said, "Abraham obeyed me and kept my requirements, my commands, my decrees, and my laws" (Gen 26:5). Knowledge of the God of Abraham was to reach the world in such a way that even "the nobles of the nations [will] assemble as the people of the God of Abraham" (Ps 47:9). God's ultimate goal has

---

[26] My translation. God's promise that, through Abraham, He will bless "all the families of the earth" (*kol mišpᵉḥot hāᵃdāmah*), is repeated in various forms in Genesis 18:18; 22:18; 26:4 and 28:14. The Hebrew phrase, *kol mišpᵉuot*, is rendered in the Septuagint as *passai hai phulai*, "all the tribes" (12:3; 28:14); but the Hebrew expression *kol goyê* is used in Genesis 18:18; 22:18; and 26:4 and is translated in the LXX as *panta ta ethnē*, "all the nations." The intention of the text envisioned the whole world with all families or clans (as this word is used in the case of Achan's tribe/family; see Josh 7:14).

[27] Paul Borgman, *Genesis: The Story We Haven't Heard* (Downers Grove, IL: InterVarsity, 2001), 124, and Nahum Sarna, *Genesis* (Philadelphia, PA: The Jewish Publication Society, 1989), 89.

[28] Kaiser, *Messiah*, 13.

[29] It is significant that the seventh promise is quoted in Acts 3:25 with reference to the Jewish people who listened to Peter's sermon, but in Galatians 3:8 it is used in reference to the Gentiles. In this way, Abraham's physical and spiritual descendants are included. The mission of the Christian church is the same: to be a blessing to the whole world (Matt 5:16; John 15:5, 16; Eph 2:10; 1 Pet 2:9).

[30] The literal translation of Isaiah 49:6 plainly highlights this point: "And he says [the Lord to His Servant]: 'It is a small thing that you be my servant to raise up the tribes of Jacob, and to restore the preserved of Israel. I will even give you for a light to the Gentiles (nations) to be my salvation to the end of the world'" (translation is mine).

always been to bless all of humanity.[31]

Genesis 10, a chapter containing a table of seventy nations (a symbolic number standing for the totality of nations), introduces the narrative about Abraham implying that Abraham was to be a blessing to the whole world. However, Abraham also needed to teach his children about the true God, instructing them concerning God's ways, and directing them to keep His law in order that they might live according to "the way of the Lord" (Gen 18:19).[32] Abraham's universal mission was repeated to Isaac ("And through your offspring all nations on earth will be blessed;" Gen 26:4), and reaffirmed to Jacob (Gen 28:13-15; 35:11-12; 46:3) and Moses (Exod 3:6-8; 6:2-8).

Mission Entrusted to Israel

Moses, together with Israel, needed to continue this universal mission to the whole world, starting as a light to the Egyptians (Exod 7:5, 17; 8:22; 14:4, 18), spreading it through the Exodus (Josh 2:8-12). God called Israel to ethical distinctiveness in order to be an effective instrument in the service of His mission (Lev 11:44-45; 18:3; 18-19; Deut 14:1-3; Micah 6:6-8). They were to be committed to a holy life, because only in this way they could live to the glory of God and be a light to the nations, resulting in the nations seeing the wisdom of God (Deut 4:6; 26:18-19; Isa 58:8; 60:1-3; 62:1-2; Ezek 36:23). Moses's exhortatory speech to Israel stressed the importance of obedience to God and His law (Deut 4:5-8; 10:17-19; 29:24-26; 31:12-13), implying the visibility of their missionary activities.

The mission of the Old Testament people can be summarized in God's ideal for Israel: "Now if you obey me fully and keep my covenant, then out of all nations you will be my treasured possession. Although the whole earth is mine, you will be for me a kingdom of priests [thus, a mediatorial role of Israel for other nations is anticipated; they should be the means of bringing people to God] and a holy nation" (Exod 19:5-6; cf. Isa 42:6). God's purpose was to bless all nations through Israel.[33]

---

[31] Christopher J. H. Wright, "Old Testament Theology of Mission," *EDWM*, 707.

[32] Abraham was to direct his family to keep "the way of the Lord," which can imply that they would be taught by Abraham not only to do "what was right and just" but also to live for others, as God's concern was to bless the whole world. Thus the "way of the Lord" becomes a missionary paradigm for God's followers to be a blessing to all people. The Old Testament Church was built, first of all, around the family circle: God's directions for life are very important for all, and, in this way, a family is to be a light to the world, not only to an individual.

[33] C. Gordon Olson, *What in the World is God Doing? The Essentials of Global Missions* (Cedar Knolls, NJ: Global Gospel, 1989), 17.

Examples of Missionary Activities

The question remains: Was Israel's witnessing passive or active? Did they actually go to foreign countries to speak about their living, loving, and holy God? Although there are only a few examples of active witnessing in the Old Testament, they are worth mentioning:

1) Joseph was brought to Egypt by the jealousy and intrigues of his brothers, but God enabled him to become a blessing for Egypt and his family and a witness for a true God (Gen 45:5-8; 50:19-21).

2) God called Moses to introduce Egypt to the true living Lord and to liberate Israel (Exod 3:10-15; Deut 34:11; 1 Sam 12:8; Ps 105:26).

3) In the case of Naaman, the commander of the army of the king of Aram, it was through the initiative and witnessing of a young Israelite slave girl in captivity in Syria that he became acquainted with the true God of heaven (2 Kgs 5:15).

4) God sent Elijah to the widow of Zarephtah in Sidon (1 Kgs 17:9-24).

5) The prophet Elisha went to Damascus. While there, Ben-Hadad, king of Aram, sent his messenger to him to inquire if he would recover from his illness (2 Kgs 8:7-15).

6) The most obvious missionary activity is recorded in the book of Jonah. This prophet was not willing to go and fulfill God's commission. Jonah saw the salvation of Ninevites as undeserved, and he refused to help with this expression of divine compassion (3:10; 4:1). In a dramatic way, God taught him about the universality of God's salvation (4:6-11), thus revealing His unselfish love for all, even for the enemies of His people.

7) Isaiah, at the conclusion of his book, declares that God will send missionaries to the whole world. The Lord "will send survivors [of the people of Israel] to the nations: Tarshish, Put, Lud, Meshech, Rosh, Tubal and Javan, to the distant coastlands that have neither heard My fame nor seen My glory. And they will declare My glory among the nations" (Isa 66:19). The result will be that "'from one Sabbath to another, shall all flesh [it means, all nations] come to worship before me,' saith the LORD" (Isa 66:23, KJV).

8) Amos, Isaiah, Jeremiah, and Ezekiel dedicated large portions of their books (even Obadiah's whole book) to pronounce judgments against other nations. This clearly suggests that God was purposefully working for these nations. They were responsible for their behavior and accountable to the Lord. The announcement of God's judgment plays an important role in the mission of God's people, because the ultimate purpose of divine judgment is redemptive.[34]

---

[34] Richard M. Davidson, "The Good News of Yom Kippur," *JATS* 2.2 (1991): 4-27; Jiří Moskala,

9) Jeremiah sent Seraiah to Babylon with a scroll containing judgments against the city and with the order to read it aloud in public (Jer 51:59–64). Seraiah's case offers a unique example of a prophetic message that could be heard in a foreign land and indicates that the oracles against foreign nations could be actually delivered in the foreign countries.[35]

10) Daniel and his three friends witnessed to Babylon's top officials and the king about the true God (Dan 1–3). They helped Nebuchadnezzar to come to the knowledge of the Most High God. After his conversion, described in Daniel 4, he wrote a letter to all nations about the mighty Most High God who would reign forever (Dan 4:1–3, 37). Daniel also witnessed to the last Babylonian king, Belshazzar (Dan 5), to Darius the Mede, the high Medo-Persian officials (Dan 6), and possibly even to Cyrus (Dan 1:21; 6:28; 10:1), who issued the decree to allow the Jews to return home from the Babylonian captivity (2 Chr 36:22–23; Ezra 1:1–4). Daniel can be described as a missionary.[36] This is strengthened by the fact that Daniel wrote chapters 2–7 in an international Aramaic language in order that everyone could understand its content. Daniel's message has an international connotation and perspective (Dan 2:31–47; 7:1–14). It is God who "changes times and seasons; sets up kings and deposes them" (Dan 2:21). Daniel 7 presents God's purpose for the whole world.[37] At the end of his book, a blessing is pronounced on those who would lead others to righteousness (Dan 12:3).

11) Ezra and Nehemiah worked and witnessed at the Persian royal court. As a result, King Artaxerxes gave them permission to rebuild the city of Jerusalem (Ezra 7:11–28; Neh 2:1–10).

12) Esther was appointed to become a queen in Persia. Through

---

"Toward a Biblical Theology of God's Judgment: A Celebration of the Cross in Seven Phases of Divine Universal Judgment (An Overview of a Theocentric-Christocentric Approach)," *JATS* 15.1 (2004): 138–165.

[35] God gave the message to Jeremiah to be proclaimed in some of the important cities of Egypt concerning the coming of Nebuchadnezzar, king of Babylon, to attack Egypt and about God's judging hand against her gods (Jer 46:13–14, 25–26). We do not exactly know how the message was delivered to Egypt, but there were Jewish settlements in Egypt at that time (see Jer 43:5–7; 44:1; compare with 2 Kgs 23:34) and some communication was going on between Israel and Egypt. Notice how another message from Jeremiah was rejected by a large assembly of Jews living in Egypt (see Jer 44:15–18).

[36] Robert H. Glover, *The Bible Basis of Mission* (Los Angeles, CA: Bible of Los Angeles, 1946), 21; see also John N. Oswalt, "The Mission of Israel to the Nations," *Through No Fault of Their Own?: The Fate of Those Who Never Heard*, ed. William V. Crockett and James G. Sigountos (Grand Rapids, MI: Baker, 1991), 93–94; and Thomas Schirrmacher, "Biblical Foundations for Missions: Seven Clear Lessons," *IJFM* 13.1 (1996): 35. See, in this volume, the chapter written by Sung Ik Kim, "Mission in Daniel."

[37] Blauw, *Missionary Nature*, 65. On "universalism" in the Old Testament, see ibid., 15–54. The universality of God's mission lies in the divine intention to establish His universal kingdom on earth (Dan 2:44; 7:26–27).

God's providence and her loyalty, she rescued God's people from massacre (Esther 4:12-14; 8:15-17).[38]

13) It is also true that the geographical location of Israel (placed at the main crossroads of Middle East international routes, between Egypt and Assyria or Babylon) was a very significant factor in witnessing for their God. Different cultures, merchants, religions, nations, and people met there and were confronted with a different system of beliefs. The importance of the worldwide mission of Israel is underlined by the temple in Jerusalem, a center for a true worship (Isa 2:2), where everyone could come and learn how to worship the true God (Isa 2:3-4; 56:2-8; 62:9-11; Jer 3:17; 33:9; Micah 4:1-2). The Israelites would become teachers of righteousness: "This is what the LORD Almighty says: 'In those days ten men from all languages and nations will take firm hold of one Jew by the hem of his robe and say, "Let us go with you, because we have heard that God is with you"'" (Zech 8:23).[39]

Additional Biblical Support

The righteous acts of God during the Exodus were heard by many other nations (see Josh 2:8-11). Hiram, the king of Tyre, spoke very highly about the Lord God of Solomon: "Because the Lord loves his people, he has made you their king. . . . Praise be to the Lord, the God of Israel, who made heaven and earth!" (2 Chr 2:11-12). The queen of Sheba visited Solomon, because Solomon's fame had reached her far country (1 Kgs 10:1-9; 2 Chr 9:1-8). These narratives suggest that other nations also heard about the God of Israel and Solomon's wisdom. Paradoxically, sometimes God's people needed to go through troubles or even be sent into exile in order to accomplish their primary mission—to be a light to the world.[40]

Mission in the Psalms

Witnessing to Gentiles is also present in the Psalms, the missionary

---

[38] See Adrinna D. Beltre, *Queen and Deliverer: An Exploration of the Missiological Implications in the Book of Esther* (M.A. thesis, Andrews University, 2007).

[39] In this context, it is significant to observe that Isaiah speaks about "Galilee of the nations/Gentiles" (Isa 9:1), because Galilee will become a part of their territory where they will worship the true living God of Israel.

[40] See the examples of Joseph as a vizier in Egypt (Gen 39:2-6, 20-21; 41:37-41); Moses as a leader of Israel in confrontation with the Egyptian pharaoh (Exod 5-15); an anonymous Israelite slave girl who witnessed to Naaman (2 Kgs 5:1-19); Daniel as a prime minister and president of the scientific academy in Babylon (Dan 1:20-21; 5-6); Daniel's three friends in the fiery furnace (Dan 3); people of God as "singers" of religious songs on the demand of Babylonians (Ps 137:1-3); Esther as a queen in Medo-Persia (Esther 4:12-16); and Nehemiah as a leader in the midst of great tensions in the Persian court (Neh 2:1-10).

book par excellence: "I will praise you, O Lord, among the nations; I will sing of you among the peoples" (Ps 57:9); "Praise the Lord, all you nations; extol him, all you peoples" (Ps 117:1-2). Two missionary Psalms, 67 and 96, express, very eloquently, a universal mission and focus on God's promise to Abraham—that he and his posterity would be a blessing to all the families of the earth. Psalm 67 is built on the Aaronic benediction from Numbers 6:24-26, in which the name of the Lord *Yahweh* (which expresses the idea of a personal God of His covenant people) is changed for God (*elohim*) to stress the universal call of God to all nations to praise Him: "May God be gracious to us and bless us and make his face shine upon us, that your ways may be known on earth, your salvation among all nations. May the peoples praise you, O God; may all the peoples praise you. May the nations be glad and sing for joy, for you rule the peoples justly and guide the nations of the earth." (Ps 67:1-7).

In Psalm 96:2-9, the psalmist calls believers to proclaim God's salvation among the nations (v. 3). There are also other texts in Psalms that call for missionary activities among the nations (e.g., 105:1-2; 119:46; 126:2-3; 145:11-12; 145:21). The psalmists declare that they will praise God among the nations (57:9; 108:3), and the kingdoms of the earth should "sing to God" (Ps 68:32). Women will be also included in the proclamation of the good news about the caring God: "The Lord gives the word; the women who announce the news are a great host" (Ps 68:11, ESV).[41] Thus the whole earth will "be filled with his glory" (Ps 72:19; cf. Rev 18:1).

As a result of these witnessing activities, Egyptians and Ethiopians will submit to the Lord (Ps 68:31), "all kings will bow down" and "all nations will serve" the Davidic King, the Messiah (Ps 72:11), God will be "feared by the kings of the earth" (Ps 76:12), God will judge all the nations as His inheritance (Ps 82:8), "all the nations . . . will come and worship" before the Lord (Ps 86:9), foreigners will be like the natives enjoying the benefits of citizenship (Ps 87:4-6), and "all men" will know of God's "mighty acts" (Ps 145:12).

Mission in the Prophets

Isaiah explained that the descendants of Israel would be a spectacle to all nations of God's goodness to them: "Their descendants will be known among the nations and their offspring among the peoples. All who see them will acknowledge that they are a people the Lord has blessed. I delight greatly in the Lord, . . . He has clothed me with garments of salva-

---

[41] The form of the Hebrew word *hambaśśᵉrôt* is in Piel participle feminine plural absolute of the root *bāśar* ("to bring good new") which means, in the context of Psalm 68:11, that "the women who proclaim/announce/bring the good news" are a great company.

tion and arrayed me in a robe of righteousness, . . . For as the soil makes the sprout come up and a garden causes seeds to grow, so the Sovereign Lord will make righteousness and praise spring up before all nations" (Isa 61:9-11). God foretells the bright future of Zion and Jerusalem in these terms: "The nations will see your righteousness, and all kings your glory; you will be called by a new name that the mouth of the Lord will bestow" (Isa 62:2). Isaiah speaks about missionaries who "will proclaim my [the Lord's] glory among the nations" (Isa 66:19), and stresses what the Lord will do: "I will select some of them also to be priests and Levites."[42] The book of Isaiah ends with the international and worldwide dimension of worship: "'From one New Moon to another and from one Sabbath to another, all mankind will come and bow down before me,' says the Lord" (Isa 66:23).[43] In this context, it is interesting to note Isaiah's rebuke of Hezekiah's failure to share God's salvation message with the Babylonian emissaries and instead choosing to show them his royal treasures (2 Kgs 20:12-19; 2 Chr 32:31; Isa 39:1-8).

Prophet Zephaniah strikingly notes that "the nations on every shore will worship him [the Lord]," not in Jerusalem but "everyone in its own land" (Zeph 2:11), and states that God will "purify the lips of the peoples, that all of them may call on the name of the LORD and serve him shoulder to shoulder" (Zeph 3:9). God projected that His worshipers, who are called His people, will come even from beyond Cush (Ethiopia) to serve Him (Zeph 3:10).[44]

God's true worshipers "will be the recipients of international fame and honor"[45] and "peoples from the most distant places . . . will experience salvation and will worship Yahweh on His day. He is the redemptive King not only of the Judahites, but also of people from many nations."[46] Thus, "on two occasions (2:11; 3:9-10) Zephaniah depicted worship of Yahweh taking place on a worldwide basis by those who are delivered from the judgment. . . . There will be so many that they will stand shoulder

---

[42] Walter Brueggemann appropriately explains: "Yahweh will dispatch 'survivors,' that is, restored Jews, to all parts of the known world. These messengers (missionaries?) will go where the news of Yahweh has never been before. . . . From among these *goyim*, these Gentiles nations, some will be designated and ordained as priests and Levites, priests to handle Jewish holy things and Levites to interpret Jewish torah" (*Isaiah 40–66* [Louisville, KY: Westminster John Knox, 1998], 258-259).

[43] See also Micah 4:1-5; Zechariah 2:11; 8:20-23; 13:8-9; 14:16-19.

[44] A note in the *NIV Study Bible* (Grand Rapids, MI: Zondervan, 1985), 1398, reads: "Israel's God will be acknowledged by the nations, and God's people will be honored by them (cf. vv. 19-20)."

[45] Greg A. King, "The Remnant in Zephaniah," *BSac* 151 (1994): 424.

[46] Greg A. King, "The Day of the Lord in Zephaniah," *BSac* 152 (1995): 21.

to shoulder, serving Yahweh unitedly (3:9)."⁴⁷ Hence, God is depicted in a unique activity (never again mentioned in the entire Old Testament): singing over His people with joy (Zeph 3:17).

The prophetic word of God was to be promulgated to others, but this word needed to be accompanied by godly behavior. In this way, the God of Israel would be attractive to all nations, and they would come and worship Him (Isa 56:6–7; 61:9–11; 62:2).⁴⁸ As a result of such activities, kings would issue edicts in favor of Jerusalem's temple (Cyrus, Darius and Artaxerxes; see 2 Chr 36:22–23; Ezra 3–7; Dan 6:25–28; Neh 2:1–10). Otherwise, the people of God would be a byword and object of scorn (Joel 2:17; Ezek 36:20–21). The deeds of God's people, rather than their words, are a stronger witness and speak louder concerning the majesty of their God (Ezek 20:41; 36:23; Hos 1:9; 2:21–23; cf. Matt 5:16).

If God's faithful remnant would accomplish His task, then people will become His dedicated followers. Isaiah and Micah prophetically envisioned a time when "many peoples/nations will come and say, 'Come, let us go up to . . . the house of the God of Jacob. He will teach us his ways, so that we may walk in his paths'" (Isa 2:3; Micah 4:2; see also Isa 27:12–13). Even the descendants of Abraham's other sons and the sons of Ishmael will come to the house of God with their offerings and praise the Lord (Isa 60:6–7).⁴⁹ Isaiah joyfully states: "From the west, men will fear the name of the Lord, and from the rising of the sun, they will revere his glory. . . . Nations will come to your light, kings to the brightness of your dawn" (Isa 59:19; 60:3). Zechariah underscored it very emphatically: "Many nations will be joined with the Lord in that day and will become my people" (Zech 2:11). Joel declares that all people who come to the Lord can be saved: "Everyone who calls on the name of the Lord will be saved; for on Mount Zion and in Jerusalem there will be deliverance" (Joel 2:32). The prophet Malachi stresses: "'My name will be great among the nations, from the rising to the setting of the sun. In every place incense and pure offerings will be brought to my name, because my name will be great among the nations,' says the LORD Almighty" (1:11).⁵⁰

---

[47] Ibid., 30.

[48] Amos mentions that nations (note the plural form) will bear the Lord's name (Amos 9:12). This text is quoted in Acts 15:17 as the fulfillment of God's promise of proclaiming the Gospel to the Gentiles, and as the confirmation of His intention to save them (Acts 15:14–15).

[49] It is worthwhile to note that Midian, Ephah, and Sheba are enumerated as descendants in Abraham's line with Keturah, according to Genesis 25:2–4; and Nebaioth and Kedar are sons of Ishmael (Gen 25:13).

[50] This verse can also be rendered into the present tense, because the first and third clauses are nominal phrases in Hebrew, and the second sentence contains a Hophal participle. Only the

God's people in the Old Testament were to be an objective lesson for other people. When nations saw what God had done for them, they should have recognized the God of Israel as a living God and followed Him. God was proving Himself holy through His people in the sight of many nations (Josh 2:9–14; Isa 61:9–11; Ezek 20:12; 36:23; 38:23; 39:7, 27–29). This is a different type of evangelism than what Christians usually have in mind. It is not so much about going outside and preaching, but about being a living example of God's intervening grace. Witnessing without practical lifestyle could be empty, harmful, and destructive (Ezek 36:23; 36:33–38).

God's Mission Outside of Israel

God called His people to a certain mission, and His people needed to fulfill that mission. But God also worked outside of Israel. The Old Testament remnant was not an elite group who would be uniquely saved. They were elected for mission. However, that does not mean that God did not also use or work for others outside of the covenant community. His methods were not always revealed to us; but it is simply stated. Examples of God's working with different peoples outside of the official body of believers include:

1) Melchizedek, king of Salem and the priest of the God Most High (Gen 14:18–20). Melchizedek appeared suddenly, blessed Abraham, and expressed his strong belief in the Creator God who gave victory to Abraham over their enemies. Abraham gave his tithe to Melchizedek as an expression of his love and gratitude to God. Melchizedek faithfully served the Lord as king and priest and became a type for Christ (Ps 110; Heb 7:1–3; 7:11–17).

2) Job, a well-respected non-Israelite sage from the East, the land of Uz (Job 1:1–3), probably lived in the time of the patriarchs. Three times it is stated that he "was blameless and upright; he feared God and shunned evil" (Job 1:1, 9; 2:3). His reputation made him a powerful witness for the true God (Job 1:3; 19:9–29; 42:10–11, 16).

3) Jethro, the priest of Midian and Moses's father-in-law (Exod 18:1). After hearing from Moses about what the Lord had done for Israel in Egypt, he praised Yahweh and added, "Now I know that the Lord is greater than all other gods, for he did this to those who had treated Israel arrogantly" (Exod 18:10–11).

4) Balaam, a prophet of God. Balaam pronounced messianic prophe-

---

context decides which translation fits best the overall message. If the text is read in the present tense, then it underscores the knowledge of the true God among nations in shocking contrast to Israel who should know Him, but dishonors Him through her unbelief, unfaithfulness, and malpractice.

cies (Num 24:17-19) while in apostasy (Num 22-24) and this cost him his life (Num 31:8; cf. Rev 2:14).

5) Rahab, the prostitute in Jericho. Rahab heard about the God of Israel, believed, helped two Israelite spies, saved her family from destruction, and joined the people of God (Josh 2:1-21; 6:17, 25; cf. Matt 1:5; Heb 11:31; James 2:25). Rahab later married Salmon, son of Nahshon, one of the prominent princes of Judah (Num 7:12; Ruth 4:18-22; 1 Chr 2:11-12; Matt 1:1, 5-6), and became an ancestor of the Messiah.[51]

6) God worked with other nations (e.g., the Cushites, Philistines, and Arameans). Amos boldly proclaims God's intervention on behalf of these nations: "'Are you not Israelites the same to me as the Cushites?' declares the Lord. 'Did I not bring Israel up from Egypt, the Philistines from Caphtor and the Arameans from Kir?'" (Amos 9:7).

7) God gave the Canaanite people 400 years of grace to repent and return to Him (Gen 15:13-16). Similarly, before the flood, God offered 120 years of grace (Gen 6:3). In both cases, rebellion against God prevailed.

8) The nations were judged by God. As was already mentioned, many prophets uttered oracles against foreign nations (Isa 13-23; 28-33; Jer 46-51; Ezek 25-32; Joel 3:1-3, 12; Amos 1-2). This suggests that God had revealed to them the truth and that they were accountable to God for their actions (see especially the books of Jonah and Obadiah; Jer 51:59-64).

9) Darius the Mede testified to many nations about the living God of Daniel who is able to rescue from perils of life. He issued a decree about this eternal God and His everlasting kingdom (Dan 6:25-27).

10) God used Cyrus to accomplish His purposes—the liberation of God's people from Babylonian exile (see especially, Isa 44:28; 45:1-4; Ezra 1:1-4; 5:13-16).

God's Ultimate Missiological Goal

God ultimately wants to bring together these two different groups—God's faithful remnant and people outside of it. For example, Melchizedek came in contact with Abraham (Gen 14:18-20); Rahab with Israel (Josh 2); Jethro with Moses (Exod 3 and 18); Naaman with Elisha (2 Kgs 5); Nebuchadnezzar with Daniel (Dan 1; 2; and 4); Ahasuerus [Xerxes] with Esther (Esth 1-9); and Ruth with Naomi (Ruth 1:16).

Isaiah describes this achievement with amazing words and vivid pictures: "In that day there will be a highway from Egypt to Assyria. The As-

---

[51] Richard M. Davidson, *In the Footsteps of Joshua* (Hagerstown, MD: Review and Herald, 1995), 52. Consider also how people from different nations were attracted to God and His people by seeking to be in the service of Israel. See, for example, the cases of Uriah, the Hittite (2 Sam 11:3), and Ebed-Melech, an Ethiopian official in the royal palace (Jer 38:7-13).

syrians will go to Egypt and the Egyptians to Assyria. The Egyptians and Assyrians will worship together. In that day Israel will be the third, along with Egypt and Assyria, a blessing on the earth. The LORD Almighty will bless them, saying, 'Blessed be Egypt my people, Assyria my handiwork, and Israel my inheritance'" (Isa 19:23-25).[52] This is a stunning, surprising, and unique statement. Not only Israel, but also Egypt and Assyria are called the people of God, and they are to worship together![53]

Conclusion

In the Old Testament, God is indeed the most glorious missionary in a mission of salvation for the whole world. In the performance of His mission, He uses human instruments and through them leads people to Himself (Isa 45:22). From the very beginning, the scope of mission for God and His people was worldwide. Adam, Seth, Enoch, Noah, Abraham, Moses, prophets, and others had their mission to fulfill. The ultimate and deliberate purpose of God in electing Abraham, or Israel, was to become a blessing, a light, and a witness on His behalf to the entire world. The Old Testament vision of mission was all-inclusive. It was not simply about going somewhere, sending someone, or doing something. It was primarily about being a special people with a special message that needed to be modeled in real life and shared.

I will briefly explore the implications of the Old Testament understanding of mission for an Adventist ecclesiology.

1) Mission requires accepting God's ultimate goal for saving humanity and, through His power, fulfilling this plan. The reason for our existence is to fulfill His mission. 2) Being is as important as sending. The call to an ethical lifestyle and living tangibly the message of God is a crucial focus that needs to be emphasized today. Only then are we able to live to God's glory.[54] Being His instrument and doing His will gives power to witnessing and gives meaning to our mission. Mission is not only being sent

---

[52] This text echoes Genesis 12:3 about the call of Abraham. The allusions to Abrahamic blessing are a key motif which is now broadened to include Egypt and Assyria. These mighty empires and close neighbors of Israel represent the civilized ancient world: "And all peoples on earth will be blessed through you" (Gen 12:3). These three nations were to form a unified league for God, and were expected to worship the Lord together.

[53] It is very important to note that the prophet Isaiah mentions, in the midst of judgment over ten nations, three positive passages regarding the Gentiles (chaps. 13-23): 14:1-2 (aliens will join God's people and unite with them); 18:7 (nations will bring gifts to the temple); and 19:17-25 (altar and pillar to the Lord will be erected in Egypt; the Egyptians will cry to the Lord; He will make Himself known to them, and they will worship Him).

[54] Lester Merklin, "The Remnant Mission: To Reveal and Proclaim God's Glory," *JAMS* 4.1 (2008): 4-17.

out into the world, but being engaged with it.

3) The worldwide scope of our mission has not changed; God's mission field has always been the whole earth. His intent to save in the Old Testament is the same today. His plan for the mission has always been inclusive of all nations, ethnic groups, and families (Gen 12:2–3; Exod 19:3–6; Acts 15:14; Gal 3:6–9, 26–29; Eph 3:6–12; 1 Pet 2:9; Rev 7:9–10; 14:6).

4) Mission and message are inseparable. The essentials of the message have not changed. It has had new and different emphases over time, but the basic concept of salvation has always been the same in the Old and New covenants. We must hold firmly to the eternal gospel, while being creative in the development of fresh and innovative methods.

5) Family is the fundamental unit where mission begins. In this way, Truth is passed from one generation to another. This stress on the family ties is emphatically presented in the last prophetic message of the Old Testament: "See, I will send you the prophet Elijah before that great and dreadful day of the LORD comes. He will turn the hearts of the fathers to their children, and the hearts of the children to their fathers; or else I will come and strike the land with a curse" (Mal 4:5–6). This inward approach to mission, centered around the family, needs to be emphasized in today's broken world and should lead to discipleship and to the upholding of the true value of Adventist education. There should be an evangelistic focus on our children and young people. To impart the values of Adventism to the next generation is evangelism par excellence.

6) The Old Testament community of faith had an eschatological dimension and was future-oriented. This biblical eschatological paradigm (cf. Gen 3:15; Ezek 36–37; Dan 2; 7–9; Jude 1:14–15) should provide a pattern for our thinking today. God is coming to establish His eternal kingdom. This eschatological focus provides powerful fuel for mission.[55] Our hope in the Second Coming of Jesus Christ is the hope of all hopes.

7) Prophets constantly spoke against false religious systems and warned against the infiltration of paganism into true worship.[56] The task of God's people today is to present first of all the true picture of God, reveal His true character, and direct the attention of all to Jesus Christ.

8) Mission engages all people—men, women, and even children—so

---

[55] Amedeo Molnár, "Eschatologická naděje České Reformace," *Od reformace k zítřku* (Praha: Kalich, 1956), 13–101; Sakae Kubo, *God Meets Man* (Nashville, TN: Southern Publishing Assoc, 1978), 105–111.

[56] Prophets spoke against idolatry and foreign gods. For examples, see Isaiah 37:16–20; 40:18–22; 41:7, 22–24; 42:17; 44:10–12; 46:5–7; 48:5; Jeremiah 32:33–35; 44:15–28; 49:1–5; Ezekiel 20:27–31; 36:18–20; 37:23; Daniel 3:16–18; 7:8, 20–26; 8:9–12; Hosea 4:6–14; Amos 5:4–6.

that they may fulfill the role God assigns to them. It demonstrates that God wants to use everyone who is willing to participate in His work and become His ambassador.

9) Mission leads to worship, praising the God who is creator of the whole world and who wants to save everyone. There is an emphasis on mission in the hymnic literature. The awareness and proclamation of God's goodness and holiness culminate in worshiping Him (Exod 33:18–19; 34:8; Isa 6:1–8; Ezek 1:28). The actual worship in the Lord's Temple was a powerful tool of witnessing about the loving-kindness of a living God and how He deals with sin in order to save repentant sinners.

10) God uses two different groups: insiders, i.e. the faithful remnant; and outsiders, i.e. those who serve God faithfully, according to the light they have. The faithful remnant have a special God-given mission. But God also has His messengers—individuals who live and proclaim important elements of His truth. The Lord desires to put these two different streams together by drawing them closer to each other. His ultimate goal is to have only one flock (Isa 14:1; 56:3–8; John 10:16; Eph 3:6).[57] The message of truth will possess all of God's people. Possessed by the truth and the power of the Spirit they would be fully equipped to faithfully proclaim God's message and fulfill His mission to the world (John 17:15).[58]

---

[57] See Richard P. Lehmann, "The Remnant in the Book of Revelation," *Studies in Adventist Ecclesiology I: Toward a Theology of the Remnant*, ed. Ángel Manuel Rodríguez (Silver Spring, MD: Biblical Research Institute, 2009), 108–112; and Ángel M. Rodríguez, "Concluding Essay: God's End-Time Remnant and the Christian Church," *Toward a Theology of the Remnant*, 217–226.

[58] Stott comments: "For we often tend to go to one or other of two opposite extremes. Either we are so determined to live in the world and maintain contact with non-Christians that we begin to assimilate non-Christian ideas and standards, and are then guilty of *becoming conformed to the world* (Rom. 12:12); or we are so determined not to lose our distinctive Christian identity that we begin to shun contact with non-Christians in the world, and then become guilty of *withdrawing from it* (John 17:15; 1 Cor 5:10). The best way to avoid these two mistakes of conformity and withdrawal is to be engaged in mission. For if we remember that we are sent into the world as Christ's representatives, we can neither conform to it or we cease to represent him, nor withdraw from it or we have no one to represent him to" (John R. W. Stott, ed., *Making Christ Known*, 11).

CHAPTER 5

MISSION IN THE NEW TESTAMENT

Clinton Wahlen

The New Testament is all about mission.[1] It begins with God sending His Son into the world to save it. It continues with the sending of the apostles by Jesus to proclaim the gospel message, first to Israel and then to the world.[2] Paul, in particular, who would gladly "spend and be spent" (2 Cor 12:15), epitomizes the indefatigable progress that characterized the earliest Christians. In the epistles, we find both setbacks and advances. The pattern persists in Revelation, first with the letters to the seven churches and then in even more thoroughgoing symbolic imagery, until the eschatological climax is ushered in, by the Word of God riding triumphantly to the earth on a white horse.

But how is mission to be defined and how is it to be done? Does the New Testament contain a unified theology of mission or does it change in accordance with the predilections of the writers and their peculiar circumstances? Should we not expect to find anything normative for the church today? To address these questions fully would require a much

---

[1] George W. Peters, *A Biblical Theology of Missions* (Chicago, IL: Moody, 1972), 131: "The New Testament is a missionary book in address, content, spirit and design." Cf. Grant R. Osborne, "New Testament Theology of Mission," *EDWM*, 682–686: "The New Testament is first and foremost a missionary document in the sense that it details the carrying out of God's plan of salvation for the world" (682).

[2] Important precursors to the New Testament concept may be found in the Old Testament (see Jiří Moskala, "Mission in the Old Testament," in this volume) and in the LXX (see, e.g., on the use of *apostellō*, T. Muraoka, *A Greek-English Lexicon of the Septuagint* [Leuven: Peeters, 2009], 83). On the role of the Septuagint, in terms of mission, see W. Richey Hogg, "The Scriptures in the Christian World Mission: Three Historical Considerations," *Missiology* 12.4 (1984): 389–396.

lengthier treatment than is possible here.[3] However, as we shall see, mission appears frequently enough in the various New Testament writings so that the major contours of the subject become clear.[4] We begin with Jesus' proclamation of the Kingdom of God as presented in the Four Gospels, noting at appropriate junctures the distinctive emphases of each, followed in turn by a consideration of Acts, Paul, the General Epistles, and Revelation.

Jesus' Proclamation of the Kingdom of God

In Mark 1:15, Jesus proclaims, "The time is fulfilled, and the kingdom of God has come near; repent, and believe in the good news" (NRS). Even from this terse summary, it seems clear that the missiological aim of Jesus is not to establish or usher in God's kingdom, but to connect people with a kingdom that has already come into existence, the manifestation of which was prophesied beforehand. God is sovereign over all the earth and over all people. Therefore, the ultimate mission aspiration of the Old Testament is for God's reign or kingdom to extend throughout the world (Isa 52:7; cf. Ps 47:8), through the coming of the ideal Davidic king (Isa 11:1–10), so that ultimately all nations will worship God (Ps 86:9–10). Jesus, at the outset of His Galilean ministry, announces the fulfillment of these prophetic expectations. In affirming that the kingdom of God "has come

---

[3] The most important treatments of the subject include Ferdinand Hahn, *Mission in the New Testament* (Naperville, IL: Allenson, 1965); Donald Senior and Carroll Stuhlmüller, *The Biblical Foundations for Mission* (Maryknoll, NY: Orbis, 1983); David J. Bosch, *Transforming Mission: Paradigm Shifts in Theology of Mission* (Maryknoll, NY: Orbis, 1991); William J. Larkin Jr. and Joel F. Williams, ed., *Mission in the New Testament: An Evangelical Approach* (Maryknoll, NY: Orbis, 1998); Ådna, Jostein, and Hans Kvalbein, ed. *The Mission of the Early Church to Jews and Gentiles* (Tübingen: Mohr Siebeck, 2000); Andreas J. Köstenberger and Peter T. O'Brien, *Salvation to the Ends of the Earth: A Biblical Theology of Missions* (Downers Grove, IL: InterVarsity, 2001); Arthur F. Glasser, *Announcing the Kingdom: The Story of God's Mission in the Bible* (Grand Rapids, MI: Baker, 2003); Michael Green, *Evangelism in the Early Church* (Grand Rapids, MI: Eerdmans, 2003); Eckhard J. Schnabel, *Early Christian Mission*, 2 vols. (Downers Grove, IL: InterVarsity, 2004); and Michael W. Goheen, *A Light to the Nations: The Missional Church and the Biblical Story* (Grand Rapids, MI: Baker, 2011). For a comprehensive bibliography, see Joel F. Williams, "Mission in the Bible: A Bibliography of Recent Research," July 2005, n.p. Online: http://www.globalmissiology.org/english/archive/williams_bibliography_recent_research_3_2005.html. (cited 6 December 2011).

[4] I. Howard Marshall has even structured this as the major theme, most clearly stated in *A Concise New Testament Theology* (Downers Grove, IL: InterVarsity, 2008), 14–15: "New Testament theology is essentially missionary theology. The documents came into being as the result of a two-part mission: first the mission of Jesus sent by God to inaugurate his kingdom; then the mission of Jesus' followers, called to continue his work by proclaiming him as Lord and Savior and calling people to faith and ongoing commitment to him, as a result of which his church grows.... In short, people who are called by God to be missionaries are carrying out their calling by the writing of Gospels, Letters and related material. They are concerned to make converts and then to provide for their nurture, to bring new believers to birth and to nourish them to maturity."

near" (*ēngiken*), He suggests a realized aspect to the kingdom already in His ministry, without overtly asserting messianic claims.[5] The call of the Twelve anticipates a successful mission, not resulting in a *new* kingdom, but a restored Israel and a reconstitution of its leadership (cf. Matt 19:28), centered on allegiance to Jesus.[6] "Missionary work and church must not be separated, since the very goal and purpose of missionary work is the creation of a community of disciples."[7] At the same time, there is clearly a sense in which the kingdom's manifestation remains future.[8] Although the Gospels recognize a connection between Israel's Davidic expectations and perceptions of Jesus as the "son of David,"[9] they also distance Jesus from such popular messianic expectations.[10] Jesus, by referring to "the son of man" (an expression found in the Gospels almost exclusively on His lips),[11] likewise seems to distance Himself from such hopes, at least in the short-term.[12] Already at His baptism by John, the voice from heaven calls Jesus to the mission of the Suffering Servant (Mark 1:11 parr.)[13] and a work of redemption (Mark 10:45). Satan offers Jesus kingly power over the nations, but He refuses to turn from His allegiance to God (Matt 4:8–10 par.).

Salvation History and the Cosmic Conflict

The Synoptic Gospels portray Jesus' life as a part of Israel's much broader story.[14] Both Matthew and Luke emphasize this salvation-histor-

---

[5] Cf. Targ. Isa 40:9 and 52:7, "The kingdom of your God is revealed!"

[6] Craig S. Keener, *The Historical Jesus of the Gospels* (Grand Rapids, MI: Eerdmans, 2009), 246, 249.

[7] Schnabel, *Early Christian Mission*, 1:356.

[8] So Robert H. Stein, *Mark* (Grand Rapids, MI: Baker, 2008), 72–73, providing also a brief summary and evaluation of the major ways the coming of the kingdom has been understood. George Eldon Ladd, *A Theology of the New Testament* (Grand Rapids, MI: Eerdmans, 1993), 181: "The messianic mission of Jesus had as its objective the preparation of men and women for the future Kingdom of God." Cf. Bosch, 31–35.

[9] E.g. Matthew 1:1; 9:27:12:23; Mark 10:47–48; 11:10; Luke 1:32.

[10] Mark 12:35–37 parr.; John 7:41–42.

[11] In John 12:34, the people twice refer to "the son of man," but do not know who he is.

[12] For discussion and references to the voluminous literature on this much-debated expression, see George W. E. Nickelsburg, "Son of Man," *ABD* 6 (1992): 137–150; John J. Collins, "The Son of Man in First-Century Judaism," *NTS* 38 (1992): 448–66; but also Craig A. Evans, *Mark 8:27–16:20* (Nashville, TN: Nelson, 2001), lxxiii–lxxviii.

[13] Cf. Ladd, *Theology*, 184: "This allusion to the servant passage in Isaiah indicates that Jesus realized from the very beginning that his messianic mission was to be carried out in terms of the Suffering Servant of the Lord rather than in terms of the ruling Davidic king."

[14] N. T. Wright, *The New Testament and the People of God* (Minneapolis, MN: Augsburg Fortress, 1992), 369.

ical perspective as well as the element of divine promise and fulfillment. Thus God is at work through Jesus to accomplish Israel's missiological purpose.[15] In John, Jesus is "the light of the world" (8:12; 9:5) that Israel was meant to be (cf. Isa 2:1–5; 60:1–3). Also, the concept of the kingdom of God is universalized as "eternal life,"[16] which reality is made possible by Christ's death and resurrection.

All four Gospels portray the establishment of God's kingdom in terms of cosmic realities, rather than in terms of the earthly expectations of many in Israel.[17] Immediately upon Jesus' acceptance of His messianic mission, that mission is challenged by Satan, in the wilderness temptations (Matt 4:1–11 par.), and by the unclean spirits and demons throughout Jesus' ministry. In Mark, Jesus' divine purity and holiness enables Him to dispatch the demons with little trouble. In Matthew and Luke, the clash of kingdoms is more evident. Jesus proves able to threaten Satan's kingdom and advance God's kingdom precisely because God is at work in Him (Luke 11:20 par.; 10:17–20). It is this direct confrontation of Satan, through miraculous healings, and the expulsion of demons by the Spirit of God, that distinguishes the messianic mission of Jesus and His disciples from that of John the Baptist (Matt 9:33; 10:1, 25; John 10:41).

The Gospel of John sublimates the cosmic conflict into a struggle between light and darkness, which is embodied in Jesus and His human adversaries.[18] Jesus' death, to which the Gospel looks forward (1:5, 29; 2:18–22), represents God's decisive victory over the cosmic "prince of this world" (12:30–31). Nevertheless, the war is not over; after Jesus returns to the Father, the Spirit will be sent to continue this conflict with the evil powers and to advance God's kingdom (16:8–11).

What it means to belong to the kingdom is arguably the entire bur-

---

[15] Bosch defines mission through a narrow, modern missiological prism through which he reads the biblical story. As a result, he finds in the Old Testament "no indication" of God sending people "to cross geographical, religious, and social frontiers in order to win others" to Israel's faith (17). See the trenchant critique of Bosch's methodology in Andreas J. Köstenberger, "The Place of Mission in New Testament Theology: An Attempt to Determine the Significance of Mission within the Scope of the New Testament's Message as a Whole," *Missiology*, 27/3 (1999): 357.

[16] Köstenberger, "Mission," 358.

[17] Much of the material for this section has been summarized from Clinton Wahlen, *Jesus and the Impurity of Spirits in the Synoptic Gospels* (Tübingen: Mohr Siebeck, 2004), 126–127, 135, 156–159 and passim. See also Susan R. Garrett, *The Demise of the Devil: Magic and the Demonic in Luke's Writings* (Minneapolis, MN: Fortress, 1989).

[18] See Rodney A. Whitacre, *Johannine Polemic: The Role of Tradition and Theology* (Chicago, IL: Scholars Press, 1982); Judith L. Kovacs, "'Now Shall the Ruler of This World Be Driven Out': Jesus' Death as Cosmic Battle in John 12:20–36," *JBL* 114 (1995): 227–247.

den of Jesus' teaching, which is gradually unpacked through His call and commissioning of the Twelve, use of suggestive images of mission such as "salt" and "light," and, even more symbolically, in the parables.

Discipleship and Commission

In calling His first disciples, Jesus said they were to be "fishers of people" (Mark 1:17 par.; cf. Luke 5:10), joining Him in His mission to rescue people for the Kingdom of God.[19] This also suggests that discipleship involves *being* as well as doing. We have already mentioned the symbolism of the number twelve. In addition, Mark 3:14 says that Jesus named them "apostles," meaning "those sent out,"[20] because He was sending them out to proclaim the nearness of the kingdom, the same message that Jesus Himself proclaimed (Matt 10:7; cf. 4:17). Furthermore, "there is a strong tradition within the Gospels that Jesus sent out His disciples to spread His message during his ministry"[21] and that they committed His teachings to memory. Even before the resurrection, Jesus sent them on a mission of preaching to Israel in His name and authority (Matt 10:1 parr.) in order to magnify the impact of His own ministry and prepare them for a more comprehensive mission of making disciples (28:19; cf. 10:5–6).[22] From the beginning, Jesus characterized His disciples by their mission.

Jesus also called them "to be with him" (Mark 3:14). The significance of this phrase is frequently overlooked.[23] The concept of being a disciple (*mathētēs*) implies learning (*manthanō*) from one's master teacher in a "teach-and-learn situation."[24] Even the wider circle of disciples could apparently take advantage of opportunities for in-depth instruction (Luke 10:39, 42) and mission (Mark 5:18–19). The importance of Jesus' example during more than three years of intimate association, in His exten-

---

[19] Eckhard J. Schnabel, "Mission, Early Non-Pauline," *DLNT,* 752.

[20] On the various nuances of *apostolos*, see Schabel, *Early Christian Mission*, 1:283.

[21] Richard Bauckham, *Jesus and the Eyewitnesses: The Gospels as Eyewitness Testimony* (Grand Rapids, MI: Eerdmans, 2006), 284; see esp. Rainer Riesner, *Jesus als Lehrer: Eine Untersuchung zum Ursprung der Evangelien-Überlieferung* (Tübingen: Mohr Siebeck, 1981), 453–475.

[22] Schnabel, *Early Christian Mission*, 1:291–292. As is frequently observed, this is the only true imperative in the Great Commission (*mathēteusate*), implying ongoing teaching both before and after baptism (ibid., 1:355).

[23] E.g., Schabel's voluminous study dwells on just about every other aspect of Mark 3:13–15, except this phrase (1:280–284), though one reason might be its common classification as a distinctive formula in Mark for discipleship (see also 5:18, 37, 40; 14:33, 67; 16:10). But the phrase is a common one in Mark (1:36; 2:25; 4:36; 5:24; 14:18, 43).

[24] Rainer Riesner, "Jesus as Preacher and Teacher," *Jesus and the Oral Gospel Tradition*, ed. Henry Wansbrough (Sheffield: JSOT Press, 1991), 191, noting on 197 the Hebrew and Aramaic correlatives (*talmîd* and *talmîdaʾ*) as equivalent to *mathētēs*.

sive outreach, dealing wisely with opposition, compassion for the poor and suffering, and winsome treatment of people in a variety of situations should not be underestimated (cf. 1 Pet 2:21-23). Being a disciple also means following His example in denying oneself and taking up one's cross (Mark 8:34 parr.).

Images of Mission

The importance of Jesus' example is underscored by several images of mission we find in the Gospels. Drawing on earlier prophetic hopes for Israel (Isa 2:2-3), Jesus called His disciples *salt* (Matt 5:13; Luke 14:33-35) and *light*—like a city on a hill (Matt 5:14).[25] They were to mingle with people from all levels of society just as Jesus did and to spread the wisdom (cf. Col 4:6)[26] of the kingdom like sunlight covers the earth.[27] The community of the disciples would be like a new Zion, whose glory would bring even the Gentiles to know the God of Israel (Isa 60:1-3; 62:1-2, 10-12).[28] Of course, they could only be such a light as followers of *Jesus*, the source of light (John 1:9; 8:12; 9:5),[29] who reached out to Gentiles and whose ministry implicitly included the Gentile mission.[30]

Arguably, the most important image of mission found in the New Testament is that of *incarnation*. In Jesus, God "tabernacled" among us by becoming flesh (1:1, 14). He is "God with us" (Matt 1:23; cf. Luke 1:35), the only one who can really show us what the Father is like (John 1:18; 14:9).[31] As the Father has sent Him, Jesus sends His disciples (17:18; 20:21); they are to reflect the character of Jesus as Jesus reflected the Father.[32] "Jesus Christ can be fleshed out in the lives of those who fol-

---

[25] Otto Betz, "Mission III. Neues Testament," *TRE* 23:25; Schnabel, "Mission," 753.

[26] Wolfgang Nauck, "Salt as a Metaphor in Instructions for Discipleship," *ST* 6.2 (1952): 165-178; R. T. France, *The Gospel According to Matthew: An Introduction and Commentary* (Grand Rapids, MI: Eerdmans, 1985), 112: "The Rabbis commonly used salt as an image for wisdom (cf. Col. 4:6)."

[27] Cf. Pliny, *Nat. Hist.*, 31.102: "There is nothing more useful than salt and sunshine."

[28] Cf. Gerhard von Rad, "Die Stadt auf dem Berge," *EvT* 8 (1948-1949): 439-447.

[29] Similarly, Joachim Jeremias, *The Sermon on the Mount* (Philadelphia, PA: Fortress, 1963), 26. Important Old Testament antecedents include Isaiah 42:6; 49:6.

[30] See Michael F. Bird, *Jesus and the Origins of the Gentile Mission* (London: T & T Clark, 2006), who argues that Jesus conceived of the salvation of Gentiles "through the mechanism of a restored and renewed Israel" (57), *which was to include the incorporation of Gentiles*, and that this salvation was already being effected through His ministry.

[31] Osborne, *Revelation*, 684.

[32] Amazingly, incarnation, as a model for mission, is absent even in the relative few discussions of mission in John (ibid.; Köstenberger, "Mission," 358-59). A notable exception is Johannes Nissen, *New Testament and Mission: Historical and Hermeneutical Perspectives* (Frankfurt: Lang, 2006).

low in Jesus' steps."³³ This so-called "passive" or "silent" witness has numerous, under-appreciated antecedents in the Old Testament.³⁴ The New Testament itself, and Paul in particular, understand witness holistically, "involving, in one seamless fabric, the Christian's gospel-determined existence, behavior, and proclamation."³⁵ This incarnational holism finds expression in mission in another way also: Just as Jesus took on humanity in its entirety, so the church is called to care for the whole person, physically as well as spiritually (1 Thess 5:23; 3 John 2). Jesus seems to have intentionally included both physical healing and reintegration into the worshipping community of Israel (Mark 2:17 parr.) as integral parts of His mission, proclaiming the kingdom of God (Matt 11:5 par.; Luke 4:18).

Parables of the Kingdom

The surpassing value of the kingdom is illustrated by the parables of the hidden treasure and pearl of great price (Matt 13:44–45). The inevitable, but often imperceptible, spread of the kingdom is depicted in the parable of leaven (Matt 13:33 par.). The kingdom begins small, like a mustard seed, but ultimately dominates the landscape and provides a place of refuge (Mark 4:30 parr.; cf. Eze 17:23). Until consummation, it encompasses both bad and good people (Matt 13:47–50). Trial, persecution, and worldly pressures test the character of each and some fall away as a result (13:19–22). At the judgment, the "tares" (which were sown not by Jesus but by the devil) will be weeded out (13:36–43). "Taken together these parables show that the spread and realization of the kingdom of God will be a process moving toward the day of judgment."³⁶

The parables Jesus told near the end of His ministry emphasize the importance of watching and waiting as faithful servants (Matt 24:43–51 par.; 25:1–13), trusting that God will reward His elect (Luke 18:1–8) and

---

[33] Alan Neely, "Incarnational Mission," *EDWM*, 474. However, the link made by Neely and others to liberation theology too narrowly circumscribes the gospel proclamation of the kingdom. While Jesus "indisputably sided with the hurting, exploited, and abused of his day," (475), His message (as with that of the Hebrew prophets) pointed to the kingdom's *future* consummation as the basis for hope (e.g., the predominant use of the future tense in the beatitudes, Matt 5:3–12 par.).

[34] Abraham, Isaac, and Jacob in Canaan; Joseph in Egypt (with the "mixed multitude" of Exod 12:38 as possible fruitage); Daniel and his three compatriots bringing a knowledge of the true God to Nebuchadnezzar (leading to his apparent "conversion," Dan 4). God's salvation of Israel is, at the same time, a call for them to be His special people—not just for their own benefit but in order that they might mediate a knowledge of the true God to the nations around them (Exod 19:5–6; Deut 4:6; Ps 67:7; Mal 3:12).

[35] Robert L. Plummer, *Paul's Understanding of the Church's Mission; Did the Apostle Paul Expect the Early Christian Communities to Evangelize?* (Waynesboro, GA: Paternoster, 2006), 72.

[36] Craig Ott and Stephen J. Strauss, *Encountering Theology of Mission: Biblical Foundations, Historical Developments, and Contemporary Issues* (Grand Rapids, MI: Baker, 2010), 35.

utilizing wisely for the kingdom the talents given (25:14–30; cf. Luke 19:11–27).[37] The generosity of God in opening the gates of the kingdom to all willing to enter it, even up to the "eleventh hour" (Matt 20:1–16), is likewise an important mission principle.

Mission in Acts

The book of Acts serves as the ecclesiological continuation of Christ's mission through His chosen apostles. "Stay in the city," Jesus had said, "until you are clothed with power from on high" (Luke 24:49, ESV). This promise of the Holy Spirit was reiterated just before the ascension. The baptism by the Spirit would enable those who were closely associated with Christ during His earthly ministry (Acts 1:12–14, 21–26) to be His witnesses in an ever-expanding mission ultimately reaching to "the ends of the earth" (Acts 1:3, 8).[38]

Mission as Witness

This notion of being a "witness" (*martyrs*) to Jesus as Savior, giving one's "testimony" (*martyria*), and "testifying" (*diamartyromai*) to what has been seen and heard assumes a prominent place immediately after the resurrection (Luke 24:48) and throughout the book of Acts.[39] When the Holy Spirit filled them at Pentecost, the gifts they received were specially designed as an aid in proclaiming the gospel message across language barriers (Acts 2:5–11). In addition, they were filled further after they prayed for greater boldness to fulfill the gospel commission (Acts 4:31). Gentiles also were to take part in the mission of the church and so received a similar outpouring of the Spirit (Acts 10:44–47). In Acts, the gift of tongues always facilitates communication of the message of salvation.[40]

---

[37] Keener, *Historical Jesus*, 188–195, argues that "Jesus' parable-telling practice is authentic," and, "barring strong evidence to the contrary," that we should accept "most" parables attributed to Him in the Gospels as authentic (194–195); also, a table shows that some of the later judgment parables cohere with earlier biblical material and the earliest Christian writings (368).

[38] While this so-called "centrifugal" model of mission permeates the New Testament, it is much more visible in the Old Testament than is often granted. See Walter C. Kaiser, Jr., *Mission in the Old Testament: Israel as a Light to the Nations* (Grand Rapids, MI: Baker, 2000), 9 and *passim*; also now Cristian Dumitrescu, "Cosmic Conflict as a Hermeneutical Framework for Mission Theology in the Old Testament" (D.Miss. diss., Andrews University, 2010), 127–131, 189–192.

[39] E.g., Acts 2:32, 40; 4:20, 33; 22:15. See Allison A. Trites, *The New Testament Concept of Witness* (Cambridge: Cambridge University Press, 1977), 137–142.

[40] Three instances are recorded: at Pentecost, the listeners heard the apostles "speaking about God's deeds of power" (2:11, NRS); the Gentiles who received the gift were heard "extolling God" (10:46); those at Ephesus "prophesied" (19:6). Further on the gift of tongues, see Gerhard F. Hasel, *Speaking in Tongues: Biblical Speaking in Tongues and Contemporary Glossolalia* (Berrien Springs, MI: Adventist Theological Society, 1991).

Challenges to Mission

From the beginning, the mission faced significant challenges—opposition from the Jewish leaders (Acts 4:1-22; 5:17-32), opposition from duplicitous disciples (Acts 5:1-11), and charges of favoritism (Acts 6:1; cf. James 2:1)—all culminating in a more systematic persecution following the martyrdom of Stephen (Acts 8:2-3). Such apparent setbacks actually furthered the mission in dramatic ways. Particularly important to notice is that persecution served to expand the geographical boundaries of outreach activity away from Jerusalem to many other important cities, including Samaria, Antioch, and beyond. The church leadership structure also expanded beyond the apostles to include deacons, elders, and missionaries like Barnabas.[41] God Himself intervened, confronting Saul on the Damascus road and sending Ananias to heal and instruct him (9:1-19; 22:12-16).

Generally, the mission focused first on those nearest to the beliefs of the early Christians and most closely acquainted with the Hebrew Scriptures—Jews, proselytes, and God-fearing Gentiles.[42] The conversion of Gentiles brought special challenges. But the issue was not *whether* they should be incorporated into the church but *on what basis*, a matter resolved by the Jerusalem Council through respectful discussion and careful study of the Scriptures (Acts 15:6-21). We do not have time to discuss the details of this decision, except to observe that there was no abrogation of the food laws in order to take the gospel to the Gentiles.[43] The issue was circumcision (Acts 15:1, 5; cf. 11:2; Gal 2:12), which, as Paul demonstrates in Romans and Galatians, was not a universal law.[44] The fact that dietary and sexual regulations are imposed on the Gentiles by the Council, based on the levitical stipulations (Lev 18-20) for resident aliens

---

[41] Cf. Schnabel, "Mission," 757.

[42] Jacob Jervell, *Luke and the People of God: A New Look at Luke-Acts* (Minneapolis, MN: Augsburg, 1972), 44-45. A variety of terminology for God-fearers is found in Acts (*phoboumenoi/sebomenoi ton theon, eusebai, prosēlutoi*). See e.g., Max Wilcox, 'The "God-Fearers" in Acts—A Reconsideration,' *JSNT* 13 (1981): 102-122; J. A. Overman, 'The God-Fearers: Some Neglected Features," *JSNT* 32 (1988): 17-26; Irina Levinskaya, *The Book of Acts in Its Diaspora Setting* (Grand Rapids, MI: Eerdmans, 1996), 1-126.

[43] See Clinton Wahlen, "Peter's Vision and Conflicting Definitions of Purity," *NTS* 51 (2005): 505-518; Markus Bockmuehl, *Jewish Law in Gentile Churches: Halakhah and the Beginning of Christian Public Ethics* (Edinburgh: T. & T. Clark, 2000), 73: "the problem . . . was not the food but the company."

[44] David J. Rudolph, *A Jew to the Jews* (Tübingen: Mohr Siebeck, 2011), 199-201, argues that the unbearable "yoke" (Acts 15:10; cf. Gal 5:10) refers not to "being 'under the yoke of Mosaic law,'" but to "being 'under the yoke of Pharisaic halakhah'" (199).

in Israel (*gerim*),⁴⁵ suggests that great care was taken to be guided by divine revelation. This point is underscored by the decree itself through the inclusion of wording that "it has seemed good to the Holy Spirit and to us. . . ."⁴⁶ Contextualization, correctly practiced, does not bend the Scriptures into conformity to culture but studies the Scriptures within their historical setting in order to understand how to communicate the truth clearly and effectively within a specific cultural context. Even Paul's sermon at the Areopagus, while utilizing philosophical arguments and literary references that would be comprehensible to his pagan audience, does not use these to camouflage his message, but as a bridge to preach biblical truth, including the resurrection of Christ and urging repentance in view of the final judgment (Acts 17:30–31). Paul's role as the dominant missionary in Acts and the importance of his epistles in the development of the church require us to give special consideration to his contribution to New Testament mission.⁴⁷

Paul and Mission

Paul was uniquely suited for advancing the early Christian mission. His knowledge of the Scriptures, the direct revelations he received from Christ, his fluency in Hebrew, Aramaic, and Greek, his education in Greco-Roman as well as Jewish circles, being a Roman citizen, and, perhaps above all, his willingness to sacrifice everything for the sake of the gospel of Christ, contributed to the efficacy of his witness and his resultant success. Sent as an apostle, just as fully as the other apostles were (Gal 1:1, 15–16),⁴⁸ Paul recognized the incorporation or "grafting in" of Gentiles into Christ, the "root" of Israel,⁴⁹ and indeed His own mission work,⁵⁰ as

---

[45] See Richard Bauckham, "James and the Gentiles (Acts 15:13–21)," *History, Literature, and Society in the Book of Acts*, ed. Ben Witherington III (Cambridge: Cambridge University Press, 1996), 172–178.

[46] The role of the Holy Spirit in Luke's writings, specifically in the sense of prophetic utterances, is widely recognized; e.g., Robert P. Menzies, *The Development of Early Christian Pneumatology with Special Reference to Luke-Acts* (Sheffield: Sheffield Academic Press, 1991), 124–126; see esp. the more nuanced view of Max Turner, "The Spirit and the Power of Jesus' Miracles in the Lucan Conception," *NovT* 33 (1991):124–152.

[47] See esp. Eckhard J. Schnabel, *Paul the Missionary: Realities, Strategies, and Methods* (Downers Grove: IVP, 2008).

[48] Ibid., 124–125 (according to Schnabel, Paul argues that there are only "differences in logistics").

[49] The word *rhizēs*, "root," in Romans 11:16–18 refers to Christ (Rom 15:12; cf. Rev 5:5; 22:16) to whom both Jews and Gentiles are united, *not* to national Israel. Paul also uses the cognate root *rhizoō* to describe Christians as "rooted" in Christ and His love (Col 2:7; Eph 3:17).

[50] Rainer Riesner, *Paul's Early Period: Chronology, Mission Strategy, Theology* (Grand Rapids, MI: Eerdmans, 1998), 236–237, observing its coherence with the portrayal of Paul in Acts (13:47, quoting Isa 49:6; Acts 26:16–18, echoing Isa 42:6, 16).

a fulfillment of some of the Old Testament's eschatological hopes mentioned above.[51] For him, the union of Jews and Gentiles in the church was the revelation of a mystery, unlocking the meaning of many Old Testament passages (Eph 2:11–3:10).

Mission Strategy

In examining Paul's strategy, we find several overarching principles. First, he went to areas where no Christian congregations yet existed to establish new and viable communities of believers. Paul's mission "found its fullest sense of completion neither in an evangelistic preaching tour nor in individual conversions but only in the presence of firmly established churches."[52] Others might build on the foundation he had laid (1 Cor 3:10), but it was not his practice to build on a foundation that others had laid (Rom 15:20; cf. Gal 2:7–9). Second, "mission was for Paul in part a geographically definable accomplishment," working "areas in roughly contiguous sequence, from east to west."[53] Third, Paul focused on large urban areas in each region, expecting that the gospel would then radiate from these centers to nearby towns and villages.[54] Fourth, in line with the larger Christian missionary practice of reaching out to those who already revered the Scriptures and in harmony with the motto, "to the Jew first and also to the Greek" (Rom 1:16; cf. 2:9–10; Acts 13:46), Paul began, wherever possible, in the synagogue, speaking to Jews and God-fearing Gentiles to create a nucleus of believers. Meeting in the homes of those he brought to Christ[55] provided encouragement for the conversion not only of individuals, but of households.[56] The *paterfamilias* seem to have pro-

---

[51] E.g., Isaiah 52:7 and 59:20 are quoted in Romans 10:15 and 11:25–26 respectively. On the complicated argumentation of Romans 9–11 relative to Jews and Christians, see Clinton Wahlen, "Will All Jews Be Saved?" *Interpreting Scripture: Bible Questions and Answers*, ed. Gerhard Pfandl (Silver Spring, MD: Biblical Research Institute, 2010), 351–354 and Richard Davidson, "Israel and the Church: Continuity and Discontinuity," in this volume.

[52] W. Paul Bowers, "Mission," *DPL*, 610.

[53] Ibid., 609 and 610 respectively. Schnabel, *Early Christian Mission*, notes the use of *kyklō* in Romans 15:19, suggesting a northern circuit "that connects Jerusalem with Illyricum and, in the context or Romans 15:24, also with Rome and with Spain" (2:1295).

[54] Roland Allen, *Missionary Methods: St. Paul's or Ours? A Study of the Church in the Four Provinces* (Grand Rapids, MI: Eerdmans, 1977), 13; cf. a more nuanced version in Schnabel, *Early Christian Mission*, 2:1300.

[55] Schnabel lists four advantages of house churches: 1) immediate availability; 2) an already familiar meeting place within Judaism; 3) included ideal facilities for "familial fellowship and common meals during which the Lord's Supper was celebrated"; 4) afforded relatively inconspicuous meetings where local synagogues were no longer an option (ibid., 2:1302).

[56] Ibid., 2:1303. E.g., in Philippi, the house of Lydia and the house of the prison official (Acts 16:14–15, 32–34; cf. Phil 1:1 where the plural forms suggest several house churches); and in

vided the natural leadership for these house-churches.[57] Fifth, while Luke details in Acts what has commonly been referred to as Paul's three missionary journeys, the itinerary was flexible enough to permit long stays, such as in the key port cities of Corinth and Ephesus, as well as drastic alterations along the way (e.g., Acts 16:9–10).[58] Sixth, Paul did not work in isolation. He worked in tandem with companions like Barnabas, John Mark, Silas,[59] and Timothy and strove to labor in harmony with the other apostles (1 Cor 9:6; Col 4:10; cf. Acts 13:2–3; 15:40). At the same time, Paul (and Barnabas) ordained leaders in the newly-established congregations (Acts 14:23).[60] One wonders whether Paul's avoidance of baptizing all but the earliest believers in Corinth (1 Cor 1:14–16; but cf. 4:15)[61] might not have been part of a more intentional strategy of delegating this work to the local overseer/elder in order to facilitate the incorporation of new believers into the local church "family." Paul also trained other missionaries[62] who would be able to carry the gospel into more distant

---

Corinth, the house of Crispus and the house of Stephanas (Acts 18:8; 1 Cor 1:16; 16:15). The latter reference, in particular, suggests that Christians were meeting in Stephanas' house and that he was its overseer (ibid.). In Corinth, Ephesus, and Rome, Priscilla and Aquila owned houses large enough to serve as churches, one of several pieces of evidence for Priscilla's high social status, on which see Robert Jewett, *Romans: A Commentary* (Minneapolis, MN: Fortress, 2007), 956–957. More generally on the role of women in Paul's missionary enterprise, see Robert Banks, *Paul's Idea of Community: The Early House Churches in Their Historical Setting* (Exeter, U.K.: Paternoster, 1980), 156–157.

[57] See Wayne A. Meeks, *The First Urban Christians: The Social World of the Apostle Paul* (New Haven, CN: Yale University Press, 1983), 76–77; Roger W. Gehring, *House Church and Mission: The Importance of Household Structures in Early Christianity* (Peabody, MA: Hendrickson, 2004), 194–195, 265, 292; and Jürgen Becker, "Paulus und seine Gemeinden," *Die Anfänge des Christentums: Alte Welt und neue Hoffnung*, ed. Jürgen Becker et al. (Stuttgart: Kohlhammer, 1987), 102–159, quoted (with no page reference) in Schnabel, *Early Christian Mission*, 2:1302.

[58] Sometimes Paul was forced to leave suddenly (ibid., 2:1308), but he always relied on divine guidance (2:1300). On the relation of Paul's journeys in Acts to his epistles, note, e.g., the observation by A. Scott Moreau, "Paul and Mission," *EDWM*, 732: "The relevant data derivable from Paul's principal letters on the geographical pattern of his mission correlate remarkably well with the more detailed data available from Acts."

[59] The shortened form of Silvanus (mentioned by Paul in 2 Cor 1:19; 1 Thess 1:1; 2 Thess 1:1). See Clinton E. Arnold, ed., *John, Acts* (Grand Rapids, MI: Zondervan, 2002), 2:146.

[60] The word used (*cheirotoneō*), unlike the other New Testament occurrence in 2 Corinthians 8:19, does not refer to selection by the congregation (Eduard Lohse, "*cheirotoneō*," *TDNT*, 9:437), but by Paul and Barnabas, and "could be rendered either 'lay hands on' or 'ordain.'" (George W. Knight III, *The Pastoral Epistles: A Commentary on the Greek Text* [Grand Rapids, MI: Eerdmans, 1992], 288; cf. Titus 1:9, v. l.). That Paul installed elders and other "servants" in the churches he established, is clear not only from Acts 20:17, 28 (referring to Ephesus), but 1 Corinthians 16:15–18; Galatians 6:6; Philippians 1:1; and his instructions in 1 Timothy 3:1–15; 4:14; 5:17, 22; 2 Timothy 1:6; Titus 1:5–9.

[61] See Gordon D. Fee, *The First Epistle to the Corinthians* (Grand Rapids, MI: Eerdmans, 1987), 62.

[62] The *euangelistēs*, "proclaimer of good news, evangelist" (Acts 21:8 [cf. use of *euangelizō* also

locales and establish congregations along similar lines (2 Tim 2:2; cf. Rom 1:8; 1 Thess 1:8).[63] By identifying missionaries from within local congregations, "Paul emphasizes the co-responsibility and the participation of the churches because he regards missionary work and ministry as a function of the entire church."[64] Seventh, thanks to Paul's Judeo-Hellenist background and education, he could approach and convey biblical truth to a variety of people groups and persuasions with sensitivity and finesse (1 Cor 9:9, 19–23).[65] This incarnational principle of having the "mind" of Christ (Phil 2:5) and becoming "all things to all men," or "accommodation-oriented ministry,"[66] applied in the case of whether or not to eat food offered to idols. This meant "asking no question" about the food; only in the case where the host makes a point of saying that the food had been offered to idols should Christians refuse to eat it (1 Cor 10:27–28).[67] The likely reason for this is that, while not abrogating the Levitical prohibitions against eating unclean foods,

> Paul wanted them to remain integrated in Corinthian Gentile society. They were to continue eating with non-Jesus-believers and not "go out of the world" (1 Cor 5:9–11). They were not to separate from unbelieving spouses (1 Cor 7:12–13). They were not to become Jews (1 Cor 7:18).[68]

---

with reference to Philip in 8:4, 12, 35, 40]; Eph 4:11; 2 Tim 4:5), "was in particular a missionary who brought the gospel into new regions" (Cleon L. Rogers, Jr. and Cleon L. Rogers III, *The New Linguistic and Exegetical Key to the Greek New Testament* [Grand Rapids, MI: Zondervan, 1998], 440); cf. Eusebius, *Hist. eccl.*, 3.37.3: the "evangelists" preached Christ "to those who had not yet heard the word of faith, and to deliver to them the divine Gospels."

[63] Cf. Schnabel, "Mission," 757: "The history of the church in Colosse [sic] indicates that churches in large centers such as Ephesus served as bases for regional outreach through other missionaries (cf. Col 1:7; 4:12)." He notes in passing that, apart from the major centers of Jerusalem, Damascus, Caesarea, Antioch, Rome, Corinth, Alexandria, and Ephesus, "there were churches in as many as fifty other towns," which he proceeds to list (ibid., 758). See also Schnabel, *Paul The Missionary*, 254.

[64] Wolfgang Schrage, *Der erste Brief an die Korinther* (Zürich: Benziger, 1991–2001), 1:101, quoted in Schnabel, *Paul the Missionary*, 255.

[65] Paul's purpose of becoming "all things to all men" that he "might by all means save some" (1 Cor 9:22) was clearly limited to doing so without sacrificing principle (v. 21; cf. 10:31–33). Cf. Paul's expedient circumcision of Timothy, whose mother was Jewish (Acts 16:1–3), with his principled opposition to circumcising Titus (Gal 2:3).

[66] Rudolph, *Jew to the Jews*, 178; cf. 167–69, based on 2 Corinthians 8:9; 6:10.

[67] The numerous linguistic connections between 1 Corinthians 9 and Luke 10:7–8 suggest that both concern "provision for the lodging and sustenance of those sent out for ministry" and that "Paul adapted Jesus' halakhic rule [which Rudolph explains earlier on the same page "probably concerned clean food of doubtful or defiled status"] to a Gentile setting" (ibid., 190).

[68] Ibid., 100.

Obviously, such a policy would encourage new converts to be "salt" and "light" to their Gentile friends and associates and result in an even greater gospel harvest. Eighth, Paul continued to encourage, nurture, and instruct the churches he established through repeated visits (cf. Acts 15:36), by sending personal envoys to speak for him when he could not be there (cf. Matt 10:40) and through the epistles from him which these envoys carried.[69]

Impact of the Gospel Message

Paul himself was a living testimony to the power of the gospel that he preached. His transformation from a zealous persecutor of the church to one of its most active, eloquent, and ardent advocates could not have been lost on those who listened to him speak, especially his Jewish listeners. He calls people to follow his example as he follows Christ (1 Cor 11:1; 4:16; Phil 3:17; 1 Thess 1:6; 2 Thess 3:6-7; cf. Acts 26:29; Heb 6:12). While he urges the Corinthians as an apostle and an "ambassador" for Christ to be reconciled to God, his appeal that *"we* are ambassadors for Christ" implicitly includes his hearers. If they are to follow his example, they must also appeal to others to exercise faith in Jesus and likewise be reconciled to God (2 Cor 5:18-21). Despite some apparent physical weakness, his "thorn in the flesh" (2 Cor 12:7)[70]—a problem his detractors avidly employed against him (2 Cor 10:10)—Paul won many converts, established churches, and trained leaders that effectively carried his work even further.

One cannot read his epistles without being impressed by the importance Paul attached to the truth of the gospel message itself. He spoke so forcefully against those who presented another gospel (Gal 1:6-9; 2 Cor 11:4) or who twisted his words to mean something quite different from that which he preached (e.g., Rom 3:8; 1 Cor 10:30). Unfortunately, while the gospel was obviously clear to Paul and his converts, it was misunderstood or misconstrued by others and has precipitated controversy and schism throughout much of church history, with vast differences in its interpretation persisting to the present (cf. 2 Pet 3:15-16). Nevertheless, it is important for us to reflect briefly on Paul's message to understand its

---

[69] Schnabel, *Paul the Missionary*, 253.

[70] The precise nature of this "thorn," about which there has been endless and myriad speculation, is not nearly as important as the perceived effect. Paul asked for its removal because it seemed to hinder his work, but ultimately it proved to be a gift of divine grace given to keep him humble, trusting, and dependent on God's resources rather than on his own. Further, see Colin G. Kruse, *The Second Epistle of Paul to the Corinthians: An Introduction and Commentary* (Grand Rapids, MI: Eerdmans, 1987), 206; U. Heckel, "Der Dorn im Fleisch. Die Krankheit des Paulus in 2 Kor 12, 7 und Gal 4,13f," *ZNW* 84 (1993): 65-92.

impact on his mission.

This message of salvation brought Paul to his senses, enabling him to read the Old Testament in the light of Jesus Christ and to understand the truth of the gospel (2 Cor 3:14–16), which was "the power of God for salvation" (Rom 1:16) for himself first of all. It revealed God's righteousness and wisdom in connection with salvation history, prophecy, and the covenant promises. In 1 Corinthians 15:1–3, Paul claims to have faithfully "delivered" (*paredōka*) and "proclaimed" (*euēngelisamēn*) to the Corinthians that which he also had "accepted" (*parelabon*),[71] thus reminding them of his own personal experience in coming to faith *and* theirs. Besides pointing to the historicity of the events connected to the gospel (Christ's death, burial, resurrection, and bodily appearances), facts reinforced by the apparent quotation of an early Christian statement of faith in verses 3–5,[72] Paul emphasizes that all this happened "according to the Scriptures." The gospel events were a fulfillment of prophecy and of the plan conceived by God in His wisdom from the beginning. The historical gospel record, the Hebrew Scriptures, Israel's experience, and prophecy combined with Paul's own personal testimony to its truthfulness, constituted a compelling message. This synthesis, together with Paul's unique capacity to communicate it effectively in pagan (Acts 14:14–18; 17:22–31) as well as Jewish contexts (13:16–43) in the power of the Spirit, helps explain the success of the Pauline mission.[73]

Missiological Insights from the General Epistles

Sprinkled through the General Epistles are additional missiological insights that should not be overlooked. While primarily pastoral in nature, they spring from a concern to advance God's purposes in the sectors of early Christianity to which they are addressed. Since the New Testament church was highly mission-oriented, it should come as no surprise that even these more generalized letters make an important contribution

---

[71] The use of *parelabon* in v. 1 for the Corinthians' acceptance suggests that its use in v. 3 should be understood similarly for Paul's acceptance of the gospel, not in the sense of it being handed down to him indirectly as a tradition, which would seem to contradict what he writes elsewhere (e.g., Gal 1:12; 2:2), but as a direct revelation from the Lord (the clear intent of *parelabon* in 1 Cor 11:23; cf. 2 Cor 12:7).

[72] That Paul here invokes an early Christian faith statement, is widely accepted as reference to the commentaries on these verses demonstrate. Such a faith statement would be immediately recognizable by his readers without further comment.

[73] Cf. Moreau, "Paul and Mission," 732: "It was the christological encounter that set in motion Paul's theological reorientation, while it was the call to Gentile mission that determined the direction of the resulting theological development."

to our topic. We begin with Hebrews,[74] followed by the other epistles in their canonical order, considering together those putatively derived from the same author.

Hebrews

The book of Hebrews is self-described as "a word of exhortation" or "appeal" (*paraklēsis*, 13:22; cf. Acts 13:15), encouraging readers to consider Jesus in His role as divine-human Son (Heb 1–2) and as apostle and high priest of their confession (3:1). The application to Jesus of the Greek word *apostolos* (only here in Hebrews) is unique in the New Testament. It supports one of the main themes of the book, Jesus as the pioneer (*archēgos*) or pattern for the Christian life, emphasizing it in terms of incarnational mission. Jesus leads the way by having identified Himself fully with humanity: in terms of their nature, their temptations, and their suffering, but also in terms of their ultimate glorification.[75] The message of salvation was spoken preeminently through Jesus (2:3), as the sent of God (cf. 1:2), just as Christians are sent by Jesus (cf. John 17:18; 20:21). However, those addressed in Hebrews are in danger of abandoning their faith in Christ (Heb 3:12) and forfeiting salvation (10:35–39; 12:3). Rather than their being active in mission, they constitute the focus of this mission appeal, being encouraged to imitate the faith of the missionaries who brought them the message of salvation (Heb 13:7; cf. 6:12). Ultimately, however, they are called to leave behind the rudimentary elements of their faith and move on to perfection, becoming teachers, like those who brought them the message, rather than merely learners with an immature and even infantile form of Christianity (5:11–6:1).

Epistles of James and Peter

Like Hebrews, both James and Peter describe the life of faith in terms of pilgrimage (James 1:1; 1 Pet 1:1; cf. Heb 11:13), with Christians "liv-

---

[74] Though guardedly classifiable as Pauline, the epistle has a unique perspective that justifies its separate treatment.

[75] The other occurrence of *archēgos* in 12:2 makes this theme explicit (cf. *metechō* in 2:14 and *metochos* in 3:1, 14). No longer wandering, as Israel did in their wilderness pilgrimage (cf. use of *archēgos* in LXX Num 13:2–3!) under the leadership of Moses, Christians follow a clear-cut pathway created for them (10:19–20) and traversed already by Jesus (9:11–12) as their forerunner (*prodromos*). Unlike Joshua (*Iēsous*), this Jesus has provided a way whereby Christians can enter into rest (4:8–9). Further, see Clinton Wahlen, "'The Pathway into the Holy Places' (Heb 9:8): Does it End at the Cross?", *JAAS* 11.1 (2008): 43–55. Cf. Ben Witherington III, *Letters and Homilies for Jewish Christians: A Socio-Rhetorical Commentary on Hebrews, James and Jude* (Downers Grove, IL: InterVarsity, 2007), 26, observing that the cameos of faith in Hebrews 11 are "meant to climax with the example of Jesus and that the audience is particularly exhorted to follow his example."

ing in the midst of an environment that was at best uninterested and at worst inimical to their faith."[76] 1 Peter, like Hebrews,[77] addresses the issue of suffering for one's faith and likewise encourages Christians to imitate Christ's example, making it an opportunity for witness so that evildoers will be led to glorify God (2:12, 15).

> Peter then shows how this works out in the three primary relationships Cristians have—to government (2:13–17), to master-slave (2:18–25) and then wife-husband (3:1–7) relationships.... For Peter mission is an eschatological journey, done in light of the blessings of salvation (1:3–12; 2:4–10) and at all times looking forward to the culmination of mission in eternity (1:4; 3:22; 4:7).[78]

The very designation *Christian*, while possibly a derogatory epithet from the standpoint of Roman officials who persecuted them, seems to have become a badge of pride among those bearing this name (1 Pet 4:14–16; James 2:7; cf. Acts 11:26; 26:28).[79] According to Peter, opposition is no reason to be silent. Believers should "be ready always to present a defense [Gk. *apologian*] to everyone who asks you concerning the hope that is in you" (1 Pet 3:15). In other words, mission through a godly lifestyle (within the biological family too, 3:1–6) "must be accompanied by the verbal witness and explanation."[80] Using Old Testament imagery (Exod 19:5–6; Isa 43:21), Christians are "a chosen people" (both Jew and Gentile); "a royal priesthood" (all having direct access to God); "a holy nation" (by making disciples from "all nations," Matt 28:19); a people saved by God (note use of *periepoiēsamen* in LXX Isa 43:21). The purpose, according to Peter, is to "proclaim far and wide"[81] the virtues of Him who called them

---

[76] I. Howard Marshall, *New Testament Theology: Many Witnesses, One Gospel* (Downers Grove, IL.: InterVarsity, 2004), 640.

[77] Those addressed in Hebrews "have been tempted to withdraw from explicit identification with Christ for fear of the hardships involved, in particular the prospect of further suffering (10:32–39; 12:1–13)" (David Peterson, *Hebrews and Perfection: An Examination of the Concept of Perfection in the "Epistle to the Hebrews"* [Cambridge: Cambridge University Press, 1982], 65–66, cf. 176).

[78] Osborne, *Revelation*, 685.

[79] How early this designation arose and what role it had within early Christian circles is not completely clear. See, most recently, David G. Horrell, "The Label Χριστιανός: 1 Peter 4:16 and the Formation of Christian Identity," *JBL* 126 (2007): 361–381.

[80] Ott and Strauss, *Encountering Theology*, Tennent, 50; 1 Pet 3:1–2 puts forth one understandable exception.

[81] The importance of the word choice in this context for both ecclesiology and missiology (*exangeilēte*, a New Testament *hapax legomenon*) has long been recognized (ibid., 51).

out of darkness into His marvelous light (1 Pet 2:9). The inclusiveness of this call to mission is emphasized by the use in this verse of almost every possible Greek word for people (*genos, ethnos,* and *laos*), its egalitarian nature by the phrase "royal priesthood" (*basileion hierateuma*). "God's calling and grace are the foundation of mission. The mercy we have received is both motivation and the content of the proclamation."[82] While setting a more polemical tone, partly explicable on the presumption of increasing persecution and, in view of the apparent delay of the *parousia*, increasing apostasy, 2 Peter also insists that God is "not willing that any should perish but that all should come to repentance" (3:9). Thus, a motivation for mission continues and even intensifies (3:12) as Christ's coming draws near.

Epistles of John

Like 2 Peter and Jude, the apostle[83] expresses concern over false teachers, identifiable through their refusal to confess that Jesus Christ has come in the flesh (2 John 7; cf. 1 John 4:2–3).[84] The importance of truth and love emphasized in 2–3 John are enlarged upon in 1 John. As in the fourth Gospel, there is a sharp dualism between light and darkness and those who belong to each realm, based on whether or not they are born of God, which is based on faith and made manifest in loving God and obeying His commandments (e.g., 1 John 5:1–5, 18–20, cf. John 3:3–8). Truth in the Johannine Epistles seems to be personified,[85] so that merely an intellectual understanding is not enough—truth comes to us through a spiritual union with the Father and the Son. Crucial to salvation and fulfilling the mission as His followers is *who* we understand Jesus to be in all His facets as Savior (as the Son of God coming in the flesh, the sacrifice for our sins, our advocate in heaven, coming again, etc.) and being led by the right "spirit" (cf. 1 John 4:1–3). According to 3 John, the apostle sent out missionaries "for the sake of the name" of Jesus[86] to other cities and towns of Asia Minor. These missionaries "accepted nothing from the pa-

---

[82] Ibid.

[83] Not important for our purposes are arguments for a different authorship of 2–3 John (distinguishing a later "Elder" John from the apostle based on their initial verses and later patristic testimony) compared with 1 John and the fourth Gospel. Notable is Marshall's contention that, based on a study of their style and content, the case for seeing a single author behind all three letters is "stronger" (*New Testament Theology*, 529 n. 1).

[84] Though cryptic, the reality of the incarnation seems to be at issue (see ibid., 541–543 for a discussion and particularly his quotation on p. 542 of Ign., *Smyrn.*, 1–3).

[85] Ibid., 530–531; cf. 1 John 5:20.

[86] So ibid., 530; Schnabel, "Mission," 769.

gans," but received room and board from the existing local congregations. By supporting them, the believers proved themselves to be "coworkers in the truth" (3 John 5–8).[87] These efforts resulted in the significant growth of Christianity throughout Asia Minor in the late first and early second centuries, evidenced by the increasing Roman concern over the movement and attempts made to hinder its further spread.[88]

Mission in the Book of Revelation

A survey of this kind would not be complete without some mention of mission as portrayed in the book of Revelation where witness is a major theme.[89] Despite its vital place, as may be implicitly recognized by the book's role as the conclusion of the biblical canon, our treatment here will of necessity be relatively brief.[90]

First and foremost, mission springs from the work of the slain Lamb.[91] From the outset, the church is assured that, although the great controversy with evil will continue for an extended period of time, the decisive battle has been won through Christ's atonement for sin and victory over death. Assurance is also given of Christ's presence and constant, watchful care over His people, with messages conveyed directly from Jesus to His church in all ages through the letters to the seven churches (Rev 1:5–6, 17–19).[92] The symbolism of the lampstands (1:20) echoes Jesus' call that His people be the light of the world and suggests their role as His witnesses through the Spirit (5:6; cf. 1:4; Zech 4:1–10). References to the "angels" or "messengers" of the churches link mission to the divine word from Jesus on the one hand (1:20; 2:1, 8, 12, 18; 3:1, 7, 14) and to the proclamation of that word throughout the world on the other (14:6, 8–9). Like Jesus' parables of the kingdom, these letters make clear that the church continues to be composed of both faithful and unfaithful followers. The various qualities of Jesus revealed through symbols in the initial vision given to John are shown in the letters to meet the specific needs of

---

[87] Ibid.; Schnabel, *Early Christian Mission*, 2:1513–1514.

[88] Similarly, ibid., 2:1514, citing Pliny the Younger, *Ep. Tra.* 10.96.8–10.

[89] Richard Bauckham, *The Theology of the Book of Revelation* (Cambridge: Cambridge University Press, 1993), 72–73, cf. 162–163. See Ekkehardt Mueller, "Mission in the Book of Revelation," in this volume for a fuller and more detailed study.

[90] For a more detailed treatment, including the book's "witness" (*marty-*) terminology (used more frequently by John than by any other New Testament author), see Ekkehardt Mueller, "Mission in Revelation," in this volume.

[91] Osborne, *Revelation*, 685.

[92] Further, see Clinton Wahlen, "Heaven's View of the Church in Revelation 2 and 3," *JAAS* 9 (2006): 145–156.

His people throughout history.

The comprehensiveness and ultimate success of Jesus' high priestly ministry to His people is implied by the fact that glorious promises to those who persevere and overcome are extended to every one of the seven churches (Rev 2–3). It becomes explicit in the vision of the "great multitude which no one could number from every nation, from all tribes and peoples and tongues" standing victorious before God's throne (7:9). This records the fulfillment of "God's promise to Abraham and Jacob that their descendants would be so numerous that no one could count them.[93] The great multitude anticipates the results of the church's mission work. More specifically, the remnant of the woman's seed, who are threatened with destruction by the dragon because they keep the commandments of God and have the testimony of Jesus (12:17), are commissioned to "proclaim the everlasting gospel . . . to every nation and tribe and tongue and people" (14:6). Living as they do, prior to the second advent of Christ (14:14–16), they announce that God's judgment has commenced; they warn earth-dwellers not to receive the mark of the beast, urging them instead to worship the Creator and give glory to God; and they convey God's call for His people to come out of Babylon (14:7–11, 18:4).[94]

The final phase of mission described in Revelation 14 is closely connected to the Great Commission in Matthew 28 and the prediction of its ultimate success given by Jesus Himself: "This gospel of the kingdom will be preached throughout the whole world, as a testimony to all nations; and then the end will come" (Matt 24:14, NRS). The word *ethnē*, "nations," like its Hebrew counterpart *'amim*, can also be translated "peoples."[95] That the closing gospel work will reach smaller population units within nations is suggested by the message of Revelation 14 being taken to "every nation and tribe and tongue and people" (v. 6). While we should anticipate many conversions as a result of this work, there is no suggestion here that the entire world will be converted. The gospel is proclaimed "as a testimony." In other words, *living* the gospel is no less important than *preaching* the gospel. Both the outward- and inward-focused aspects of mission are comprehended in Matthew 24:14; 28:19 and Revelation 14:6–12 and are essential to the mission's final success.

The catalog of vices (21:8) and conditions for access to the New Je-

---

[93] Observed by Schnabel, *Early Christian Mission*, 2:1514 and the several commentators listed there.

[94] Further, see Ekkehardt Mueller, "The End Time Remnant in Revelation," *JATS* 11.1–2 (2000): 188–204.

[95] The same word form occurs in Matthew 28:19 and in the singular in Revelation 14:6.

rusalem (21:27; 22:15), the vision of the final judgment (20:11–15), and the depiction of God's covenant people established on the recreated earth (22:1–5) exclude the redemptive universalism suggested by some.[96] The "nations" who are saved (21:24; 22:2) "are the believers in Jesus who came from all nations" and "who have been liberated from the curse of the wrath of God (Rev 22:3)."[97] They are variously described as clothed in white robes (7:9), worshipping God and the Lamb (7:15; 22:3), written in the book of life (20:15; 21:27), victorious over the beast and his image (15:2; 20:4), able to stand through the time of trouble (6:14–7:4; Rev 14:1, 3), and keeping the commandments of God and the faith of Jesus (12:17; 14:12).[98] The fact that the earth-dwellers as a whole refuse to repent and give God glory in the face of the seven last plagues (16:9, 11; contrast 9:20; 11:13) indicates that the mission work of the church has been completed by this time and that even God's mercy has its limits (22:11). However, like the day and hour of Christ's return (Mark 13:32 par.), exactly when probationary time will expire is not disclosed (cf. Acts 1:6–7). The church is to work "while it is day," because the time will come when no one can work (cf. John 9:4).

Conclusion

Mission in the New Testament is based on the work of Jesus himself. Jesus announced the fulfillment of prophetic hopes through His kingdom, ministry, suffering, and death. And yet, though it was God's mission being fulfilled, Jesus could only accomplish it through the incarnation—becoming human. This fact underscores a vital principle found throughout the New Testament and, indeed, Scripture as a whole: Mission is only possible as a result of God's initiative and yet should not happen apart from human involvement. A divine-human partnership is essential. Thus Jesus called others, including Paul, to join Him in His mission of rescuing people for the kingdom of God.

Mission is incarnational. As Jesus revealed the Father, so Christ's followers are to reveal Jesus. This work involves both being and doing. One's way of life is itself a witness to the truth of the gospel being proclaimed. In order to be communicated to others, salvation must first be experienced—through faith in Christ and by being born of the Spirit. Extending the church's proclamation to new areas may require crossing barriers

---

[96] So Schnabel, *Early Christian Mission*, 2:1519–1520; Bauckham, *Theology of Revelation*, 139: "Unrepentant sinners have no place in the New Jerusalem."

[97] Schnabel, *Early Christian Mission*, 2:1520.

[98] Similarly, ibid., 2:1521.

of language, culture, and prejudice. It may also require a Spirit-led application of the message to the hearers' understanding, communicating the truth clearly, without changing the essential features of the message or concealing its potentially offensive elements for fear of rejection or persecution. Surprisingly, persecution, rather than hindering mission, tends to advance it—geographically and organizationally as the church is forced to adapt to new circumstances.

Mission reaches outward and draws inward. Like salt, followers of Jesus are sent out to make a difference. Their purpose and mission reaches outward. In order to influence the people with whom they mingle, they cannot act like everyone around them—thus the warning for salt not to lose its flavor. This is not about being different for the sake of being different, but about being different as in the manner Jesus was in treating people. Jesus' followers are also like light— attracting people's attention, modeling a better way, and drawing them inward toward the Savior. Jesus casts these two images of salt and light as indicative rather than imperative statements: not "Be salt" or "Be light," but "You are . . . ." Wherever His followers go, their lives bear witness to the faith they profess.

Mission is holistic. Jesus ministered to the *whole* person, showing concern for what people think and feel as well as what they say. He cared for their physical and spiritual well-being. Mission cannot compartmentalize humanity as though ministry to the "soul" has nothing to do with the body. Medical recognition of mind-body interdependence, interaction, and integration suggests that a similar relationship exists between the physical and the spiritual aspects of a person. Just as Christian love and hospitality,[99] forgiveness, and acceptance can positively impact people physically, so can encouraging people toward a healthier diet, avoidance of harmful substances, and physical activity have a positive spiritual impact and is an important component in Christian mission.

Mission is egalitarian. Jesus calls *everyone* to follow Him. Implicit in that call is the commission to invite others to become a disciple. Jesus sends His church into *all* the world, to *every* nation, kindred, tongue, and people. Just so, His church is composed of both Jew and Gentile, rich and poor, slave and free, male and female, and *all* are called and endowed with spiritual gifts to participate in this mission, in fulfillment of the divine "mystery," so that the church will reflect the universal character of God himself. So inclusive is this work that it requires a final judgment to sepa-

---

[99] On which, see Christine D. Pohl, "Biblical Issues in Mission and Migration," *Missiology* 31.1 (2003): 3–15.

rate true followers from pretenders, a judgment possible only in retrospect and which only God Himself can ultimately perform.[100]

Mission is strategic and systematic. Effective evangelization begins with those "nearest to the kingdom" before extending to those farther away from God and His Word. Mission can only expand as it remains subject to God's Word, sensitive to God's providential guidance, and in harmony with the Spirit-led decisions of the church as a whole. It must be intentional and constant as well as strategic and systematic, anticipating challenges and seeking divine wisdom to overcome them. Ideally, it focuses on offense rather than playing defense and yet continually works at reinforcing existing gains through spiritual nurture, additional biblical instruction, and mission training. Even missionary work carried forward at a distance maintains close ties to established congregations, enabling them to participate in the mission through their prayerful support, financial contributions, and spiritual encouragement.

Mission originates from, and must remain faithful to, the truth of the Gospel. Mission is, by definition, a divine-human partnership. It can only really operate within the parameters of Scripture, revealing God's work in history as illuminated by the life and teachings of Jesus and as foretold in prophecy. It is not enough just to receive the gospel message and live out its principles; the truth must be proclaimed, in its fullness, for it to have the divinely designed effect. Any narrowing or constriction of the truth, regardless of how apparently sincere and altruistic the motivation, eviscerates the message because the Spirit cannot bless such a patently human-inspired (and ultimately human-dependent) endeavor. "Speaking the truth in love" is the only way to let the light of God shine in a darkened world.

Mission is victorious in the end. The mission of the church reflects the character of the Lord, not only in word and deed, but also in its ultimate victory. Christ's defeat over Satan and sin is the assurance that, as the church relies on Him for wisdom and strength, willingly following His path of self-denial even to death, God's purposes will come to full and perfect fruition. Although the church is now comprised of both the faithful and the unfaithful, it will not always be so. God will hasten His work, cutting it short in righteousness (Rom 9:28). Likewise, His people will hasten the coming of the day of God as they carry out His work and will, and eagerly await the consummation (2 Pet 3:12). As Jesus crushed the head of the serpent on the cross, God will use the final remnant to crush

---

[100] Only three exceptions to retrospective judgment appear: 1) Enoch, representing the antediluvian world; 2) Elijah, representing Israel as well as prefiguring; 3) the eschatological remnant which will be translated/redeemed from the earth (Rev 14:3) as the culmination of God's work for and through his people.

the work of the dragon soon (Rom 16:20; Rev 12:17; 14:12). At the final judgment, Satan and all who cling to his kingdom will be brought to ashes and God will recreate a new earth for those who have chosen His kingdom (Rev 20:9–21:5). Then and only then can the voice of God proclaim "It is done!" (Rev 21:6), mission accomplished.

CHAPTER 6

MISSIOLOGICAL PERSPECTIVES IN THE BOOK OF DANIEL

Sung Ik Kim

Scholars pay little attention to the salvation-historical foundation of mission (*missio Dei*, "God's mission,"[1]) or its cross-cultural context in the book of Daniel. The book has not attracted much attention from missiologists despite Daniel's missionary status.[2] It has also been suggested that the book is "a remarkable illustration of the nature and effect of mission."[3] In Daniel 7:1–14, we find a universal message of God's purpose for the whole world.[4] Nevertheless, there is no explicit missiological study on the cross-cultural perspectives of witnessing in the book of Daniel.

Since theology can be defined as reflecting about God, it should seek to understand God's mission, His intentions, purposes, and His use of hu-

---

[1] In Latin, *missio Dei* means "the sending of God." Originally, it was used (from Augustine on) in Western discussions of the Trinity for the "sentness of God (the son)" by the Father. It is translated in English as "God's Mission." I support a comprehensive definition of *missio Dei* as everything God does for the communication of salvation (John A. McIntosh, "*Missio Dei*," *EDWM*, 631–632).

[2] Robert H. Glover, *The Bible Basis of Missions* (Los Angeles, CA: Bible House of Los Angeles, 1946), 21.

[3] John N. Oswalt, "The Mission of Israel to the Nations," *Through No Fault of Their Own?: The Fate of Those Who Never Heard*, ed. William V. Crockett and James G. Sigountos (Grand Rapids, MI: Baker, 1991), 93–94.

[4] Johannes Blauw, *Missionary Nature of the Church: A Survey of the Biblical Theology of Mission* (Grand Rapids, MI: Eerdmans, 1974), 65. Blauw uses the term "universalism" to denote the fact that the message of the Old Testament has the whole world in view and that it has validity for the whole world (ibid., 17).

man instruments in His mission.[5] If it is true that the Bible has been the blueprint throughout history for Christian missionary activity and has provided criteria for the establishment of Christian mission,[6] then the book of Daniel should be seriously considered as one of its missionary documents.[7]

Awareness of Mission

Even in tragedy, God placed Daniel and his friends in circumstances that enabled them to witness in ways that extended far beyond their family circle in Judah.[8] Through their awareness of God's initiative in the exile, they understood that God sent them to Babylon just as He sent Joseph to Egypt (Gen 45:5, 8).[9] Ellen G. White also mentions this missionary motif in Daniel:

> Through the Hebrew captives the Lord was made known to the heathen in Babylon. This idolatrous nation was given knowledge of the kingdom the Lord was to establish, and through His power maintain against all the power and craft of Satan. Daniel, and his fellow-companions, Ezra and Nehemiah, and many others were witnesses for God in their captivity. The Lord scattered them among the kingdom of the earth that their light might shine brightly amid the black darkness of heathenism and idolatry. To Daniel, God revealed the light of His purposes, which had been hidden for many generations. He chose that Daniel should see in vision the light of His truth, and reflect this light on the proud kingdom of Babylon.[10]

The context of the exile also shows the missiological impact of the book Daniel. Israel was to be a blessing to "all peoples on earth" (Gen 12:3; cf. Ps 67) and a "kingdom of priests" (Exod 19:6).[11] Although Is-

---

[5] Charles Van Engen, "Theology of Mission," *EDWM*, 949.

[6] Robert J. Schreiter, foreword to *The Biblical Foundations for Mission*, ed. Donald Senior and Carroll Stuhlmueller (Maryknoll, NY: Orbis, 2001), xi.

[7] C. Gordon Olson, *What in the World is God Doing? The Essentials of Global Missions* (Cedar Knolls, NJ: Global Gospel, 1989), 29.

[8] William H. Shea, *Daniel 1–7: Prophecy as History* (Boise, ID: Pacific Press, 1996), 35.

[9] Note the similarities in the process of interpretation of dreams in the accounts of Joseph and Daniel (cf. Gen 41:16, 25, 38–40; Dan 2:27–30, 45–49; 4:25, 34–37).

[10] Ellen G. White, Letter 32, 1899 (published, in part, in *AdvBibComm*, 4:1169).

[11] The NIV has been used in this research unless otherwise indicated. For a more detailed discussion of mission in the Old Testament, see Jeří Moskala, "Mission in the Old Testament,"

rael was not successful in its mission, the Lord used the exile for His own purpose. Yahweh sent "his people into exile in order for them to act in accordance with his desire that the nation of Israel should be his agents whereby he could bless all the families of the earth."[12] With this understanding, the exile forced the Jews into a situation where the godly remnant bore powerful witness to the true God.[13]

There seems to be a connection between mission awareness and Daniel's insights into the secrets of a universal future. These insights not only motivated Jewish missionary consciousness in the Diaspora, but also impacted the New Testament church.[14] It has been suggested that Daniel "and his fellow Jews of the captivity and later Dispersion were theistic missionaries among the peoples of the East as well as of southern Europe and northern Africa, right to the time of Christ."[15] It was during this period that "Israel's missionary role completely changed and became centrifugal."[16] Recognizing the impact of Daniel at the time of the exile allows us to approach the book from a missiological perspective, investigating "God's salvific purpose for all people"[17] and the cross-cultural context of *missio Dei*.

The subject of God's sovereignty and His desire to bring salvation to the nations is especially dominant in the book of Daniel. This is *missio Dei*,

---

in this volume.

[12] Walter C. Kaiser, Jr., *Mission in the Old Testament: Israel as a Light to the Nations* (Grand Rapids, MI: Baker, 2000), 13.

[13] Hicks explains how the development of the synagogue during this period impacted Jewish missions: "The temple was too far away (and they were in bondage), so these exiles began meeting in small groups (synagogues) to celebrate and cultivate their religious life. The community-centered institution was much more accessible to outsiders than the temple had been" (Bryant Hicks, "Old Testament Foundations for Mission," *Missiology: An Introduction to the Foundations, History, and Strategies of World Missions*, ed. John Mark Terry, Ebbie Smith, and Justice Anderson [Nashville, TN: Broadman & Holman, 1998], 61–62).

[14] Blauw, *Missionary Nature*, 60.

[15] Glover, "Bible Basis," 21.

[16] J. Herbert Kane, *Christian Missions in Biblical Perspective* (Grand Rapids, MI: Baker, 1976), 30. Blauw also indicates the exile as a turning point in the history of Israel second only to the Exodus (Blauw, *Missionary Nature*, 29).

[17] To describe this concept, Donald R. Dunavant uses the term "universality of mission" to denote the mandate of mission that the gospel of salvation should be proclaimed to all peoples and nations as well as Israel (Donald R. Dunavant, "Universality of Mission," *EDWM*, 989–990). To avoid the general concept of "universalism," which denotes that "salvation is not only available to all, it is applicable to all and ultimately will be realized by all" (*idem*, "Universalism," *EDWM*, 988), Dunavant uses the term "universality of mission." However, because of the ambiguous connotation of the expression "universality of mission," I prefer to use the expression "God's salvific purpose for all people" or "God's universal mission" to designate the same idea.

"God's mission."[18] The term *"missio Dei"* defines mission as "an activity of God himself, which he has begun in the sending of his son"[19] and one that looks forward to the establishing of the kingdom.[20] Daniel informed the heathen king that the most important thing is "to know that the Most High is sovereign over the kingdoms of men" (Dan 4:17; cf. vv. 25, 32; 5:21).

Daniel's Awareness of the Purpose of the Exile

Daniel 1 echoes Nebuchadnezzar's perception that the fall of Jerusalem was the result of his own action: He "came," "besieged," and "took" (vv. 1–2). However, according to Daniel, Nebuchadnezzar did not defeat Jehoiakim through his own skill or power. He was a recipient of God's gift: "The Lord gave Jehoiakim into his hand" (v. 2). By attributing the exile to the Lord, Daniel constructed a worldview in which the Lord was in control of history and was capable of using foreign rulers for His own purpose.[21] God's sovereignty was fully revealed in the visions of Daniel 7–12 and the stories in chapters 3–6. They disclose the whole spectrum of future world history and portray a God who works actively behind the scenes to grant unexpected favors or remarkable insight to His servants. These manifestations of God's sovereignty encouraged Daniel to commit his life to fulfilling God's mission.

Jeremiah and Daniel's Understanding of the Exile

Daniel 9 helps us understand Daniel's awareness of God's purpose in the exile (v. 2). He had studied the scroll of Jeremiah and knew about the prophecy of the seventy years of Israelite captivity in Babylon (Jer 25:8–14). One of Jeremiah's major messages is Israel's exile to Babylon (Jer 20:4; cf. 20:5–6; 21:7, 10; 22:25). In Jeremiah 27:22, the removal of the "vessels of the Lord's house" was foretold. Although the vessels became a distinct sign of "God's judgment," in the context of Jeremiah 27 and 28,[22] they were also a sign of the "hope of restoration"[23] of the temple and of

---

[18] For linguistic considerations of *missio Dei*, see H. H. Rosin, *"Missio Dei:" An Examination of the Origin, Contents, and Function of the Term in Protestant Missiological Discussion* (Leiden, Nederland: Interuniversity Institute for Missiological and Ecumenical Research Department of Missiology, 1972), 3–5. Rosin translated the Latin *"missio Dei"* into English as "God's mission" or "the mission of God" (ibid., 3).

[19] George F. Vicedom, "Missio Dei," *CDCWM*, 387.

[20] See Johannes C. Hoekendijk, "The Church in Missionary Thinking," *IRM* 41.3 (July 1952): 324–336.

[21] Ibid., 35–36.

[22] Winfried Vogel, "Cultic Motifs and Themes in the Book of Daniel," *JATS* 7.1 (1996): 30.

[23] See Peter R. Ackroyd, *Studies in the Religious Tradition of the Old Testament* (London: SCM,

"the reign of God" (Jer 27:22). Daniel had seen the fulfillment of the first part of the prophecy. The vessels were in Babylon. Because of his knowledge of prophecy, Daniel could say, "The Lord delivered Jehoiakim king of Judah into his hand, along with some of the articles from the temple of God" (Dan 1:2). This was strong evidence that God was involved in the exile. He had a purpose for the nation of Israel and He was sovereign Lord over other nations.

Jeremiah declares that God cares for the Babylonians as well as the Israelites, although the major messages of the prophets were about God's judgment against Babylon. This concern was clearly portrayed in God's explanation of judgment on Babylon: "We would have *healed* Babylon, but she is *not healed*" (Jer 51:9, emphasis supplied). This understanding was clearly expressed in Daniel's speech to Belshazzar (Dan 5:18–28). Belshazzar knew of God's judgment upon Nebuchadnezzar, his grandfather, and how Nebuchadnezzar had acknowledged that the Most High God is sovereign over human kingdoms (5:21). Daniel told Belshazzar that he had sinned against the God of Heaven: "Instead, you have set yourself up against the Lord of heaven. . . . You did not honor the God who holds in his hand your life and all your ways" (5:23). Daniel's message to the heathen kings shows that even the Babylonian king was expected to serve and glorify the God of Heaven. This missiological conviction was probably strengthened by Daniel's reading of Jeremiah.

God's Salvific Purpose for All People

The concept of God's universal purpose is the "basis for the missionary message of the Old Testament."[24] The book of Daniel shows, in different ways, God's salvific purpose for all people and what He expected from them.

Instrument of Salvation: Son of Man

The "Son of Man" in the book of Daniel is an "individual, eschatological, and celestial figure with messianic characteristics" (7:13, 14).[25] The divine salvific purpose for all people is dominant in the vision of the Son of Man. This apocalyptic vision predicts the coming of the Son of Man, whose kingdom shall put an end to the kingdoms of the world, and whose domain shall include all people, nations, and languages (7:1–29). It is notable that there are two different characteristics of judgment in Daniel 7:

1987), 54–55.

[24] Blauw, *Missionary Nature*, 17.

[25] Arthur J. Ferch, "The Apocalyptic Son of Man in Daniel 7" (Th.D. diss., Andrews University, 1979), 184.

a favorable judgment for the saints in the context of suffering (vv. 21–22) and an unfavorable judgment against the little horn (vv. 11, 26).

With the coming of the Son of Man (vv. 13, 14), all "peoples, nations, and languages" might offer Him their reverent service and the saints will possess the kingdom of God (vv. 22, 27). Daniel anticipated the moment when "all peoples, nations, and languages, should serve him" (vv. 13–14). He was an eyewitness to "God's salvific purpose for all people" through the "Son of Man."[26] He presented an apocalypse in which the flow of history, culminating in the triumph of God's salvific purpose for the nations, is unraveled.

Instrument of Salvation: The Promised Messiah

In response to the prayer of Daniel, Gabriel was sent to announce the restoration of Jerusalem and the coming of the Anointed One (Dan 9:25). Although the tone of some of the prophecies in the Old Testament is overwhelmingly negative in proclaiming impending and unavoidable judgment, the Messianic visions point to a future hope centered on the Messiah.[27] It is notable that the Messiah appears in the context of wars (9:24–27). Although Daniel was concerned about the restoration of the temple, the vision concluded with a conflict that culminates in the victory of the saints led by the great prince, Michael, during the time of the end (12:1). The focus was not simply on the restoration of the earthly temple. It centered on the revelation of God's salvific plan, whereby the Messiah, who would appear as a warrior for His people, would be first "cut off" (9:25). The vision of the Messiah was given to announce the gospel, the great missiological truth that God Himself becomes the incarnate missionary to be cut off for the salvation of humans.

The work of the universal Messiah also affects the "many" (*rabim*) mentioned in Daniel 9:27: "He will confirm a covenant with many for one 'seven.' "[28] In 12:2, the "many" is divided into two different groups: First,

---

[26] Shea also sees a universal salvific scene here: "Everyone who lives on the surface of the earth in those days will worship and serve him" (William Shea, *Daniel 7–12: Prophecies of the End Time* [Boise, ID: Pacific Press, 1996], 149). Zdravko Stefanovic points out that "all peoples, nations, and languages" express the concept of universality of Daniel's worship of the true God (Dan 7:14), contrasting to the Babylon's universal rule on earth (3:4; 4:1; 5:19) (Zdravko Stefanovic, *Daniel: Wisdom to the Wise* [Nampa, ID: Pacific Press, 2007], 265).

[27] M. Daniel Carroll R., "Old Testament Prophets," *EDWM*, 705. For different passages offering several pictures of the person and ministry of Yahweh's Anointed One, see Walter C. Kaiser Jr., *Toward an Old Testament Theology* (Grand Rapids, MI: Zondervan, 1978), 182–261.

[28] In the book of Daniel, "many" occurs thirteen times (8:25; 9:18, 27; 11:10, 14, 18, 26, 33, 39; 12:2–4, 10). It refers to people, except for 9:18, where it refers to the mercy of God. The discussion of "many" in the book of Daniel is taken from Brempong Owusu-Antwi, *The Chronology of*

"multitudes [many] who sleep in the dust of the earth will awake: some to everlasting life, others to shame and everlasting contempt;" and second, in 9:27, the "many" is more definitive, denoting those to whom the Messiah confirms the covenant. The parallel to this usage is found in 12:10: "Many will be purified, made spotless and refined, but the wicked will continue to be wicked; none of the wicked will understand, but those who are wise will understand." The same meaning is found in Isaiah 53:11: "After the suffering of his soul, he will see the light of life and be satisfied; by his knowledge my righteous servant will justify many, and he will bear their iniquities."[29] Just as in Isaiah 53:11, "many" specifies those who are "justified" through the ministry and death of the suffering Servant. Similarly in Daniel 9:27, the Messianic being would "confirm a covenant" with "many." In fact, the word "many" in the Bible often carries a connotation of universality (cf. Ezra 3:12) and is used to designate the peoples and the nations involved in the universal adoration of God (Micah 4:2).[30] Thus, the Messiah in Daniel 9:27 is "the Messiah of all peoples, the Messiah who will save the world."[31]

Universal Dimension of the Covenantal Relationship

Daniel 9 begins with one of the longest prayers in the Bible. Daniel offered this intercessory prayer for the remnant of Judah in exile after studying the scroll of the prophet Jeremiah (Jer 25:10–14; Dan 9:1–3). The designation of God as the "One who keeps the covenant" (9:4) indicates Daniel's awareness of the permanent covenantal relationship between God and Israel. His prayer for mercy and the restoration of Israel is based on the fulfillment of the covenantal relationship (cf. vv. 10, 13; cf. Lev 26:40–45; Deut 27–29). The prophet also prayed for God's people; the city, which is called by God's name (Dan 9:18); and the holy mountain of God (9:16, 18, 20). Daniel's prayer alludes to Solomon's prayer (1 Kgs 8).

Solomon's prayer was also based on the covenantal relationship with God: "You who keep your *covenant of love* with your servants who continue wholeheartedly in your way" (v. 23, emphasis supplied). Daniel used the same expression, "covenant of love" (Dan 9:4). Solomon's prayer clearly shows that God's purpose for the temple is to welcome all nations to worship there.[32] The phrases, "because of your name" (1 Kgs 8:41) and

---

Daniel 9:24–27 (Berrien Springs, MI: Adventist Theological Society, 1995), 184–185.

[29] For the connections between Daniel 9 and Isaiah 53, see Owusu-Antwi, *Daniel 9:24–27*, 166.

[30] Doukhan, *Daniel*, 150–151.

[31] Ibid., 141.

[32] Steven C. Hawthorne, "The Story of His Glory," *Perspectives on the World Christian Movement:*

"all the peoples of the earth may know your name" (v. 43), are similar to the phrase, "for your sake ... because your city and your people bear your Name" in Daniel 9:19 (cf. vv. 17–18). Through the comparison of Daniel's similar expressions with Solomon's, we can suggest that Daniel was likely aware of Solomon's prayer and understood the universal aspects of the covenantal relationship.[33] By forgiving the people and restoring His temple and nation, God would cause His name to be honored among all the nations of the world and all the peoples would realize His greatness and mercy (cf. Exod 32:11, 12; Num 14:15, 16).[34]

The expression "under the whole heaven" (Dan 9:12) indicates that the destruction of Jerusalem was not a regional issue, but a universal one. It impacted God's purpose for the salvation of all the nations.[35] The universal nature of the catastrophe is revealed more clearly in Daniel's confession: "Our sins and the iniquities of our fathers have made Jerusalem and your people an object of scorn to all those around us" (v. 16). The tragedy is universal because Israel's fate in some way involves the fate of the neighboring countries. Daniel's prayer seems to imply that if the city and the temple of God remain desolate and the people in permanent exile, the neighboring people would not change their attitude of scorn toward God's temple or His people and could not be drawn to the temple to meet the God of Heaven.

God's Instruments: The Wise

The wise (*maśkîlîm*) who will instruct many (11:33) hints at Christ's commission: "Therefore go and *make disciples* of all nations, baptizing them in the name of the Father and of the Son and of the Holy Spirit, and *teaching* them to obey everything I have commanded you" (Matt 28:19, 20, emphasis supplied).[36] The expressions "those who lead to righteousness" and "those who are wise" in Daniel 12:3 illustrate that "believers generally who are spiritually wise themselves make others wise through their life and witness."[37] Thus, the wise are the ones who will be teach-

---

A Reader, ed. Ralph D. Winter and Steven C. Hawthorne (Pasadena, CA: William Carey Library, 2000), 41.

[33] C. Mervyn Maxwell, *God Cares* (Nampa, ID: Pacific Press, 1981), 1:203.

[34] William H. Shea, *Daniel: A Reader's Guide* (Nampa, ID: Pacific Press, 2005), 146–147; Stefanovic, *Daniel*, 349.

[35] Jacques B. Doukhan, *Secrets of Daniel: Wisdom and Dreams of a Jewish Prince in Exile* (Hagerstown, MD: Review and Herald, 2000), 139.

[36] "Daniel," *AdvBibComm*, 4:874.

[37] Miller, *Daniel*, 319.

ers under God's guidance.[38] In fact, Daniel and his three friends were called wise (cf. Dan 1:4, 17, 20; 2:20-24). As exemplified by Daniel and his friends, the "sharing" by the eschatological wise goes beyond simple testimony. The wise will stand firm on the side of God with not only an understanding of the end-time prophecies, but also with concern for the salvation of others.[39]

Repentance and Social Justice

When King Nebuchadnezzar asked Daniel to interpret his dream of the tree, Daniel advised him saying, "Renounce your sins by doing what is right and your wickedness by being kind to the oppressed. It may be that then your prosperity will continue" (4:27). Daniel was suggesting that the heathen king practice social justice.[40] By requesting that the king do what is right, Daniel was telling the king to correct his sinful life by conducting himself righteously.[41] In other words, it was a strong request for repentance.[42] The main message of Daniel's advice is that God has a universal interest and concern for the oppressed, even in a foreign land.[43] Daniel, with his understanding of God, strongly urged the king to reflect on his critical position before God and to seriously consider the warning message God was sending.[44]

Strategic Perspectives

From a strategic point of view, the book of Daniel clearly shows that God not only calls human workers in different ways to participate in *missio Dei*, but it also shows how God directly intervenes in human history

---

[38] "Daniel," *AdvBibComm*, 4:879.

[39] Doukhan, *Daniel*, 108.

[40] The Aramaic word "renounce" (*pᵉruq*) is often translated as "atone" (e.g., NRSV). This rendering has contributed to the misconception that salvation could be obtained by good works. See John J. Collins, *Daniel* (Philadelphia, PA: Fortress, 1993), 230; Stephen R. Miller, *Daniel* (Nashville, TN: Broadman & Holman, 1994), 138. The textual or contextual evidence supports the meaning, "tear away" or "break off."

[41] Leon Wood, *Commentary on Daniel* (Grand Rapids, MI: Zondervan, 1973), 117.

[42] "Daniel," *AdvBibComm*, 4:792.

[43] The "oppressed" motif was also important in the ancient Near East. In the code of Hammurabi which was written by Hammurabi, King of Babylon in 19th century B.C., the king showed the same concern in the purpose of the code: "to cause justice to prevail in the land, to destroy the wicked and the evil, that the strong might not oppress the weak" (*ANET*, 164). See also M. E. J. Richardson, *Hammurabi's Laws: Text, Translation and Glossary* (Sheffield: Sheffield Academic Press, 2000), 123.

[44] Roland S. Wallace, The Lord Is King: The Message of Daniel (Downers Grove, IL: InterVarsity, 1998), 81.

to fulfill His purpose. God's intervention is also closely connected with spiritual conflict in the book of Daniel and illustrates how the church today should deal with the issue of supernatural evil forces.[45]

Committed Individuals

Although most theories of mission strategy focus on means, principles, or ways to accomplish a predetermined goal, the book of Daniel shows that God's strategy focuses more on human partners who commit their lives to Him and His purpose. In the context of the exile, God chose Daniel and his companions to fulfill His salvific purpose for the nations as well as for Israel. It could be that by reading Jeremiah (Dan 9:2), Daniel has become aware of God's purpose for the "healing" (salvation) of Babylon, foretold by Jeremiah (Jer 51:9). He most likely knew of the predictions of Isaiah, nearly one hundred years earlier, that the descendants of Hezekiah would be taken to Babylon and forced to serve in its court (Isa 39:6–7; 2 Kgs 20:17–18). Daniel and his companions were fulfilling that prediction (cf. Isa 43:14–21).[46] Daniel boldly declared to which kingdom he was dedicated (2:44; cf. 7:27).

This explains how Daniel and his friends could testify about their faith in God in exile. We could say that "a key to understanding this [missionary] call is to understand the necessity of our sensitivity to His [God's] sovereign work in our lives."[47] When Daniel and his friends recognized "God's authority as the guiding principle," they decided to stand for God and be missionaries in a cross-cultural context.[48]

Spiritual Individuals

Another reason why God was able to use Daniel to achieve His salvific purpose was that Daniel took time to develop his spirituality.[49] He was

---

[45] Peter Wagner says that spiritual warfare is a crucial factor in missions today because Satan works to thwart *missio Dei* (C. Peter Wagner, "On the Cutting Edge of Mission Strategy," *Perspectives in the World Christian Movement*, 531). In this study, "spiritual conflict" and "spiritual warfare" will be used interchangeably.

[46] Gammie claims that linguistic, thematic, and theological parallels exist between Dan 1–6 and Isa 40ff. This, according to Gammie, suggests that the writer of the Danielic stories believed that a number of Isaiah's sayings, predicting that Israel's sons would serve in foreign courts, had been fulfilled (John G. Gammie, "On The Intention and Sources of Daniel 1–4," *VT* 31.3 [1981]: 282–292).

[47] William E. Goff, "Missionary Call and Service," *Missiology: An Introduction to the Foundations, History, and Strategies of World Missions*, ed. John Mark Terry, Ebbie Smith, and Justice Anderson (Nashville, TN: Broadman & Holman, 1998), 334.

[48] Alan Neely, "Sovereignty of God," *EDWM*, 900.

[49] Gordon Wakerfield describes spirituality as "the attitudes, beliefs and practices which animate

described by two heathen kings and a queen as one who had "the spirit of the holy gods in him" (4:8, 9, 18; 5:11).[50] He also possessed "an excellent spirit" (5:12; 6:3, KJV). Although "spirit" in this expression is sometimes translated as "mind" (NAB, NIV), or "ability" (TEV), based on 5:11 it seems to be connected to "the ability to interpret dreams."[51] Without a strong spiritual life, Daniel would have been unaware of God's calling in his life and unable to interpret the king's dreams and visions.[52] Daniel's whole life was a process of "spiritual formation" and reveals the importance of prayer in the life of a missionary.[53]

Commitment to a Holy Life

The expression "Daniel resolved not to defile himself" (Dan 1:8) indicates his conscious purposefulness to be holy in a cross-cultural context. His commitment to holiness shows that he was a man of deep convictions and with the courage of a martyr.[54] He decided to live undefiled in all ways, including his diet. This allowed God to use his consecrated life to save nations. Although one of the primary claims in Daniel 1 is the "general affirmation of the trustworthiness of God even in the remote and difficult circumstances of the exile,"[55] an important aspect was the decision of Daniel and his friends to maintain their religious identity. Their radical obedience in terms of holiness, even in the area of diet, allowed them to be a witness in a foreign nation.

---

people's lives and help them reach out towards supersensible realities" (Gordon Wakerfield, "Spirituality," *NDCT*, 539).

[50] In the Theodotion version, it is rendered as "the spirit of God." Compare this with Pharaoh's designation of Joseph as "one in whom is the spirit of God" (Gen 41:38), suggesting that the spirit of God was the source of all the skills Joseph possessed (Robert Davidson, *Genesis 12–50* [Cambridge: Cambridge University Press, 1979], 247). In Daniel 4:9 Nebuchadnezzar used the same expression to designate the ability of Daniel to interpret his dream as having a supernatural origin.

[51] See Collins, *Daniel*, 249.

[52] Geoffrey Wainwright suggests that to improve spirituality, one must have a "combination of praying and living."(Geoffrey Wainwright, *Principles of Christian Theology* [New York: Scribners, 1977], 592].

[53] Jim Plueddmann defines "spiritual formation" as "a process that takes place inside a person, and is not something that can be easily measured, controlled, or predicted;" that is, "a lifelong process" (Jim Plueddmann, "Spiritual Formation," *EDWM*, 901–902).

[54] René Péter-Contesse and John Ellington, *Handbook on the Book of Daniel* (New York: United Bible Society, 1993), 15.

[55] W. Sibley Towner, *Daniel* (Atlanta, GA: John Knox, 1984), 27.

Excellence of God's Agents

Daniel and his friends were "Israelites from the royal family and the nobility" (Dan 1:3). They were "young men, without any physical defect, handsome, showing aptitude for every kind of learning, well informed, quick to understand, and qualified to serve in the king's palace" (v. 4). Their qualifications suggest they had already received a considerable amount of education in their home country.[56] In addition to their former education, Nebuchadnezzar ordered his officials "to teach them the language and literature of the Babylonians" (v. 4). Although divination, magic, and exorcism were widespread among the people of the ancient Near East, it is a mistake to believe that the wise men of Babylon were only diviners and magicians. It is important to understand what was involved in "the learning of the Chaldeans" (1:4, KJV). In Chaldean culture, learning was the privilege of the scribes because only they were literate.[57] Babylonian learning included vast areas of knowledge under the headings of astrology, extispicy (reading omens from entrails of animals, a form of divination), anatomy, medicine, mathematics, lexicography, historiography, and commentaries.[58] Thus, it seems evident that any of these areas of "scientific" knowledge could be involved in the course of learning undertaken by Daniel and his friends.

That Daniel and his friends were ten times better than all the magicians and astrologers in all matters of wisdom and understanding and without mention of magical or supernatural activity in the passage (1:20), it is possible to speculate that the test in front of Nebuchadnezzar was more "scientific" than religious.[59] Because Daniel and his friends demonstrated excellence in the area of science, they were appointed and considered as members of the wise men in the Babylonian court.[60] It is notable that they were placed in high positions of administration rather than in the religious system (2:48; 3:30).[61]

At the same time, it is possible that Daniel and his friends studied the Babylonian polytheistic literature because the religion of Mesopota-

---

[56] See, Maxwell, *God Cares*, 1:23.

[57] A. Kirk Grayson, "Mesopotamia: History and Culture of Babylonia," *ABD*, 4:772, 775.

[58] Ibid., 4:773.

[59] "Daniel," *AdvBibComm*, 4:763.

[60] Ibid.

[61] For more on the large and extensive clergy system of Mesopotamia, see William W. Hallo, "Mesopotamia and the Asianic Near East," *The Ancient Near East: A History*, ed. John M. Blum (New York: Harcourt Brace Jovanovich, 1971), 171–172.

mia was closely connected with its culture. Even their scientific literature found application in the ritual needs of court, priesthood, and laity.[62] From a missiological perspective, one could say that "in order to witness to their God in Babylonian court they had to understand the cultural presuppositions of those around them, just as the Christian today must work hard at the religions and cultures amongst which he lives, if different thought-worlds are ever to meet."[63] However, based on Daniel's handling of the food issue (1:8), it is not necessary to suppose that they allowed their study to undermine their faith.[64]

A most impressive thing is that "what the Babylonians think to be the result of their own effort is, in actuality, the result of God's intervention."[65] Knowing that it was God who was the provider of grace, wisdom, and protection, Daniel continually witnessed to the superiority of his God in the heathen court (1:9, 17; 2:28-30, 45; 6:22).[66] Excellence in service was a part of God's strategy to reach the people in the heathen court to achieve *missio Dei*.

Ironically, the four Hebrew youths, who refused to align themselves religiously with the king by their decision on the matter of food, were chosen for royal service because of their excellence (1:19). After the interpretation of his dream in Daniel 2, Nebuchadnezzar placed Daniel in a high position as ruler over the entire province of Babylon and of all his wise men. The king also appointed Daniel's friends as administrators over the province of Babylon (vv. 48-49; 4:9). Belshazzar appointed Daniel as the third ruler in the kingdom (5:29). Darius appointed him as one of the three highest administrators of the kingdom (6:2). These appointments show Daniel's excellence in service, which provided opportunity to witness for his God. His moral excellence, honesty, and the protecting power and care were further illustrations of the superiority of the living God. He transformed Daniel and his friends into competent government administrators and counselors to allow His work through them and to achieve His purpose for Babylon as well as for His own people.

---

[62] Ibid., 169-170.

[63] Joyce G. Baldwin, *Daniel: An Introduction and Commentary* (Downers Grove, IL: InterVarsity, 1978), 80-81.

[64] Ibid.

[65] Danna N. Fewell, *Circle of Sovereignty: A Story of Stories in Daniel 1-6* (Decatur, GA: Almond, 1988), 22.

[66] It is also notable that the Babylonian king and queen compared his wisdom to that of the gods (4:9, 18; 5:11).

Special Revelations: Dreams and Visions

Dreams and visions were important ways through which God conveyed His message to heathen kings as well as to Daniel.[67] In Daniel 5, God used a vision to declare His judgment on Belshazzar and to reveal His sovereignty over history. Today, in about two-thirds of the world, religious dreams and visions play an important part in people's lives. One cannot rule out the possibility that God may choose to speak through dreams and visions to those who have not yet been reached by the gospel.[68]

Involvement in Spiritual Conflict

In the book of Daniel, the concept of spiritual conflict between God and the powers of evil is a very important theme. Because of its common occurrence in many parts of the world, the issue of spiritual conflict is of great concern to missiologists and missionaries. In an effort to build a biblical foundation and understanding, some missiologists have used Daniel 10:13, 20–21 as a supporting reference for regional or territorial spirits.[69] However, this is very speculative and lacks clear biblical support. The book of Daniel shows that God intervenes in the history of this world through His angels, and that the concept of spiritual conflict between God and the powers of evil is a very distinctive theme. Angels appear in scenes connected with God's judgment and in the context of spiritual conflict (Dan 3:25, 28; 4:17; 6:22; 7:10, etc.). In the vision of the four beasts and the Son of Man, a description is given of the persecution of the saints by the little horn (7:25) who will also speak against the Most High.

In the vision of Daniel 8:11–12, the little horn casts down the sanctuary and its system and truth. The vision of Daniel 9 prophesies an attack against the temple by one who causes desolation (9:26–27). The vision of Daniel 10–12 deals with a great war (10:1). Some significant aspects of spiritual conflict between God's angelic powers and evil powers appear in chapter 10 (vv. 13, 20–21). The archangel Michael appears in the context of fighting, contention, and liberation. Michael is also referred to

---

[67] In the book of Daniel, dreams and visions are used as synonyms. See Daniel 1:17; 2:28; 4:9; 7:1. Compare the dream of the heathen king and its interpretation by the servant of God in Joseph's case (Gen 41).

[68] Richard Love, "Dreams and Visions," *EDWM*, 291–292.

[69] Cf. C. Peter Wagner, *Confronting the Powers: How the New Testament Church Experienced the Power of Strategic-Level Spiritual Warfare* (Ventura, CA: Gospel Light, 1996), 172–173; Anna Gimenez, "Battle in the Heavenlies," *Engaging the Enemy: How to Fight and Defeat Territorial Spirits*, ed. C. Peter Wagner (Ventura, CA: Regal, 1991), 78–79.

as a "prince," suggesting that in these passages the princes of Persia and Greece do not refer to human rulers, but to "satanic angelic forces" who work to influence the kings of Persia and Greece. Thus, the prophecies of Daniel can be designated as the divine portrayal of "the age-old conflict between good and evil."[70]

However, it is notable that Daniel 6, 10, and 11:1 indicate that an angel worked to influence the king's heart. Behind the scenes of world history, angelic powers are working to influence human decisions. The earthly kings of Persia and Greece can be thought of as representatives of Satan, if they are under his influence. Satan also can be designated as the prince of the kingdoms he controls. But ultimately, the battlefield is found in the heart of the people.

Daniel was a successful witness in the course of spiritual conflict in a cross-cultural context because he had faith in the sovereignty of God. His experience can be categorized under three encounters of spiritual conflict: truth encounters, allegiance encounters, and power encounters.[71] Daniel was a successful witness in his cross-cultural setting because he experienced victory in all three areas of encounters. The fact that Daniel prayed only for the restoration of the sanctuary, and that it was Gabriel and Michael who fought against the Prince of Persia to answer Daniel's prayer, indicates that the foremost spiritual weapon is God Himself.

Cross-Cultural Witness

The book of Daniel is full of illustrations of God using cultural elements to efficiently communicate His salvific purpose in a cross-cultural setting. The book also shows how Daniel witnessed his faith in the God of Heaven before heathen kings by using their language and cultural forms. We will comment on some of the examples.

Cultural Perspectives

The prophets in the Old Testament were masters at using local cul-

---

[70] Leroy E. Froom, *The Prophetic Faith of Our Fathers* (Washington, DC: Review and Herald, 1954), 4:1054. Froom also called this conflict "the personalized war between Christ and Satan for the winning of the human race" (ibid.).

[71] Charles H. Kraft, "Three Encounters in Christian Witness," *Perspectives on the World Christian Movement*, 410–412. Kraft defines three encounters: 1) truth encounters, in which the mind is exercised and the will is challenged, seem to provide the context within which the other encounters take place; 2) allegiance encounters, involving the exercise of the will in commitment and obedience to the Lord, are the most important of the encounters because there is no spiritual life without commitment and obedience; and 3) power encounters, which focus on freedom from the captivity of Satan who attempts to keep people from allegiance to God and from knowing the truth (ibid.).

tural processes, and their messages were often communicated orally or by symbolic actions that were clearly understood by their audience (cf. Ezek 3:15; 4:4–8; 5:1–4).[72] In like manner, Daniel was also very sensitive to the culture in which he worked.

Use of Foreign Names

The master of eunuchs gave Babylonian names to Daniel and his friends (1:6–7). It was an ancient practice for names to contain an appellation or reference to pagan deities, in the same way that many Hebrew names refer to the true God.[73] There is no indication that Daniel and his friends resisted their Babylonian names, although Daniel used his Hebrew name consciously whenever he refers to himself.[74] The fact that the new names referred to Babylonian deities suggests not only pressure to convert them to the worship of Babylonian gods (1:7; cf. 4:8), but also additional pressure to assimilate them into the Babylonian culture.[75] This may have had a pragmatic goal: "The Babylonians simply wanted to give these captives names which would be easy to recognize by the Babylonians with whom they would be working."[76] But from the perspective of the captives, they received their new names from their captors and not by choice.[77]

It is true that a "name" is a "distinguishing mark" which makes it possible to differentiate, to structure, and to order.[78] Knowledge of a name can give power because it has to do with ontological identity.[79] Therefore, having a native name as a foreigner is often a first step toward acceptance as an insider in a foreign culture. The Babylonians' calling the four captives by their familiar Babylonian names might have been an indication that the outsiders were in the process of building personal relationships

---

[72] Arthur F. Glasser, "Old Testament Contextualization: Revelation and Its Environment," *The Word Among Us: Contextualizing Theology for Mission Today*, ed. Dean S. Gilliland (Dallas, TX: Word, 1989), 42.

[73] Miller, *Daniel*, 65.

[74] In the book of Daniel, Daniel used 75 times and Belteshazzar 10 times.

[75] In the ancient world, "a byname may be adopted to signify a shift in a religious adherence" (G. H. R. Horsley, "Names, Double," *ABD*, 4:1015).

[76] Shea, *Daniel 1–7*, 60. Montgomery also suggests that Ashpenaz had no intention to degrade or humiliate these captives by this name change (Montgomery, *Daniel*, 123).

[77] André Lacocque, *The Book of Daniel* (Atlanta, GA: John Knox, 1979), 29. We should add that in the Hebrew Bible, the new names are misspelled to damage or eliminate the reference to the Babylonians gods (see, Doukhan, *Daniel*, 18–19).

[78] Martin Rose, "Names of God in the Old Testament," *ABD*, 4:1002.

[79] Ibid.

with the insiders. However, it is evident that they were forced to assimilate into Babylonian religion and culture. The new names made it easier for Daniel and his friends to be accepted into the new culture, whether or not the four captives intended it to be so.

Conflict Resolution

Daniel expressed his rejection of the king's food by offering a religious reason: The avoidance of defilement. The food issue could have caused a cultural conflict between two very different cultures and religions.[80] Daniel's handling of this crisis illustrates some steps in solving cross-cultural conflicts.[81] First, Daniel did not make the food problem an ongoing issue. Instead, he suggested a ten-day test. Second, the reason Daniel was in "favor and sympathy" with the prince of the eunuchs (1:9) was most likely that he had shown respect to his guardian and maintained a good relationship with him.[82] Third, Daniel used a win-win approach.[83] When the results of the test were in, Daniel and his friends were able to maintain their allegiance to God and Daniel's suggestion for a ten-day trial made the guardian feel that there was little risk for him.

However, in Daniel 3, the three friends of Daniel were unable to solve a conflict with Nebuchadnezzar. Their refusal to bow down to the image, which the king had built, shows that conflict resolution has its limits and no one should sacrifice fundamental, scriptural truths to avoid or solve conflicts.

Empathy

When the king ordered the death of all the wise men, the king's guard came to Daniel and his friends This indicates that they were regarded as part of the group of wise men, though they had not been called by the king to help interpret the dream (v. 13).[84] After the mystery was revealed

---

[80] Ibid.

[81] According to Duane Elmer's "general rules for dealing with conflict" to resolve cross-cultural conflict, first of all, we need to "ask whether this is worthy of attention or should be let go" (Duane Elmer, *Cross-Cultural Conflict: Building Relationships for Effective Ministry* [Downers Grove, IL: InterVarsity, 1993], 180).

[82] Elmer emphasizes the importance of building relationships in cross-cultural contexts. He says: "Make your approach one of concern for the person and for the preservation of the relationship (ibid.).

[83] Elmer also suggests: "'Believe a win-win resolution' is possible if both parties can remain calm, understand each other's interests, and negotiate with integrity and fairness" (ibid., 181).

[84] The reason why they were not called to the court to interpret the king's dream seems to be that they had but only recently graduated and the monarch only summoned the high-ranking wise men ("Daniel," *AdvBibComm*, 4:769).

to Daniel in a vision, he went to Arioch and interceded for the wise men (2:19, 24). This case demonstrates that God wants to save everyone, even heathen religious leaders.[85] Daniel did not see the wise men of Babylon as his religious enemies. Through his identification with them, he created a situation that allowed him to witness to them. However, Daniel's identification with them never caused him to sacrifice his religious identity, showing that empathy with people for the purpose of cross-cultural witness is never an excuse for compromise.

Language Skills

Daniel and his friends were chosen by Ashpenaz, the chief officer who served the king, because they were "skillful in all wisdom and cunning in knowledge, and understanding science" (1:4). They were taught the language and literature of the Chaldeans. For Daniel, overcoming the language barrier was the first step in communicating and reaching Babylonians with a message from the true God.[86] In order to truly identify with people in a mission field, cross-cultural workers must make every effort to reach them in their own language and culture.[87]

The book of Daniel uses various languages in different ways. Most of the historical parts were written in Aramaic (2:4b–7:28), which was the language used for official correspondence during the Neo-Babylonian era. Most of the prophetic chapters, as well as chapter 1, were written in Hebrew (1:1–2:4a; chaps. 8–12).[88] Aramaic begins when the wise men made their speech to the king and it stops when the focus moves away from the politico-religious interests of 2:4b–7:28 and gives way to primarily religious concerns (chaps. 8–12).[89] Others have seen a missiological implication in the use of Aramaic in the book of Daniel: "Aramaic was reserved for the parts of the book that had universal appeal or special relevance to the Gentile nations."[90] If that is true, then the shift to Aramaic in the book of Daniel did have a missiological purpose.

---

[85] The subtitle for this section in Maxwell's book is "God's Love for Astrologers" (Maxwell, *God Cares*, 1:42).

[86] Sherwood Lingenfelter says that learning the local language is crucial if one is to understand the people in a different culture (Sherwood Lingenfelter, "Cultural Learning," *EDWM*, 255).

[87] Pat Gustin, "Learning the Language," *Passport to Mission*, ed. Erich W. Baumgartner et al. (Berrien Springs, MI: Institute of World Mission of Andrews University, 1999), 95.

[88] Shea, *Daniel 1–7*, 21.

[89] Gehard F. Hasel, "Establishing a Date for the Book of Daniel," *Symposium on Daniel*, ed. Frank B. Holbrook (Silver Spring, MD: Biblical Research Institute, 1986), 143.

[90] Miller, *Daniel*, 48.

Cultural Symbols

In the king's dream, God used a well-known cultural reference: a great *image*. God chose to reveal coming events to the heathen monarch by means of an immense and dazzling statue because, in ancient times, people performed public worship at the feet of their gods and some of these images were very large.[91] Furthermore, ancient Near Eastern cultures occasionally connected a statue of a human being with the world's destiny.[92]

The scheme of the four world empires also reflects a process of contextualization. The use of the metals assigned to the four kingdoms in the book of Daniel is similar to the order of metals referred to in the Great Triumphal Inscription of Sargon II.[93] The "different metals were assigned by Babylonians to different gods."[94] Daniel also related the metals to idolatry: "the gods of gold and silver, of bronze, iron" (5:4, 23). It has also been suggested that there is some parallelism between Daniel's prophecies and some of the Akkadian historical prophecies. Daniel's prophecies shared with the Uruk prophecy and the Dynastic prophecy not only the feature of a historical outline, but also the motif of an ideal era for Babylon within such an outline.[95] One could recognize a point of contact between the "Akkadian prophecies"[96] and the book of Daniel in the concept of the rise and fall of empires.[97]

Although there are some differences between the prophecies of Daniel and ancient Near Eastern prophecies, the use of a human statue shows God's sensitivity to culture. The book of Daniel contains a message of God's sovereignty through a symbolism familiar to Babylonian culture.

The *"huge mountain"* in the king's dream (2:35) was originally a title of Enlil, the patron god of Nippur, to whom the most ancient Babylonian temple was dedicated. Later Enlil was replaced by Marduk, the patron god of Babylon.[98] In Babylonian mythology, the gods were supposed to

---

[91] Maxwell, *God Cares*, 1:35.

[92] Doukhan, *Daniel*, 29.

[93] Charles Boutflower, *In and Around the Book of Daniel* (Grand Rapids, MI: Kregel, 1977), 24.

[94] Ibid., 34.

[95] Roy Gane, "Genre Awareness and Interpretation of the Book of Daniel," *To Understand the Scriptures: Essays in Honor of William H. Shea*, ed. David Merling (Berrien Springs, MI: Institute of Archaeology and Siegfried H. Horn Archaeological Museum, 1997), 143.

[96] See A. Kirk Grayson and W. G. Lambert, "Akkadian Prophecies," *JCS* 16.1 (1964): 7–30.

[97] Gerhard F. Hasel, "The Four World Empires of Daniel 2 Against Its Near Eastern Environment," *JSOT* 12.1 (May 1979): 21.

[98] Boutflower, *Daniel*, 45. See also William J. Fulco, "Enlil," *ABD*, 2:507–508; Lowell Handy, "Marduk," *ABD*, 4:522–523.

dwell in a sacred mountain called "the Mountain of the Lands," and Enlil, as chief of the gods, became identified with the mountain itself.[99] For the Hebrew hearers, the mountain symbolized Zion and Jerusalem (Dan 9:16, 20; 11:45). The mountain of Zion is a technical expression, designating the heavenly place of God (Isa 14:13). The stone also symbolizes God Himself (e.g., Isa 8:14). The use of the mountain shows how careful God is to speak in culturally relevant terms when communicating His message to the peoples of the world.

In the dream of Daniel 4, Nebuchadnezzar saw a big *tree*. The symbolic meaning of a tree was well known in the ancient Near East.[100] The tree represented the divine world order maintained by the king as the representative of his god.[101] Sometimes the king took the place of the tree as the "human personification of the Tree."[102] Interestingly, "Nebuchadnezzar himself, in an inscription, compares Babylon to a great tree sheltering the nations of the world."[103] Thus, the imagery of the big tree was also a vehicle God used to enable the recipient of the message to retain the meaning and importance of the message longer than if the message had been communicated in any other way.[104]

In Daniel 7, Daniel saw in his vision "the four winds of heaven churning up the great sea" (v. 2). This scene is similar to the Babylonian myth, *Enuma Elish*, which tells of rebellious monsters born from the primordial ocean (Tiamat) and who were destroyed by the winds Marduk stationed to defeat Tiamat and her monsters.[105] In Babylonian tradition, *animals* often symbolized upcoming historical events.[106] The first beast, "a winged lion," is depicted in Babylonian sculptures, again suggesting that the symbolism would have been easily recognized. The combination of a lion

---

[99] Boutflower, *Daniel*, 45. In Sumerian Hymns to Enlil, it says, "In Nippur, the beloved shrine of the father, the Great Mountain" (*ANET*, 574).

[100] Pfandl says: "Sacred or cosmic trees were a major element of the iconography of ancient Mesopotamia" (Gerhard Pfandl, *Daniel: The Seer of Babylon* [Hagerstown, MD: Review and Herald, 2004], 40).

[101] S. Parpola, "The Assyrian Tree of Life: Tracing the Origins of the Jewish Monotheism and Greek Philosophy," *JNES* 52.3 (July 1993): 167.

[102] Pfandl, *Daniel*, 40.

[103] S. Langdon, *Building Inscriptions of the Neo-Babylonian Empire* (Paris: Leroux, 1905), 34.

[104] "Daniel," *AdvBibComm*, 4:789.

[105] *ANET*, 60–72, 501–503. In *ANET*, 66, the four winds are divided into the south wind, the north wind, the east wind, and the west wind. For the biblical and cultural influences on the vision of Daniel 7, see Jüng Eggler, *Influences and Traditions Underlying the Vision of Daniel 7:2-14: The Research History from the End of the 19th Century to the Present* (Göttingen: Vandenhoeck und Ruprecht, 2000).

[106] Doukhan, *Daniel*, 101.

and an eagle was a common object of art—most often a lion with eagles' wings.[107] The other beasts have often been likened to Babylonian engravings, sculptures, reliefs, and sphinxes, but they are not exact images.[108] Babylonian readers, however, would have understood the meaning of the beasts used for the various kingdoms because they were already familiar with mythical animal motifs. In Mesopotamia, there was a custom of describing a king as having characteristics of various animals.[109] It is thus reasonable to assume that most Babylonians would have readily understood the meaning of the animals in Daniel's vision.

Cross-Cultural Witness to Kings

Being a document with missionary concern, the book of Daniel shows how he and his three friends witnessed in the land of their captivity, fulfilling God's purpose of giving to heathen nations the blessings that come through the knowledge of the God of Heaven.[110]

Witness to Nebuchadnezzar

Daniel's prayer, offered after God had revealed the content and meaning of the king's first dream, indicates that Daniel already possessed a correct understanding of God that allowed him to witness about the "God in Heaven" and the "Great God" to King Nebuchadnezzar (Dan 2). It has been indicated that "a God in Heaven" parallels "the Most High" (3:26; 4:2, 25; 5:1, 21; 7:25, 27) both in general meaning and in resembling pagan titles for the gods.[111] The term ꜥelyôn, "the Exalted One," was "a title given

---

[107] Montgomery, *Daniel*, 287; "Daniel," *AdvBibComm*, 4:820. See also picture 534 in *ANEP*, 180. Pfandl says, "Representations of lions appear on the walls of the great processional way to the Ishtar Gate as well as the gate itself. They occur also on the outer wall of the throne room in Babylon" (Pfandl, *Daniel*, 62).

[108] John E. Goldingay, *Daniel* (Dallas, TX: Word, 2002), 151; cf. *ANEP*, 212–217. See also Eggler, *Influences*, 45–54, for the efforts by scholars to see any iconographic influences of the Near East in the animal vision of Daniel 7.

[109] *ANET*, 585–586.

[110] Ellen G. White, *Prophets and Kings* (Boise, ID: Pacific Press, 1917), 479.

[111] Goldingay, *Daniel*, 47; Rose, "Names," 1004. For other cases where "Most High," *Elyôn*, parallels Yahweh, see 2 Samuel 22:14; Psalms 18:14; 21:8. Psalm 47:2 clearly identifies the two phrases: "How awesome is the LORD [Yahweh] Most High, the great King over all the earth!" For the further usage of God in Heaven in the Old Testament, see Genesis 2:3; 24:7; Nehemiah 1:5; Jonah 1:9; Psalms 47:2; 83:18; 91:9; 92:1; 97:9. "The name of God" (2:20) is another reverential substitute for Yahweh just as "heaven" is later used as a reverential substitute for "God." The phrase "God in Heaven" is also reminiscent of the Canaanite title "lord of heaven," which was apparently an epithet of the high god *El* (Goldingay, *Daniel*, 47). In fact, in the ancient Near East and in Greece and Persia, worship of "the lord of heaven" was widespread (ibid.).

to the highest of the gods in the Canaanite pantheon."[112] The ancient Near Eastern gods were also designated as the great gods.[113] Although there were disputes as to the supremacy between different gods, Marduk was most certainly at the head of the Babylonian pantheon during Daniel's time.[114] Thus, by using the phrase "Great God," Daniel put his God in the place of Marduk.[115] Using terms for God that were similar to the terms used for the gods of Babylon, Daniel may have created common ground, while contrasting his God with the other gods.

Nebuchadnezzar's motive in erecting the golden image was both political and religious. Through the dramatic rescue of His servant, God made it clear to Nebuchadnezzar that Judah's defeat was not because Israel's God was incompetent. Although the king designated Daniel's God as the "Most High God," he did so in a polytheistic sense. He was not ready to admit that his power should be subject to God's divine power. In his decree, he only required people to respect, or not despise, the God of Daniel's friends.

The narrative in Daniel 4 is mainly Nebuchadnezzar's personal testimony. After his encounter with God through the dream and after spending seven years living with wild animals, the king used the phrase "the Most High God" in an absolute sense—a deity superior to other gods, even as a personal God (vv. 2–3). His conversion became widely known to "all peoples, nations, and languages" through a royal decree. This was as important as his conversion. God's original plan to appoint Israel to be a light to the nations was being fulfilled through the witness of a converted heathen king.

Witness to Belshazzar

In Daniel's interpretation of the handwriting on the wall, he used the term "the Most High God," which was used by Nebuchadnezzar in Daniel 3 and 4. It was the Most High God (Yahweh of Judah, not the idols of Babylon) who had given Nebuchadnezzar a great kingdom, power, and honor among the nations (5:18).[116] In witnessing cross-culturally to King Belshazzar, Daniel contrasted the true "Most High God" and "Lord of Heaven" with the Babylonian gods that cannot see or hear or understand (v. 23). Daniel's faithful witness included a message of judgment given in front of thousands of officials (as well as the king) in a heathen kingdom,

---

[112] Frederick W. Schmidt, "Most High," *ABD*, 4:922.

[113] E.g., Marduk (*ANET*, 66); Ashuramazda (ibid., 316).

[114] Boutflower, *Daniel*, 93.

[115] Ibid., 98.

[116] Miller, *Daniel*, 162.

suggesting that modern cross-cultural witnesses should also include a judgment message as part of a cross-cultural mission.

Witness to Darius

Daniel's religious belief was well known even in the Median kingdom. Darius may not have had a strong faith in God, but his statement expressing God's power to save Daniel from the lions reveals that Darius was somewhat acquainted with the God and religion of Daniel. In response to Darius' call, Daniel testified about how his God had saved his life. Darius acknowledged Daniel's miraculous deliverance was because Daniel had trusted in his God (v. 23). Darius then wrote a decree to all the peoples, nations, and speakers of every language throughout the land to testify concerning the "living God" of Daniel. Daniel's faithful witness, through life and word, brought unexpected results through the confession of King Darius.

Conclusions

In this study, several missiological perspectives in the book of Daniel have been noted and it has been shown that the theology of *missio Dei* is prominent in the book. Daniel and his friends were aware of God's sovereignty in human history and of His salvific purpose for all people. The book of Daniel demonstrates some strategies used in *missio Dei* such as God's use of committed individuals, dreams and visions, prayer and spiritual formation, power encounters, and spiritual conflict. From a cross-cultural perspective, Daniel and his friends were sensitive to their surrounding culture as they communicated the truth of God in relevant ways to people in a heathen kingdom. The book of Daniel can be used as a valid missionary document, from which can be drawn relevant missiological implications for today.[117] Ellen G. White emphasizes that possibility:

> Great light shone forth from Daniel and his companions.... Thus the Lord designs that spiritual light shall shine from His faithful watchmen in these last days. If the saints in the Old Testament bore such a decided testimony of loyalty, how should God's people today, having the accumulated light of centuries, shine forth, when the prophecies of the Old Testament shed their veiled glory into the future![118]

As we near the close of cosmic conflict, the missiological perspectives,

---

[117] For the detailed implications, see Sung Ik Kim, "Proclamation in Cross-cultural Context: Missiological Implications of the Book of Daniel" (Ph.D. diss., Andrews University, 2005), 246–281.

[118] Ellen G. White, Letter 32, 1899, *AdvBibComm*, 4:1169.

as well as the prophecies recorded by Daniel, demand special attention for the achievement of God's mission. Like Daniel, we are called to reveal the true character of God to the world as manifested in a unique way in His Son, calling everyone to worship Him as Creator and Redeemer.

CHAPTER 7

MISSION IN THE BOOK OF REVELATION

Ekkehardt Mueller

Revelation's missiological themes are easily overlooked. "In the myriad of studies of Revelation, both scholarly and popular, almost no attention has been paid to its contributions to the theology of mission."[1] At first glance, the Apocalypse seems to describe the church almost exclusively involved in internal and external difficulties. By emphasizing the inner struggles of the church and outside threats, we get the impression mission is not a primary concern in the book. Even vocabulary traditionally associated with mission tends to be absent.[2]

---

[1] Johnny V. Miller, "Mission in Revelation," *Mission in the New Testament: An Evangelical Approach*, ed. William J. Larkin Jr. and Joel F. Williams (Maryknoll, NY: Orbis Books, 1998), 227.

[2] The language related to mission in the Apocalypse differs to some extent from the language used in non-Johannine literature. For instance, the Great Commission in Matthew 28:19–20 uses the words "to go" (*poreuomai*), "to make disciples" (*mathēteuō*), and "to teach" (*didaskō*). Only the last term is used in Revelation, but in a negative context: The false prophets "teach" (Rev 2:14, 20). *Didaskō* is used in the Gospel of John ten times, mostly in a mission-related context. The term "disciple" (*mathētēs*) occurs 261 times in the New Testament, but only in the Gospels (78 times in John) and Acts. Revelation does not employ it. The parallel commission found in Mark 16:15 uses the verb "to preach"(*kerussō*), a term occurring frequently in the synoptic Gospels and the Pauline literature to describe the proclamation of the gospel or of God's kingdom. Apart from Revelation 5:2, it is not used in the Johannine literature. It is found in Revelation 5:2 but even here, the term does not point to missionary activity. According to Matthew 10:5 and John 20:21, Jesus sent out (*apostellō*) His disciples. The term occurs frequently in the Gospels and in Acts, but also in some New Testament letters. It can be mission-related and is found in Revelation 1:1; 5:6; 22:6. However, in these texts those that are sent out are not human beings. The verb "to bring good news"/"to preach the gospel" (*euangelizō*) and the noun "the gospel" (*euangelion*) are employed frequently in the New Testament (Luke's material uses the verb most frequently [25 of the 54 occurrences] followed by Paul [23 times]. The noun is employed most often by

In spite of this, Revelation does have a mission perspective. This perspective is not limited to certain words, but is evident in the use of mission-related concepts. Our purpose is to examine the presence and meaning of mission in Revelation. We will explore the message that the church should proclaim and its mission. Finally, we will summarize the results of God's mission in Revelation.

Mission Activity in Revelation

Mission runs throughout the Apocalypse and expresses itself in two closely related ways. One can be called "the mission of God." The other is the mission of the church. Though God remains in charge of both, for our purpose we will separate the two. God's mission can be understood as His direct involvement in this world to bring about His desired purpose. The church's mission stresses the responsibility of human agents.

God's Mission

The Book of Revelation portrays, as no other book in the Bible, a cosmic conflict between good and evil.[3] In this conflict, God is especially concerned with the salvation of humanity. It is His mission "to reclaim both the lost territory and its inhabitants for fellowship with him, to his own glory."[4] In order to achieve this goal, the Godhead is personally involved.

God the Father

According to Revelation 10:7, it is God who "preached [*euangelizō*] to His servants—the prophets."[5] He proclaims "the message of God's redemption to those who love Him and judgment for those who hate Him. God gives this message to his servants, whom He expects to pass it on to all people (vv. 10–11; 11:3, 10)."[6] *Euangelizo* is found once more in Rev-

---

Paul [60 of the 76 occurrences]), but occur neither in John's Gospel nor in his letters, but only in two verses in Revelation (10:7; 14:6 use the verb; the noun is found in 14:6). This word family is always mission-oriented. In any case, John seldom uses common mission-related vocabulary. However, he uses the word family *martu-* quite frequently, surpassing all other authors. This word family includes the terms 1) "to bear witness"/"to testify"/"to be a witness" (*martureō*); 2) "testimony"/"witness"/"reputation" (*marturia*); and 3) "witness" (*martus*) from which the word "martyr" is derived. A martyr is one who testifies to the truth with his life. The word family does not always denote a mission-oriented situation, although in Revelation it seems it does.

[3] Stephen Pattemore, *The People of God in the Apocalypse: Discourse, Structure and Exegesis* (Cambridge: Cambridge University Press, 2004), 97, mentions also a cosmic conflict that "John certainly describes..." but, he does not think that this is "his primary interpretative direction."

[4] Miller, "Mission," 227.

[5] Bible texts are quoted from the NASB, unless otherwise noted.

[6] Richard Bauckham, *The Theology of the Book of Revelation* (Cambridge: Cambridge University

elation 14:6, where the good news is to be proclaimed by an angel. God uses messengers to carry out His mission.

This is also stressed in Revelation 22:6, which takes us back to the very beginning of the book (Rev 1:1). God gave Revelation to His people and did it using, among others, an angel.[7] He is not a distant God who, like a watchmaker, has wound up the clock of this world and now leaves it to itself. He has a plan and a goal. He allows heavenly beings and humanity to be part of that plan and has shown them what will take place. God's mission will also be accomplished through the rider on the white horse, the Spirit, and the two witnesses.

Jesus and the Gospel

The Rider on the White Horse.[8] According to the symbolic or historicist view, the rider on the white horse represents Jesus and the proclamation of the gospel.[9] The next seals then describe the events that follow a

---

Press, 1993), 314.

[7] Cf. Ulrich B. Müller, *Die Offenbarung des Johannes* (Gütersloh: Gütersloher Verlagshaus Gerd Mohn, 1984), 367–368; Grant R. Osborne, *Revelation* (Grand Rapids, MI: Baker, 2002), 780–781, states: "In his sovereignty God revealed the book..."

[8] Representatives of the preterist view suggest to take the first seal literally and apply it to the Parthians, who were a threat to the Roman empire. Cf. Müller, *Offenbarung*, 167; Ronald L. Farmer, *Revelation* (St. Louis, MO: Chalice Press, 2005), 74; Simon J. Kistemaker, *New Testament Commentary: Exposition of the Book of Revelation* (Grand Rapids, MI: Baker, 2001), 222–224. Others among them apply it to Rome itself; e.g., David J. Hawkin, "Globalization, the American Empire, and the Four Horsemen of the Apocalypse," *Ch* 118.4 (2004): 320–321.

[9] Cf. Kistemarker, *Revelation*, 224–225. Michael Bachmann, "Noch ein Blick auf den ersten apokalyptischen Reiter (von Apk 6.1–2)," *NTS* 44 (1998): 278, understands this rider as a hypostasis of the epiphany of God and closely linked with the Christ of Revelation 19. However, another symbolic view regards the first horseman as the antichrist; see Allen Kerkeslager, "Apollo, Greco-Roman Prophecy, and the Rider on the White Horse in Rev 6:2," *JBL* 112 (1993): 116–121; Kistemaker, *Revelation*, 221; Mathias Rissi, "The Rider on the White Horse," *Interp* 18 (1964): 407–418. This view is very unlikely because: 1) The corresponding rider on the white horse in Revelation 19:11–16 is Jesus. 2) In Revelation, the white color is always positive. George Eldon Ladd, *A Commentary on the Revelation of John* (Grand Rapids, MI: Eerdmans, 1991), 97–98. John C. Poirier, "The First Rider: A Response to Michael Bachmann," *NTS* 45 (1999): 259 states, "By my reckoning, Bachmann, and other exegetes of this passage, are wrong to insist upon the determinative bearing of the symbolic value of the horse's colour for the identity of the first horseman." However, Stephen Smalley, *The Revelation of John: A Commentary on the Greek Text of the Apocalypse* (Downers Grove, IL: InterVarsity, 2005), 147, maintains: "The motif of coloured horses (red, black, white, dappled grey) appears again at Zech. 6.1–8... In Zechariah the colours seem to have no particular significance; whereas in the context of Rev. 6 they reflect the character of the rider, and symbolize specific causes." 3) The bow seems to be God's bow that he uses (Ps 7:12; Lam 2:4; 3, 12; Hab 3:9; and esp. Ps 45, 2–6). 4) In the Apocalypse, the wreath/crown of victory is predominantly positive (Rev 2; 10; 3;11; 4:4, 10; 12:1; 14:14); the one exception are the locusts of Revelation 9:7. Yet their victory is transient and not long-lasting. Cf. Kistemaker, *Revelation*, 225; Bachmann, "Blick," 257–278. 5) In Revelation, the verb "to conquer" is predominantly positive. Conquering is attributed to Jesus (Rev 5:5; 17:14) and is used in connection with

rejection of the gospel. In Revelation, the symbolic understanding is the predominant one.[10] The context of Revelation 6 favors this understanding. The phrase "conquering and to conquer" fits Jesus' victory well and points to His complete triumph. The gospel horseman began His ministry in the first century A.D., and the message is proclaimed till our own days.[11]

Jesus as Witness. The word family *mart-* is important in Revelation. We find two nouns, namely *martus*,[12] designating the "witness" as an individual, and *marturia*, the "witness" or "testimony" as the message proclaimed by a witness. We also find the verb *martureō*, "to witness."[13] Jesus, as true witness, revealed the Father, testified to the truth that He received from Him, and remained faithful until death.[14] He calls attention to Scripture as embodied in the book of Revelation (22:18–20)[15] and guarantees the reliability of the eschatological hope it describes.[16] Revelation most often uses the term *marturia*,[17] particularly in the phrase "testimony of Jesus" (*marturia Iēsou*; Rev 12:17). It refers to Christ's self-revelation through the

---

believers (Rev 2:7, 11, 17, 26; 3:5, 12, 21; 12:11; 15:2; 21:7). Only in Revelation 11:7 and 13:7 evil powers enjoy some type of victory. Cf. Kistemaker, *Revelation*, 222.

[10] This may be indicated in Revelation 1:1 by the term *sēmainō* which points to Jesus "symbolizing" the Apocalypse to John.

[11] Ranko Stefanovic, *Revelation of Jesus Christ: Commentary on the Book of Revelation* (Berrien Springs, MI: Andrews University Press, 2002) 228, writes, "With the coming of the Holy Spirit at Pentecost, the proclamation of the gospel was propelled into motion. It was then that Christ went forth overcoming and that he might overcome. This conquering evidently has to do with spiritual matters."

[12] *Martus* is found five times in Revelation. It refers to Jesus (Rev 1:5; 3:14) and his followers (Rev 2:13; 17:6), as well as the two witnesses (Rev 11). In the New Testament, Jesus as the faithful witness appears only here and in Revelation 3:14.

[13] Those who bear witness (*martureō*) are John (Rev 1:2), the angel sent by Jesus (Rev 22:16), and Jesus himself (Rev 22:18, 20).

[14] Cf. G. K. Beale, *The Book of Revelation*, The New International Greek Testament Commentary (Grand Rapids, MI: Eerdmans, 1999), 190; Smalley, *Revelation*, 34; and Osborne, *Revelation*, 62. Ben Witherington III, *Revelation* (Cambridge: Cambridge University Press, 2003), 76, connects the different descriptions of Jesus in Revelation 1:5 and notes: "The close association of his faithful witness and his resurrection implies that the witness entailed his death." Gerhard A. Krodel, *Revelation* (Minneapolis, MA: Augsburg, 1989), 83, concludes that because of Jesus' exemplary witness that led Him to the cross, believers must be faithful in an uncompromising way, even if they have to suffer for their obedience.

[15] Miller, "Mission," 236, states that "Revelation itself is part of that witness (1:1–3)."

[16] U. B. Müller, *Offenbarung*, 73.

[17] It is found ten times in nine verses (Rev 1:2, 9; 6:9; 11:7; 12:11, 17; 19:10; 20:4). It is the most important term of the word family in Revelation, found six times in the phrase "testimony of Jesus" (Rev 1:2,9; 11:17; 19:10 twice; 20:4). Repeatedly, it appears in connection with other expressions, predominantly the "word of God" (Rev 1:2, 9; 20:4). *Marturia* has also to do with prophecy. And indeed, the parallel text to Revelation 19:10 replaces the phrase "testimony of Jesus" with the "prophets" (Rev 22:9).

prophets; His testimony, not the believer's testimony about him.[18]

Jesus and the Two-Edged Sword out of His Mouth. Revelation 1 describes Jesus with majestic imagery. He holds in His hand the seven stars. A sharp, two-edged sword comes out of his mouth. The sword is particularly important (Rev 1:16). It is found again in Revelation 2:12, 16, in the messages to the seven churches. It also occurs in 19:15, 21.

The description of the rider in Revelation 19 resembles the description of the one like a son of man in Revelation 1b. He is called "the Word of God" (Rev 19:13; see John 1:1–3 and 1 John 1:1–3) and a sharp sword comes out of His mouth.

This sword is the Word of God (Heb 4:12).[19] It has been suggested that "throughout Revelation, it is made clear that Jesus' power is the 'sword of his mouth' (1:16; 2:12, 16; 19:15, 21). The Word of God is truly powerful. But it is a power that, unlike the sword of empire, operates without bloody violence."[20] Jesus is also described as having an iron scepter (Rev 12:5; 19:15), which seems to parallel the sword out of His mouth.[21] The Word of God will cause the destruction of the wicked.[22]

A study of the term "mouth" in Revelation indicates that the main emphasis is on its use for propaganda and counter-propaganda purposes—for the promotion of the message of evil powers and the message of God.[23] This suggests that the final events have to do with God's mission

---

[18] For a discussion of the term "testimony of Jesus," see Gerhard Pfandl, "The Remnant Church and the Spirit of Prophecy," *Symposium on Revelation - Book II*, ed. Frank B. Holbrook (Silver Spring, MD: Biblical Research Institute, 1992), 295–333. He shows that the genitive in "testimony of Jesus" is a subjective genitive, describing Jesus' activity in His self-revelation. Richard Bauckham, *The Climax of Prophecy: Studies on the Book of Revelation* (Edinburgh: T & T Clark, 1993), 161, supports this conclusion. The witness of Jesus is the witness Jesus bore. Loren L. Johns, *The Lamb Christology of the Apocalypse of John: An Investigation into Its Origins and Rhetorical Force* (Tübinben: Mohr Siebeck, 2003), 173, however, suggests that "both the objective and the subjective are envisioned in the book." He is supported by Olutola K. Peters, *The Mandate of the Church in the Apocalypse* (New York: Peter Lang, 2005), 83.

[19] See Ian Boxall, "Violence in the Apocalypse," *ScrB* 35.2 (2005): 78–79.

[20] Wes Howard-Brook and Anthony Gwyther, *Unveiling Empire: Reading Revelation Then and Now* (Maryknoll, NY: Orbis, 1990), 140.

[21] Mark Bredin, *Jesus, Revolutionary of Peace: A Nonviolent Christology of the Book of Revelation* (Carlisle, OK: Paternoster, 2003), 208.

[22] Ibid.

[23] Jesus uses the Word of God that comes out of His mouth (Rev 1:16; 2:16; 19:15, 21). God's two witnesses have power in their mouth (Rev 11:15). His people, the 144,000, have no lies in their mouth (Rev 14:5). But the demonic horses of the sixth trumpet have power in their mouths and destroy people (Rev 9:17–19). "The thrice repeated reference to the 'mouth'... of the creatures from which the spirits emerge suggests the 'persuasive and deceptive propaganda' which will drive the secular unfaithful at the end-time to be committed to the cause of evil and isolated from the source of truth." The serpent has power in his mouth (Rev 12:15). The sea beast has a

and the proclamation of His message. It could be suggested that "those who receive the messages of the three angels [in Rev 14] unite with God and the true gospel. But those who respond to the three frogs join with Babylon . . ."[24] In this final conflict, Jesus plays a crucial role. God's mission is carried out by the rider on the white horse. His association with the Word of God makes clear that the final showdown will be about more than persecution, but the rival messages of good and evil.

The Spirit

The Holy Spirit is introduced under the symbol of seven spirits (Rev 1:4).[25] These seven spirits are clearly part of the divine Trinity (Rev 1:4–5). They are linked to Jesus (Rev 3:1; 5:6) and to God the Father who sits on the throne (Rev 4:5).[26] They are also "sent out into all the earth" on an all-encompassing mission (Rev 5:6). According to John 14:26; 15:26; and 16:7, the Holy Spirit was sent out by Father and Son to accomplish their mission. G. R. Osborne states:

> . . . here that mission theme is extended further. It is a major motif in the book focusing on what Bauckham calls "the conversion of the nations." Elsewhere, "the whole world" is deceived by Satan (12:9), follows him (13:3; 16:14), and is soon to come under judgment (3:10). At the same time "the eternal gospel" is proclaimed to "the inhabitants of the earth" (14:6–7) . . . The Spirit thus begins the universal mission of God to "the whole earth" . . .[27]

The Holy Spirit, simply called "Spirit" (*pneuma*),[28] is found throughout the Book of Revelation. Obviously, the Holy Spirit is involved in the

---

mouth like a lion blaspheming God, His tabernacle, and those who dwell in heaven (Rev 13:2, 5, 6). Finally, three unclean spirits come out of the mouth of the satanic trinity in order to deceive humanity and gather the kings of the earth for the final battle of Armageddon.

[24] Jon Paulien, *Armageddon at the Door* (Hagerstown, MD: Review and Herald, 2008), 172.

[25] See John Sweet, *Revelation* (Philadelphia, PA: Trinity, 1990), 65.

[26] Dan Lioy, *The Book of Revelation in Christological Focus* (New York: Peter Lang, 2003), 132, comments on Revelation 5:6 saying: "It is worth noting that the fullness of the divine in His Trinitarian presence is unmistakable in Revelation 5. The 'one seated on the throne' (vss. 1, 7, 13) refers to the Father; the 'Lamb' (vv. 6, 8, 12–13) points to the Son, and 'the seven spirits of God" (v. 6), 'who is the horns and eyes of the Lamb,' refers to the Holy Spirit."

[27] Osborne, *Revelation*, 257.

[28] While *pneuma* seems to refer to the Holy Spirit in Revelation 1:10; 2:7, 11, 17, 29; 3:6, 13, 22; 4:2; 14:13; 17:3; 19:10; 21:10; 22:17, it also designates evil spirits (Rev 16:13–14; 18:2), humans (Rev 22:6), and life/breath (Rev 11:11; 13:15). In any case, the term is predominantly employed for the Holy Spirit.

communication of the message of the Book of Revelation, because John is repeatedly "in the Spirit" (Rev 1:10; 4:2; 17:3; 21:10); this is "a formula of prophetic commission."[29] Additionally, the Holy Spirit addresses the believers in the seven churches, because all of Christ's messages to the seven churches end with a reference to the Holy Spirit. One could say that:

> The writer does not distinguish between the exalted Christ and the work of the Spirit . . . The revelation comes from God through Jesus Christ, and is mediated to John by his angel (1.1). Now the voice of Christ in victory is heard, as the Spirit speaks to the churches. He speaks continuously (. . . present tense) to the churches. In the first place, the word is directed toward the seven churches of Asia, including Ephesus. But, as with Revelation in general, the scope of the message is far reaching. Christ addresses the Church as a whole, and for all time.[30]

The Holy Spirit is also the Spirit of prophecy that speaks through genuine prophets (Rev 19:10; 22:9), "bringing the word of the exalted Christ to his people on earth . . ."[31] His message is not only future-oriented, but has implications for the life of humanity here and now. The Holy Spirit is twice described as speaking.[32] In Revelation 14:13, He confirms the heavenly voice.[33] According to Revelation 22:17, the Holy Spirit, together with the bride of the Lamb (the church),[34] utters a final invitation to humanity to come and freely receive the water of life. God's mission is carried out by the Holy Spirit.

The Word of God

The Two Witnesses. The two witnesses are participants in the procla-

---

[29] Beale, *Revelation*, 850. Cf. Osborne, *Revelation*, 609–610. Leon Morris, *Revelation* (Grand Rapids, MI: Eerdmans, 1988), 198, understands "*in the Spirit* as a state of exaltation and special receptivity brought about by the Spirit . . ." However, David Aune, *Revelation 1–5* (Dallas, TX: Word, 1997), 82–83, opts for what he calls a vision trance and does not take *pneuma* as the Holy Spirit. Bauckham, *Climax*, 150–159, rejects the view that *pneuma* refers to the human spirit.

[30] Smalley, *Revelation*, 63–64; cf. Aune, *Revelation 1–5*, 151.

[31] Bauckham, *Climax*, 160.

[32] For a discussion whether or not this is the Holy Spirit and who is speaking, see Osborne, *Revelation*, 793.

[33] Ulrich B. Müller, *Offenbarung*, 268–269, suggests that the speech by the Spirit is what the Holy Spirit communicates through the visionary.

[34] See Bauckham, *Climax*, 167.

mation of God's message and in suffering. The frequent association of witness with the Word of God demonstrates a strong affinity with Scripture. This is important because according to Old Testament law, two or three witnesses were required to build a case in court (Deut 19:15).[35] They are also described as two olive trees. The background, found in Zech 4:1–10, clearly connects the two olive trees with the work of the Holy Spirit.[36] Whereas the number of the lampstands in Revelation has been increased from one to two, the olive trees in Zechariah and Revelation remain two. K. A. Strand argued that because of this continuity, the olive trees allude to the work of the Spirit: "the Holy Spirit's role in providing the word of God, in both the Old Testament and New Testament aspects."[37] They are also two lampstands,[38] a source of light. In the Old Testament God's Word is called a lamp (e.g., Ps 119:105).

They are also described as two prophets. The word family, *prophēt-*, focuses on genuine prophecy in the narrow sense and on the product of this prophecy as found in the book of Revelation. The two witnesses are the only entity that is described with all three major words of this word family. Prophecy is the most prominent characteristic of the two witnesses. The fact that they stand before the Lord of the earth (Rev 11:4) suggests their "heavenly origin."[39]

> The legal nature of the testimony is intensified by the position of the witnesses as they bear their testimony in an unseen courtroom, 'standing before the Lord of the earth.' . . . This proximity to

---

[35] See Beale, *Revelation*, 581; Morris, *Revelation*, 143.

[36] See Beale, *Revelation*, 577–578; Morris, *Revelation*, 144.

[37] Kenneth A. Strand, "The Two Olive Trees of Zechariah 4 and Revelation 11," *AUSS* 20 (1982): 260.

[38] Lampstands are mentioned seven times in Revelation. Six of these occurrences are found in the letter frame of Revelation, in this case in Revelation 1:12–13, 20 (twice); 2:1, 5. They depict the seven golden lampstands and are identified with seven churches (1:20). The only other place where lampstands occur is 11:4. Scholars have argued that the two witnesses of Revelation 11 must refer to the church, since the seven lampstands are clearly identified as churches (see Beale, *Revelation*, 574–577). Although words are normally used with the same meaning throughout the Apocalypse, there are exceptions. While according to Revelation 22:5 there will no longer be a need for the light of the lamp, according to Revelation 21:23, Jesus the Lamb is the lamp. A change of meaning may also occur with the lampstands. In Revelation 11, they are identified as two olive trees, two witnesses, and two prophets. There is a difference with regard to location. While the seven lampstands are on earth (Rev 2:1), the two lampstands of Revelation 11 are standing before the Lord, possibly being connected to His heavenly sanctuary (see David E. Aune, *Revelation 6–16* [Nashville, TN: Thomas Nelson, 1998], 613). It must also be kept in mind that the motif of the lampstands is not the predominant one in Revelation 11. More important are the motifs of witness and prophecy. Obviously, again the work of the Holy Spirit is emphasized.

[39] Ibid.

the Lord also emphasizes the witnesses' direct divine inspiration and commission. Though they live in a world of danger, they are never far from their Lord's sovereign presence.[40]

The two witnesses share the fate of their Lord (Rev 11:8), participating in His death.[41] But after three and a half days, they also share in His resurrection and ascension. They have to encounter difficulties and must face enemies and temporary defeat. Still, they are powerful. For instance, fire proceeds out of the mouths of the demonic horses (Rev 9:17–18). The two witnesses are very active during the 1260 days/years.

K. A. Strand has argued in favor of understanding the two witnesses as the Old Testament message and New Testament witness.[42] He arrived at this conclusion by noticing 1) that the two witnesses "do not function as two individual entities, but only as *one entity*–always in unity and in absolute union;"[43] 2) that "the two witnesses constitute a symbolism drawn from *several prophetic backgrounds* beyond the obvious allusions to Moses and Elijah, just as in 11:8 'the great city' also embraces a blend of symbolic references . . . ;" and 3) that Revelation contains an extensive two-witness theology.

God's mission is carried out through the ministry of the two witnesses, the Old and New Testaments. "Confronted with a world addicted to idolatry and evil (9:20–1), they proclaim the one true God and his coming judgment on evil (cf. 14:7), but they do so *as a call to repentance*."[44]

The Book of Revelation. God's mission is carried out by giving the book of Revelation to His people (1:1–3). The phrase "testimony of Jesus" occurs for the first time in Revelation 1:2 and seems to include the Apocalypse.[45] According to Revelation 1:3, those who read or hear the message

---

[40] Beale, *Revelation*, 576.

[41] Cf. Aune, *Revelation 6–16*, 587.

[42] Kenneth A. Strand, "The Two Witnesses of Rev 11:3–12," *AUSS* 19 (1981): 134.

[43] While in Revelation 9:18, 20 fire comes out of the mouths of the strange horses—plural—in Revelation 11:5, fire comes out of the mouth—singular—of the two witnesses. Although there are two witnesses, nevertheless they have only one mouth. Although they are two, they have one prophecy (Rev 11:6) and one testimony/witness (Rev 11:7). The word "corpse/body" is found three times in 11:3–13. Their body—singular—lies in the street of the great city (Rev 11:8). People see their body—singular—three and a half days long (Rev 11:9), and their bodies–plural–are not buried (Rev 11:9). A tomb–singular–is not available for them (Rev 11:9). It seems that the singular is used intentionally in order to stress the unity of the two witnesses. The usage of both singular and plural within the very same verse may point to the unity in duality. This feature fits best the interpretation of the two witnesses as Scriptures.

[44] Bauckham, *Theology*, 86.

[45] See Hubert Ritt, *Offenbarung des Johannes* (Würzburg: Echter Verlag, 1988), 17; Morris,

are blessed. Revelation 1:11 records John's clear commission to write to the seven churches. God, through Jesus and this written document, has important messages to share with His children. This process reminds us of the calling of the prophets of the Old Testament and the prophetic authority which is also associated with the Apocalypse.[46] In Revelation 1:19, "the instruction to write is recapitulated from v. 11 and made specific."[47] John "is to describe God's saving activity through his exalted Christ, in the Church and in the world, as this is relevant for today and for all the days to come."[48]

God's Angels

Finally, God employs His angels to advance His mission. In Revelation, the term "angel" occurs sixty-seven times, underscoring their importance. However, there are other angelic beings not designated as angels in the Apocalypse. The four living beings, found for the first time in Revelation 4 are cherubim (cf. Ezek 1, 10; Isa 6). The angels appearing in Revelation can be divided in four groups:

1) God's angel(s) (Rev 1:1; 3:5; 5:2, 11; 7:2, 11, etc.), depicted as His messengers (e. g., Rev 14:10).

2) Some angels in Revelation may represent Jesus Christ (Rev 8:3–5; 10:1, 5, 8–10). The angel in Revelation 8:3–5 mediates the prayers of the saints. This points to Jesus functioning as the angel (Rom 8:34; 1 John 2:1).[49] John may be referring to the Old Testament, where the angel of the Lord is a divine person (cf. Exod 3:2–4). The strong angel of Revelation 10, clothed with a cloud, could also be Jesus.[50]

3) Satan's evil angels (Rev 9:11; 12:9).

Revelation, 47.

[46] See Beale, *Revelation*, 203–204.

[47] Smalley, *Revelation*, 57.

[48] Smalley, *Revelation*, 57. For a discussion of "the things which you have seen, and the things which are, and the things which will take place after these things," see Osborne, *Revelation*, 97; Beale, *Revelation*, 216; and Aune, *Revelation 1–5*, 105–106.

[49] Cf. Beale, *Revelation*, 454, Jacques B. Doukhan, *Secrets of Revelation: The Apocalypse Through Hebrew Eyes* (Hagerstown, MD: Review and Herald, 2002), 80, and *AdvBibComm*, 7:787.

[50] Notice that a rainbow surrounds his head. His face shines like the sun and his feet resemble pillars of fire. The last two characteristics remind us of Jesus in Revelation 1b. The cloud was mentioned in Revelation 1:7 in connection with Jesus, while the rainbow is linked to the throne of God (Rev 4:3). Furthermore, the angel resembles the heavenly being in Daniel 10–12. This angel has divine attributes and therefore is either Christ or the angel of the Lord, who again would be Jesus. Other scholars admit the similarity with Revelation 1b, but avoid identifying the angel with Jesus. See Beale, *Revelation*, 522; Kistemaker, *Revelation*, 308–309; Robert H. Mounce, *The Book of Revelation* (Grand Rapids, MI: Eerdmans, 1998), 201–202; and Osborn, *Revelation*, 393. Mounce admits: "The phrases by which he is described are elsewhere used of deity" (201).

4) Angels may stand for human beings (Rev 1:20; 2:1, 8, 12, 18; 3:1, 7, 14; 14:6, 8-9). "In Malachi, the priests and messengers of God's people are referred to as angels (Mal 2:7; 3:1), an idea that also appears in the New Testament (cf. Matt 11:10). The context here [Rev 2-3] suggests that the angels stand for the leaders of the churches."[51] The angels in Revelation 14:6, 8, 9 should be also understood as representatives of human beings.[52]

In Revelation, the majority of the angels are involved in heavenly worship and relate to earth and humanity. They "mediate revelation and interpret visions (1:1; 10:1-10; 14:6-11; 17:1, 7-18)." But they are also "agents of God by implementing divine and saving judgment (7:1-3; 8:2-3; 9:1, 13; 11:15; 12:7-12; 14:15-20; 15:1, 6-7; 18:1-2; 19:17-18; 20:1-3)."[53] The appearances of angels in the Apocalypse can be grouped as those who speak (e.g., Rev 7:2-3) and those who act (e.g., Rev 7:1). In other words, angels are involved in carrying out God's plan of salvation.

The book of Revelation is a book about God's mission, involving God the Father, Jesus Christ, the Holy Spirit, Scripture as the Word of God, and God's angels. This mission is very crucial and is set in the context of the Great Controversy. While humans are called to repent and while life is offered to them, mission deals also with the character of God, His rule, and the consummation of all things.

The Mission of the Church

Jesus provides an open door of opportunity for the church of Philadelphia (Rev 3:8). This door has been understood as a door to salvation (Matt 7:13-14) and/or a door to service which means proclamation of the Gospel.[54] The phrase is used in other places to express the ideas of ministry and service (Acts 14:27; 1 Cor 16:9; 2 Cor 2:12; Col 4:3).[55] If John has this vocabulary in mind, the open door has clear missiological connotations. "Wherever he [Jesus] opens doors for his workers, there he blesses their work of presenting the gospel..."[56] This interpretation is not only supported by the usage of "door" in Pauline writings but also by the

---

[51] Stefanovic, *Revelation*, 97. See also Kistemaker, *Revelation*, 102-103; similarly, Isbon T. Beckwith, *The Apocalypse of John* (Grand Rapids, MI: Baker, 1967), 440.

[52] Cf. Stefanovic, *Revelation*, 440; *AdvBibComm*, 7:827.

[53] Smalley, *Revelation*, 29.

[54] For more details, see Osborne, *Revelation*, 188-189.

[55] Cf. John R. W. Stott, *What Christ Thinks of the Church: An Exposition of Revelation 1-3* (Grand Rapids, MI: Baker, 2003), 99-100.

[56] Kistemaker, *Revelation*, 159.

close proximity of the open door to "works" which appear in the beginning of the same verse (Rev 3:8). Further, the salvation theme seems to be found in v. 11. The open door points to assurance and provides "a stimulus to evangelism,"[57] and requires specific instruments to continue it.

Witnesses

In the Book of Revelation *martus* (witness) refers to Jesus and His followers (Rev 2:13; 17:6). "The witness of Jesus is the witness that he bore through his life, death, resurrection and exaltation. . . . The mission of the faithful is to share in the witness of Jesus (6, 9; 12, 17; 19, 10). Jesus is the witness par excellence (1, 5; 3, 14) and others in their witness can only imitate him."[58] Jesus is the role model and provides a pattern for the church.[59]

In the church of Pergamum, where some church members began to follow heretical teachings, Antipas was martyred. He is praised for his public profession of faith in Jesus. Jesus calls him "my faithful witness." According to Revelation 1:5, Jesus himself is "the faithful witness." The term "witness"(*martus*) points to proclamation, but it begins to take on the additional idea of martyrdom.[60] Antipas was a true witness and missionary. He died for what he believed—for the One in whom he believed. But he is not the only martyr. The great harlot Babylon is portrayed as being "drunk with the blood of the saints, and with the blood of the witnesses of Jesus" (Rev 17:6).

In addition to being called "witnesses," the faithful followers of the Lamb have the testimony or witness of Jesus (*marturia Iēsou*). They include the apostle John (Rev 1:9), the martyrs (Rev 6:9;[61] 20:4), the remnant (Rev 12:17), and the brothers (Rev 19:10), namely the prophets (Rev 22:9). Believers overcame the dragon "because of the blood of the Lamb and because of the word of their testimony, and they did not love their life even when faced with death" (Rev 12:11). It is clear that "the dragon conquers through killing whereas God conquers through the dying of his witnesses and their testimony (12:11)."[62] This text, more than those

---

[57] Colin J. Hemer, *Letters to the Seven Churches of Asia in Their Local Setting* (Grand Rapids, MI: Eerdmans, 2001), 162.

[58] Johnson Puthussery, *Day of Man and God's Day: An Exegetico-Theological Study of hēmera in the Book of Revelation* (Rome: Editrice Pontificia Università Gregoriana, 2002), 51.

[59] Cf. Peters, *Mandate*, 11.

[60] Cf. Morris, *Revelation*, 66.

[61] Morris, *Revelation*, 106, notes "John is probably referring to the testimony Christ gave to them (cf. Jn. 3:32) rather than to the testimony they bore to him . . ."

[62] Mark Bredin, "Ecological Crisis and Plagues (Revelation 11:6)," *BThB* 39.1 (2009): 35.

mentioning the testimony of Jesus, emphasizes that Christians proclaim Christ.[63] Witnessing is not just "a passive acceptance of suffering,"[64] but nonviolent resistance to evil and defense of truth.[65] Witnessing is living an obedient life without compromise.[66] Although by overcoming their fear of death they were willing to lay down their lives for Jesus, it is not necessary to equate witnessing with martyrdom alone.[67] "The 'witness' of the believers is first a lifestyle of faithfulness to Christ and second a verbal witness during the period of their suffering. It is clear that the church at this final period of terrible persecution does not go into hiding so as to avoid the wrath of the beast but maintains its evangelistic effort to the very end."[68]

Priests

Three texts are found in Revelation which directly call Christians "priests" (Rev 1:6; 5:10; and 20:6). The first two describe kingship and priesthood of the saints as a present reality. Revelation 20 applies kingly reign and priesthood to the future. Revelation 1:6 is part of the introduction to Revelation, which summarizes the book's overarching message. In vv. 4–5 the divine trinity is introduced. Jesus comes last, because the following verses focus on Him. They describe Him as "the faithful witness, the firstborn of the dead, and the ruler of the kings of the earth" and state what He does and has done: 1) He loves us (Rev 1:5); 2) He has saved us by His blood (Rev 1:5); and 3) He has made us a kingdom and priests (Rev 1:6). The statement about the kingdom and priests is based on Exod 19:6 and recalls 1 Pet 2:9. The language describes installment to one's office.[69] The term "kingdom" should be seen in the active sense, namely as "reigning."[70]

How should one understand the priestly and kingly role of Christ's

---

[63] Beale, *Revelation*, 664. Bauckham, *Theology*, 92, states: "... John's message is not, 'Do not resist!' It is, 'Resist!—but by witness and martyrdom, not by violence."

[64] Adela Yarbro Collins, "The Political Perspective of the Revelation to John," *JBL* 96 (1977): 247.

[65] Johns, *Lamb*, 173–174.

[66] See Pattemore, "Discourse," 115; Peters, *Mandate*, 84, 86.

[67] Smalley, *Revelation*, 328. Miller, "Mission," 235, supports this view by saying: "Some witnesses are protected throughout their mission, while others die for their boldness (6:9–12; 14:1–5)."

[68] Osborne, *Revelation*, 476.

[69] The term *epoiēsen* is used in this sense in Mark 3:14–19 and Acts 2:36. Cf. Beale, *Revelation*, 194.

[70] Cf. Osborne, *Revelation*, 65. Beale, *Revelation*, 195, mentions that in Revelation, the term "kingdom" is used most of the time in the active. Furthermore, Revelation 20:6 lacks the term "kingdom" (*basileia*), but uses the verb *basileuō*, thus pointing to an active sense of *basileia*. See also Revelation 5:10 which contains both the noun and the verb.

followers? This is not directly specified. But we certainly cannot go wrong by saying that the priestly and kingly role of God's people is following the model of Jesus. It means to serve God (Rev 7:15) and the world, to be His representatives, and witnesses of His work for humanity's salvation.[71] The priestly aspect includes also "direct access to God."[72] However, the priesthood of Christians does not involve offering real sacrifices, representing the community of believers, or being religious specialists of some sort.[73]

Apostles and Prophets

God has sent (*apostellō*) His angel (Rev 1:1; 22:6) and the Holy Spirit (Rev 5:6), but he also uses apostles (*apostoloi*) and prophets (*prophētai*) in his mission (Rev 18:20). Prophets are mentioned quite often (Rev 10:7; 11:10, 18; 16:6; 18:20, 24; and 22:6, 9) and connected to witnessing (Rev 19:10). The remnant who have the testimony/witness of Jesus (Rev 12:17) have the "spirit of prophecy," the Holy Spirit who speaks through the gift of prophecy.[74] And John, as a representative of the true church on earth at the end of time, is called to "prophesy again concerning/about/to/against[75] many peoples and nations and tongues and kings" (Rev 10:11) as the two witnesses of Revelation 11 had prophesied during the period of 1260 prophetic days (Rev 11:3).[76]

---

[71] See Beale, *Revelation*, 193. Christopher J. H. Wright, *The Mission of God's People: A Biblical Theology of the Church's Mission* (Grand Rapids: Zondervan, 2010), 121–122.

[72] Osborne, *Revelation*, 66.

[73] Cf. Aune, *Revelation 1–5*, 49.

[74] David E. Aune, *Revelation 17–22* (Nashville, TN: Thomas Nelson, 1998), 1039, concludes that "since true prophecy witnesses to Jesus, any witness to Jesus can be identified as prophecy, and thus prophecy is not limited to those who are designated 'prophets' in a special sense." This argument may go too far and seems to be based on an interpretation of the genitive in "the testimony of Jesus" as an objective genitive.

[75] Some take the term *epi* in the negative sense as "against." So Aune, *Revelation 6–16*, 574; Beale, *Revelation*, 554; Kistemaker, *Revelation*, 31, although most translations prefer the neutral "about."

[76] The word group *prophēteia/prophēteuō/prophtēs* is found twice in Revelation 10 and three times in Revelation 11a. On prophecy, see Gerhard A. Krodel, *Revelation*, 212; S. Minear, *I Saw a New Earth: An Introduction to the Visions of the Apocalypse* (Washington, DC: Corpus Books, 1968), 96; and Pierre Prigent, *L'Apocalypse de Saint Jean* (Paris: Delachaux & Niestlé, 1981), 149–150. Jürgen Roloff, *The Revelation of John: A Continental Commentary* (Minneapolis, MN: Fortress, 1993), 122, maintains: "A key for the entire thematic focus of this section is found in the observation that allusions to prophets and prophetic speech run through it like a scarlet thread (10:7, 11; 11:3, 11; cf. also 11:18)." Similarly, Kenneth A. Strand, "The 'Spotlight-On-Last-Events' Sections in the Book of Revelation," *AUSS* 27 (1989): 208–209, views the interlude as twofold. On p. 208, he declares: "The theme of prophetic proclamation which is so basic and central to chapter 10 continues, under different imagery, in chapter 11: namely, the imagery of a temple setting. Here we find . . . a temple-measuring scene . . . followed by the periscope concerning two

Why would we suggest the apostle John functions as a representative of the church in Revelation 10:11 and that prophesying should be understood in the sense of proclaiming God's message? The experience of John recorded in Revelation 10—the eating of the little scroll and the new commission to prophesy about many peoples, nations, languages, and kings—is part of the sixth trumpet which precedes the establishment of God's kingdom on earth under the seventh trumpet. In other words, Revelation 10 describes events that will be part of the final events of earth's history. They did not take place in the time of John, the first century A.D. As such, they describe the experience of the church. Revelation 14 is a parallel account found in another vision of Revelation. As in Revelation 10:11, the church is "concerning many peoples and nations and tongues and kings." In Revelation 14:6, the first angel's message is addressed "to every nation and tribe and tongue and people." The universal character[77] of the commission makes impossible the completion of the task by one individual only. The church is called to address the nations, warn them of judgment, and call them to repentance.[78]

Lampstands

The seven churches are compared to seven golden lampstands (Rev 1:20). The imagery of lampstands may suggest that the churches are to be seen as light bearers or witness bearers.[79] It is likely "that the witness of the seven churches is the prevailing theme of the seven letters."[80]

> The loss of 'first love' in the Ephesian church 'was tantamount to becoming unzealous witnesses" . . . As for the churches of Smyrna

---

prophetic witnesses (vv. 3–13) who are introduced in terms of the temple imagery of two olive trees that are also two lampstands (vv. 3–4)."

[77] Aune, *Revelation 6–16*, 574.

[78] That the experience of John describes the experience of the church is recognized by some expositors. G. R. Osborne talks about "the prophetic ministry of John and the church" and adds: "Through John the church is called to the same ministry of preaching repentance and judgment to a generation that has turned their backs on God" (Osborne, *Revelation*, 405–406). When talking about the sweetbitter experience, U. B. Müller mentions the preservation of the Christian church and her sufferings (U. B. Müller, *Offenbarung*, 203. See also *AdvBibComm*, 7:799). And while discussing the seven churches, Bauckham states that "the churches [have] to fulfill their prophetic ministry to the world, which is their indispensable role in the coming of God's kingdom, the task to which it is the function of Revelation to call them" (Bauckham, *Theology*, 121).

[79] See Peters, *Mandate*, 112–113.

[80] Peters, *Mandate*, 113. See Robert L. Thomas, *Revelation 1–7: An Exegetical Commentary* (Chicago, IL: Moody, 1992), 277–278 and Beale, *Revelation*, 289. On page 227, Beale suggests that "all of the letters deal generally with the issue of witnessing for Christ in the midst of a pagan culture."

and Pergamum, both of them are commended for their suffering which was provoked by their witnessing openly to their faith in Christ. In the case of the church of Thyatira, the 'works' for which it is complimented are not merely general deeds of 'Christian service,' but 'works of persevering witness to the outside world.' As for some of the Christians that were castigated in Sardis, the problem with them was their failure to witness to their faith before the unbelieving culture . . . With regard to the church of Philadelphia, its commendation for 'not denying the name of Christ' is an indication of persevering witness. And in the case of the Laodicean church, criticisms are leveled due to the church's 'innocuous witness'—a witness which was either non-existent or consistently compromised by participation in idolatrous facets of the Laodicean culture.[81]

The Remnant and Their Message

The remnant is particularly prominent in the center of the book. The dragon makes war against the remnant of the woman's seed (12:17). He also attacks her through the sea beast. In this case, the remnant are called the saints. He makes war against them through the beast out of the earth. They are those who do not worship the beast or its image and who will not accept the mark of the beast. They are also called the 144,000.[82] Revelation 13 emphasizes being the object of attack rather than being active in ministry. Yet, they are those involved in God's mission. This is indicated in Revelation 14:6–12, under the symbol of three angels proclaiming a universal and final message. Who are these angels? As demonstrated, angels can stand for human beings. This seems also to be true for the angels in Revelation 14:6, 8, and 9.[83] Some scholars seem to move into that direction.[84]

---

[81] Peters, *Mandate*, 114.

[82] For more details, see Ekkehardt Mueller, "The End Time Remnant in Revelation," *JATS* 11.1–2 (2000): 188–204.

[83] *AdvBibComm*, 7:827, talks about a symbolic vision. Charles H. Talbert, *The Apocalypse: A reading of the Revelation of John* (Louisville, KY: Westminster John Knox, 1994), 62–64, takes some space to develop a short but incomplete angelology of Revelation. He calls the angels in Revelation 14 seven agents of judgment. However, the angels involved in the three messages of Revelation 14:7–12 are not only proclaiming judgment but also seem to call humanity to return to God.

[84] Elisabeth Schüssler Fiorenza, *Revelation: Vision of a Just World* (Minneapolis, MN: Fortress, 1991), 89, notes that the first angel's message uses "expressions of early Christian missionary preaching (cf. 1 Thess 1:9f and Acts 14:15ff; 17:24ff). According to the Synoptic apocalypse, the Gospel had to be preached to all the nations before the end would come (Mark 13:10; Matt 24:14). This expectation is shared by Revelation." G. B. Caird, *The Revelation of St. John the Divine* (Peabody, MS: Hendrickson, 1987), 182, connects the proclamation of John's eternal gospel to what he calls "the great martyrdom" which would certainly not apply to heavenly beings. Craig S. Keener,

A typological connection has been found between the Elijah message, mentioned in Malachi 4:5 in connection with the day of judgment, and the proclamation of the three angels' messages. This means that Revelation 14:6–12 is "the final awakening call . . . It brings the hour of decision, just as Elijah and John the Baptist led apostate Israel to a new commitment. . . . The voice of Elijah is increasingly needed in our decadent civilization. It will reverberate throughout all society and is reflected in a worldwide movement of Christian Sabbath-keepers."[85] The angel flying in midheaven has been taken as "a symbol for a group of people on earth,"[86] identified as God's end-time remnant, the Adventist movement, to whom God entrusted the proclamation of the three angels' messages to the world.[87]

The three angelic messages of Revelation 14:6–12 are set within the context of the conflict between the dragon and the remnant. They are introduced in the context of a clear reference to the remnant (Rev 14:1–5; 14:12). Therefore, the messages must be related to them. The remnant have accepted and proclaim these messages. Structurally, they come in the same place as John's re-commissioning in Revelation 10:11, namely just prior to the establishment of God's kingdom and the judgment in connection with the Second Coming which separates the wheat from the grapes. John and his message represent the church at the end of time (Rev 10:7), so the angels in Revelation 14 represent earthly messengers with a final message of God to humanity.

Mission and Message

After dealing with the agents of mission, we now turn to the message itself. Message and mission should always go together because without content there is nothing to proclaim.

False Teachers and Prophets

The book of Revelation not only relates to us God's final message and

---

Revelation: The NIV Application Commentary (Grand Rapids, MI: Zondervan, 2000), 372, states, "The 'eternal gospel' proclaimed by the angel to all peoples (14:6) probably does not imply an angel literally spreading the saving gospel to all the nations before the end, which is the work of the church (Matt. 24:14; Rev. 6:9–11). Because angels in Revelation often correspond to earthly realities (12:5–7), the angel's flight may correspond to the spread of the gospel through martyrs."

[85] Hans K. LaRondelle, *How to Understand the End-time Prophecies of the Bible* (Sarasota, FL: First Impressions, 1997), 361. Prigent, *Apocalypse*, 438, points out that the Elijah interpretation is already found with Victorinus who understands the evangelist angel as Elijah.

[86] C. Mervyn Maxwell, *God Cares, Vol. 2: The Message of Revelation For You and Your Family* (Boise, ID: Pacific Press, 1985), 351. Cf. Stefanovic, *Revelation*, 440.

[87] Ángel Manuel Rodríguez, *Future Glory: The 8 Greatest End-Time Prophecies in the Bible* (Hagerstown, MD: Review and Herald, 2002), 129.

call, but is also filled with references to false messages, heresy, and deceptive and coercive propaganda. In the letters to the churches in Ephesus and Pergamum, we encounter the Nicolaitans (Rev 2:6 and 15). We are not completely sure who the Nicolaitans were and what they taught. In any case, Jesus and the church members in Ephesus hated their works. They could perhaps be identified with the followers of Balaam (Rev 2:14–15).[88] If that is true, they would be libertarians and antinomians with hardly any interest in theology. The church members in Pergamum are reminded of Balaam (Num 22–25) who, after having been prevented from cursing Israel, finally revealed how to overcome the people of God (Num 31:16). A similar situation arose in the church of Pergamum (Rev 2:14). Sexual immorality may actually refer to idolatry more than to sexual acts.[89] The question was how far to go with regard to cultural adaption.[90]

The Phoenecian princess Jezebel, wife of King Ahab, was notorious for her idolatry. As Ahab's wife, she was instrumental in introducing Israel to the worship of Baal. She also persecuted the prophets of God, Elijah among them. The church of Thyatira is accused by Jesus to accommodate His enemy, the false prophetess (Rev 2:20). This modern Jezebel openly supported idolatry and fornication (*porneia*). The "deep things of Satan" (Rev 2:24) have been interpreted in various ways.[91] It is possible that the followers of Jezebel claimed they needed to investigate the deep things of Satan and were protected in doing so. In their search for the deep things of God (1 Cor 2:10), they ended up teaching that which was of satanic origin.

The seven seals report an increasing perversion and darkening of the gospel.[92] The seven trumpets describe apostasy and judgment from another perspective leading to the Age of Enlightenment, which "ended the rule of Christians faith over the Western mind. This new phenomenon rejected traditional religion and led to the outgrowth of rationalism, skepticism, humanism, and liberalism. Its final product was the birth and

---

[88] In this case, Jude 1:11 and 2 Peter 2:5 should also been taken into consideration.

[89] This is supported by Morris, *Revelation*, 67.

[90] Cf. Ronald L. Farmer, *Revelation*, 47–48.

[91] Cf. Aune, *Revelation 1–5*, 207; Hemer, *Letters*, 122.

[92] Jon Paulien, "The Seven Seals," in *Symposium on Revelation-Book 1*, ed. Frank B. Holbrook, (Silver Spring, MD: Biblical Research Institute, 1992), 233–234, declares, "It is noteworthy that the thematic progression of the four horses fits well with the history of the first thousand years of the Christian Era. First, there was the initial rapid expansion of the church throughout much of the then-known world. The succeeding period brought division and compromise in the face of persecution. The loss of a clear understanding of the gospel followed as the church settled into an earthly kingdom in the years after Constantine. Finally, the Dark Ages of spiritual decline and death engulfed Christendom."

rise of secularism." Secularism did not allow for supernatural events and "replaced the authority of the Bible . . . with human reason."[93]

However, the climax of apostasy is in the center of the Book of Revelation where John talks about events which, from our present perspective, are still future. Repeatedly, the apostle points to almost universal, yet forced, worship of the dragon, the sea beast, and the image of the beast (Rev 13:4, 8, 14–17). There is an immense propaganda going on and a counter-gospel being preached (13:14b, 16–17), supported by deceptive signs including the falling of fire from heaven (13:13–15). No wonder that the beast coming out of the earth is called the false prophet (16:13; 19:20; 20:10). Finally, evil spirits, like frogs, go forth to the rulers of the world to gather them for the final battle against the Lamb and his followers (16:14, 16).

The Divine Message and Its Content

Revelation's divine message is found in the initial greeting and doxology of Revelation 1 and sets the tone for the entire book.

Message of the Prologue and the Book

Revelation 1:4–8 stresses Jesus as the faithful witness, the firstborn from the dead, and the ruler of the kings of the earth who 1) loves us (1:5); 2) has redeemed us through his substitutionary death (1:5); 3) has set us in a new position—we are a kingdom and priests (1:6); and 4) will come again (1:7). Revelation 1:5–6 "is the first doxology in the New Testament addressed only to Jesus."[94] After the doxology, His Second Coming is described. Verse 8 returns to God the Father, who as the Almighty and as the Alpha and Omega, cares for His people. John changes his address from "to the seven churches that are in Asia" (v. 4) to "us" (v. 5), thus getting more personal and more comprehensive.[95]

While the statement that Jesus loves us is found in the present tense and emphasizes the continual, neverending love of Jesus toward us, salvation and the privilege to be a kingdom[96] and priest have already been realized in the past[97] and are a present reality. Obviously they are dependent

---

[93] Stefanovic, *Revelation*, 297.

[94] Osborne, *Revelation*, 63. Cf. U. B. Müller, *Offenbarung*, 74.

[95] Revelation 1:3 calls those blessed who hear and read Revelation, which does not limit the audience to the first century A.D.

[96] This term should be understood actively, i.e. in the sense of kingly rule.

[97] John uses the aorist indicative. Cf. Beale, *Revelation*, 194.

on Jesus' death on the cross.[98] These verses can be understood as a summary of the message of Revelation. Revelation has to do with the Godhead, Jesus, and salvation through Him. Its aim is Christ's Second Coming and God's kingdom of glory thereafter.

In Revelation 3:9, 19, we read again about Jesus' *love*. Because Jesus loves his church, the church loves him (2:19; 12:11). The major title used for Jesus in the Apocalypse is "Lamb." Because Jesus was crucified (11:8), slaughtered (5:6, 9, 12; 13; 8), and shed his blood (1:5; 5:9; 7:14; 12:11), he is able to save humans. Salvation is described using wonderful images such as being purchased, having washed one's robe, and having one's name written in the book of life (5:9; 7:14; 12:11; 14:3-4; 21:27). The Second Coming of Jesus permeates the entire Apocalypse and is described through the verb "to come" and various images at the end of major visions in Revelation.[99] Already in Revelation 1:7 a dual aspect is recognizable. The Second Advent is the blessed hope of believers and a threat to God's enemies. It is connected with the concept of reward (22:12) and various phases of judgment.[100] It brings about long-expected final salvation and a paradise without evil, suffering, and death as described in Revelation 21 and 22.

Three Angels' Messages

The message of Revelation climaxes in the three angels' messages in the center of the book. An outline of Revelation 13 and 14a shows that the remnant, portrayed as 144,000, and their message form the contrast to the evil powers and their message.

A. The beast out of the sea (Rev 13:1-10)
  (1) "*I saw* ... "
  (2) Description of the beast and its activity
  (3) "**HERE IS** patience and faith ... "
B. The beast out of the earth (Rev 3:11-18)
  (1) "*I saw* ... "
  (2) Description of the beast and his activity
  (3) "**HERE IS** wisdom ... "
C. The 144,000 and the three angels' messages (Rev 14:1-12)

---

[98] Osborne, *Revelation*, 64, declares: "Here the ecclesiological aspect of Christ's work is described..."

[99] See Ekkehardt Mueller, "Jesus and His Second Coming in the Apocalypse," *JATS* 11.1-2 (2000): 205-215.

[100] They include the investigative judgment (Rev 6:9-11; 14:7), the judgment during the Millennium, and the execution of the verdict after the Millennium (Rev 20). Historical judgments are found in various parts of the book such as the seven churches, the seven seals, and the seven trumpets.

(1) *"I saw..."*
(2) Description of the 144,000
(3) *"I saw..."*
(4) Three angels' messages
(5) "**HERE IS** patience ... faith ... "

This outline reveals also the close relation between the 144,000 and the message of the three angels. In contrast to the previous passages, only one "here is" is used in Revelation 14:1-12 despite two visionary elements. By means of this structure, the 144,000 and the end-time message are closely connected. William Johnsson has focused on Revelation 13b and Rev 14b and has outlined these passages in the following helpful way, showing that the message of the three angels is the divine antidote against the deceptions of the evil powers:

A. Propaganda of the beast out of the earth (13:11-15)
    B. Followers of the beast out of the sea (13:16-18)
    B'. Followers of the lamb (14:1-5)
A'. God's last message (14:6-12)[101]

Revelation 12-14 portrays the final conflict in earth's history. From Revelation 15 onward, the last moments of this drama are revealed through God's intervention for His saints in the form of seven plagues. Plague number six and seven depict the collapse of Babylon in the battle of Armageddon. Revelation 17 and 18 describe in more detail this fall of Babylon, and Revelation 19 pictures the intervention of Jesus as the rider on the white horse. This is followed by the Millennium (Rev 20) and the new heaven and new earth, including the New Jerusalem (Rev 21-22). Throughout Revelation, the three angels' message is the final and universal message addressed to all people.

The first angel introduces his message as the eternal gospel.[102] In the

---

[101] William G. Johnsson, "The Saint's End-Time Victory over the Forces of Evil," *Symposium on Revelation - Book II*, ed. Frank B. Holbrook (Silver Spring, MD: Biblical Research Institute General, 1992), 14. For a useful exposition of the significance of the proclamation of the gospel in Revelation, see Mario Veloso, "Lo específico del evangelio en el tiempo del fin," *La iglesia, cuerpo de Cristo y plenitud de Dios*, ed. Mario Veloso (Argentina: Editorial Universidad Adventista del Plata, 2006), 209-216.

[102] It has been argued by various scholars that gospel has to be understood in a restricted sense pointing primarily to judgment. Mounce, *Revelation*, 270-271, for instance, suggests that "it is not the gospel of God's redeeming grace in Christ Jesus but, as the following verse shows, a summons to fear, honor, and worship the Creator.... It relates to judgment and salvation in the coming eternal age (cf. Smalley, *Revelation*, 361)." Kistemaker, *Revelation*, 407, states: "The angel proclaims the gospel not necessarily as good news but as a reminder of God's abiding truth; the angel calls men and woman to respond to God's message before the judgment comes." Caird, *Revelation*, 182, disagrees: "For whether it has an article or not, the word *euangelion* can only mean

context of Revelation, and especially in view of the prologue, *euangelion* should indeed be understood as good news. In other words, the prologue of the Apocalypse contains a clear description of the gospel. The author knows and understands the gospel. When he refers to it, he has in mind the major features of the gospel including the details that he will mention in the next verse. It is good news that, even in this late hour of world history, salvation is still available. People can still accept redemption. They can commit their lives to God and give glory to Him, that is, repent (11:13; 16:9) and "acknowledge Him as the most important person in the universe."[103] Glory is associated with creation (4:11), but also with salvation (1:6; 5:12; 19:1). It is good news because the investigative judgment is still in progress and "Christ is still working in the heavenly sanctuary on our behalf . . ."[104] It is good news because people can leave behind deception and come out of Babylon (18:4). On the other hand, the executive phase of the judgment mentioned later assures believers that there will be justice, vindication, and a bright future for them. Summarizing the final divine message, we can say: The *first message* emphasizes worship of the creator in contrast to worship of man-made systems and worship of Satan. It accentuates the pre-advent judgment and obedience to God in keeping the biblical Sabbath.[105]

The *second message* proclaims the fall of Babylon.[106] In the *third mes-*

'good news', and it is improbable that John should have thought of using it in a cynical sense. Moreover, he says nothing about the gospel being good news for Christians; this is a gospel to proclaim to the inhabitants of earth . . . Nor is it any casual or ephemeral news; it is an eternal gospel, a gospel rooted and grounded in the changeless character and purpose of God. If the angel carried a gospel which was eternal good news to every nation, tribe, tongue, and people, it is hard to see how this could differ from *the* gospel."

[103] Rodríguez, *Glory*, 131.

[104] Ibid.

[105] The wording in Revelation 14:7 points back to the fourth commandment. To worship God as the creator also implies keeping His day holy, the day that He instituted at creation as a commemoration of creation. While the healing of the fatal wound of the beast leads to a new conflict on earth, heaven is conducting the pre-advent judgment and actively sides with the true believers.

[106] In order for us to understand the meaning and significance of the term Babylon, we have to examine this expression in the Old Testament (e.g., Gen 11; Isa 14; Daniel) as well as in its New Testament context. In the New Testament, it is used as a code name for Rome (1 Pet 5:13). In the book of Revelation, Babylon is described in detail in chapters 17–18. The great city Babylon stands in contrast to Jerusalem, the city of God (Rev 11:2, 8; 14:1, 8; 16:19). In 17:1–5, Babylon is depicted as a harlot. Thus, it also stands in contrast to the woman clothed with the sun in Revelation 12, a symbol of the faithful church. Babylon represents a religious system that has fallen away from God. Its destruction is announced, and God's people are called to separate from it in order to avoid judgment (Rev 18:2, 4). The remnant have nothing to do with Babylon. Cf. Ekkehardt Müller, *Der Erste und der Lehre: Studien zum Buch Offenbarung* (Frankfurt: Peter Lang, 2011), 381–416.

sage, the angel announces God's final judgment on those who worship the beast or its image and carry the mark of the beast. God responds to the Babylonian wine of wrath with His own wine of wrath (Ps 75:9). The followers of the beast have persecuted God's people who persevere and keep the commandments and the faith of Jesus. God intervenes on behalf of His children.[107] The blessing that follows in v. 13 indicates that, although some may have to pay for their loyalty to Jesus with their life, they are blessed and will rest until the resurrection.

Results of Mission Activity in Revelation

The biblical message, particularly the message of Revelation, splits humanity in two sides. There are those who, touched by it, decide to give their lives a new direction. But, there are others who disregard the good news, become less receptive to the voice of God, and harden their hearts.

Unknown and Negative Outcomes

There are some cases in which the result of the proclaimed message is not indicated. For instance, Jesus addresses the seven churches and challenges most of them to repent, but we are not told whether or not repentance occurred. In other cases, we hear about negative outcomes. Revelation 9:20–21 tells us that the seven trumpets did not reach their intended goal to bring about repentance. In the case of the almost universal worship of the evil powers (Rev 13), the implication is that many will reject the message of the three angels. They are depicted as being deceived by evil powers (13:13–14) and fascinated by the sea beast (13:3–4; 17:8). According to Revelation 17:2, they became intoxicated with Babylon's wine. Although all inhabitants of the earth are deceived, the saints are not included (13:7). The phrase "inhabitants of the earth"[108] is always used in a negative way. The people of God are "those who dwell in heaven" (13:6). The earth dwellers are "all, both small and great, both rich and poor, both

---

[107] The mark of the beast is indirectly defined in Revelation 14:12. Those who receive this mark are contrasted with the saints. The saints are characterized by patience, faith in Jesus, and the keeping of the commandments. Evidently, these characteristics are lacking in the first group. These people are not faithful to Jesus and His commandments or they partially respect the law found in the ark of the covenant of the heavenly sanctuary (Rev 11:19). Yet partial obedience still counts as disobedience (James 2:10–12). This is supported by the understanding of the seal of God in Revelation 7, the counterpart of the mark of the beast. John may have had in mind Ezekiel 9:4–6 when he wrote about the seal of God. Those who will receive the seal of God are the brokenhearted because of the sins of God's people and those who turn away from their sins and turn to God with all earnestness. They do not disregard God's will because they love their Lord (John 14:15) and expect salvation only from Him. Those who are not sealed by God will eventually be left to the "sealing" by the beast and its image.

[108] Revelation 3:10; 6:10; 11:10; 13:8, 12; 17:2, 8.

free and slave" who receive the mark of the beast on their right hand or their forehead (13:16). They seem to form the tribes, peoples, tongues, and nations of Revelation 13:7. They will experience the wrath of God and are presented as grapes in a bloody harvest (14:17–20).

Positive Outcome

However, there is also a positive outcome. The Apocalypse knows groups of faithful people: the pure church (Rev 12), the remnant (2:24; 12:17), and some who have laid down their lives for their Lord (2:13; 6:9). There are also the converted. Although the trumpet judgments were originally not able to bring about repentance, the ministry of the two witnesses brought about a change. People "were terrified and gave glory to the God of heaven" (11:13). Since the same phrase is used for repentance (14:7; 16:9), their reaction should also be understood as repentance and conversion.[109]

In Revelation 18:4, God's people are still in Babylon and are called to come out of it. Although the outcome is not reported, on account of its parallelism with Judah's partial return from the Babylon exile,[110] it may be assumed that some will leave Babylon. In any case, Revelation 7 pictures a large multitude standing before the throne of God and serving in the heavenly sanctuary (7:15), indicating that God's mission was successful. This also applies to the bride of the Lamb (Rev 19) and the New Jerusalem (Rev 21). There will be a redeemed people among whom God will dwell (21:3).

Conclusion and Implications

The Book of Revelation paints the last events in such a way that gray areas will disappear and only two groups of people will remain—the end-time remnant and the followers of harlot Babylon. These two groups will be in conflict with each other. It will be a deadly war. One side will be fought with deception, force, and violence; and the other side with patience, suffering, love, and justice. There will be no middle ground. Today, people can still decide, and Revelation urges them to make a decision for God. Although the book is realistic enough to inform us that universal salvation will not take place, it challenges us to proclaim with fervor and urgency God's last message to the human race.

---

[109] This is debated among expositors. For a discussion, see Osborne, *Revelation*, 433–436. Aune, *Revelation 6–16*, 628, opts for conversion while Beale, *Revelation*, 603–604, and Mounce, *Revelation*, 223–224, seem to deny it.

[110] See the call to leave Babylon in Jeremiah 51:45; Isaiah 48:20; and the subsequent exodus described in Nehemiah and Ezra.

What are some of the results and implications of our study? First, the Book of Revelation is a book about mission, although one may not be aware of it at first. Second, the mission is God's mission, a divine enterprise, and He is responsible for it. The Trinity is involved in this mission that is fulfilled in the context of a cosmic controversy. This controversy has various dimensions. One of them is God's desire for people to be saved and to bring sin to an end. As the controversy heightens, so does the proclamation of God's final message. Third, God involves human instrumentalities in His mission. Being His people, they become His witnesses and share with humanity His final message (14:6–12). Not only is there a universal challenge, but also a great urgency. Fourth, the outcome of any mission could vary. Even if the outcome may be undesirable, the proclamation of the message is not affected by it. In fact, victory is assured. Fifth, by becoming witnesses, God's people participate in His mission and enjoy a close relationship with Him. The remnant "follow the Lamb wherever He goes" (14:4). Sixth, being faithful witnesses involves intentionally sharing one's faith, "maintaining authenticity and truthfulness . . . showing patient endurance . . . giving obedience to the commandments of God . . . and expressing purity of devotion to Christ through worship, lifestyle, teachings and beliefs . . ."[111] Seventh, it is not our duty to worry about the success of the mission. We are asked to do our part with vigor, earnestness, enthusiasm, and urgency, faithfully employing the gifts God has given to us.

---

[111] Peters, *Mandate*, 117–118.

CHAPTER 8

Understanding Apostasy in the Christian Church

John W. Reeve

When a Seventh-day Adventist visualizes the great apostasy predicted in the New Testament (Matt 24:9–12, 24; 2 Thess 2:3–12; 1 Pet 2:8; 1 John 4:1; Rev 14:8–11), it seems obvious that it has already happened.[1] For Adventists, the conceptual and practical differences between the theology of the later Middle Ages and the first-century apostolic Church are so vast it is hard to believe that the roots of the first are in the second. Nowhere is this distance so apparent as in the areas of forgiveness, repentance, and ecclesiology. Johann Tetzel selling indulgences in Germany, Albert of Mainz buying his ordination as archbishop from Pope Leo X, repetitive prayers of the rosary, and merits achieved by pilgrimages to martyrs' graves are examples of the great divide between the actions of the medieval church and the concept of direct access to Christ presented in Hebrews 4:13–16 and 1 John 1:9. But are these excesses and abuses of a fundamentally-sound set of doctrines, or is the system of grace as it developed into the Roman Catholic system irrevocably blemished?

The standard Protestant answer has been that the system is blemished to its core. This paper does not focus on the political system, with

---

[1] We are not arguing that the apostasy of the church was absolute and final because this would deny the care of the Risen Lord through the Spirit for His church. Throughout the history of God's people, He has always preserved a faithful remnant even in cases when there was widespread or national apostasy among them. The history of the Christian church points to the damaging effects of widespread apostasy in the church while also indicating the existence of a faithful remnant. On this topic, see Ángel M. Rodríguez, ed., *Studies in Adventist Ecclesiology—I: Toward a Theology of the Remnant: An Adventist Ecclesiological Perspective* (Silver Spring, MD: Biblical Research Institute, 2009).

its inadequate checks on the political power of popes, cardinals and bishops as these interacted with the relative strengths of monarchs, princes and emperors. Instead it highlights the social and human forces which eventually led to the establishment of two underlying principles that I see as the center of Christian apostasy: the Church hierarchy's perception of itself as 1) effectively in control of salvation and 2) essentially correct in all it teaches and practices. These two ecclesiological principles have their roots in scriptural interpretation. The first arises from a literal reading of Matthew 16:19 and John 20:23, where Jesus gives authority to His followers to forgive sin. The second derives from such passages as Matthew 16:18, where the church is built on the solid rock of Christ, and Matthew 28:18-20, where Jesus assures His followers that He has all power and will always be with them as they teach and baptize throughout the world.

Despite both principles' biblical underpinnings, they have been pushed to an extreme and caused many New Testament scholars to see them as unbiblical. To the first, the argument is made that no human is in charge of forgiveness and salvation, not even the Church. Only God can forgive sins. And to the second, it has been argued that there is no human institution without error. The forces shaping theology and practice need to be tested regularly (cf. 1 John 4:1). However, we should recognize that in the early centuries of Christianity, there were forces at work moving Christians to define the church as the conduit of grace and as being infallible in doctrinal declarations.

The one idea that most succinctly demonstrates what went irrevocably wrong in the early church can best be expressed as follows: The Scriptures must be interpreted according to what the church has defined to be true. With the use of this hermeneutical principle, the church began a journey that would protect it from heretical teachings, but that at the same time made it impossible for the Scripture to correct the church. This understanding led to the doctrine of the infallibility of the church—that it cannot err in matters of truth. The first part of this study will describe the development of this hermeneutic in the second and early third centuries and its use in the fifth century to support the idea of an infallible church. The second part of the study will show five of the theological and sociological underpinnings that allowed this mindset to grow unchecked.

Development of the Hermeneutic of Tradition as Truth

Irenaeus (130-200)

In the second century of the Christian era, much about Scripture and its interpretation remained undefined. In the middle of the century, we find Justin Martyr discoursing with a Jew named Trypho on christological and Christianized readings of the Hebrew Scriptures.[2] We hear from Melito of Sardis about his trip to Palestine to see what books should be included in the Hebrew Scriptures.[3] We overhear Marcion giving his "canon," the first defined listing of the Christian Scriptures, which only included portions of the letters of Paul and the parts of Luke/Acts with which he agreed.[4] We bemoan the upside-down readings of the many gnostic groups, as they twist the Scriptures into secret meanings. Then, we listen to Irenaeus of Lyon defending the writings of Paul and the other writers of the Christian Scriptures against Marcion.

Irenaeus asserts a straightforward reading of Scripture over and against Valentinus and the other gnostics. His confident listing of the four, and only four, Gospels[5] and his wide quoting of the writings of Paul, Peter, and John as authoritative Scriptures seems like a breath of fresh air. His definition of the one, right reading of Scripture[6] tends to tame the wild readings of the gnostic interpreters. In many ways, Irenaeus saves the day for what seems a correct and literal reading of the Hebrew and Christian Scriptures. His confidence and consistency contributes to establish the rule of faith, which defines the main tenets of Christianity. However, in this very assurance of correctness, lie the seeds of a hermeneutic that grew into the assertion that the Church is always right.

In the opening chapters of book three of his *Adversus haereses* (*Against Heresies*), Irenaeus argues that the correct reading of Scripture is defined by the tradition of the Church—the tradition of the apostles as declared by the Church. Irenaeus is fighting against gnostics who assert, according to him, that the Scriptures and even Christ before His resurrection, cannot be the final arbiter of truth. They believe only the gnostics, who have the secret *gnosis* directly from the *pleroma*,[7] can actually know the truth. Irenaeus had no choice but to use Scripture as the authority to refute them (2.1). And when the gnostics asserted their tradition for the interpretation of the Scriptures, which agreed with their secret *gnosis*, Irenaeus felt compelled to counter with "the tradition which originates from the apostles and which is preserved by means of the successions of the presbyters in the Churches" (2.2). Irenaeus goes on to argue that

---

[2] Justin Martyr, *Dialogue with Trypho*, ANF, 1.194–270.
[3] As reported in Eusebius, *Ecclesiastical History*, 4.26.13, 14, NPNF 2nd Series, 1.206.
[4] As reported in Tertullian, *Against Marcion*, 4, ANF, 3.345–423.
[5] Irenaeus, *Against Heresies*, 3.1, ANF 1, 414.
[6] Mary Ann Donovan, *One Right Reading: A Guide to Irenaeus*, (Collegeville, MN: Liturgical Press, 1997), 50–56.
[7] See Donovan, *Guide to Irenaeus*, 29–33.

those the apostles left in charge of the churches are the ones who received the truth firsthand and, therefore, can be trusted to have the correct understanding of truth. He names a few, specifically Clement of Rome (3.3), Polycarp of Smyrna (3.4), and John in Ephesus (3.4) as true witnesses of the tradition of the apostles. He then concludes, in chapter four, that the truth is secured in the Church: "Since, therefore, we have the proofs, it is not necessary to seek the truth among others which it is easy to obtain from the Church" (4.1). He goes on to give a creedal statement which he identifies as the "tradition of truth" or the "tradition which they handed down to those to whom they did commit the Churches" (4.1) and as the "ancient tradition" (4.2):

> Believing in one God, the Creator of heaven and earth, and all things therein, by means of Christ Jesus, the Son of God; who, because of His surpassing love towards His creation, condescended to be born of the virgin, He Himself uniting man through Himself to God, and having suffered under Pontius Pilate, and rising again, and having been received up in splendor, shall come in glory, the Saviour of those who are saved, and the judge of those who are judged, and sending into eternal fire those who transform the truth, and despise His Father and His advent (4.2).

The problem with this statement is not with the list of beliefs,[8] but its source of authority. The statement is considered to be true because it is what the Church teaches and not because it is the teaching of Scripture. Of course, for Irenaeus there was no difference between the two. The teaching of Scripture equals the teaching of the Church. However, his argument suggests that the teaching of the Church guarantees a correct reading of Scripture. This may not be a massive difference, but it certainly sets a dangerous precedent.

Origen (185-254)

In the third century, Origen continues the hermeneutic of tradition-as-truth with more nuances. In the preface to his work *peri archōn* (*Concerning the Archons*),[9] Origen sets out his three working hermeneutics of

---

[8] It is true that I believe much the same as this statement, though his nuance concerning eternal fire is moving in the wrong direction. See my interpretation of Irenaeus' understanding of soul and judgment in John W. Reeve, "The Theological Anthropology of Theophilus of Antioch: Immortality and Resurrection in the Context of Judgment" (Ph.D. diss., University of Notre Dame, 2009), 239-247.

[9] This complete work has come down to us only in the fifth century Latin translation of Rufinus

biblical interpretation. In the fourth book of this same work, he details his three-level interpretation: 1) the level of history, or literal interpretation; 2) the level of moral interpretation; and 3) the highest level of spiritual interpretation, most often referred to as allegorical interpretation. He also presents the cue which indicates what was intended by the Holy Spirit as having a spiritual interpretation. I contend the cue of "impossibilities or incongruities" (4.1.15) represents his fourth hermeneutic. Here in the preface, however, Origen contents himself by stating his overall principles for reading Scripture, which are a fair representation of the basic hermeneutics used by most early church fathers in their reading of Scripture.

The first of his three basic principles of interpretation identified all Scripture as christological. Origen argued that Christ, as the Word of God, was both the source and the object of all the scriptures—from the writings of Moses on through Christian scriptures.[10] His third basic principle hints at the multivalence he pursues at the beginning of book 1 and in most of book 4 by suggesting that the Scriptures have a "spiritual" meaning beyond the "first sight." This spiritual meaning "is not known to all, but to those only on whom the grace of the Holy Spirit is bestowed in the word of wisdom and knowledge" (Preface, section 8). These first and third principles are not only employed throughout Origen's writings, but are reflected in the writings of many other early Christian authors. However, it is the second of his basic principles that concerns us here— the same principle we found in Irenaeus, that truth is defined by tradition.

Origen's second principle is, for him, the antidote to the greatly varied beliefs of professed Christians. He argued that the beliefs must be brought into a more uniform system of "truth." According to him, "it seems necessary first of all to fix a definite limit and to lay down an unmistakable rule." He adds that "as the teaching of the Church, transmitted in orderly succession from the apostles, and remaining in the Churches to the present day, is still preserved, that alone is to be accepted as truth which differs in no respect from ecclesiastical and apostolic tradition" (Preface, section 2). Origen then goes on to suggest that the church has clearly defined the tradition of many things, but remained silent on others. He lists a fairly full creed of Christian tenets defined by the church, including a description about the one God, followed by a description of Jesus Christ and the Holy Spirit, and a relatively lengthy description of the human and the soul of the human, including free will and judgment.

---

entitled, *De principiis* (*On First Principles*).

[10] Origen, *De principiis*, "Preface," section 1, *ANF* 4, 239.

Next, he gives a list of things included in the apostolic tradition, but only in an undefined way (e.g., the devil and his angels; that the world was made and will have an end; that the author of Scripture is the Holy Spirit; and that certain angels are good and have a part in God's salvation of humans). He describes his intent to give fuller wisdom on all these areas in the work to follow, but that he will in no way differ from the established truth of apostolic tradition.[11]

Origen, like Philo of Alexandria before him, often interprets Scripture from a Platonic perspective. His conception of the pre-existence of souls is an example of this. Interestingly, his conception of a personal devil, outlined in book 3.2, is incompatible with a Platonic worldview. Yet Origen maintains it as part of the tradition of the church,[12] which for him is the rule for establishing truth. Neither Plato, nor Scripture, nor Scripture interpreted through a Platonic context, is as important to Origen as an arbiter of truth in the apostolic tradition retained by the church. For Origen, as for Irenaeus before him, church tradition establishes truth.

Augustine (354–430)

Many other authors in the early Christian centuries assigned authority to the developing tradition of the beliefs of the church. Major evidence of the ingrained power of this thought surfaces in the beginning of the fifth century, in the writings of Augustine of Hippo. We will concentrate our discussion in what is found in *De civitate Dei* (*City of God*), book 20, chapters 7 and 8. Though the whole work is rather discursive, in book 20, Augustine turns his attention to the final judgment of God and other eschatological matters. In chapter 7, he addresses issues surrounding the two resurrections in Revelation 20, specifically the 1000-year period. He begins by chastising the *chiliasts*, denouncing both their interpretation of the passage and the physicality with which they envision the feasting during that 1000-year Sabbath rest. His main concern is not to expose wrong teaching, but to establish right teaching concerning the millennium.

Augustine addresses the millennium in terms of a stage in the battle

---

[11] Unfortunately for Origen's legacy, many of the speculative thoughts he gives in *De principiis* get him in trouble later when more doctrines are clearly defined within the growing tradition of the Church. So much so that he is condemned as a heretic nearly two centuries later, especially on account of his speculation on the definition of Christ and on the eventual salvation of all. This universal salvation includes those beings whom he suggests were only for a time the devil and his angels, but by the changing power of God ceased to be evil. Herein lies the difficulty of tradition rather than Scripture being the rule of what is true. As the tradition changes, so does the truth by which all is to be judged.

[12] Sigve Tonstadt, "Theodicy and the Theme of Cosmic Conflict in the Early Church," *AUSS* 42.1 (2004): 169–202.

between Christ and the devil for the souls of humans. He begins by quoting the words of Christ in Matthew 12:29: "No man can enter into a strong man's house, and take his property, except he first bind the strong man." He identifies the strong man as the devil and his house as his domain in which he has held humans captive. He pictures Christ as taking the "possessions" which are those who were held by the devil through sin, "but who were to become Christ's faithful people." The binding of the devil by the angel with the key to the bottomless pit represents the devil being "restrained and bridled . . . , so that he should not seduce and gain possession of those who were to be redeemed."

The next part of his interpretation needs some background to make sense. In the LXX, *goyyim* is translated as *toi ethnoi* (the nations). This was a designation to separate the Israelites as the people of God from all other people. Thus, "the nations" was a pejorative term from the perspective of the Jews. However, during the second century of the Christian era, when the Christians were trying to separate themselves from the Jews, Christian apologists embraced this term for themselves as a positive appellation. In a supersessionist move, "the nations" are now considered the true people of God, not the Jews. With this understanding of "the nations," Augustine applies the portion of the text about "no longer seducing the nations" to the church. The binding of the devil means that the church cannot be seduced, by which Augustine means the church cannot be deceived. The timing of this protection against deception by the devil is during the millennium of the church, which Augustine defines as the time between Christ's first and second comings: "Thus the devil is bound throughout the whole period embraced by the Book of Revelation, that is, from the first coming of Christ to the end of the world, which will be Christ's Second Coming" (20.8).

Of course, this presents a problem at the time of the loosing of the devil. But Augustine anticipates that difficulty and slides the meaning of "the nations" back to the "enemies of the Church" after the devil's loosing. In fact, he allows for the current seduction of all the nations who are not "predestined to eternal life." For Augustine, it is only the church, the "Christian nations," who receive God's predestination and are protected from being deceived by the devil. He also shifts the binding from a literal and historical series of events into a spiritual binding at the conversion of each individual. The main point is that Augustine strengthens the idea of salvation within the church and the impossibility of the deception of the church. In fact, by the time the devil is "loosed for a little while" the church will be so strong as to defeat him when he is at full force. The church, as presented by Augustine, provides the security of salvation and truth.

This nearly universally accepted hermeneutic of tradition-as-truth allowed the thought and praxis of the church to move farther and farther away from its biblical foundation without raising much opposition. As such, I hold it to be primarily responsible for the growing difference and distance between the Bible and the church. However, there were other factors that contributed to this difference and distance. There were theological factors that allowed the hierarchy of the church to take effective control of salvation. Sociological factors also contributed to the rise of a separate clergy as a particular priesthood and to a mystagogical understanding of the priesthood and the sacraments.

Theological and Sociological Underpinnings of Soteriology

Overview

There are three sets of theological tensions that I perceive to be involved in the establishment of the church hierarchy and its effective control of salvation. The first is between repentance and penance. The second deals with *Ordo* and church order. The third involves earned authority and official authority within the Church. There are also two areas of societal pressure which provide overarching pressure in one direction regarding each of these three tensions: a popular respect towards a lifestyle based on rigorist, ascetic ethics and an overzealous shift from a proper reverence of holy things toward a perception of an objective holiness shaped into mystagogical and sacerdotal terms. I will deal with each of these as five separate sections, but they are inseparably intertwined.

Repentance and Penance

The first of the three tensions involved in the establishment of the Church hierarchy and its effective control of salvation is the tension between light repentance leading to forgiveness and weighty penance leading to forgiveness. The late-second century pagan Celsus in his work, *A True Discourse*, accused the Christians of bringing in any wretch who had committed any crime and forgiving them freely and openly, without ever having any good people come into their sect. Of course, when Origen answered for the Christians in his *Contra Celsum* (*Against Celsus*), he made it clear that Christian forgiveness was not cheap, just free. Moreover, he argued that Christians lived lives that were more righteous than even the lives of the philosophers. But in reality, we find a constant tension between repentance and penance and the meanings of those words from the earliest times until the Middle Ages.

For instance, in *De paenitentia* (*On Repentance*), Tertullian, the early third-century North African best known as the first Latin-speaking Christian theologian, interprets Hebrews 6:4–6 as meaning there is only one chance for salvation. According to him, baptism provides the forgiveness of all previous sins. But if you fall after baptism, your salvation is gone. The opening chapters of the *Shepherd of Hermas* paint a similar picture, though there is allowance for one repentance after baptism. This led to a very stringent view of falling. Of course, the fall they are talking about is not just making a small mistake. They are talking about rejecting Christ in the context of persecution or committing an egregious sin. This belief that baptism voided all previous sins, but that a person was vulnerable to falling irrevocably after baptism, led many who were becoming Christians to put off baptism until near death. Constantine I is perhaps the most famous example of this practice. Several other emperors followed suit. There seemed to be a fear that many of the things required of an emperor—conducting wars, ordering death penalties, carrying out the traditional functions of a pagan state—might cause the Christian emperor to be lost. Saving baptism until after an emperorship would ensure their salvation. Such was the force believed to exist in the ritual of baptism. But what about those who were baptized young? Is there any repentance and forgiveness for sins after baptism? If so, how does one guard against cheap grace? Tertullian argued that the way to guard against cheap grace is to enforce serious penance.

So the question arises: What is the difference between repentance as taught in the New Testament, using the Greek terminology of *metanoia* and *metanoeō*, and penance as taught in the Middle Ages, using the Latin term *paenitentia*? One frustrating circumstance is that in the writings of Tertullian, who sets the tone and terminology for Latin Christian theology and communication, the Latin term he uses for both repentance and penance is *paenitentia*. This suggests that, for Tertullian, there was no major difference between penance and repentance. Much later, a different Latin term, *expio* ("to make amends") is added to show that penance was making amends for the sin that was committed. The initial term, *paenitentia*, was used in Latin to suggest grief for sin, or grieving for having sinned. This is the understanding that Tertullian brings to the concept of repentance/penance. He wants it to be more than just a light repentance. He wants it to be something that is weighty, something that is not trite. And so he introduces the untranslated, but transliterated, Greek terminology, *exomologēsis* ("confession"), into his Latin writing to insist on a form of public confession. Now *exomologeō* is the basic verb used to denote confessing in the New Testament, but the noun form *exomologēsis*, as used by Tertullian in his book *On Repentance*, is used specifically to show an overt and very public indication of the knowledge of one's sin. Furthermore, he equates the Greek term, *exomologēsis*, with his Latin term, *paenitentia*, making it clear that, for Tertullian, one has not really repented until the completion of what came to be known as penance: a public expression and action. For Tertullian, this included wearing sackcloth and ashes in public. Specifically, if one were being penitent for a sin, he or she would dress not as a rich, comfortable person but as a poor, wretched beggar, publicly grieving for personal sin. This became the beginning for understanding a weighty repentance as doing penance.

Now as far as the interpretation of Hebrews 6, Tertullian does allow, along with the *Shepherd*, for one more chance after baptism. Just one fall and you are out of salvation may have been too stringent. So, in deference to the *Shepherd of Hermes*, Tertullian presents the possibility of one more chance after baptism and, if you do not fall again a second time, you are still within salvation, still a member of God's people. But that is all. For Tertullian, there were never more than two chances. This whole concept of how many falls are allowed after baptism is based on what is, in my opinion, a misinterpretation of Hebrews 6:4–6 in connection with Hebrews 10:26. Hebrews 10:26 is suggesting that outside the sacrifice of Jesus Christ there is no sacrifice for sin. If you try to go back to Judaism, to the sacrifice of the lambs, goats, and bulls, they are no longer a valid sacrifice once you have understood Jesus to be the true sacrifice. If you attempt to use any pagan sacrifice, there is no merit. Jesus is the only true sacrifice.[13] That, I believe, is the meaning of Hebrews 6, but it is interpreted in the early church as an issue of how many times you can fall and still remain within the church. This disregards the teaching of Jesus when Peter asks him: "How many times must I forgive my brother? As many as seven times?" (Matt 18:21). Of course, Jesus answers with seventy times seven, a number too high to easily keep score. If this is an example of how God forgives, then an unlimited amount of forgiveness is available for the repentant sinner. This can become very embarrassing on the human level. In the early church, especially with the apologists like Tertullian, it was imperative that public scandal would not impugn the new religion. As a result, they did not want light repentance and easy forgiveness. They pushed toward a weighty penance and a weighty forgiveness to counteract the accusations of Celsus and others.

A few short decades after the death of Tertullian, Cyprian became the metropolitan bishop in Carthage in North Africa. This made him the most influential Christian in the official hierarchy of the entire North African Church. Shortly after his controversial election, the Decian persecution began with all the difficulties caused by hundreds, if not thousands, of Christians falling. When Decius demanded all people in the world offer incense as an act of loyalty to the divine essence of the new emperor,

---

[13] See William L. Lane, *Hebrews 9–13* (Dallas, TX: Word, 1991), 292–293.

many complied. Cyprian himself left town in order to remain alive. He was accused by many back in Carthage of running away. After the persecution abated, Cyprian returned to an extreme ecclesiastical mess that had to be cleaned up.

Not only had many fallen by offering the incense, others had retained their family homes by sending a slave to offer it in their name. Others purchased a *libellus*, a document to certify performance of a pagan sacrifice showing loyalty, on the black market. This would allow them to "prove" to the public officials that they had offered the incense when they had not actually done so. Still others, however, stood strong and lost all their possessions, supported by the church while awaiting, imprisoned, the potential of dying for their faith. These were referred to as the confessors, martyrs-in-waiting. A few had actually been martyred. Some of the confessors were approached by those who had fallen outright or who were viewed as fallen because of their devious means of appearing legal, to have them pray to God for their forgiveness. Based on the merits of those would-be martyrs, it was popularly understood that the fallen could be fully reinstated in the church.

There were also five presbyters who had been jealous of Cyprian becoming the bishop when each of them thought they should have been selected instead.[14] In Cyprian's absence, they started offering the Eucharist and its assumed guarantee of salvation to those who had fallen, even while the persecution continued. This, in spite of the fact that Cyprian was writing letters from his hideout in his family home in Ithaca, urging against too quick a forgiveness to those who had fallen, especially while those who were in prison were still suffering for their brave faithfulness. So upon his return, he faced these two difficult situations of quick and easy forgiveness, one by the confessors and the other by the self-important presbyters overplaying their leadership functions in the Church in the absence of their bishop. Cyprian, having lost influence on account of his perceived cowardice and needing to regain control of a deteriorating situation, called a council of some 180 bishops in North Africa to reassert his official authority as well as to bring some order to the situation of forgiveness within the Church.

This bishops' council, under the leadership of Cyprian, adopted three principles that he popularized in bold statements in a theological treatise. First, Cyprian stated in *De Unitate Ecclesiae* (*On the Unity of the Church*), 6: "You cannot have God as Father unless you have the Church as moth-

---

[14] This next section on Cyprian is based on a reading of his extant correspondence, a series of over 80 official letters to and from Cyprian, as Bishop of Carthage.

er." The primary meaning of this is, of course, that God's salvation comes through the church. Second, in this same work, Cyprian concludes that to act apart from your bishop is to act outside of the church: The church is defined as the bishop. This suggests that the bishops not only represent the church, but to be in communion with the bishop is the definition of being in the church. Third, is the bold statement: Only the bishops can forgive sins. By offering the Eucharist to an individual, the bishop is recognizing and conferring salvation on that individual. Further, bishops outlined a standard of penitential activity to be practiced by those who had fallen during the persecution. It consisted of spending the rest of their lives doing public penance, including the abstinence from fancy dress or careful attention to grooming, in order to demonstrate their sorrow for their fall and their seriousness of wanting God's acceptance through the church. On their deathbeds, if the bishop has deemed their penance as sufficient, they were to receive the Eucharist and the full forgiveness of the church.[15]

All of this, both problem and solution, hinges upon the idea that forgiveness comes through the church or through the rites or elements provided by the church: baptism and the Eucharist. Everybody in North Africa, from Tertullian on, including Cyprian and those on all sides of the Decian persecution, believed that the Eucharist and baptism secured forgiveness and, therefore, salvation. It is important to note that Cyprian has a caveat. He suggests that if the church were to make a mistake and not offer forgiveness to someone whom God forgives, God would make amends. Vice versa, if the church were to make a mistake and offer forgiveness to one who should not have it according to God, God would make the correction. This caveat is lost. But the three statements remain, given credence by the later martyrdom of Cyprian during the Valerian persecution. They become the normative understanding within the sacramental theology that developed during the Middle Ages. They are used in the presentation of the sacraments in book four of the *Sentences* of Peter Lombard, without the caveat.

The system of confession to a priest, performance of penance, and absolution given by the authority of the Holy Spirit received through the bishop, had a positive goal. But it also had a negative side. On the positive side, this system was intended to disallow cheap grace by requiring that a representative of the church supervise the processes of repentance. This

---

[15] It is important to note that in actual practice at the first sign of a new persecution, less than three years after the cessation of the Decian persecution and the bishops' council, it was deemed prudent to offer the Eucharist to all the fallen, to prepare them and strengthen them to not fall again. The Council of Nicea later set the standard to seven years of penance as the norm for a fall during a persecution before being readmitted to full fellowship and receiving the Eucharist.

provides a check on individuals who may have thought that their sins are of no real significance or consequence. It can also help those who would be too hard on themselves, doubting that Christ's blood can actually take away their guilt and allow them to stand before God with the assurance of forgiveness. However, this system puts another human in control of one's accountability to God. This subjects the system to all the weaknesses of humanity and the abuses in both directions of over-leniency or never-enough sorrow for sin. It also subjects the forgiveness of God to the possibility of human manipulation for greed or power. The system also allows a penitent the option of deceiving the priest and yet feel assured of salvation by receiving absolution and the Eucharist. Additionally, they may feel that the penance, rather than the blood of Christ, pays for the guilt of sin. Finally, the biggest problem of the system is that it seems to put human beings in the place of God.

At the crucial times, when the direction of the development of church practices was being set, it was considered right to put these protections into place. The understanding of the essential correctness of church traditions as passed down (the hermeneutic of tradition as truth) kept the system from being overthrown when its inevitable weaknesses became evident. These weaknesses include abuses of the system, like simony and the sale of indulgences; but also the faults of the system itself, such as dependence on human actions for salvation in the form of merit received from saints and forgiveness received from bishops and priests.

Ordo *and Order*

The second tension contributing to the establishment of church hierarchy and its effective control of salvation is the tension between the various forms of leadership ministry in the church. I call this *ordo* and order because of the need to establish and maintain order in the churches (*ordo*) and the consolidation of power and authority into a centralized and objectively ordained group of official leaders (order). After the apostles, there were at least three major groups of leaders striving to be the highest human authority in the churches: prophets, presbyters, and bishops. During the first few centuries A.D., these three seemed to have varying rank, respect, and function in the Christian churches in different cities. The prophets were the first to lose out.

The first difficulty for the prophets arises in the pages of the *Didache*. This early second-century work is the first in a long line of Church orders, books on how to run the church and its services. Chapter 11 of the *Didache* warns against false prophets and teaches to distinguish a prophet by their actions. The approach is pragmatic: A true prophet will not stay for more than two or three days in any one place, depending on the hospitality of the people, and he will not ask for money. Anyone who stays longer or asks for money is a false prophet. This suggests, of course, that there were lots of prophets roaming around preaching to the different churches and groups of Christians and expecting both hospitality and respect. So the prophets were the first to fall under the guise of not being orderly in function. Also, as direct spokespersons for God, prophets did not lend themselves to orderly control by the local church authorities. Montanus and the Montanist prophetesses, Priscilla and Maximilla, were cases in point of prophets who would not submit their testimony to the traditional interpretations of the Scriptures. These and other prophets tended to cause havoc in local congregations and, by the late second century, were largely bypassed as authoritative leaders in Christianity.

The New Testament left instructions on the appointment of bishops and other sets of instructions for presbyters as local Christian authorities. There is good reason to think that in the New Testament these two terms refer to the same office of local leaders. They continue to be used synonymously in the early church as evidenced by their usage in *1 Clement*.[16] In chapters 44, 47, and 52, Clement makes it clear that local leaders who have been recognized by the congregation and assigned by church leadership, in this case the apostles, should not lightly be put aside. His issue is not whether they are bishops or presbyters, but whether they should be put aside lightly. He urges the upstarts in Corinth to continue to respect the presbyters. He never urges them to continue to respect the bishops because, apparently, there were none in Corinth. But in chapter 44, he either equates the office of bishop (overseer) with that of presbyter or denotes that the function of oversight belongs to the presbyters. Clement does not identify himself as a bishop in Rome, which would tend to suggest that there were also presbyters, rather than a single bishop, in Rome and that he is writing as one among many.

Polycarp, who was often referred to as the second century bishop of Smyrna, never refers to himself as such and, in fact, never uses the term bishop. Instead he uses the term presbyters in the plural. In his letter to the Philippians, he makes it clear that the Christians in Philippi should be carefully subject to the presbyters. In contrast, Ignatius of Antioch, who wrote a series of letters to various churches in Asia Minor, states in the letters to the *Magnesians* and the *Trallians*, that one bishop is to be in charge of the rest of the church.[17] He compares the bishop to Jesus Christ

---

[16] This is a very late first-century or early second-century letter from Clement, a presbyter in Rome, to the Corinthian Church on the occasion of their having an insurrection against the established local leadership.

[17] This is particularly the case in *Trallians*, chapter 2.

and the presbyters to the apostles, suggesting that the one bishop should have the respect and obedience of all.[18] This is the first suggestion that bishops would eventually take precedence over presbyters in the early Christian church.

The tensions within the different offices in the church concerning who would ultimately be in charge are eventually resolved through the use of a typology of the priesthood from the Old Testament.[19] It seems more than coincidental that this takes place during a time when a single emperor was effectively replacing the Roman senate. Church hierarchy tends to follow secular governmental hierarchy in structure. The first leaders to function as priests in the Christian Churches were the bishops, but eventually the presbyters acted as priests in subjection to their bishops. This was necessary because the priestly duties were more than one person could handle. The presbyters were pressed into service and eventually became the priesthood with the bishops being the high priests, in accordance with the adopted Old Testament typology.

We can reason that using the typology of the priesthood became the normal way of expressing the Christian ministry in the medieval church. We will return to this when discussing the transition from Eucharist to Mass and the sacerdotal understanding of sacrificial language.

The writings of Irenaeus of Lyon (130–200)[20] seem to have introduced the concept of apostolic succession in Christian thinking. We have seen, in the discussion of the hermeneutic of tradition-as-truth, how Irenaeus argues that true Christianity must be received from the apostles. The underlying assumption is that all the apostles had the same doctrines, which they received from Christ and the Holy Spirit and that they communicated it unaltered to those they taught. It also assumes that the second generation passed it on without change to the third, etc. It was convenient for Irenaeus that he was one of those still alive who had known a man (Polycarp of Smyrna) who had known an apostle (John). He was probably the only one left in the West who had received direct

---

[18] Although Ignatius is consistent in his placing a single bishop over the plural presbyters, he is not consistent with his typology. In *Magnesians* 6, he interchanges God with Jesus Christ as the type of the bishop and adds the deacons as the ministers of Jesus Christ. All references here are, of course, to the shorter versions of his letters rather than to the longer recension, which is clearly from a post-Nicean date and has a considerably more complex ecclesiology.

[19] For greater detail, see John W. Reeve, "The Presbyter: Jewish Elder to Christian Priest" (M.A. thesis, Andrews University, 1997).

[20] He was a late second-century bishop in Gaul (now southern France) who is best known for his fighting against gnosticism and for being an early advocate for a christology that insisted that Christ was both fully God and fully human.

knowledge from an "apostolic man."[21] This identified him as the most authoritative of his colleagues and he was not reticent about using his clout to combat heresies. Though this advantage served him well, there was an unintended result that has hindered Christianity ever since. It is said that your greatest strength is also your greatest weakness. That certainly is true of Irenaeus' concept of apostolic succession. The very thing that, according to him, adds continuity to the beliefs of the Church through the generations also tends to resist corrective ideas from overturning old mistakes. This is as true in establishing the authority of bishops as it is in dealing with scriptural truth. Augustine of Hippo, probably the most influential Christian theologian after Paul, continues the same idea of apostolic succession, adding to the succession of teaching suggested by Irenaeus; the succession of ordination; and the handing on of the Holy Spirit through the *ordo*. Augustine is certainly not the first to suggest this connection of ordination through time, but he is the most lasting authoritative voice among the early doctors of the church. When he equates the ordination to receiving the authority of the Holy Spirit by the action of the church, he sets the norm in the Roman Catholic Church for the whole of the Middle Ages. He also establishes that the action of the church is effective regardless of the personal qualities of the officers involved: *ex opere operato* ("from the work which is done").[22]

Now, however, we direct our attention once again to Cyprian of Carthage in the middle of the third century, this time on the current discussion of the Christian ministry. For Cyprian, the bishop is the minister of the church, the high priest. By this time, the office of the bishop had been split into three different levels: the first, most authoritative level was comprised of the metropolitan bishops, who were in charge of whole areas such as Carthage and the surrounding North African countries or the whole area of the city of Rome and the surrounding countryside, etc. The second level was made up of the regular bishops who were in charge of the church in their town, but were subject to their metropolitan superiors. The third level of bishops was the local leaders in small and rural villages where small groups of Christians recognized a bishop without the full authority afforded the first two levels (the ability to initiate churches or to ordain other bishops). All three levels of bishops tended to be, by

---

[21] Irenaeus writes of his connection to John through Polycarp in *Against Heresies* 3.3.4, and in his lost work, *On the Ogdoade*, this fragment is preserved in Eusebius of Caesarea, *Ecclesiastical History*, 5.20.

[22] See discussion in Alistar E. McGrath, *Christian Theology: An Introduction* (Malden, MA: Wiley-Blackwell, 2011), 406; and Maxwell E. Johnson, *The Rites of Christian Initiation: Their Evolution and Interpretation* (Collegeville, MN: Liturgical, 1999), 151–158.

this time, above the presbyters and above the deacons. The bishops were the central ministers of the churches and were more and more perceived as the high priests in a priesthood of presbyters. They were definitely in charge of the *ordo* and the order of the church.

Bishops as the head of the church hierarchy allowed local practice and interactions between churches to be more nimble. These interactions were not tied down to a group of presbyters trying to run everything by committee. Also, the model of bishops/elders in charge of churches is a solid biblical model. However, the introduction of the Old Testament priesthood typology into Christian ministry misdirects the function of the Christian ministry into priestly duties rather than pastoral duties, the core of ministry. The dynamic of apostolic succession adds a component of solidarity through time that practically makes it impossible for a new generation of leaders to correct old mistakes. This placed the onus needed for more than a surface reform out of reach of most generations of leaders.

Earned Authority Versus Official Authority

The third set of tensions involved in the establishment of the church hierarchy and that hierarchy's effective control over salvation is the tension between official authority and earned authority. There is an authority that comes from holding an office, either from the inherent respect accorded to the office itself or from the change of status resulting from an initiation such as ordination. This official authority is in contrast to authority that is earned. That is, authority which is derived in the eyes of the people by merit, apart from any office held. Those who were viewed by the populace of the early church as having earned religious authority can be summarized by three words: martyrs, money, and monks.

Martyrs

The earliest Christian martyrs that we know by name are big names from the Bible: Steven, Peter, and Paul and many of the other apostles as well. But in *1 Clement* 5, Peter and Paul are described as martyrs, already in heaven by virtue of their martyrdom. This, together with the biblical account of Steven's martyrdom, according to which he was looking into the very gates of heaven while he was being stoned, set the stage within Christianity for the belief that martyrs immediately go to heaven after death. Of course, this relationship had been established in Judaism back in the second century B.C. in 2 Maccabees 7, where the seven Jewish brothers are martyrs in Antiochus Epiphany's court. Their pain was great, but their faith, virtue, and bravery were even greater. Their story became the model for martyr stories *par excellence* and was often copied by other Christian martyr stories. There are Christian martyr stories from Nero's time, including those of Peter and Paul, and martyrdoms during Domitian's persecution at the end of the first century, including references in the book of Revelation. Early in the second century A.D. there are three other famous Christian martyrs—Ignatius of Antioch, Polycarp of Smyrna, and Justin called the Martyr. All three of these, if indeed Ignatius was actually martyred when he reached Rome, have martyr stories that are often told and greatly revered. These early martyr stories set the stage for martyrs to be associated with the apostles Peter and Paul as well as with heaven, giving them great earned authority. This continues on with Blandina and the martyrs of Lyon near the end of the second century and, under Septimius Severus at the beginning of the third century, Perpetua and Felicitas in North Africa, as well as the many martyrs killed in Alexandria. They all became Christian heroes and are considered the truest Christians, those who have the greatest impact in heaven. This line of Christian martyrs continues on in the mid-third century with the Decian persecution, followed shortly afterwards by the Valerian persecution, in which Cyprian was killed. I have already spoken of the issues that came up concerning the authority of martyrs, and particularly of confessors, the martyrs-in-waiting, during the Decian persecution. These Christians who were imprisoned for their faith, but not actually killed, were given almost equal authority in the minds of the people as the martyrs who were actually killed. Of course, in the early portion of the fourth century, we have the greatest persecution of all: that of Diocletian, which was the most universal and claimed the most lives of Christians. For nearly 300 years, there was persecution of Christians by the Roman Empire, producing thousands of martyrs with hundreds of well-known stories. Many of these martyrs have been officially beatified, sainted, and are honored yearly by both Orthodox Christian and Roman Catholics.

Two Christian practices arose in the face of these Christian martyrdoms. The first was the practice of suppliants praying at tombs. This started as early as the martyrdoms of Peter and Paul. In the catacombs, just outside of Rome, there are numerous inscriptions posted to the walls, where it was believed that Peter and Paul's bodies had originally lain, asking Peter and Paul for assurances. There were requests for assurance of salvation, for health and wealth, and well-being. They were not just praying and thanking God for the examples of the martyrs. They were praying to the martyrs themselves, counting on them to act as mediators before God. The devotees, counting on the martyrs' presence in heaven, their sainthood, their merits, and their extra power before God, asked for answers to their prayers.

A second practice developed with respect to the martyrs-in-waiting.

They were asked to pray to God interceding on behalf of the supplicants. This has already been mentioned in regards to Cyprian's situation during the Decian persecution. Many who had fallen during this persecution requested martyrs-in-waiting to intercede on their behalf and ask for God's forgiveness. This represented a great level of earned authority, ascribed by church members to these saints for their willingness to die for their faith in Christ. Often, in the wake of their death, stories of their previous righteous living would surface along with stories of healing and supernatural events interpreted as signs of God's special favor.

This great authority in the eyes of the Christian congregations became a very direct threat to the official authority of the Church hierarchy. This was especially true in cases where martyrs were perceived to be at odds with the official church authorities. However, in those cases where official authority aligned with earned authority, official authority was enhanced, thus encouraging the hierarchy to join in honoring the saints, attempting to bring the earned authority within the sphere of official authority. Of course, the greatest authority was derived for those who, like Cyprian, had both official and earned authority. The martyred bishop gave great clout both to what he taught while in office and to his office itself.

Martyrs, with their earned authority, and the martyr cults that rose up around the popular practice of praying to these martyrs became such a force that the Church had to harness it in order to keep its own authority and control over salvation. The activities of Cyprian and the 180 bishops who gathered together after the Decian persecution in North Africa addressed the need to make martyrs and confessors part of the church structure. They limited the power of martyrs so that the church was in charge of salvation. This is based upon a misunderstanding of the relationship between believers and their God. Martyrs provided a level of protection from the unpredictable world and from God or, more precisely, protection from a misunderstanding of God as too transcendent, too impassable, and too immutable to be touched by compassion for our human needs. This highlights a perceived need for human mediation, a patron to protect from the divine and fate.

Money

The second "m" is money, which divides easily into two categories. Money itself is simply an agreed upon representation of value or a more easily transportable symbol of property, and in this context has to do with patronage and almsgiving. Since the time when the rich man who came to Jesus and went away sorrowful when told to give all his money to the poor, (Matt 19:16–22), there has been a deep understanding in Christianity that you could not serve both God and mammon. In other words, it was very difficult to be rich and still be a Christian. The way out of this dilemma was the abundant giving of alms. The giving of alms was viewed very highly, both within Judaism and Christianity, as a way to separate yourself from the temptation to be selfish with your riches.

Almsgiving, as portrayed in the story of the rich man and Lazarus (Luke 16:19–31), is a unidirectional action of the rich giving the poor a portion of their plenty so that the poor could have their most basic needs filled. In practice, however, it is often a bidirectional transaction where the rich person expects something in return for an investment of value. It may be as intangible as gratitude, or a blessing, or a prayer said on behalf of the donor, but there is often the expectation of an exchange of value. When this exchange becomes a socially expected norm approximating *quid pro quo*, then it is no longer almsgiving, but patronage. The patronage system of the Mediterranean basin, under Greco-Roman influence, was well-known and well-developed throughout the region and came into play within the Christian communities. Patrons were necessary in society, providing things that day laborers and farmers and even tradesmen could not provide for themselves. These included public utilities, bath houses and temples, wood for fuel, alms to the poor, and even jobs for security in case of economic downturn, to ensure people had money for food. All these things came from the few rich in each community. In return, they expected to be respected, honored, and served.

The church was no different. In spite of the clear biblical directions to be no respecter of persons (James 2), it inevitably became important to take care of the rich people in the church. They provided the support for church buildings and functions as well as for the many poor people in the church. Cyprian, again, makes a fine example. He gave all of his money to the church when he was converted, and since he was from a rich, old-money family in Carthage, it was a substantial gift. While bishop, he spoke of the many dependents for whom the church was providing care. He tells of 1500 widows that were on the church dole during the decade of the 250s A.D. in Carthage. The number of people receiving goods and services from the church required large amounts of money, and the patronage system was the standard way in which money was gathered and used for these types of activities. In other words, the rich donors in the church were the ones who provided the sustenance of the poor as well as the upkeep of the church, etc.

One of the times where this became problematic was in the middle of the second century when the very rich Marcion in Rome gave the proceeds from the sale of his shipping company to the Roman Church. As other great patrons of the church, he was recognized as having earned authority separate from the official authority of the presbyters who were ruling in the Roman Church at that time. As such, he gained a great following as a teacher, and his theology and his understanding of Scripture was given great respect. It was an extreme embarrassment and hardship to the Roman Church when they were forced to recognize that his theology was sadly heretical and that his understanding of Scripture was simply unacceptable. In the end, his earned authority was so great that to overcome it, the Church hierarchy found it necessary to collect and repay the entire fortune. This was a major setback to the Church in Rome and it took a major commitment to reclaim the authority of the official church away from the earned authority of the heretic Marcion.

Once again, these few illustrations portray the tension between the earned authority of the patrons and alms givers within the church and the official authority of the bishops, presbyters, and deacons. If it was only the bishop who could forgive sins, then the rich could not use their influence with the righteous poor, the martyrs-in-waiting or any other class of believers who may have better access to God; they had to depend on the bishops. The bishops, then, became the patrons of the ultimate value, namely salvation. In the eyes of the laity and the developing Christian tradition, they wielded the keys to the kingdom of heaven.

Monks

The third "m" in earned authority is the monks. The proliferation and organization of Christian ascetics developed at a later time than the martyrs and Christians with money. During the latter half of the third century, Anthony of the Desert became the first of the desert monks near Nitria and Scetis, south of Alexandria, to go away from the river and out into the main desert itself. There he lived a life of isolation and for twenty years struggled with the devil until he returned victorious. His story is told by Athanasius,[23] who became acquainted with Anthony during his many exiles for his Trinitarian beliefs. In his *Vita Antonii*, Athanasius portrays Anthony as starting out as a rich young man who gave away his wealth in response to hearing Jesus' admonishment to the rich young ruler. He quickly overshadowed that early attainment by living successfully for so many years as a monk in the desert, as an ascetic with high ethics and no impediments or controls over him by the things of this world. He had left behind family ties, dependence upon other people, money, etc.

Those following in the footsteps of Anthony, both south of Alexandria and up in Palestine and even farther up in Syria, set the stage for

---

[23] Athanasius (*c.* 296–373) is most famous for his single-minded adherence to the *homoousios*, "of one substance," formula describing the Father and the Son as sharing the same nature in the Trinitarian controversies of the fourth century.

what would happen once the martyrdom under the Diocletian persecution ended and Christianity became legal under Constantine. Then the possibility of proving yourself to be a true Christian of the highest order by martyrdom became very improbable. The monks became the most serious Christians. They were now the ones who would live the most righteous of lifestyles, the ones who would gain the most earned authority in the eyes of the people, both Christian and non-Christian. It was the monks that everyone would expect to have the ear of God. Monks became a force that had to be reckoned with over and over again because of their earned authority. Their authority with the people often outstripped the local authority of church officials.

So, as with the martyrs and those with money, the official church authorities had to work continually to bring the earned authority of the monks under the auspices of the church. The trump card again was the sacraments. The records of the sayings of the monks of the desert make it clear that it was normal for the monks to have a great deal of respect for the ordination of the priests and the Eucharist that they distributed. The only regular meetings of the loosely confederated monks, before official orders became the norm, was at the *synobium*, literally "the gathering," on Sabbaths and Sundays when they gathered for the communal partaking of the Eucharist. Men and women who devoted their lives to the pursuit of holiness and salvation were committed to availing themselves of the salvation-engendering elements, even if they eschewed the more public commitments of congregations within the towns. The ascetic movement as a whole was committed to receiving salvation through the church. Many of the most famous bishops and other official church leaders were first monks.

Toward a Rigorous Ascetic Ethics

So far it has been suggested that the tensions between the various authority figures in the church community and the official church leadership led to the need for the bishops to be in charge of salvation. These tensions include those felt among the earned authorities, including martyrs, money, and monks, and the official church authorities. It also includes the tensions between perceived sources of forgiveness and the person by whom repentance/penance can be offered. Historically, the solution to these frictional and potentially factional situations has been a system where the bishops wield the keys of the kingdom as benevolent dictators, as it were, so that there would be no disorder or contention in the church. This solution has become an integral part of the Christian tradition and has been seen by most Christians through history as the God-ordained pattern of church order and soteriology.

It is true that church political environments portrayed the need for bishops to function as benevolent dictators or emperors, and it is also true that they eventually took the titles of secular dictators and emperors, such as *Pontifex Maximus*, as titles for the bishops in Rome. It is not true, however, that it was only for political reasons that the bishops became in charge of salvation. There also were religious and social pressures constantly pushing toward an ever greater reverence for ethical rigor and all things holy. These were important factors in the development of a system which placed the church hierarchy in effective control of the dispensation of salvation. These two dynamics are referred to in this paper as a bias toward rigorous ascetic ethics in Christian lifestyle and an exaggeration from reverence of the sacred toward an elevation to objective holiness. Both seem to be constant pressures from the Greco-Roman super-culture from which Christianity grew. These issues involve what we would now term religious sociology, which I have attempted to identify through primary case studies rather than through formal sociological methods. As such, the presentation is intended to be descriptive and hopefully useful, even though it is incomplete.

The first of these religious social pressures is most obviously recognized in the lives and deaths of the martyrs. They have a rigorous ethic in refusing to forsake their faith in the face of death. In a more general sense, the lives of the monks portray this pressure toward rigor as they have a very controlled lifestyle. They experimented with rigor and self-control not just in the one area of never giving up their faith, but in all areas (e.g., what they ate and drank, how much they slept and in what conditions, what they thought and said, their interactions with society, and in their disconnection from the world). These two groups, the martyrs and the monks, portrayed this societal value of ethical rigor. But this bias may also be recognized in the writings of Tertullian, who takes a very conservative view of the traditional Roman values and mores and essentially pushes them within Christianity.

Tertullian's attitude seems to suggest that the more rigorous a person is, the closer he or she is to God. It was this respect for rigor in lifestyle that was probably as influential in causing the Roman Church to accept Marcion as a local Christian. Marcion talked, and apparently lived, a very rigorous ethic. It was probably also this rigorous ethic that attracted Tertullian to the Montanist movement.

Living a rigorous ethic brought public respect in the wider society. It was an attempt to enlist this public respect that caused the second century apologists to point out the rigorousness of the Christian lifestyle. This was taken a step further by Clement of Alexandria, Origen, and others when they equated the lifestyle of Christians with that of the philosophers. Christ and Christians, Clement argued in *Stromata* (*Miscellanies*),

1.20–28 and throughout *Paedagogus* (*The Teacher*), were the true philosophers living a more philosophic lifestyle than the philosophers themselves. The constant push for rigor eventually became so severe among the Syrian monks, as reported by Theodoret of Cyrrhus in his work *Historia religiosa*, that death and ruination of health almost became the norm. Theodoret commended their extremes. In contrast, many of the desert fathers of Egypt urged some moderation and even spoke out against the spiritual pride of those who would be too extreme. Theodoret consistently used praise and encouragement for yet more rigor, no matter how extreme the asceticism. Future generations of monks, largely Basil of Caesarea and later Benedict of Nursia, in their respective *Rules*, had to mediate the rigor of the monks into something more physically tolerable for the human body.

The two-fold attraction of this ascetic rigor would be the desire for personal holiness and assurance of salvation on the one hand and earned authority on the other. While officially eschewing the public eye, many times the monks would come out of the desert to Alexandria to place their authority on one side of a public debate, especially during the christological controversies. The politically adept bishops of Alexandria, such as Athanasius[24] in the fourth century and Cyril[25] in the fifth, often used the earned authority of the monks on behalf of their theological agendas. All bishops in areas with many monks had to deal carefully with them to make sure that the monks' considerable earned authority was useful, rather than hurtful, to them. Many bishops, like John Chrysostom, were monks themselves, having been elevated from among the ranks of the ascetics. Many of those considered good candidates for bishoprics in these early centuries were personal participants in the push toward a rigorous, ascetic life of holiness. There was certainly constant pressure toward choosing leaders that were positive public representatives of Christianity. Those who lived a rigorous ethic were able to fill the need for respectability and the desire to be well thought of among the greater society because, whether pagan or Christian, all of Roman society admired the ethic of those who lived rigorously.

The church came to depend on those who lived rigorous lives to rep-

---

[24] Athanasius' *Life of Anthony*, 69 places Nicean Trinitarian arguments into the mouth of the old man. The book was one of the most widely read books in the world for centuries afterward. Athanasius gained a lot of local and international authority by his use of Anthony.

[25] Cyril, Bishop of Alexandria, brought boatloads of monks (officially, 50 clerics and their servants) with him to the Council of Ephesus, ensuring that Nestorius, Bishop of Constantinople, did not have a chance of a fair hearing for his christology, especially since John of Antioch and his entourage arrived late. See detailed description of the council in John Anthony McGukin, *St. Cyril of Alexandria: The Christological Controversy: Its History, Theology, and Texts* (Crestwood, NY: St. Vladimir's Seminary Press, 2004), 53–62; esp. 55–56.

resent or illustrate the virtue of its religion to the greater society, thereby garnering public support for the whole of Christianity. This two-tiered Christianity became normative within Christian tradition with the super Christians being pushed out of the realm of normal humans into the realm of the holy as saints. It was just a series of small steps to move from recognizing extra virtue on the part of the saints to recognizing extra merit. If righteous living was part of the plan of salvation, then these saints had it in overabundance. They came to be viewed as patrons of virtue and merit like the financial patrons in the surrounding society. The rich were expected to use their means for the public good in towns and cities; in like manner, the saints were tapped for the public good in the church. The saints became a storehouse of merit for those in need of it. But who should mind the bank to keep the flow of spiritual patronage orderly and efficient? Those who held the keys to the kingdom of heaven—the bishops.

Ambrose of Milan, a statesman within the Roman government, before he was elevated to bishop of Milan, was part of the process, which brought the relics and tombs of the saints under the control of the bishops.[26] His strategy included creating shrines controlled by the church at significant sites of miraculous happenings ascribed to the saints or where they died or were buried. Also, he extended the practice of the bishops' certification of bones, pieces of wood, or metal as authentic body parts of the saints or pieces of the cross, etc. to be used as relics. The sanctification process was developed in such a way as to make the bishops the only ones who could certify the righteous life of a candidate and the posthumous miracles necessary for the beatification. And, of course, only a council of bishops could declare sainthood. This placed the virtue and merit of the saints and their earned authority, firmly under the control of the bishops.

It was tragic when holy living became a necessary ingredient in salvation, made available through the church from the storehouse of the saints' merits. This created a dependence on humans (the saints) to provide what only the merits of Christ through His blood can provide. It also forged another dependence on humans (the bishops) to provide what only the mediation of Christ our High Priest can provide. Humans were usurping God's role in order to preserve the momentum and fruits of religious tradition. Each step may have seemed right at the time, but the

---

[26] See Neil McLynn, *Ambrose of Milan: Church and Court in a Christian Capital* (Berkley, CA: University of California Press, 1994) and Collin Garbarino, "Resurrecting the Martys: The Role of the Cult of the Saints, A.D. 370–430" (Ph.D. diss. Louisiana State University, 2010), 82–103.

Ambrose never specifically outlines his strategy on the incorporation of the saints and martyrs in an extant work, but his use of their earned authority on his side of arguments show up in several places in his other works. Examples include: *De fide ad Gratianum Augustum* (*On the Faith to Gratias Augustus*), 2.24, 3.128 and *De Bono Mortis* (*On Death as a Good*), 3.8.

collective distance between the simplicity of the thief receiving Christ on the cross and the multitude of structures of the system of grace built up within the Christian tradition by late antiquity (about the fifth century A.D.) is almost unbelievable. The difference and the distance between the writings of the apostles and the practices of the church grew so great that the apostles would hardly recognize their teachings within the structures.

Reverence and Sacerdotalism

Just as the bias toward rigorous Christian living turned into a patronage system of merit and saints, pagan influences were clearly part of the pressure toward objective holiness and sacerdotalism. Edward Gibbon in *The History of the Decline and Fall of the Roman Empire*, chapter 15, argued that Christianity, on account of passivism, was a major cause in destroying the classical world. I would suggest that the inverse may actually have been closer to the truth. The classical world may have nearly destroyed Christianity by the pagan influences that came into the church in the push for an objective holiness.

Reverence is a good thing, called for in numerous biblical texts, but there is something in human nature that wants to push reverence for a person, place, or thing that has been set aside for a holy use into revering, or even adoring the person, place, or thing. This is what I call objective holiness, which is so apparent in the saints, relics, and icons of late antiquity and in the Middle Ages. It was also applied to what is now called the sacraments of the church. In the early church, there were only two or three sacraments: baptism, the Eucharist, and probably penance, depending on the definition of sacrament being used. The next two sections of this paper will show how baptism and the Eucharist became the focal points of pressure toward an objective holiness that resulted in securing the control of the distribution of salvation into the hands of the bishops in the Christian sacramental system. The last section will show how it has stayed this way.

Baptism

This pressure toward objective holiness is obvious when we look at the dynamics of Christian initiation or baptism as it developed through the early centuries of the church.[27] In the earliest extant Christian writ-

---

[27] For recent overviews of the development of baptism in the Early Church, see Max Johnson, *The Rites of Christian Initiation: Their Evolution and Interpretation, Revised and Expanded Edition* (Collegeville, MA: Liturgical, 2007); Max Johnson, "Christian Initiation," *The Oxford Handbook of Early Christian Studies*, ed. Susan Ashbrook Harvey and David G. Hunter (Oxford: University Press, 2008), 693–710.

ings discussing baptism after the New Testament, namely the *Didache* and Justin Martyr, there is a reflection of the New Testament understanding of baptism being by immersion. Justin does more than just describe the physical mechanics of baptism. He goes into an understanding of the theology of baptism, identifying two major meanings. Baptism is about the forgiveness of past sins and it is about the regeneration of the new birth, or as he terms it in *First Apology*, chapter 61, in his description and his understanding of the baptism, "intellectual illumination." These two aspects of baptism, as illustrated by Justin, are extremely important.

The idea of guilt being washed away from past sins and the idea of illumination or regeneration are both clearly found in the New Testament. Passages like Mark 16:16 and Acts 22:16 talk about forgiveness and the resulting salvation. Romans 6 and numerous other passages talk about regeneration, the baptism of regeneration into Christ's death, and living a new life with Him. It is clear, then, that in the early church there is a two-part theological understanding of what baptism represents: the forgiveness of sins and the regeneration of the life by the Spirit. But the practice of baptism changes rapidly. It does not remain what we find in the New Testament or in Justin Martyr. The timing of baptism changes in two ways. First, there are those who argue that since baptism should be primarily for the forgiveness of past sins, then baptism should be put off until all sins have been committed. And if baptism and the forgiveness of sin assures salvation up to that point, why not be baptized on your death bed to ensure you are saved from all the sins you have committed in your life? This end-of-life baptism was practiced, as mentioned before, by emperors and many others. Given the beliefs about salvation, it made sense.

The second temporal extreme for baptism takes us to the very beginning of life. If baptism insures salvation, then we should get this salvation as soon as possible. Do not tempt fate by trying to live your whole life, facing the possibility of an accidental death or a sickness that may take you so quickly that you would not have time to arrange a baptism. So the safest time to be baptized, this argument suggests, is at the beginning of life, at birth. Baptism at birth makes regeneration and newness of life somewhat pointless. The same can be said for baptism at the end of life. There is no life left to live a new life. The focus of baptism in both these extremes has dwindled to only the securing of salvation. Baptism, under these circumstances, becomes the ritual means of insuring salvation rather than being a symbol of that which has taken place in the life of the person. It becomes the thing rather than symbolizing the thing; an objective holiness which is automatic, a holiness that is secure and unambiguous. In this stark understanding, baptism is very similar to the conceptualization of appeasing God through a ritual rather than having a relationship with God and the ritual symbolizing that relationship.

Ramsay MacMullen, who has done much study on paganism within the Roman Empire, considers the conversion of Augustine probably the single most famous Christian conversion after that of the Apostle Paul. In his chapter, "How Complete was Conversion,"[28] illustrating the understanding of Christian dynamics that were related to paganism, MacMullen concludes that Augustine's conversion is essentially pagan in its understanding. The circumstances under which Augustine describes the situation of his actual point of conversion being closer to pagan divination than to Christian revelation: the random thumbing through a text and the prattle of a child's voice. We tend to think that God can use anything in His favor, but MacMullen suggests that divination was the methodology that Augustine celebrates as his conversion and points out that Augustine is still essentially pagan in mindset.

In his next chapter, "Conversion by Coercion,"[29] MacMullen discusses the extended anecdotes entitled *The Life of Porphyry* purported to be written about an otherwise unknown bishop in Gaza around 390 A.D. Whereas it is not clear whether Porphyry or such a person ever existed, the descriptions are no doubt useful in pointing out the changing understanding of Christian initiation. Included in this work is a call by Porphyry for the use of troops to convert his pagan population into a Christian population. There is even the description of the use of force and coercion that sounds very much like torture used to convince people to convert to Christianity from paganism. The end result of almost all the anecdotes, whether anecdotes of miracles or of coercion, seems to be the same: many pagans chose to recognize "the God of the Christians" and were hustled off to be baptized. Baptism would not mean anything in a circumstance like this, unless it was understood that baptism was both the forgiveness of sins and the giving of salvation. Such is the description of conversions in this possibly fictive book purporting to be from the late fourth century. Clearly, for at least some Christians, the focus of baptism moves from a combination of forgiveness and illumination or regeneration leading toward eternal life to an understanding of baptism which itself provides forgiveness and eternal life. The focus of baptism, whether of infants or of the dying, becomes an objective ritual viewed as effective for forgiveness and salvation. It is no longer a sym-

---

[28] Ramsey MacMullen, *Christianizing the Roman Empire: A.D. 100–400* (New Haven, CT: Yale University Press, 1984), 74–85.

[29] Ibid., 86–101.

bol of a reality; it has become the reality.

Eucharist, Priesthood, and Sanctuary

The Eucharist, as it developed along with the priesthood, moved from the idea of reverence and objective holiness, based on the use of Old Testament sacrificial typology and terminology, toward a mystagogical understanding of the Eucharist, priesthood, and sanctuary. The first step in this development was the understanding of the universal sacrifice in Malachi 1:11 in the writings of Justin Martyr, specifically in his *Dialogue with Trypho*, 41,117. He argues, based on Malachi's prophecy, that Judaism was to bring about universal salvation and draw all nations to God, but that this never happened until the Christian church came on the scene as the New Israel. It is through Christianity, comprised of all the nations, that this universal sacrifice is to be found. According to Justin, this typological application of the universal sacrifices is fulfilled in the Eucharist as a sacrifice of praise offered in all cities of the earth, i.e. the Roman world. While it is true that Justin couches his equation of the Eucharist as a sacrifice in the context of a remembrance of Jesus, his cultic terminology and typology opens the way for conceptualizing the Eucharist as a sacrifice itself. And, of course, a sacrifice requires a priesthood and a sanctuary. More and more, with application of Old Testament sacrifice typology of the Eucharist, the ministry, i.e. the bishops and the presbyters in the church, were beginning to be viewed not primarily as a ministry but as priests functioning within a sanctuary. The church buildings themselves were built and viewed as sanctuaries with altars, as places of sacrifice.[30]

In Cyprian's time, the middle of the third century, we find typological application of the bishops being equated with the high priests and the presbyters being equated with the priests.[31] That which they were offering as the sacrifice was no longer the praise associated with the name of the Eucharist, but the elements of the Eucharist themselves. Just as the sacrifices of the Old Testament provided the atonement to the supplicant, these sacrifices offered by the Christian priests provided atonement to the communicants. This universal sacrifice offered in all the nations is now offering salvation to the individuals in the church.

A particular priesthood making propitiation well suited the needs of Cyprian as he faced the confusion left after the Decian persecution. The particular priesthood was exclusive, fitting his vision that only the bish-

---

[30] See John W. Reeve, "The Presbyter: Jewish Elder to Christian Priest" (M.A. thesis, Andrews University, 1997).

[31] Ibid. 18–25; 63–80. See esp. Cyprian, *Epistle* 3.1.1.

ops can forgive sins. This control over salvation through giving or withholding the Eucharist by the bishops develops into the understanding of what it means for the church to have the keys to the kingdom, a misappropriation of Matthew 16:18–19.[32] What follows is the development of the Eucharist, priesthood, sanctuary, and the elements within the sanctuary such as the altar, etc., into more and more revered terminology. This is the development of sacerdotalism.

So from Cyprian and his exclusive forgiveness, we move to Ambrose of Milan and what has come to be known as his mystagogical preaching. Concerning the ordinary bread and the wine and their transfiguration, Ambrose, bishop of Milan at the end of the fourth century, says that consecration changes nature. Thus, we see the beginning of the movement toward transubstantiation and a mass. Henry Chadwick, in his chapter on Ambrose of Milan in his *magnum opus* on the early church, summarizes the message of Ambrose and his mystagogical preaching as such: "The catechetical lectures on the sacraments and on the mysteries are shot through with awe at the word of Christ in the institution of the daily sacrifice, bringing divine transfiguration of ordinary leavened bread to be in faith Christ's body and blood."[33] But even Ambrose, who certainly helped develop a more objective holiness and a mystagogical understanding of things ecclesiastical, occasionally put on the brakes. In his *Hexameron* and his *Instruction to the Virgins* regarding the increasing glorification of Mary, Ambrose insisted that "one remember that Mary was God's temple not the God of the temple. She is to be held in high honor but not to be worshiped as divine." Chadwick then comments that the need for such a warning was instructive.[34]

There was a constant pressure to make things more holy: to make Mary more holy, to make the saints more holy, to make the Eucharist more holy, to make the priesthood more holy, to make the sanctuary and the altar table more holy. Another case in point, in the generation concurrent with Ambrose of Milan, is Gregory of Nyssa's Epiphany sermon on the baptism of Christ. While describing the transforming power of God in regard to the altar table, Gregory inadvertently describes a late fourth century conception of the Christian priesthood and sacrifice:

> For this holy altar, too, by which I stand, is stone, ordinary in its nature, nowise different from the other slabs of stone that build

---

[32] See Cyprian, *On the Unity of the Church*, 4–5.

[33] Henry Chadwick, *The Church in Ancient Society: From Galilee to Gregory the Great* (New York: Oxford, 2003), 348–378.

[34] Ibid.

our houses and adorn our pavements; but seeing that it was consecrated to the service of God, and received the benediction, it is a holy table, an altar undefiled, no longer touched by the hands of all, but of the priests alone, and that with reverence. The bread again is at first common bread, but when the sacramental action consecrates it, it is called, and becomes, the Body of Christ. So with the sacramental oil; so with the wine: though before the benediction they are of little value, each of them, after the sanctification bestowed by the Spirit, has its several operation [sic]. The same power of the word, again, also makes the priest venerable and honourable, separated, by the new blessing bestowed upon him, from his community with the mass of men. While but yesterday he was one of the mass, one of the people, he is suddenly rendered a guide, a president, a teacher of righteousness, an instructor in hidden mysteries; and this he does without being at all changed in body or form; but, while continuing to be in all appearance the man he was before, being, by some unseen power and grace, transformed in respect of his unseen soul to the higher condition.[35]

John Chrysostom, in the next generation, while he was still a presbyter in Antioch before becoming the bishop of Constantinople, wrote a series of six books on the priesthood. As the rhetorical master of his age, he gets carried away in showing the absolute difference of nature between those who have been ordained as priest and those who remain still sheep. He says, "Let the difference between shepherd and sheep be as great as the distinction between rational and irrational preachers, not to say even more, since matters of much greater moment are at stake."[36] And commenting on the glory of the priesthood he says, "When you see the Lord sacrificed and lying before you and the high priest standing over the sacrifice and praying and all who partake being tinctured by the precious blood, can you think that you are among men and still standing on earth? Are you not at once transported to heaven?"[37] And further he speaks of the priest as holding God in his hands in the elements representing Jesus Christ, "He who sits above with the Father is at that moment held in our hands."[38]

---

[35] Gregory of Nyssa, *On the Baptism of Christ*, NPNF, 5:519.

[36] John Chrysostom, *De Sacerdotio* (*On the Priesthood*), 2.2 in Graham Neville, *St. John Chrysostom: Six Books on the Priesthood* (New York: St Vladimir's Seminary Press, 1984), 54.

[37] Ibid., 70–71.

[38] Ibid., 73.

And again in speaking of the Holy Spirit, contrasting the physical fire that Elijah brought down in front of the vast crowd standing before the sacrifice and the stone altar, he talks of the "much greater thing that is happening in our present rites when you see not only marvelous things but things that transcend all terror. The priest stands, bringing down not fire, but the Holy Spirit. He offers prayer at length, not that some flame lit from above may consume the offerings, but that grace may fall on the sacrifice through that prayer, set alight the souls of all and make them appear brighter than silver, refined by fire."[39] And yet again, with another rhetorical flourish, illustrating that the Eucharist, which the priests handle and hand out, is the greatest way to understand the reception of salvation on the part of people, he says, "And all these things can happen through no other agency except their sacred hands, the priests I mean. How can anyone without their help escape the fire of gehenna or win his appointed crown?"[40] It may be that Chrysostom is using these statements as rhetorical flourish, pushing the understanding of the awesomeness of the ritual of the Eucharist, and could be understood as overstating the case for persuasive rhetorical reasons. But these types of quotes from Ambrose, Gregory of Nyssa, and John Chrysostom became the quotes that are used as normative during the Middle Ages to denote the objective holiness of priesthood and Eucharist, the handling of God by priests, and the control of salvation by the hierarchy of the church.

In summarizing Chrysostom's emphasis of the awe-inspiring nature of the priest's duties at the Eucharist, Frances Young suggests that "Christian worship, it appears, was increasingly assimilating the religious features of a dying paganism."[41] She argues that whereas it was almost inevitable that the Christian ministry should take the projection of the Old Testament models of kingship and priesthood, but in so doing Christianity also adopted the pagan understanding of sacrifice and worship.[42] It may have been that this generation in the later part of the fourth century and the first part of the fifth was using rhetorical flourishes of arguing, in very mystical terms, the awesome holiness of the priesthood and of the Eucharist in order to combat the continual attraction of paganism. However, as it turned out, they adopted much of the pagan understanding of sacrifice that they were trying to combat. Reverence is good, but wor-

---

[39] Ibid.

[40] Ibid.

[41] Frances Young, "The Ministerial Forms and Functions in the Church Communities of the Greek Fathers," *Community Formation in the Early Church and in the Church Today*, ed. Richard N. Longenecker (Peabody, MA: Hendrickson, 2002), 173.

[42] Ibid., 174.

ship belongs only to God. Reverence of people, places, and things set aside for holy purposes was pushed to extreme, usurping the honor due only to God. This pressure to view things with a more and more heightened sense of holiness certainly backfired in the early church.

The Staying Force of Religious Tradition

This section need not be long as the dynamics have been pointed out throughout this paper. Three additional illustrations will demonstrate the constant force toward maintaining tradition. First, a reading of church orders followed by an interpretation of the age of the church as presented by Augustine in his *City of God*. Finally, the attitude toward the relationship between Scripture, tradition and truth represented in the Papal encyclical "*Fides et ratio*," released in 1998 shows the continuation of this momentum of tradition into the present.

The church orders, starting with the *Didache* in the first half of the second century and progressing through the *Didascalia Apostolorum*, an early third-century Syrian text; the so-called *Apostolic Traditions*, a work with its beginnings in third-century Rome and/or Egypt;[43] the *Canons of Hippolytus*; the *Apostolic Constitutions*, a late fourth-century text; and various Acts and Canons all purport to record the original instructions of how to run the church and its services as given from Jesus Christ to His apostles. Every one of them contains new information, new practices, and changes to old practices, but report everything to be the original, unchanged tradition. "The more things change the more they claim to be the same." That seems to be the dictum of change within a conservative religious setting. This allows change, without the evaluation of what has come before. In such a setting, there is no room to ask where tradition went wrong. To make matters worse, the appeal to tradition is considered safe from error. This is forcefully claimed by Irenaeus in his battle against the new gnostic systems. An appeal to tradition is both the making and breaking of Origen, whose *On First Principles* was originally viewed as a reservoir of ancient tradition until, 150 years after his death, it was condemned along with its author as an originator of new errors outside tradition. Augustine, in his *City of God*, gives a historical summary of the church and its enemies that progresses into a then-current summary of the church tradition and into a view of the triumphal future of the church. As part of this view of church tradition as the guarantee of safety, a tradition with a secure future, he suggests that Satan cannot tempt the Church to err. Augustine's argu-

---

[43] See discussion in Max Johnson, "Christian Initiation," *The Oxford Handbook of Early Christian Studies*, ed. Susan Ashbrook Harvey and David G. Hunter (Oxford: University Press, 2008), chapter 34.

ment, which he undertakes while interpreting the 1000 years of Revelation 20:2ff in *City of God* 20.7, is that the binding of Satan and his inability to tempt the nations was to be understood as God binding Satan from being able to attack the church (the church universal comprising all nations). Augustine draws the conclusion that since Satan is bound during the age of the Church, the Church cannot err. This sums up the prevailing attitude of most church leaders throughout the history of the church: the tradition is where the safety against current attacks on truth resides. Unfortunately, unless you think you might be wrong, you will never inspect the very roots of tradition and consequently the ancient errors are secure.

Even in our own time, the momentum of tradition over Scripture as the safeguard of truth continues. Note the interplay between Scripture, philosophy, and church tradition in chapter five of "*Fides et ratio*" by Pope John Paul II:

> There are also signs of a resurgence of *fideism*, which fails to recognize the importance of rational knowledge and philosophical discourse for the understanding of faith, indeed for the very possibility of belief in God. One currently widespread symptom of this fideistic tendency is a "biblicism" which tends to make the reading and exegesis of Sacred Scripture the sole criterion of truth. In consequence, the word of God is identified with Sacred Scripture alone, thus eliminating the doctrine of the Church which the Second Vatican Council stressed quite specifically. Having recalled that the word of God is present in both Scripture and Tradition, the Constitution *Dei Verbum* continues emphatically: "Sacred Tradition and Sacred Scripture comprise a single sacred deposit of the word of God entrusted to the Church. Embracing this deposit and united with their pastors, the People of God remain always faithful to the teaching of the Apostles." Scripture, therefore, is not the Church's sole point of reference. The "supreme rule of her faith" derives from the unity which the Spirit has created between Sacred Tradition, Sacred Scripture and the Magisterium of the Church in a reciprocity which means that none of the three can survive without the others.[44]

---

[44] Pope John Paul II, "*Fides et ratio*" (Vatican Encyclical, 1998), 5.55.3 of the English Version. http://www.vatican.va/holy_father/john_paul_ii/encyclicals/documents/hf_jp-ii_enc_15101998_fides-et-ratio_en.html. (accessed April 24, 2012)

Conclusion

There is no doubt that from the perspective of a Seventh-day Adventist, the Christian tradition handed down from Late Antiquity and the Middle Ages contains errors so integral to the core of soteriology that nearly the whole sacramental system needs to be uprooted and reconfigured—precisely what the Protestant reformation attempted. This study clearly identifies the perceived forces that contributed to the development of the faulty system and follows that development in summary form. It includes ecclesiological ramifications that point to the dangers of assigning too much of God's work into human, institutional hands. It suggests that the force of religious conservation of belief and practice needs to be constantly open to the corrective and enhancing light of Scripture. It suggests that we should be cautious in judging those from the past who are faced with their own set of circumstances. We can critique faulty actions, decisions, and beliefs, but not motives.

CHAPTER 9

THE SIXTEENTH CENTURY PROTESTANT REFORMATION AND ADVENTIST ECCLESIOLOGY

Darius Jankiewieck

For the early Seventh-day Adventist pioneers, the years immediately following the Great Disappointment on October 22, 1844 were marked by vigorous and intense theological activity. The most important item on the agenda, of course, was the explanation of the Great Disappointment itself. Other doctrinal breakthroughs, such as the Sabbath and the state of the dead, soon followed. Conspicuously absent from the theological agenda of these early pioneers was discussion concerning the church. With the passing of years marked by an increasing doctrinal maturity, the attention of the pioneers turned toward the mission and protection of the newly fledged community. This new emphasis spawned the need for an efficient organization that could oversee missionary activity as well as shield the church from any illicit activity on the part of troublesome individuals. Thus, in 1863, despite vigorous opposition, the leaders of the movement decided to establish a formal organization. It appears, however, that the search for an appropriate organizational structure did not happen in a vacuum. In the manner of the primitive church, which viewed the leadership system already present within the synagogue as best suited to fulfill the mission of the Christian community, the early Adventist pioneers must have examined various organizational options available within the existing Christian denominations.

Naturally, any attempt at forming a religious organization must presuppose a reflection on the nature, purpose, and theology of the community. Such presuppositions must have guided the Adventist pioneers in forming an organizational structure that would both serve the needs of the young denomination and conform to its theology. This theology, while unique and fresh, finds its roots in the teachings of the 16th century Protestant Reformation.

It is the purpose of this paper, first, to briefly explore the Medieval Catholic ecclesiology that forms the background of the Protestant Reformation. Second, it will explore the ecclesiology of the Lutheran, the Reformed, and the Radical branches of the Reformation respectively. Finally, it will relate these findings to modern Adventist ecclesiology.

The Medieval Ecclesiology of the Catholic Church

It is evident that post-biblical ecclesiology has developed as a corollary to Christian soteriology. Consequently, it is expected that a well-thought-through ecclesiology should go hand in hand with a given soteriology. It follows that a challenge to soteriology will be accompanied by an inevitable re-evaluation of the ecclesiology that goes with it. It comes as no surprise, therefore, that while primarily driven by soteriological concerns, the 16th century Reformation was also forced to respond to medieval Catholic ecclesiology, a daunting task considering that Catholic ecclesiology had few rivals in Western Christianity at the time.

The medieval Catholic Church inherited a nearly complete ecclesiological system from the Patristic era,[1] which tended to conceive the church primarily in terms of a visible, hierarchically structured reality, organized around its bishop and his ministry.[2] The chief purpose of the church was to mediate the benefits of Christ's sacrifice to the individual members.[3] The most important pre-condition for this mediation to take place was the presence of the episcopally ordained priesthood that had to be historically linked with the New Testament church.[4] Thus the episcopally ordained ministry was considered as indispensable, not only for the essence and identity of the church but also for the salvation of its members.

While the organizational aspects of the Catholic Church were certainly soteriologically fine-tuned, this was even more evident in the area of sacramental theology. Through various medieval controversies, sacramental theology was developed and refined. By the time the scholastic

---

[1] Bernard J. Otten, *A Manual of the History of Dogmas: The Development of Dogmas During the Middle Ages* (St. Louis, MO: B. Herder Book, 1918), 214.

[2] Yves Congar, *Lay People in the Church* (Westminster, MD: Newman, 1967), 37–38; cf. Hans Küng, *The Church* (New York: Sheed and Ward, 1967), 9–10, and Bernard Cooke, *Ministry to Word and Sacraments* (Philadelphia, PA: Fortress, 1976), 113.

[3] Congar, *Lay* 113.

[4] Cooke, *Ministry*, 258–260.

era ended, it presented the bulwark against any new theological innovations.[5] It was during medieval times that the sacraments received their final and authoritative definition and their number was limited to seven.[6] Aided by the newly rediscovered Aristotelian philosophy, the medieval theologians were able to work out the mechanism of sacramental efficacy, explaining how sacraments convey upon the believer a special seal that allows them to receive God's grace.[7] Like the presence of an episcopally ordained ministry, the sacraments were considered to be absolutely necessary for salvation.

Medieval theologians saw the church as the divinely appointed instrument of peace on earth, necessary for human beings if they were to prepare for heaven,[8] outside of which there was no possibility for the forgiveness of sins or for true sacraments—in short, no possibility of salvation.[9] This exclusive identification of the visible church with the kingdom of God made the spiritual life of believers completely dependent upon the mediation of the church. Separating oneself from this one true visible church on earth, was a development of catastrophic proportions, as it automatically meant exclusion from salvation.

The Lutheran Reformation

While a challenge to the soteriological conventions of medieval Catholicism was at the heart of the Lutheran Reformation,[10] the inevitable challenge to medieval ecclesiology had to necessarily follow. Thus, while Luther's early years as the Protestant Reformer were primarily dedicated to fighting the obvious soteriological abuses perpetrated by medieval Catholicism, it soon became apparent that he also needed to address issues such as the nature and identity of God's church.[11]

---

[5] For a detailed description of some of these controversies, see Justo González, *A History of Christian Thought: From Augustine to the Eve of the Reformation* (Nashville, TN: Abingdon Press, 1987), 1:119–123.

[6] Jaroslav Pelikan, *The Christian Tradition: A History of the Development of Doctrine: The Growth of Medieval Theology (600–1300)* (Chicago, IL: University of Chicago Press, 1978), 3:210.

[7] This continues to be the official position of the Roman Catholic Church. Joseph Pohle states, for example, that "the justification of the sinner . . . is ordinarily not a purely internal and invisible process or series of acts, but requires the instrumentality of external visible signs instituted by Jesus Christ, which either confer grace or augment it. Such visible means of grace are called Sacraments" (*The Sacraments: A Dogmatic Treatise* [Saint Louis, MO: Herder, 1915], 1:1).

[8] Ian McNeill, "Attitudes to Authority in the Medieval Centuries," *Problem of Authority*, ed. John M. Todd (Baltimore, MD: Helicon, 1962), 159; cf. Cyprian, *De Unitate Ecclesiae* 6, ANF 5:423.

[9] Cyprian *Epistle* 72.21, ANF 5:384.

[10] Otto W. Heick, *A History of Christian Thought* (Philadelphia, PA: Fortress, 1973), 318.

[11] Bernard Lohse, *Luther* (Edinburgh: T & T Clark, 1986), 177.

Nature of the Church

Luther addressed some of these issues in one of his earliest works, *On the Papacy in Rome* (1520). He posited the existence of the oft-mentioned distinction between the "two Christendoms:"[12] the "true," inner one and the "man-made and external."[13] This true or "essential Christendom," he believed, was not visible to the human eye because only God knows who belongs to it. This is the genuine church that has its origins with God. On the other hand, Luther believed that there is also another church, the visible one. Luther's purpose was not to juxtapose two separate "churches," but to pose a challenge to medieval thinking, which identified the kingdom of God with the visible forms of the hierarchical church, giving it a divine sanction.[14] To this, Luther emphatically asserted that the institutional church of his day was too corrupt to be identified with the kingdom of God.[15] Through his distinction between the visible and invisible church, Luther intended to highlight Christianity's need to find a firmer foundation for their faith and salvation than a mere trust in the earthly institution.[16]

Despite his criticism of the 16th century visible, institutional church, Luther nevertheless recognized the need for the objective, real presence of the visible church on earth.[17] But having argued that the true visible church of God was not found in the structures of Catholicism of his day, Luther was ultimately forced to define what it was and where it can be found. So, what is the "church" in Luther's opinion?

In contrast to the prevalent institutionalism of his day,[18] Luther tended to consistently refer to the true church of God as the "congregation of believers," "spiritual assembly," "assembly of saints," "communion of

---

[12] Eric W. Gritsch, "Introduction to Volume 39," *Luther's Works*, ed. Eric W. Gritsch (Philadelphia, PA: Fortress, 1970), 39:xiii.

[13] Martin Luther, "On the Papacy in Rome," *Luther's Works*, 39:70.

[14] Cf. Augustine, *The City of God Against the Pagans* (Cambridge, MA: Cambridge University Press, 1998), 982; cf. John F. Walvoord, *The Millenial Kingdom* (Grand Rapids, MI: Zondervan, 1983), 49; and Carl E. Braaten, "The Kingdom of God and Life Everlasting," *Christian Theology: An Introduction to Its Traditions and Tasks*, ed. Peter Crafts Hodgson and Robert Harlen King (Philadelphia, PA: Fortress, 1994), 336.

[15] Martin Luther, "On the Papacy in Rome," *Luther's Works*, 39:70: cf. Millard Erickson, *Christian Theology* (Grand Rapids, MI: Baker, 1985), 1044; G. C. Berkouwer, *The Church* (Grand Rapids, MI: Eerdmans, 1976), 37.

[16] Berkouwer, *Church*, 38.

[17] Paul Althaus, *The Theology of Martin Luther* (Philadelphia, PA: Fortress, 1966), 288.

[18] Ibid.

saints," "community of holy people," or "holy believers."[19] The church was no longer conceived as the depository of God's blessings, but rather as a gathering of people who had *already* been blessed and justified by God's grace. This was a momentous paradigm shift that constituted one of the main points of difference between Protestantism and Roman Catholicism at the time. But how was such an assembly to be recognized?

In his early writings, Luther argued that the presence of the true church of God could be discerned by three marks: the preaching of the gospel, baptism, and the Lord's Supper. These, he wrote, "are the signs by which the existence of the church in the world can be noticed externally."[20] The Augsburg Confession of 1530, written by Melanchthon and approved by Luther, struck a similar note when it stated, "The Church properly is the congregation of saints, in which the Gospel is rightly taught and the Sacraments rightly administered."[21]

His later writings expanded on the *notae ecclesiae* found in his earlier writings.[22] As in the early years, the Word of God continued to hold preeminence. "First," Luther wrote, "the holy Christian people are recognized by their possession of the holy word [sic] of God.... Now, wherever you hear or see this word preached, believed, professed, and lived, do not doubt that the true *ecclesia sancta catholica*, 'a Christian holy people' must be there, even though their number is very small."[23] Thus, the true church exists only where the Scripture holds a primary place, "for since the church owes its birth to the word, is nourished, aided and strengthened by it, it is obvious that it cannot be without the word."[24] This, he contended, was no longer true of the Catholicism of his day, where the emphasis upon human additions replaced the primacy of the Scripture.[25] Second, God's holy people are recognized as possessing the sacrament of baptism, "wherever it is taught, believed, and administered according to

---

[19] Such wording is also found in one of the earliest Lutheran definitions of the church found in the *Augsburg Confession*. Written by Melanchthon, it was certainly written with Luther's consent.

[20] Luther, "On the Papacy in Rome," *Luther's Works*, 39:75.

[21] *Augsburg Confession* 7 (Philadelphia, PA: United Lutheran Publication House, 1913), 10. Cf. Martin Luther, *Sermons on the Catechism in Martin Luther: Selections from His Writings*, ed. John Dillenberger (New York: Anchor, 1961), 212–213, where Luther defines the church as the gathering where the gospel is preached and the sacraments are administered.

[22] Luther, "On the Councils and the Church," *Luther's Works*, 41:143–167 and, idem., "Against Hanswurst," *Luther's Works*, 41:194–198.

[23] Luther, "On the Councils and the Church," *Luther's Works*, 41:148, 150.

[24] Luther, "Concerning the Ministry," *Luther's Works*, 40:37.

[25] Thus Luther writes: "Some possess the word in its complete purity, others do not." Luther, "On the Councils and the Church," *Luther's Works*, 41:148–149; cf. Bernhard Lohse, *Martin Luther's Theology: Its Historical and Systematic Development* (Minneapolis, MN: Fortress, 1999), 285.

Christ's ordinance." Next, God's people may be recognized "by the holy sacrament of the altar, wherever it is rightly administered, believed, and received, according to Christ's institution."[26] What, by the standards of the 16th century, made Luther's theology most controversial, however, was the fourth mark, namely, "the power of the keys." This mark of the visible church flowed from Luther's most important principle that put him on a collision course with Rome right from the outset of his ministry, namely, "the priesthood of all believers."[27] Building his argument on Matthew 18:15–20 and 1 Peter 2:9, Luther maintained that all true Christians share a common priesthood and are called to use the "office of the keys," which is the ministry of reproving, forgiveness, reconciliation, and salvation. These keys, Luther proclaimed emphatically, "are the pope's as little as baptism, the sacrament, and the word of God are, for they belong to the people of Christ and are called 'the church's keys' not 'the pope's keys.'"[28] It is the entire church, he argued, that has been called to the gospel ministry. There is no ontological difference between "layman and priest, princes and bishops, between religious and secular, except for the sake of office and work, but for the sake of status . . . all are truly priests, bishops, and popes."[29] Did that mean, however, that the church was supposed to be devoid of duly constituted ministry?

Leadership of the Church

Despite his enthusiastic endorsement of the idea of the "priesthood of all believers," Luther clearly saw a need for ordained ministry in the church and, in his later years, provided guidance for the selection of church leadership. For the church to function according to Christ's design, he believed, the church's membership must include those who would "publicly and privately give, administer and use . . . [the] holy possessions, viz. Word, baptism, sacrament of the altar, keys, in behalf of and in the name of the Church."[30] Luther's injunction, however, goes beyond the desire for order in the church, as argued by the radical followers of

---

[26] Luther, "On the Councils and the Church," *Luther's Works*, 41:152.

[27] This principle is also built upon some strands of medieval thought where it was emphasized that all the baptized believers share in the priestly office of Jesus Christ. Wolfhart Pannenberg, *Systematic Theology* (Grand Rapids, MI: Eerdmans, 1997), 3:373.

[28] Luther, "On the Councils and the Church," *Luther's Works*, 41:154. In another place, he proclaimed that "the keys of the pope are not keys but husks and shells of the keys" (Luther, "The Keys," *Luther's Works*, 40:349).

[29] Luther, "To the Christian Nobility," *Luther's Works*, 44:127; cf. Alister McGrath, *Reformation Thought* (Oxford: Blackwell, 2000), 203–204.

[30] Luther, "On the Councils and the Church," *Luther's Works*, 41:154.

the Reformation.[31] The ministry was necessary, as it existed *jure divino* and, as such, functioned as another mark by which the true church of God might be recognized in the world.[32]

Sacramental Theology and the Church for Salvation

Notwithstanding his critique of the prevalent ecclesiology of his day, Luther struggled to move beyond the conventions of Catholic medievalism in some ways. A careful perusal of his writings dealing with sacramental theology reveals a surprising, if not disconcerting, tension between his emphasis on justification by faith alone and the role the sacraments play in the life of a believer. This has not been unnoticed by some students of Luther who argue that, in essence, Luther's sacramental theology did not differ much from the Catholic view.[33]

While in his early writings Luther tended to emphasize the believer's faith as central to salvation,[34] the mature Luther repeatedly underscored the necessity of sacraments in the life of a believer,[35] as they—the sacraments of baptism and the Eucharist[36]—represented the promises of God mediated through material objects of everyday use.[37] Ideally, the Word of God and its promises should come to believers through Jesus Christ, the Scripture, and the preaching of the gospel.[38] Because of human sinfulness and a reluctance to accept God's promises, preaching needed to be supplemented by the external signs of God's favor, whose purpose was to enhance the believer's trust in God. Thus, while closely related to faith, sacraments functioned as another form in which the Word was heard in faith.[39] While Luther strongly affirmed the idea that salvation was through

---

[31] James F. White, *Protestant Worship: Traditions in Transition* (Louisville, KY: Westminster John Knox, 2006), 41.

[32] Luther, "On the Councils and the Church," *Luther's Works*, 41:154.

[33] Paul Enns, *Moody Handbook of Theology* (Chicago, IL: Moody, 1989), 453–454; cf. Alister McGrath, *Christian Theology* (Oxford: Blackwell, 2007), 427, and Linwood Urban, *A Short History of Christian Thought* (New York: Oxford University Press, 1995), 293.

[34] Martin Luther, "Concerning Rebaptism," *Luther's Works*, 40:252–253.

[35] E. G. Schwiebert, *Luther and His Times* (Saint Louis, MO: Concordia, 1950), 448.

[36] Early on in his ministry, Luther challenged much of Roman Catholic sacramental theology and concluded that, on the basis of the Scripture, there were only two sacraments: baptism and Eucharist. The church, he believed, had no authority to institute sacraments for which there was no explicit command in the Scriptures. Luther, "The Babylonian Captivity of the Church," *Luther's Works*, 36:93–94.

[37] Luther, "Babylonian Captivity of the Church," *Luther's Works*, 36:63–66.

[38] Justo Gonzales, *A History of Christian Thought: From the Beginnings to the Council of Chalcedon* (Nashville, TN: Abingdon Press, 1987), 3:64.

[39] Ibid.; cf. McGrath, *Christian Theology*, 427.

faith alone and did not depend on human works, he continued to insist that the sacraments were still necessary for salvation.[40]

With his Catholic opponents, Luther agreed that a person becomes a Christian and enters the church through baptism.[41] At the same time, he rejected the Catholic teaching that it created a permanent seal or conferred a permanent character upon the soul of a believer. This did not mean that nothing happened during the rite. While baptism was unbreakably bound with faith, the centerpiece of Luther's soteriology, it was also the means through which "the Holy Trinity recreated the natural man's soul."[42] Moreover, the water used in baptism became, through the words of consecration, "godly, blessed, fruitful water full of grace."[43] For Luther, therefore, the regeneration that came with baptism eventually became essential for salvation.[44] Faith did not necessarily need to precede baptism. Instead, baptism was the initiative of God, who bestowed His faith upon those who believe.[45] This explains why Luther stringently opposed the Anabaptist rejection of infant baptism.[46] Denial of such a baptism on the grounds that an infant did not have faith would amount to the negation of the power of baptism and to the affirmation that the sacrament depended on human ability to receive it, thereby implying a new form of justification by works.[47]

With regard to the Lord's Supper, it is well documented that Luther emphatically rejected the Catholic teachings that considered it a sacrifice. He also rejected the medieval notion of transubstantiation and the doctrine of priestly mediation (sacerdotalism).[48] At the same time, he strongly affirmed the traditional Catholic idea that Christ's body and blood are physically present in the elements. Thus, he proposed a theory of the simultaneous presence of both the bread and the wine and the body of

---

[40] Martin Luther, *The Large Catechism* (Minneapolis, MN: Fortress, 1995), 80–86; cf. *idem.*, *Commentary on Galatians* (Grand Rapids, MI: Kregel, 1979), 221–222, where Luther insisted that "baptism is a thing of great force and efficacy;" cf. Schwiebert, *Luther*, 448.

[41] Luther, *The Large Catechism*, 80.

[42] Luther, quoted in Schwiebert, *Luther*, 448.

[43] Ibid., 448–449.

[44] Martin Luther, *Commentary on Peter and Jude* (Grand Rapids, MI: Kregel, 1990), 169; cf. *idem.*, *Commentary on Romans* (Grand Rapids, MI: Zondervan, 1954), 101, and *idem.*, *The Large Catechism*, 86.

[45] Luther, "Concerning Rebaptism," *Luther's Works*, 40:252.

[46] Ibid., 252–253.

[47] Ibid., 252–254.

[48] Urban, *History*, 283–286; cf. Roger Olson, *The Story of Christian Theology* (Downers Grove, IL: InterVarsity, 1999), 391–394, and Schwiebert, *Luther*, 449.

Christ. This view became known as consubstantiation, although Luther never used this term.[49] Through partaking in the Eucharist, Luther maintained, a believer received forgiveness of sins and was given strength to lead a Christian life.[50]

The sacraments, thus, were extremely important for Luther's ecclesiology, as they conveyed God's grace and were constitutive of the church.[51] Through baptism, people were received into the kingdom of God and their faith was initiated; through the Eucharist, their faith was maintained. Thus, it appears that Luther did not intend for the *sola* in *sola fide* to exclude the Word of God as it comes to believers through the sacraments.[52]

Taking into consideration Luther's sacramental theology, it is not surprising to find echoes of the early Catholic belief that outside of the church there is no salvation.[53] One of the most explicit statements on the matter is found in his *Confession Concerning Christ's Supper:* "Outside this Christian Church there is no salvation or forgiveness of sins, but everlasting death and damnation."[54] Being a part of the true church of God on earth, according to Luther, was part of God's grand design for the salvation of humanity.[55] Thus, in spite of his emphasis on the priesthood of all believers, justification by faith, and individual relationship with God, Luther continued to insist on the need for an institutional church, albeit not in the Roman Catholic sense,[56] that would mediate individual

---

[49] Luther used an analogy of a heated iron to illustrate the mystery of the presence of Christ at the Eucharist. When iron is placed in a fire and heated, it glows, and in the glowing iron, both the iron and heat are present ("The Babylonian Captivity of the Church," *Luther's Works*, 36:32, 35).

[50] Luther, *Large Catechism*, 98.

[51] This was clearly understood by Luther's radical critics. Caspar Schwenckfeld, for example, wrote: "I do not know how to agree with Luther [when] he writes that the revered sacrament imparts life, grace, and salvation, yea, that it is a fountain of life and salvation" ("An Answer to Luther's Malediction," *Spiritual and Anabaptist Writers*, ed. George Huntston Williams [Philadelphia, PA: Westminster, 1957], 170).

[52] Jaroslav Pelikan, *The Christian Tradition: A History of the Development of Doctrine: Reformation of Church and Dogma (1300–1700)* (Chicago, IL: University of Chicago Press, 1985), 4:178; cf. Enns, *Handbook*, 452.

[53] This expression can be directly traced to Cyprian of Carthage (d. 258), who also tied it with his sacramental theology. This view was eventually incorporated into Catholic theology.

[54] Martin Luther, "Confession Concerning Christ's Supper," *Luther's Works*, 37:368; cf. Luther, *Large Catechism*, 56–62.

[55] "Sermon, October 5, 1544," *Luther's Works*, 51:337; cf. Martin Luther, "Commentary on Psalm 68," *Luther's Works*, 13:14; cf. Martin Luther, "The Gospel for the Early Christmas Service," *Luther's Works*, 52:39–40 (emphasis mine); cf. *idem.*, "Confession Concerning Christ's Supper," *Luther's Works*, 37:368; cf. Lohse, *Luther's Theology*, 280; and Althaus, *Theology*, 291.

[56] Alister McGrath notes that while Luther and the other Reformers "rejected the definition of the church offered by Catholicism, . . . the magisterial Reformation found itself defending a more

access to the Word of God and regulate the spiritual and moral lives of believers.

The Reformed Tradition

While the Reformed branch of the Reformation traces its beginnings to the teachings of Huldrych Zwingli (1484–1531) and his successor Heinrich Bullinger (1504–1575), it became most closely associated with the Genevan Reformer, John Calvin (1509–1564). The two branches of the 16th century Reformation share much of its theological heritage. All of its leaders committed themselves to the principal teachings of Lutheranism known as the Reformation's *solas*: *sola Scriptura*, *sola fide et gratia*, *solo Christo* and *soli Deo Gloria* as well as the foundational principle of Protestantism: the priesthood of all believers.[57] The differences between the German and the Reformed branches of the Magisterial Reformation were not necessarily theological, but rather in certain emphases they placed upon various aspects of their theology. Consequently, while Luther placed a great emphasis upon the doctrine of justification by faith, John Calvin and his followers tended to emphasize the sovereignty of God.[58] The change in emphasis did, to some extent, influence Calvin's ecclesiology.

Luther Versus Calvin

There are many areas in which Calvin's ecclesiology resembles that of Luther.[59] In agreement with the latter, he made a distinction between the visible and invisible church,[60] defined the church as a "communion of saints,"[61] and enumerated similar marks of the church.[62] He also agreed with Luther that the visible church of God can be found "wherever we see the Word of God purely preached and heard, and the sacraments administered according to Christ's institution."[63] In tune with 16th century mentality, he also concurred with Luther and Zwingli, that the civil government, or the magistrates, must be supportive of Christian endeavors

---

'institutional' definition of the church against their radical opponents" (McGrath, *Reformation Thought*, 198).

[57] G. C. Berkouwer, *Holy Scripture* (Grand Rapids, MI: Eerdmans, 1975), 302–303.

[58] Bruce L. Shelley, *Church History in Plain Language* (Nashville, TN: Thomas Nelson, 1995), 257.

[59] Louis Berkhof, *The History of Christian Doctrines* (London: Banner of Truth, 1937), 237–238.

[60] John Calvin, *Institutes of the Christian Religion*, ed. John T. McNeill (Philadelphia, PA: Westminster, 1960), 2:1021 (iv.i.7).

[61] Ibid., iv.i.3 (2:1014–1016).

[62] Ibid., iv.i.9 (2:1023–1034).

[63] Ibid., (2:1023).

and at times play a decisive role in ecclesiastical affairs.[64] It is from this belief that the Reformation has received the adjective, "Magisterial."

While there was a significant consensus between Calvin and Luther on the essentials of the Reformation's theology, there were some notable differences. Most importantly, Calvin clearly perceived the threat of individualism and looked to provide a theological and practical remedy. He sought to make Geneva a place where Protestant theology could be expressed in the daily life of its citizens.[65] It is not surprising, therefore, that a significant section of the *Institutes* (Book IV) is entirely devoted to ecclesiology.[66]

Predestination and the Visible Church

Differing in emphases from Luther, Calvin placed his doctrine of the church firmly within the framework of predestination.[67] It could be argued, however, that placing the doctrine of the church within the overarching scheme of God's eternal decrees would render the visible church redundant, its structures and ministry unnecessary to those whose fate was sealed by the *a priori* decision of God.[68] Calvin solved the problem by insisting that the existence of the visible church has been decreed by God as the way the elect are saved. It was within the bounds of the visible church that the faith of the believers was to be born, nurtured, and sanctified.[69] Hence, while the membership of the visible church of God on earth consisted of both the elect and the reprobate, this membership was a necessity for the elect.[70]

---

[64] Thanks to Calvin's work, the state-church relationship in the territories influenced by the Reformed churches was much more fine-tuned than in the Lutheran territories. On Calvin and his views regarding the state-church relationship, see the last chapter of the *Institutes* iv.xx (McNeill, 2: 1485–1521).

[65] J. S. Whale, *The Protestant Tradition: An Essay in Interpretation* (Cambridge, MA: Cambridge University Press, 1955), 145; cf. Ronald Bainton, *The Reformation of the Sixteenth Century* (London: Hodder and Stoughton, 1953), 111.

[66] It must be recognized that during Calvin's life, the *Institutes* went through five editions, each adding to the previous one as he attempted to respond to the various controversies that arose during his time in Geneva. Thus there seems to be a distinction between the more idealistic Calvin of the first, 1536, edition of the *Institutes* and the much more realistic Calvin of the subsequent editions (see McGrath, *Historical Theology*, 205). Whale further points out, for example, that while the first edition focuses on the invisible church, the subsequent editions tend to emphasize the visible church and its marks. Whale, *Tradition*, 155–158.

[67] Geddes MacGregor, *Corpus Christi: The Nature of the Church According to the Reformed Tradition* (Philadelphia, PA: Westminster, 1958), 48–49.

[68] Whale, *Tradition*, 145.

[69] Calvin, *Institutes* iv.i.4–7 (McNeill, 2:1016–1022).

[70] Ibid., iv.i5 (2:1017–1018).

The Church as the Means of Salvation

Calvin's predestinarian ecclesiology allowed him to unabashedly designate the church as the means of salvation. It is perhaps for this reason that Calvin is at times referred to as the "Cyprian of the Reformation," for he considered the visible church as the place where the predestination of believers is completed.[71] The elect were gathered in the church, not to abandon it, believing that they were a part of the invisible church. If they did leave the church, it was a sure indication that they were not elected in the first place. For Calvin, there was no salvation outside of the church. Having, in Cyprianic fashion, affirmed the necessity of the visible church at the very outset, Calvin wasted no more time discussing the invisible church and spent the rest of Book IV focusing on the various aspects of the church's visibility.

Ecclesiastical Order and Ministry

Having firmly grounded the visible church's existence in the eternal decrees of God, Calvin proceeded to provide fledgling Protestantism with a structure and an ecclesiastical order. He moved beyond Luther, as the latter was more hesitant in nominating a specific order for the church. Calvin insisted that the ecclesiastical structure he was setting forth in the *Institutes* was not a humanly devised order, but one he believed was directly laid down in the New Testament and thus directly instituted by God.[72] While, for Luther, the organization of the church depended on historical circumstances, Calvin understood it as belonging to the very nature of the church.[73] As in Catholicism, church organization was made to be a matter of doctrine.

Calvin found biblical support for the model he championed in the Pauline metaphor of the church as the "Body of Christ," where Christ functions as the head of the organization in which each member fulfills its God-given task.[74] The church, as an organization, will not function according to God's design, however, unless it is bound "together with a knot that he [Christ] foresaw would be the strongest means of keeping unity."[75] For Calvin, this bond of unity was the ministry of the church. Function-

---

[71] Donald K. McKim, *The Cambridge Companion to John Calvin* (Cambridge, MA: Cambridge University Press, 2004), 87; cf. Calvin, *Institutes* iv.i.4 (McNeill, 2:1016).

[72] Calvin, *Institutes* iv.iii.1 (McNeill, 2:1053).

[73] McGrath, *Reformation Thought*, 210.

[74] Calvin, *Institutes* iv.iii.1 (McNeill, 2:1054).

[75] Ibid., iv.iii.1 (McNeill, 2:1054).

ing as the agents of the church's unity, the ministers "represent [Christ's] person" and distribute "his gifts to the church," the end of their ministry being the renewal of the church.[76] As pastors govern the church, "God himself appears in our midst, and, as Author of this order, would have men recognize him as present in his institution."[77]

At their ordination, pastors received "the power of the keys," which enabled them to serve their congregation in a manner that would "strengthen godly consciences by the gospel promises in the hope of pardon and forgiveness."[78] This was in contrast to Luther, who taught that the "keys" were given to the entire congregation. Reading through the sections of the *Institutes* dealing with church ministry gives the clear impression that Calvin placed the ordained ministry in the church on a higher, almost distinct, level than the remainder of the congregation.[79]

Calvin also provided instructions for the choice and ordination of ministers. Before they are allowed by the congregation to exercise their ministry, they must show evidence of having both an "outer and inner call." They must be selected from among those who "are of sound doctrine and of holy life" by other ordained ministers, "for no one could duly perform this ministry unless he had been called by God."[80] They must first carefully examine the candidates and present them to the people for acceptance.[81] In Calvin, as in Luther, we see the reversal of the Catholic model of ministry and a move towards democracy, although clearly not, as Kenneth Latourette points out, towards equalitarianism.[82] Once approved, the specially gifted male candidates for ministry were to be ordained through the laying on of hands by previously ordained ministers.[83] In contrast to medieval Catholicism, Calvin insisted that ordination binds the pastor to the local church.[84]

Calvin may thus be recognized as the first Christian theologian to establish the representative model of church government, also known as government by presbytery. While the ministry of the church constituted a separate order within the membership of the church, its authority was

---

[76] Ibid., iv.iii.2 (McNeill, 2:1055).

[77] Ibid., iv.i.5 (McNeill, 2:1017).

[78] Calvin, *Institutes* iv.i.22 (McNeill, 2:1035).

[79] Cf. Eric G. Jay, *The Church* (Atlanta, GA: John Knox, 1978), 174.

[80] Calvin, *Institutes* iv.iii.13 (McNeill 2:1064).

[81] Ibid., iv.iii.15 (McNeill, 2:1066).

[82] Kenneth Scott Latourette, *History of Christianity* (New York: Harper and Brothers, 1953), 757.

[83] Ibid., iv.iii.16 (McNeill, 2:1067).

[84] Ibid., iv.iii.7 (McNeill, 2:1059–1060).

derived from below, rather than from above as in the Catholic model of ministry. In agreement with the Catholicism of his day, however, only the ministers were allowed to administer the sacraments of the church. And like the ministry and order in the church, Calvin's sacramental theology was firmly placed within the framework of predestinarian ecclesiology.

Sacramental Theology of the Reformed Tradition

Regarding the sacraments, Calvin found himself much in agreement with Luther.[85] However, a perusal of the sections of the *Institutes* dealing with the sacraments reveals an interesting tension in Calvin's sacramental theology. On the one hand, he described the sacraments as tokens, or signs, of belonging to God's elect as well as of His gracious favor on behalf of those who are decreed to be saved. By receiving them, the elect were to be assured that God's promises regarding their election would be fulfilled.[86] On the other hand, Calvin stressed the efficacy of the sacraments and considered them as the genuine means of salvific grace.[87]

In accord with Luther, Calvin affirmed that baptism is more than a simple sign of forgiveness. Instead, it offers God's power of forgiveness to save those who were baptized. This does not mean that all who receive baptism were to be saved, but rather that those who were elected must be baptized. If they were not, this was a sure sign of their reprobate status.[88] Consistent with his view on baptism as the means of grace, Calvin claimed that while baptism's efficacy requires the presence of faith in the believer,[89] this is not always so because the primary purpose of baptism (and the sacraments in general) is to arouse, nourish, and confirm our faith. Through the rite of baptism, he wrote, the Lord "effectively performs what it symbolizes."[90] Thus it is self-evident that Calvin would find himself in agreement with Luther on infant baptism.[91] Baptism, he claimed, need only be performed once. In its secondary function, baptism was seen as the sign of "initiation by which we are received into the society of the church."[92] Like circumcision, baptism thus confirmed that

---

[85] *Institutes* iv.xiv.7–8.14.17 (McNeill, 2: 1281–1284; 1289–1290; 1292–1293).

[86] Ibid., iv.xiv.14 (McNeill, 2:1289–1290)

[87] Ibid., iv.xiv.16–17; iv.xv.1–2 and iv.xv.15 (McNeill, 2:1291–1294; 1303–1304, and 1315).

[88] Ibid., iv.xv.1–3 (McNeill, 2:1303–1306).

[89] Ibid., iv.xv.15 (McNeill, 2:1315).

[90] Ibid., iv.xv.14 (McNeill, 2:1314). Thus, we find Calvin in strong agreement with Augustine's views on baptismal regeneration. *Idem*, iv.xv.16 (McNeill, 2:1316).

[91] Ibid., iv.xvi.1 (McNeill, 2:1324–1325).

[92] Ibid., iv.xv.1 (McNeill, 2:1303).

the infant belonged to the "household of God"[93] and allowed for further growth in faith.[94]

Regarding the Lord's Supper, the only true disagreement between Calvin and Luther was in the area of Christ's bodily presence. Calvin believed that Christ's body was in heaven and therefore could not simultaneously be present during the Lord's Supper. Thus he spoke of a spiritual or, as it is sometimes described, a dynamic presence[95] of Christ during the Eucharistic meal where the partakers were spiritually nourished by the bread and wine.[96] Through the sacrament, the Holy Spirit brought them into a closer relationship with Christ, the head of the church and the source of spiritual vitality.[97]

To further elucidate Calvin's understanding of the Lord's Supper, his views must be compared to those of Huldrych Zwingli's, as the position of the former represented the middle ground between Luther and Zürich's Reformer. In agreement with Luther and Calvin, Zwingli viewed the sacraments as signs of belonging to the Christian community.[98] Baptism, like circumcision in the Old Testament, was a public declaration that an infant (or an adult) was now a member of the church. Likewise, participating in the Lord's Supper symbolized a continuing loyalty to the Christian community.[99] Like Calvin, Zwingli rejected Luther's views regarding the real presence of Christ in the elements, but he would most likely have found himself in disagreement with Calvin's teachings on dynamic presence.[100] For Zwingli, the Eucharist was no more than what it meant: "the remem-

---

[93] Ibid., iv.xvi.4–5 (McNeill, 2:1327–1328).

[94] In another context, Calvin says of baptism: "The Holy Spirit . . . is he who brings the graces of God with him, gives a place for the sacraments among us, and makes them bear fruit" (ibid., iv.xiv.17; McNeill, 2:1293).

[95] The phrase, "dynamic presence," in reference to Calvin's doctrine of Christ's presence in the Eucharist, was first used by the Princetonian theologian Charles Hodge (Charles Hodge, *Systematic Theology* (Grand Rapids, MI: Eerdmans, 1946), 3:628, 645.

[96] John Calvin, "Best Method of Obtaining Concord," *Calvin: Theological Treatises*, (London: SCM Press, 1954), 328; cf. Calvin, *Institutes* iv.xvii.3 (McNeill, 2:1362).

[97] Ibid., iv.xiv.5.12 and 20 (McNeill, 2:1280, 1287, 1296–1297).

[98] "Zwingli," *Oxford Dictionary of the Christian Church*, ed. F. L. Cross, and Elizabeth A. Livingstone (New York: Oxford University Press, 2005), 1797; cf. Huldreich Zwingli, "Of Baptism," *Zwingli and Bullinger: Selected Translations*, (Philadelphia. PA: Westminster, 1953), 131.

[99] Ibid., 131–132, 148.

[100] By the time Calvin produced the first edition of the *Institutes*, Zwingli was no longer alive, having died in the Second Kappel War in 1531. Calvin, on the other hand, was strongly critical of Zwingli and his views regarding the Eucharist. See Calvin, *Institutes* iv.xv.1 (McNeill, 2:1304) and Calvin's letter to André Zebedee, May 19, 1539, in *Calvin's Letters*, ed. Jules Bonnet (New York: B. Franklin, 1973), 4:402. Huldreich Zwingli, "On the Lord's Supper," *Zwingli and Bullinger: Selected Translations*, (Philadelphia, PA: Westminster, 1953), 216.

brance of that deliverance by which he [Christ] redeemed the whole world . . . that we might never forget . . . but that we might publicly attest it with praise and thanksgiving."[101] The Eucharist was a *memorial* of the historical event leading to the establishment of the Christian church and a public declaration of membership in the church.[102] Notwithstanding his memorialism and a clear departure from Luther's views on the real presence, Zwingli appears to be in agreement with Luther and Calvin with regard to sacramental efficacy. He believed, especially in regard to the Lord's Supper, that physical eating might still be a means of grace through which the believer's "soul [is] being strengthened by the faith which [he/she] attests in the tokens." In Zwingli's theology, the sacraments "augment faith and are an aid to it. This is particularly true," he writes, "of the Supper."[103] In contrast, for Calvin, mere "head knowledge" was most assuredly insufficient to communicate eternal life into the lives of the believers and nourish their faith. Through participation in the rite, the believer's soul was "quickened to spiritual life."[104] These vestiges of Catholic sacramentalism remaining in the teaching of the Magisterial Reformers were strongly opposed by the more Radical Reformers, whose sole desire was a complete return to biblical ecclesiology.

The Radical Reformation

In contrast to the Magisterial branch of the Reformation, many 16th century Radical Reformers, fiercely opposed by Luther, Calvin, and Zwingli, appear to have recognized the radical implications of the foundational Protestant principles and brought them to their ultimate conclusion. While the various groups that came under the umbrella of the Radical Reformation may have had different agendas, they all tended to agree that the success of the Reformation depended on a complete return to biblical Christianity. As such, they argued that although the Magisterial Reformers had emphasized the role of Scripture in the life of the church, they had not sufficiently freed themselves from Catholic thinking in their sacramental theology and their continual support of the alliance between church and state.[105] "A true Church cannot exist where the secular rule

---

[101] Ibid., 234.

[102] Ibid., 235.

[103] Huldreich Zwingli, "Exposition of the Faith," *Zwingli and Bullinger: Selected Translations* (Philadelphia, PA: Westminster, 1953), 259, 263.

[104] Ibid., iv.xvii.5 (McNeill, 2:1365).

[105] Michael Novak, "The Free Churches and the Roman Church: The Conception of the Church in Anabaptism and in Roman Catholicism: Past and Present," *JES* 2 (1965): 429. While the various groups that were part of the Radical Reformation had this one goal in mind — complete

and the Christian Church are blended together."[106] All Radicals fiercely opposed such an alliance, which, they asserted, tended to curtail religious liberty by allowing the use of force to coerce doctrinal uniformity.[107] Salvation, they argued, in no way depended on church membership or assent to doctrinal formulations handed down from above. Thus, while some radical groups produced confessions of faith, such as the *Schleitheim Confession* (1527), for the most part they were "reluctant to issue writings of dogmatic content."[108]

Nature of the Church

In relation to medieval Catholicism, the Radicals tended to find themselves at the other ecclesiological extreme. Many of them believed that the true church of God was in heaven,[109] while the church on earth was just an assembly of baptized and regenerated Christians who were allowed to interpret Scripture according to the leading of the Holy Spirit.[110] The believers were certainly encouraged to gather together in bands, but the emphasis was upon an individual, unmediated relationship with Jesus Christ, rather than on association with a visible, organized body.[111] One could not be baptized into the church, as both Catholics and the Magisterial Reformers taught, but only accepted on the basis of certain qualifications. This did not mean another form of merit but rather a willing submission "to the humbling concept of grace." Such humbling would certainly lead to an internal renewal of a believer. The church, thus, had a right to search for such signs of internal regeneration. "In this sense, a 'walk worthy of the calling' [was] a prerequisite

---

return to biblical Christianity — they tended to differ on the methods by which this goal was to be achieved. While the more conservative Anabaptist groups were satisfied with freedom to worship, others, such as the leaders of the Münster Rebellion, embraced a much more radical agenda, which called for the establishment of a theocratic state. For a concise overview of the Anabaptist movement and its agenda, see Daniel Liechty, *Sabbatarianism in the Sixteenth Century: A Page in the History of the Radical Reformation* (Berrien Springs, MI: Andrews University Press, 1993).

[106] Leonard Verduin, *The Reformers and Their Stepchildren* (Grand Rapids, MI: Eerdmans, 1964), 37.

[107] Williston Walker, *A History of the Christian Church* (New York: Charles Scribner's Sons, 1959), 327; Bainton, *Reformation*, 99–101. It is to be noted that prior to gaining the state's backing, the Reformers also argued for freedom of religion according to the individual's conscience.

[108] Pelikan, *Reformation of Church and Dogma*, 314.

[109] Sebastian Frank, quoted in Alister McGrath, *Christian Theology*, 400.

[110] F. H. Littell, *The Origin of Sectarian Protestantism: A Study of the Anabaptist View of the Church* (New York: Macmillan, 1964), 69, 86–87, 89, 95–98; cf. Verduin, *Reformers*, 116.

[111] Pelikan, *Reformation of Church and Dogma*, 316.

for membership."¹¹² Such membership, however, in no way guaranteed salvation.

Local congregations could choose their ministers. They, while not receiving any remuneration or authority other than that which was delegated to them by the congregation, facilitated the celebration of communion and baptism. The ministry of the church was simply a matter of order and nothing else.¹¹³ The Anabaptist notion of the church went hand in hand with their views on the sacraments, an area in which they subjected the Magisterial Reformers' teachings to vigorous criticism.

Sacramental Theology

The Radical Reformers were critical of Luther, Calvin, and Zwingli, asserting that although these Reformers had emphasized the *sola fide* principle, they had not sufficiently freed themselves from Catholic thinking by continuing to hold to the concept of sacramental efficacy, thus relying on external works. The Radicals argued that just as good works did not secure salvation but were a result of faith, so the Lord's Supper did not constitute the means of grace but, rather, signified the grace already given.¹¹⁴ Contrary to Luther's assertion that "baptism effects forgiveness of sins," the Anabaptists believed that baptism simply bore testimony to the already changed life.¹¹⁵ For such reasons, they argued against Catholicism and the Magisterial Reformation that the church could not and must not hold any ecclesiastical control over the means of grace. This conviction was at the center of their rejection of infant baptism, as salvation could only be obtained through a personal relationship with Christ.¹¹⁶

Anabaptist theology constitutes a complete departure from any form of institutional ecclesiology prevalent in the 16th century. The rejection of such an ecclesiology, however, often resulted in the elevation of "the private judgment of the individual . . . above the corporate judgment of

---

[112] Verduin, *Refromers*, 118.

[113] Littell, *Sectarian*, 91–93, 99; González, *History*, 3:90–91; Erickson, *Theology*, 1045; Pelikan, *Reformation of Church and Dogma*, 313–322.

[114] Conrad Grebel, "Letter to Thomas Müntzer," *The Radical Reformation*, ed. Michael G. Baylor (Cambridge, MA: Cambridge University Press, 1991), 39 (emphasis mine); cf. Littell, *Sectarian*, 52, 68, 80.

[115] Menno Simons, "Christian Baptism," *The Complete Writings of Menno Simons*, ed. J. C. Wenger (Scottdale, PA: Herald, 1984), 244; cf. Menno Simons, "Christian Baptism," *Main Currents of Western Thought: Readings in Western Europe, Intellectual History from the Middle Ages to the Present*, ed. Franklin Le Van Baumer (New Haven, CT: Yale University Press, 1978), 206.

[116] Pelikan, *Reformation of Church and Dogma*, 317–319; cf. Martin Luther, *Small Catechism* (Adelaide: United Evangelical Lutheran Church in Australia, 1941), 13; cf. Littell, *Sectarian*, 69, 100.

the church."[117] This, in turn, resulted in many factions among the Radical Reformers.[118] Thus the implications of *sola Scriptura* and the "priesthood of all believers" appear to have been fully realized in the Radical Reformation.

The Reformation of the 16th century proved to be a watershed moment in the history of the Christian church. By its insistence on *sola Scriptura* and the return to biblical Christianity, it offered a formidable challenge to the soteriological-ecclesiological conventions of the time, ushered in a new era in biblical studies, and led to a new understanding of the church with its ordinances and government. However, it became evident that while the Magisterial Reformers repudiated much of the Catholic ways of understanding and doing church and attempted to harmonize ecclesiastical structures and sacramental theology with the foundational principles of Protestantism, in some ways they were unable fully to break away from the medieval ways of thinking.[119] The Radical Reformation challenged both medieval Catholicism and the Magisterial Reformers with a bold departure from the medieval ways of thinking about the church. At the same time, and as a result of the inherent individualism that permeated the Anabaptist vision of the church, the movement spearheaded further fragmentation of Western Christianity. As a result, "the monopoly of a single confession" was forever broken and denominationalism was born.[120] Out of the melting pot of Protestant confessions, which traced its theological roots to the 16th century Reformation, the 19th century saw the birth of the Seventh-day Adventist movement.[121]

Adventist Ecclesiology in Relation to the Sixteenth Century Reformation

Faced with the continuing delay of the Second Coming and influenced by the Protestant search for greater understanding of the nature of the church,[122] the Seventh-day Adventist Church has initiated its own ecclesi-

---

[117] McGrath, *Historical Theology*, 182.

[118] Pelikan, *Reformation of Church and Dogma*, 314–315.

[119] Ernst Troeltsch, *Protestantism in Progress: A Historical Study of the Relation of Protestantism to the Modern World* (Boston, MA: Beacon Press, 1958), 48, 70; cf. Bainton, *Reformation*, 115–116; McGrath, *Reformation Thought*, 197–98; and Steven Ozment, *The Age of Reform: 1250–1550* (New Haven, CT: Yale University Press, 1980), 261–262.

[120] Bainton, *Reformation*, 211.

[121] While at this point I may be charged with making a huge historical leap that ignores almost three centuries of theological developments, the scope of this paper calls only for a search for the 16th century Reformation roots of Adventist ecclesiology.

[122] In recent years, a steady flow of studies dealing with the church has appeared. See Edmund P. Clowney, *The Church* (Downers Grove, IL: InterVarsity, 1995) and Mark Husbands and Daniel J. Treier, ed., *The Community of the Word: Toward an Evangelical Ecclesiology* (Downers Grove, IL:

ological exploration. Until recent years, ecclesiology received scant attention within Adventist literature, pushed aside by more urgent theological issues. This is now changing, and attempts are made to discover the essence of Adventist ecclesiology and fine-tune it to the extent that it would reflect the soteriology of the denomination.[123]

In their theology, Adventists find themselves much in agreement with what was worked out during the travails of the 16th century. With Luther, Calvin, and the Radical Reformers, mainstream Adventist theology confidently affirms the traditional Protestant principles of *sola Scriptura* and *sola gratia et fide*.[124] Adventists also find themselves agreeing with the Protestant principle of the priesthood of all believers and reject any form of institutional mediation in the process of salvation.[125] This principle, Adventists believe, is directly related to ecclesiology and stands in clear and decisive disagreement with Catholic ecclesiology, where the emphasis lies on the visible institution, which, with its hierarchical structures, functions as the "ark of salvation" for humanity.

Visible Church Versus the Invisible Church

Notwithstanding the Magisterial Reformers' rejection of the Catholic emphasis on the visible church, they struggled to free themselves from the reliance on institutional structures for salvation. In the end, both Calvin and Luther strongly affirmed the necessity of the visible church for

---

InterVarsity, 2005).

[123] See, for example, Raoul Dederen, "The Church," *Handbook of Seventh-day Adventist Theology*, ed. Raoul Dederen (Hagerstown, MD: Review and Herald, 2000), 538–581 and Herbert Kiesler, "The Ordinances: Baptism, Foot Washing, and Lord's Supper," *Handbook of Seventh-day Adventist Theology*, ed. Raoul Dederen, 582–609. A helpful review of Adventist writings on ecclesiology is provided by Gerald A. Klingbeil, "Ecclesiology in Seventh-day Adventist Theological Reseach, 1995–2004," *AUSS* 43 (2005): 11–29. Moreover, during the last decade, many articles dealing with ecclesiology have appeared in a variety of Adventist journals and books published throughout the world. See, for example, Gerald A. Klingbeil, ed., *Pensar La Iglesia Hoy: Hacia una Ecclesiología Adventista* (San Martin: Editorial Universidad Adventista del Plata, 2002) and three volumes of *Studien zur Adventistischen Ekklesiologie* published in Germany from 1990 to 2002. See, particularly, the important collection of studies in Ángel Manuel Rodríguez, ed., *Studies in Adventist Ecclesiology 1: Toward a Theology of the Remnant* (Silver Spring, MD: Biblical Research Institute, 2009).

[124] Having affirmed as much, one must be aware that there are limits to Adventists' acceptance of these principles as 16th century Protestant soteriology was deeply rooted in the thought of Augustine and his predestinarianism. Thus, while Adventist soteriology shares much with classic Protestantism, for the most part, it is not Augustinian. Instead, it finds its immediate roots in the Arminian/Wesleyan synthesis, which made room for the exercise of human free will in the process of salvation. For a clear exposition of the fine lines separating Adventist soteriology from that of the Reformers, see *Questions on Doctrine* (Washington, DC: Review and Herald, 1957), 404–420.

[125] *AdvBibComm*, 7:561–562.

the salvation of humanity. They believed God decreed the church to be the sole means of grace, without which no one could be saved. While a person could be in the church and be unsaved, God demanded His elect be part of the visible church. Abandonment of the church was a sure sign that a person was not among the elect in the first place. In this, they were challenged by the various groups of Anabaptists, many of whom took the Protestant principles of *sola Scriptura* and the priesthood of all believers to their radical extremes and had little use for any form of institutional ecclesiology, be it Catholic or that of the Magisterial Reformers. The true church of God, in their beliefs, was in heaven while the earthly church appeared to be no more than a grouping of like-minded individuals who gather together to study the Bible, pray, and evangelize.

Like the Reformers, Adventists struggle at times to keep their perspective on the church and its relationship to the kingdom of God in balance. On the one hand, Adventists firmly disagree with Catholic institutionalism and support the notion that the kingdom of God must not be identified with any earthly organization. Membership in an earthly organization is certainly not viewed as equivalent to belonging to the kingdom of God, and thus guaranteeing salvation.[126] In agreement with Matthew 13 and the 16th century Reformers, Adventists also assert that until the eschaton, we will find in the church both true believers and those who have not given their heart to Jesus.[127] However, Adventists have always viewed themselves as the remnant of God and a gathering of those who have "covenant[ed] to keep the commandments of God, and the faith of Jesus Christ."[128] They also believe that this is not to be restricted to those who are part of that visible remnant.[129] For the most part, however, Adventists agree with Ellen G. White when she states that "in every age the Lord Jesus has had His witnesses, a remnant who trusted in the Word of God. And today, in every place, there are those who hold communion with God."[130]

---

[126] See, for example, Marvin R. Thurber, "The Life and Times of Martin Luther," *RH*, May 2, 1929, 16; cf. Ellen White, *Upward Look* (Washington, DC: Review and Herald, 1982), 315; and *idem.*, *Great Controversy* (Nampa: Pacific Press, 1950), 383.

[127] Ellen G. White, *Maranatha* (Washington, DC: Review and Herald, 1976), 203; and *AdvBibComm*, 5:408.

[128] Such were the words of the first Adventist confession of faith. Quoted in George Knight, *A Search for Identity* (Hagerstown, MD: Review and Herald, 2000), 22.

[129] See, for example, *AdvBibComm*, 6:489–490.

[130] Ellen G. White, "'They Shall be Mine, Saith the Lord of Hosts'," *Signs of the Times* 30 (Nov 23, 1904), 1.

Importance of the Visible Church

Should Adventist rejection of institutional mediation, either Catholic or Magisterial, lead to a reductionistic ecclesiology? I believe not. In recent decades, sociologists and health practitioners have come to recognize the importance of community over the Western inclination toward individualism. Like-minded individuals are encouraged to form genuine, all-inclusive communities to foster their personal growth and to protect them from the world's evils.[131] Although the Christian community could be involved in all of this, the Bible implies that the "church" is more than just a collection of like-minded individuals who come together for betterment of self and the world. According to the New Testament, the *ekklesia* had its beginning in Christ, who not only established it to be His agent in the world but also promised His continual presence within it (Matt 28:20). When Christians prayerfully gather together in submission to the Holy Spirit, Jesus Himself becomes dynamically present in their midst.[132] Being a part of the church allows the believers to experience Christ in ways that may not be possible otherwise.[133]

Moreover, Ellen White states, "God has made His church on the earth a channel of light, and through it He communicates His purposes and His will."[134] The church is a group of individuals who come together for the purpose of discerning the will of God through the study of the Scriptures. While the study of the Scriptures benefits the individual, its primary purpose is to benefit the church, and its goal is fulfilled when the church listens, receives, and responds to its message (Rev 2:7). It is the task of the whole community, under the guidance of the Holy Spirit, to interpret the divine message, to formulate its doctrinal boundaries, and to defend itself against the attacks of its opponents. The importance of the visible church of God on earth was clearly accentuated by Paul when he concludes that the church, not the individual, is "the pillar and foundation of the truth" (1 Tim 3:15, NIV). Of course, to protect the integrity of the Scriptures, this statement must be balanced by Paul's other sayings, such as that found in Galatians 1:9 (NIV): "If anybody is preaching to you a gospel other than what you accepted, let him be eternally condemned" (cf. 2 Cor 11:4). The latter

---

[131] M. Scott Peck, *The Different Drum* (New York: Simon and Schuster, 1987), 328.

[132] Ellen G. White, *Desire of Ages* (Mountain View, CA: Pacific Press, 1940), 414, 166; cf. Ellen G. White, *Testimonies for the Church* (Mountain View, CA: Pacific Press, 1948), 6:418–419.

[133] Ibid., 418.

[134] Ellen G. White, *Gospel Workers* (Washington, DC: Review and Herald, 1948), 443.

statement emphasizes the authority of Scripture over the community,[135] while the former stresses the authority of the church over the individual.[136]

Therefore, it may be concluded that Adventists place themselves somewhere in the middle between the sacramental or the predestinarian vision of the church and the one that seems to have been espoused by the various Anabaptist groups. Adventists reject the view that the earthly church is the effective instrument of salvation and affirm that it is an agency of salvation.[137] Being a part of the organized church on earth is considered to be an extremely important aspect of the Christian experience that directly contributes to spiritual growth and to the fulfillment of the mission of the church.

Theology of the Ordinances

There seems to be little doubt that, in the area of ordinances, Adventists find themselves in general agreement with their Protestant predecessors, with special affinity to the teachings of the Anabaptist branch of the Reformation. It needs to be noted that, in general, Adventists tend to avoid the term "sacrament" because of its historical connotations. The term "ordinances" (from Latin *ordo*, "an order, a row") is preferred, and it refers to certain definite rites instituted by Christ for the benefit of His followers. In agreement with the Magisterial Reformation, Adventists believe that only two of seven Roman Catholic rites can be traced to Christ. These rituals are of key importance to Christian worship. Properly administered, they can elevate the worship experience to its highest levels as they promote a spirit of communion, forgiveness, and humility.[138] Adventists also find a firm scriptural foundation for the practice of other religious rites, such as ordination, marriage, and the anointing of the sick. The manner in which these rites are administered is regulated by church policy and may be adapted to the needs of local cultures, as long as scriptural principles are maintained.

Adventists are firmly within the Anabaptist tradition when they categorically reject the view that Christian ordinances convey grace in and of themselves. In contradistinction to the traditional Roman Catholic

---

[135] This, according to Bernard Ramm, is the genius of Protestantism, which excludes the possibility of any scriptural interpretation from having the same authority as the Scriptures themselves (Bernard Ramm, *The Pattern of Religious Authority* [Grand Rapids, MI: Eerdmans, 1968], 56). Ramm adds that the authority of the church "is never final, never unquestionable, and never primary. [It] must always be under the supremacy and lordship of the revelation itself" (ibid., 60).

[136] Anthony Campolo, *A Reasonable Faith: Responding to Secularism* (Waco, TX: Word, 1983), 108.

[137] See Rodríguez, "Unity, Message and Mission of the Church," in this volume.

[138] Ellen G. White, *Evangelism* (Washington, DC: Review and Herald, 1946), 278.

teaching, participation in the church's rites is not what saves. Instead, the New Testament emphasizes faith, rather than works, as the true means of salvation. In other words, a person is declared righteous before God, not because of having participated in the church's rituals, but because of having believed (Rom 3:28; Gal 3:11; Eph 2:8-9). This faith commitment expresses itself in the participation in the rituals within the community of faith.

While most Catholics and Protestants view baptism as a necessary rite of Christian initiation, they disagree on the appropriate age of the person being baptized or the meaning of the rite. As discussed above, Catholics and the Magisterial Reformers assigned sacramental qualities to baptism and insisted upon infant baptism.[139] Adventists are firmly within the Anabaptist tradition when they insist that baptism is essentially a symbol of the renunciation of the old life and the adoption through the power of the Spirit of a new life in Christ. For the ceremony to have any meaning, it must be evident that the candidate has a living relationship with Christ. Thus, Adventists disagree with the teaching that baptism is to be viewed as the means by which God imparts His saving grace and effects the remission of sins with or without conscious participation by the believer. Instead, the emphasis is placed on the existing, rather than latent, faith and on a personal relationship with Christ prior to baptism. This is in agreement with the New Testament, where only adults are specifically mentioned as being baptized. As to the mode of baptism, in agreement with the Anabaptists, Adventists believe that the Greek word *baptizo* clearly means "to dip in or under" the water.[140] In the Adventist tradition, the rite of baptism is recognized as a condition of entrance into church membership. For practical rather than theological reasons, the rite is usually administered by an ordained minister, or, in the absence of such, by an authorized local church elder.[141]

Regarding the Lord's Supper, Adventists object to the Catholic and Lutheran view of Christ's real presence in the elements. Instead, they find themselves in agreement with the position advocated by the Reformed branch of the Reformation, especially that of Zwingli and the Anabaptists. They see the bread and wine as "symbols of the body and blood of Christ,

---

[139] Space restricts me from a detailed treatment of baptism and its relation to original sin in both Catholic and the Magisterial Reformation theology. For a detailed history and meaning of the issues surrounding the problem of the original sin, see Erickson, *Theology*, 629-639.

[140] Albrecht Oepke, "*Baptizo*," *TDNT*, 1:529.

[141] For a detailed exposition of the history and meaning of baptism, see Herbert Kiesler, "The Ordinances: Baptism, Foot Washing, and Lord's Supper," *Handbook of Seventh-day Adventist Theology*, ed. Raoul Dederen, 583-591.

as reminders of Christ's passion and death. The Lord's Supper is also a witness to the believer's acceptance of Christ as his Savior and of his faith in the Second Advent."[142] The Lord's Supper, thus, is seen essentially as a memorial of what Christ accomplished on the cross. According to Paul's account of the Lord's Supper, Jesus twice said: "Do this in remembrance of me" (1 Cor 11:23–26). Participating in the Lord's Supper brings forth a memory of what Christ has done for me, personally, on the cross. The communal orientation of the Last Supper focuses on a sense of fellowship, as believers gather together and express their dependence on Christ.[143]

Finally, in contrast to much of the Christian world, Adventists teach that Christ instituted the ordinance of foot washing as a perpetual rite to be practiced by all of His followers as prescribed by Christ in John 13:14. While most Christians simply sidestep this ordinance, this ritual symbolizes true servanthood extended especially to fellow believers. The act of washing feet with water also represents cleansing from sin and union with Christ. Within Adventism, this ordinance is considered as an ideal preparation for the communion meal and is usually practiced immediately prior to it.[144]

Government and Ministry in the Church

In their choice of government and ministry in the church, the early Adventists appeared to be eclectic, and elements of all Christian systems of governance are found in the Adventist way of doing church. Motivated primarily by pragmatic, rather than theological, reasons, the pioneers tended to select and adapt those ways of church governance that appeared to be in line with the New Testament and their missionary goals. However, being the heirs of the 16th century Reformation, they rejected any form of government that would promote the flow of authority from above.

From the Reformed tradition, Adventists inherited the emphasis upon the representative form of church government pioneered by John Calvin in Geneva. The fundamental presupposition underlying such a system of governance is the headship of Christ who, through a succession of various representative bodies, oversees the work of the church. These bodies are comprised of delegates who are chosen by the members of

---

[142] Siegfried H. Horn, "Lord's Supper," *The Seventh-day Adventist Bible Dictionary* (Washington, DC: Review and Herald, 1979), 680.

[143] Kiesler, "Ordinances," 604; White, *Desire of Ages*, 656; and White, *Evangelism*, 278.

[144] Dederen, "Church," 558. For an extended discussion on the ordinance of feet washing as well as its biblical and historical background, see Kiesler, "Ordinances," 592–595.

individual churches.[145] In contrast to Calvin, and in agreement with Luther, Adventists do not accept the theory that the Scriptures determine every detail of the representative system of church governance. Instead they hold that, while such a system is broadly based upon the principles gleaned from the New Testament, it can, and should, be adapted, depending on historical contingencies.[146]

The Methodist tradition provided the early Adventists with the strong episcopal element of church governance, which they amalgamated with the representative model of the Reformed tradition. Adventist conferences are thus organized in such a way that the conference president effectively functions as overseer of the work of the church within a specific geographical region. In contrast to the Catholic model, however, Adventist pastors who function as regional leaders are selected by delegates chosen by individual churches that belong to a given Conference of Churches. Such a procedure clearly reflects the Adventist desire to promote an ecclesiology from below.

Finally, Seventh-day Adventism rejects those forms of congregationalism that advocate the complete autonomy of each local congregation. Instead, in contrast to many other Protestant denominations and more like Roman Catholicism, they have adopted a centralized organizational form of government that promotes a close interrelationship among various worldwide congregations. This unique system allows for a certain measure of local autonomy, for example, in matters of local evangelism and discipline, while at the same time promoting a worldwide fraternity of churches. This unusual combination of local autonomy and worldwide support and oversight allows the Church to bring widespread collective resources to bear in a manner that is sensitive to local situations. Those who have studied it feel that this is one of the reasons for Adventism's remarkable international growth.[147] This organizational system, Adventists believe, is in harmony with the New Testament and best serves the church's missionary goals.[148]

In their view of the ministry in the church, Adventists find themselves in agreement with both the Magisterial and the Radical branches of the Reformation—strongly advocating the principle of the priesthood of all believers. Adventists, however, reject Calvin's notion that the "power of

---

[145] Cf. G. D. Henderson, *Presbyterianism* (Aberdeen: University Press, 1954), 162.

[146] Cf. Louis Berkhof, *Systematic Theology* (Grand Rapids, MI: Eerdmans, 1941), 581.

[147] For a thoughtful analysis of the development of Adventist organizational structures and their impact upon the mission of the church, see Barry D. Oliver, *SDA Organizational Structure* (Berrien Springs, MI: Andrews University Press, 1989).

[148] White, *Gospel Workers*, 444.

the keys" belongs exclusively to the ministry in the church. In agreement with Luther, they affirm that the "power of the keys" belongs to the entire church. They thus reject any form of clericalism that would in any way separate ministers from other believers.

In the New Testament, only those individuals who were spiritually qualified and sound in doctrine were chosen as leaders in the community. The authority of such leaders depended far more on the quality of their character and their spiritual gifting than on any position they may have held. Adventists are in agreement with other Protestant Christians that it is appropriate for the body of believers to carefully select its leaders and recognize their spiritual gifts by the laying on of hands, as prescribed in the New Testament. However, ordained ministerial leadership is an institution of the church and the ministers are its representatives, chosen on the basis of their particular spiritual gifting and set apart to serve the community. Thus, in contrast to Catholic tradition and in agreement with all branches of the Reformation, it is the endowment of the Holy Spirit, rather than ordination that qualifies ministers to fulfill the task of ministry. The emphasis is upon spiritual servanthood rather than on the authority of position (Mark 9:35; Rom 16:1; 1 Cor 3:5, 4:1).[149]

Conclusion

Between 1844 and 1863, the movement later known as Seventh-day Adventism moved from vigorous anti-organizationalism, realizing the lack of an effectively functioning organization would hamper its missionary goals and threaten the wellbeing of the community. The aforementioned years were filled with intense debate as to what form such organization should take. In their search for appropriate organizational structures, the early pioneers tended to be eclectic and pragmatic, drawing from the variety of Christian traditions, adopting and adapting only those elements of ecclesial reality grounded in the Scriptures. While their ecclesiology was not systematically articulated at the time, it is beyond doubt that its ultimate roots can be traced to the ecclesiology of the Reformation. While not in complete agreement with the 16th century Reformers, the ecclesiology of early Adventism reflected its grounding in the principle of priesthood of all believers, while at the same time rejecting any form of sacramentalism.

---

[149] Cf. Ibid., 441–445.

CHAPTER 10

SEVENTH-DAY ADVENTIST ECCLESIOLOGY, 1844–2012: A BRIEF HISTORICAL OVERVIEW[1]

Alberto R. Timm

Mainstream Seventh-day Adventists have always seen themselves as God's end-time remnant, people called out of the world to proclaim the three angels' messages of Revelation 14:6–12 to "those who live on the earth—to every nation, tribe, language and people" (v. 6). In order to effectively dialogue and gain better understanding of the historical trajectory of this ecclesiological self-understanding, we need examine how it was generated, developed across time, and is perceived today. There are helpful studies that can assist in such an endeavor.[2]

The present study provides a brief historical overview of the development of Seventh-day Adventist ecclesiology from 1844 to 2012. After some reflection on the historical background, it explores the following three major periods: 1) Adventist Ecclesiology (1844–1888); 2) Adven-

---

[1] A preliminary version of this paper was published under the title, "Seventh-day Adventist Ecclesiology, 1844–2001: Brief Historical Overview," *Pensar la iglesia hoy: hacia una eclesiología adventista,* ed. Gerald A. Klingbeil, Martin G. Klingbeil, and Miguel Ángel Núñez (Libertador San Martín, Entre Ríos, Argentina: Editorial Universidad Adventista del Plata, 2002), 283–302.

[2] See, for instance, Richard W. Schwarz and Floyd Greenleaf, *Light Bearers: A History of the Seventh-day Adventist Church,* 2nd ed., rev. (Nampa, ID: Pacific Press, 2000); George R. Knight, *A Search for Identity: The Development of Seventh-day Adventist Beliefs* (Hagerstown, MD: Review and Herald, 2000); Malcolm Bull and Keith Lockhart, *Seeking a Sanctuary: Seventh-day Adventism and the American Dream,* 2nd ed. (Bloomington and Indianapolis, IN: Indiana University Press, 2007), 259–272; and Carmelo L. Martines, "El concepto de remanente en la Iglesia Adventista del Séptimo Día: razones subyacentes en el debate contemporáneo" (Th.D. diss., Universidad Adventista del Plata, Argentina, 2002).

tist-Evangelical Ecclesiology (1888–1950); and 3) Ecclesiological Challenges (1950–2012). The overall discussion highlights basic components of the Seventh-day Adventist message, organizational structure, and missionary endeavor, with some glimpses into the denomination's self-understanding.

Ecclesiological Background

The Seventh-day Adventist movement was derived from Millerism, the North American expression of the worldwide Advent revival of the late 18th and early 19th centuries. At that time, many Protestant interpreters were convinced, from their study of these prophecies, that Christ's Second Coming would take place in their own time, specifically the 1840s (1843, 1844, and 1847).[3] The Baptist William Miller provided some of the most "elaborate and refined" chronological calculations of biblical prophecies,[4] showing that the 2,300 days of Daniel 8:14 would end in the Jewish religious year of 1843. Then the "sanctuary," understood by him as both the earth and the church, would be cleansed through the literal, visible, and premillennial Second Coming of Christ.[5] Later, Samuel S. Snow more precisely stated that the 2,300 days would be fulfilled on the tenth day of the seventh month of the Jewish religious year of 1844 (i.e. on October 22, 1844).[6]

The eschatological preaching of Miller and his associates launched a fast-growing interdenominational movement that flourished mainly on the east coast of North America between 1839 and 1844. They had no intentions of separating themselves from the Protestant denominations to which they belonged.[7] Nevertheless, the North American Protestant

---

[3] See LeRoy E. Froom, *The Prophetic Faith of Our Fathers* (Washington, DC: Review and Herald, 1946–1954), 4:402–410 and Alberto R. Timm, *The Sanctuary and the Three Angels' Messages: Integrating Factors in the Development of Seventh-day Adventist Doctrines* (Berrien Springs, MI: Adventist Theological Society Publications, 1995), 21–24.

[4] Whitney R. Cross, *The Burned-over District: The Social and Intellectual History of Enthusiastic Religion in Western New York, 1800–1850* (Ithaca, NY: Cornell University Press, 1950), 291.

[5] A synopsis of Miller's chronological calculation of biblical end-time prophecies can be found in "Synopsis of Miller's Views," *ST*, Jan. 25, 1843, 145–150.

[6] S. S. Snow to [N.] Southard, *MC*, Feb. 22, 1844, 243–244; *idem*, "Death Warrant of Jesus Christ," *MC*, May 2, 1844, 334–335; *idem* to [N.] Southard, *MC*, June 27, 1844, 397; *idem*, "Prophetic Chronology," *AH*, Aug. 14, 1844, 15; *idem*, "Prophetic Chronology," *MC*, Aug. 22, 1844, 51; and *idem*, [untitled], *True Midnight Cry*, Aug. 22, 1844, 1–4.

[7] The Millerites clearly stated, "Our fellow laborers are among the choicest of the faithful in Christ from among all denominations. We know no sect, or party as such, while we respect all; and wish them to have an equal privilege to our columns, to address the people and diffuse their views on the advent near.... '*Our object* is to revive and restore the ancient faith, to renew the ancient landmarks, to 'stand in the ways and see and ask for the old paths, where is the good way' in which

denominations would not tolerate very long the expansion of such an interconfessional revival of the premillennial hope in the Second Coming of Christ.[8] In the early 1840s, Millerites were increasingly forced to abandon their faith in the soon coming of Christ or risk disfellowship from their original churches. Many of them were driven out of their churches just "for believing and teaching, testifying and singing, the advent hope."[9] For Charles Fitch, this was clear evidence that not only the Roman Catholic Church but also "all sects into which the Protestant church is divided" had become Babylon and Antichrist.[10] Although Miller himself was somewhat reluctant to endorse this idea,[11] it "spread extensively" in the ranks of the Millerite movement after the summer of 1843.[12]

Expelled from their original churches, the Millerites were forced to develop an "Adventist" identity for themselves. But when Christ did not come on October 22, 1844, it shook the very foundation of that identity, fragmenting the Millerite movement into several different branches.[13] Many Millerites gave up their hope in the soon coming of Christ and returned to their former churches or other mainstream churches. Those who continued upholding their faith in the Second Advent eventually became polarized around the "open door" and the "shut door" (cf. Matt 25:10–12; Rev 3:7–8) interpretations of the 1844 experience.

The open-door Adventists usually continued relating the cleansing of the sanctuary of Daniel 8:14 to the Second Coming of Christ, and saw

---

our fathers walked and the martyrs 'found rest for their souls. We have no purpose to distract the churches with any new inventions, or to get to ourselves a name by starting another sect among the followers of the Lamb. We neither condemn, nor rudely assail, others of a faith different from our own, nor dictate in matters of conscience for our brethren, nor seek to demolish their organizations, nor build new ones of our own; but simply to express our convictions like a Christian" ("Our Course," *ST*, Nov. 15, 1840, 126; the single quotation marks, which do not always close, appear in the original).

[8] See Wayne Judd, "From Ecumenists to Come-outers: The Millerites, 1831–1845," *Adventist Heritage* 11 (Spring 1986): 3–12.

[9] Froom, *Prophetic Faith of Our Fathers*, 4:449.

[10] C[harles] Fitch, "Come out of Her, My People," *A Sermon* (Rochester, NY: J. V. Himes, 1843), 9–15; idem, "'Come out of Her, My People,' A Sermon," *MC*, Sept. 21, 1843, 34–35.

[11] Cf. Editorial, "The Conference," *AH*, Feb. 14, 1844, 9; William Miller, *Remarks on Revelations Thirteenth, Seventeenth and Eighteenth* (Boston: Joshua V. Himes, 1844), 30–47; idem, *Apology and Defence* (Boston: Joshua V. Himes, 1845), 24–25, 30–31.

[12] Miller, *Apology and Defence*, 25.

[13] For further study of the post-1844 fragmentation of Millerism, see David T. Arthur, "'Come out of Babylon': A Study of Millerite Separatism and Denominationalism, 1840–1865" (Ph.D. diss., University of Rochester, 1970), 84–379; George R. Knight, *Millennial Fever and the End of the World* (Boise, ID: Pacific Press, 1993), 217–325.

the October 1844 Disappointment as the result of a chronological error—choosing too early a date to end the 2,300 days. The shut-door Adventists regarded October 22, 1844, as the correct date for ending the 2,300 days. One of the major branches of shut-door Adventists formed around the belief that on October 22, 1844, a change took place in Christ's priestly ministry in the heavenly realms. They understood that change as Christ's going to the presence of His Father to receive the kingdom of this world (cf. Dan 7:13–14; Matt 25:1–13) and/or Christ's moving from the Holy Place into the Most Holy Place of the heavenly sanctuary (cf. Heb 8:1–2; Rev 11:19), fulfilling the antitype of the Day of Atonement ritual of the earthly sanctuary (cf. Lev 16; 23:26–32). Out of this branch of shut-door Adventists came Sabbatarian Adventism, which eventually became the Seventh-day Adventist Church.

Adventist Ecclesiology (1844–1886)

The second half of the 1840s was a period of intense Bible study in early Sabbatarian Adventist circles. Two significant realities helped to initiate and feed that study. First, the disruptive effect of the October 1844 Disappointment challenged the founders of Sabbatarian Adventism to search the Scriptures further for convincing answers to the disappointment. Second, the "shut door" theory led early Sabbatarian Adventists to believe their mission to the world had been accomplished during the first half of the nineteenth century through the great Second Advent movement. With a missionary endeavor that did not go much beyond the task of strengthening the faith of some ex-Millerites friends, the Sabbatarians spent much time praying and searching the Scriptures for further light.

By studying the Bible, early Sabbatarian Adventists not only found a biblical answer to the October 1844 Disappointment, but also discovered many other overlooked biblical teachings. This led them to revise and expand the Millerite system of prophetic interpretation into a far broader doctrinal system of "present truth." The Millerite message focused exclusively on the end-time prophecies of Scripture, emphasizing the fulfillment of the 2,300 day prophecy in Daniel 8:14. The Sabbatarians kept this end-time eschatological emphasis as the basic hermeneutical framework for developing a unique doctrinal system *integrated* by the concept of the cleansing of the sanctuary of Daniel 8:14 and *proclaimed* by the three angels' messages of Revelation 14:6–12.

The doctrinal components of that system of "present truth" comprised both the "*eschatological* doctrines derived from the historical and/or supra-historical fulfillment of specific end-time prophecies of Scripture" and the "*historical* doctrines of Scripture that had been overlooked and disregarded by the larger Christian church, but which would be restored at the end of time."[14] The eschatological doctrines were 1) the personal, visible, premillennial Second Coming of Christ; 2) the two-phase priestly ministry of Christ in the heavenly sanctuary, with special emphasis on the second phase that began on October 22, 1844; and 3) the modern manifestation of the gift of prophecy in the person and writings of Ellen G. White. And the historical doctrines included 4) the conditional immortality of the soul and the final annihilation of the wicked; and 5) the perpetuity of God's law and the seventh-day Sabbath.

Small Bible-study groups flourished shortly after the October 1844 Disappointment. Their contributions were crucial for the formation of this doctrinal system. The following groups are worthy of special mention: Port Gibson, New York, who were concerned with Christ's heavenly ministry; Portland, Maine, where Ellen G. Harmon (later White) received her first prophetic vision; and Washington, New Hampshire, who emphasized the abiding nature of the seventh-day Sabbath. Joseph Bates, James White, and Ellen G. White were of special influence in the process of integrating the discoveries of those groups into a single doctrinal platform. Publications and Bible conferences held between 1848 and 1850 helped to spread these teachings within ex-Millerite circles, expanding the newly-formed community of believers.[15]

The growth of the Sabbatarian Adventist movement brought the need for organizational developments beyond the level of the personal leadership of Joseph Bates, James White, and Ellen G. White. Till 1863, the development of an organizational structure took place at three basic levels: 1) local churches, which started to elect their first local leaders in the early 1850s;[16] 2) State conferences, the first seven of which were established in the United States between 1861 and 1862;[17] and 3) a General Confer-

---

[14] Timm, *The Sanctuary and the Three Angels' Messages*, 116 (italics supplied).

[15] See ibid., 77–91.

[16] The first local church leaders included 1) a committee of seven (cf. Acts 6) "to attend to the wants of the poor" ("Our Tour East," *RH*, Nov. 25, 1851, 52); 2), church deacons (H. S. Gurney, "From Bro. Gurney," *RH*, Dec. 27, 1853, 199; M. E. Cornell, "From Bro. Cornell," *RH*, Jan. 24, 1854, 7; *idem*, "Conference at Rosendale, Wisconsin," *RH*, May 23, 1854, 101; Joseph Bates, "Communication from Bro. Bates," *RH*, May 30, 1854, 148); 3), church elders (Joseph Bates, "Church Order," *RH*, Aug. 29, 1854, 22–23; "Church Order," *RH*, Jan. 23, 1855, 164); and 4) church treasurers (J[ames] W[hite], "Systematic Benevolence," *RH*, Feb. 3, 1859, 84; Henry E. Carver, "Report of Meetings, &c.," *RH*, Mar. 3, 1859, 120).

[17] Joseph Bates, "Doings of the Battle Creek Conference, Oct. 5 & 6, 1861," *RH*, Oct. 8, 1861, 148–49; H. C. Whitney and R. S. Patterson, "Southern Iowa Conference," *RH*, Apr. 1, 1862, 142; J. T. Mitchell and M. B. Smith, "Proceedings of the Northern Iowa Conference," *RH*, May 27, 1862, 206; Albert Stone and Stephen Pierce, "Doings of the Vermont Conference, June 15, 1862," *RH*, July 1, 1862, 40; W. S. Ingraham and Joseph G. Wood, "Illinois and Wisconsin Conference," *RH*, Oct. 14, 1862, 155;

ence, which was established in Battle Creek, Michigan, in May 1863, with John Byington as its first president.[18] Although the denomination adopted a representative form of church organization, the leadership of the General Conference was centralized to a large degree in the authority of its president.

Early Sabbatarian Adventist identity was largely influenced by the Millerite view of other Christian denominations. The Millerites started their religious movement with the idealistic intention of keeping a friendly relationship with other Protestant denominations. But this intention vanished as Protestant intolerance increased against the Millerite preaching of the Second Coming. This eventually led the Millerites to identify those denominations as part of the spiritual "Babylon" of Revelation 14:8 and 18:1–24. Sabbatarian Adventists kept this basic concept of Babylon, but suggested a far broader spectrum of doctrinal reasons to place the Protestant denominations into that category. While the Millerites saw the spiritual Babylon as formed by the religious opposition to the biblical teaching of the Second Coming, the Sabbatarians viewed that entity as antagonistic not only to that specific teaching but also to all other major components of the doctrinal system of "present truth."[19]

With such a broad doctrinal spectrum, Sabbatarian Adventists excluded from God's end-time "remnant" people (cf. Rev 12:17; 14:12) the Roman Catholic Church, non-Adventist Protestant denominations and even the non-Sabbatarian branches of Millerism. Up to 1860, Sabbatarian Adventists referred to themselves as the "little flock" (cf. Luke 12:32);[20] the end-time "remnant" (cf. Rev 12:17);[21] the "Sabbath and shut door believers;"[22] "God's peculiar people that Keep the Commandments of God,

---

Calvin Kelsey and F. W. Morse, "Business Proceedings of the Minnesota Conference," *RH*, Nov. 4, 1862, 182–183; J. N. Andrews and J. M. Aldrich, "Doings of the N.Y. Conference," ibid., 182.

[18] John Byington and U. Smith, "Report of General Conference of Seventh-day Adventists," *RH*, May 26, 1863, 204–206.

[19] See Timm, *The Sanctuary and the Three Angels' Messages*, 81–83, 182–187.

[20] Joseph Bates, *The Seventh Day Sabbath, a Perpetual Sign, the Beginning to the Entering into the Gates of the Holy City, according to the Commandment* (New Bedford, MA: Benjamin Lindsey, 1846), i; [James White], idem, *Word to the "Little Flock"* (Brunswick, ME: [James White], 1847), 1; E. G. White, "To the 'Little Flock'," *Present Truth*, no. 9, Apr. 1850, 71.

[21] Bates, *The Seventh Day Sabbath, a Perpetual Sign*, 2nd ed., 52, 59; J. White, *The Third Angel's Message* (Oswego, NY: James White, 1850), 7.

[22] Joseph Bates, *A Vindication of the Seventh-day Sabbath, and the Commandments of God: With a Further History of God's Peculiar People, from 1847 to 1848* (New Bedford, MA: Benjamin Lindsey, 1848), 86; cf. idem, *A Seal of the Living God: A Hundred Forty-four Thousand, of the Servants of God Being Sealed, in 1849* (New Bedford, MA: Benjamin Lindsey, 1849), 56.

and the Faith of Jesus;"[23] "God's covenant keeping people;"[24] "the church of God who keep[s] the Sabbath—the seal of the living God;"[25] and the "Philadelphia church" (cf. Rev 3:7-13).[26] By contrast, such expressions as the "remnant scattered abroad"[27] and "scattered remnant"[28] were used in reference to the disappointed Millerites who kept their faith in the seventh-month movement of 1844, while the expression "rebellious house of Israel" (cf. Ezek 12:25)[29] was applied to those former Millerites who gave up their faith in the seventh-month movement.

In his *Second Advent Way Marks and High Heaps* (1847), Joseph Bates defined a "Christian Church" as "an assembly or congregation of *faithful men*," and an "anti-Christian Church" as "an assembly or congregation of *unfaithful* men." For him, Christianity became "corrupt and anti-Christian," among other reasons, "by disregarding or renouncing any of the fundamental truths of the Bible."[30] Regarding the creed-bondage of the churches as a major characteristic of mystic Babylon (Rev 14:9),[31] Sabbatarian Adventist did not accept any formal creed.

On October 1, 1860, the name "Seventh-day Adventists" was officially adopted by the Sabbatarian Adventists that would organize themselves as

---

[23] James White, *Hymns, for God's Peculiar People, That Keep the Commandments of God, and the Faith of Jesus* (Oswego, NY: Richard Oliphant, 1849).

[24] H. Edson, "Appeal to the Laodicean Church," *AR* Extra, Sept. 1850, 4.

[25] Ellen G. White, "Dear Brethren & Sisters," [T]Ms 3, Jan. 18, 1849, Ellen G. White Research Center-Andrews University.

[26] Joseph Bates, *Second Advent Way Marks and High Heaps, or a Connected View, of the Fulfillment of Prophecy, by God's Peculiar People, from the Year 1840 to 1847* (New Bedford, MA: Benjamin Lindsay, 1847), 33-35, 65, 68; idem, *Vindication*, 53, 63, 72, 107-108.

By the mid-1850s, Sabbatarian Adventists came to the conclusion that they were the Laodicean church (Rev 3:14-22) rather than the Philadelphian church (Rev 3:7-13), as pointed out, for example, in J[ames] W[hite], "Watchman, What of the Night?" *RH*, Oct. 9, 1856, 184; R. F. C[ottrell], "Are We in Laodicea?" *RH*, Jan. 8, 1857, 77; and J. N. Loughborough, "A Letter to a Friend, on the Seven Churches," *RH*, Mar. 26, 1857, 162-163. For further study on this subject, see P. Gerard Damsteegt, *Foundations of the Seventh-day Adventist Message and Mission* (Grand Rapids, MI: Eerdmans, 1977), 148, 244-248.

[27] Ellen G. Harmon, *To the Little Remnant Scattered Abroad* (Portland, ME: [James White], 1846).

[28] [James White, Introductory remarks], *Present Truth*, no. 1, July 1849, 1; J. Bates, "New Testament Seventh Day Sabbath," *RH*, no. 4, Jan. 1851, 32.

[29] Bates, *Vindication*, 6, 85-86; [J. White], "The Voice of God," *A Word to the "Little Flock,"* 5-6; Joseph Bates, "Midnight Cry in the Past," *RH*, no. 3, Dec. 1850, 23-24.

[30] Joseph Bates, *Second Advent Way Marks and High Heaps, or a Connected View, of the Fulfillment of Prophecy, by God's Peculiar People, from the Year 1840 to 1847* (New Bedford, MA: Benjamin Lindsay, 1847), 25.

[31] See Timm, *The Sanctuary and the Three Angels' Messages*, 189, 227, 238, 262-263.

the Seventh-day Adventist Church.[32] Until the early 1870s, Adventist authors continued to believe that their commission to preach "before many peoples, and nations, and tongues, and kings" (Rev 10:11) could be fulfilled simply by preaching in the United States to representatives of those nations.[33] But in the early 1870s the denomination became convinced of their responsibility to develop an overseas mission program. In 1874, J. N. Andrews was sent to Europe as the first official Seventh-day Adventist missionary overseas, with the purpose of consolidating the work M.B. Czechowski had started on that continent.[34] After 1874, many other missionaries expanded the Adventist presence in Europe, Africa, Australia, Latin America, the South Pacific Islands, and India, among others.[35]

The first "S. D. A. Church Manual" was published as an 18-part series in the *Review* between June 5 and October 9, 1883.[36] It spoke of the church as

> an assembly of persons who believe in the religion of the Lord Jesus Christ, and who have voluntarily associated themselves together for the purpose of maintaining his worship. When fully organized, it consists of the body of the church, or laity, and the proper officers,—an elder, a deacon, a clerk, and a treasurer.[37]

---

[32] Joseph Bates and Uriah Smith, "Business Proceedings of B. C. Conference," *RH*, Oct. 23, 1860, 179. In 1861, Ellen G. White made the following statement about that specific name: "The name, Seventh-day Adventist, is a standing rebuke to the Protestant world. Here is the line of distinction between the worshipers of God, and those who worship the beast, and receive his mark. The great conflict is between the commandments of God and the requirements of the beast [cf. Rev 14:9–12]" (*Testimony for the Church*, no. 6 [Battle Creek, MI: Steam Press of the Review and Herald Office], 1861, 22–23; idem, *Testimonies for the Church* [Mountain View, CA: Pacific Press, 1948], 1:223). See also J. W[hite], "Seventh-day Adventists," *RH*, Apr. 30, 1861, 192.

[33] See e.g., "The World's Conversion" (reprint), *RH*, June 26, 1856, 69; [Uriah Smith], "Note," *RH*, Feb. 3, 1859, 87; [idem], editorial note, *RH*, Jan. 1, 1867, 48; John Matterson, "Report," *RH*, Mar. 24, 1868, 237; James White, "Our Faith and Hope; or, Reasons Why We Believe as We Do. Number Two," *RH*, Dec. 27, 1870, 9–10; Editorial, "The Gospel Preached in All the World," *RH*, July 16, 1872, 36.

[34] Harry Leonard, ed., *J. N. Andrews: The Man and the Mission* (Berrien Springs, MI: Andrews University Press, 1985).

[35] For a chronological list of countries and territories entered by Seventh-day Adventists between 1862 and 1976, see Borge Schantz, "Development of Seventh-day Adventist Missionary Thought: Contemporary Appraisal" (Ph.D. diss., Fuller Theological Seminary, 1983), 765–769.

[36] See [W. H. Littlejohn], "The S. D. A. Church Manual," 18-part series in *Advent Review and Sabbath Herald*, June 5, 1883, 361–362; June 12, 1883, 377–378; June 19, 1883, 393–394; June 26, 1883, 409; July 3, 1883, 426–427; July 10, 1883, 441–442; July 17, 1883, 457–458; July 24, 1883, 474; July 31, 1883, 491; Aug. 7, 1883, 505–506; Aug. 14, 1883, 521–522; Aug. 21, 1883, 537–538; Aug. 28, 1883, 553–554; Sept. 4, 1883, 569–570; Sept. 11, 1883, 586–587; Sept. 18, 1883, 602–603; Sept. 25, 1883, 618; Oct. 9, 1883, 631–632.

[37] Ibid., June 5, 1883, 361.

J. H. Waggoner's *The Church: Its Organization, Ordinances, and Discipline* (1886) defined the church as 1) "an *organized body*, meeting from time to time by regular appointment"; 2) having "a *regular membership*; each member being known as such to officers and to the fellow-members"; and 3) being "not only clothed with the *power of discipline*, but upon it is laid the *duty of discipline*."[38] To this he added,

> A church should be well *indoctrinated*. We have no confidence in this sensationalism now called religion in which "only believe" is the sole standard of duty, and frequent ejaculations of "Praise the Lord," and "Glory to God," are taken as sufficient evidences of deep piety . . . But no amount of indoctrinating, of preaching, of exhorting to duty, will ever keep a church in a healthy, prosperous condition without proper and prompt administration of discipline.[39]

But the church was not yet ready to formally accept a Church Manual, and Waggoner's project did not prosper.

Between the late 1840s and the early 1860s, Sabbatarian Adventists defined their doctrinal system with emphasis on their distinctive teachings, and established an organizational structure able to maintain unity of faith and facilitate the mission of the church. The next stage, following the same doctrinal and organizational pattern, took place between the late 1880s and early 1900s when Seventh-day Adventists enriched their doctrinal system with a more Christ-centered emphasis, and revised their organizational structure to assist more efficiently its worldwide expansion and growth.

Adventist-Evangelical Ecclesiology (1888–1950)

New denominations usually demonstrate the reason for their existence through their unique, singular contribution to the religious experience of their believers. Hence, the founders of Seventh-day Adventism gave much attention to components of their system of beliefs neglected by other Christian denominations. But four decades of such one-sided emphasis led Seventh-day Adventism into an existential crisis regarding the basic components of the Evangelical faith. As early as 1857, Albert Stone

---

[38] J. H. Waggoner, *The Church: Its Organization, Ordinances, and Discipline* (Oakland, CA: Pacific Press, 1886), 6–7. Typeset printed copies of this book were provided only for the members of the Pacific Press Book Committee, which seem not to have approved it for publication. A copy of it is available in the White Estate Vault.

[39] Ibid., 61. The term "ejaculation" was used in the sense of shouts of religious excitement.

wrote, "we have talked much of the Commandments of God, and the Testimony of Jesus Christ, but we have had too little of Christ in our hearts."[40] Later in 1890, Ellen White stated, "as a people, we have preached the law until we are as dry as the hills of Gilboa that had neither dew nor rain."[41]

The 1888 General Conference session in Minneapolis, Minnesota was of special significance in giving a more explicitly evangelical tenor to the Adventist message.[42] E. J. Waggoner, A. T. Jones, and Ellen G. White challenged the delegates towards a more Christ-centered emphasis on salvation by grace through faith (see Eph 2:8–10). Throughout her prophetic ministry, Ellen White uplifted "the matchless charms of Christ,"[43] and at Minneapolis she stated emphatically, "Now, brethren, we want the truth as it is in Jesus" (cf. Eph 4:21).[44] But, unfortunately, there was much dispute among the delegates on the topic of righteousness by faith. Since no official action was taken on this matter at the end of the meetings, the delegates left Minneapolis "divided into three groups: 1) those who gladly accepted the message; 2) those who opposed it; and 3) those who, neither accepting nor rejecting it, preferred to remain neutral or undecided."[45] However, the post-1888 era saw a significant Adventist revival on the preaching of righteousness by faith.

With a more Christ-centered doctrinal emphasis in place, the denomination began to revise its organizational structure. When the General Conference of Seventh-day Adventists was organized in 1863, the denomination had only 3,500 members and no official overseas mission work. But significant growth and territorial expansion towards the end of

---

[40] Albert Stone, "Letter from Bro. Stone," *RH*, Jan 29, 1857, 101.

[41] E. G. White, "Christ Prayed for Unity Among His Disciples," *RH*, March 11, 1890, 146.

[42] For further study of the major discussions about the events related to the 1888 General Conference session in Minneapolis, see *The Ellen G. White 1888 Materials: Letters, Manuscripts, Articles, and Sermons Relating to the 1888 Minneapolis General Conference*, 4 vols. (Washington, DC: Ellen G. White Estate, 1987); Ellen G. White Estate, comp., *Manuscripts and Memories of Minneapolis: Selections from Non-Ellen White Letters, Articles, Notes, Reports, and Pamphlets Which Deal with the Minneapolis General Conference Session* (Boise, ID: Pacific Press, 1988). See also Norval F. Pease, *By Faith Alone* (Mountain View, CA: Pacific Press, 1962); A. V. Olson, *Thirteen Crisis Years, 1888–1901: From the Minneapolis Meeting to the Reorganization of the General Conference* (Washington, DC: Review and Herald, 1981); Arnold V. Wallenkampf, *What Every Adventist Should Know about 1888* (Washington, DC: Review and Herald, 1988); George R. Knight, *Angry Saints: Tensions and Possibilities in the Adventist Struggle over Righteousness by Faith* (Washington, DC: Review and Herald, 1989); idem, *A User-friendly Guide to the 1888 Message* (Hagerstown, MD: Review and Herald, 1998).

[43] [Ellen G. White], "Christ and the Law," *The Ellen G. White 1888 Materials*, 1:348.

[44] Ellen G. White, "Morning Talk by Ellen G. White, Minneapolis, Minnesota, October 24, 1888," A. V. Olson, *Thirteen Crisis Years*, 302.

[45] A. V. Olson, *Thirteen Crisis Years*, 41–42.

the 19th century called for major revisions of the original organizational structure.

According to Barry D. Oliver, two different ecclesiological models of church organization were being fostered within the denomination in the 1890s. There were men like A. T. Jones, E. J. Waggoner, D. J. Paulson, P. T. Magan, and, for a time, W. W. Prescott arguing for a more *ontological,* "cristocentric model of organization," which "emphasized the *local* nature of the church" and overlooked, to a large extent, its universal nature. For them "the priesthood of believers, the headship of Christ, the church as the body of Christ, and spiritual gifts should determine the form of organization." Conversely, A. G. Daniells, W. C. White, W. A. Spicer, and others advocated a more *functional* model in which "the *universal* unity of the church took priority over the individuality and diversity of its constituent local congregations and individual members."[46]

The Seventh-day Adventist organizational adjustments that took place between 1901 and 1918 followed the functional model more closely, emphasizing the universal unity of the church. The 1901 General Conference session in Battle Creek, Michigan, made at least six important changes: 1) the establishment of Union Conferences and Union Missions in those parts of the world where possible; 2) the centralization, within a departmental structure, of leading disconnected branches of the church; 3) the decentralization of leadership from the General Conference president to a General Conference Executive Committee of 25 members; 4) the transfer of ownership and management of institutions, previously under General Conference jurisdiction, to the respective unions; 5) the creation of a fund-sharing plan providing better financial support to the worldwide work; and 6) the coordination of the mission work by the General Conference committee.[47] A.G. Daniells became the "chairman" of the General Conference Executive Committee (instead of "president" of the General Conference), and W. A. Spicer, the secretary of the Mission Board.

New modifications were added to the organizational structure of the church at the 1903 General Conference session in Oakland, California. Among them were 1) the reinstatement of the function of General Conference president; 2) the election of two General Conference vice presidents, one for Europe and one for North America; and 3) the decision that all institutions operated by the denomination should become its direct property. A. G. Daniells assumed the renewed function of General Confer-

---

[46] Barry D. Oliver, *SDA Organizational Structure: Past, Present and Future* (Berrien Springs, MI: Andrews University Press, 1989), 136–140, 219–221 (italics supplied).

[47] Ibid., 173–75. Cf. A. G. Daniells, "A Statement of Facts Concerning Our Present Situation–No. 8," *RH*, Mar. 29, 1906, 6–7.

ence president, and W. A. Spicer became the General Conference secretary. Later, at the 1913 General Conference session in Washington, D. C., the first three Divisions were organized, with their own independent constituencies, under the names of "European Division Conference,"[48] "North American Division Conference,"[49] and "Asiatic Division Mission."[50]

By 1913, the denomination was organized under the following five levels: 1) local churches, 2) local Conferences and local Missions, 3) Union Conferences and Union Missions, 4) Division Conferences and Division Missions, and 5) a General Conference. In 1918, the Division Conferences were abolished as independent conferences and became extensions of the General Conference so that "the General Conference constituency would appoint the leadership in each division and the president of each division would be a vice president of the General Conference."[51] With this adjustment, the Seventh-day Adventist organizational structure reached the standard that would continue, basically unchanged, into the twenty-first century.

After the General Conference reorganization in 1901, the denomination saw a significant explosion in its mission work. "Between 1901 and 1926, included, 2,937 missionaries were sent, i.e. an average of 112 per year."[52] This expansion was fostered by the Adventist conviction to go out and preach the three angels' messages of Revelation 14:6–12 "to every nation, tribe, language and people" (v. 6; NIV) before the end could come (Matt 24:14).[53]

---

[48] "Fourteenth Meeting, May 22, 2:30 P.M.," *RH*, June 5, 1913, 536; "The European Division Conference," ibid., 552.

[49] "Eighteenth Meeting, May 26, 10 A.M.," *RH*, June 5, 1913, 538–541; "North American Division Conference," ibid., 552.

[50] "Twenty-fifth Meeting, May 30, 2:30 P.M.," *RH*, June 12, 1913, 564.

[51] George R. Knight, *Organizing to Beat the Devil: The Development of Adventist Church Structure* (Hagerstown, MD: Review and Herald, 2001), 139.

[52] Werner Vyhmeister, *Misión de la Iglesia Adventista* (Brasilia: Seminario Adventista Latinoamericano, 1980), 58.

[53] During the first 70 years of its history, Seventh-day Adventism was assisted by the prophetic voice of Ellen White. But after she passed away in 1915, her writings continued to provide guidance and stability for the denomination. Her most significant statements on the church are found, for instance, in her books *Testimonies to Ministers and Gospel Workers* (Mountain View, CA: Pacific Press, 1923), 15–62; *Selected Messages from the Writings of Ellen G. White* (Washington, DC: Review and Herald, 1980), 3:15–26; *Counsels for the Church: A Guide to Doctrinal Beliefs and Christian Living* (Nampa, ID: Pacific Press, 1991), 240–248. Among her prolific allusions to the church, one finds several noteworthy statements. For example, she defined the church as "God's appointed agency for the salvation of men. It was organized for service, and its mission is to carry the gospel to the world" (Ellen G. White, *The Acts of the Apostles in the Proclamation of the Gospel of Jesus Christ* [Mountain View, CA: Pacific Press, 1911], 9).

Basic reasons for establishing a Seventh-day Adventist organization are found in following statement by Ellen G. White:

> From the first our work was aggressive. Our numbers were few, and mostly from the poorer class ... As our numbers increased, it was evident that without some form of organization, there would be great confusion, and the work would not be carried forward successfully. To provide for the support of the ministry, for carrying the work in new fields, for protecting both the churches and the ministry from unworthy members, for holding church property, for the publication of the truth through the press, and for many other objects, organization was indispensable.[54]

In regard to the relationship between church and culture, she warns, "Conformity to worldly customs converts the church to the world. It never converts the world to Christ."[55] Yet,

> although there are evils existing in the church, and will be until the end of the world, the church in these last days is to be the light of the world that is polluted and demoralized by sin. The church, enfeebled and defective, needing to be reproved, warned, and counseled, is the only object upon earth upon which Christ bestows His supreme regard. The world is a workshop in which, through the cooperation of human and divine agencies, Jesus is making experiments by His grace and divine mercy upon human hearts.[56]

Ellen White placed much emphasis on the unity of the church (cf. John 17:21), as reflected in the following statement:

> God is leading a people out from the world upon the exalted platform of eternal truth—the commandments of God and the faith of Jesus. He will discipline and fit up his people. They will not be at variance, one believing one thing, and another having faith and views entirely opposite, each moving independently of the body. Through the diversity of the gifts and governments he has placed

---

[54] [Ellen G.] White, "Dear Brethren of the General Conference," *Daily Bulletin of the General Conference*, Jan. 29, 1893, 22.

[55] E. G. White, "Workers for God," *RH*, June 20, 1882, 386; *idem*, *The Great Controversy between Christ and Satan* (1888), 509.

[56] E. G. White, *Testimonies to Ministers and Gospel Workers*, 49–50.

in the church, they will all come to the unity of the faith.[57]

Somewhat in line with J. H. Waggoner's *The Church: Its Organization, Ordinances, and Discipline* (1886), two other books were published in the early 1900s. One was H. M. J. Richards's *Church Order and Its Divine Origin and Importance* (1906). Speaking of "The Authority of the Gospel Ministry," Richards made ecclesiastical and ministerial authority directly dependent on loyalty to God's Word. He argued that,

> The true ministry has, in the church of Christ, authority supreme in all spiritual matters because it is the authority of the Word of God. 2 Tim. 3:15–17; 4:1–5 ... But, since the "all authority" is dependent upon the speaking of "these things"—the Word—therefore, when any minister or ministry departs from the Word, that minister or ministry has lost all authority in that thing in which departure exists. Since the authority is in the Word, therefore, when the Word of God is absent, there can be no authority.[58]

The second (and more influential) book was J. N. Loughborough's *The Church: Its Organization, Order, and Discipline* (1907), which addressed the church and its organization more doctrinally through biblical metaphors such as a building, the head and the body, the shepherd and his flock, the vine and its branches, the light of the world, the rulers, and the ambassadors.[59]

A new *Church Manual* came off the press in 1932, justifying its publication in the following terms:

> As the work of the church has grown and spread into many lands, it has become increasingly evident that a Manual on church government is needed to set forth and preserve our denominational practices and polity. An ever-increasing number of men are being called into positions of responsibility as ministers and church officers. To all these a work of this kind should prove helpful in the administration of church work.[60]

---

[57] Ellen G. White, *Testimony for the Church*, No. 24 (Battle Creek, MI; Steam Press of the Seventh-day Adventist Publishing Association, 1875), 164; idem, *Testimonies for the Church* (Mountain View, CA: Pacific Press, 1948), 3:446.

[58] H. M. J. Richards, *Church Order and Its Divine Origin and Importance* (Denver, CO: Colorado Tract Society, 1906), 16–17.

[59] J. N. Loughborough, *The Church: Its Organization, Order, and Discipline* (Washington, DC: Review and Herald, 1907).

[60] General Conference of Seventh-day Adventists, *Church Manual* (Washington, DC: General Confer-

Defining the church from a pragmatic perspective, the *Manual* stated:

> The church is an organization of individuals who hold the same faith and doctrines in common. If all such individuals lived in one locality, the form of organization would be simple, but being scattered in many lands, other steps in maintaining unity of faith and action are necessary.[61]

In the late 1930s and early 1940s, two new titles dealt with church organization. First, C. C. Crisler's 265-page *Organization: Its Character, Purpose, Place, and Development in the Seventh-day Adventist Church* (1938) provided an extensive compilation of Adventist sources dealing with the subject, with special emphasis on the Ellen White writings.[62] Second, Oliver Montgomery's 296-page *Principles of Church Organization and Administration* (1942) mentioned that the apostolic church was operated with the following six fundamental principles: 1) "ecclesiastical authority," 2) "delegated authority," 3) "representative government," 4) "recognition of autonomy, limited and unlimited," 5) "recognition of relationship to other congregations, the general interests of the whole body of churches," and 6) "the holding of general councils or conferences representing the entire sisterhood of churches." He suggested that these principles should also inform "the church of Christ today." In regard to the Seventh-day Adventist Church, Montgomery affirmed that it has "an organization that is second to none in the religious world."[63]

From 1888 to 1950, Seventh-day Adventists continued to consider themselves God's end-time remnant people and viewed other Christian denominations as upholding the "false doctrines" of Babylon, which include "the natural immortality of the soul, the eternal torment of the wicked, the denial of the pre-existence of Christ prior to His birth in Bethlehem, and advocating and exalting the first day of the week above God's holy and sanctified day."[64] Those teachings were perceived as the core of the end-time eschatological polarization between those who "keep the commandments of God, and the faith of Jesus" (Rev 14:12) and those who

---

ence of Seventh-day Adventists, 1932), 5.

[61] Ibid., 8.

[62] C. C. Crisler, *Organization: Its Character, Purpose, Place, and Development in the Seventh-day Adventist Church* (Washington, DC: Review and Herald, 1938).

[63] Oliver Montgomery, *Principles of Church Organization and Administration* (Washington, DC: Review and Herald, 1942), 69, 85.

[64] Ellen G. White, *Testimonies to Ministers and Gospel Workers* (Mountain View, CA: Pacific Press, 1923), 61.

"worship the beast and his image, and receive his mark" (Rev 14:9–11).

Seventh-day Adventists kept their view of Roman Catholicism as the end-time religious power that will persecute those who "keep the commandments of God and have the testimony of Jesus Christ" (Rev 12:17). But over the years, Adventists assumed a "more conciliatory" position toward the Evangelicals.[65] First, the post-1888 emphasis on salvation by grace through faith brought the Adventist message closer to the evangelical views on the subject. Second, during the 1920s and 1930s, Seventh-day Adventists explicitly supported Evangelical Fundamentalism in uplifting the trustworthiness of the Bible in the context of the Modernist-Fundamentalist controversy.[66] F. M. Wilcox even suggested that "Seventh-day Adventists, with their historical belief in the Divine Word, should count themselves the chief of Fundamentalists today."[67]

Between 1888 and 1950, Seventh-day Adventists moved from a more restricted Adventist-distinctive-doctrine approach to a broader, more balanced Adventist/evangelical doctrinal emphasis. The functional adjustments of the Adventist organizational structure took place in the first two decades of the 20th century, helping this international fast-growing denomination to maintain its basic doctrinal unity and to move more effectively into a true worldwide mission endeavor. However, the post-1950 era would see many voices challenging the Adventist identity from within the church itself.

Ecclesiological Challenges (1950–2012)

Seventh-day Adventism coped with defiant apostasies and offshoot movements throughout its history.[68] Traditionally, challengers to the church tended either to reconcile themselves with it or leave and criticize from outside its membership. But from the 1950s onward, the pattern changed considerably. Many critics remained as church members, criticizing it from within. This brought about a much more challenging reality because, as a general rule, criticisms from *outside* tend to unite the church, while criticisms from *within* tend to divide it.

---

[65] Reinder Bruinsma, *Seventh-day Adventist Attitudes toward Roman Catholicism, 1844–1965* (Berrien Springs, MI: Andrews University Press, 1994), xi, 299–300.

[66] For a comparative study between Seventh-day Adventism and Fundamentalism, see Carl Walter Daggy, "A Comparative Study of Certain Aspects of Fundamentalism with Seventh-day Adventism" (M.A. thesis, Seventh-day Adventist Theological Seminary, 1955).

[67] F. M. W[ilcox], "Forsaking the Foundations of Faith," *RH*, Nov. 28, 1929, 14. See also George McCready Price, "The Significance of Fundamentalism," *RH*, May 12, 1927, 13–14.

[68] Some of those Adventist apostasies and offshoot movements are treated by Lowell Tarling in *The Edges of Seventh-day Adventism* (Bermagui South, Australia: Galilee Publication, 1981).

One of the most significant and enduring criticisms gravitated around the understanding of the 1888 Minneapolis General Conference Session. In early 1950, Robert J. Wieland and Donald K. Short, missionaries to Africa, questioned the General Conference's supposed antagonistic position of the church at that conference session. For them, the church had committed a corporate sin, and it would not receive the blessings of the loud cry of the third angel until it repents corporately at a future General Conference session. Wieland and Short exposed their views in a 208-page document titled, "1888 Re-examined,"[69] to which the General Conference responded the next year.[70] But even so, Wieland and Short continued to promote the idea that since 1888 the church has been guilty of a corporate sin.

1957's *Seventh-day Adventists Answer Questions on Doctrine* (usually known only as *Questions on Doctrine*)[71] brought to the surface a struggle developing within the church, one with long-lasting ecclesiological implications. The book contained revised answers by Adventist scholars (LeRoy E. Froom, Roy A. Anderson, W. E. Read, and others) to evangelical ministers (Walter R. Martin, George E. Cannon, and Donald G. Barnhouse) who participated in the Seventh-day Adventist-Evangelical conferences of 1955–1956.[72] Those conferences led Barnhouse and Martin to appeal to the larger evangelical community to start viewing the Seventh-day Ad-

---

[69] Robert J. Wieland and Donald K. Short, "1888 Re-examined" (Manuscript presented to the GC leaders, 1950). See also *idem*, *1888 Re-examined*, rev. and updated ed. (Uniontown, OH: 1888 Message Study Committee, 1987); *idem*, *1988 Re-examined: A Review of What Happened a Hundred Years After 1888* (Paris, OH: 1888 Message Study Committee, 1989).

[70] W. E. Read and Frank H. Yost (for the Defense Literature Committee) to R. J. Wieland and D. K. Short, Dec. 4, 1951, White Estate; "Further Appraisal of the Manuscript '1888 Re-examined'" (Mimeographed document, General Conference, 1958), White Estate. See more recent responses in footnote 45, above.

[71] *Seventh-day Adventists Answer Questions on Doctrine: An Explanation of Certain Major Aspects of Seventh-day Adventist Belief* (Washington, DC: Review and Herald, 1957).

[72] For further study about the 1950s dialogues between Evangelicals and Seventh-day Adventists, which led to the publication of *Questions on Doctrine* (1957), see Roy A. Anderson, "Brief Story of the Origin of *Questions on Doctrine*" (unpublished manuscript, n.d.), T. E. Unruh, "The Seventh-day Adventist Evangelical Conferences of 1955–1956," *Adventist Heritage* 4 (Winter 1977): 35–46; Schwarz, *Light Bearers to the Remnant*, 542–546; Jerry Moon, "M. L. Andreasen, L. E. Froom, and the Controversy over *Questions on Doctrine*" (research paper, Andrews University, 1988); George R. Knight's "Historical and Theological Introduction to the Annotated Edition" and notes, in *Seventh-day Adventists Answer Questions on Doctrine*, annotated ed. (Berrien Springs, MI: Andrews University Press, 2003); A. Leroy Moore, *Questions on Doctrine Revisited! Keys to the Doctrine of Atonement and Experience of At-one-ment* (Ithaca, MI: AB Publishing, 2005); and Juhyeok Nam, *Reactions to the Seventh-day Adventist Evangelical Conferences and* Questions on Doctrine, *1955–1971* (*Questions on Doctrine* 50th Anniversary Conference Limited Edition, [Andrews University, Berrien Springs, MI, 2007]).

ventist Church as a true Christian denomination.[73] Their appeal was so clear that even *Time Magazine's* December 31, 1956 issue included an unsigned article titled "Peace with the Adventists."[74]

But not everyone was pleased with the conferences and the content of *Questions on Doctrine*, published under the sponsorship of the General Conference Ministerial Association. M. L. Andreasen, a former professor of the Seventh-day Adventist Theological Seminary and the father of modern Adventist perfectionism,[75] blamed the church leadership for teaching a "new" anti-Adventist theology. He spread his criticisms within the church between 1957 and 1960, first, in a mimeographed nine-part series called "The Atonement"[76] (for ministers) and, later, in a new series of six, "Letters to the Churches"[77] (for church members in general). Disagreeing specifically with the concepts of an unfallen human nature of Christ and the atonement based on the cross,[78] Andreasen did not hesitate to call *Questions on Doctrine* "a most dangerous heresy."[79] His bellicose attitude towards the General Conference leadership set the tone for the so-called "independent ministries" that would assume a similar stance from the late 1980s on.

The last three decades of the 20th century saw an increasing polarization of the edges of Seventh-day Adventism.[80] On one side, liberal revi-

---

[73] See e.g., Donald G. Barhouse, "Are Seventh-day Adventists Christians? A New Look at Seventh-day Adventism," *Et*, Sept. 1956, 6–7, 43–45; Walter R. Martin, "The Truth About Seventh-day Adventism," 3-part series in *Et*, Oct. 1956, 6–7, 38–40; Nov. 1956, 20–21, 38–43; Jan. 1957, 12–13, 38–40; Donald G. Barnhouse, "Postscript on Seventh-day Adventism," *Et*, Nov. 1957, 22–23, 45; Walter R. Martin, *The Truth About Seventh-day Adventism* (Grand Rapids, MI: Zondervan, 1960).

[74] "Peace with the Adventists," *Time*, Dec. 31, 1956, 48–49.

[75] For a critical exposition of M. L. Andreasen's "last generation" theology, see Knight, *A Search for Identity*, 144–152.

[76] See *The M. L. Andreasen File: Manuscripts and Letters Pertaining to the Evangelical Conferences of 1955–1956* (St. Maries, ID: LMN Publishing, 1988), 1–88.

[77] See M. L. Andreasen, *Letters to the Churches* (Conway, MS: Gems of Truth, n.d.).

[78] Cf. Knight, *A Search for Identity*, 164–173.

[79] [M. L. Andreasen], "A Most Dangerous Heresy," *L. Andreasen File*, 89.

[80] For further study on those tensions within the Seventh-day Adventist Church since the early 1970s, see e.g., William G. Johnsson, *The Fragmenting of Adventism* (Boise, ID: Pacific Press, 1995); A. Leroy Moore, *Adventism in Conflict* (Hagerstown, MD: Review and Herald, 1995); Samuel Koranteng-Pipim, *Receiving the Word: How New Approaches to the Bible Impact Our Biblical Faith and Lifestyle* (Berrien Springs, MI: Berean Books, 1996); Alberto R. Timm, "A History of Seventh-day Adventist Views on Biblical and Prophetic Inspiration (1844–2000)," *JATS* 10 (1999): 513–541; Laura L. Vance, *Seventh-day Adventism in Crisis: Gender and Sectarian Change in an Emerging Religion* (Urbana and Chicago: University of Illinois Press, 1999); Knight, *A Search for Identity*, 160–97; Richard W. Schwarz and Floyd Greenleaf, *Light Bearers: A History of the Seventh-day Adventist Church*, rev. ed. (Nampa, ID: Pacific Press, 2000), 633–641; Alberto R. Timm, "Issues on Ellen G. White and Her Role in the Seventh-day Adventist Church" (Lecture presented at the General Con-

sionists, with a late 20th-century socio-cultural agenda, tried to modernize the denomination to a more-*evangelical*-than-Adventist perspective. On the other side, some traditionalists, with a nineteenth-century historical agenda, would like to push the church back to a more-*Adventist*-than-evangelical approach.[81] Without overstating or generalizing such polarization, it has resulted in some challenges to the identity of the church in some parts of the world.

Despite challenges, Seventh-day Adventism is a very stable Christian denomination, with a well-defined prophetic self-consciousness. Even without any formal ecclesiological statement in their pre-1980 statements of beliefs (1872, 1889, and 1931),[82] over the years Seventh-day Adventists operated with what could be called an "implicit ecclesiology" that would be systematized more explicitly from the early 1980s on. Especially meaningful in this process were three official/representative doctrinal expositions intended to preserve and strengthen the doctrinal unity of the denomination. The first was the 1980 Statement of "27 Fundamental Beliefs of Seventh-day Adventists,"[83] officially approved by the delegates to the 1980 General Conference session in Dallas, Texas. Three of those beliefs explicitly deal with ecclesiology:

Church

The church is the community of believers who confess Jesus Christ as Lord and Saviour. In continuity with the people of God in Old Testament times, we are called out from the world; and we join together for worship, for fellowship, for instruction in the Word, for the celebration of the Lord's Supper, for service to all mankind, and for the worldwide proclamation of the gospel. The church

---

ference Field Conference in Theology, Greece and Turkey, April 29–May 7, 2002); and Richard W. O'Ffill, *Lord, Save My Church: Tackling the Tough Issues* (Nampa, ID: Pacific Press, 2007).

[81] The non-official church magazine *Adventist Today* even spoke in 1993 about the existence, in North America, of 1) "Mainstream Adventism;" 2) "Evangelical Adventism;" 3) "Progressive Adventism;" and 4) "Historic Adventism;" ("A Gathering of Adventisms," special section in *Adventist Today*, Jan.–Feb. 1993, 4–16).

[82] See *A Declaration of the Fundamental Principles Taught and Practiced by the Seventh-day Adventists* (Battle Creek, MI; Steam Press of the Seventh-day Adventist Publishing Association, 1872); reprinted in "Fundamental Principles," *Signs of the Times*, June 4, 1874, 3; "Fundamental Principles of Seventh-day Adventists," *Seventh-day Adventist Year Book of Statistics for 1889* (Battle Creek, MI: Review & Herald, 1889), 147–151; reprinted in "Fundamental Principles of Seventh-day Adventists," *Word of Truth Series*, No. 5—Extra (July 1897); "Fundamental Beliefs of Seventh-day Adventists," *1931 Year Book of the Seventh-day Adventist Denomination* (Washington, DC: Review & Herald, 1931), 377–380.

[83] "Section Actions," *AtR*, May 1, 1980, 23, 25–27; *Seventh-day Adventist Church Manual*, rev. 1981 (Washington, DC: General Conference of Seventh-day Adventists, 1981), 31–46; *Seventh-day Adventist Yearbook — 1981* (Washington, DC: General Conference of Seventh-day Adventists, 1981), 5–8.

derives its authority from Christ, who is the incarnate Word, and from the Scriptures, which are the written Word. The church is God's family; adopted by Him as children, its members live on the basis of the new covenant. The church is the body of Christ, a community of faith of which Christ Himself is the Head. The church is the bride for whom Christ died that He might sanctify and cleanse her. At His return in triumph, He will present her to Himself a glorious church, the faithful of all the ages, the purchase of His blood, not having spot or wrinkle, but holy and without blemish. (Gen 12:3; Acts 7:38; Eph 4:11–15; 3:8–11; Matt 28:19–20; 16:13–20; 18:18; Eph 2:19–22; 1:22, 23; 5:23–27; Col 1:17–18.)

Remnant and its Mission

The universal church is composed of all who truly believe in Christ, but in the last days, a time of widespread apostasy, a remnant has been called out to keep the commandments of God and the faith of Jesus. This remnant announces the arrival of the judgment hour, proclaims salvation through Christ, and heralds the approach of His second advent. This proclamation is symbolized by the three angels of Revelation 14; it coincides with the work of judgment in heaven and results in a work of repentance and reform on earth. Every believer is called to have a personal part in this worldwide witness. (Rev 12:17; 14:6–12; 18:1–4; 2 Cor 5:10; Jude 3, 14; 1 Pet 1:16–19; 2 Pet 3:10–14; Rev 21:1–14.)

Unity in the Body of Christ

The church is one body with many members, called from every nation, kindred, tongue, and people. In Christ we are a new creation; distinctions of race, culture, learning, and nationality, and differences between high and low, rich and poor, male and female, must not be divisive among us. We are all equal in Christ, who by one Spirit has bonded us into one fellowship with Him and with one another; we are to serve and be served without partiality or reservation. Through the revelation of Jesus Christ in the Scriptures we share the same faith and hope, and reach out in one witness to all. This unity has its source in the oneness of the triune God, who has adopted us as His children. (Rom. 12:4, 5; 1 Cor. 12:12–14; Matt. 28:19–20; Ps. 133:1; 2 Cor. 5:16–17; Acts 17:26, 27; Gal. 3:27, 29; Col. 3:10–15; Eph. 4:14–16; 4:1–6; John 17:20–23.)[84]

---

[84] *Seventh-day Adventist Church Manual*, rev. 1981, 36–38; *Seventh-day Adventist Yearbook—1981*, 6.

A second official/representative document was an exposition of each of those 27 Fundamental Beliefs in a 392-page book produced by the General Conference Ministerial Association and published in 1988 under the title *Seventh-day Adventists Believe...*[85] In this book the end-time remnant people are described as coming into existence after the end of the 1,260 prophetic days in 1798 (Rev 12:6, 14), and as characterized by keeping 1) the faith of Jesus, 2) the commandments of God, and 3) the testimony of Jesus (Rev 12:17; 14:12; 19:10).[86] It places the Adventist identity in line with the original Adventist self-understanding.

The third far more comprehensive doctrinal exposition was the scholarly 1,027-page volume published in 2000 as *Handbook of Seventh-day Adventist Theology*.[87] This *Handbook* was produced under the sponsorship of the Biblical Research Institute Committee of the General Conference and edited by Raoul Dederen. Some sections of those documents deal specifically with the nature of the church (Raoul Dederen)[88] and the end-time remnant (Hans K. LaRondelle).[89] LaRondelle summarized the Seventh-day Adventist ecclesiological identity in the following terms:

> Adventists see themselves as a fulfillment of apocalyptic prophecy, a prophetic movement called to prepare a people in all parts of the earth to be ready for Christ's appearance. They consider themselves collectively to be the fulfillment of the promised Elijah in Malachi 4:5, 6, sent by God "to restore all things" (Matt 17:11). Therefore, they are committed to restoring all the neglected Bible truths of the new covenant. They see their message as the ultimate fulfillment of Isaiah 58:12–14, combining ideas of restoration and preparation.

They emphasize certain truths revealed in the end-time prophecies as testing truths, which reflects their understanding and historical applications of the three angels' messages. They emphasize the restored gospel truths of justification by faith in Christ Jesus and sanctification in willing obedience from a redeemed heart to the covenant law of God, the

---

[85] *Seventh-day Adventists Believe... A Biblical Exposition of 27 Fundamental Doctrines* (Washington, DC: Ministerial Association of the General Conference of SDAs, 1988). A 2nd revised and updated version of the book came out in 2005.

[86] Ibid. (1988), 161–163.

[87] Raoul Dederen, ed., *Handbook of Seventh-day Adventist Theology* (Hagerstown, MD: Review and Herald, 2000).

[88] Raoul Dederen, "The Church," ibid., 538–581.

[89] Hans K. LaRondelle, "The Remnant and the Three Angels' Messages," ibid., 857–892.

law by which God will judge His covenant people (James 2:12; Rom 2:13; 2 Cor 5:10). They believe that the seventh-day Sabbath of the fourth commandment, altered into the Sunday-Sabbath by the postapostolic church, now should be restored as the appointed sign of worshiping the Creator in truth and in the Spirit (Isa 56; 58; Dan 7:25; Mal 4:5–6). They view the restored Sabbath as a providential testing truth to counteract the modern dogma of evolution, one of the key heresies of the end-time. To them the Sabbath celebration is not an isolated test of the correct day of the week, but an appointed sign of true worship of the Creator by a redeemed and sanctified people. They honor the biblical teaching that professed believers are saved by grace and judged by the works produced by their relation with Christ.

Seventh-day Adventists believe it is their appointed role as the remnant church to restore revealed truth in worshiping God as Creator-Redeemer by restoring the seventh-day Sabbath as the memorial of His creation and the sign of giving Him glory. Based on the urgency of this message, they summon God's children in all churches to flee from the historic apostasy to escape punishment for Babylon's sins under the seven last plagues, and instead, to receive the fullness of God's Spirit and be ready for meet Christ in His glory (Rev 18:1–5).[90]

Insightful Adventist responses to the ecumenical movement were penned by Walter R. Beach, proposing that the Apostles' Creed could provide the "basis of ecumenical agreement among divided Christians today."[91] And Bert B. Beach demonstrated the dangers of modern ecumenism.[92] The Seventh-day Adventist self-understanding as God's end-time remnant was addressed with a more liberal approach in Jack W.

---

[90] Ibid., 887–888. Helpful insights into Seventh-day Adventist ecclesiology are found in other ecclesiological works. See for instance, Johannes Mager, ed., *Die Gemeinde und ihr Auftrag*, Studien zur adventistischen Ekklesiologie, vol. 2 (Bern: Saatkorn-Verlag, 1994); G. A. Klingbeil, M. G. Klingbeil, and M. A. Núñez, ed., *Pensar la iglesia hoy*, Mario Veloso, ed., *La Iglesia, cuerpo de Cristo y plenitud de Dios*, Serie Monográfica de Estudios Bíblicos y Teológicos de la Universidad Adventista del Plata (Libertador San Martin, Entre Rios, Argentina: Editorial Universidad Adventista del Plata, 2006); The ecclesiology of Reinder Bruinsma is largely based on four church characteristics of the Apostles' Creed, namely 1) unity, 2) universality, 3) holiness, and 4) apostolicity. For him, "God's church does not coincide with one particular denomination or religious tradition" (*The Body of Christ: A Biblical Understanding of the Church*, Library of Adventist Theology [Hagerstown, MD: Review and Herald, 2009], 59–70, 154). By contrast, George R. Knight, in his book *The Apocalyptic Vision and the Neutering of Adventism* (2008), states forcefully that, if Adventism loses its apocalyptic vision, there is no reason for its existence as a denomination.

[91] Walter R. Beach, *The Creed that Changed the World* (Mountain View, CA: Pacific Press, 1971), back cover.

[92] Bert B. Beach, *Ecumenism: Boon or Bane?* (Washington, DC: Review and Herald, 1974).

Provonsha's *A Remnant in Crisis* (1993),[93] and from a more conservative perspective in Clifford Goldstein's *The Remnant: Biblical Reality or Wishful Thinking?* (1994);[94] Carmelo L. Martines's Th.D. dissertation, "El concepto de remanente en la Iglesia Adventista del Séptimo Día" (2002);[95] and the book *Toward a Theology of the Remnant* (2009), edited by Ángel M. Rodríguez.[96]

Important bilateral conversations between the Lutheran World Federation and the Seventh-day Adventist Church were held between 1994 and 1998. The final report and scholarly papers presented at those conversations were published in 2000 in the book, *Lutherans & Adventists in Conversation: Report and Papers Presented, 1994–1998*.[97] The Adventist chapters of the book emphasize the Adventist soteriological-eschatological emphasis. Accepted by the representatives of both denominations, the final report states, "We recommend that Lutherans in their national and regional church contexts do not treat the Seventh-day Adventist church as a sect but as a free church and a Christian world communion."[98]

Conclusion

The present study provided a brief historical overview of the development of Seventh-day Adventist ecclesiology across time. Seventh-day Adventist ecclesiology was divided into following periods: 1) Adventist Ecclesiology (1844–1886), 2) Adventist-Evangelical Ecclesiology (1886–1950), and 3) Ecclesiological Challenges (1950–2012). The discussion showed some developments of the Seventh-day Adventist message, organizational structure, mission, and identity in each of those periods.

Previous attempts to develop a Seventh-day Adventist ecclesiology have oscillated between approaches that were more Adventist and those more Evangelical. Those who see the denomination as a prophetic movement usually look for ecclesiological allusions in the apocalyptic writings of the Bible. Those who consider the denomination as a mere Christian

---

[93] Jack W. Provonsha, *A Remnant in Crisis* (Hagerstown, MD: Review and Herald, 1993).

[94] Clifford Goldstein, *The Remnant: Biblical Reality or Wishful Thinking?* (Boise, ID: Pacific Press, 1994).

[95] Martines, "El concepto de remanente en la Iglesia Adventista del Séptimo Día."

[96] Ángel M. Rodríguez, ed., *Toward a Theology of the Remnant: An Adventist Ecclesiological Perspective*, Adventist Ecclesiology, vol. 1 (Silver Spring, MD: Biblical Research Institute, 2009).

[97] *Lutherans & Adventists in Conversation: Report and Papers Presented, 1994–1998* (Silver Spring, MD, and Geneva: General Conference of Seventh-day Adventists and Lutheran World Federation, 2000).

[98] "Adventists and Lutherans in Conversation, 1994–1998: Report of the Bilateral Conversations between the Lutheran World Federations and the Seventh-day Adventist Church," ibid., 22.

church tend to define it by means of the church metaphors found in the gospels and the epistles. However, by recognizing Seventh-day Adventism both as a prophetic-eschatological movement as well as an organized church, one has to look for an ecclesiology that, going beyond the various ecclesiologies of the Christian tradition,[99] is able to merge and harmonize both of those basic characteristics.

---

[99] See e.g., Veli-Matti Kärkkäinen, *An Introduction to Ecclesiology: Ecumenical, Historical & Global Perspectives* (Downers Grove, IL: InterVarsity, 2002).

CHAPTER 11

Oneness of the Church in Message and Mission: Its Ground

Ángel Manuel Rodríguez

Probably one of the most damaging effects of sin has been its fragmenting impact on the very structure of creation and particular on human nature. Practically everything we know is characterized by fragmentation and lack of real unity or wholeness. We find in the cosmos, among many other things, good and evil, order and disorder, violence and peace, love and hatred, justice and injustice, and life and death. These phenomena lack integration and in fact cannot be integrated into a harmonious system. Sin and evil fragmented everything and we find ourserlves surrounded by fragments of creation moving around us without cohesiveness. Everything is finally possessed by total disintegration and death. But the most damaging effect of sin has been on human nature. The fragmentation of sin constituted every person into his or her own center of existence obsessed with self-preservation. Each one has become an independent cell seeking to survive at almost any cost. The unity that we seem to find in political structures or in the field of business is a superficial one that disintegrates as soon as the self-interest of those holding it together or living under the system are seriously damaged. We come together in order to satisfy our urge for personal survival or for the survival of the group from which we derive what we need. Even when working together we still remain fragmented: independent cells seeking self-satisfaction.

But the fragmenting impact of sin is also present in the deepest chambers of our own being. We exist in tension with ourselves being pulled in different directions by our emotions, our will, our reason, and our love and hatred. We are fragmented cells lacking a unifying center and pretending that our ego holds us together as individuals when in reality our ego is disoriented. It lacks a nucleus to orient itself and to provide cohesiveness to our inner being. Hence, it is difficult for humans to understand the nature of the unity promoted by the Scriptures and the need to seek it. Often the unity of the church is defined along the lines of a social club that contributes to my self-interest and as long as it fulfills that need we remain attached to it. But the nature of unity in the Bible requires relinquishing our obsession with our ego by finding a center outside ourselves that can hold us together in our inner being and in our social interaction.

The Bible unambiguously states that without Christ, humanity is enslaved by sin and under its lordship, each one doing the desires of the flesh as selfish fragments of life. The common Christian understanding of salvation—salvation is ours by faith in Christ as Savior—frees us from that condition and unites us. This unity becomes immediately visible within the community of believers, the church, established by Christ where individualism as an expression of fragmentation comes to an end and we learn to be united around the Lord.[1] In order for the church to remain united it is important for its members and leaders to understand what it is that holds us together as a global church and that nurtures and expresses that unity. In what follows we will explore the nature and expression of the unity of the church, hoping that this will help us to work together as one people in a world characterized by fragmentation.

Christ and the Unity of the Church

The Scripture states that church unity is not the result of human ingenuity or cleverness, but the manifestation of God's creative power through His Son and the work of the Spirit. The Bible indicates that fragmentation is caused by forces opposed to God and to the cosmic order established by Him. Self-preservation is almost the natural condition of human existence. Consequently, we exist in a state of inner isolation, despite constant interaction with others. Therefore the oneness of the church is an anomaly in a world fragmented by sin. But more than an anomaly, it

---

[1] It is important for church members to recover the biblical concept of the solidarity of the people of God found in the Bible. It is, as we will discuss, firmly grounded in the mystery of the unity of the Godhead. For an important ecclesiological discussion of the tension between individualism and collectivismo, see Gerald A. Klingbeil, "Entre individualismo y colectivismo: hacia una perspectiva bíblica de la naturaleza de la iglesia," *Pensar la iglesia hoy: hacia una eclesiología adventista*, ed. Gerald A. Klingbeil, Martin G. Klingbeil, and Miguel Ángel Núñez (Argentina: Editorial Universitaria Adventista del Plata, 2002), 3–23.

is a manifestation of the grace and power of God in the life of those who, after listening to the message of salvation through Christ, embrace it with joy and gratitude.

The Incarnation and the Unity of the Church

The unity that the Bible promotes is grounded in the fact that God sent into this world a center, a nucleus, around which the whole cosmos, including the human race, can be reintegrated into wholeness, bringing to an end the fragmentation of the universe. The Son of God came into our world united to the Father and remained united to Him. He never became in Himself a fragment in a fragmented world. Consequently He became the unifying center of the church and of the cosmos. The mystery of the unity of the church is rooted in its union with the Risen Lord who is the very center of its existence (Eph 5:32). Therefore, unity is to be understood as a spiritual experience and then as an issue of organizational structure. Jesus placed the unity of the church at the very core of the nature and role of the church (John 17). This was probably based on the conviction that the origin of the church is located in the unity of the essence, will, and action of the Father and the Son.

It could be suggested that the church is the result of a theophany, namely the manifestation of the glory of God in human flesh (John 1:14; 11:40) that transforms individuals into the one people of God. In the Old Testament the people of Israel came into existence through theophany (Exod 19:10-11). It was at Sinai that God transformed the tribes of Israel into one people through the most majestic theophany recorded in the Old Testament (19:16-19). God descended, revealing Himself to the Israelites as their Redeemer, and entered into a covenant relationship with them. He became their God and they became His people (19:3-6). In the New Testament, Christ pulls together the Israel of faith through an even more majestic theophany—the incarnation.

The New Testament occasionally refers to the incarnation as an "epiphany" (Greek, *epiphaneia*, "appearing, appearance"). This term was used in secular Greek to indicate "the appearance of the saving deity and the experience of the saving act."[2] These same ideas are found in 2 Tim

---

[2] P. G. Müller, "*Epiphainō* to Appear," *EDNT* 2:44. This usage of the term is similar in meaning to the significance of the apparitions of God or the theophanies recorded in the Old Testament. In the Bible, the theophanies are moments when God gloriously revealed Himself as a warrior fighting against evil powers, manifesting His control over the powers of nature, and bringing salvation, guidance, and instruction to His people. On this topic, see J. Jeremias, "Theophany in the Old Testament," *IDBSupp*, 896-898; J. E. Alsup, "Theophany in the New Testament," ibid., 898-900; and particularly, Theodore Hiebert, "Theophany in the Old Testament," in *ABD* 6:505-511. Cf. Jeffry J. Niehaus, *God at Sinai: Covenant & Theophany in the Bible and Ancient Near East*

1:10: "But it [grace] has now been revealed through the appearing [*epiphaneia*] of our Savior." Here the appearance of God in Christ is also a revelation of His saving grace for us. The verb *epiphainō* ("to appear") is used in Luke 1:79, in a quote from Isaiah 9:1; 42:7 that is applied to the birth of Jesus, to indicate that Christ is "the light of the presence of God in the world."[3] Both the noun *epiphaneia* and the verb *epiphainō* ("to appear") are employed in the New Testament to refer to Jesus' earthly ministry (2 Tim 1:9–10; Titus 2:11; 3:4) as well as to His Second Coming (2 Tim 4:8; Titus 2:13; 2 Thess 2:8). John indicates that the Father moved individuals to come to Jesus and He, in turn, *revealed* to them the glory of the Father (17:6). Those who apprehended that glory—those who saw the epiphany—constituted His church. Consequently, the church now exists between two divine epiphanies: one in the incarnation and the other at the Second Advent—anticipated in hope—and they both contribute to hold the church together.

Unity in Christ

Through the incarnation Jesus became the center around which fragmented humans beings found wholeness and harmony. Jesus' understanding of the ground of the oneness of the church reveals the unique and even mysterious nature of this experience. During His intercessory prayer on behalf of the disciples, He specifically said to the Father: "I pray . . . that all of them may be one, Father, just as you are in me and I am in you. May they also be in us so that the world may believe that you have sent me" (John 17:20–21). As already indicated, Jesus was totally and absolutely untouched by the fragmentation that characterizes a world of rebellion. Herein lays the uniqueness of this Man, in Him the divine was incarnated and, while in that condition, He remained inseparably connected to the Father. A unifying nucleus entered our world, making it possible for sinful and disjointed human beings to find oneness in Him. This unifying center is found in the very being of Jesus who, in His own person, permanently reunited God with humanity. He revealed the saving and reconciling love and power of the Father. Those who see Jesus and believe that He is the only Son of God, full of grace and love, are being incorporated into this new creation of fellowship with Him, the Father, and one another (1 John 1:3).

According to Jesus, the church does not simply proclaim His message

---

(Grand Rapids, MI: Eerdmans, 1995); and George W. Savran, *Encountering the Divine: Theophany in Biblical Narrative* (New York: T & T Clark, 2005).

[3] Müller, "*Epiphainō*," 44.

of salvation; it is an essential expression of it. In a world split by sin and rebellion, the church stands as a visible witness to the saving work and power of Christ, who brought to an end the divisiveness of sin. Consequently, fragmentation in the church would evidence a worldly influence, a distancing from Christ, the incursion of the fragmenting nature of sin within the church itself, and a denial of the reconciling power of the cross. In other words, the unity of the church witnesses to the world that God sent His Son to reconcile us to Him and to one another. Without the oneness of the church, the saving power of the cross would hardly be apparent in this world.[4]

In His prayer for the church, Christ asks the Father to keep believers united to Him and to each other as He and the Father are united in the mystery of the trinity (John 17:21). The church participates in some way in the unity of the Godhead. Through the Spirit Christ establishes a union between Himself and believers as real as the union between the different parts of our bodies. In Scripture, this union is compared to the vital connection between the branches and the vine (John 15:4-5).[5] Here, we face a profound mystery that we will not be able fully to comprehend but which is of defining value in the development of an ecclesiology:

> The Holy Spirit, which proceeds from the only-begotten Son of God, binds the human agent, body, soul, and spirit, to the perfect, divine-human nature of Christ. This union is represented by the union of the vine and the branches. Finite man is united to the manhood of Christ. Through faith human nature is assimilated with Christ's nature. We are made one with God in Christ.[6]

The very existence of the church as the community of believers, its very life (John 12:23-24), its power to move and act in oneness, is determined by its union with the Lord (1 Cor 12:12-13, 27-28).

---

[4] Ellen White wrote: "Unity with Christ establishes a bond of unity with one another. This unity is the most convincing proof to the world of the majesty and virtue of Christ, and of His power to take away sin" ("Comments—John," *AdvBibComm* 5:1148). In another place she wrote, "In the oneness of Christ's church it will be proved that God sent His only-begotten Son into the world" (*Selected Messages* [Washington, DC: Review and Herald, 1958], 1:385).

[5] "We are to be attached to the parent stock, and to receive nourishment from the Vine. Christ is our glorified Head, and the divine love flowing from the heart of God, rests in Christ, and is communicated to those who have been united to Him. This divine love entering the soul inspires it with gratitude, frees it from its spiritual feebleness, from pride, vanity, and selfishness, and from all that would deform the Christian character" (Ellen G. White, *Fundamentals of Christian Education*, 178-179).

[6] White, *Selected Messages*, 1:251.

Once separated from God by the lying devices of Satan, they [God's children] are reunited to him by learning the lesson of redeeming love, as manifested in the great sacrifice of Christ in giving his precious life for mankind. *The human is united to the divine by a tie so strong that unfallen worlds, angels, and men are amazed*, for those who believe in the love of God to them are secure in the refuge of his love, ...[7]

This is a new community, a new humanity born from above, from the Spirit (John 3:5-7). Believers no longer belong to a disjointed world.[8] They exist in union with Christ and with one another as co-participants of the saving revelation of God in Christ.[9] The church is the mystery of the heavenly union of its members with its Savior and Lord.[10] What holds the church together is its union with the Risen Lord made possible by Him, through the work of the Holy Spirit, in the human heart. Only those who have been united to Christ through faith in the power of the Spirit will find in Him the center of a new life and will also find in the unity of the church their joy.

---

[7] Ellen G. White, "Revelation of God Through Christ," *Signs of the Times*, April 11, 1895 (italics mine).

[8] Commenting on Paul's views on ecclesiastical unity, Raoul Dederen states: "Such a unity toward which Paul strove transcends the divisive elements of race, class, and gender (Gal. 3:28). It is not the result of a voluntary act of uniting on the part of the members of Christ's body, but a unity enabled by the Spirit, for the church has found oneness in Christ (Eph. 5:2-15)" ("The Church," *Handbook of Seventh-day Adventist Theology*, ed. Raoul Dederen [Hagerstown, MD: Review and Herald, 2000], 562).

[9] This type of union is rooted in the Christian experience of the new birth. At that moment, the Spirit implants in us new emotions and values, thus beginning in us a new life in union with Christ. Ellen G. White connects the new birth with the privilege of partaking of the divine nature: "The new birth consists in having new motives, new tastes, new tendencies. Those who are begotten unto a new life by the Holy Spirit have become partakers of the divine nature" (Ellen G. White, *Lift Him Up* [Hagerstown, MD: Review and Herald, 1988], 123). The life of the new birth is "a new life derived from His [Jesus] own life..." (*Sons and Daughters* [Washington, DC: Review and Herald, 1955], 299). We become part of the body of Christ; one with Him in heart, soul, and spirit—"As soon as the human agent becomes united with Christ in heart, soul, and spirit, the Father loves that soul as a part of Christ, as a member of the body of Christ, He himself being the glorious head" (*Fundamentals of Christian Education* [Nashville, TN: Southern Publishing, 1923], 466). It is not that God did not love the person before, but that now love reaches new potentials of intimacy because the believer is united to Christ.

[10] After commenting on the mystery of this union, Ellen G. White is only able to use doxological language: "God in Christ, and Christ in God, and Christ abiding by faith in man, is so large a truth that the mind cannot fully comprehend it. It is so great a theme, so grand a conception, so far beyond the power of reason to explain, that, as we speak of it, we feel our insufficiency. Our comprehension is too restricted, our language too limited, to unfold this great truth. The mind fails and sinks down weary under the effort, and we can speak of this truth only in softened, subdued tones, acknowledging our helplessness, and bowing in adoration before the infinite love that has provided so great a salvation" (*Signs of the Times*, May 18, 1891).

The importance Christ places on the unity of the church provides the Adventist Church a motivation for mission. The fragmentation that characterizes the Christian church is symptomatic of its spiritual condition and contributes to weaken the efficacy of its witness. God's end-time remnant seeks to bring healing to this condition through a constant emphasis on the imperative return to Scripture as the foundation of any permanent reunification of Christianity. In the performance of that task the remnant must be vigilant against any spiritual seismic experience within itself that could fragment its own unity in Christ.

The unity that Christ has made possible for the church finds expression and is nurtured by the message, the unity, the lifestyle, the biblical worldview, the mission, and the organizational structure of the church.[11]

Unity in Message

The written Word and the incarnated Word are deeply connected. Therefore, our spiritual union with Christ brings with it a new self-perception and convictions that flow from Scripture (Eph 4:4–6). These convictions constitute a common and unique body of beliefs that defines us and is one of the most important unifying elements within the Seventh-day Adventist Church—God's end-time remnant. Although we have so much in common with other Christian bodies, it is clear that our set of beliefs forms a unique system of biblical truth, framed by the biblical understanding of reality.[12] Our system of doctrine produces something that is larger than the sum of its parts. What we have found to be biblically true in the Christian world has been placed within the context of other biblical truths that were overlooked, ignored, or rejected. The result has been a system of truth that integrates creation, sin, soteriology, pneumatology, and eschatology in unique ways. What makes this body of beliefs significant and authoritative is its biblical foundation.[13] It is the result of careful biblical study affirmed by the global community of believers. It is not the product of a few individuals working in isolation from the world church. It is what is called, in Christian theology, the expression of the *consensus fidelium*, that is to say the global consensus of the faithful ones created within the community of faith through the study of the Scripture and the work of the Spirit.

---

[11] Since some of these topics are fully treated in other chapters in this book, our discussion of some of them will be brief.

[12] See Fernando Canale, "The Mission and the Message of the Remnant: A Methodological Approach," in this volume.

[13] On the nature and role of the Adventist Statement of Fundamental Beliefs, see Kwabena Donkor, "The Role of the Statement of Fundamental Beliefs in the Church," in this volume.

This means that truth is not defined by a small group of individuals, but by the work of the Spirit in the global community of believers. This requires that believers be in constant touch with Scripture, listening and willing to submit to it. This also requires that no one claim to be the exclusive depository of biblical truth—such truth belongs to the community of believers. Believers should be characterized by a spirit of humility, a willingness to set aside personal views that do not conform to the biblical witness and to the work of the Spirit within the church. These are not two different sources of truth for the church but one, in that the Scripture was the result of the work of the Spirit and that the Spirit is the best interpreter of Scripture. Any claim of truth based on a subjective experience of the Spirit should be tested by the content of Scripture.

Since the Lord holds our church together, we find Him at the very center of this body of beliefs, revealing through them different aspects of His work and His genuine concern for the human race. He is the one who integrates the different doctrinal elements into a truth relevant for the last days. When we proclaim them, we are in fact proclaiming Christ in them and not just the biblical and rational foundation of the doctrine. This body of beliefs contributes to unite us around the world as a community of believers. Obviously, the depth of knowledge is not the same everywhere, but the message is. Adventists around the world will know about the substitutionary death of Jesus on the cross, His ministry in the heavenly temple, His Second Coming, etc. These doctrines are dear to all of them and meaningful enough to be shared with others.

Unity in Lifestyle[14]

Our union with Christ expresses itself in all aspects of our lives. A Christian lifestyle seeks to answer this question: How should a follower of Christ live in a world of sin and evil while eagerly waiting for the coming of the Lord? The Bible clearly teaches that the Christian life should be lived a certain way (Eph 4:1–3; 2 Pet 3:11). Consequently, it provides specific and abundant guidance on how to live this life. The Christian church has always taught the value and need of biblical standards for the Christian life. Adventists are well known because of their particular lifestyle. It makes their identity quite visible.[15] There is some diversity in the details

---

[14] For a more detailed discussion of the Christian lifestyle and church standards, see Miroslav M. Kiš, "Christian Lifestyle and Behavior," *Handbook of Seventh-day Adventist Theology*, ed. Raoul Dederen (Hagerstown, MD: Review and Herald, 2000), 675–723.

[15] Adventist church standards address different aspects of the Christian life: *Spiritual Life* (prayer, Bible study, the proclamation of the gospel of salvation, attendance to church services, Sabbath observance, and proper use of our time); *Moral Life* (being careful with what we watch, read,

of our lifestyle, but this is to be expected in a world church formed by people of different cultures. However, there are some specific elements that are common to the global church and that contribute to strengthen and manifest the unity of the community of faith.

Biblical standards for the Christian life are not the gospel. Salvation is only and exclusively through the sacrificial death of Jesus. Nevertheless, church standards are not against the gospel but rather have the gospel as their center. They contribute to the unfolding of the meaning of the cross and embody the power and significance of the gospel in the life of the believer. It is this connection with the saving work of Christ that makes it possible for church standards to contribute to the visible unity of the church as a global community. The standards are our response to God's love revealed on the cross of Christ. They fundamentally spell out the nature of the Christian life.

In order to be a true Christian, Christ has to be accepted not only as Savior but also as Lord. Church standards provide the setting within which the lordship of Jesus is manifested in our lives. They are established by the world church as the minimum expression of the Lordship of Christ in the lives of church members.[16] They are required from those who are going to be baptized as indicating that they have made Christ not only their Savior, but their Lord.

Ignoring the biblical lifestyle can be risky. The road to apostasy is paved with disregard toward what may appear to be small matters (e.g., hardly praying, irregular church attendance, rarely studying the Bible) and could signal that church members are slowly drifting away from the lordship of Jesus. It is almost impossible to know at which point in life a person has drifted so far away from her commitment to Christ that He is no longer the lord of her life. Church standards alert us to the quality of our relationship with the Lord and are of great value in our spiritual pilgrimage.

God did not leave it up to us to decide how we should live the Chris-

---

listen, and think; proper entertainment; modesty and simplicity in dress and adornment; submission to the Decalogue; and above all imitating Jesus); *Physical Life* (proper diet and exercise); *Social Life* (properly relating to others, including the family, and proper use of our skills); and *Material Resources* (practicing biblical stewardship). For a more detailed exposition of the church standards, consult *Seventh-day Adventist Church Manual* (Silver Spring, MD: Secretariat of the General Conference, 2005), 171–184.

[16] There are what we could call personal or individual life standards. Church members could have some other personal standards for the Christian life that are not necessarily promoted by the world church, but are based on what they feel the Bible teaches and that is good for them to put into practice. For instance, a person may conclude that it is important to follow Daniel's example and pray three times a day. In such cases, they should not try to impose their personal decision on other believers.

tian life. He has modeled it for us in the life of Jesus, His Son, and through the Scriptures and the guidance of the Spirit. One of the fundamental characteristics of biblical religion is its impact on every aspect of our life; it is a way of life, not simply a way of thinking or a set of concepts and beliefs. The Adventist faith has appropriated this biblical understanding of religion and sees the Christian life holistically. Biblical standards deal with the totality of Christian life because, according to biblical anthropology, we are an indivisible unity of life in bodily form. Therefore, church standards point to and assume the biblical understanding of human nature. Through these standards, and under the powerful guidance of the Spirit, we are transformed into the likeness of Jesus.

Adventists promote the importance of prayer and Bible study around the world, creating instruments and occasions that facilitate implementation of these two elements in our lifestyle. Adventists also go to church every Sabbath and observe it from sunset to sunset. This element of our lifestyle expresses in a very specific and concrete way our identity. Adventists around the world wake up Sabbath morning and get ready to go to church, to worship the Creator and Redeemer. This is who we are. We also promote a healthy lifestyle. Not all of us are vegetarians, but we all accept the distinction between clean and unclean foods and the importance of temperance in all we do. We also know, all over the world, about modesty and simplicity in dress and personal adornment,[17] even though the application of these principles may slightly differ in different cultures. These things are important for the identity of the remnant and contribute to keeping Adventists united as one world family. This lifestyle is not embraced because we lack assurance of salvation; we do so *because* we have experienced the joy of salvation in Christ.

Unity in Worldview[18]

The uniqueness of our body of beliefs is directly related to our understanding of the presence of good and evil in the universe and the conflict it entails. Many other Christians believe in a cosmic conflict, but we have placed it in direct relation to the work of Christ, the law of God, and to challenges launched against His character. Its origin in the heavenly family (Isa 14:12–15; Ezek 28:11–19; Rev 12:7–12)—in a fallen angel— and its resolution through the atoning death of Christ and His ministry

---

[17] On the standard of the church on jewelry, see Ángel Manuel Rodríguez, *Jewelry in the Bible* (Silver Spring, MD: Biblical Research Institute, 1999).

[18] For a more detailed discussion of the biblical worldview as reflected in the cosmic conflict, consult Frank B. Holbrook, "The Great Controversy," *Handbook of Seventh-day Adventist Theology*, 969–1009.

of mediation and judgment in the heavenly sanctuary creates a profile of a uniquely biblical and peculiarly Adventist cosmic conflict. This worldview transforms our system of beliefs into a metanarrative. We proclaim a story that begins with cosmic harmony that moves from the origin of evil and sin in the universe to humanity's fall into sin and the redemption announced and realized in Christ's ministry, death, resurrection, ascension, and mediation for us. The narrative also includes the conflict within the history of the Christian church and concludes with Christ's return in glory and the re-creation of the world.

At the center of this biblical worldview is Christ, the One who confronted the forces of evil and defeated them on the cross (Col 2:15). This biblical worldview provides an excellent frame of reference for better understanding Adventist doctrines. Since this worldview is upheld by the world church, it contributes to making believers around the world one body of faith. We hold this cosmic understanding to be biblically reliable and it reaffirms our hope in Christ. We all understand the role of Lucifer in this conflict, his rebellion in heaven and his expulsion from it. We know well the narrative of the fall of Adam and Eve, and above everything else, we know about Jesus' victory over this cosmic enemy through His ministry, death, and resurrection. We also know about the final resolution of the cosmic conflict at the Second Coming and after the Millennium. We all have these convictions in common and they contribute to nurture the unity we have in Christ and to manifest it to the world.

There are many worldviews available to humans in the fragmented world in which we live but none of them come close to the biblical one. In the western world the worldview that seems to predominate is called natural evolution. It also begins with creation, or rather with the natural origin of the cosmos, most probably through a big bang. Through millions of years the universe formed itself and, at least in one planet, life originated by itself and continues to develop through natural selection and the survival of the fittest. This metanarrative attempts to provide an integrated view of the cosmos as it seeks to explain its fragmented nature. But it lacks hope. It talks about a self-produced cosmos that will return by itself into nothingness. It is one of the darkest worldviews available to humans.

In this particular context, Adventists proclaim a biblical worldview that is deeply embedded in a hope made possible by our Lord, in whom we find perfect union.

Unity in Mission

The words of Jesus continue to resonate within the church and form the basis of its mission: "As you sent me into the world, I have sent them into the world" (John 17:18). There are two important concepts in this text. First, the church's mission is the entire world, the whole human family in a state of rebellion against God. This clearly affirms the universality of the church and its task of addressing the universal problem of sin by proclaiming its universal remedy through Christ. The second concept defines the church in terms of its relationship to Christ and to the world. By sending the church into the world, Jesus constituted it, through the Spirit, into *His representative*. He had been sent into the world, and now He sends the church. His mission continues to be fulfilled through the mission of the church. The unity of the church finds expression in its dynamic *universality* (catholicity), enabling it to fulfill its God-given global mission as God's end-time remnant.

Therefore, the unity of the church is particularly visible in its collective journey toward a common goal, namely the fulfillment of the gospel commission in the human sphere (Matt 28:18–20; 24:14; Rev 14:6–12) and its impact at the cosmic level (Eph 3:10). This specific mission should not only be understood as simply something the church does, as if the church could still be the church without accomplishing this most important task. Mission, like its union with Christ, belongs to the essence of the church. It is not something it does; it is what the church is.[19] So to the question, "What is the church?", one could answer:

> *The church is God's appointed agency for the salvation of men. It was organized for service*, and its mission is to carry the gospel to the world. From the beginning it has been God's plan that through His church shall be reflected to the world His fullness and His sufficiency. The members of the church, those whom He has called out of darkness into His marvelous light, are to show forth His glory. *The church is the repository of the riches of the grace of Christ*; and through the church will eventually be made manifest, even to "the principalities and powers in heavenly places," the final and full display of the love of God. Ephesians 3:10.[20]

This is a significant theological statement that deserves careful attention. According to it, the church interacts with two spheres of exis-

---

[19] Obviously, we may distinguish between the church and its mission and, in that respect, say that the church has a mission to the world. This distinction is useful for analysis and dialogue, but when we look at the nature of the church, it becomes obvious that mission is part of that nature. The church is or exists in the realization of its mission. Otherwise, the church would have corrupted itself, becoming a human social entity, a type of social club without a heavenly identity.

[20] Ellen G. White, *Acts of the Apostle*, 9 (italics supplied).

tence—the earthly and the heavenly. In that interaction, it manifests its very nature.

Mission to the World

The *first* thing we should notice in the statement quoted above is that the church is "God's appointed agency for the salvation of men [humans]."[21] This brief statement suggests several important thoughts. It makes clear that, as we indicated earlier, the church is of divine origin and therefore belongs to God. It is a new creation of God in a world fragmented by sin. It has a task directly assigned to it by God, namely to be the agency for the salvation of the human race. It is not the effective cause of salvation, but the agency of salvation. Its existence presupposes Christ's work of salvation. Finally, the phrase "the church is God's appointed agency for the salvation of men" implies that there is no other agency for the salvation of humans; it points to the uniqueness of the church. God's purpose for the salvation of humankind is now operative through the church of Christ. Theologically speaking, this is the church in its visible and invisible expression—visible in the end-time remnant and invisible in the silent but genuine conversion of individuals in the religious world who are not yet part of the end-time remnant.[22]

Second, in order for the church to reach its goal, organization is essential. God's appointed agency "was organized for service. Its mission is to carry the gospel into the world." The church is not a mystical entity, amorphous or without borders. It has a structure that facilitates the expression of its nature in service to others through the proclamation of the gospel. *Third*, the church is formed by "those whom God has called out of darkness into His marvelous light." Since the church is God's agency, the effectiveness of its mission is in His hands. He is the One who calls men and women out of darkness into His light. The church is never left to itself in the fulfillment of its mission. The transfer from darkness to light radicalizes the distinction between the church and the world.

Fourth, the church exists "to show forth God's glory." The mission of the church does not only consist of proclaiming the gospel through the spoken word, but through the transformation of lives. This was Jesus'

---

[21] She also wrote, "The church of Christ is God's agency for the proclamation of truth; she is empowered by Him to do a special work" (*Sons and Daughters of God*, 218).

[22] For a more detailed discussion of the church of Christ as composed of a visible remnant and the other sheep that already belong to Jesus, but that are not yet within His sheep pen (invisible to the human eye), see Ángel Manuel Rodríguez, "Concluding Essay: God's End-time Remnant and the Christian Church," *Toward a Theology of the Remnant*, ed. Ángel M. Rodríguez (Silver Spring, MD: Biblical Research Institute, 2009), 217–226.

understanding of the church as a community of individuals who experienced a transforming revelation of His grace in the mystery of the incarnation (John 1:14). The revelation of the glory of God now takes place in the transformation of the lives of those who have joined the body of Christ (2 Cor 3:18).

Fifth, "the church is the repository of the riches of the grace of Christ." There is a close relationship between the church and the grace of Christ. How is the church the repository of grace? Christ is unequivocally the only source of grace and the exclusive means for its dispensation to humans. We all have access to God through Christ, without the mediation of any human being. The church is simply and only the *repository* of grace. This repository should not be thought of as a container filled with grace to be distributed to others, but rather as a living organism in which the richness of Christ's grace is exhibited in the transformed lives of its members.[23] This same grace is available to those who, in response to the divine call to come to Jesus, join the church. The church shows Christ's glory and grace to the human race.

Mission to the Cosmos

The church also interacts with the heavenly realm: "Through the church will eventually be made manifest, even to 'the principalities and powers in heavenly places,' the final and full display of the love of God. Ephesians 3:10."[24] The church's witnessing to the heavenly beings is so formidable that they will eventually see in it a full display of God's love. Ellen G. White is referring to the final and full display of God's love in the life of church members.[25] We are not dealing with an abstract understanding of the love of God, but with an evidential and concrete expres-

---

[23] This is clearly expressed by Ellen White in another place: "The church, endowed with the righteousness of Christ, is His depositary, in which the riches of His mercy, His grace, and His love, are to appear in full and final display. Christ looks upon His people in their purity and perfection, as the reward of His humiliation, and the supplement of His glory,—Christ, the great Center, from whom radiates all glory," (*Desire of Ages* [Mountain View, CA: Pacific Press, 1940], 680).

[24] White, *Acts of the Apostles*, 9.

[25] She also wrote, "The Lord Jesus is making experiments on human hearts through the exhibition of His mercy and abundant grace. He is effecting transformations so amazing that Satan, with all his triumphant boasting, with all his confederacy of evil united against God and the laws of His government, stands viewing them as a fortress impregnable to his sophistries and delusions. They are to him an incomprehensible mystery. The angels of God, seraphim and cherubim, the powers commissioned to co-operate with human agencies, look on with astonishment and joy, that fallen men, once children of wrath, are through the training of Christ developing characters after the divine similitude, to be sons and daughters of God, to act an important part in the occupations and pleasures of heaven" (*Christian Experience and Teachings of Ellen G. White*, [Mountain View, CA: Pacific Press, 1940], 208).

sion of it in the life of human beings. All heavenly intelligences will be fully enlightened with the display of the love of Christ in the mystery of the church and specifically in the transformation of repentant sinners into the likeness of the image of the Son of God.

The mission of the church should be clearly focused on these two objectives, the earthly and the heavenly. The oneness of the church is expressed in its common witnessing to the content and transforming power of the sacrificial love of God in Christ.

Mission in Oneness

This understanding of mission is one of the most important aspects of Adventism, nurturing its unity in Christ and exhibiting it to the world. The church is a global remnant movement with a very strong sense of mission. Adventists are persuaded that we are on this planet of sin, suffering, and death for a very specific reason. This is directly connected to our apocalyptic awareness in the context of the cosmic conflict. There is a strong sense of urgency in the fulfillment of the mission of the church, based on the conviction that Christ is coming soon. Millions of Adventists around the world are actively involved in the mission of the church, giving Bible studies, participating in evangelistic campaigns, using modern technology, or simply announcing to others the soon return of our Lord. Consequently, this is a very dynamic, rapidly growing church. For Adventists, mission is the very breath of life. God has incorporated the church into His mission to the world.

The oneness of the church is essential to its mission. The gospel of salvation needs to be heard by the human race in the context of the final conflict. Humans need to prepare to meet last-day demonic deceptions and be victorious. The mission is one of service to others and requires that church members see themselves as servants of the Lord, placed by Him at the service of a perishing and fragmented world. This understanding of mission is shared by the church around the world.

Global Organization

Our global identity and unity come to visible expression through an efficient global organization. We have already indicated that order belongs to the essence of the church and this requires a functional and structured ecclesiastical organization. Such an organization has at least three main functions. *First*, it promotes and coordinates global planning and projects for mission. In other words, it is at the service of the mission of the church. The community of believers, the church, needs to be constantly reminded by its leaders that we exist for mission. Therefore, organizational structures and institutions at all levels of the church are expected to be directly involved in planning and executing mission projects for their territories.

Second, part of the responsibility of the ecclesiastical global organization is to make sure that the financial contributions of church members are properly distributed and used by the world church. This includes, among other things, defining, based on the Scriptural principles, how tithe is to be used by the church and the percentage of tithe that will be shared with the different administrative levels of the church. *Third*, the organizational structure of the church is responsible to oversee the administrative operations of the church. This is achieved by developing general, operational, or administrative policies. All of this is done in order to ensure that the mission of the church is being fulfilled and that church leaders, at all administrative levels, are performing their assigned responsibilities to achieve this goal.

Finally, organizational structure should be the vehicle through which the voice of the global church is heard speaking to itself and to others. One of its most important functions is properly articulating the biblical message entrusted to us without adulterating it. This global, corporate voice of the church is important in that it serves to express an oneness in message, mission, and identity.

Church members around the world, though they may not fully understand its administrative complexity, are fully aware of the Adventist global organizational structure. They know that the church is more than its limited expression in their town or city. They know that they belong to a global family and have been called by God to work together to advance the gospel of salvation. They provide financial resources, in obedience to the Lord, knowing that they are contributing not only to the mission of the church in their local field, but also to the global fields. They belong to something larger than themselves; something that came into existence by the power of the Holy Spirit.

Conclusion

The different elements that we have discussed directly contribute to define and preserve the unity that the church has found in Christ, the very center of our lives. The unity in message and mission that characterizes the world church is a miracle of the grace of God, performed in the midst of a fragmented world, and testifies that God sent His Son to reconcile the world to Him. It is indeed the result of the work of the Spirit among us uniting us to the Son of God in whom there is no fragmentation. The cultural, social, and ethnic differences in the world church have great potential for conflict and fragmentation. In order to avoid such tragedy, church members and leaders should cooperate with the Spirit making everything necessary to stay together in Christ. Unity requires a disposition to make significant efforts to achieve it and to nurture it. In that process we should not seek uniformity in non-essentials because the cultural, social, and ethnic differences would not allow for this to take place. Through the power of the Spirit we were brought into union with Christ and His body, the church, and now, empowered by Him, the church must remain one in the message and the mission entrusted to it.

CHAPTER 12

THE MESSAGE AND THE MISSION OF THE REMNANT: A METHODOLOGICAL APPROACH

Fernando Canale

My approach to the message and mission of the church may appear unconventional, but it is not. It will contribute to clarify the divine intervention in the rise of the Adventist movement and the true biblical nature of our message and mission. The two are inseparable from our understanding of Scripture and biblical worldview, both of which have confronted serious challenges throughout the history of the Christian church. To gain a better understanding of the relevance and urgency of our message and mission, it is important to place the rise of the Adventist movement within the history of scriptural interpretation and the theological and philosophical forces that have shaped Christian thinking. By examining the message and mission of the church from this broad perspective, we will be able to perceive elements of the Adventist mission that are not usually noted. We will discuss the Adventist message and mission in the context of the cosmic conflict, as it has developed within the theological and philosophical assumptions incorporated within the Christian church by merging Scripture, tradition, and Greek philosophy into a theological system.

The Emergence of Tradition

In order to better appreciate the significance of the Adventist message it is necessary to examine the emergence of Christian tradition. Soon after the apostles preserved the revelation of God in Jesus Christ in the New Testament writings, Christians began to use them not only as rules of faith but also as spiritual food. Together with God's Old Testament revelations, they became the theological and spiritual ground for the Christian church. The process of receiving, appropriating, and spiritually internalizing God's word, however, always involves interpretation. Due to many complex historical reasons early in its history, the Christian church progressively adapted its teachings and liturgical forms to Greek ontological categories—their understanding of reality.[1] Christian leaders facing a world of culture, science, and reason decided, for various reasons, not to reject the leading scientific culture of their days, namely Greek philosophy, in its Neoplatonic format. Historians of Christian theology label this process the "hellenization"[2] or alternatively the "de-Judaization"[3] of Christianity. By adapting to the cultural trends of their days, early Christians progressively and radically replaced the macro hermeneutical presuppositions[4] that the New Testament writers took from the Old Testament canon. In doing so, Christians thought they were faithful to God and desired to advance His mission on earth. Unfortunately, they progressively neglected Isaiah's injunction to use scriptural teachings as interpretive principles when evaluating new spiritual events (Isa 8:20). Moreover, they failed to follow Christ's hermeneutical practice of using the Old Testament teachings and categories as interpretive principles necessary for a proper explanation of His salvific ministry and death on the cross (Luke 24:27).

The replacement of Old Testament macro interpretive principles with interpretative principles derived from Greek philosophical categories led to the development, consolidation, and dominance of Christian tradition in all levels of Christianity, including scriptural interpretation, theological constructions, ministerial practices, liturgical forms, and mis-

---

[1] Adolph Harnack describes the Christian Church of the middle of the third century as "a new commonwealth, politically formed and equipped with fixed forms of all kinds. We recognize in these forms few Jewish, but many Greco-Roman features, and finally we perceive also in the doctrine of faith on which this commonwealth is based, the philosophic spirit of the Greeks." Consequently, "the Christian Church and its doctrine were developed within the Roman world and Greek culture in opposition to the Jewish Church" (Adolf Harnack, *History of Dogma*, [New York: Dover, 1961], 1:45–46).

[2] Harnack popularized the notion of "Hellenization" to describe the gradual adaptation of Christian doctrine to Greek, Neoplatonic ontological patterns. See for instance, ibid., 1: 41–50. See also Jaroslav Pelikan, *The Christian Tradition: A History of the Development of Doctrine*, (Chicago, IL: Chicago University Press, 1971–1989), 1:45.

[3] Pelikan, *Christian Tradition*, 1:21.

[4] By this, I mean the broadest philosophical assumptions that the interpreter brings to the interpretation of the Scripture and of reality itself. They include the way in which theologians understand the reality of God of human beings (Ontology), the world (Cosmology), the whole of reality (Metaphysics), and knowledge (Epistemology).

sionary strategies. As this situation ruled unopposed for over a thousand years, a systematic mingling of philosophical views about God, human nature, reason, and the world permeated all levels of Christian thought, life, and action, becoming ingrained in Christianity itself. An attentive reading of Christian doctrinal history reveals that Christianity soon developed a theological tradition that consolidated throughout the Middle Ages.[5] Guided by Neoplatonic and Aristotelian hermeneutical principles, Augustine and Aquinas respectively are perhaps the most distinguished systematizers of Christian tradition. For spiritual purposes, Scripture was replaced by the sacramental system of liturgy and worship. Although Scripture was never absent from Christian tradition, the new philosophical hermeneutics decisively distorted many of its teachings and weakened its power.

The Emergence of Scripture and Protestantism

The synthesis between Greek macro hermeneutical interpretive principles and biblical data, on which Christian tradition stands, sheltered a fateful conflict bound to create theological and spiritual inconsistencies along the way. For example, Luther noticed a glaring irregularity: the system of meritorious works clearly did not fit experience or the clear teachings of Scripture. With God-given conviction and staunch determination he turned to Scripture to fight against unbiblical tradition and to reform the church. Scripture was emerging from tradition.[6] With the passing of

---

[5] See John Reeve, "Apostasy," in this volume.

[6] Perhaps, the analysis of change in scientific thought and practices advanced by the philosopher of science, Thomas Kuhn, could help us to better understand the thinking and practice of the Christian church and particularly what emerged as a result of the Reformer's "turn to Scripture." (For an introduction to and evaluation of Kuhn's thought, see, for instance, Frank Hasel, "Scientific Revolution: An Analysis and Evaluation of Thomas Kuhn's Concept of Paradigm and Paradigm Change for Theology," *JATS* 2 [1991]: 160–177). Kuhn argues that "normal" science produces discoveries that become the foundation guiding the search and interpretation of new data and discoveries (Thomas S. Kuhn, *The Structure of Scientific Revolutions* [Chicago, IL: University of Chicago Press, 1970], 10). With the passing of time, accumulation and refinement of knowledge produce a body of information forming a "tradition of normal science." Normal science, in turn, becomes the interpretative paradigm guiding scientific interpretation, knowledge, and, practice (42). Yet, when the paradigm cannot interpret or assimilate new data or discoveries, anomalies arise that lead to crisis in scientific interpretation and to a period of "extraordinary science" (82). When this happens, the interpretive paradigm is challenged, studied, and eventually replaced by a new one, giving rise to a "scientific revolution." We should keep in mind that the new interpretive paradigm is not the articulation or extension of the old one. It is rather "the reconstruction of the field from new fundamentals, a reconstruction that changes some of the field's most elementary theoretical generalizations as well as many of its paradigm methods and applications" (85). A group of Christian theologians recognized the value of Kuhn's analysis of scientific revolutions and applied it to the field of Christian theology with the purpose of interpreting Christian traditions and advancing the development of ecumenical theology and practice (See

time, Luther and Calvin's "turn to Scripture" intensified and disseminated throughout Europe and America. In the process, mainline and radical reformations progressively rediscovered and integrated forgotten biblical teachings into the fabric of Christianity. Notably, English Puritan theologians during the 17th century and John Wesley during the 18th century used Scripture to challenge tradition. Simultaneously, the discovery of further biblical teachings produced an ever-increasing doctrinal and theological fragmentation of Protestant Christianity.

In fact, the "turn to Scripture" by mainline and radical reformations did not challenge but assumed and used the interpretative principles Christian tradition had drawn from Greek philosophical ideas. This little-known fact buried deep in the history of Protestant and evangelical histories may explain why the emergence of Scripture that followed in the wake of the Reformation did not produce a unified alternative to Roman Catholicism, but rather an ever-increasing fragmentation of Christian doctrines, practices, and denominations that still goes on unabated.

Because faithfulness to Scripture and its mission belong to the essence of the remnant, we will focus our brief analysis on theological change, that is to say, change in the understanding of the doctrines of Christianity—the message of the church. As mentioned above, Martin Luther noticed a glaring inconsistency between Paul's teachings on justification by faith and the traditional teachings of the church on meritorious works and assurance of salvation through plenary papal indulgences. In his attempt to solve these anomalies, however, Luther was still thinking inside the box of normal theology, using tradition and Scripture. The system of normal theology did not like the "fixing" Luther advanced with his proposal of justification by faith alone and placed him outside its community.

As Luther's insight caught the imagination of his time, anomalies rising from Scripture to challenge the system of normal theology multiplied. This trend gave rise to a period of "theological crisis" stemming from the Protestant "turn to Scripture." However, after almost five centuries of "theological crisis" and fragmentation, no "theological revolution" has

---

Hans Küng, *Theology for the Third Millennium* [New York, NY: Doubleday, 1988], 123–127; Hans Küng and David Tracy, ed., *Paradigm Change in Theology: A Symposium for the Future* [New York: Crossroad, 1991]; Hans Küng, *Christianity: Essence, History, and Future* [New York: Continuum, 1995]). Clearly, they understood that the questions facing Christianity in the third millennium were about hermeneutical macro interpretive principles (Küng, *Theology*, xii). However, their theological commitment to tradition (47–63) did not allow them to properly recognize the true nature of the "anomalies" that the emergence of Scripture brought about by Luther and the Protestant Reformation introduced into the fabric of Christianity. Obviously, they did not understand the true nature of the theological crisis and hermeneutical revolution facing Christianity. I will apply Kuhn's approach to the field of historical theology to address issues of hermeneutics and the synthesis of tradition and Scripture.

taken place. What was needed was a period of "extraordinary theology" to replace the old hermeneutical paradigm (the normal theology drawn from Greek philosophical ideas) with a new one. This theological revolution has not happened yet. Why not?

A main reason for the absence of extraordinary theology and the onset of a theological revolution is that the Protestant turn to Scripture never challenged the macro hermeneutical principles of normal or common theology. With the passing of time, the Protestant Reformation rediscovered a veritable wealth of scriptural teachings and practices, but it never challenged traditional philosophical interpretations of foundational macro hermeneutical principles. Hence, the much-heralded Reformation principle of Scripture alone ("*sola Scriptura*") never actually challenged the interpretive role of tradition based on Greek philosophical ideas on the reality of God, human nature, the world, the whole of reality (ontology and metaphysics), and reason (epistemology).

More precisely, mainline Reformers used Scripture to challenge doctrinal points in tradition, but never the hermeneutical and methodological basis on which Christian tradition stands. On the contrary, tradition is the explicitly recognized source of biblical hermeneutics.[7] Even when Radical Reformers like the Anabaptists departed from mainline Reformation, explicitly applying the "*sola Scriptura*" principle and leaving tradition further behind, they never challenged the macro hermeneutical principles of normal theology.

In conclusion, because the church stands on Christ as revealed in Scripture, the Protestant turn to Scripture initiated the emergence from tradition to a people fundamentally oriented by the Scripture itself. But the Protestant commitment to Scripture did not challenge the ontological, metaphysical, and hermeneutical presuppositions on which Christian traditions built their theological and ecclesiological systems. Because Protestantism still shares these basic guiding assumptions with Roman Catholicism, its turn to Scripture is only partial and tends to produce systemic and theological inconsistencies. This unavoidably generates an ever-increasing ecclesiological fragmentation. Due to this situation Protestantism became unable to fully emerge as the end-time Biblical remnant people of God. Instead it became shaky and in need of theological answers and ecclesiological stability. With the passing of time this search for answers will cause Protestantism to pave the way for the rise of the end-time remnant.

---

[7] Keith A. Mathison, *The Shape of Sola Scriptura* (Moscow, ID: Canon Press, 2001), 48.

The Emerging Eschatological Remnant

During the 18th century, Protestantism expanded throughout the American frontier, beyond the restraints imposed by tradition, and established denominations. In this environment, the Protestant "turn to Scripture" generated two revivals of practical piety that shaped the culture of the times.[8] During this period, growing grassroots dissatisfaction with doctrinal inconsistencies within the Protestant Reformation motivated serious Bible students to find a way to overcome tradition and ecclesiological fragmentation through a deeper and more inclusive understanding of Scripture. Unlike the Magisterial Reformers (16th century) and the English Puritans (17th century), this search did not originate from clergymen or theologians, but from the laity. It grew from the basic, naïve conviction that Scripture can interpret itself. This radical view, implicitly departed from the hermeneutical perspective of the Magisterial Reformers, set the patterns, limits, and hermeneutical principles of current Protestant or evangelical theology. The rejection of tradition as a source of theology and hermeneutical guide could be traced back to the Radical Reformers' call for a restoration of biblical (mostly New Testament) Christianity. In the 18th century, various restorationist groups in America embraced this approach to Christian theology,[9] in an attempt to overcome what had gone wrong with the Catholic Church[10] and the historical churches of the Reformation.[11]

---

[8] See Alister McGrath, *Christianity's Dangerous Idea: The Protestant Revolution–A History from the Sixteenth Century to the Twenty-First* (New York: Harper Collins, 2007), 156–166.

[9] Mark G. Toulouse, "Restoration Movements," *The Encyclopedia of Christianity*, vol. 4, ed. Erwin Fahlbusch (Grand Rapids, MI: Eerdmans, 2005), 659–664.

[10] According to Steven L. Ware, "restorationism may be viewed primarily as an interpretive framework used to varying degrees by nearly every Protestant group." He goes on to explain: "Stated bluntly, there was a widespread but not always consciously articulated perception among early radical holiness leaders (as well as among many other Protestants) that something went very wrong early in the history of the church. Following the apostolic era of the first century, during which time the church was marked by the purity of apostolic teaching, the exemplary character of sanctified lives, and the power of the Holy Spirit's demonstrations among them, the church slowly sank into corruption. Over the next few centuries pure apostolic Christianity was corrupted through the development of ecclesiastical hierarchies, the addition of pomp and splendor to worship, and the wide acceptance of Platonic philosophy. The result was a medieval Roman Catholicism which was marked by moral laxity, persecution of non-conformists, and continual dissension with kings and emperors in a struggle for political power. The church became a religious system in which, as viewed by restorationists, much of the truth of Christianity is 'buried beneath the rubbish,' buried so deep that it has been 'scarce seen or heard of for a thousand years'" (Steven L. Ware, "Restoring the New Testament Church: Varieties of Restorationism in the Radical Holiness Movement of the Late Nineteenth and early Twentieth Centuries," *Pneuma* 21.2 [1999]: 235).

[11] Ibid., 236.

In this environment and out of the second American revival (1800–1830),[12] interest in the study of the long forgotten apocalyptic prophecies of the Old and New Testaments intensified and attention shifted to the Second Coming of Christ. Through careful application of the well-established historicist method of prophetic interpretation to Daniel chapter 8 and 9, an ecumenical movement emerged. This movement, born mostly out of the laity of various Protestant denominations, announced the visible and historical coming of Christ on October 22, 1844. From the Great Disappointment that crushed the sincere expectations of the Advent Movement, a very small number of believers sought answers in Scripture for their predicament. When on October 23 they turned their eyes to the reality of the heavenly sanctuary, where Christ since His resurrection and ascension had been ministering the benefits of His death to human beings, they found the explanation for their disappointment. Christ was not coming to earth but entering into the Most Holy Place of the heavenly sanctuary. Eventually, this discovery gave rise to the Seventh-day Adventist Church and its claim as God's remnant people of biblical prophecy.

However, in turning their attention to Christ in the heavenly sanctuary, the group of evangelical believers, who later became the Seventh-day Adventist Church, did not discover a new doctrine or information unknown to Christians. To the contrary, the historicist method used in the interpretation of Daniel was commonly used by Protestant theologians.[13] These theologians had also recognized the New Testament belief that Christ ascended to heaven and was sitting at the right hand of His Father in the heavenly sanctuary continuously advocating for our salvation.[14] Adventist historians have long recognized that their doctrines were known in earlier periods of church history, notably during the emergence of Protestantism.[15] Thus, it is necessary to examine the theological and ecclesiological experience of the early Adventist pioneers.

During the first six formative years that followed the Great Disappointment, early Adventist pioneers continued their search for biblical truths beyond the interpretation of prophecies and the doctrine of the

---

[12] McGrath, *Dangerous Idea*, 164.

[13] Ware, "Restoring the New Testament Church," 237.

[14] Bryan W. Ball, *The English Connection: The Puritan Roots of Seventh-day Adventist Belief* (Cambridge: James Clarke, 1981), 103–107.

[15] See for instance, *Seventh-day Adventists Answer Questions on Doctrine: An Explanation of Certain Major Aspects of Seventh-day Adventist Belief*. (Washington, DC: Review and Herald, 1957). Le Roy Edwin Froom, *The Conditionalist Faith of our Fathers: The Confict of the Ages over the Nature and Destiny of Man* (Washington, DC: Review and Herald, 1965–1966). And the more detailed exposition by Ball, *The English Connection*.

sanctuary.[16] Their genius was not discovering new truths—most had already been recognized and accepted by many other Protestants. Instead, they took a small step that was to generate a gigantic theological revolution in Christianity. They used their newfound insights into the relationship between prophecy and the sanctuary as hermeneutical presuppositions that were needed to understand the entire Bible, the whole range of Christian doctrines, and the mission of the Church.[17] Perhaps Ellen White summarized this epoch changing experience best when she explained:

> The subject of the sanctuary was the key which unlocked the mystery of the disappointment of 1844. It opened to view a complete system of truth, connected and harmonious, showing that God's hand had directed the great advent movement, and revealing present duty as it brought to light the position and work of His people."[18]

In their determination to understand prophecy, the Protestant "turn to Scripture" had finally advanced from the initial phase to a decisive time of "extraordinary theology" when the old paradigm was replaced. In other words, when Adventist pioneers used their understanding of apocalyptic prophecies and the Sanctuary as an interpretive paradigm, they effectively replaced the interpretive paradigm that Christian tradition had drawn from extra-biblical philosophical ideas. This paradigmatic epochal shift made possible the emergence of the end-time remnant. The remnant church had finally arrived to challenge the theological and ecclesiological status quo. The Protestant "turn to Scripture" eventually had given way to the "biblical hermeneutical turn" embraced by the emerging end-time remnant.

Protestants face a dilemma. By embracing tradition, evangelical leaders attempt to overcome the theological contradictions and ministerial anomalies dividing fragmented traditions. By failing to apply the turn to Scripture to their hermeneutical principles and by embracing the non-biblical interpretation of the ontological, metaphysical, and hermeneuti-

---

[16] "Thus the Sanctuary truth, so long 'cast down' and trodden underfoot throughout much of the Christian Era—until the prophesied end of the 2300 years—began to be recovered in 1844. *That was the demand of Biblical Prophecy. That was the significant fulfillment of history.* It is tremendously impressive. With the coming of the time came the people called of God, and the recovered message of the Sanctuary truth foretold in holy writ" (Leroy Edwin Froom, *Movement of Destiny* [Washington, DC: Review and Herald, 1971], 80).

[17] C. Mervyn Maxwell, "A Brief History of Adventist Hermeneutics," *JATS* 4.2 (1993): 214–215.

[18] Ellen White, *The Great Controversy Between Christ and Satan During the Christian Dispensation* (Oakland, CA: Pacific Press Publishing Co., 1888), 423.

cal principles of "early" Christian tradition, they appear to be returning to Rome.[19] Nonetheless, at this time a large sector of Protestants remains wholly committed to "turn to Scripture" and yet they still implicitly and inadvertently assume the hermeneutical paradigm of Christian tradition. This sector remains unstable because it is unable to overcome the contradiction between theological data and hermeneutical presuppositions.

The biblical hermeneutical turn of the early Adventist pioneers, though revolutionary, only signaled the birth of the remnant—not its full-developed existence. To properly understand the meaning of being the emerging, visible, biblical remnant church in the context of the end times of the history of salvation, we need to consider its message and mission. We need to highlight how the "biblical hermeneutical turn," embraced and advanced by early Adventist pioneers, relates to the essence of the Christian remnant church.

Christ, Hermeneutics, and the Remnant

How does the hermeneutical turn from tradition to Scripture relate to ecclesiology? More specifically, how do the hermeneutics of Christian tradition (Catholic and Protestant) and the hermeneutics of Adventist pioneers shape their understanding of the church? Let's examine the influence of hermeneutical presuppositions on the doctrinal system of the church. Hermeneutics relates to ecclesiology by generating alternate understandings of the entirety of Christian doctrines and practices thereby producing two competing and incompatible understandings.

The incompatibility between the traditional and the Adventist theological systems stems from the conflicting views that Christian tradition and Adventists assume about the nature of reality. Christian tradition embraces a reality inspired and mediated by Greek Neoplatonic ontology and articulated by Aristotelian metaphysics. Adventists embrace the view of reality expressed and assumed by biblical writers. The former places the reality of God, His acts, and human spirituality outside the realm of time, space, and history. The latter places the reality of God, His acts, and human spirituality inside the realm of time, space, and history. These opposite views of reality (ontology of God, human beings, and the world), and the whole (everything in the universe in relation to God) become unavoidable assumptions when interpreting Scripture, understanding its doctrines, and fulfilling God's will and mission. The difference and conflict between them could not be greater.

---

[19] Fernando Canale, "The Emerging Church: What Does it Mean? And Why Should We Care?," *Adventist Review*, June 10, 2010; and John Jovan Markovic, "The Emerging Church: Voices of Confussion (Part 2 of 2)," *Ministry* 82.5 (2010).

Churches based on tradition tend to ignore and replace the view of reality (ontology) and the whole (metaphysics) revealed in Scripture. In so doing, they may distort the biblical teachings about God, Christ, and salvation. This fact disqualifies them to represent the God of Scripture and to claim to be Christ's visible church on earth. This approach deals with ecclesiology indirectly, via the doctrine and practices of the church. Yet, there is a direct way in which hermeneutics conditions the essence of Christian ecclesiology.

In general, most Christians agree that the church is, in essence, the spiritual community of Christ on earth, existing through its faith-relationship with the real presence of Christ through the Spirit. Ecclesiological disagreements revolve around the way in which Christians interpret the real presence of Christ, which is the center of the Christian church. Clearly, any exposition of the presence of Christ depends on the interpreters' preunderstandings of the nature of God, human beings, and Christ. And these, in turn, depend on the preunderstanding the interpreter assumes about the general nature of reality as a whole (ontology and metaphysics). Let us consider, as an example, the way in which hermeneutical presuppositions influence the understanding and experience of the presence of Christ. This approach will help us to see how hermeneutics relates to ecclesiology by generating alternate understandings of the presence of Christ, thereby producing two competing and incompatible grounds for the Christian church.

Roman Catholics and a large sector of mainline Protestant denominations believe that after Christ's ascension to heaven, we have access to His real presence in or through the sacraments.[20] Christ's presence in the sacraments then, is the essence, center, and foundation of the Christian church. This belief springs from the hermeneutical assumption that God's spiritual reality and our spiritual realities are neither temporal nor material. Within this hermeneutical assumption, God can relate directly to separate souls (souls without a body, as the angels are according to tradition) but not to souls in material bodies. Since human souls exist in essential connection to a material body, God needs to use a material element to reach the soul. Thus, to interact with embodied souls, God uses a material element to bridge the material historical gap that exists between His non-historical reality and the non-historical reality of the human soul. In the case of Christ, His body is the material vehicle God used to make His spiritual, non-historical nature present in the times of the disciples. After the ascension of Christ's body to heaven, God uses other material vehicles

---

[20] Although Christians have developed various ways to understand the sacraments, they see the presence of God in or through them.

(wine, water, bread, etc.) to communicate the presence of Christ's divinity to the Christian Church.

Tradition teaches that Christ's spiritual, non-historical, divine presence becomes real to us through the material signs and symbols (sacraments) that we apprehend with our spirits. It is important to bear in mind that the divine presence mediated by the sacraments is the same that the disciples experienced through the human body of Jesus Christ. This relation takes place in the "spiritual" timeless realm, outside the everyday flow of historical events. The sacraments provide the material element God needs to become present to our embodied souls.

According to tradition, God relates to our immaterial souls without the need for the historical mediation of Christ, as revealed in the New Testament. The human Christ is not the Son of God incarnated now ministering in the heavenly sanctuary, but the material component of the sacrament necessary for the eternal timeless God to communicate His spiritual presence directly to our souls, presently embodied in space and time. Thus, through the sacraments, Christian believers do not relate to the incarnated Christ ministering for them in heaven but directly to God's own transcendent unmediated non-historical being.

Radically departing from this view, Seventh-day Adventists believe that after Christ's ascension to heaven, believers experience His real historical presence in the heavenly sanctuary through the historical teaching ministry of the Holy Spirit, His representative on earth, who operates through prayer, Bible study, and obedience to His words (Scripture). Adventists are not the first Christians to accept this view,[21] but are the first to take the revolutionary step of using this biblical belief as a hermeneutical presupposition for their entire theological system and for the real presence of Christ who is the center and ground of the church. By taking this small step, Adventists effectively rejected the Neoplatonic-Aristotelic-Augustinian-Thomistic ontological ground on which traditional churches stand, and replaced it with the ontology-metaphysics of God in His sanctuary relating historically to historical temporal beings (biblical ontology of human nature). In so doing Adventists radically depart from traditional conservative and modern Protestant and evangelical theolo-

---

[21] Early in the Protestant Reformation, Zwingli understood that Christ's presence was tied to His body in heaven. See for instance, W. P. Stephens, "Zwingli's Theology," *The Encyclopedia of Christianity*, ed. Erwin Fahlbusch and Geoffrey William Bromiley (Grand Rapids, MI: Eerdmans, 2008), 5:864. He used this idea as a presupposition to reject the traditional view that Christ was present in the bread and wine of the Holy Communion. Thus, he "argued that Christ's body could not be present on many altars at one and the same time, since after the ascension it was restricted to one location at God's right hand" (Scott Hendrix, "Luther's Theology," *Encyclopedia of Christianity*, 3:373).

gians. Clearly, the incarnated, resurrected, and ascended Christ cannot be at the same time present in or through the sacraments and bodily in the heavenly sanctuary. The claim that He is present in the sacraments involves the spiritualization of Christ.[22]

Therefore, in Adventism, the heavenly-sanctuary-word-prayer-personal relational dynamics replaces the impersonal ritualistic mechanics of the sacraments as the essence, center, and foundation of the Christian church. Believers no longer experience the presence of Christ in and through the mediation of the liturgical rituals of the church. Instead, through the understanding of Scripture, prayer, and the work of the Spirit, believers encounter the presence of Christ as a historical, living person in heaven—the only mediator between God's transcendent being and His creatures. Moreover, He is also the merciful high priest ministering salvation and providentially guiding believers. In this ontological context or understanding of reality, the remnant church exists and stands as the spiritual and visible community that grows out of Christ's redemptive-mediatory work in the heavenly sanctuary. By accepting His love and sovereignty in faith and obedience, it accepts Christ's given mission to proclaim His gospel of the kingdom of God to the world.

Unquestionably, the turn to biblical hermeneutics belongs to the macro historical level of theological and ecclesiological developments. The acceptance of the biblical teachings of Christ's historical and bodily presence in the heavenly sanctuary produced a radical change at the on-

---

[22] To say that Christ is present in the sacraments necessarily involves the spiritualization of the historical reality of Christ in heaven, which the implicit ontologies of God's timeless being and the immortal soul require. Wolfhart Pannenberg represents well-known theologians working from the perspective of "normal" traditional theology when he considers Zwingli's hermeneutical use of Christ's bodily presence in the Heavenly Sanctuary as a "hindrance" to a correct understanding of the sacraments. "On the matter of the real presence Zwingli was hampered by this idea of the exalted Christ being tied corporeally by his session at the right hand of God" (Wolfhart Pannenberg, *Systematic Theology* [Grand Rapids, MI: Eerdmans, 1991–1998], 3:310–311). Calvin, though, following Scriptural evidence from the Gospels argues that Christ's real body presently exists in heaven but makes room for his presence to be real in the sacrament through the Holy Spirit, not bodily as Roman Catholic dogma affirms, but in the mode of "majesty, providence, and ineffable grace" (John Calvin, *Institutes of the Christian Religion* [Bellingham, WA: Logos Research Systems, 1997], IV, xvii, 26). Although Calvin goes further than Luther in challenging traditional thought on the real presence of Christ in the bread and wine, he remains closer to tradition than Zwingli by embracing the ontology of tradition that "hampers" (to use Pannenberg wording) him from accepting the ontological implications of the biblical teaching by which Christ's presence is indivisibly in heaven and tied to His body in space and time. In the final analysis, with some caveats, Calvin embraces Christ's real presence in the bread and the wine. He concludes, "[b]ut when these absurdities are discarded, I willingly admit anything which helps to express the true and substantial communication of the body and blood of the Lord, as exhibited to believers under the sacred symbols of the Supper, understanding that they are received not by the imagination or intellect merely, but are enjoyed in reality as the food of eternal life" (ibid., IV, xvii, 19).

tological foundations of Christian theology and ecclesiology. The temporal, historical ontological framework of Scripture definitively replaces the timeless, non-historical ontology of Christian tradition. The hermeneutical consequences of this ontological shift are momentous. Its consistent application by Adventist believers to the entire system of Christian theology, worship, and ministerial practices amounts to a macro paradigm shift at the very foundation of Christian theology.

Since, according to Christ, believers feed from His words of revelation in Scripture, the spirituality of the remnant church is essentially and indissolubly connected to its message.[23] Adventists talk much about their "message." But what is a message? A message is a communication addressed to a recipient. Clearly, the recipient is the world, but what is the content of the communication God expects the remnant to deliver to the world? Some believers may find it difficult to identify our message. Others may readily identify the message of the church with some of the so-called distinctive truths (e.g., the seventh-day Sabbath, the Second Coming, health reform, the gospel, or the three angels' messages). Is the message of the church something short that can be delivered quickly? Let us reflect for a moment on the message of the church as it relates to the essence and mission of the church.

---

[23] Spirituality has also been impacted by non-biblical tradition. The Church as a spiritual visible community exists because it is nurtured by Christ, its center and foundation. Christ taught: "I am the bread of life.... The one who eats this bread will live forever" (John 6:35, 58; NRSV). Traditional ontology dictating the hermeneutics of traditional churches led them to interpret Christ's teachings on the "Bread of Life" in a sacramental way. Accordingly, by partaking of the bread and wine, Christians actually eat His real spiritual being "spiritually" present "in" the bread and wine. According to this view, the soul of the believer actually "feeds" from the very substance of the transcendent God. It "feeds" from the actual power of divine life. The "feeding" does not take place in the realm of everyday life but in the parallel realm of spiritual substances (God and the soul). This transaction, therefore, is mechanistic and impersonal.

The radical paradigm shift in ontological views that generated the remnant church dictates a different hermeneutical commitment that leads us to interpret Christ's teachings on the "Bread of Life," historically and personally. According to biblical ontology, the "bread of life" is the real incarnated Christ that came down from heaven (John 6:33, 39) and, as he went back up to heaven (John 6:62), now feeds us the words of life He spoke personally and through the prophets (John 6:63) through the teaching ministry and providences of His representative, the Holy Spirit. According to Scripture, then, the "feeding" on Christ that generates the church does not take place mechanically in and through the sacraments as an impersonal encounter with God's transcendent reality. Instead, the "feeding" on Christ that generates the remnant church takes place as a historical experience that involves the whole being in and through the words of Scripture as a personal encounter with the incarnated Christ in heaven. The spiritual feeding Christ speaks about, then, takes places in the realm of our everyday lives within the sequence of time and the spatiality of our bodies, not in the ethereal, non-historical, non-spatial realm of traditional Christian spirituality. In short, a personal spirituality centered in Christ's words and historical acts replaces an impersonal spirituality centered in the transcendent, non-historical substance of the divinity.

Message: An Overview

Ellen White frequently wrote about the church's message. According to her, God gives the remnant church the same Gospel Commission Christ gave to the disciples.[24] Hence, one wonders about the contents of Christ's commission to the church. Is the Gospel Commission the proclamation of divine grace? Certainly. But the proclamation of "the mysteries of the grace of God" requires the inclusion of "the whole counsel of God,"[25] "the saving truths of the third angel's message,"[26] and "the special truths that have separated us from the world and made us what we are."[27] Let us explore these rather succinct and technical points further to appreciate their spiritual and practical meaning.

The message the church proclaims is God's grace. But grace is not just a thing or a power; it is an essential characteristic of God's person (Exod 34:6; Deut 4:31, Ps 116:5). Grace is revealed and experienced through His divine actions. Consequently, the mission of proclaiming God's grace requires the church to make all of God's acts known to the world. The proclamation of God's grace coincides with the proclamation of His acts.

According to Paul, the message the church proclaims includes nothing less than "the whole counsel of God" (Acts 20:27; ESV). "God's counsel" refers to the "plans of his heart" for all generations (Ps 33:11; NRSV). In His eternal wisdom and understanding, God designed (Job 12:13; Prov 1:25; 8:14) and, by His will, planned for our salvation before the foundation of the world (Eph 1:11). The "counsel of God" or "plan of salvation" includes, among other things, Christ's incarnation and ministry (2 Cor 2:7; 1:30); the goal that human beings should become holy (Eph 1:4) and transformed into the image of Christ (Rom 8:29) through Christ's redemptive sacrifice (Eph 1:7); forgiveness of sins (Eph 1:7); and adoption in the family of God (Eph 1:5). The proclamation of "the entire counsel" of God coincides with the proclamation of the entire plan of salvation.

The "saving truths of the third angel's message" include, among other things, the eternal gospel, the fear of the Lord, God's judgment hour, the worship of God the Creator, the commandments of God, and the faith of Jesus (Rev 14: 6–13). The proclamation of the saving truths of the third angel's message identifies aspects of God's message which His Church

---

[24] Ellen G. White, "The Great Commission: A Call to Service," *RH*, March 24, 1910, par. 8.

[25] Ellen G. White, *Life Sketches of Ellen G. White* (Mountain View, CA: Pacific Press, 1915), 329.

[26] Ellen G. White, *Testimonies for the Church* (Mountain View, CA: Pacific Press, 1855–1909), 8:24.

[27] White, *Life Sketches*, 329.

will emphasize before His Second Coming. "The special truths that have separated us from the world and made us what we are" include doctrines like the sanctuary, the non-immortality of the soul, the law of God, the Sabbath, and the three angels' messages.[28] These truths are "special" because they provide the biblical, hermeneutical foundations to interpret the "saving truths of the third angel," the "whole counsel of God," and the "mysteries of God's grace."

This succinct exploration of the remnant message shows that it is not something that can be swiftly processed and disseminated without much personal involvement. Yet this may cause many to find this extended notion of the message complicated because its various parts require closer attention. This negative feeling normally awakens when we become aware of its unavoidable complexity: the message has many truths. But these truths are interconnected and form a perfect, complete, and harmonious system. Anyone can, through Bible study and prayer, perceive the complete and perfect harmony of the biblical message, as the pioneers did. Its complexity leads into a rich and satisfying personal encounter with Christ.

How do we come to apprehend the inner theological, spiritual, and experiential harmony that exists between the components of the Adventist message? We do it by using the "landmarks" or "pillars" truths of Adventism as hermeneutical tools to understand how the Bible "unfolds a complete system of theology and philosophy."[29] This biblical system of theology and philosophy articulates the remnant church's message. The message of the remnant is a complete system of theological and philosophical truths that replaces the system of theological and philosophical truths of tradition.

Message: Presuppositions

The biblical message of the remnant church stands on three major methodological principles of theology and the practice of ministry. The first fundamental principle makes Scripture the normative source of our knowledge of God—the *sola, tota, prima Scriptura* principles.[30] Its application leads to a second and third principles, both of them are macro

---

[28] White, *Counsels to Writers and Editors* (Nashville, TN: Southern Publishing, 1946), 30.

[29] Ellen White, *Christian Education* (Batle Creek, MI: International Tract Society, 1894), 106.

[30] *Sola scriptura* means that the teachings of the Bible, not of science, philosophy, tradition, or experience, are the source of special revelation we have to know God, His thoughts, will, and work for us. *Tota scriptura* means the Bible in its totality—Old and New Testaments—and in its historical continuity is the normative source for Christian theology. *Prima Scriptura* means that natural revelation (Rom 1: 19-20) must be interpreted and understood from the teachings of the totality of Scripture and not from science, philosophy, tradition, or experience.

hermeneutical principles. The second principle is the principle of reality. According to this principle, ultimate reality is historical rather than timeless/spaceless and non-historical, as tradition assumes. The third principle is the principle of articulation. This principle deals with the way in which the manifold components of historical reality interconnect, forming a whole. The historical Christ "connects" the whole of reality historically, thereby replacing the "chain of being," "order of being," or "pyramid of being" that tradition uses to articulate biblical contents and spiritual realities. The consistent application of the second and third principles helps the remnant church go beyond the theological and ecclesiological fragmentation that followed the Protestant "turn to Scripture"[31] and its failure to overcome the hermeneutical rule of Christian tradition.[32]

The conviction that the Bible is the only source from which the community can derive its knowledge of God is clearly stated in the first fundamental belief of the Seventh-day Adventist Church. In scholarly circles, we refer to this principle under the label of the *sola* and *tota Scriptura* principles. These principles replace the multiplicity of sources of Christian tradition and unleash the two methodological principles that give rise to the end-time people of God. Meanwhile, the leading sector of Prot-

---

[31] Through the centuries, radical Protestants experienced the "turn to Scripture" as what some historians call "primitivism," a going back to a golden age before the distortion brought about by tradition. This, they argued, was impossible. The implication is that Christians cannot reach unity by working from Scripture alone. "Primitivism . . . in its search for a pristine fount in biblical time and especially for the simpler, less complicated realities of the New Testament, makes two misjudgments. It underestimates the hold of our own times on our vision of the Scriptures. And it overestimates our ability to get back, to recover that ideal time—the Old Testament for some Puritans, the Gospels for the Anabaptists, the Acts for the pentecostals, or the Epistles for fundamentalists—in its original purity" (Noll, "Rethinking Restorationism: A Review Article," 21). The last portion of Noll's comment, however, seems to indicate that fragmentation originates from the inability to grasp the entire system of scriptural truth. They failed to find in Scripture the principle of reality and the principle of articulation.

[32] According to Mathison, the *sola Scriptura* principle, as experienced by the Radical reformers, destroys the authority of Scripture because it calls for an individualistic hermeneutics to decide its meaning. As you read the following quotation, you should bear in mind that Mathison uses the label "*solo scriptura*" to refer to the Radical Reformation claim to get the truth without the help of tradition. He reserves the "*sola Scriptura*" label for the Magisterial Reformers who used the hermeneutical guidance of tradition. "The doctrine of sola *scriptura*, despite its claims to uniquely preserve the authority of the Word of God, destroys that authority by making the meaning of Scripture dependent upon the judgment of each individual. Rather than the Word of God being the one final court of appeal, the court of appeal becomes the multiplied minds of each believer. One is persuaded that Calvinism is more biblical. The other is persuaded that dispensationalism is more biblical. And by what standard does each decide? The standard is each individual's opinion of what is biblical. The standard is necessarily individualistic, and therefore the standard is necessarily relativistic" (Keith A. Mathison, *The Shape of Sola Scriptura* [Moscow, ID: Canon Press, 2001], 246-247). Individualism, in turn, ends up creating new human traditions (253).

estantism still grounds its hermeneutical principles on tradition, failing to see the need for the "biblical hermeneutical turn."[33]

At this point a question arises: Does Adventism have a principle of reality and a principle of articulation? Yes, Adventism has them; although, so far Adventist theologians have not explicitly identified and formulated them as such. Adventists are not used to thinking about the reality and articulation of their message. But they have, since early days, operated assuming biblically defined notions about them. These understandings arose from the pioneers' hope in Christ's personal, historical Second Coming and, after the Great Disappointment, by following Him into the heavenly sanctuary.

In synthesis, Adventists assume that reality is historical, both for human beings and for God (ontology). They also presuppose implicitly that the whole of reality is the common history of God with His creatures (metaphysics). By understanding reality as existing in one single historical level where God, angels, and humans as spiritual beings interact, Adventists effectually rejected and replaced the Neoplatonic cosmological dichotomy between the realms of spirit (heaven) and history (creation). Finally, Adventists have always assumed that the historical, incarnated, resurrected, and ascended Christ is the principle of articulation of all realities in the vast universe from past to future eternity.

Message: System of Truth

By using these principles, Adventist pioneers discovered a "complete system of truth, connected and harmonious."[34] The remnant came into existence not only because they came to a correct understanding of prophecy but because the beauty and power of the harmonious and interconnected system of truth they discovered in Scripture left them no other option before God.[35] The system brings all the teachings of Scrip-

---

[33] "Instead of advocating chaos, the Evangelical church must regain an understanding of the Reformation doctrine of sola scriptura, which is essentially nothing more than the early Church's doctrine of Scripture and tradition framed within a different historical context. The Church must affirm that Scripture is the sole source of revelation. The Church must affirm that Scripture is the sole, final, and infallible norm of faith and practice. And the Church must affirm that Scripture is to be interpreted in and by the communion of saints within the theological context of the rule of faith. Only by rejecting all forms of autonomy, institutional or individual, can any branch of the Church be in obedience to Jesus Christ the Lord" (ibid., 347).

[34] White, *The Great Controversy*, 423.

[35] This is what Ellen White briefly summarized by stating that the complete system of truth they were able to experience showed them that God had directed the great Advent Movement revealing to them their position (to be the Remnant Church) and duty (their mission to the world as the Remnant) (ibid.).

ture together into a harmonious whole, centered and articulated by the living historical person of Christ; the historical incarnated Christ who died, resurrected, and ascended to heaven, ministers for our salvation, and will come to take us home. Adventists know this system as "the Great Controversy theme." Yet, the Great Controversy is much more than a biblical "theme" or "motif." The Great Controversy is the gospel message, because it unfolds the history of God's love for the world and the universe.[36]

Adventists preach the same gospel the disciples proclaimed after the resurrection. "They had a Gospel to preach—Christ in human form, a Man of sorrows; Christ in humiliation, taken by wicked hands and crucified; Christ resurrected, and ascended to heaven, into the presence of God, to be humans' Advocate; Christ to come again with power and great glory in the clouds of heaven."[37] The incarnated Christ, "His character and work, is the center and circumference of all truth. He is the chain upon which the jewels of doctrine are linked. In Him is found the complete system of truth."[38] From before creation to the consummation of salvation in the restoration of the new earth, the cross is the great central truth around which clusters 1) all biblical truths;[39] 2) Christ's work of atonement that transforms sinners;[40] and 3) the history of the church in heaven and

---

[36] For an introduction to the broad and all inclusive reach of the Great Controversy, see Herbert E. Douglass, *The Heartbeat of Adventism: The Great Controversy Theme in the Writings of Ellen White* (Nampa, ID: Pacific Press, 2010).

[37] Ellen G. White, *God's Amazing Grace* (Washington, DC: Review and Herald, 1973), 49.

[38] Ellen G. White, *Our High Calling* (Washington, DC: Review and Herald, 1961), 16.

[39] "The Sacrifice of Christ as an atonement for sin is the great truth around which all other truths cluster. In order to be rightly understood and appreciated, every truth in the Word of God, from Genesis to Revelation, must be studied in the light that streams from the cross of Calvary. I present before you the great, grand monument of mercy and regeneration, salvation and redemption,–the Son of God uplifted on the cross. This is to be the foundation of every discourse given by our ministers"(Ellen G. White, *Gospel Workers* [Washington DC: Review and Herald, 1948], 315). However, the cross should not be reduced to justification by faith. Instead, "[t]he atoning sacrifice, the righteousness of Christ, is to us the vital center of all truth. In the cross of Calvary, mercy and truth are met together, righteousness and peace have kissed each other. The law and the gospel are in perfect harmony; they are interwoven as the warp and the woof. They shed a flood of light amid the moral darkness of the world, stimulating, renovating, sanctifying, all who will believe the truth, all who will gladly and gratefully accept the light coming from the throne of God" (Ellen G. White, "Missionary Work," *Review and Herald*, September 29, 1891, par. 8).

[40] The cross is the center of Christ's work of atonement that transforms the soul of the believer: "The atonement of Christ is the great central truth around which cluster all the truths that pertain to the great work of redemption. The mind of man is to blend with the mind of Christ. This union sanctifies the understanding, giving the thoughts clearness and force..." (Ellen G. White, *Lift Him Up* [Hagerstown, MD: Review and Herald, 1988], 229).

earth.⁴¹ In short, the historical, resurrected Christ as "the Son of God is the center of the great plan of redemption which covers all dispensations."⁴² He is the center of all doctrines.⁴³ The "completeness" of the system of truth revealed in Scripture includes everything Christians need to know in faith and practice.⁴⁴

This system is more than an intellectual understanding of doctrines. Through it, there is a spiritual union of the soul with Christ, on which the biblical church stands and exists. The biblical system of truths Christ articulates into a harmonious whole is the spiritual bread that nourishes and unites the soul with Christ, thereby generating the existence of the church.⁴⁵ Through the teaching ministry and providences of the Holy Spirit, the complete system of divine living truths centered in Christ penetrate, cleanse, and sanctify the soul.⁴⁶ The church gathers around Christ,

---

⁴¹ Finally, the cross, as the center of Christ's work of atonement, is the center of church history and of the church of the redeemed in heaven: "The church history upon the earth and the church redeemed in heaven all center around the cross of Calvary. This is the theme, this is the song,— Christ all and in all,— in anthems of praise resounding through heaven from thousands and ten thousand times ten thousand and an innumerable company of the redeemed host. All unite in this song of Moses and of the Lamb. It is a new song, for it was never before sung in heaven" (Ellen G. White, *Testimonies to Ministers and Gospel Workers* [Mountain View, CA: Pacific Press, 1962], 433).

⁴² Ellen G. White, "Inexpressible Joy," *Signs of the Times*, December 22, 1914, par. 9.

⁴³ "Christ is the center of all true doctrine. All true religion is found in His word and in nature. He is the One in whom our hopes of eternal life are centered; and the teacher who learns from Him finds a safe anchorage" (Ellen G. White, *Counsels to Parents, Teachers, and Students* [Mountain View, CA: Pacific Press, 1943], 453).

⁴⁴ "The Lord has uttered His voice in His Holy Word. Those blessed pages are full of instruction and life, harmonious with truth. They are a perfect rule of conduct. Instructions are given, principles are laid down, which apply to every circumstance in life, even though some particular case may not be stated. Nothing is left unrevealed which is essential to a complete system of faith and a correct line of practice. Every duty that God requires at our hands is made plain; and if anyone fails of eternal life, it will be because he was self-sufficient, self-confident, full of vain conceit, and did not rely solely upon the merits of the blood of Christ for salvation. None will err from the right path who meekly and honestly take the Bible as their guide, making it the man of their counsel" (Ellen G. White, *Mind, Character, and Personality* [Nashville, TN: Southern Publishing, 1977], 2:784).

⁴⁵ "The cause of division or discord in the church is separation from Christ. The secret of unity is union with Christ. Christ is the great Center. We shall approach one another just in proportion as we approach the Center. United with Christ, we shall surely be united with our brethren in the faith." (White, *Manuscript Releases* [Silver Spring, MD: E. G. White Estate, 1993], 15:301).

⁴⁶ "The oil so much needed by those who are represented as foolish virgins, is not something to be put on the outside. They need to bring the truth into the sanctuary of the soul, that it may cleanse, refine, and sanctify. It is not theory that they need; it is the sacred teachings of the Bible, which are not uncertain, disconnected doctrines, but are living truths, that involve eternal interests that center in Christ. In Him is the complete system of divine truth. The salvation of the soul, through faith in Christ, is the ground and pillar of the truth" (Ellen G. White, *Ye Shall Receive Power* [Hagerstown, MD: Review and Herald, 1995], 16).

"the center of all love and light."[47]

Mission and the History of God's Love

Adventists have a message to tell to the world. The biblical history of God's love is their message. By living this message everyday, they become part of God's history of salvation as the eschatological biblical remnant. They are God's visible remnant church, because they experience it spiritually and proclaim it to the world. This history is the complete harmonious system of biblical truths centered in the historical acts of Christ from before the creation of the world to the unending ages of eternity. As already indicated, Adventists refer to this history as the Great Controversy between Christ and Satan.

Christian denominations have, to a large extent, neglected, forgotten, or perhaps rejected this history, or portions of it, because hermeneutical assumptions led them to spiritualize it. The ontologies or understanding of God and the soul that Christian tradition assumes have no place for God acting historically as an agent among other historical agents as Christ did during His life and ministry. Thus, the Great Controversy became spiritualized as the "story" of Christ ontologically "descending" from the Father (incarnation) and "ascending back" to the Father (decarnation). The history of God became a story.

In this "story," the personal, historical relationship that Christ had with His disciples is replaced by the platonic idea of communion as participation.[48] After the resurrection, believers are thought to relate directly with God by "participating" in its being. Tradition understands "participation" as a "sharing-in-being," "mutual indwelling," and "mutual interpenetration" of the timeless non-historical reality of God with the soul.[49] Participation then defines communion as the relationship of the soul with the timeless God through the ascended Christ. Thus, communion with

---

[47] "The more closely we walk with Christ, the center of all love and light, the greater will be our affection for His light-bearers. When the saints are drawn close to Christ, they must of necessity be drawn close to each other, for the sanctifying grace of Christ will bind their hearts together. You cannot love God and yet fail to love your brethren" (Ellen G. White, *Manuscript Releases*, 15:88).

[48] Irenaeus and later tradition used "to describe the kind of relationship that humanity enjoys with the triune God" (Julie Canlis, *Calvin's Ladder: A Spiritual Theology of Ascent and Ascension* [Grand Rapids, MI: Eerdmans, 2010], 6).

[49] George Hunsinger explains that according to Christian tradition, *koinonia* "means that we are not related to God or to one another like ball bearings in a bucket, through a system of external relations. We are rather, something like relational fields that interpenetrate, form, and participate in each other in countless real tough often elusive ways" (George Hunsinger, *Disruptive Grace* [Grand Rapids, MI: Eerdmans, 2000], 257; quoted by Canlis, *Calvin's Ladder: A Spiritual Theology of Ascent and Ascension*, 7–8).

God frees human souls from their present association with matter and historical events and unites them with the timeless realm of the Trinitarian life.[50] Clearly, participation in the being of God replaces the biblical, personal, social, spiritual, face-to-face, fellowship (communion/*koinonia*) with the incarnated, historical Christ that lies at the foundation of the Great Controversy.

Calvin also spiritualized the history of the Great Controversy, by translating it into Neoplatonic ontological categories. For example, Calvin spiritualized the historical meaning of communion with Christ in Scripture by embracing the traditional notion of "participation." Communion with Christ, according to Calvin, cannot be understood in terms of fellowship or society, basic to the Great Controversy, but rather in terms of the "unity by which the Son of God engrafts us into His body, so that He communicates to us all that He is. We so draw life from His flesh and His blood, that they are not improperly called our food."[51] However, more conservative and biblically-minded evangelical denominations still think historically and have not surrendered completely to the spiritualization of God's history of love.[52] The influence of traditional hermeneutical ideas still operates in the background of these denominations, leading them to reduce the history of God to the history of Christ's incarnation on earth. In the practice of spirituality, the history of God's love is reduced to Christmas and Easter. And even this is understood as a symbol of a non-historical, spiritual reality that transcends and leaves behind human history.

At the antipodes of tradition, the history of God's love takes place within the temporal, spatial, and material realm of creation. Spiritual communion with God is a historical, social relationship between humans and the ascended, incarnated, historical Christ ministering from the heavenly sanctuary. Christ is the center of human reality, and therefore of human and cosmic history. Ellen White's massive five volumes, called the Great Controversy series, starts and ends with the words "God is love" thereby indicating that God's history reveals His loving merciful being and character.

---

[50] Canlis, *Calvin's Ladder*, 3, 43–44, 177–178.

[51] Clavin Letter to Martyr (8 August, 1555), quoted by ibid., 13.

[52] See for instance, Henry M. Morris, *The Long War Against God: The History and Impact of the Creation/Evolution Conflict* (Grand Rapids, MI: Baker Book House, 1989), 199, where he states: "...the modern creation-evolution conflict is more than a mere scientific controversy, or even a battle between science and religion, as evolutionists pretend. It is nothing less than a new and critical phase in the agelong conflict between the only two basic world views. One is centered in the Creator of the world and his redemptive work on behalf of that lost world; the other is centered in the creatures of that world, not only man and his self-oriented goals, but also in the devil himself, who is ultimately behind all rebellion against God."

According to Scripture, the history of God's love in creation and redemption is an extension of the eternal history of love of the Godhead. We can trace the origins of this history to before Creation. It was then, through divine, infinite wisdom, the Trinity planned the design of the universe. From love and through love, they sought to share their life by opening themselves to their creation.

At the beginning, before God created the universe, the Trinity designed the universe and the plan of salvation. At that time, Christ was appointed to be the great center of creation (Prov 8:22–23; ESV), to play the role of mediator between the infinite transcendence of the being, life, and history of the Trinity and the limited reach of the life, being, and history of the future creatures.[53] According to God's design, all things in the universe will hold together in Christ (Col 1:17). He was appointed as the center of God's system of reality. God's love prompted Him to relate directly to His creatures through the mediatory presence of Christ in their future life and history. God's love is direct, personal, and historical. Through Christ's mediation, God's wisdom and law will become the basis of spiritual order among free beings created in the image of God.

God knew in detail what would take place after He created the universe. He knew His creatures would rebel against the spiritual order centered in Christ and challenge His sovereignty. God also knew about the suffering and death that would follow. Yet, God created the universe anyway. Many question God's love, forgetting that God decided that Christ, the center around which all things cohere in the universe, should become a human being and die in the place of His rebellious creatures. God's love in Christ's incarnation and death was the way to respond to the creatures' challenge to Christ's work.

In the beginning God created the heavens and the earth even when He did not need to do it. Yet, in love He did. When God created the historical reality of the universe, perfect spiritual harmony existed until controversy arose in heaven and on earth. In love, He allowed the other to ex-

---

[53] "I suggest that according to Prov 8, at the beginning of creation, we find a situation of equal members of the Godhead as Co-creators. There is no reference to a time before which One of the Members of the Godhead did not exist, nor a reference to the eternal subordination of One Member of the Godhead to Another Member. Rather, there is described a time, before the creation of the universe, when, presumably by mutual consent, one Person of the Godhead is "installed" (*nsk* III) in a role of Mediator. While the Person we call the Father continued to represent the transcendent nature of the Godhead, the Person we know as the Son condescended in divine *kenosis* to represent the immanent aspect of divinity, coming close to His creation, mediating between infinity and finitude, even before sin. This is not a subordination of the Son to the Father, but a voluntary condescension to be installed into a mediatorial role, representing the divine love in an immanent way to His inhabited universe" (Richard Davidson, "Proverbs 8 and the Place of Christ in the Trinity," *JATS* 17.1 [2006]: 54).

ist even when His sovereignty, wisdom, love, law, and government were challenged. Only a God of love could create a universe that will cause Him infinite suffering while pursuing the well-being of His creatures. Through the rebellion of His creatures, the history of God's love became the history of the Great Controversy between Christ and Satan.

Ever since the rebellion against God's government, the history of God's love carried on with the aim to restore creation back to its original spiritual harmony. Beginning with Satan's rebellion in heaven and its expansion to the Garden of Eden, Christ has continued to be the heart around which all things cohere.

Christ is the historical agent of God's covenant of salvation. The preaching of the Gospel before the flood; the call to Abraham; Christ's presence and revelation at Sinai; and His incarnation, ministry, death, resurrection, ascension, and heavenly ministry are just some of the events He used to achieve full restoration of the perfect spiritual harmony that existed at the beginning of Creation. The history of the universe revealed in Scripture and articulated by Jesus Christ helped the biblical, visible remnant understand the history of God's love for His creatures. It integrates all the teachings of Scriptures and doctrines of Christianity into a comprehensive, harmonious whole.

Understanding this history has profound implications for Christian theology as it replaces the macro hermeneutical perspective that tradition draws from classical and modern metaphysics or postmodern metanarratives and metahistories.[54] The history of God's love reinforces the "biblical hermeneutical turn" that helped Adventist pioneers free themselves from the hermeneutical dominion of Christian tradition and overcome the inconsistencies and ambiguities generated by the Protestant attempt to "turn to Scripture." The theological and spiritual strength of the historical metanarrative of the Great Controversy brought about the emergence of the biblical, visible remnant church. This ensures faithfulness to the gospel of Christ and the apostolicity of the Church.[55]

Understanding the history of God's love also has profound implications for Christian spirituality, because it facilitates a deep and steady personal relationship with God. When by faith the believer understands

---

[54] The word "metahistory" refers to the overarching narrative or "grand récit" that gives order and meaning to the historical record, especially in the large-scale philosophies of history of writers such as Hegel, Marx, or Spencer.

[55] The apostolicity of the Church, according to Scripture, is not based on apostolic succession, but on faithfulness to the gospel of Christ. See for instance, Raoul Dederen, "The Church," *Handbook of Seventh-day Adventist Theology*, ed. Raoul Dederen (Hagerstown, MD: Review and Herald, 2000), 563–564.

and obeys God's words he or she feeds on Christ, the Bread of Life. God's words, through the teaching ministry of the Holy Spirit, penetrate deep in the heart of believers transforming them in the image of Christ. Communion with God is no longer participation in His being, experienced through the liturgical mechanics of the sacraments, leaving the heart empty. Instead, communion with God is a personal, ongoing dialogue with the incarnated, ascended Christ ministering in the heavenly sanctuary. This dialogue is very real and takes place in everyday life through Bible study, prayer, obedience, and mission. This experience unites each believer in fellowship with Christ and simultaneously with one another and becomes the spiritual ground on which God's visible remnant church on earth stands.

Summary and Conclusions

The Christian church has progressively abandoned the hermeneutical presuppositions that New Testament writers took from the Old Testament, replacing them with the Greek understanding of reality. This hermeneutical turn to Greek philosophy distorted biblical teachings and produced a reinterpretation of Scripture and its teachings. Moreover, it led Christian tradition to replace Christ's presence in the heavenly sanctuary with the liturgy and sacraments of the church. Although Scripture was never absent from Christian tradition, the new philosophical hermeneutics decisively distorted its teachings and weakened its power. Eventually, it contributed to the church's self-understanding as the replacement of Israel rather than its remnant, and to ground its existence on the sacraments and on the claim of apostolic succession, rather than on Scripture.

Although the mainline and radical reformations "turn to Scripture" led to the discovery of forgotten biblical teachings they stopped short of challenging the macro hermeneutical principles of Christian tradition. This prevented the churches of the Reformation from becoming a unified theological and ecclesiological alternative to Roman Catholicism. Instead, the Protestant "turn to Scripture" fragmented the Christian church into an increasing number of denominations.

This turn to Scripture intensified, leading to the unavoidable biblical hermeneutical turn of early Adventist pioneers. This means that Seventh-day Adventist identity as the remnant church stands on more than the scriptural marks of the remnant and its distinctive doctrines. It primarily stands on Scripture alone (*sola*), completely (*tota*), and hermeneutically (*prima*). According to Scripture, this remnant exists in spiritual union with Christ. This union flows from the discovery, acceptance, and spiritual internalization of the complete and harmonious biblical system of theology. More precisely, the "biblical hermeneutical turn" replaced the "philosophical hermeneutics" embraced by Christian tradition. The spirituality of Scripture, centered in the presence of the historical incarnated Christ in the heavenly sanctuary, replaced the spirituality of Christian tradition, centered in the assumed presence of Christ in the liturgy and sacraments of the church.

The biblical remnant is not a possession or badge of honor to brag about, but responsibility, service, and mission. It exists as the unfinished process of reviving and reforming the Christian church in the wilderness of human traditions. The remnant church stands on the same biblical and spiritual ground on which the remnant of Israel in the New Testament stood, eating the same spiritual food (1 Cor 10:1–5). We can, then, suggest that the biblical remnant of Israel, as found in the New Testament and as represented by the remnant of the woman in Revelation 12:17, has reemerged from Scripture and history in eschatological times.

Being the remnant is the spiritual experience of being-in-message. This means that the message of the remnant belongs to its very existence. It is the process of historically appropriating the complete system of theology and philosophy identified by Adventists as the Great Controversy between Christ and Satan. The message of the Church coincides with the history of God's love and salvation. The spirituality of the remnant is the internalization of Christ's teachings and of His history of love. As believers unite with Christ in spirit, they become completely dedicated to His laws, teachings, and promises. Because being-in-the history of God is an existential, spiritual experience of the whole being, it involves a radical departure from the spirit of the world and human cultures.

Being-in-message requires Adventists to articulate, in detail, the contents and power of the "complete system of theology and philosophy" the early pioneers discovered and outlined. The Great Controversy theology and philosophy, masterfully developed by Ellen White, should be presented on the basis of the *sola, tota,* and *prima Scriptura* principles at the scholarly level of systematic theology and philosophy. Adventists should present to the church and the world the complete system of biblical doctrines, without using human traditions or the writings of Ellen White (*sola Scriptura*), and show the beautiful inner historical and systematic coherence of Christ's acts of redemption and teachings throughout the entire Bible *(tota Scriptura)*.

Being the remnant is the spiritual experience of being-in-mission. This means that the mission of the remnant is its very existence and life. The mission of the remnant church is to proclaim the message and mission of Christ. In its essence, the remnant is a call to repentance extended to Christian tradition and Protestantism for neglecting and replacing the real living Christ with human traditions and teachings. It is also an invitation addressed to every human being to leave the ways of the world and follow the Christ of Scripture. The mission of the remnant church is to share the experience of understanding and belonging to the history of Christ's love, making and gathering a community of spiritual disciples ready to share the same experience and meet Christ in His coming glory. By fulfilling its mission, the remnant is destined to become the ecumenical, biblical alternative to the ecumenical, traditional alternative.

Being-in-mission requires Adventists to uplift the Christ of Scripture by experiencing and sharing the complete and harmonious system of philosophy and theology to the church and to the world. This message/system (the three angels' messages, present truth, platform of truth) is powerful because it includes the doctrines and data of Scripture in a coherent all-encompassing spiritual and historical metanarrative centered in Christ. In this metanarrative, the cross is the center of attraction, and the incarnate, resurrected Christ, ministering in the Heavenly Sanctuary, is the center of spirituality and salvation.

Being the remnant is the spiritual experience of being-in-hope. This means that hope belongs to its very existence and life of the remnant and that the remnant lives in anticipation of eternity. Believers eagerly expect to meet Christ face to face, exactly as the disciples did, when He returns back historically, visibly, in glory and majesty. At that time, He will restore everything in heaven and on earth back to the original perfect harmony of love. The controversy will be over: "Sin and sinners are no more. The entire universe is clean. One pulse of harmony and gladness beats through the vast creation. From Him who created all, flow life and light and gladness, throughout the realms of illimitable space. From the minutest atom to the greatest world, all things, animate and inanimate, in their unshadowed beauty and perfect joy, declare that God is love."[56]

---

[56] White, *The Great Controversy*, 678.

CHAPTER 13

Role of the Fundamental Beliefs in the Church

Kwabena Donkor

There has been little reflection among Adventist theologians on the nature and role of the Statement of Fundamental Beliefs. In 2005, the addition of a 28th statement to the official list brought with it a renewed interest in the topic. A traditional Adventist concern has been the danger of transforming the Statement into a creed, which it is not. But this concern has not been accompanied by a systematic discussion on the positive role of the Statement of Fundamental Beliefs. This discussion is long overdue. Here, we will focus on the positive role of the Statement in the church while addressing the matter of creedalism.

Statement of Beliefs, Not a Creed

Throughout the development of their statements of fundamental beliefs, Seventh-day Adventists have insisted that they have no creed but the Bible.[1] In other words, the Statement of Fundamental Beliefs is not a creed. Defining the difference between a statement of fundamental beliefs and a creed is difficult. Webster's New Collegiate Dictionary (1979) defines a creed as "a set of fundamental beliefs." The difference between the two is not immediately evident by formal analysis. The question is whether the difference resides in their nature or in their function? Looking at the writings of the pioneers, especially Ellen White, we see that the difference resides in both the *nature* of the *existing* creeds of the Christian church at the time and in their *use*. A few statements illustrate this point.

---

[1] See Ellen G. White, *Selected Messages* (Washington, DC: Review and Herald, 1958), 1:416.

First, as documents of human creation, the existing creeds of Christendom at the time were found to contain errors:

> There are tower builders in our time. Infidels construct their theories from the supposed deductions of science, and reject the revealed word of God.... In the professedly Christian world many turn away from the plain teachings of the Bible and build up a creed from human speculations and pleasing fables, and they point to their tower as a way to climb up to heaven....[2]

Furthermore, the nature of creeds as such, for the pioneers, had the potential to stifle the further unfolding of biblical truth:

> Thus early in the experience of the emerging church, light new to herself and others, yet in full harmony with the Scriptures, was given by the Lord through His chosen messenger. The pioneers were conscious of this; a decade and a half later, when organizing the church, *they refrained from the adoption of a creed, which could stand in the way of God giving new light through the visions.*[3]

Second, the pioneers felt that the way the creeds of Christendom were employed left much to be desired. As the pioneers saw it, the creeds were being used in place of the Bible, which did not encourage personal encounter with Scripture or a vital, personal experience of truth. Such understanding put at risk the function of the Bible as the only source of faith and practice. Ellen G. White wrote,

> The question is, "What is truth?" It is not how many years have I believed that makes it the truth. You must bring your creed to the Bible and let the light of the Bible define your creed and show where it comes short and where the difficulty is. The Bible is to be your standard, the living oracles of Jehovah are to be your guide. You are to dig for the truth as for hidden treasures... You know how it is with the papal power. The people have no right to interpret the Scriptures for themselves. They must have someone else interpret the Scriptures for them. Have you no mind? Have you no reason? Has not God given judgment to the common people

---

[2] Ellen G. White, *Conflict and Courage* (Washington, DC: Review and Herald, 1970), 42.

[3] Arthur L. White, *Ellen G. White Biography: The Early Years, 1827–1862* (Hagerstown, MD: Review and Herald, 1985), 1:100.

just as well as He has to the priests and rulers? . . . Until you can see the reason for it yourself and a "thus saith the Lord" in the Scriptures, don't trust any living man to interpret the Bible for you. And when you can see this, you know it for yourself, and know it to be the truth of God. You will say, "I have read it, I have seen it, and my own heart takes hold upon it, and it is the truth God has spoken to me from His Word." *Now this is what we are to be—individual Christians. We need to have an individual, personal experience.*[4]

It seems clear that the pioneers frowned upon creeds, not just because of the way they had been used but also because their very nature as documents of human creation requires they always stand under the critical judgment of the Bible. The pioneers' attitude on creeds has continued to characterize the Seventh-day Adventist Church throughout its history. As we address the role of the Statement of Fundamental Beliefs in the church, we do so with the understanding that it is not a substitute for the Bible—neither as the absolute definition of truth, nor as the primary means of encountering the life-altering truths of the Bible. However, a real question remains as to whether a statement of fundamental beliefs is of any significant value to the life of the church. This question becomes even more important in contemporary times when there is a decided depreciation of officially-defined doctrines.[5]

The Role of the Statement of Beliefs

The pioneers' view on creeds, by implication, shows how they saw the beliefs which they themselves were formulating. While we are clear on what their beliefs were *not* (i.e. not to be looked upon as a creed), it is not very clear what they understood them to *be*. It is not enough to say creeds are statements of fundamental beliefs. In order to assess the role

---

[4] Ellen G. White, *Faith and Works* (Nashville, TN: Southern Publisher, 1972), 77.

[5] The Enlightenment of the 17th century, embodying a general aversion to "authority" as it did, and capitalizing on the disaffection with Protestant scholasticism, introduced a radical subjectivism that remains a defining characteristic of our times. From Adolf von Harnack, through Rudolf Bultmann, Paul Tillich, and Gordon Kaufmann, to many contemporary postmodernists, there is a decided contempt for officially defined systems of doctrine. Evidently, contemporary aversion to officially defined systems of doctrine goes beyond the historic creeds of Christendom to include confessions of faith and statements of beliefs from more recent vintage. Among the reasons for the declined confidence in creeds, confessions and statement of beliefs are the following: belief in the subjective nature of truth in the post-enlightenment climate: the stress of orthopraxis over orthodoxy: the appeal to cultural relativism: and a revised concept of revelation (i.e. revelation as an ongoing reality) that leads to a new overemphasis on the understanding of doctrine as an organism that ever evolves and matures.

of a statement of fundamental beliefs in the church correctly, we need to more clearly understand what it is. To do so, we will examine three issues: its *formal* essence, its *material* connection to the Scriptures, and the nature of its authority.

The *Formal* Essence of the Statement of Fundamental Beliefs

The first part of the analysis of the nature of a statement of fundamental beliefs will deal with its essence. By referring to the *essence* of the statement of beliefs, a very formal idea is in view.

A Formal Set of Doctrines

A statement of fundamental beliefs is a set of doctrines or teachings (Greek, *didaskalia*). The focus is *not* on teaching as an activity but as a system of beliefs. Two important points emerge from a biblical understanding of *doctrine* or *teaching*. Unlike the Greek usage of *didaskalia* outside of the Bible which emphasized the communication of intellectual or technical knowledge, the New Testament usage stresses *content*, usually of ethical instruction. Thus "sound doctrine" in the pastoral epistles is contrasted with immoral living (1 Tim 1:10; Titus 2:1–5). Furthermore, the ethical dimension of biblical *doctrine/teaching* is connected to preaching as the means by which people are brought to faith in Jesus, to be instructed in the ethical principles and obligations of the Christian life.[6]

Yet, since God's will is the focus of ethical instruction in the Bible, *doctrine/teaching* becomes closely identified with the "essential data of the faith," taking on a meaning which includes the essential beliefs of the Christian faith.[7] Knowing doctrine in the Bible is not a mere accumulation of pieces of data; rather, knowing doctrine results in the love of God (2 John 6–10).

Great care should be exercised to note that biblical teaching is useful only when it leads to conversion.[8] The goal of the Bible and its teachings is to lead people to a saving knowledge and a relationship with God through Christ. Biblical teaching and truth all aim at building a community around

---

[6] G. D. Fee, "Doctrine," *ZPEB*, 2:152.

[7] Ibid.

[8] "All, high or low, if they are unconverted, are on one common platform. Men may turn from one doctrine to another. This is being done, and will be done. Papists may change from Catholicism to Protestantism; yet they may know nothing of the meaning of the words, 'A new heart also will I give you.' Accepting new theories, and uniting with a church, does not bring new life to anyone, even though the church with which he unites may be established on the true foundation. Connection with a church does not take the place of conversion. To subscribe the name to a church creed is not of the least value to anyone if the heart is not truly changed...." (Ellen G. White, *Evangelism* [Washington, DC: Review and Herald, 1946], 290).

Christ. We are told that by *"speaking the truth* in love," we may grow into Christ (Eph 4:15-16). It is in this sense of growing up in Christ in "all aspects or things" (v. 15) that a statement of fundamental beliefs is so wholistic, reaching into practically all aspects of life. A statement of beliefs is helpful in pointing to Christ as the center of belief and practice. Clearly, Christ should remain the ultimate essence of a statement of fundamental beliefs, since He is true teacher (John 14:6).

The Statement of Fundamental Beliefs is to be understood as a set of *didaskalia*. The very essence of such a statement is *content*, comprising data of the faith which, when embraced, eventuates in love and obedience to God through Jesus Christ.

A Reflection of Faith-Consciousness Based on Scripture

A statement of fundamental beliefs can also be used as a means of instruction.[9] It implies some measure of "sameness" with regards to belief within the ranks of the Adventist community of faith. In other words, a statement of fundamental beliefs reflects a group's corporate faith-consciousness, *based solely on Scripture.* It is a consensus document that mirrors the belief commitments garnered from Scripture that the group regards as essential to its identity and mission.

However, this reflects a consensus on "truth." This point is of pivotal importance as we seek to reflect on the role of the Statement of Fundamental Beliefs in the Seventh-day Adventist church. The issue as to whether one can indeed speak about "the truth" is very much debated today. The question is, does the Statement represent the church's consensus on "truth" or is it an "in-house" understanding of reality? The position taken on this question has profound implications on one's valuation of the Statement of Fundamental Beliefs. From the Seventh-day Adventist perspective, it appears that from the very beginning, a definite conception of "truth" underlies the effort to formulate a statement of fundamental beliefs.[10]

---

[9] *Seventh-day Adventist Church Manual* (Silver Spring, MD: General Conference, 2010), 209–213.

[10] See James White, "Resolution of the Seventh-day Baptist Central Association," *Advent Review and Sabbath Herald*, Aug. 11, 1853, 52. "As a people we are brought together from divisions of the Advent body and from various denominations, holding different views on some subjects; yet, thank Heaven, the Sabbath is a mighty platform on which we can all stand united. And while standing here, with the aid of no other creed than the Word of God, and bound together by the bonds of love—love for the truth, love for each other, and love for a perishing world—'which is stronger than death,' all party feelings are lost. We are united in these great subjects: Christ's immediate, personal second Advent, and the observance of all of the commandments of God, and the faith of his Son Jesus Christ, as necessary to a readiness for his Advent."

The Connection between Scripture and a Statement of Beliefs

The second part of the analysis of the nature of a statement of fundamental beliefs has to do with its *relation* to Scripture. The Seventh-day Adventist understanding presupposes an ongoing, dynamic relationship with Holy Scripture. Not only does the church see its Statement of Fundamental Beliefs as grounded in the Bible, it also explicitly and purposefully subordinates the statement of beliefs to the Bible by giving the Bible magisterial oversight on its future expressions. The Statement of Fundamental Beliefs is prefaced as follows:

> Seventh-day Adventists accept the Bible as their only creed and hold certain fundamental beliefs to be the teaching of the Holy Scriptures. These beliefs, as set forth here, constitute the church's understanding and expression of the teaching of Scripture. Revision of these statements may be expected at a General Conference session when the church is led by the Holy Spirit to a fuller understanding of Bible truth or finds better language in which to express the teachings of God's Holy Word.[11]

Indeed, the church claims the Bible as its only creed. The notion of "no creed but the Bible" is certainly not unique with Seventh-day Adventists, but their perspective on the idea is to emphasize the need to go to the Bible for new vistas on truth as well as to help us be "individual Christians".[12]

In spite of the foregoing, Seventh-day Adventists have also emphasized the need for correct doctrine and truth expressed in their adoption of a statement of fundamental beliefs. This is not designed in any way to

---

[11] *Seventh-day Adventist Church Manual* (Silver Spring, MD: General Conference, 2010), 156.

[12] White, *Faith*, 77. Jehovah's Witnesses also make the claim 'no creed but the Bible,' but traditionally, the Adventist claim has a hermeneutical focus. It intends to defend the normative status of the Bible over against any interpretations of men that are set up to interfere with the Bible from functioning as ultimate authority. Ellen White noted clearly about Protestant churches of her time: "They are taught to accept its teachings *as interpreted by the church;* and there are thousands who dare receive nothing, however plainly revealed in Scripture, that is contrary to their creed or the established teaching of their church" (*Great Controversy* [Mountain View, CA: Pacific Press, 1911], 596). The following statement by Ellen White again shows that the concern was to ensure that the Bible has the final word: "But God will have a people upon the earth to maintain the Bible, and the Bible only, as the standard of all doctrines and the basis of all reforms. The opinions of learned men, the deductions of science, the creeds or decisions of ecclesiastical councils, as numerous and discordant as are the churches which they represent, the voice of the majority—*not one nor all of these should be regarded as evidence for or against any point of religious faith. Before accepting any doctrine or precept, we should demand a plain 'Thus saith the Lord' in its support*" (ibid., 595, emphasis mine). On the other hand, a fundamentalist may make the claim sometimes to defend a crude literalism over against responsible interpretation.

diminish the role of Scripture in the life of the Adventist community of faith. Indeed, the very fact of the *adoption* of a statement of fundamental beliefs brings out two implications on the church's stand on Scripture: the need for careful, open, and responsible reflection on Scripture; and the desire to emphasize the importance for doctrine. When Seventh-day Adventists make the assertion "no creed but the Bible," they do not in any way endorse the position of those who use the same slogan to express a crude, fundamentalist literalism. On the other hand, the church's adoption of a statement of beliefs runs contrary to the sentiment behind the other equally popular slogan, "No Creed but Christ" which sometimes represents a liberal, reductionist approach to the Bible. Underlying the fundamentalist's disapprobation of creed-like documents is the fear that such documents undermine the sufficiency of Scripture. The liberal dissatisfaction with creed-like documents sometimes results from a concern for non-coercion and freedom of belief and even from a relativistic, existential perspective. Therefore, the Statement of Fundamental Beliefs, while consistent with scriptural sufficiency, prevents a decline into relativism that may deny Scripture its legitimate authority in the church.

The Authority of the Statement of Fundamental Beliefs

Before we discuss more directly the role of the statement of fundamental beliefs in the church, we need to explore one more aspect of the statement of fundamental beliefs. The issue here concerns the authority of the statement of fundamental beliefs, namely, the power that enables it to be what it is, and to accomplish its desired goal. Views on the nature and scope of a statement of fundamental beliefs' authority can be quite broad and raise difficult questions, but its power will rarely be denied. The question is, in what does the authority and power reside? It seems that an understanding of what gives a statement authority will help determine its role in the church.

In view of the relation between the Bible and the statement of fundamental beliefs, whatever authority the latter has is a derivative authority. One of the sources of the power that attends a Statement of Fundamental Beliefs seems to be the fact that it is rooted in history.[13] The rootedness in history that is of interest here relates specifically to the faith community's perception of God's action in their midst and in their history. Such were the confessions and declaratory affirmations of Israel about God's activity in history (Deut 26:5–9; Deut 6:4–5) that some consider to be the

---

[13] Ibid., 2.

basis of Christian creeds.[14] The power of a document such as a statement of fundamental beliefs as a reflection of its rootedness in history is manifested in the fact that once they come into being, they influence historical developments. Creeds, confessions, and statement of beliefs shape history by providing the context for future theological decisions as well as the defining of denominational practice.

Statement of Beliefs as Tradition

Obviously, the comment made above raises the question of tradition in doctrinal definition. Tradition must be distinguished in its various meanings. It is important to distinguish tradition as the teaching and practice of a church, as this teaching and practice has been carried on continuously from the beginning—from tradition as defined by the decrees of the Council of Trent (1545–63).[15] No denomination can exist without a tradition in the former sense. Whereas the former may be a helpful, even an unavoidable and indispensable theological resource, the latter has been rejected by Protestants as contrary to the *sola scriptura* principle. Even within an acceptable view of tradition, care ought to be taken not to neccessarily equate the church's interpretation of Scripture with Scripture.[16] Using the statement of fundamental beliefs as a theological resource in the sense of tradition defined above shapes history without necessarily stultifying further theological activity.

Among Seventh-day Adventists for example, the events prior and subsequent to 1844 were instrumental in the development of their beliefs, which in turn informed and continues to inform Adventist theology, worship, and mission today. For Adventists, this rootedness in history shapes their philosophy of history and their place along cosmic lines in what is generally known as the Great Controversy motif. In that sense, the Statement of Fundamental Beliefs is not any mere collection of biblical truth. It also represents "present truth" in the Seventh-day Adventist philosophy of history within an apocalyptic setting.

A careful look at the history of confessions or statements of beliefs leads to the conclusion that their relation to history is often a dialectical relationship. While they shape history, they are also judged by it. This

---

[14] J. N. D. Kelly, "Creeds," *The Westminster Dictionary of Christian Theology*, ed. Alan Richardson and John Bowden (Philadelphia, PA: Westminster, 1983), 131.

[15] R. P. C. Hanson, "Tradition," *Westminster Dictionary*, 574.

[16] Such for example, is the view taken by Thomas Oden when he argues: "It is not necessary to decide between Scripture and what the church historically teaches in order to define the rule of faith. For what the church, at its best, teaches is precisely what the Scriptures teach" (*The Living God* [San Francisco, CA: Harper and Row, 1987], 344).

is so because, as an expression of a faith community's understanding of God's Word, confessions and statement of beliefs are examined, clarified, and confirmed in the history of the community. It is important to emphasize that community's historical reflection and clarification is an attempt to more accurately reflect the will of God expressed in Scripture. Thus, we are pointed back to the ultimate source of the authority of the statements of fundamental beliefs, namely, the Bible. The Statement of Fundamental Beliefs is really the church's reading and reception of Scripture and it is authoritative only to the extent that it accurately depicts the message of Scripture.

The Statement of Beliefs as the Work of the Spirit

Historical rootedness is not the only source of power for a statement of fundamental beliefs. The faith community ascribes authority to the statement mainly because it sees in it an expression of God's activity among them, where they find Christ's promise regarding the Holy Spirit fulfilled (John 16:13). In this sense, the statement of beliefs is regarded as one of the results of the work of the Spirit. The consensus expressed in the statement is seen as the presence and work of the Spirit within the church, leading it to a biblically-based consensus.

The Value of the Statement of Beliefs

From our analysis, we can define a statement of beliefs as *a faith community's definitive, Spirit-directed consensus on biblical truth based on its reading of inspired Scripture, which defines the community's identity, message, and mission.* The question we face now is the following: What possible value does such a statement have for the community and, in this case, the Seventh-day Adventist Church?

An Indicator of Hermeneutical Concern

The nature of a statement of beliefs as the community's reading of Scripture points to one of its key roles, namely, as an indicator of the community's concern for hermeneutics. By putting out a statement of beliefs, the community declares that 'this is the way we read Scripture' and 'we are not indifferent to any reading of Scripture.' The statement of beliefs as a system of beliefs, becomes the collective principle of interpretation for the community in organizing the disparate data of Scripture. In this way, the statement not only declares the interpretational stance of the community in the past, but also provides a guide for present interpretational efforts. At a time in the history of theology when things appear uncertain and changing, the methodological value of a statement of beliefs in providing theological identity cannot be underestimated.

It should be quite evident that in fulfilling the foregoing role, the statement begins to function as a "rule." Anti-creedalism objects to this. The same attitude may be shown towards a statement of fundamental beliefs. Edward Farley, for example, objects to this function of a creed, arguing that we should refuse "to make anything human and historical a timeless absolute, dwelling above the flow of contexts and situations." Indeed, "one refuses to give this status . . .to one's denomination, to one's confessions, to one's heritage, even to one's Scripture." For him, this stance is a positive expression of the "conviction that God's presence and truth come through human, but historical and fallible vessels."[17] Farley's assessment is even more radical: "If we need certainty about salvation, modernism would direct that to God and God alone, not to the vessels that deliver it".[18] If our analysis of the nature of the creed or statement of beliefs is correct, then two divergent, but equally inappropriate attitudes on this issue need to be addressed. Bruce Demarest's thoughts on creeds apply much better to a statement of fundamental beliefs: "If we desist from divinizing the creed, neither do we depreciate its intrinsic worth and relevance."[19]

On the one hand, the statement should be viewed as *norma normata*, that is "a rule that is ruled," nonetheless a "rule." The indispensability of biblical interpretation means that at any time the role of Scripture will be as interpreted. To the extent that a statement of beliefs represents what has been dubbed a record of the "central convictions" of earlier generations, it deserves a wider utilization in the church. Individual explorative interpretations, as important as they are, may not, without some risk, treat interpretations in a statement of beliefs lightly. We should be aware that some voices against statements of fundamental beliefs may be due to a loss of confidence in Scripture's authority or uniqueness due to its inspiration. Equally, such positions may be the result of a loss of confidence in human ability to know "*the* truth."

On the other hand, a statement of beliefs is still a rule that is ruled. The desire to maintain this principle has always been the cornerstone of the Seventh-day Adventist apprehension of creeds. However close the statement purports to represent biblical teaching, the *sola scriptura* principle should be maintained, in matters of doctrinal controversy, inspired Scriptures is the ultimate court of appeal. Obviously, in the eventuality of any such process of appeal, the critical issue becomes the science of

---

[17] Edward Farley, "The Modernist Element in Protestantism," *TT* 47 (1990): 141.

[18] Ibid.

[19] Bruce A. Demarest, "Christendom's Creeds: Their Relevance in the Modern World," *JETS* 21/4 (1978): 355.

hermeneutics. It is for this reason that a broad-based community effort in establishing hermeneutical principles beforehand is indispensable for the community's theological health and existence.[20]

An Aid to the 'Critical' Task

Closely related to the role of the Statement of Fundamental Beliefs as an indicator of the community's hermeneutical concern, the Statement helps make decisions concerning doctrine. Traditionally, the rise of heresy was one of the reasons why the need for a rule of faith arose. The statement of beliefs, being a faithful summary of biblical truth, could function as a standard to judge new teachings in the church. It is not only descriptive of biblical truth but also prescriptive. Of all the roles that the statement of beliefs may play, this attracts the greatest fear and concern. The history of the Christian church is filled with inquisition and persecutions that were carried out on the basis of creedal formulations. Hence, any fear about the critical use of the statement of beliefs is well-founded.

Still, in assessing a statement of beliefs in this regard, the question that lies close to the heart of the matter is: Can the question of heresy still be asked?[21] If the answer is yes, then we are faced with a situation where, in spite of the potential for abuse, the critical role of the statement of beliefs cannot be avoided. The biblical perspective is quite clear, placing a high priority on maintaining sound teaching and avoiding heresy by guarding the pure content of the true gospel (1 Tim 1:3; 6:3; 2 Tim 1:13; 1 Cor 11:2; Gal 1:8).

Attempts to reject the prescriptive dimension of biblical doctrines often embody a certain degree of ambivalence. While the value of theological self-definition is applauded, there is apprehension about what may happen to those whose theological convictions fall short of what is consensually defined. Some have detected an irony in the situation. It is acknowledged that a statement of beliefs "can be appropriately 'authoritative' in the sense of representing the church family as a whole and expressing its theological consensus. A church needs to define itself theologically; this is a matter not only of identity, but also of 'truth in advertising' .... But—

---

[20] The General Conference Executive Committee of the Seventh-day Adventist Church voted a document on "Methods of Bible Study" at the 1986 Annual Council in Rio de Janeiro, Brazil. It is found in *Understanding Scripture: An Adventist Approach*, ed. George W. Reid (Silver Spring, MD: Biblical Research Institute, 2005), 329–337.

[21] S. W. Sykes, "Heresy," *Westminster Dictionary*, 249. Sykes observes: "The radical denial that heresy could exist, or if it existed, could be identified, seems to be based on a sociological misunderstanding. The fact that the boundaries of a religion may be difficult to determine with precision does not mean that a religion has no boundaries. Religious commitment depends upon both affirmations and denials."

and here is the irony— ... as soon as we produce a statement of belief ... some people will use the statement to judge others, and to try to exclude from the community those who don't measure up ...."[22]

Does theological self-definition in formulating a statement of beliefs *necessarily* involve the judging and exclusion of those who do not accept the terms of self-identification? Historically, with regard to creeds, the answer appears to have been yes. "The task of the creed was to defend the Church against heresy. The creed has the negative role of shutting the heretic out and setting the boundaries within which authentic Christian theology and life can take place."[23] When we address the question from the perspective of the Adventist Statement of Fundamental Beliefs, the emphasis is not necessarily there but on the truth that the human race needs to hear as we approach the closing moments of the cosmic conflict. But this emphasis does not exclude the discriminatory or judging aspect of the Statement of Beliefs. Why? If it is a faithful expression of biblical truth, then, it is bound to be used to distinguish between truth and error. In the setting of the biblical concept of a cosmic conflict, such a distinction is of supreme importance. The criterion to be employed in that task is God's revelation as found in Scripture.

The point being made here is that a statement of fundamental beliefs has what may be called, for lack of a better word, a legitimate *juridical* role in settling doctrinal disputes, and even possibly avoiding them. Whether this role always leads to exclusion raises questions beyond this basic point. In any case, we would be dealing with the self-exclusion of the individual because the church by its very nature does not seek to exclude, but to include. The decision for inclusion or exclusion is located in the will of the individual. Nevertheless, the juridical significance of the statement of beliefs needs to be underlined. Perhaps the question is simply this: In our postmodern context, does the church subscribe to belief in *the truth*? Is this question still a legitimate one? At this point, the question has very little to do with the material expression of our doctrines in the Statement of Fundamental Beliefs. The question is a formal one about the other side of the question about heresy. The answer to this question is positive—The church opening itself up for future redefinition and clarification of truth does not mean it does not express itself definitively on questions of biblical truth at any one time. To take such a stance would amount to a virtual

---

[22] Fritz Guy, "Uncovering the Origins of the Statement of Twenty-seven Fundamental Beliefs," *Spectrum* 32.3 (2004), 28.

[23] John Leith, ed., *Creeds of the Churches* (Atlanta, GA: John Know, 1982), 9.

"agnosticism"[24] which would undermine the very existence of the church.

A Promoter of Church Unity and Mission

The role of a statement of beliefs in detecting heresy highlights its positive role in promoting unity. The relationship between heresy and unity is clear because *hairesis* denotes schism or faction (1 Cor 11:19; Gal 5:20), and Paul's use of the adjective *hairetikos* (Titus 3:10) characterizes the heretic as a divisive or factious person. The absence of heresy, then, is conducive to the promotion of unity. Stated positively, the statement of beliefs serves as a rallying point for all those who make the same confession of the truth.

Total unity of the church goes beyond theological concerns to include matters that may be more appropriately described as ecclesiological, as well as cultural and sociological. Nevertheless, the fundamental dependence of denominational unity on biblical doctrine cannot be denied since it is usually the case that theological matters create separate denominations in the first place. Herein lays the importance of affirming the statement of fundamental beliefs. It is one of the strong evidences of the unity of the church. Since the document is put together on the basis of definite historical, hermeneutical, and methodological presuppositions, affirming such a document signals not only a unity and continuity with the faith community's historic past and biblical foundation, but with its present theological and missiological goals.

Important as theological unity is, achieving that goal is not an end in itself. The initial analysis of the essence of the statement of beliefs made the connection between the biblical concept of 'teaching' and ethics. It was noted that the ethical dimension of biblical *doctrine/teaching* is connected to preaching as the means by which people are brought to faith in Jesus, to be instructed in the ethical principles and obligations of the Christian life. Thus the role of a statement of belief in preserving the church's theological unity is significant because that unity contributes to the promotion of the mission of the church. It is quite evident that community effort is better performed in that community that possesses a homogenous faith. Ellen G. White certainly saw the "truth-unity-mission" connection:

> God is leading out a people to stand in perfect *unity upon the platform of eternal truth*. Christ gave Himself to the world that

---

[24] It has been noted that agnosticism may not only be identified with denial of belief, but could be compatible with "that strand in Christian thought recognized in an earlier age through stress on the *via negativa*, or throughout the history of theism in recognition of the transcendence and mystery of God" (Steward Sutherland, "Agnosticism," *Westminster Dictionary*, 10).

He might 'purify unto Himself a peculiar people, zealous of good works.' This refining process is designed to purge the church from all unrighteousness and the spirit of discord and contention, *that they may build up instead of tear down, and concentrate their energies on the great work before them.*[25]

The statement of beliefs not only unifies the church for mission, it is also a witness to those outside the church. The statement, as a document, performs this function in a number of ways: it clearly outlines and expounds on the fundamental assertions of the faith; it witnesses to the unity and systematic nature of the faith; and it demonstrates the rational, objective, biblical content of the truth as believed in the community. It does all these things in such a systematic, yet concise manner that what the community believes is made readily clear to those who stand outside the community of faith. In this way, the statement of fundamental beliefs performs an invaluable *apologetic* function.

An Aid to Theological/Biblical Education

The statement of beliefs discloses intent on the part of the faith community to interpret and apply the biblical message. For contemporary theologians, understanding the interpretational dynamics of the statement of beliefs provides useful insight into how it may be preserved for both the present and future.[26] At a popular level within the community of faith, the statement of beliefs is an invaluable pedagogical aid to believers. By compiling, systematizing, and summarizing biblical teaching on many subjects, it is easier for the church to fulfill its instructional mandate within the faith community.[27] The value of a statement in facilitating biblical education is based on the fact that a growing understanding of the Bible comes from reading, systematizing, and applying it. The State-

---

[25] Ellen G. White, *Testimonies for the Church* (Mountain View, CA: Pacific Press, 1948), 4:16, emphasis mine.

[26] The discussion over the wording of Fundamental Belief #11 at the 2010 General Conference Session in St. Louis, Missouri highlights this point. Critical to the debate over the correct semantic formulation of the statement was the principle of striking a responsible balance between theology and mission. Underlying the whole discussion on phraseology was a difference of opinion in expressing the intent of the statement, a difference that indicated perceptions of how far it was thought that statement should correctly reflect biblical teaching or whether it was felt that 'relevance' to mission should be the proper intent of the statement.

[27] This was one of the roles of creeds. With particular reference to children and new believers, Philip Schaff comments: "In the form of Catechisms they are of especial use in the instruction of children, and facilitate a solid and substantial religious education, in distinction from spasmodic and superficial excitement" (Philip Schaff, *The Creeds of Christendom* [Grand Rapids, MI: Baker], 1:8).

ment of Fundamental Beliefs, as a distilled exposition of biblical themes, facilitates education in Scripture. But this is to be done by moving from the statement, which functions as a summary, to the biblical text in order to fully explore the biblical foundation of the Statement.

An Instrument of Initiation

The teaching role of the statement of beliefs in the case of new believers requires further comment. On the basis of Romans 10:9-10, a connection may be made between a statement of beliefs and a new believer's covenant initiation into the family of God. It is only natural that the first step towards Christianity entail a confession of some kind, however rudimentary. Speaking in the context of confessional statements, Glenn Hinson comes to the conclusion that the confession with the lip that Jesus is Lord, and the belief with the heart that God raised Him from the dead (Rom 10:9), "represented in an external and visible way the making of an inward covenant: 'For man believes with his heart and so is justified, and he confesses with his lips and so is saved.'"[28] In Hinson's view, it is this connection between confession and the personal covenant-making process that made a statement of beliefs a *sine qua non* of the initiation rites in the early church.[29] In this way, the statement, although only one part of the initiation process, plays a critical role in the convert's total cognitive and affective commitment to be faithful in all circumstances.

The significance of this role goes back to our analysis of it as "teaching." One of the implications of that analysis was that "content" is the essence of a statement of beliefs. The use of a statement of beliefs as a means of incorporation into the body of Christ is an indication of how the Seventh-day Adventist Church understands the nature of the Christian life and experience. The Christian life is nourished and flourishes mainly through the Word and not in a sacramental manner. A proper use of the Statement of Fundamental Beliefs offers a powerful avenue for an individual's personal incorporation into, and private appropriation of the ethos of the faith community.

The Seventh-day Adventist Church requires the newly baptized or those received into fellowship by profession of faith to publicly affirm their acceptance of the doctrinal beliefs of the Seventh-day Adventist Church. Although the practice of incorporation into the body may vary, the connection between belief and incorporation into the body of Christ

---

[28] E. Glenn Hinson, "Confessions or Creeds in Early Christian Tradition," *RE* 76 (1979): 6.
[29] Ibid.

is, in principle, acknowledged.[30] It should be mentioned that public confession of faith only takes place after the new believer has studied the Bible itself. This is done to ground faith in the Scripture and not on the summary of biblical teachings contained in a document.

Other Uses of a Statement of Beliefs

There are a few other uses that may be derived from a statement of beliefs. For example, homiletical and liturgical purposes. Thus, there are Seventh-day Adventist ministers who have developed preaching schedules around the Fundamental Beliefs of the church. The purpose of such preaching has always been to set forth in the church the truths that are held together in the community, and thereby to ground the people of God in the truth. Similarly, portions of a statement may be incorporated into the worship of the church as an "affirmation of faith."

Conclusion

The "phenomenon" of the statement of belief has been analyzed to discern what legitimate role the Seventh-day Adventist Statement of Fundamental Beliefs may play within the community of faith. A statement of beliefs clearly has a useful role to play, some of which have been outlined above. It is an indispensable instrument of the church as it seeks to accomplish its mission in an imperfect world. Seventh-day Adventists hold to biblical landmarks of truth that may not be moved while leaving room for the possibility of their expansion. The fullness of biblical truth cannot be adequately summarized in a statement of fundamental beliefs. Openness to truth will always characterize God's end-time remnant.

---

[30] The *Church Manual,* on "Baptismal Vows and Baptism," introduces some degree of flexibility in the administration of the vow in the baptismal service (see 46–49). Whether a public, detailed, verbal affirmation of *all the contents* of the Statement of Beliefs should be required will probably continue to attract theological discussion. On the one hand, while the recently voted alternative vow does not expressly and specifically spell out the teachings of the Statement, it does require a full, formal, and public affirmation of "the teachings of the Bible as expressed in the Statement of Fundamental Beliefs of the Seventh-day Adventist Church." On the other hand, although the existent vow expressly spelled out specific teachings in the Statement of Beliefs, it fell short of outlining all the beliefs in the Statement. While the existent vow appears to create a hierarchy of beliefs, the alternate vow seems to fall short on details. It may be that in all of this, the principle to preserve is a reasonable measure of both cognitive and affective elements in the initiatory service.

CHAPTER 14

THE HOLY SPIRIT AND THE CHURCH

Denis Fortin

This paper will study the Holy Spirit's role in early Christianity and provide an understanding of His role and guidance in the church today. The focus will be on ecclesiology rather than soteriology or eschatology. Even a cursory reading of the New Testament reveals the importance of the Holy Spirit in the early church. Before His death, and immediately before His ascension, Jesus promised His disciples a Comforter, the Holy Spirit (John 14:16–17), who was to guide (John 14:26; 15:26; 16:13) and empower them to proclaim the good news of salvation to all parts of the earth (Acts 1:8). The presence of the Holy Spirit in the early church was crucial to its development and growth. After Jesus' ascension, His apostles were a loosely organized group of people in need of the Holy Spirit's guidance to fulfill the great commission (Matt 28:19–20). Not only would the Spirit influence the conversion of thousands of individuals, but His presence would be felt as the church developed its organizational structures.

The Holy Spirit's Work in the Old Testament

The Spirit is introduced to us in the very first passages of the Bible. As God began His work of creation, the Spirit is described as "moving over the surface of the waters" (Gen 1:2).[1] When God formed human beings "of dust from the ground" (Gen 2:7), the Holy Spirit was also involved (Job 33:4). Psalm 104 celebrates God's creation of the world, and the giving of life is attributed to the Spirit. In reference to the creation of all the animals, it is said, "You send forth Your Spirit, they are created; and You re-

---

[1] All Bible texts are quoted from the NASB unless otherwise indicated.

new the face of the ground" (Ps 104:30). The psalmist not only attributes the creation of life to the Spirit of God, but also its maintenance.

In the Old Testament, the Holy Spirit was active in the salvation of God's people. He strove with people before the flood (Gen 6:3). The Spirit also used judges and prophets to communicate God's will to His people. The Spirit came upon Othniel (Judg 3:10), Gideon (6:34), Jephthah (11:29), and Samson (13:25). God filled Joshua (Exod 31:3) and Ezekiel (Ezek 11:5) with His Spirit and He rested upon the seventy elders (Num 11:25). The Spirit also used kings to deliver Israel. After Samuel anointed David, "the Spirit of the Lord came mightily upon David from that day forward" (1 Sam 16:13). Thus in the Old Testament the Holy Spirit was active in the world in general and also among God's people. A similar pattern of influence is visible in the New Testament, beginning with Jesus, whose Spirit-led ministry was predicted by the prophet Isaiah (Isa 61:1–2).

The Promise of a Helper

The Holy Spirit was uniquely active in the life and ministry of Christ. The Savior of the world was conceived of the Holy Spirit (Luke 1:35), baptized by the Spirit (John 1:32–33), led by the Spirit (Luke 4:1), anointed by the Spirit (Luke 4:18), and empowered by the Spirit (Matt 12:27–28). Later, the apostle Paul would encourage all Christians to let the Holy Spirit guide their lives (Gal 5:16, 18) as He had guided Jesus. As His death neared, Jesus promised His disciples that the Holy Spirit would succeed Him (John 14:16–17). His promise included details about the role of the Holy Spirit: "But the Helper, the Holy Spirit, whom my Father will send in My name, He will teach you all things, and bring to your remembrance all that I said to you" (John 14:26). The Holy Spirit would also testify about Jesus (John 15:26) and "convict the world concerning sin and righteousness and judgment" (John 16:8). He would guide the disciples "into all the truth; for He will not speak on His own initiative, but whatever He hears, He will speak; and He will disclose to you what is to come" (John 16:13).

These passages portray the Spirit as Christ's representative. Just as Jesus did not speak or act on His own initiative, instead reflecting the will of the Father (John 5:19, 30; 8:28; 12:49), so the Holy Spirit would not speak on His own initiative but would be sent by the Father to be a witness of Jesus' words and mission. The harmony of purpose among all persons of the Godhead is evident in this context. John also tells us that the work of the Holy Spirit is both external and internal in relation to the work of the church. This two-pronged activity of the Spirit will continue until the end. The Spirit is present in the world and actively engaged in the lives of people who are not part of the church, who are not Christ's disciples.

The experience of Cornelius (Acts 10:1–48) and the conversion of Paul (Acts 9:1–19) demonstrate the Holy Spirit's ability to work outside the church in order to lead people to Christ. Jesus said the Holy Spirit would come to "convict the world concerning sin and righteousness and judgment" (John 16:8). This work of the Spirit would become more pronounced after the ascension of Christ. In connection with His work, the Spirit actively brought people to a conviction of sin, urging men and women to accept the righteousness of Christ, warning them of the judgment to come. "Thus the Spirit convicts men of their sin, points them to the salvation and righteousness that is in Jesus, and warns them of the consequences of continuing in their sins and of neglecting the salvation freely proffered."[2]

Jesus' promise of a Helper emphasized that the Spirit would be also active in the church. Speaking directly to the disciples, He said, "I will ask the Father, and He will give you another Helper, that He may be with you forever; that is the Spirit of truth" (John 14:16–17). The promise of the Comforter points to the continuing work of the Spirit within the church (John 14:26). The Spirit would be given to the church to teach and guide it to a fuller understanding of the teachings of Jesus. He would assist the church to recall what Jesus said and to clarify His teachings. "He will guide you into all the truth" as it has been revealed in Jesus (John 16:13). "When the Helper comes," added Jesus, "He will testify about Me" (John 15:26). It could be said that "the witness which Jesus had borne, by his words and works, to the grace of God would not come to an end when he was no longer in the world. The Spirit would take up this ministry of witness and carry it on, and he would do so not least through the disciples."[3] In a sense, these promises indicate that the Spirit would oversee the direction the church would take in formulating its Christ-centered teachings and outreach to the world. The Spirit would solidify the meaning of Jesus' life and ministry in the minds of the disciples. They, in turn, would go on to witness their faith to the world. Indirectly, we also find in these promises an indication that the Spirit inspires the disciples in their writings about the story of Jesus.

---

[2] *AdvBibComm*, 5: 1048. For a discussion of the role of the Spirit as the prosecutor of the world in John 16:8–11, see Craig S. Keener, *The Gospel of John: A Commentary* (Peabody, MA: Hendrickson, 2003), 2:1030–1035.

[3] F. F. Bruce, *The Gospel of John* (Grand Rapids, MI: Eerdmans, 1983), 315. We are not suggesting that the revelation of God that Jesus brought was incomplete and that it now needs to be supplemented by the revelatory work of the Spirit. The work of the Spirit is to take that revelation and make it relevant and meaningful to the church and, through it, to the world.

The Coming of the Holy Spirit

The promise of the Holy Spirit was repeated just before Jesus' ascension into heaven (Acts 1:5, 8) and found its immediate fulfillment at Pentecost (Acts 2:33). As promised, the Holy Spirit came to the disciples with power and they proclaimed with boldness the resurrection of Jesus Christ and salvation in Him. Thousands of people were convicted by the gospel message. The coming of the Holy Spirit at Pentecost was a fulfillment of God's promises in the Old Testament (Joel 2:28–32; Acts 2:16). At Pentecost, the many nations were made one by the Spirit (Acts 2:7–11). Faith in Christ destroys the walls of division and creates a new people, the people of God (Eph 2:11–22). Christ's followers are the living stones of the temple of the Holy Spirit (1 Pet 2:5; Eph 2:21–22; 1 Cor 6:19–20). The central work of the Spirit in the church is clear. Through Him people become God's children (Rom 8:14–15; Gal 4:5–7), have the hope of everlasting life (2 Cor 1:22; Eph 1:14), are joined to Christ (1 Cor 12:3), and receive a new heart (Ezek 36:25–28). As a result of the indispensable presence of the Spirit in the church, it is described as the fellowship of the Spirit (2 Cor 13:14; Phil 2:1).

The Presence of the Holy Spirit and the Word of God

As Jesus is the truth (John 14:6), the Comforter is described as the Spirit of truth (John 14:17) who bears testimony to Jesus (John 15:26). His role is not to bring new truth but to teach the truth and bring to remembrance the teachings of Jesus. The Holy Spirit's work therefore is closely connected with the truth as found in Scripture. "Through the Scriptures the Holy Spirit speaks to the mind, and impresses truth upon the heart," comments Ellen White. "Thus He exposes error, and expels it from the soul. It is by the Spirit of truth, working through the word of God, that Christ subdues His chosen people to Himself."[4]

According to Peter, the Holy Spirit inspired the Word of God in the Old Testament (1 Pet 1:10–12). Paul claimed the Spirit reminded the apostles of Jesus' words and deeds (1 Cor 2:10–16; Eph 3:3–5). The Spirit, who inspired the Scriptures, illumines the minds of believers to understand them (2 Tim 3:15–17; 2 Pet 1:20–21) and also uses the Scriptures as His sword to convict and sanctify believers (Eph 6:17; Heb 4:12). Clearly, for Peter and Paul, it is the Spirit who speaks through the Scriptures. This relationship between the Holy Spirit, the Scripture, and the church is a vital

---

[4] Ellen G, White, *Desire of Ages*, (Mountain View, CA: Pacific Press, 1898), 671. In *Acts of the Apostles*, (Mountain view, CA: Pacific Press, 1911), 284, Ellen White also states that "the operations of the Spirit are always in harmony with the written word."

one. How do we know where and when the Spirit speaks to the church? The church is indeed governed by the Holy Spirit, but in order that guidance might not be vague or unstable, the Spirit works with the Word of God to provide light and direction.

The Role of the Holy Spirit in the Early Church

Acts illustrates the role of the Holy Spirit in shaping the life and ministry of the early church.[5] At the time of Jesus' ascension, there were many things still left to be organized. During the period between the ascension and the day of Pentecost, 120 disciples were assembled together in Jerusalem as they prepared their hearts to receive the promised Holy Spirit (Acts 1:14–15). That group would grow by thousands within a few years. It is in this context that the work of the Holy Spirit operates. As the church grows, the Holy Spirit provides guidance and direction, new structures are put in place, new ministries begin, new leadership roles appear. The Spirit does not work alone, but in the context of the teachings of Scripture and in relation with the community of believers. The Spirit guided the community and its leaders in making appropriate decisions. Some of the narratives in Acts reveal interesting insights into God's activities in the early church. How the church made decisions in these narratives reveals elements significant to our theological reflection on the role of the Holy Spirit in the church today.

The Selection of Matthias (Acts 1:15–26)

The Holy Spirit's first appearance in the book of Acts is in conjunction with finding a replacement for Judas. After Judas' betrayal, his place among the twelve apostles had to be filled by someone who had been a disciple "beginning with the baptism of John until the day He was taken up from us—one of these must become a witness with us of His resurrection" (Acts 1:22). The reconstitution and completeness of the apostolic circle of twelve was crucial for Peter and the other apostles. In fact, according to Peter, the Holy Spirit had predicted this through David in the Scripture. "The Scripture had to be fulfilled" (Acts 1:16), and the fulfillment of this prophecy was the main purpose for the assembly. Peter's argument is simple: Judas was a member of the twelve apostles, his place is now vacant, and therefore needs to be filled. But why was it necessary to do so then, so soon after the ascension of Jesus?

Most early Christians were Jews and the first organizational structures of the early Christian church was modeled on synagogue assem-

---

[5] See Luke Timothy Johnson, *Scripture and Discernment: Decision-Making in the Church* (Nashville, TN: Abingdon, 1996), 82–108.

blies common in Judaism in the first century (Acts 2:46; 3:1; 9:2, 20). At first, the apostles appear to have been the primary group of leaders (Acts 1:13–14). This group resided mainly in Jerusalem, and by the time of the council of Jerusalem, included elders (Acts 15:2, 6). Elders were leaders in synagogue assemblies. Paul and Barnabas appointed elders in the local congregations they formed in various cities such as Pamphylia and Pisidia (Acts 14:23). The book of Acts gives evidences of strong affinities between the organizational structures of the early church and the Jewish synagogue.

Numerical symbolisms in the New Testament are also indicative of this affinity between the church and the synagogue. The apostolic circle of twelve men is reminiscent of the twelve tribes of Israel. The 120 disciples in the upper room (Acts 1:15) happens to be the minimum number of people required by rabbinic tradition to constitute a local Sanhedrin of twelve.[6] Peter's call for replacing Judas was a valid request in this context, which he believed Scripture supported. According to Luke Timothy Johnson, "Judas had to be replaced before Pentecost, because the integrity of the apostolic circle of Twelve symbolized the restoration of God's people."[7]

Peter laid down the qualifications for a new apostle. The criteria of selection were: 1) one who has been a disciple the whole period of time from John the Baptist to the ascension of Jesus and 2) one who is a witness of Jesus' resurrection (Acts 1:21–22). Here we have the basic understanding of the apostles' role. They were primarily witnesses to Jesus' life, teaching, ministry, and resurrection. And, as such, the role of apostle was limited to the Twelve. Then why was Judas replaced and none of the others after that? The truth is that no other apostle was replaced after his death. No such procedure was felt necessary after the martyrdom of James (Acts 12:2). This can only mean that the function of the apostles was not that of an ecclesiastical magistracy or permanently constituted court of appeal, where the loss of a member means that a replacement must be erected at once. Their importance as a group was of a very different nature.[8] Others would not take their place within the church. It

---

[6] John B. Pohill, *Acts* (Nashville, TN: Broadman Press, 1992), 91. See also William Neil, *Acts* (Grand Rapids, MI: Eerdmans, 1973), 68–69.

[7] Luke Timothy Johnson, *The Acts of the Apostles* (Collegeville, MN: Liturgical Press, 1992), 39.

[8] Hans von Campenhausen, *Ecclesiastical Authority and Spiritual Power in the Church of the First Three Centuries* (Peabody, MA: Hendrickson, 1969, 1997), 16. Campenhausen further states: "As witnesses to Jesus the Twelve have become the 'foundation' of the Church, and this significance, which they had acquired for the very first generation of Christians, they retain to all eternity, corporately providing the solid base on which the whole structure rests." Ibid., 17.

has been correctly stated that the apostolic office of the Twelve "was a unique, irreplaceable office (Eph 2:20; Rev 21:14). There could be no apostolic succession, since there were no further eyewitnesses to succeed them."[9]

Peter led the assembly to select one of two possible candidates to replace Judas: Joseph and Matthias. The selection process continued with prayer. "As the assembly prayed for God's direction in the selection of the twelfth apostle, it was following a precedent already set by Jesus, who also prayed before he chose the original Twelve (Luke 6:12f.)."[10] Then lots were cast and the lot fell to Matthias as, who was added to the eleven apostles (Acts 1:26). The casting of lots was a practice used in the Old Testament to assign portions of land in Canaan (Num 26:55; 33:54) or to determine who would fulfill a particular responsibility (1 Chron 24:5; 25:8; 26:13). The underlying assumption of this practice is that the decision was always determined by God, free from human manipulation. The same assumption should be considered in this case. The lot fell to Matthias and he became God's choice to replace Judas, according to the Word of Prophecy spoken by the Holy Spirit through David.

There is no record of hands laid upon Matthias to "ordain" him to this responsibility. Evidently, the assembly of 120 believers understood that the Holy Spirit had shown His approval in the selection. "In this choice of Matthias, we have early and significant evidences of church organization: (1) an official meeting of believers, (2) the discussion of an important item of church business, (3) the decision and its execution. The church was organized and now awaited divine power."[11]

The Selection of Seven "Deacons" (Acts 6:1–6)

In Acts 4:32–5:11, we read about a plan of communal support for believers in need of food and other necessities. Christian believers gave of their means to the apostles, who redistributed the funds to those in need. In Acts 6, Christians from a Greek-speaking, Jewish heritage complain that their widows appear to be regularly neglected during the daily distribution of food. The overtones of ethnic and cultural discrimination are apparent, and the complaint prompts the apostles to find a better system. The apostles gathered all the disciples together and explained to them

---

[9] Pohill, *Acts*, 93. These qualifications and basic understanding of apostleship are likely at the root of Paul's continuous difficulties to be accepted as a genuine apostle. Although a witness of the resurrected Christ, he was not a disciple of Jesus from the beginning.

[10] Ibid., 94.

[11] *AdvBibComm*, 6:131.

that they preferred the teaching of God's Word to serving food, a task that they did not appear to fulfill very well (Acts 6:2). The Twelve suggested that a group of seven men be appointed to do the ministry of food distribution, relieving the apostles from this task. Clear qualifications for this ministry are given, one of them being "full of the Spirit and of wisdom." While the group of Seven will perform the ministry of food distribution, the Twelve will attend to the ministry of prayer and the Word (Acts 6:3–4). This is the beginning of a distinction of roles of ministry among early believers. We see twelve apostles, seven "deacons," and other disciples. This is not necessarily a hierarchy of offices and people, but a distinction of functions according to the responsibility given to each by Jesus (this applies in particular for the Twelve).

The word "deacon" (servant or minister, *diakonos*) is not used in direct reference to these seven men but only in reference to their function—they serve (*diakonein*) tables. But it is also remarkable that a form of the same word (*diakonia*) is used in reference to the ministry of the Word of the apostles. Both groups are servants or ministers. One is doing the ministry of distribution of food, the other is doing the ministry of the Word of God. This proposal pleased the whole assembly and seven men were chosen. They were "brought before the apostles; and after praying, they laid their hands on them" (Acts 6:6).

The community of early Christians in Jerusalem came together as they faced a problem that could have divided them. The apostles took the lead in suggesting a solution. They proposed a plan: seven men to take over the ministry of food distribution to widows while the Twelve pray and minister the word of God. The community agreed with the idea. They selected seven men and the apostles laid hands on them. Although this is not a true democracy, there is a shared participatory approach to solving this problem. Implied in the narrative is the discernment the Holy Spirit gave to the early church to find a workable solution to the problem.

In her comments on this story, Ellen White highlights the role of the Holy Spirit in the resolution of this conflict.

> Under the wise leadership of the apostles, who labored unitedly in the power of the Holy Spirit, the work committed to the gospel messengers was developing rapidly. The church was continually enlarging, and this growth in membership brought increasingly heavy burdens upon those in charge. No one man, or even one set of men, could continue to bear these burdens alone, without imperiling the future prosperity of the church. There was necessity for a further distribution of the responsibilities which had been borne so faithfully by a few during the earlier days of the church.

The apostles must now take an important step in the perfecting of gospel order in the church by laying upon others some of the burdens thus far borne by themselves. Summoning a meeting of the believers, the apostles were led by the Holy Spirit to outline a plan for the better organization of all the working forces of the church.[12]

What becomes intriguing in the following chapters of the book of Acts is the ministry performed by two of the seven men appointed by the church. We read nothing further regarding the distribution of food, but we read that Stephen who was "full of grace and power, was performing great wonders and signs among the people" (Acts 6:8). Stephen was a bold witness of the resurrected Jesus and became the first martyr for the gospel. One wonders if Stephen's selection as one of the Seven, based on the fact that he was full of the Spirit and of wisdom, readily qualified him to serve in any form of ministry for the gospel. In Acts 8, we encounter another of the Seven, Philip, who is also being led by the Spirit to preach the good news in Samaria and to the Ethiopian eunuch (Acts 8:4–40). Not only did he minister the word of God (Acts 8:4)—a function attributed to the apostles (Acts 6:4)—but he preached the gospel in Samaria and Caesarea (Acts 8:5, 40), did signs and wonders (Acts 8:6–7), and baptized the eunuch (Acts 8:38). Evidently, Philip's ministry had become similar to that of the Twelve.

The Holy Spirit played a part in the lives of Stephen and Philip as well. "Philip's openness to the Spirit's leading enabled this major progress toward fulfilling Christ's commission for a worldwide gospel."[13] The lines of distinction between various functions of ministry and service in the early church were fluid and do not appear to have been clearly drawn. Even in Acts 1, the place left vacant by Judas is referred to as a ministry of service (*diakonia*, 1:17) and of oversight (*episkopē*, 1:20,), which suggests that the two terms are synonymous. And in Titus 1:5, 7 and in Acts 20:17, 28, the terms elder (*presbyteros*) and overseer (*episkopos*) are also seen as synonymous. Categorical distinctions between functions in ministry (*diakonos, presbyteros* and *episkopos*) come later in the history of the church.

The Conversion of Paul (Acts 9:1–30)

Paul's encounter with the resurrected Christ on the road to Damascus is a turning point in the early church. His conversion brings up some

---

[12] Johnson, *Acts of the Apostles*, 88–89.

[13] Pohill, *Acts*, 227.

interesting insights into early church organization. The encounter with Christ left Paul blind and confused. But Christ's instructions, "Get up and enter the city, and it will be told you what you must do" (Acts 9:6), confused him even more. Strangely, Christ's instructions are rather succinct and embarrassingly vague for someone who will become such a pillar of the church. Three days later, Ananias had a vision in which Christ tells him, "Get up and go to the street called Straight, and inquire at the house of Judas for a man from Tarsus named Saul, for he is praying, and he has seen in a vision a man named Ananias come in and lay his hands on him, so that he might regain his sight" (Acts 9:11–12). Ananias, who had heard about Saul, resisted this command. But Christ continued, "Go, for he is a chosen instrument of Mine, to bear My name before the Gentiles and kings and the sons of Israel; for I will show him how much he must suffer for My name's sake" (Acts 9:15–16). In Acts 22, Luke gives us a second version of this meeting between Ananias and Paul in which Ananias explains Paul's new commission. "The God of our fathers has appointed you to know His will and to see the Righteous One and to hear an utterance from His mouth. For you will be a witness for Him to all men of what you have seen and heard" (Acts 22:13–15).

That Christ called on Ananias, an unknown disciple in Damascus, to officially usher Paul into the church, baptize him, and give him his lifelong commission is significant. Christ could have said much more during the encounter outside Damascus. But He did not. The unspoken reasons for His process heighten the importance of the role of the local congregation in Damascus and of one of its leaders. The local Christian community was the instrument God uses to officially bring Paul into the community and to give him his commission.

Reflecting upon this story in the context of her own struggles with Adventist leaders who felt a need to carry on their work according to their own independent judgment, Ellen White comments that Christ "did not give Paul an experience, in his conversion to truth, independent of His church recently organized upon the earth."[14] Christ had done the initial work of revelation and conviction, but He placed Paul in contact with the church to complete the process. Christ could have given all His instructions directly to Paul, but He "respects the means which He has ordained for the enlightenment and salvation of men." White believes that,

---

[14] White, *Testimonies for the Church*, 3:430. For more insights into this story, see the entire section, 428–434.

In the conversion of Paul are given important principles which we should ever bear in mind. The Redeemer of the world does not sanction experience and exercise in religious matters independent of His organized and acknowledged church, where He has a church. Many have the idea that they are responsible to Christ alone for their light and experience, independent of His acknowledged followers in the world."[15]

Ananias obeyed the Lord's command and found Paul, who received healing and was baptized (Acts 9:17-18). Christ, Ananias of Damascus, and the Holy Spirit joined together in the salvation of Paul and commissioned him to his lifelong ministry.

The Sending of Barnabas and Paul (Acts 13:1-2)

Following his conversion, Paul began a life of ministry for the Lord. A few years after his conversion, we find Paul with Barnabas in Antioch: "While they were ministering to the Lord and fasting, the Holy Spirit said, 'Set apart for Me Barnabas and Saul for the work to which I have called them.' Then, when they had fasted and prayed and laid their hands on them, they sent them away" (Acts 13:2-3). We are not told how the Holy Spirit communicated with the church at Antioch, but we know that it is while the community is worshiping and praying. We get the distinct impression that worship and call to ministry are closely intertwined; that sometimes it is in moments of worship that calls to ministry are heard; that it is through worship that God reveals new opportunities for mission. In this case, as in the others we have seen so far, it is individuals already involved in the activities of the community and with gifts of ministry from God who are selected for a new, special mission.[16]

The mission called for a fresh commission and a blessing from the church: "Then, when they had fasted and prayed and laid their hands on

---

[15] Ibid., 433. See also *Acts of the Apostles*, 120-122.

[16] Barnabas had been active in Jerusalem where he was among those who gave of their means to support the poor (Acts 4:36-37), and he had been sent by the church in Jerusalem to Antioch after the Christian faith was first established there (Acts 11:19-26). Paul also had been active in ministry. After his conversion in Damascus, he remained there for a few days and witnessed of his faith (Acts 9:19-22). He then went to Jerusalem "speaking out boldly in the name of the Lord" (Acts 9:28). Sometime during these early years, Paul spent three years in Arabia (Gal 1: 17-18). Barnabas was the first disciple to really have confidence in Paul and to introduce him to the apostles in Jerusalem (Acts 9:27) and later to bring him to Antioch to serve as a colleague in ministry (Acts 11:25-26). It is while they were both active in ministry at Antioch that the Holy Spirit revealed their new mission. They had been partners in ministry in a local church, now they would be partners in missionary work in distant places.

them, they sent them away" (Acts 13:3). This service of laying on of hands is a commissioning and a blessing of the church at Antioch for the work they will do for the sake of the gospel. Who laid their hands on Barnabas and Paul? In a sense the Holy Spirit already had by calling them to this mission and evidencing in their lives their God-given call. More specifically, we are not told who laid hands on them. Perhaps it was the entire congregation that did so, or at least some of its leaders.

In this story, we get a clear indication that ministry and calls to ministry operate within the local church community and under the guidance of the Spirit. Servants and ministers of the gospel work within the church community, they are not independent of it, but within it. The social and communal dimension of this setting apart for ministry is important. "In commissioning Barnabas and Saul by the imposition of hands, the other office-bearers invest them with authority to act on behalf of the Christian community at Antioch, and symbolically identify the whole community with their enterprise."[17] The Holy Spirit's active role is just as important. "Their mission is validated by the direct intervention of the Holy Spirit. . . . And in case we miss the point, Luke repeats that they were sent out 'by the Holy Spirit' (13:4)."[18]

In her comments on this story, Ellen White discusses the setting apart of Paul and Barnabas and emphasizes the intimate relationship between the work of the Holy Spirit and the church.

> The circumstances connected with the separation of Paul and Barnabas by the Holy Spirit to a definite line of service show clearly that the Lord works through appointed agencies in His organized church. . . . God has made His church on the earth a channel of light, and through it He communicates His purposes and His will. He does not give to one of His servants an experience independent of and contrary to the experience of the church itself. Neither does He give one man a knowledge of His will for the entire church while the church—Christ's body—is left in darkness. In His providence He places His servants in close connection with His church in order that they may have less confidence in themselves and greater confidence in others whom He is leading out to advance His work."[19]

---

[17] Neil, *Acts*, 154.

[18] Johnson, *Acts of the Apostles*, 226.

[19] Ellen G. White, *Acts of the Apostles*, 162–163. Along the same line of thought, Ellen White continues her argument against independent judgment in ministry. "Those who are inclined to

The Council of Jerusalem (Acts 15)

The council of Jerusalem is perhaps one of the most important ecclesiological events in the apostolic Christian church.[20] It was held for two primary reasons: 1) to sort out some theological differences of opinions between church leaders and 2) to unify the church. Regarding the conversion of Gentiles and their inclusion in the people of God in Luke's chronicles of the events that led to the convening of this council, we are left with the indubitable impression that the Holy Spirit was responsible for calling this council.

After the proclamation of the gospel to the Gentiles by Peter (Acts 10:19), Paul, and Barnabas (13:2, 4), a dispute arose among early Christians over whether Gentile Christians should be circumcised in order to be saved and participate in the covenant promises made by God to His people—a clear indication that Christianity, up to that point, was a subgroup of Judaism and that Peter, Paul, and Barnabas did not seem to have required circumcision of their Gentile converts. Yet, it is also evident that in the ministry of these three apostles, the Holy Spirit was especially active. But as Johnson explains, many crucial questions regarding this development needed to be answered.

> Whether Gentiles can be preached to or even baptized is settled rather quickly. But the deeper human difficulty of fellowship between Jewish and Gentile believers is far harder to resolve. If both Jews and Gentiles are to be considered part of "God's people," will

---

regard their individual judgment as supreme are in grave peril. It is Satan's studied effort to separate such ones from those who are channels of light, through whom God has wrought to build up and extend His work in the earth. To neglect or despise those whom God has appointed to bear the responsibilities of leadership in connection with the advancement of the truth, is to reject the means that He has ordained for the help, encouragement, and strength of His people. For any worker in the Lord's cause to pass these by, and to think that his light must come through no other channel than directly from God, is to place himself in a position where he is liable to be deceived by the enemy and overthrown. The Lord in His wisdom has arranged that by means of the close relationship that should be maintained by all believers, Christian shall be united to Christian and church to church. Thus the human instrumentality will be enabled to cooperate with the divine. Every agency will be subordinate to the Holy Spirit, and all the believers will be united in an organized and well directed effort to give to the world the glad tidings of the grace of God" (Ibid., 164).

[20] Johnson comments: "No reader can miss the obvious importance Luke attaches to this Jerusalem Council. Preparation for it began already in Acts 10–11, with Peter's conversion of Cornelius and his household. The first mission of Paul and Barnabas among the Gentiles continued that preparation through Luke's repeated emphasis on faith as the basis for salvation. Luke's capacity for composing a sustained narrative is nowhere impressively displayed than in the way he weaves these earlier thematic strands together in this scene" (Johnson, *Acts*, 267–268).

it be on even or uneven footing? On what basis will Gentiles be recognized and associated with? On the basis of their belief in the Messiah and the gift of the Holy Spirit, or on the basis of being circumcised and observing the law of Moses? Will the church split into two ethnically and ritually distinct bodies? Is Yahweh a tribal deity, or Lord of all? Will fellowship be determined by faith, or by precedent; by the experience of God, or by the rules of the community? At stake is the church's identity as witness to the work of God. Will the church decide to recognize and acknowledge actions of God that go beyond its present understanding, or will it demand that God work within its categories?[21]

According to the narrative, "some men came down from Judea [to Antioch] and began teaching the brethren, 'Unless you are circumcised according to the custom of Moses, you cannot be saved.'" This dispute provoked a dissension and debate between Paul and Barnabas and the men from Judea (Acts 15:1–2)[22] and it got so heated that they decided to appeal to the church in Jerusalem for a solution. Paul and Barnabas were appointed by the church at Antioch to go to Jerusalem and discuss this issue with the apostles and elders.

The delegation was welcomed by the church, the apostles, and the elders and gave a report to the whole group. An assembly was convened to resolve the problem (Acts 15:5–6). The solution was based on two kinds of evidence. First, Peter, Paul, and Barnabas testified to the role of the Holy Spirit in the conversion of Gentiles without the prior requirement of circumcision. This was experiential evidence. The second evidence came from the Word of God in the prophet Amos which predicted the conversion of Gentiles (Amos 9:11–12, quoted by James in Acts 15:16–18). The experience of faith, ministry, and the Word of God confirmed that what was happening was a fulfillment of prophecy and in agreement with God's will.

The decision of the members of the council was reached by consensus. They were convinced by the evidence. The process is summarized

---

[21] Johnson, *Discernment*, 90–91.

[22] If the conflict referred to by Luke in Acts 15:1–2 is the same one referred to by Paul in Galatians 2:11–14, then the effect of Peter's example and concession was bound to have a most disastrous effect on other Jewish Christians, such as Barnabas. "Paul was clear-sighted enough to see that in the long run the concession on the question of fellowship compromised the fundamental principle of salvation by grace. Ultimately, the only valid reason for making circumcision a condition of social intercourse was if it was necessary for salvation. Peter's concession was the thin end of the wedge; refusal to have fellowship at table with uncircumcised believers would be followed ere long by refusal to admit them to church fellowship or to regard them as really saved" (Bruce, *Acts*, 288).

as follows: "It seemed good to us, having become of one mind . . ." (Acts 15:25). This was the consensus guided by the Holy Spirit. "For it seemed good to the Holy Spirit and to us to lay upon you no greater burden than these essentials," stated James in his epistolary decree (Acts 15:28). These essential matters that James references are from Mosaic Law in Leviticus, where God commanded aliens living among the people of Israel to abstain from eating flesh with its blood (17:8–16). Immediately before and after this text in Leviticus, God also forbade the sacrifice of animals to idols (Lev 17:7) and all types of sexual immorality (Lev 18). Since "Moses from ancient generations has in every city those who preach him, since he is read in the synagogues every Sabbath" (Acts 15:21), Gentile Christians should already be aware of these restrictions—in other words this should not be something new to them. These restrictions were intended to enable both groups to fellowship together.[23]

This is not an either/or solution: Either one needs to be circumcised or not in order to be saved. The solution is both/and: One can be saved both with and without circumcision. The decision was reached by a consensus guided by the Holy Spirit. No one needs to decide whether the law of Moses (Scripture) or the Holy Spirit (experience) are at odds or whether one is superior to the other. According to Peter, there is only one way to be saved: "We believe that we [Jews] are saved through the grace of the Lord Jesus, in the same way as they [Gentiles] also are" (Acts 15:11).

The apostles, elders, and the church chose official delegates to carry this decision to Antioch—Paul, Barnabas, Judas Barsabbas, and Silas. The letter was from "the apostles and elders" of Jerusalem. This letter or decision was not merely a recommendation. Soon afterward, on their second missionary journey, Paul and Silas, passing through various cities on their way to the region of Phrygia and Galatia (Acts 16:6) delivered "the decrees [*dogmata*] which had been decided by the apostles and elders who were in Jerusalem" (Acts 16:4). Clearly, the decision was perceived as universally applicable to all Christians.

The Holy Spirit and Spiritual Gifts

As we have seen, the Holy Spirit guides and works with the church and its leaders to make appropriate decisions in order to fulfill the mission of the church. Whether it is the guidance given to leaders during the council of Jerusalem (Acts 15:28), energizing the ministry of evangelists

---

[23] See Johnson, *Acts*, 273; Ernst Haenchen, *The Acts of the Apostles: A Commentary* (Philadelphia, PA: Westminster Press, 1971), 468–470.

(Acts 18:25), or appointing church leaders to their functions (Acts 13:2, 4; 20:28), true to the mission He is given (John 16:13), the Holy Spirit is the divine agent who leads the church.[24]

The Bible makes it clear that the Spirit is given to all members of the community and not only to its leaders or ministers. The gift of the Holy Spirit is given as a natural consequence of believing in Christ as Lord and Savior and/or of baptism (Acts 2:38; 9:17; 10:44; 19:6). The outpouring of the Spirit is on the entire community of believers. How are we to understand the role of spiritual gifts individual members receive? How do these gifts function within the context of the church community? Is a spirit of individualism and independence justifiable? A true doctrine of spiritual gifts as presented in 1 Corinthians 12 and Ephesians 4 helps us realize the Holy Spirit works through more than one person or group of people. But at the same time, the operations of the Spirit are always in harmony with the Word of God to foster unity of doctrine, purpose, and mission.

Besides the well-known metaphors such as "people of God" and "body of Christ," the church is also described as a "temple of the Holy Spirit" or a "dwelling [place] of God in the Spirit" or a "spiritual house" (1 Cor 3:16; Eph 2:21–22; 1 Peter 2:5). It is through the gift of God's grace, in Christ, that Christians, in one Spirit, have access to the Father and membership in God's household (Eph 2:18–19). Together, God's children form the church, which is built on the apostles and prophets, with Christ Jesus himself as the cornerstone (Eph 2:19–20). It is within this community that Christians receive the gifts of the Spirit that equip them for the work of service and to build up the body of Christ (Eph 4:12). The gifts of the Spirit are given for the common good and the uplifting of the community of faith (1 Cor 12:7). No gift should create feelings of superiority within the community (1 Cor 12:14–26) because one person's gifts differ from another according to the grace given to all (Rom 12:6; Eph 4:7).

There are three lists of spiritual gifts in Paul's writings (Rom 12:6–8; 1 Cor 12:6–8, 28–30; Eph 4:11). Paul does not group these gifts by category and no arrangement of the gifts seems to be totally satisfactory. Yet, there appear to be three basic categories of gifts: functional gifts (apostles, prophets, evangelists, pastors, teachers, service, administration, and leadership), gifts of spiritual insight (love, wisdom, knowledge, faith, dis-

---

[24] Hans Küng comments, "The Spirit bestows power, authority and legitimacy. The Spirit as divine authority links communities to the one Church and gives continuity; he guides the early Church and its missionaries, gives offices (Acts 20:28); sends out ecclesiastical decrees through the Church (15:28); is connected with the laying-on of hands (6:6; 13:2 f.) and legitimizes the testimony of the Church (5:32)" (Hans Küng, *The Church* [New York: Sheed and Ward, 1967], 165).

cernment, exhortation, mercy), and sign gifts (healing, miracles, tongues, interpretation of tongues). These gifts are evidence that the Holy Spirit is present in the life of the church. Categorizing the gifts of the Spirit helps us understand their role within the church, although not all of them have the same priority. In 1 Corinthians 13 and 14, Paul acknowledges that some gifts have superior quality and benefit for the church. He invites the Corinthians to aspire to the greater gifts and, in particular, the gift of love which he describes as the "more excellent way" (12:31) and "greatest" gift (13:13). Love is said to be superior and of more lasting significance than the gifts of prophecy, tongues, or knowledge (13:8). The gift of tongues is less useful than the gifts of prophecy, teaching, or knowledge (14:6). In fact, some gifts, such as speaking in tongues, are essentially for one's personal spiritual benefit and encouragement (unless there is the accompanying gift of interpretation for the benefit of others), while the gifts of prophecy, knowledge, and teaching benefit the entire community of believers (14:4, 6, 28). Paul's exhortation is clear: All the gifts are to be used in one way or another for the edification of the church (14:4, 12, 26).

In Ephesians 4, Paul lists only the functional gifts that are particularly needed for the "equipping of the saints for the work of service, to the building up of the body of Christ" (4:12). "And He gave some as apostles, and some as prophets, and some as evangelists, and some as pastors and teachers" (4:11). According to Luke, Paul also included among the gifts the one of overseer or elder (Acts 20:28). Would this be an indication of a growing emphasis on the institutionalization of the church by the time the books of Acts and Ephesians were written? Perhaps. This institutionalization would therefore not be an aberration, but a normal process, taking place in the church and guided by the Holy Spirit. In the end, the functional gifts of the Spirit are crucial to the survival of the church community. Without them, the believers would be susceptible to being "tossed here and there by waves and carried about by every wind of doctrine, by the trickery of men, by craftiness in deceitful schemes" (Eph 4:14).

The Holy Spirit and Church Leadership

For many Adventists and many Protestants in general, it is difficult to understand that the Holy Spirit has anything to do with the institutional and organizational character of the church. Such attributes of the church are perceived as accommodations to the modern world. In fact, it is widely believed that all one really needs is the presence of the Holy Spirit in one's heart. The church itself is sometimes perceived as a handicap or hindrance to personal fulfillment or success. Many have an individualistic understanding of the role of the Holy Spirit and spiritual gifts. They do not understand that God created the organization of the church and that, in His saving work, He is interested in both people and the structures of the church insofar as they can serve His purposes. The New Testament does not have the slightest trouble in indicating that the Spirit is connected with various ministries, the appointments of people to serve the congregations and to do missionary work and organize the church for service. The Holy Spirit plays an important role in the baptism of people, the laying of hands on the servants of the gospel, the proclamation of the gospel to new nations, authority and discipline in the church, and various kinds of ministry. The Holy Spirit creates and works with the church to ensure the fulfillment of the gospel commission. Without the Spirit, the church would be spiritually dead. "The gift of the Spirit is not just for individual believers but aims at the building of the fellowship of believers, at the founding and the constant giving of new life to the church."[25]

The New Testament teaches us that the work of the Holy Spirit forms a new community of believers by bringing people to Christ. The Spirit connects believers with Christ and works with the community to accomplish the mission of the church. Leaders, either apostles or elders, are led by the Holy Spirit, but never in isolation from the community of believers. The Spirit guides leaders *and* the community in making appropriate decisions. Later on in the history of the Christian church, the situation changed and the work of the Holy Spirit came to be associated only with the ministry of leaders, such as bishops or popes, and not with the whole community of believers. This limitation of the work of the Holy Spirit to the clergy is a development absent from the New Testament. The issue of authority in the church has been a point of discussion for centuries. Jesus contrasted human authority with the authority that should be exercised among His people: "The kings of the Gentiles lord it over them; and those who have authority over them are called 'Benefactors.' But it is not this way with you, but the one who is the greatest among you must become like the youngest, and the leader like the servant" (Luke 22:25–26). By faith in His death, resurrection, and in baptism, all believers are in Christ; by the power of the Holy Spirit, they are integrated into the fellowship of believers in a spirit of genuine service to one another and to humanity.

Appropriate and harmonious relationships between church leaders are also a concern emerging from the New Testament. Commenting on the work of Apollos and Paul in Corinth, Ellen White highlighted their contributions to the growth of the church and their dependence on the influence of the Holy Spirit. Quarrels arose in Corinth regarding the preeminence of some gospel workers over others. These unfortunate discus-

---

[25] Wolfhart Pannenberg, *Systematic Theology* (Grand Rapids, MI: Eerdmans, 1998), 3:12.

sions created dissension among the believers. Paul noted this in his first letter to the Corinthians and appealed for unity in Christ (1 Cor 1:10–13; 3:21–23). "God's servants do not all possess the same gifts, but they are all His workmen," Ellen White noted. "There is a diversity of gifts, but all the workers are to blend in harmony, controlled by the sanctifying influence of the Holy Spirit."[26] "God has placed in the church, as His appointed helpers, men of varied talents, that through the combined wisdom of many the mind of the Spirit may be met."[27]

Conclusion

The narratives recorded in Acts illustrate a variety of activities accomplished by the Holy Spirit's ever-active role. With respect to the church, His primary tasks are both internal—what He does within the church; and external—what He does through the church in the fulfillment of the mission of the church and what He does in a direct way independent of the church but leading to the church (e.g., the conversion of Paul). The work and activities of the Holy Spirit cannot be circumscribed in a radical way to the activity and existence of the church. The Spirit works where the physical presence of the church is not yet visible (e.g., the experience of Cornelius), but His aim is the building up of the community of faith and bringing people into fellowship with Christ.

Within the church, Scripture illustrates how the Holy Spirit guided the early church in its decision-making process. This is done in at least three closely interconnected ways: revelations (e.g., the Spirit told the people what to do; Cornelius, Ananias, Philip; and perhaps the casting of lots), Scripture (the church reached a conclusion in which the Scripture was used), and consensus (the Spirit worked from within the community, almost imperceptibly, creating a consensus through dialogue and study at the end of which the church realizes that the Spirit was working within it). It appears that when faced with cultural, doctrinal, and theological controversies among the community of believers, the Holy Spirit worked through consensus in its decision-making process. In this process, we see the active role of the community of believers and not just its leaders, and the importance of prayer for discernment. The guidance of the Holy Spirit is sensed through the community's understanding of the Word of God, the experience of the community and its needs, and through the experience of its leaders as they minister. Various church decisions were made through a process guided by the Holy Spirit in which Scripture, prayer,

---

[26] White, *Acts of the Apostles*, 274–275.

[27] Ibid., 279.

and experience were elements of theological reflection.

Additionally, the internal work of the Holy Spirit is also accomplished through the giving of spiritual gifts and empowering leaders to guide the church. This internal and crucial work of the Spirit is also for the purpose of building up the church and giving it power to fulfill its mission. It is the Holy Spirit who fills people with His presence and wisdom and guided the early church to appoint people for various kinds of ministry. The Holy Spirit guided early Christians to sense the needs of the church and to find the best answer to these needs. Local communities of believers actively participated in the process of selecting leaders and thus leaders were empowered to make the right decisions or to select the right individuals. The harmonious synergy between the Holy Spirit, the community of believers, and its leaders sets in place an important ecclesiological paradigm of how decisions are to be made.

CHAPTER 15

THE ROLE OF THE CHURCH IN THE INTERPRETATION OF SCRIPTURE

Richard Davidson

Most scholarly studies of biblical hermeneutics deal primarily with individual interpretations of Scripture. Aside from the Roman Catholic perspective (where the magisterium plays a dominant role), little has been published dealing specifically with the church's role as a corporate body in biblical interpretation. In this study, I seek to address the question: How should we *collectively* approach and interpret Scripture? Or to phrase the question differently: What is the relationship between the church and Scripture? A number of inter-related issues are connected with the role of the church and the interpretation of Scripture. We will attempt to shed some light on the role of the church in the interpretation of the Bible.

Foundational Concepts

The Church and sola Scriptura ("By Scripture Alone")

A fundamental principle set forth by Scripture is that it alone is the final norm of truth, the foundational and absolute source of authority, the ultimate court of appeal, in all areas of doctrine and practice. The classic text expressing this basic premise is Isaiah 8:20 (NIV): "To the law and to the testimony! If they do not speak according to this word, they have no light of dawn."[1] The two Hebrew words *tōrāh* ("Law") and *tᵉʿûdāh*

---

[1] All Bible texts are quoted from the NASB unless otherwise indicated.

("testimony") point to the two loci of authority in Isaiah's day which now constitute Holy Scripture: the Pentateuch (the Torah or Law of Moses) and the testimony of the prophets (the books of the Prophets) to the previously revealed will of God in the Torah. Jesus similarly referred to the two divisions of Old Testament Scripture when He spoke of the "Law and the prophets" (Matt 5:17; 11:13; 22:40). The New Testament adds the authoritative revelation given by Jesus and His apostolic witnesses (see Eph 2:20; 3:5).

Isaiah warned apostate Israel against turning from the authority of the Law and the Prophets to seek counsel from spiritist mediums (Isa 8:19). In biblical times, other sources of authority threatened to usurp the final authority of the biblical revelation. Some of these sources include human philosophy and science/knowledge (Col 2:8; 1 Tim 6:20), nature (Rom 1:20–23; 2:14–16; 3:1–2), reason (Prov 14:12), and experience (Gen 3:1–6). But what concerns us in this study is the authority of ecclesiastical tradition. Jesus and Paul clearly affirm that Scripture is the authority over tradition, including the tradition of the religious authorities (Matt 15:3, 6; Col 2:8). This does not deny the usefulness of Judeo-Christian tradition as some wrongly interpret *sola Scriptura*,[2] but rather upholds the authority of Scripture over all tradition as the final truth. Tradition, even ecclesiastical tradition, must be judged by Scripture.

The Bible stands alone as the unerring guide to truth; it is sufficient to make one wise unto salvation (2 Tim 3:15). It is the standard by which all doctrine and experience must be tested (2 Tim 3:16–17; Ps 119:105; Prov 30:5, 6; Isa 8:20; John 17:17; Acts 17:11; 2 Thess 3:14; Heb 4:12). Scripture thus provides the framework, divine perspective, and foundational principles, for every branch of knowledge and experience. All additional knowledge and experience, or revelation, must build upon and remain faithful to the foundation of Scripture. The appropriate human response must be one of total surrender to the ultimate authority of the Word of God (Isa 66:2). Ellen White states this principle succinctly:

> But God will have a people upon the earth to maintain the Bible, and the Bible only, as the standard of all doctrines and the basis of all reforms. The opinions of learned men, the deductions of science, the creeds or decisions of ecclesiastical councils, as numerous and discordant as are the churches which they represent, the voice of the majority—not one nor all of these should be

---

[2] The Reformation rallying cry *sola Scriptura* should be translated as "*by* Scripture alone" (ablative), not just "Scripture alone" (nominative), in parallel with the two other Reformation slogans, *sola fide* ("*by* faith alone") and *sola gratia* ("*by* grace alone).

regarded as evidence for or against any point of religious faith. Before accepting any doctrine or precept, we should demand a plain "Thus saith the Lord" in its support.³

The Church and the Biblical Canon

Adventists join many other Protestants in affirming that the canonization of the books of the Bible is not a product of the church or other human agencies, but of the Holy Spirit, with internal, self-authenticating and self-validating qualities recognized by the community of faith.⁴ Regarding the Old Testament, Adventists, along with other Protestants, accept only 39 canonical books and not the so-called deutero-canonical books of the Apocrypha. The latter books, while containing some helpful historical information, were not written by inspired prophets, but came after the close of the Old Testament prophetic period (ca. 400 B.C.).⁵ Adventists accept a sixth-century date for the writing of Daniel (in harmony with the internal claims of the book), and place the canonization of the Old Testament in the time of the prophets, Ezra and Nehemiah (ca. 400 B.C.), both of whom played a role in popularizing and affirming the canonized books among the Jewish people (Ezra 7:10; Neh 8:2–8). Jesus Himself recognized the three-part Hebrew canon (Luke 24:44), which was later reaffirmed at the Council of Jamnia (ca. 90 A.D.).⁶

Regarding the New Testament, we have already noted above the apostolic witness inherent in all of these writings—all written by an inspired apostle or an inspired apostle's direct disciple—and thus the canon of the New Testament was closed by the end of the first century when the last inspired apostolic document had been written. Such inspired apostolicity/canonicity was eventually recognized by the New Testament covenant community. The church "came to recognize, accept, and confirm the self-authenticating quality of certain documents that imposed themselves as

---

³ Ellen G. White, *Great Controversy* (Mountain View, CA: Pacific Press, 1911), 595.

⁴ See esp. Gerhard F. Hasel, "Divine Inspiration and the Canon of the Bible," *JATS* 5.1 (1994): 68–105.

⁵ For further discussion of additional reasons why Protestants (including Adventists) do not accept the canonicity of the Apocrypha, see e.g., Norman L. Geisler and Ralph E. MacKenzie, *Roman Catholics and Evangelicals: Agreements and Differences* (Grand Rapids, MI: Baker, 1995), 157–175; Hasel, "Inspiration," 74–75.

⁶ For discussion of the new scholarly consensus that rejects the older theory that the Old Testament canon was not fixed till the Council of Jamnia, see Hasel, "Inspiration," 90–96; and Jack P. Lewis, "Jamnia Revisited," *The Canon Debate*, ed. Lee Martin McDonald and James A. Sanders (Peabody, MA: Hendrickson, 2002), 146–162.

such upon the Church."[7] In sum, the church did not *determine* the canon, but *discovered* it; did not *regulate* the canon, but *recognized* it; the church is not the *mother* of the canon, but the *child* of the canon; not its *magistrate*, but its *minister;* not its *judge*, but its *witness;* not its *master*, but its *servant*.[8]

Formal Authority of the Church

Based on the Church as the Repository of the Oracles of God

Paul describes the Jewish people as "entrusted with" the oracles of God" (Rom 3:2), i.e. the Old Testament. For the apostolic church, the "Scriptures" or "oracles of God" included the Old Testament (see Luke 24:17, 32, 44–45; Rom 1:2; 3:2; 2 Pet 1:21; etc.), and also the writings which became known as the New Testament. Paul's use of the word "scripture" (*graphē*, "writing") in his first epistle to Timothy (5:18) points in this direction. He introduces two quotations with the words "Scripture says," one from Deuteronomy 25:4, and one from the words of Jesus recorded in Luke 10:7. The word "scripture" thus is used simultaneously and synonymously to refer to both the Old Testament and the gospel accounts in the technical sense of "inspired, sacred, authoritative writings."

The gospels assert their truthfulness and authority on the same level as the Old Testament Scriptures (e.g., John 1:1–3 paralleling Gen 1:1; John 14:26; 16:13; 19:35; 21:24; Luke 1:2–4; Matthew 1 paralleling Genesis 5; Matt 23:34). Peter's use of the term "scriptures" for Paul's writings supports this conclusion (2 Pet 3:15–16; NIV). By comparing Paul's letters to the "*other* Scriptures," Peter implies that Paul's correspondence is part of Scripture.

The New Testament is the apostolic witness to Jesus and to His fulfillment of the Old Testament prophecies. Jesus promised the twelve apostles the Holy Spirit to help them remember His teachings (John 14:26). Paul states that "the mystery of Christ" was "revealed to his holy apostles and prophets by the Spirit" (Eph 3:4–5). The twelve apostles held a unique, singular position in history (Eph 2:20) as first-hand witnesses of the humanity of Christ (Luke 1:2; Gal 1:11–17; 2 Pet 1:16; 1 John 1:1–4). This certainly validates the writings of apostles such as Peter, John, and Matthew. Paul also was called to be an apostle (see Rom 1:1, 1 Cor 1:1), and he indicates that his writings are given under the leadership of the Holy

---

[7] Bruce M. Metzger, *The Canon of the New Testament: Its Origin, Development, and Significance* (Oxford: Clarendon, 1987), 287.

[8] Adapted from Geisler and MacKenzie, *Catholics and Evangelicals*, 173.

Spirit and have full apostolic authority (1 Cor 7:40; 12:13; 14:37; 2 Cor 3:5–6; 4:13; Gal 1:11–12; 1 Thess 5:27; 2 Thess 3:6–15). The New Testament embodies the witness of the apostles, either directly or indirectly through their close associates and eye-witnesses Mark, Luke, James, and Jude (see Luke 1:1–3; Acts 12:12, 25; 15:37; 16:11; Col 4:10, 14; 2 Tim 4:11; Philem 24). Therefore the church served as the "repository of the oracles of God." Beyond New Testament times, the church's responsibility as the "repository of the oracles of God" continues in its role to preserve the Word of God. As L. Berkhof states it:

> By giving His Word to the Church, God constituted the Church the keeper of the precious deposit of the truth. While hostile forces are pitted against it and the power of error is everywhere apparent, the Church must see to it that the truth does not perish from the earth, that the inspired volume in which it is embodied be kept pure and handed on faithfully from generation to generation.[9]

The responsibility to preserve the Word involves not only fostering a sound interpretation of Scripture, but also ensuring the Bible is made available for study by all people in faithful and clear modern translations, and that copies of Scripture are plentiful and affordable. But what constitutes the Bible? What "authorized" the various biblical writings to become canonical? How was the church involved in this process?

Based on the New Testament Model

The New Testament provides numerous examples where Jesus and the apostles interpreted Old Testament Scripture. Elsewhere, I have examined the claim that Jesus and the New Testament writers often took Old Testament passages out of context, reinterpreted, and reapplied them in light of the Christ-event, and thus imposed a New Testament meaning upon the Old Testament, foreign to the original meaning. After examining major examples of New Testament citations of Old Testament passages where it has been claimed that the New has not remained faithful to the Old Testament meaning in its original context, I have joined other biblical scholars who have concluded that the New Testament writers did not take Old Testament Scriptures out of context in their citations. Neither did they read back into it what was not originally there, but rather consistently remained faithful to the Old Testament intention, and consistently engaged in solid exegesis of the Old Testament passages using sound her-

---

[9] L. Berkhof, *Systematic Theology* (Grand Rapids, MI: Eerdmans, 1939), 595.

meneutical principles.[10]

But this study focuses upon the church as a whole in its interpretation of Scripture. Acts 15's description of the Jerusalem Council gives us an apostolic model of ecclesiastical authority within the church at large: representatives of the various local churches (v. 3) met in a general assembly under the direction of church leaders ("the apostles and elders"; vv. 2, 6) to consider a matter of vital significance for the world church (vv. 5–6).

It has been claimed that this is a model of ecclesiastical authority in which the church, empowered by the freedom of the Spirit, is able to reach back into the Old Testament and select passages still relevant to the current situation, and with that same authority of the Spirit, move beyond other portions of the Old Testament that are no longer applicable and that even add new stipulations not contained in the Old Testament.[11] In other words, it is suggested that the New Testament church, and by implication, the church today, has authority to determine the best path to unity by rejecting some Old Testament instructions and adding new ones as it sees fit under the sanctified guidance of the Spirit.

Such a position, however, does not square with the data of Acts 15. It is true that the Jerusalem Council did allow for vigorous debate (v. 7) on the issues that were faced. The basic issues were: should Gentiles become Jews in order to become Christians, and what Jewish practices beyond the moral law of the Ten Commandments were to be required for these Gentiles who became Christians. There was spirited discussion (v. 7a), and personal testimonies were given (vv. 7b–12). But the ultimate deciding factor, in the end, was the authoritative testimony of Scripture. James' concluding statement was in essence based upon an exegesis of crucial Old Testament passages. In Amos 9:11–12 they found the answer to the issue of whether Gentiles had to become Jews to become Christians: They did not.

And in Leviticus 17–18 was found the biblical basis for deciding which laws of the Jewish ceremonial law applied to Gentiles. Acts 15 lists four prohibitions for Gentile Christians given by the Jerusalem Council: "That you abstain from things offered to idols, from blood, from things strangled [i.e. with the blood coagulated and not drained away],[12] and

---

[10] For further discussion and examples of other scholars who have come to a similar conclusion, see e.g., Richard M. Davidson, "New Testament Use of the Old Testament," *JATS* 5.1 (1994): 14–39.

[11] See e.g., Alden Thompson, *Inspiration: Hard Questions, Honest Answers* (Hagerstown, MD: Review and Herald, 1991), 147–150.

[12] The Greek adjective, *pniktos*, usually translated "strangled" or "choked," actually refers precisely to the situation described in Leviticus 17:13–16. See H. Bietenhard, "*Pniktos* Strangled," *NIDNTT*, 1:226: "The command [of Acts 15:20, 29] goes back to Lev. 17:13 f. and Deut. 12:16, 23.

from sexual immorality [*porneia*]" (v. 29). Particularly striking is that this is the same list, *in the same order*, as the four major legal prohibitions explicitly stated to be applicable to the stranger/alien as well as to native Israelites in Leviticus 17–18. In these Old Testament chapters, we find 1) sacrificing to demons/idols (Lev 17:7–9); 2) eating blood (Lev 17:10–12); 3) eating anything that has not been immediately drained of its blood (Lev 17:13–16); and 4) various illicit sexual practices (Lev 18). Numerous scholars have recognized this intertextual connection.[13] In this clear case of intertextuality, the Jerusalem Council undoubtedly concluded that the practices forbidden to the stranger/alien in Leviticus 17–18 should be prohibited to Gentile Christians in the church. Scripture ultimately provided the basis for the church's decision.

The Jerusalem Council involved a multi-faceted process that may shed light on the way the church today should work through crucial issues. There was vigorous debate, personal testimony, and testing of views and experience by Scripture. As the study and application of Scripture proceeded, a consensus began to emerge under the guidance of the Spirit and the leadership of the apostles. This Spirit-led consensus is apparent from the wording of the Jerusalem Decree: "The apostles and the brethren who are elders" (v. 23); "it seemed good to us, having become of one mind" (v. 25); "it seemed good to the Holy Spirit, and to us" (v. 28). The consensus was articulated by James, the brother of Jesus (v. 19), formalized in writing (vv. 23–29) and circulated among the churches by delegated representatives (vv. 22, 30; 16:4).[14]

An animal should be so slaughtered that its blood, in which is its life, should be allowed to pour out. If the animal is killed in any other way, it has been 'strangled'." Cf. *idem.*, "*Pnigō*," *TDNT* 6:457: "The regulations in Lv. 17:13 f. and Dt. 12:16, 23 lay down that an animal should be slaughtered in such a way that all the blood drains from the carcass. If it is put to death in any other way, it 'chokes,' since the life seated in the blood remains in the body."

[13] For scholarly concurrence and further discussion, see Richard M. Davidson, "Which Torah Laws Should Gentile Christians Obey? The Relationship Between Leviticus 17–18 and Acts 15," paper presented at the Evangelical Theological Society 59th Annual Meeting, San Diego, CA, 15 November 2007. Cf. the articles by H. Reisser, "*Porneuō* Practice Prostitution," *NIDNTT* 1:497–501; and F. Hauck and S. Schulz, "*Pornē, Pornos*," *TDNT* 6:579–595.

[14] Some claim that this decision on the part of the Jerusalem Council was only advisory, not binding, inasmuch as Paul is seen to consider its ruling as a nonissue in his dealings with food offered to idols (1 Cor 10:19–33; see, e.g., Thompson, *Inspiration*, 150). But again, such readings overlook both the wider New Testament data and the Old Testament basis for the Jerusalem Council's ruling. According to Acts 16:4, in Paul's journeys after the Jerusalem Council, Silas and he upheld the rulings of the Council and considered them binding upon the churches. Paul did not change his basic position in his counsel to the Corinthians. Rather, he apparently recognized that the Old Testament basis for not eating food offered to idols was found in Leviticus 17:7–9, which prohibits the sacrificing of food to demons/idols. Paul seems to have understood the intent of this Old Testament passage that formed the basis of the Jerusalem Council prohibition, and, thus,

Acts 15 reveals that the church, in its assembly of representative members, may indeed speak not merely in an advisory capacity, but with binding authority upon the whole church, as it is based upon the authority of the written Word.[15]

Based on the Bible's Emphasis on a Corporate Reading

In contrast to the Roman Catholic doctrines of apostolic succession (the uninterrupted transmission of spiritual authority from the apostles and perpetuated through the bishops) and the magisterium, the biblical principle is that the Bible is perspicuous and does not require any human ecclesiological magisterium to pronounce its meaning. The biblical testimony upholds the priesthood of all believers (1 Pet 2:9; Rev 1:6) and encourages them to study the Bible for themselves in order to understand God's message (e.g., Deut 30:11–14; Luke 1:3, 4; John 20:30–31; Acts 17:11; Rom 10:17; Rev 1:3).

Likewise, Ellen White continually encourages personal searching of the Scriptures. For example, she writes: "The one book that is essential for all to study is the Bible. Studied with reverence and godly fear, it is the greatest of all educators. Its pages are filled with truth. Would you gain a knowledge of God and of Christ, whom the Father sent into the world to live and die for sinners? An earnest, diligent study of the Bible is necessary in order to gain this knowledge."[16] Again, White urges:

> Let everyone who has been blessed with reasoning faculties take up the Bible and search its pages, that he may understand the will of God concerning him. In this Book divine instruction is given to all. The Bible is addressed to every one—to every class of society, to those of every clime and age. Everyone should read the Bible for himself. Do not depend on the minister to read it for you. The

---

correctly upheld the prohibition against offering food to idols/demons (1 Cor 10:20–21). At the same time, he appears to have recognized that a Gentile Christian not personally offering food to idols would not be going against the Old Testament prohibition (hence, against the Jerusalem Council ruling based upon that Old Testament prohibition), if he ate food that, unknown to him, someone else had offered to an idol (vv. 25–29).

[15] Acts 15 is an illustration of the principle set forth by Jesus regarding the authority of the church in Matthew 16:19: "I will give you the keys of the kingdom of heaven; and whatever you bind on earth shall have been bound in heaven, and whatever you loose on earth shall have been loosed in heaven." As the NASB correctly translates, using the perfect passive participle of the verbs "bind" and "loose," what the church decides is not independent and arbitrary; rather its "binding" and "loosing" is dependent upon recognizing what already "has been bound" and "has been loosed" in heaven, as revealed in Scripture through the Spirit.

[16] "God's Word: Our Guide," *Signs of the Times*, March 21, 1906, par. 1.

Bible is God's Word to you. And Christ has made this Word so plain that in reading it, no one need misunderstand.[17]

White warns individuals not to allow any other source of authority take precedence over the Bible. While the Bible and Ellen White's counsel underscore the importance of individual study of Scripture, there is also the need to recognize the validity of corporate study of Scripture. The passages cited above encouraging personal study are almost all set within the context of corporate study in the faith community. Moses' appeal to his hearers to internalize Scripture (Deut 30:11-14) must be seen within the context of the community leaders' public teaching of the Torah (Deut 33:10). Jesus' promise to the church that the Spirit "will guide you into all the truth. . . . He will teach you all things" (John 16:13; 14:26), also has the "you" in plural; the Spirit directs interpreters together in the fellowship of the church body, where they can benefit discourse with other believers. Likewise, the "you" in John's appeal to study his gospel is also in the plural, implying corporate study (John 20:30-31). The noble Bereans are commended for their study of Scripture (Acts 17:11) in the context of their corporate hearing of the Word in the synagogue (v. 10). The call by Paul to "hearing by the word of God" (Rom 10:17) is in the corporate context of hearing a preacher (v. 14). John the Revelator's blessing to those who hear and read the Apocalypse (Rev 1:3) is in the setting of the public reading of his book in the seven churches (v. 4).

Many other passages in Scripture uphold the corporate element in the study and interpretation of Scripture. The psalmist proclaims to God that he is "a companion of all those who fear You, And of those who keep Your precepts" (Ps 119:63). The book of Acts describes the experience of the early church as "continually devoting themselves to the apostles' teaching and to fellowship, to the breaking of bread and to prayer" (Acts 2:42). The various lists of spiritual gifts in the church (Rom 12:4-8; 1 Cor 12; Eph 4:3-13) emphasize their corporate exercise in connection with the study and ministry of the Word. And all of these passages are to be seen in the larger context of strong emphasis upon corporate solidarity in the biblical worldview.[18]

---

[17] "A Sure Guide," *Signs of the Times*, July 11, 1906, par. 6.

[18] See e.g., Joel S. Kaminsky, *Corporate Responsibility in the Hebrew Bible* (Sheffield: Sheffield Academic Press, 1995); Gerald A. Klingbeil, "Entre el individualismo y el colectivismo: hacia una perspectiva bíblica de la naturaleza de la iglesia," *Pensar la iglesia hoy: hacia una eclesiología adventista*, ed. Gerald A. Klingbeil, Martin G. Klingbeil, and Miguel Nunez (Entre Rios, Argentina: Editorial Universitaria Adventista, 2002), 3-23; cf. Richard Davidson, "Corporate Solidarity in

The Bible calls the church to come into "the unity of the faith" (Eph 4:13). The body of Christ must take a definite and unified stand in interpreting the fundamentals of the Christian faith, recognizing that there is "one body and one Spirit, . . . one Lord, one faith, one baptism" (Eph 4:4–5). The spiritual gifts given to the corporate church (apostles, prophets, evangelists, pastors-teachers, Eph 4:11) are for the purpose of bringing all in the church "to the unity of the faith and the knowledge of the Son of God . . . We are no longer to be children, tossed here and there by waves and carried about by every wind of doctrine" (vv. 13–14).[19] Biblically-based tension must be maintained between an individual Christian's right and responsibility to stand alone before the Word (if necessary, even in the face of established doctrine, as did Martin Luther and William Miller) and his/her loyal and submissive stance with regard to church authority.

Even in the area of doctrinal beliefs there is ongoing need to deepen our understanding of the Word. There is also need for a corporate faith-consciousness, a corporate consensus on the truth that defines the community's identity and mission. The Bible alone must always be the basis of church unity. The importance of corporate unity in interpreting Scripture is especially evident when faced with those who claim to have discovered "new light," an issue to which we turn next.

---

the Old Testament," Unpublished paper, 44, December 2004.

[19] Ellen White writes: "God is leading a people out from the world upon the exalted platform of eternal truth, the commandments of God and the faith of Jesus. He will discipline and fit up His people. They will not be at variance, one believing one thing and another having faith and views entirely opposite, each moving independently of the body. Through the diversity of the gifts and governments that He has placed in the church, they will all come to the unity of the faith. If one man takes his views of Bible truth without regard to the opinion of his brethren, and justifies his course, alleging that he has a right to his own peculiar views, and then presses them upon others, how can he be fulfilling the prayer of Christ? And if another and still another arises, each asserting his right to believe and talk what he pleases without reference to the faith of the body, where will be that harmony which existed between Christ and His Father, and which Christ prayed might exist among His brethren? Though we have an individual work and an individual responsibility before God, we are not to follow our own independent judgment, regardless of the opinions and feelings of our brethren; for this course would lead to disorder in the church. It is the duty of ministers to respect the judgment of their brethren; but their relations to one another, as well as the doctrines they teach, should be brought to the test of the law and the testimony; then, if hearts are teachable, there will be no divisions among us. Some are inclined to be disorderly, and are drifting away from the great landmarks of the faith; but God is moving upon His ministers to be one in doctrine and in spirit" (*Testimonies to Ministers* [Mountain View, CA: Pacific Press, 1923], 29–30).

The Expression of the Church's Reading of Scripture

In the Statement of Fundamental Beliefs

The basic Adventist understanding of the relationship between its Statement of Fundamental Beliefs and Scripture is set forth in the Preamble to the "Fundamental Beliefs of Seventh-day Adventists":

> Seventh-day Adventists accept the Bible as their only creed and hold certain fundamental beliefs to be the teaching of the Holy Scriptures. These beliefs, as set forth here, constitute the church's understanding and expression of the teaching of Scripture. Revision of these statements may be expected at a General Conference session when the church is led by the Holy Spirit to a fuller understanding of Bible truth or finds better language in which to express the teachings of God's Holy Word.[20]

Seventh-day Adventists recognize that church creeds, even among Protestant churches, can often function like tradition in the Roman Catholic Church, placing the authority of the church over that of the Bible. Ellen White warned of this:

> Though the Reformation gave the Scriptures to all, yet the selfsame principle which was maintained by Rome prevents multitudes in Protestant churches from searching the Bible for themselves. They are taught to accept its teachings as interpreted by the church; and there are thousands who dare receive nothing, however plainly revealed in Scripture, that is contrary to their creed or the established teaching of their church.[21]

The Adventist Statement of Fundamental Beliefs represents the church's current consensus on biblical truth, a corporate faith-consciousness based solely upon Scripture. This statement reflects the ongoing relationship between the church and Scripture, in which the Scripture is given final authority in any future expression of the church's fundamental beliefs.[22] Therefore, the statement of fundamental beliefs is authoritative to the extent that the statement accurately represents the message of Scripture. The statement is regarded as authoritative because the com-

---

[20] *Seventh-day Adventist Church Manual* (Hagerstown, MD: Review and Herald, 2010), 156.

[21] White, *Great Controversy*, 596.

[22] See Kwabena Donkor, "The Role of the Statement of Beliefs and Creeds," in this volume.

munity of faith sees it as representing a Spirit-directed consensus, in fulfillment of Jesus' promise that the Spirit would guide into all truth (John 16:13). It constitutes a derived authority, a *norma normata*, a "rule that is ruled," and is open to further modification as the Spirit leads into deeper understanding of biblical truth. The Adventist Statement of Beliefs, while always provisional, and derivative in authority, under the Word of God, nonetheless is to be accepted as authoritative for God's people. It was voted by the General Conference in session, which follows the model of Acts 15 in setting forth the interpretation of Scripture under the leading of the Holy Spirit.

Following the pattern established in Acts 15, the Seventh-day Adventist Church assigns its highest authority, under the Word of God, to the General Conference in session. In 1877, the General Conference session took the following action:

> *Resolved*, that the highest authority under God among Seventh-day Adventists is found in the will of the body of that people, as expressed in the decisions of the General Conference when acting within its proper jurisdiction; and that such decisions should be submitted to by all without exception, unless they can be shown to conflict with the word of God and the rights of individual conscience.[23]

Ellen White discusses the authority of the General Conference in session, in the following counsel written in 1909:

> I have often been instructed by the Lord that no man's judgment should be surrendered to the judgment of any other one man. Never should the mind of one man or the minds of a few men be regarded as sufficient in wisdom and power to control the work and to say what plans shall be followed. But when, in a General Conference, the judgment of the brethren assembled from all parts of the field is exercised, private independence and private judgment must not be stubbornly maintained, but surrendered. Never should a laborer regard as a virtue the persistent maintenance of his position of independence, contrary to the decision of the general body.

---

[23] *Review and Herald*, 50.14, 1877, 106.

At times, when a small group of men entrusted with the general management of the work have, in the name of the General Conference, sought to carry out unwise plans and to restrict God's work, I have said that I could no longer regard the voice of the General Conference, represented by these few men, as the voice of God. But this is not saying that the decisions of a General Conference composed of an assembly of duly appointed, representative men from all parts of the field should not be respected. God has ordained that the representatives of His church from all parts of the earth, when assembled in a General Conference, shall have authority. The error that some are in danger of committing is in giving to the mind and judgment of one man, or of a small group of men, the full measure of authority and influence that God has vested in His church in the judgment and voice of the General Conference assembled to plan for the prosperity and advancement of His work.

When this power, which God has placed in the church, is accredited wholly to one man, and he is invested with the authority to be judgment for other minds, then the true Bible order is changed. Satan's efforts upon such a man's mind would be most subtle and sometimes well-nigh overpowering, for the enemy would hope that through his mind he could affect many others. Let us give to the highest organized authority in the church that which we are prone to give to one man or a small group of men.[24]

The *Church Manual* summarizes the nature and extent of the authority of the General Conference in session:

The General Conference in session, and the Executive Committee between sessions, is the highest organization in the administration of the church's worldwide work, and is authorized by its constitution to create subordinate organizations to promote specific interests in various sections of the world; it is therefore understood that all subordinate organizations and institutions throughout the world will recognize the General Conference as the highest authority, under God, among Seventh-day Adventists. When differences arise in or between organizations and institutions, appeal to the next higher organization is proper until it reaches the General

---

[24] Ellen G. White, *Testimonies for the Church* (Mountain View, CA: Pacific Press, 1909), 9: 260–261.

Conference in session, or the Executive Committee at the Annual Council. During the interim between these sessions the Executive Committee shall constitute the body of final authority on all questions where a difference of viewpoint may develop. The committee's decision may be reviewed at a session of the General Conference or at an Annual Council of the Executive Committee.[25]

The authority of the church, exercised by the assembled General Conference in session, in voting a statement of fundamental beliefs, as in other decisions, is a derived authority, always under the authority of Jesus Christ expressed in the truths of Scripture. This does not nullify the responsibility and privilege of individual interpretation of Scripture to determine one's personal duty to God.

In Procedures to Deal with "New Light" and with Heresies

Both the Bible and Ellen White encourage the ongoing searching of Scriptures. "The earth itself is not so interlaced with golden veins and filled with precious things as is the word of God."[26]

> We have seen only the glimmering of divine glory and of the infinitude of knowledge and wisdom; we have, as it were, been working on the surface of the mine, when rich golden ore is beneath the surface, to reward the one who will dig for it. The shaft must be sunk deeper and yet deeper in the mine, and the result will be glorious treasure. Through a correct faith, divine knowledge will become human knowledge.[27]

Again, White emphasizes:

New light will ever be revealed on the word of God to him who is in living connection with the Sun of Righteousness. Let no one come to the conclusion that there is no more truth to be revealed. The diligent, prayerful seeker for truth will find precious rays of light yet to shine forth from the word of God. Many gems are yet scattered that are to be gathered together to become the property of the remnant people of God.[28]

---

[25] *Church Manual*, 31.

[26] Ellen G. White, *Christ's Object Lessons* (Washington, DC: Review and Herald, 1900), 104.

[27] White, *Christ's Object Lessons*, 113.

[28] Ellen G. White, *Counsels on Sabbath School Work* (Washington, DC: Review and Herald, 1938), 34.

However, at times individuals who study Scripture discover what they consider "new light" contrary to the established positions of the Seventh-day Adventist Church. The *Church Manual,* building upon biblical principles, urges that those who think they have discovered "new light" contrary to established doctrinal or procedural Adventist positions to seek counsel from responsible leaders. Three times in Proverbs, the principle is stated: "In a multitude of counselors there is safety" (Prov 24:6; NKJV; cf. 11:14; 15:22). Ellen White elaborates:

> There are a thousand temptations in disguise prepared for those who have the light of truth; and the only safety for any of us is in receiving no new doctrine, no new interpretation of the Scriptures, without first submitting it to brethren of experience. Lay it before them in a humble, teachable spirit, with earnest prayer; and if they see no light in it, yield to their judgment; for 'in the multitude of counselors there is safety.'[29]

In the early church, when a difference of opinion arose over an important issue, the believers sent representatives to Jerusalem, and the question was submitted for considertation to those assembled under the leadership of the apostles and elders. The decision of this council was accepted by the believers in Antioch, and unity was preserved in the church.

This counsel and paradigm from inspired sources must not be seen as a deterrent to diligent study of the Scriptures, but as a protection against the introduction of false theories and doctrines into the church. God encourages individual study of the Word for gems of truth, but does not wish any to be led astray by erroneous teachings. New light from God's Word does not make void a particular teaching of the Word. Instead it harmonizes with the old, causing it to shine brighter with greater luster. As the inspired wise man puts it, "the path of the righteous is like the light of the dawn, that shine brighter and brighter until the full day" (Prov 4:18).

"Progressive revelation" does not imply the acquisition of new light that contradicts the old, but denotes a progressive understanding of truth which coheres with what has been revealed in the past. While the individual interpreter of Scripture must be ready to accept the progressive understanding of the Word, such understanding will not contradict previous light. This position is supported by the fundamental biblical principle of testing claims in Isaiah 8:20: "To the law and to the testimony! If they do not speak according to this word, it is because there is no light in

---

[29] White, *Testimonies,* 5:293.

them" (NKJV). Although this principle speaks primarily to testing claims of competing sources of authority, it also implies that new light will not contradict previous light. The special light God gave the Seventh-day Adventist Church in its formative years, hammering out a system of truth with its distinctive foundational doctrines (the "old landmarks"), will not be overthrown by further explorations of the Word.[30]

The church has various venues where those who have discovered potential new light may test these ideas and receive biblically-based feedback: private interviews with a pastor or teacher or colleague, informal discussion groups involving academic peers or papers presented to theological societies, correspondence with scholars in such church entities as the Biblical Research Institute or other academic institutions. People who present the results of their study should be treated with respect and not looked upon with suspicion.

These policies allow for a process for those who claim to have new light. The process allows them to have their ideas examined by those of experience, beginning at the local (conference/institution) level and allowing for appeal to committees at the union and division levels.[31] During this process of investigation by the "multitude of counselors," it is urged that the one claiming new light refrain from presenting publicly any questions not in full harmony with the views of the established body, in order to "preserve the unity of the Spirit in the bond of peace" (Eph 4:3). The church pulpit or class lecture room is not the place for a pastor or teacher to work through his/her questions regarding the teachings of the Bible or promote new ideas that contradict the fundamental beliefs of the church.

With regard to those who seek to bring false doctrine into the church, and who will not accept the counsel of the "multitude of counselors," the church has a corporate responsibility to protect its doctrinal purity. In the Bible, high priority is given to maintaining sound teaching and avoiding heresy (1 Tim 1:3; 6:3; 2 Tim 1:13; 1 Cor 11:2; Gal 1:8–9; 2 John 7–11).

---

[30] Ellen White gives the following warning: "We are not to receive the words of those who come with a message that contradicts the special points of our faith. They gather together a mass of Scripture, and pile it as proof around their asserted theories. This has been done over and over again during the past fifty years. And while the Scriptures are God's word, and are to be respected, the application of them, if such application moves one pillar from the foundation that God has sustained these fifty years, is a great mistake. He who makes such an application knows not the wonderful demonstration of the Holy Spirit that gave power and force to the past messages that have come to the people of God" (*Counsels to Writers and Editors* [Nashville, TN: Southern Publishing, 1946], 32).

[31] See the voted document, "A Statement on Theological and Academic Freedom and Accountability," especially, the section "Guidelines for Assessing Divergent Views," accessible on the website of the General Conference of Seventh-day Adventists (www.adventist.org), under "Adventist Beliefs–Official Statements."

The church was charged by the apostles to "test the spirits to see whether they are from God" (1 John 4:1) or, in Paul's terms, to "examine everything" and "hold fast to that which is good" (1 Thess 5:21). The same is true in regard to the exercise of church discipline (Matt 18:15–17), ranging all the way from private admonition (cf. Matt 18:16; Gal 6:1) to removal from church membership (Matt 18:18; 1 Cor 5:11, 13; 2 Cor 2:5–11). The church, as a corporate body, has established specific biblically-based policies and procedures for dealing with church discipline. However, in practice, there is considerable variation in their application as situations dealing with individual church discipline and/or membership status are ultimately handled by local congregations. The church is given authority to deal with church discipline, based upon Bible principles.[32] The church is also given authority, under Scripture, to establish various working policies, an issue to which we now turn.

In the Formulation of Church Policies

The Bible gives basic direction that the church is to formulate plans so that "all things must be done properly and in an orderly manner" (1 Cor 14:40). In the formative years of the Advent movement, Ellen White consistently urged the application of this biblical principle. In 1875 she wrote: "The church of Christ is in constant peril. Satan is seeking to destroy the people of God, and one man's mind, one man's judgment, is not sufficient to be trusted. Christ would have His followers brought together in church capacity, observing order, having rules and discipline, and all subject one to another, esteeming others better than themselves."[33]

As indicated above, the General Conference in session, in its role as the "highest authority" on earth, under the Word of God, and following the model of Acts 15, has authority to settle the conditions of membership and the rules governing the church. It has well-defined rules and various policies derived from principles set forth in Scripture. The content of the various voted policies set forth in the *Church Manual* is "the expression

---

[32] White comments: "The world's Redeemer has invested great power with His church. He states the rules to be applied in cases of trial with its members. After He has given explicit directions as to the course to be pursued, He says: 'Verily I say unto you, Whatsoever ye shall bind on earth shall be bound in heaven: and whatsoever [in church discipline] ye shall loose on earth shall be loosed in heaven.' Thus even the heavenly authority ratifies the discipline of the church in regard to its members when the Bible rule has been followed. The word of God does not give license for one man to set up his judgment in opposition to the judgment of the church, neither is he allowed to urge his opinions against the opinions of the church. If there were no church discipline and government, the church would go to fragments; it could not hold together as a body" (*Testimonies*, 3:428).

[33] *Testimonies*, 3:445.

of the Seventh-day Adventist Church's understanding of Christian life and church governance and discipline based on biblical principles."[34] It expresses the authority of a duly assembled General Conference session.

These church policies, presented in the *Church Manual* and the broader *Working Policies*, while representing the best thinking of the church, are not static. The 1946 General Conference Session voted that all "changes or revisions of policy" in the *Church Manual* and Church *Working Policies* shall be "authorized by the General Conference session."[35] In practice, numerous such changes have been made at each succeeding General Conference session, as they are re-evaluated in light of biblical principles and the needs of the global church.

Teaching the Scriptures

In the Old Testament church the institution of the priesthood was given the responsibility of teaching God's Word to the people (Lev 10:11; Deut 24:8; 33:10; Mal 2:7), instructing them on how to distinguish between the holy and the common and the unclean and the clean, and interpreting the law of God for individual case situations (Ezek 44:23–24; Deut 17:8–11). In the days of Samuel, special schools of the prophets were established, which "proved a great blessing to Israel, promoting that righteousness which exalteth a nation, and furnishing it with men qualified to act, in the fear of God, as leaders and counselors. . . . The chief subjects of study were the law of God with the instructions given to Moses, sacred history, sacred music, and poetry. . . . Sanctified intellects brought forth from the treasure house of God things new and old."[36] In the days of Ezra and Nehemiah, the Levites "read from the book, from the law of God, translating to give the sense so that they understood the reading" (Neh 8:8).[37]

Jesus indicated the need for biblical interpretation, in light of the misapprehension of truth in His day. After His resurrection, Jesus walked with the two disciples on the road to Emmaus and "explained [*diermēneuō*] to them the things concerning Himself in all the Scriptures" (Luke 24:27). Later that night, He met with the rest of the disciples and "opened their minds to understand the Scriptures" (Luke 24:45). Jesus taught the first hermeneutics course to the early church. And the record of the sermons

---

[34] *Church Manual*, 18.

[35] Ibid., 19.

[36] Ellen G. White, *Fundamentals of Christian Education* (Nashville, TN: Southern Publishing, 1923), 96–97.

[37] This involved both translation from Hebrew to the more familiar language of Aramaic and explanation of the meaning to the Jewish people recently returned from Babylonian Exile.

in the book of Acts evidence Jesus' hermeneutical teaching being passed on by the apostles to the wider community of faith in Israel and beyond.

The New Testament is clear that the interpretation and application of Scripture is the task of the entire church, and not restricted to an elite cadre of biblical specialists (see Acts 17:11; Eph 3:18-19; 4:13-14; 5:10, 17). We find the example of Philip interpreting the meaning of Isaiah 53 to the Ethiopian eunuch (Acts 8:30-31). The apostle Paul instructs Timothy to be sure he is "rightly dividing" (KJV), "rightly handling" (RSV), or "handling accurately" (NASB) [*orthotomeō*, literally, "to cut straight"] the Word of God. In 2 Cor 2:17, Paul affirms that he is not like many who "adulterate" God's word. The Greek word here is *kapēleuō*, literally "to peddle," alluding to the peddlers of the day who so often used such deceptive tricks that the term "peddle" came to signify "adulterate." The presence of those who adulterate or corrupt the Word implies the need for careful interpretation and application on the part of church members and leaders alike.

It is still the responsibility of church leaders today to instruct church members, pastors, professors, and administrators on the proper interpretation of the Bible.[38] The Scripture should be at the center of the church in all its expressions, e.g., in academic institutions, hospitals, administrative offices. Proper hermeneutical principles in the study of the Scripture should be supplied through seminars and publications addressing this important topic. Each church should be a place where the message of Salvation is clearly proclaimed and church members are instructed on the nature of the Christian life and their involvement in mission.

The Spirit and Unity in Biblical Interpretation

In modern hermeneutical approaches toward the Bible, especially among liberal/critical scholars but also sometimes among conservative/evangelicals, it is assumed that the original intent of the Bible writer can be ascertained by the rigorous application of hermeneutical principles and exegetical tools, quite apart from the assistance of the Spirit. This

---

[38] The church has taken the lead in clarifying sound methods of biblical interpretation, in contrast to unbiblical methodologies. A landmark Bible Conference in 1974 and publication of a basic book on hermeneutics in the same year (Gordon M. Hyde, ed., *A Symposium on Biblical Hermeneutics* [Washington, DC: Review and Herald, 1974]) both sponsored by the Biblical Research Institute, began this process in earnest. In 1986, the "Methods of Bible Study" document, voted by the Annual Council, gave impetus to this project (Published in the *Adventist Review*, January 22, 1987). Two other volumes on hermeneutics have been published by the Biblical Research Institute, under the guidance of the Biblical Research Institute Committee (George W. Reid, ed., *Understanding Scripture: An Adventist Approach* [Silver Spring, MD: Biblical Research Institute, 2006] and Gerhard Pfandl, ed., *Interpreting Scripture: Bible Questions and Answers* [Silver Spring, MD: Biblical Research Institute, 2010]).

assumption is made with the intention of maintaining a degree of objectivity in interpreting the biblical text.[39] However, scriptural data lead to a different conclusion. Paul indicated, "For who among men knows the thoughts of a man except the man's spirit within him? In the same way no one knows the thoughts of God except the Spirit of God. . . . The man without the Spirit does not accept the things that come from the Spirit of God, for they are foolishness to him, and he cannot understand them, because they are spiritually discerned" (1 Cor 2:11, 14; NIV).[40]

"Spiritually discerned," means that, since the Bible is ultimately the product of the mind of God revealed through the Spirit (cf. 1 Cor 2:12-13), it is not possible to separate "what it meant" to the human writer (to be studied without the aid of the Holy Spirit) from "what it means" (to be applied by the help of the Spirit). Both the original meaning and its present application involve the thoughts of God and can only be adequately comprehended with the aid of His Spirit (cf. John 6:45; 16:13; 1 Cor 2:13-14; 2 Cor 3:14-18). And this same Spirit, who has inspired the prophets (2 Tim 3:15, 16; 2 Pet 1:19-21), has been promised to illumine the minds of those who seek to understand the meaning of the divine revelation.

It is true that "spiritual exegesis" *alone*—that is, an attempt to rely totally on the Spirit without conscientiously applying principles of exegesis and hermeneutics arising from Scripture—can lead to subjectivism. But the proper combination of dependence upon the Spirit with rigorous exegesis, based upon sound hermeneutical procedures, constitutes the only way of escaping subjectivity. Modern scholars are increasingly more willing to recognize that all come to the Scripture with their own presuppositions and bias. This cannot be remedied by approaching the text "scientifically" without a "faith bias." In fact, since the Scriptures call for a response of faith, an attempted "neutral" stance is already at cross-currents with the intent of Scripture (cf. Matt 13:11-17; John 6:69; Acts 2:38).

Spirit-led interpreters also come with their own biases and are not impervious to error (cf. Acts 11:15). But for Christians who believe the promises of Scripture, it is possible to ask God to transform their minds so that they increasingly adopt and incorporate the presuppositions of Scripture and not their own (see Rom 12:1). The Spirit of Truth was promised to the disciples and to us corporately (John 16:13; 14:26). Interpreters within the church must make a collective decision that their pre-understandings will derive from and be under control of the Bible itself,

---

[39] See the classical presentation of this position by Krister Stendahl, "Biblical Theology, Contemporary," *IDB* 1: 418-432.

[40] See also, e.g., 2 Corinthians 3:8, which speaks of the "ministration of the Spirit;" and Psalm 36:9, "In Your Light we see light."

and constantly be open for modification and enlargement on the basis of Scripture. They must consciously reject any external keys or systems to impose on Scripture from without, whether it be naturalistic (closed system of cause and effect, without any room for the supernatural), evolutionary (the developmental axiom), humanistic (man, the final norm), or relativistic (rejection of absolutes). They must ask the Spirit who inspired the Word to illuminate, shape, and modify their pre-understandings, and to guard their understandings to remain faithful to the Word.

"Spiritually discerned" also means that the Spirit not only illuminates the mind, but also transforms the interpreter's heart. The approach of the interpreter, in both corporate and individual settings, must embrace an attitude of consent or willingness to follow what Scripture says, if we are to understand Scripture's meaning (John 7:17). There must be diligent, earnest prayer for understanding, corporate as well as private, after the example of David: "Teach me, O Lord, the way of Your statutes, And I shall observe it to the end" (Ps 119:33; cf. vv. 34–40; Prov 2:3–7). There must be an acceptance by faith of what the prophets say (2 Chr 20:20; cf. John 5:46–47).

Conclusion

The church has a God-given responsibility to interpret the Scriptures under the guidance of the Spirit. The value of the interpretation is to be determined by its adherence to the teaching of the biblical text itself. One must keep in mind that the Bible cannot be studied as any other book, coming merely "from below" with sharpened tools of exegesis and honed principles of interpretation. At every stage of the interpretive process, both by the individual interpreter and in the corporate interpretation of the church body, the Book inspired by the Spirit can only be correctly understood "from above," by the illumination and transformation of the Spirit. Perhaps the best encapsulation of the interpreter's appropriate stance, and of the collective attitude of the church, before Scripture, is the divine assessment recorded by Isaiah: "But this one I will look, To him who is humble and contrite in spirit, and who *trembles at My word*" (Isa 66:2; emphasis mine).

CHAPTER 16

THE ROLE OF ELLEN G. WHITE IN THE LIFE OF THE ADVENTIST CHURCH

Alberto R. Timm

The Seventh-day Adventist Church has recognized Ellen G. White as a genuine, non-canonical prophetess called by God to assist in the final restoration of truth at the eschatological end time. She played a crucial role in the formation of the Seventh-day Adventist Church and the definition of its mission to the world. So significant was her ecclesiological contribution that it has been suggested that "the ministry of Ellen White and the emergence of the Seventh-day Adventist Church are inseparable. To try to understand one without the other would make each unintelligible and undiscoverable."[1] Yet, her ecclesiastical leadership was "of a charismatic rather than of an administrative nature."[2]

Different aspects of Ellen White's ecclesiology are considered in some major works on her prophetic ministry.[3] Helpful insights on this subject can be found also in a few studies trying to build a Seventh-day Adventist ecclesiology[4] and in other works on the development of Seventh-day Adventist

---

[1] Herbert E. Douglass, *Messenger of the Lord: The Prophetic Ministry of Ellen G. White* (Nampa, ID: Pacific Press, 1998), 182.

[2] George R. Knight, *Meeting Ellen White: A Fresh Look at Her Life, Writings, and Major Themes* (Hagerstown, MD: Pacific Press, 1996), 61.

[3] See, e.g., Roy E. Graham, *Ellen G. White, Co-Founder of the Seventh-day Adventist Church* (New York: Peter Lang, 1985), 69–139, 223–354, 410–435; Knight, *Meeting Ellen White*, 13–87; Douglass, *Messenger of the Lord*, 133–370.

[4] See, e.g., Johannes Mager, ed., *Die Gemeinde und ihr Auftrag, Studien zur adventistischen Ekkle-*

doctrines,[5] organizational structure,[6] and missionary thought.[7] But there is still room for a more specific thematic reflection on this topic.

This paper appraises Ellen G. White's role in 1) the formation of Seventh-day Adventist doctrines and lifestyle; 2) the formation and organization of the Seventh-day Adventist Church; 3) the development of Seventh-day Adventist missiology; as well as 4) the role of her writings in the church today.

Formation of Seventh-day Adventist Doctrines and Lifestyle

The Millerite disappointment of October 22, 1844 led many Millerites to look for the reason Christ did not return as expected on that day. By studying the Scriptures, the founders of Sabbatarian Adventism discovered not only a biblical answer to the disappointment, but also many other biblical teachings overlooked by the Christian tradition. Several truths were restored and integrated into the so-called system of "present truth." Once the theoretical foundation (doctrines) of the emerging movement was established, efforts were concentrated in the development of the practical dimension of faith (lifestyle). Crucial in the whole process was the prophetic assistance of Ellen White.

---

siologie, vol. 2 (Lüneburg: Saatkorn-Verlag, 1994); Raoul Dederen, "The Church," *Handbook of Seventh-day Adventist Theology*, ed. Raoul Dederen (Hagerstown, MD: Review and Herald, 2000), 538–581; Gerald A. Klingbeil, Martin G. Klingbeil, and Miguel Ángel Núñez, ed., *Pensar la iglesia hoy: hacia una eclesiología adventista* (Libertador San Martín, Entre Ríos, Argentina: Editorial Universidad Adventista del Plata, 2002); Carmelo Martines, "El concepto de remanente en la Iglesia Adventista del Séptimo Día: razones subyacentes en el debate contemporáneo" (Th.D. diss., Universidad Adventista del Plata, Libertador San Martín, Entre Rios, Argentina, 2002).

[5] See, e.g., LeRoy E. Froom, *Movement of Destiny* (Washington, DC: Review and Herald, 1971); P. Gerard Damsteegt, *Foundations of the Seventh-day Adventist Message and Mission* (Grand Rapids, MI: Eerdmans, 1977); Alberto R. Timm, *The Sanctuary and the Three Angels' Messages: Integrating Factors in the Development of Seventh-day Adventist Doctrines* (Berrien Springs, MI: Adventist Theological Society, 1995); Rolf J. Pöhler, *Continuity and Change in Adventist Teaching* (Frankfurt am Main: Peter Lang, 2000); George R. Knight, *A Search for Identity: The Development of Seventh-day Adventist Beliefs* (Hagerstown, MD: Review and Herald, 2000).

[6] See, e.g., Andrew G. Mustard, *James White and SDA Organization: Historical Development, 1844–1881* (Berrien Springs, MI: Andrews University Press, 1987); Barry D. Oliver, *SDA Organizational Structure: Past, Present and Future* (Berrien Springs, MI: Andrews University Press, 1989); George R. Knight, *Organizing to Beat the Devil: The Development of Adventist Church Structure* (Hagerstown, MD: Review and Herald, 2001).

[7] See, e.g., *Historical Sketches of the Foreign Missions of the Seventh-day Adventists* (Basle: Imprimerie Polyglotte, 1886); Damsteegt, *Foundations*; Werner Vyhmeister, *Mision de la Iglesia Adventista* (Brasilia: Seminario Adventista Latinoamericano, 1981); Borge Schantz, "The Development of Seventh-day Adventist Missionary Thought: Contemporary Appraisal" (Ph.D. diss., Fuller Theological Seminary, 1983); George R. Knight, "From Shut Door to Worldwide Mission: The Dynamic Context of Early German Adventism," *Die Adventisten und Hamburg: Von der Ortsgemeinde zur internationalen Bewegung*, ed. Baldur Ed. Pfeiffer, Lothar E. Träder, and George R. Knight (Frankfrut am Main: Peter Lang, 1992), 46–69.

Of the overall doctrinal-lifestyle contributions Ellen White left for the church, at least four foundational elements deserve special consideration. First, she helped the church build a *solid doctrinal-lifestyle platform* based on the principle of "the Bible, and the Bible only, as the standard of all doctrines, and the basis of all reforms."[8] Seeing her own prophetic mission in terms of confirming biblical truth and reproving error, White wrote in 1851:

> I recommend to you, dear reader, the word of God as the rule of your faith and practice. By the Word we are to be judged. God has, in that Word, promised to give visions in the "LAST DAYS;" not for a new rule of faith, but for the comfort of his people, and to correct those who err from [B]ible truth.[9]

In the process of doctrinal-lifestyle formation, Seventh-day Adventist pioneers devoted themselves to a prayerful study of the Bible until reaching a general consensus on the topic under consideration. Then, Ellen White sometimes received a vision on that subject that would "reaffirm the consensus" and "help those who were still out of harmony with the majority to accept the correctness of the group's biblically derived conclusions." Thus, "we can best view Mrs. White's role in doctrinal development as confirmation rather than initiation."[10]

With many doctrinal-lifestyle components already in place, Ellen White helped the church build a *major theological framework* based on the all-encompassing Great Controversy motif (see Rev 12). The first major step in this direction was, undoubtedly, her 1858 Great Controversy vision.[11] In contrast to other previous descriptions of a spiritual conflict between good (truth) and evil (error),[12] Ellen White's vision placed obedience to God's Law and the seventh-day Sabbath at the very core of that controversy (cf. Rev 12:17; 14:6–12). Satan's continuous efforts to lead humanity away from God are clearly reflected in the Israelite idolatry,

---

[8] Ellen G. White, *The Great Controversy* (Washington, DC: Review and Herald, 1888), 595.

[9] Ellen G. White, *A Sketch of the Christian Experience and Views of Ellen G. White* (Saratoga Springs, NY: James White, 1851), 64.

[10] George R. Knight, *A Brief History of Seventh-day Adventists* (Hagerstown, MD: Review and Herald, 1999), 37.

[11] See Ellen G. White, *Spiritual Gifts*, vol. 1 (Battle Creek, MI: James White, 1858).

[12] A classical example of a nineteenth-century exposition of the non-Sabbatarian Christian view of the cosmic controversy is found in H. L. Hastings, *The Great Controversy Between God and Man: Its Origin, Progress, and End* (Rochester, NY: H. L. Hastings, 1858). This book was critically reviewed in "Book Notice," *Advent Review and Sabbath Herald*, Mar. 18, 1858, 144.

Jewish legalism, and Christian antinomianism.

The Great Controversy theme could be considered as "Ellen White's unifying principle," which "provided a coherent framework for her theological thought as well as for her principles in education, health, missiology, social issues, and environmental topics."[13] The prophetic gift she received from the Lord allowed her to illuminate many historical events not clearly understood by mere human perceptions. Behind those scenes, she saw two contending supernatural powers disputing the ground. On one side, God tries to save, through His loving grace, as many human beings from the bondages of Satan as possible. On the other side, Satan keeps the vast majority of humanity bound to sin, using a great variety of strategies to mislead. This controversy has cosmic, historical, and personal dimensions that permeate all doctrinal-lifestyle discussions.

Ellen White also encouraged Bible study from an *exegetical-systematic perspective*. The relevance of exegetical studies trying to unfold the true meaning of a passage is highlighted in the following statement from her pen:

> But there is but little benefit derived from a hasty reading of the Scriptures. One may read the whole Bible through and yet fail to see its beauty or comprehend its deep and hidden meaning. One passage studied until its significance is clear to the mind and its relation to the plan of salvation is evident, is of more value than the perusal of many chapters with no definite purpose in view and no positive instruction gained.[14]

Systematic studies of Scripture are seen by the same author as the key to discover the "beauty and harmony" of truth. She declares:

> When you search the Scriptures with an earnest desire to learn the truth, God will breathe His Spirit into your heart and impress your mind with the light of His word. The Bible is its own interpreter, one passage explaining another. By comparing scriptures referring to the same subjects, you will see beauty and harmony of which you have never dreamed. There is no other book whose perusal strengthens and enlarges, elevates and ennobles the mind, as does the perusal of this Book of books. Its study imparts new vigor to the mind, which is thus brought in contact with sub-

---

[13] Douglass, *Messenger of the Lord*, 256.

[14] Ellen G. White, *Steps to Christ* (Mountain View, CA: Pacific Press, n.d.), 90.

jects requiring earnest thought, and is drawn out in prayer to God for power to comprehend the truths revealed. If the mind is left to deal with commonplace subjects, instead of deep and difficult problems, it will become narrowed down to the standard of the matter which it contemplates and will finally lose its power of expansion.[15]

A fourth major contribution by Ellen White for the development of Seventh-day Adventist doctrines and lifestyle was her *concentric concept of theological center*. It appears that in Ellen White's all-integrated understanding of truth, the various entities she regards as theological centers are not of an isolated or self-exclusive nature, but rather complementary concentric centers that vary according to the level of broadness or narrowness of the theological perspective involved. One could regard the Great Controversy as "the grand central theme of Scripture" and the Sanctuary as the "window into the Biblical System of Truth." One could displace concentrically, from a narrower to a broader perspective, 1) the cross, 2) substitutionary atonement, 3) Christ, and 4) the plan of redemption—all regarded as theological centers.[16]

Ellen White confirms her systemic-integrative view of truth. She mentioned, for instance, that "the truth for this time is broad in its outlines, far reaching, embracing many doctrines; but these doctrines are not detached items, which mean little; they are united by golden threads, forming a complete whole, with Christ as the living center."[17] "Christ, his character and work, is the center and circumference of all truth, he is the chain upon which the jewels of doctrine are linked. In him is found the complete system of truth."[18]

Thus, Ellen White helped Seventh-day Adventism to 1) build a solid doctrinal-lifestyle biblical platform; 2) develop a major theological framework based on the Great Controversy motif; 3) study the Scriptures from an exegetical-systematic perspective; and 4) uncover a concentric concept of theological center. These four major contributions not only gave strength and coherence to the Adventist message during Ellen White's

---

[15] Ellen G. White, *Testimonies for the Church* (Mountain View, CA: Pacific Press, 1948), 4:499. See also *idem*, *Fundamentals of Christian Education* (Nashville, TN: Southern Publishing, 1923), 126–127.

[16] See R. M. Davidson, "The Grand Central Theme of Scripture" (unpublished class handout, 1996).

[17] Ellen G. White, *Selected Messages* (Washington, DC: Review and Herald, 1958), 2:87.

[18] Ellen G. White, "Contemplate Christ's Perfection, Not Man's Imperfection," *RH*, Aug. 15, 1893, 513; reprinted in *idem*, *Our High Calling* (Washington, DC: Review and Herald, 1961), 16.

own lifetime, but also provided helpful guidelines for future refinements of that message.

Formation and Organization of the Seventh-day Adventist Church

Ellen White played a crucial role in the formation and organization of the Seventh-day Adventist Church. Instead of selfishly calling attention to herself, she used her prophetic influence to unite the growing body of Sabbatarian Adventist believers around God's Word. Since the very beginning of her prophetic ministry, the divine message was far more important than the human messenger, and she tried to bring as many disappointed Millerites as possible to the emerging Sabbatarian platform of truth.

Early Sabbatarian Adventism was kept together mainly by the leadership of Joseph Bates, James White, and Ellen White as well as by the publications carrying their message. In 1854 Mrs. White's booklet titled, *Supplement to the Christian Experience and Views,* came off the press with a special section on "Gospel Order." Without prescribing any specific church organization, she challenged her fellow believers to move towards the establishment of an organizational structure. She argued:

> The Lord has shown that gospel order has been too much neglected and feared. That formality should be shunned; but in so doing, order should not be neglected. There is order in heaven. There was order in the church when Christ was upon earth; and after his departure, order was strictly observed among his apostles. And now in these last days, while God is bringing his children into the unity of the faith, there is more real need of order than ever before. For as God is uniting his children, [S]atan and his evil angels are very busy to prevent this unity, and to destroy it.[19]

Significant steps toward organization were taken in the late 1850s and early 1860s, under the prophetic guidance of Ellen White. When the plan of Systematic Benevolence was established in 1859 to finance the Sabbatarian cause, she stated, "God is leading His people in the plan of systematic benevolence, and this is one of the very points to which God is bringing up His people which will cut the closest with some."[20] When the name "Seventh-day Adventists" was adopted in 1860, she declared, "No

---

[19] Ellen G. White, *Supplement to the Christian Experience and Views of Ellen G. White* (Rochester, NY: James White, 1854), 15.

[20] White, *Testimonies for the Church,* 1:191.

name which we can take will be appropriate but that which accords with our profession and expresses our faith and marks us a peculiar people."[21] And she had no difficulty rebuking those who opposed the organizational process. In August 1861 she stated that, due to the lack of organization, "the churches in Central New York have been perfect Babylon, confusion," and unless they are "so organized that they can carry out and enforce order, they have nothing to hope for in the future."[22] Despite such challenges, the organizational process culminated with the establishment of a General Conference in May 1863.

Ellen White did not write much on church organization during that period, though that does not mean she did not play a major role in the process. From her later reminiscences, we might infer that she influenced the process more personally and orally, than literarily. In 1892 she explained,

> We had a hard struggle in establishing organization. Notwithstanding that the Lord gave testimony after testimony upon this point, the opposition was strong, and it had to be met again and again. But we knew that the Lord God of Israel was leading us, and guiding by his providence. We engaged in the work of organization, and marked prosperity attending this advance movement.... The system of organization has proved a grand success. Systematic benevolence was entered into according to the Bible plan.... As we have advanced, our system of organization has still proved effectual.... Let none entertain the thought, however, that we can dispense with organization. It has cost us much study, and many prayers for wisdom that we know God has answered, to erect this structure. It has been built up by his direction, through much sacrifice and conflict. Let none of our brethren be so deceived as to attempt to tear it down, for you will thus bring in a condition of things that you do not dream of. In the name of the Lord, I declare to you that it is to stand, strengthened, established, and settled.[23]

But in this very same document, she pointed out that in some parts of the work the machinery has been made too complicated. Especially has this been the case in the tract and missionary work; the multiplication of rules and regulations made it needlessly burdensome. An effort was to be

---

[21] White, *Testimonies for the Church*, 1:223.
[22] Ellen G. White, "Communication from Sister White," *RH*, Aug. 27, 1861, 101.
[23] Ellen G. White, quoted in *General Conference Daily Bulletin*, Jan. 29, 1893, 24.

made to simplify the work, so as to avoid needless labor and perplexity. The business of our Conference session had sometimes been burdened down with propositions and resolutions, and that would never have been presented if the sons and daughters of God had been walking carefully and prayerfully before him. The fewer rules and regulations that we can have, the better will be the effect in the end."[24]

During the 1890s, she spoke more openly about the need for a major revision of the church's organizational structure. Her own missionary experience in Australia and the South Pacific helped her understand the challenges of the mission fields and to foresee structural changes that could solve those challenges. In a special meeting at the Battle Creek College Library just before the opening of the 1901 General Conference Session, she stated to the church leaders that "new blood" should "be brought into the regular lines" and that "an entire new organization" was needed.[25] The reorganization that took place at that meeting included the creation of Union Conferences and Union Missions, the decentralization of the General Conference president's authority, auxiliary organizations became departments of the denomination's organizational structure, and a fund-sharing plan provided "a more substantial financial base for the missionary enterprise of the church."[26]

Reflecting on the organizational-structural revisions made at the 1901 General Conference Session, Mrs. White declared, "I was never more astonished in my life than at the turn things have taken at this meeting. This is not our work. God has brought it about. Instruction regarding this was presented to me, but until the sum was worked out at this meeting, I could not comprehend this instruction."[27] However, in neither the organizational process of the late 1850s and early 1860s[28] nor in the reorganizational endeavors that took place between 1888 and 1903[29] did Ellen White provide any specific model of organization. She just presented basic principles which, when implemented, helped the denomination fulfill

---

[24] Ibid.

[25] Ellen G. White, "Kingly Power," *Spalding & Magan's Unpublished Manuscript Testimonies of Ellen G. White* (Payson, AZ: Leaves-of-Autumn Books, 1975), 163.

[26] Oliver, 175; see also pp. 173–175.

[27] Ellen G. White, *General Conference Bulletin*, Apr. 25, 1901, 464.

[28] Mustard, 129, n. 1: "… at no time did Ellen G. White express herself before 1863 on the precise form of organization to be adopted."

[29] Oliver, *Structure*, 166, 169: "While she [Ellen White] often referred to broad principles of organization, she did not prescribe structures." "Consistently, it was her contention that her role related to principle rather than form. The needed structures were always a function of the principles, and in no case could that dependency be reversed."

more efficiently its double task of keeping the unity of faith and carrying the advent message to the world.

Besides her contribution to the organization and reorganization of the church, Ellen White also counseled many church leaders over the years.[30] Not everybody gladly accepted her counsels, and sometimes the final outcome was unfortunate. Much can be learned from the contrasting attitudes of General Conference Presidents George I. Butler and Arthur G. Daniells. Butler did not attend the 1888 Minneapolis General Conference Session, but his warnings against the teachings of justification by faith helped to nourish the polemic and divisive spirit of that conference. On the other hand, Daniells' acceptance and implementation of Mrs. White's advice brought to the 1901 Battle Creek General Conference Session an overall tenor of unity and improvement. The difference between both occasions was not merely a matter of attitude about personal opinions, but rather the acceptance or rejection of divine counsels communicated by a prophetic voice (cf. 2 Chr 20:20; Luke 10:16). Although such counsels were given to specific people living in a world different than ours, they are grounded on universal principles applicable to all subsequent generations of church leaders.

Ellen White assured her fellow believers that the Seventh-day Adventist Church, although militant and faulty, would never apostatize to the point of having to be replaced by some other "holier" church or independent movement. She stated in the 1890s that "God has a church upon the earth who are His chosen people, who keep His commandments. He is leading, not stray offshoots, not one here and one there, but a people."[31]

> There is no need to doubt, to be fearful that the work will not succeed. God is at the head of the work, and he will set everything in order. If matters need adjusting at the head of the work, God will attend to that, and work to right every wrong. Let us have faith that God is going to carry the noble ship which bears the people of God safely into port.[32]

Thus, the formation and consolidation of the Seventh-day Adventist message and organizational structure gave the denomination conditions

---

[30] Some of Ellen G. White's most important counsels on organizational and local church leadership are found in her books *Gospel Workers* (Washington, DC: Review & Herald, 1915); *Testimonies for Ministers and Gospel Workers* (Mountain View, CA: Pacific Press, 1923); *Christian Leadership* (Washington, DC: Ellen G. White Estate, 1985); *Pastoral Ministry* (Silver Spring, MD: Ministerial Association of the General Conference of Seventh-day Adventists, 1995).

[31] White, *Testimonies to Ministers and Gospel Workers*, 61.

[32] E. G. White, "Walk Not in Darkness," *RH*, Sept. 20, 1892, 594.

to expand its outreach program. Ellen White was the key figure in transforming the Seventh-day Adventist Church from a small New England and New York movement into a worldwide missionary denomination.

Development of Seventh-day Adventist Missiology

The mission of the Seventh-day Adventist Church has been shaped largely by the theological-practical contribution of Ellen White. On the *theological* level, her missiological thinking was the convergence and interplay of three basic concepts. One is that God's saving grace is universally accessible to all sincere Christians and even non-Christians who live according to the light available to them (see Rom 2:14).[33] She explained:

> Our standing before God depends, not upon the amount of light we have received, but upon the use we make of what we have. Thus even the heathen who choose the right as far as they can distinguish it are in a more favorable condition than are those who have had great light, and profess to serve God, but who disregard the light, and by their daily life contradict their profession.[34]

> Those whom Christ commends in the judgment may have known little of theology, but they have cherished His principles. Through the influence of the divine Spirit they have been a blessing to those about them. Even among the heathen are those who have cherished the spirit of kindness; before the words of life had fallen upon their ears, they have befriended the missionaries, even ministering to them at the peril of their own lives. Among the heathen are those who worship God ignorantly, those to whom the light is never brought by human instrumentality, yet they will not perish. Though ignorant of the written law of God, they have heard His voice speaking to them in nature, and have done the things that the law required. Their works are evidence that the Holy Spirit has touched their hearts, and they are recognized as the children of God.[35]

---

[33] Some of Ellen White's most meaningful statements on the salvation of the Gentiles to whom the gospel was never preached are found in her books *Desire of Ages* (Mountain View, CA: Pacific Press, 1898), 238–239, 638; *Christ's Object Lessons* (Battle Creek, MI: Review and Herald, 1900), 385–386; *Education* (Mountain View, CA: Pacific Press, 1903), 28–29, 262–263; and *The Story of Prophets and Kings* (Mountain View, CA: Pacific Press, 1917), 376–378. See Ángel M. Rodríguez, in this volume.

[34] White, *Desire of Ages*, 239.

[35] Ibid., 638.

Another basic theological and missiological concept is that all children of God are responsible for sharing the light they receive with others. Reflecting on the experience of the Samaritan woman (John 4:1–42), White argues:

> Every true disciple is born into the kingdom of God as a missionary. He who drinks of the living water becomes a fountain of life. The receiver becomes a giver. The grace of Christ in the soul is like a spring in the desert, welling up to refresh all, and making those who are ready to perish eager to drink of the water of life.[36]

A third basic concept is that the Seventh-day Adventist Church is God's end-time remnant church with the prophetic mission of restoring and preaching all biblical truths to the entire world (see Matt 4:4; 24:14; 28:18–20; John 16:13; Rev 14:6–12). She declares:

> In a special sense Seventh-day Adventists have been set in the world as watchmen and light bearers. To them has been entrusted the last warning for a perishing world. On them is shining wonderful light from the word of God. They have been given a work of the most solemn import – the proclamation of the first, second, and third angels' messages. There is no other work of so great importance. They are to allow nothing else to absorb their attention.
>
> The most solemn truths ever entrusted to mortals have been given us to proclaim to the world. The proclamation of these truths is to be our work. The world is to be warned, and God's people are to be true to the trust committed to them.[37]

By interrelating these basic concepts, one might conclude that although God's saving grace is available to all humanity, it becomes effective only for those who follow, with integrity of heart, the light they receive from Him. However, God's ideal for human beings is not that they remain in ignorance, but rather that "the earth shall be full of the knowledge of the Lord, as the waters cover the sea" (Isa 11:9). While other Christians might help to restore some biblical teachings, the Seventh-day Adventist Church was called into existence by God as an end-time prophetic move-

---

[36] Ibid., 195.

[37] White, *Testimonies for the Church*, 9:19.

ment with the mission of restoring biblical truth as a whole, in preparation for the Second Coming of Christ. This particular *theological* conviction moved Ellen White to motivate church leaders at the *practical* level to expand missionary outreach program over the years.

After the October 1844 Millerite disappointment, many "shut-door" Adventists (cf. Matt 25:10–12), including Ellen White, believed that their mission to the world was already fulfilled and that there was no reason to preach the Adventist message outside the ex-Millerite circles for Christ would come very soon. But in that context, she received some visions describing the preaching of the Seventh-day Adventist message in a worldwide scope. For example, on November 18, 1848, she saw the spreading of Seventh-day Adventist publications "like streams of light that went clear round the world."[38] On July 29, 1850, she received a vision showing that "others who had not heard the Advent doctrine and rejected it would embrace the truth."[39]

But far beyond the mere expansion of the Adventist presence within North America, White foresaw and encouraged increasing the number of missionaries overseas. Church leaders' failure to support the Polish minister M. B. Czechowski's missionary move back to Europe in 1864 was not rebuked by Mrs. White because she knew of his financial problems and temperament instabilities.[40] In 1866, the leadership refused to send the newly-converted missionary, Hannah More, to Africa. In 1875, nine years after More's death, Mrs. White declared with deep sorrow,

> Already a great deal of time has been wasted, and angels bear to heaven the record of our neglects. Our sleepy and unconsecrated condition has lost to us precious opportunities which God has sent us in the persons of those who were qualified to help us in our present need. Oh, how much we need our Hannah More to aid us at this time in reaching other nations! Her extensive knowledge of missionary fields would give us access to those of other tongues whom we cannot now approach. God brought this gift among us to meet our present emergency; but we prized not the gift, and He took her from us. She is at rest from her labors, but

---

[38] Ellen G. White, *Christian Experience & Teachings of Ellen G. White* (Mountain View, CA: Pacific Press, 1922), 128.

[39] Ellen G. White, "A Vision the Lord Gave Me at Oswego [N.Y.]," Ms 5, 1850, published in *Manuscript Releases* (Silver Spring, MD: Ellen G. White Estate, 1993), 18:13.

[40] See K. F. Mueller, "Ellen G. White and M. B. Czechowski," *Michael Belina Czechowski, 1818–1876*, ed. Rajmund L. Dabrowski (Warsaw, Poland: Znaki Czasu, 1979), 360–405 (even pages in English).

her self-denying works follow her. It is to be deplored that our missionary work should be retarded for the want of knowledge how to gain access to the different nations and localities in the great harvest field.[41]

Finally, in 1874, the church sent John N. Andrews to Europe as its first official overseas missionary. Writing to the brethren in Switzerland, not initially supportive of his journey, Ellen White stated, "We sent you the ablest man in all our ranks; but you have not appreciated the sacrifice we made in thus doing. We needed Elder Andrews here. But we thought his great caution, his experience, his God-fearing dignity in the desk, would be just what you needed."[42] This reflects Ellen White's deep conviction for mission outreach. She felt so strongly about this that she set the example by leaving her home country to serve two years in Europe (1885–1887) and almost ten years in Australia and the South Pacific (1891–1900).

By the end of the 19th century there was already an Adventist presence in all continents of the world. But for Ellen White, church leaders were still too narrow-minded in their missionary plans. So at the 1901 Battle Creek General Conference Session, she gave a powerful speech entitled, "In the Regions Beyond," in which she spoke directly to the point,

> I told the Lord that when I came to Battle Creek this time, I would ask you why you have withheld means from the work in Australia. The work there should have been pressed with ten fold greater strength than it has been, but we have been hindered on the right hand and on the left.... Why am I telling you this? Because we desire that at this meeting the work shall be so established that no such thing shall take place again. Two or three men, who have never seen the barren fields where the workers have had to wrestle with all their might to advance an inch, should not control matters....
>
> There are many barren places in America, many places that have not been worked. What is the matter with the church here? It is congested. This is the reason why there is so little of the deep moving of the Spirit of God. There is a world perishing in sin, and again and again the message has come to Battle Creek, God wants

---

[41] Ellen G. White, *Testimonies for the Church*, 3:407–408.

[42] Ellen G. White, To "Dear Brethren in Switzerland," Aug. 29, 1878, published in *Manuscript Releases*, 16:324.

> you to move out into places where you can labor for the salvation of souls. . . .
>
> The people in Battle Creek are dying of inaction. What they need is to impart the truth which they believe. Every soul who will impart will receive from God more power to impart. This is what we are in the world for – to bring souls to a knowledge of the truth as it is in Jesus. Before the way is hedged up, it is for every one to realize his accountability to proclaim the message that God has given him. . . . The work is one. Do not think that because you are here in Battle Creek, God is not supervising the work in any other parts of the field. The world is the field; the world is the vineyard; and every spot must be worked. God desires every soul to put on the harness.[43]

In addition to her role in the formation of Seventh-day Adventist doctrines-lifestyle and in the organization and reorganization of the Church, Ellen was also the driving ideologist and champion of worldwide mission service. So, how relevant is her advice in these areas for the church today?

The Role of Ellen G. White Writings in the Church Today

The prophetic ministry of Ellen White is as important for the church today as it was in the formative years of the denomination. Her long-term prophetic ministry brought significant doctrinal, administrative, and lifestyle stability to the Seventh-day Adventist Church. After her death in 1915, her writings have continued to provide the same stability for the denomination. In 1907 she stated,

> Abundant light has been given to our people in these last days. Whether or not my life is spared, my writings will constantly speak, and their work will go forward as long as time shall last. My writings are kept on file in the office, and even though I should not live, these words that have been given to me by the Lord will still have life and will speak to the people.[44]

In the early days of Sabbatarian Adventism, she provided significant prophetic assistance to the end-time *restoration* of biblical truths. Today, her writings are needed to help contemporary believers *persevere* in the

---

[43] Ellen G. White, "In the Regions Beyond," *General Conference Bulletin*, Apr. 5, 1901, 84–86.
[44] White, *Selected Messages*, 1:55.

already-restored biblical faith. In both restoration and perseverance, Ellen White's writings have served "three basic purposes: 1) to direct attention to the Bible, 2) to aid in understanding the Bible, and 3) to help in applying Bible principles in our lives."[45] At any rate, those writings are not intended to replace the Bible, but rather to free its interpretation from the large amount of anti-biblical traditions accumulated over the centuries.

The need of a prophetic assistance for us to persevere in the faith comes from the fact that all religious movements tend to lose over the years their early restorationist commitment. Such movements are usually launched with the purpose of reforming culture. But in the second century of their existence, after the pioneers and those who knew them passed away, those very same movements tend to lose their own identity and to be reabsorbed by the same culture they originally intended to reform.[46] The original message and lifestyle of the movement are reread into a new cultural setting and end up losing much of their prophetic meaning. The acculturation process obfuscates the ability to distinguish between the holy and the profane.

Seventh-day Adventism came into existence as an end-time restorationist movement, but it is not invulnerable to the threat of losing its identity. That risk can be minimized and even overcome by unconditional commitment to the same prophetic guidance that assisted the rise and early development of the movement. Proverbs 29:18 (RSV) warns: "Where there is no prophecy the people cast off restraint." The word "prophecy" stands here for the Hebrew *chazon*, which actually means a "prophetic vision." Underlying this statement is the foundational principle that whenever God's people disregard genuine prophetic revelations, they are susceptible to unbiblical ideologies of contemporary cultures (cf. 2 Chr 36:11–16). Conversely, the acceptance of God's true prophets helps believers to overcome anti-biblical cultural temptations (see 2 Chr 20:20).

The stability fostered by Ellen White's writings can be distorted whenever the interpreter does not clearly distinguish universal principles from the temporal applications of those principles. The difficulty is largely caused by the fact that those writings are frequently interpreted just from the perspective of the contexts in which they were penned and to which they were addressed, leaving the interpretation too open to the subjective views of the interpreter. Any serious interpretation should

---

[45] T. Housel Jemison, *A Prophet Among You* (Boise, ID: Pacific Press, 1955), 371.

[46] Alberto R. Timm, "Podemos ainda ser considerados o 'povo da Bíblia'?" *Revista Adventista* (Brazil), June 2001, 14.

consider not only such contexts but also the interaction of those writings with the whole content of the Scriptures. While contextual knowledge helps one to better understand her temporal applications, the interaction with Scripture helps to more precisely identify the universal principles that flow throughout her writings.

Conclusion

The Seventh-day Adventist Church has been shaped by Ellen White's prophetic guidance. In the formation of its message, she helped the church build a solid doctrinal-lifestyle biblical platform, develop a major theological framework based on the Great Controversy motif, study the Scriptures from an exegetical-systematic perspective, and uncover a concentric concept of theological center. The full meaning of these concepts can be better understood by a more comprehensive study of her writings.

The formation and organization of the Seventh-day Adventist Church was assisted by Ellen White's personal, charismatic leadership; then, by her efforts to convince her fellow believers to develop a church organization; later on, by her appeals and advice in the process of reorganizing the structure of the church; and through her counsels to the leadership of the church.

With a defined message to preach and an organization to facilitate that task, the Seventh-day Adventist Church began to expand its outreach program. Ellen White played a major role in this process. She helped build a missionary awareness and concentrated her efforts in convincing church leaders to send an increasing number of missionaries overseas. As part of the endeavor, she went as a missionary to Europe and the South Pacific. She never tired of preaching the Adventist message to the entire world.

Ellen White's prophetic legacy in these areas will be more helpful to those who are able to identify in her writings a constant dialogue between universal principles and cultural applications of those principles. While the cultural contexts might vary significantly, the principles involved are applicable to all times and cultures, and are still relevant for the church today. More likely, the Seventh-day Adventist Church will be able to preserve its prophetic identity only by remaining loyal to the prophetic voice that personally guided the denomination during the first seven decades of its history.

CHAPTER 17

Adventist Mission Among World Religions: Some Theological Foundations

Ganoune Diop

There is a need for biblically-based mission in our interaction with other world religions. This goes beyond the confines of interfaith dialogue, community services, or humanitarian assistance. Ecumenical validations of various paths to God are increasingly present in popular discourse. For the sake of clarity, there is an urgent need to delineate, as accurately as possible, the rationale for the beliefs of world faiths in light of biblical revelation. Protology, soteriology, and eschatology play a significant role in this process.

The Adventist message points back to creation, and forward to the Second Coming when the world will be recreated in justice, righteousness, and peace. The creation story provides a frame of reference by which we can assess cosmogonies developed in world religions. Biblical eschatology could also be used to evaluate their convictions of the end. In the realm of ethics, there is much to be commended in people of other faiths. However, in reference to protology, eschatology, soteriology, and theology, the differences are too far apart to be ignored.

There is a difference between respecting and loving people of other faiths and validating or endorsing beliefs, values, and practices in conflict with biblical truth. Considering other world religions' cosmogonies and cosmologies, their eschatology and ultimate goals give us perspective into their worldviews. It helps us understand the underlying logic of their problems, values, taboos, goals, and culture. Love, respect, discernment, and tact are essential in the interaction with members of other faiths. The outcome of interfaith relations and mission depends on this awareness.

The Uniqueness of the Biblical Narrative

The three angels' messages entrusted to Adventists uniquely capture the various components of the biblical message (Rev 14:6–12). These messages connect protology with eschatology in significant ways. The hour of judgment calls for the worship of the Creator of heaven and earth. The great controversy, the righteousness by faith in Jesus Christ, and the Second Coming are all within these messages. They constitute God's last call for unswerving allegiance in the last days.

Protology, Soteriology, and Eschatology

The biblical creation story is only properly understood in light of the covenant between God and humanity, and between God and Israel. This covenant and the implication of a personal God who freely chooses to reveal and engage His faithfulness, is unique to the biblical record. Consistent with the overarching goal of Scripture to reveal God, the biblical creation story is inseparable from the revelation of the triune God—Father, Son, and Holy Spirit. The Father, The Word, and the Spirit acted in creation as well as redemption. This perspective is unique to the Bible. "In the beginning God created the heavens and the earth" (Gen 1:1) echoes the revelation that "in the beginning was the Word" and "through him all things were made" (John 1:1a, 3a). The Spirit that brings new life, the life of God, the love of God, and the fellowship of God was active at creation (Gen 1:2). He is also active in recreation. The new spiritual birth is not biblically conceivable without the Spirit (John 3:5).

The account of the intrusion, the reality of evil, and the great controversy show the scope of the human predicament—humanity's problems and deliverance. They are fundamentally evil, sin, curse, and death. All the ills listed in the first chapters of the Bible are symptoms of this condition: fear, hiding, shame, guilt, suffering, violence, murder, exile, and separation from God. The atonement, an integral part of reconciliation and restoration of God's cosmic sovereignty, reveals a trajectory unique to the biblical faith. Redemption from sin, the curse, death, Satan, and evil through Christ's atonal sacrifice at the cross and ministry in the heavenly Sanctuary gives a perspective found only in the Bible.

Christ's atoning and substitutionary sacrifice on the cross was not just a life offered for the world; it also inaugurated the end of a lost world. The signs of the times signaling the coming of the last days of world history and the consummation of the history of salvation in the Second Com-

The Overarching Storyline

The Bible portrays the beginning and the end of a cosmic drama, with human beings as the climax of God's creation. The story moves from perfection, harmony, and fellowship to the tragedy of separation, expulsion, and exile. We then find reunion and the consummation of world history at the Second Coming of Jesus Christ. Besides Buddhism, which denies altogether the concept of beginning and end in favor of a perpetual cycle of aeons,[1] the beginning and ending of world stories, as depicted in other world religions, fundamentally differ from the biblical account. We will focus on Islam's articulation of protology, eschatology, and cosmic conflict as they shape both biblical and Islamic faith, worship, goals, and hopes.

The following assumptions have informed our approach: Each religion is a unique world of thoughts irreducible to common grounds with other religions and philosophies. While building bridges of understanding, it is advisable to establish a good rapport with one's neighbors and respect and honor the dignity of every human being. But uncritical generalizations of commonalities between world religions and philosophies should be avoided because they tend to dumb down the claims of Jesus Christ. Moreover, they do not do justice to the claims of each world religion and philosophy either.

Fundamental Differences in the Storyline

It is important to develop a critical awareness of the irreconcilable trajectories of thinking between biblical Christianity and other world religions. Even in the area of ethics, where much communality can be found, the foundation and justification for biblical ethical principles are rooted in different values. The foundation for biblical ethics is God Himself: His character and righteousness. This is unique. The sanctity of every human life, because it is created in God's image, is endowed with unparalleled dignity in the created order. The love owed to everyone, even an enemy, the celebration of the Sabbath, are all grounded on God's being and His acts. The Christian is called to bring every thought in captive obedience to Jesus Christ. Everything, therefore, is measured on the basis of its conformity to the model provided in Jesus Christ.

---

[1] According to Buddhists, our present existence is one cycle characterized by formation, evolution, dissolution, and destruction. Another way to account for this is that there is no beginning. The end will be another beginning. It is a perpetual cycle.

Since the foundation of ethics and worldviews differ among religions, one must deconstruct popular beliefs or assumptions of similarities between them. If, for example, one assumes Abraham is a common figure among monotheistic religions, such a shortcut deprives each monotheistic tradition of its unique perspective. The figure and functions of Abraham vary in detail for reasons and purposes specific to each monotheistic religion. Labeling all monotheistic religions as religions of the book is not very helpful either, because each one of them defines divine revelation and its content from different perspectives. Strictly speaking, Christianity is not a religion of a book, but of a Person—Jesus Christ. It is subversive of the very idea of religion as the means to gain access to the divine being. Access to God became a reality in Jesus Christ. God came and dwelt among human beings. Furthermore, He indwells believers in Jesus Christ through His Holy Spirit.

Even to postulate that Jesus Christ is a figure common to Christians and Muslims creates difficult interpretive issues. For Christians, who worship Jesus, recognizing people of other faiths claim to respect Jesus while carefully stripping Him of any allusion to His divine identity creates uneasiness in reference to the legitimacy of the path they offer. Even the assumption that theological or ecclesiological concepts can be used and applied to people of other faiths without critical thinking, may present some pitfalls. Words extracted from their biblical roots and contexts and placed in new setting can create new semantic trajectories that depart from their intentions. This cannot form the basis of intelligent interfaith relations.

Careful contextual studies provide safeguards against the distortion of meaning and significance. Blending belief systems creates entirely new systems depriving each of its uniqueness and coherence. Moreover, syncretistic models of interfaith relations are exclusivist in their claims. At their core they betray the faith of Jesus Christ, which no religious wineskin can contain.

Genuine respect for members of other religions, therefore, requires allowing them to define their religions on their own terms. Authentic dialogue takes place on the platform of openness. Significant contributions from a Jewish world of thought have considerably enriched such conversation.[2] Honesty in relating to people of other faith traditions is the best platform for genuine encounters. And faithfulness to the content of biblical revelation is a safeguard against syncretistic alliances.

---

[2] Jonathan Sacks, *To Heal a Fractured World: The Ethics of Responsibility* (New York: Continuum, 2005), 32.

The world religions considered in this paper provide accounts of creation and the end of the world at variance with the Bible. At times, there are similarities in vocabulary. But, they are isolated threads from various narratives and differ in content. When stories contradict each other, as is the case with the denial in Islamic circles of the divinity of Jesus Christ, His incarnation, death, and resurrection, there is no hesitation to postulate the corruption and abrogation of previous Scriptures. This obviously seems, at first, a convenient way to account for the differences in content. Most Muslims position themselves against the authenticity and veracity of the Bible. An example of this is the belief that Jews and Christians misunderstand their own prophets and Scriptures. Muslim tradition maintains that Jesus comes to judge and correct the misunderstanding about His nature and teachings.

Because the causes for the human predicament are diverse, so are the solutions. In the prevailing struggle against evil, Christianity has but one response: the need for God, the only Lord and Savior. The logic of the Christian faith is entirely based on the fact that it takes God to be a Savior. Only God, in His incomparable sovereignty, possesses intrinsic immortality and can master time, space, matter, and energy. He alone has access to the whole of reality. Because nothing is able to restrain or constrain His movement, God is able to deliver humans from predicaments generated by a sinful human existence.

Overarching Findings

Throughout history, there is a gradual devolution of biblical truth. God's antidote to reverse this religious and spiritual entropy is special revelation. God has revealed the Bible through His chosen prophets to correct and redirect religious trajectories. As the Bible is the measure of conformity to God's truth, Jesus is the absolute criterion to God's will and character. The truth of creation provides a solid ground for truth of the Second Coming of the Creator. He comes to recover His creation.

In reference to salvation, the options are the following: Extinction or survival, submission or fellowship? That is the question. World religions have their own stories of the beginning and end of the world. These narratives reflect the distinct characteristics, claims, and aims of each world religion. These stories are articulated differently, based on core beliefs and needs of that particular faith.

Hinduism focuses on deliverance, fusion, and infinite divine bliss. In this religious tradition, the need for salvation and for a savior allows for the idea of incarnation connected to a cosmic conflict.[3]

---

[3] In the Bhagavad Gita, 4:7–8, Krishna says: "When righteousness is weak and faints, and un-

Buddhism is framed in terms of compassion, harmlessness, and awakening from illusion to extinction.

Islam's story centers around divine sovereignty in terms of power, greatness, and submission. We will now look more specifically at the metanarrative of Islam, its view of protology, eschatology, and the conflict that perpetuates the reality of evil.

Case Study: Islam

Protology in Islam: Pre-Historic Covenant

In reference to protology, the main function of the Qur'anic creation narrative is to assert that Islam is the natural religion of all human beings. The story of origins does not place an emphasis on the depravity of human nature, but rather on its perfection, which has been forgotten and buried under layers of negligence. This explains the need for two of the core values in Islam—remembrance and diligence to perform worship.

A major aspect of protology that helps us understand Islamic faith is the pre-historic covenant that God made with the human race, in which future descendants of Adam pledge to be Muslims. This covenant occurred before the actual creation. The traditional belief is that in pre-eternity (*azal*), before the creation of the bodies, God caused human beings to testify about His sovereignty.[4] In Surah 7:172

> And when thy Lord brought forth from the children of Adam, from their loins, their descendants and made them bear witness about themselves: Am I not your Lord? They said: Yes, we bear witness. Lest you should say on the day of Resurrection: We were unaware of this.

The "call" (*al-da'wa*) of Islam received and accepted, fundamentally aimed at vivifying the memory of this *mithaq* (covenant). The core concept of

---

righteousness exults in pride, then I come to earth. For the salvation of those who are good, for the destruction of evil in men, for the fulfillment of the kingdom of righteousness, I come to this world in the ages that pass." The themes of incarnation, cosmic struggle, the need to preserve righteousness and salvation, are all mentioned in this passage as central beliefs in Hinduism. Krishna is considered an avatar or descent of Vishnu who has incarnated nine times: "The first three were in the form of animals who saved the world, then came a half-lion and half-man, and a dwarf. The remainder included Rama, Krishna and the Buddha. One Kalkin is yet to come." He concludes: "This teaching about god descending into living forms to rescue the world in times of crisis is superficially like the Christian doctrine of the incarnation but the differences are more important than the similarities. It is easy to see how Jesus could be incorporated into such a scheme and so misunderstood."

[4] Louis Gardet, *L'Islam: Religion et communauté* (Paris: Desclée de Brouwer, 2002), 33.

"Shahada" that expresses the first pillar of Islam is connected to this primordial testimony.

This Quranic discourse about protology is characterized by an attempt to make a case for the natural disposition of all humanity toward Islam. The primordial covenant between God and humanity is framed in a form of theodicy. Its purpose is to make manifest that human beings are inexcusable if they are not Muslims. Islam is their true nature, the fitrah, the true nature with which humans were created (Q. 30:30)

> The human caliphate began when the first couple and the disobedient jinn descended to earth. The souls of the children of Adam and his wife, that is all subsequent persons, are questioned by God before their birth as to whether they confessed that God was the Lord who gave them life. The souls, apparently invariably, confessed and thereby entered into a general covenant with their Creator: When thy Lord drew forth from the children of Adam from their loins their descendants and made them testify concerning themselves (saying): "Am I not your Lord (who cherishes and sustains you)? They said: "Yea! We do testify! (This) lest ye should say on the Day of Judgment: 'Of this we were never mindful' (Surah 7:172). Every individual in every time and place, therefore, is oriented and accountable to the One-Only God. In other words, humans are naturally disposed towards Islam.[5]

These concepts of natural religion, the religion of the Hanif, are the reasons Muslims place themselves on a trajectory that bypasses the need for a savior and for atonement. The coming of the Messiah and the understanding of righteousness, without which, according to Jesus, no one will enter the kingdom, are also transferred to another web of meaning and significance.

The revelation of sin as deep-seated antagonism against God's sovereignty and the fatal consequences it generated in human nature should not be overlooked. According to the biblical narrative, this depravity in human nature and its symptoms are not curable through rites and rituals, not even through remembrance or obedience. Jesus was unequivocal about the need to be born again to see and be in the kingdom of God. From a biblical perspective, it is only through death and new birth to a new life—the divine gift of life lived in complete reverence to God and in

---

[5] Walter H. Wagner, *Opening the Qur'an: Introducing Islam's Holy Book* (Notre Dame, IN: University of Notre Dame Press, 2009), 65.

gratitude to His gift of eternal life—that salvation is articulated.

Protology in Islam: Satan's Refusal to Prostrate Before Adam

According to the Qur'an, when God created Adam, He presented him to the angels and asked them to prostrate themselves (Surah 15:26–44). They all did it, except Iblis, leader of the Jinn, known as Shaitan. He refused, disobeying and defying God. The controversy that follows in this passage focuses on Satan vowing to cause human beings to deviate from obeying God. God told Satan (v. 42 of the same surah) that He has no authority over His servants but only upon those who follow him.

God forewarned Adam that Satan is their enemy and would try to deceive him. But, all they would need is God's guidance. He promised: "There will surely come to you guidance from Me, then whoever follows My guidance, he will not go astray nor be unhappy And whoever turns away from My Reminder, for him is surely a straitened life, and We shall raise him up blind on the day of Resurrection" (Q. 20:123). The story of the conflict between God and Satan in the Qur'an is at variance with the biblical account. The book of Hebrews, referring to the incarnation of the Son of God, specified that "when God brings his firstborn into the world, he says, 'Let all God's angels worship him'" (Heb 1:6).

The Qur'anic rendering of the great controversy is inseparably connected to the logic of the religion of Islam, especially in reference to prayer and worship.

> To the present time, when Muslims gather in prayer throughout the world, facing towards the Ka'aba and circumambulating it on the great pilgrimage of the Hajj, they believe themselves to be performing the eternal rite of prostration and worship performed by the heavenly hosts. Final victory over Shaitan will come when all human beings join in true obeisance to the Creator by circumambulation of the Ka'aba in the final days. Thus a cosmic struggle ensued: a fight for the heart of the human being. On one side, there is the "respited" Iblis, freed from the confines of death, allowed to retain his great power and ability until the battle is ended. On the other side, there is Allah, who in his mercy sends assistance to human beings through revelation; a clear reminder of the "straight path" that leads back to him.[6]

The Qur'anic version of the story is consistent with the Islamic world-

---

[6] Ron Geaves, *Islam Today* (London: Continuum International, 2010), 3.

view, theology, hamartiology, and soteriology. In Islamic perspective, there is no need for atonement. Adam erred; hence, the temptation for humans is to err. What is needed, therefore, is guidance, obedience to divine stipulations recorded in the Qur'an, and the worship of the only God, Allah. The promise of guidance is what Islam is about. The Qur'an is called such a guidance (Q. 2:1). This role of the Qur'an has decisive bearings upon Islamic eschatology.

Eschatology in Islam

Major themes of biblical eschatology are found in Islam. According to Muslim traditions, before the end of time there will be global chaos and apostasy. Unique events will occur, battles will be fought, antichrists will be manifested, the Mahdi will bring justice, and the Christ will descend to earth.

Cosmic Signs

The Qur'an occasionally mentions end-time catastrophes. The trumpet will sound and there will be signs in the natural order: the sky ripped apart, the earth leveled out, the mountains raised high and then crushed in one stroke (Q. 69:13-16; 84:1-5). The skies will be rolled up as a writer rolls up his scrolls, the sun shrouded in darkness, the stars dimmed, and the seas boiled over (70:8-9; 52:9-10; 50:44, 21:104; 81:1-2, 81:6). The response of unbelievers is repeated several times to heighten the urgency to heed the warning of the prophet of Islam. The literature devoted to the signs that precede the last days of the world are numerous. There are 143 hadiths devoted to the last days of the world. Ten among them are considered major signs occurring in chronological order.

> First there will be three entombments (*khasf*), which is to say three places—in the east, in the west, and in the Arabian Peninsula—where the earth will open up and people will be buried alive. These events will be followed by the appearance of smoke, and then the Antichrist. The Beast will then crawl out of the earth, followed by Gog and Magog, who will break through the wall that isolates them from the civilized world and run wild. The three last signs will be the rising of the sun in the west, the supernatural fire originating in Yemen, finally the gathering of humanity driven by the fire to the place of the Final Judgment.[7]

---

[7] Jean-Pierre Filiu, *Apocalypse in Islam* (Berkeley, CA: University of California Press, 2011), 15.

The Antichrists

Specifically, Islamic sources announce the appearance of more than thirty Dajjals (antichrists); two of these antichrists are connected to end-time issues. Muslim traditions speak about two antichrists: one designated as Dajjal, who will appear in the non-Muslim world; and the other as Sufyan, who will appear in the Muslim world and struggle against Islam. According to Islamic sources, the Dajjal will claim divinity and people will worship him.

Mahdi and the Messiah

Shia Muslims give special emphasis to the figure of the Mahdi whom they believe is the "hidden Imam," the twelfth and last Imam. Some Muslims, such as Fethulah Gullen, think that the Mahdi is actually a corporate phenomenon, a global Islamic revival. Muslims, who identify the Mahdi as a human being, postulate that Jesus will descend to the world, cooperate with the Mahdi and follow him. The belief in the coming of an eschatological leader who will guide the Muslim community is also present in popular Sunni Islam.

> The whole of Islam wait for the coming of a ultimate guide of the community, who will lead it into the straight path, his reign of justice will prepare the annihilation, the resurrection and the judgment, *fana'*, *qiyama*, and *din*. For some it will be Muhammad himself, for others (a significant number) Jesus, for others al-khidr, the companion who did the initiation of Moses the prophet. For the Shia`, it will be `Ali or one of his descendants.[8]

In popular Islam, the coming of the Mahdi will restore the caliphate and lead the whole world into Islam.

Death of the Messiah at the End of time

The dominant Islamic tradition teaches that Jesus did not die on the Cross.
Q. 4:157–159:

> That they said (in boast), "We killed Christ Jesus the son of Mary, the Messenger of Allah but they killed him not, nor crucified him, but so it was made to appear to them, and those who differ therein are full of doubts, with no knowledge but only conjecture to follow. For a surety, they killed him not. Nay, Allah raised him up

---

[8] Louis Gardet, *L'Islam: Religion et Communauté* (Paris: Desclée de Brouwer, 2002), 162.

unto Himself; and Allah is exalted in power, wise. And there is none of the people of the book but must believe in him before his death and on the Day of Judgment He will be a witness against them."

The belief is that when Jesus comes back at the end of time, He will taste death Himself before the day of the resurrection, the last day.

Gog and Magog

The Qur'an 18:94–98 and 21:94 mention entities designated as Gog and Magog. There is no consensus among Muslim interpreters as to their identifications. Some find here an allusion to a major end-time battle, initiated by invading forces to overcome the Muslim world just as it had occurred in the 13th century.[9]

Interrogating Angels

Vivid in the consciousness of popular Islam is the belief that at death, in the tomb, two angels named Munkar and Nakir interrogate the dead. Islamic traditions add that believers who have not sinned will meet two other angels, Mubashshar and Bashir. Since no one can claim a sinless life, these beliefs tend to nurture fear among Muslims.

Islam and Christianity: Shared Values and Irreducible Differences

Between a hostile attitude toward Islam and a naive, uncritical endorsement of unchecked so-called similarities based on presumed universal values, there is room for a more lucid and honest understanding of both common grounds and irreducible differences between Islam and Christianity. Values and beliefs that especially resonate with Adventism are in the Mekkan chapters (surahs) of the Qur'an that focus on the following themes: call to purification, fear of God, charity, perseverance; challenge of paganism through persuasion and affirmation of the belief in the resurrection, the omnipotence of God, and the threat destined to all who refuse God's messages. Some texts on prayer and exhortation to patiently wait on God are moving too.

However, Adventists have difficulty identifying themselves with the last part of the carrier of the prophet Muhammad, when he migrated to Medina in 622. There, the legislative and military components of his message were added to his status of warner about the Day of Judgment. After his death, the conquests for the expansion of Muslim territories posed a formidable dissonance with Jesus' pacifistic stand.

---

[9] Said Nursi, Sualar (The Rays,), "The Fifth Rays," 574, cited in Ali Unal, *Introduction*, 125.

In Mecca

Muhammad initiated a religious movement that changed the face of seventh century Arabia and the world since. Initially,
- He was a warner, a reminder, and a religious reformer.
- He was in the minority.
- He was persecuted.
- He was a sufferer.
- His message was directed against the idolaters of Mecca.
  - He preached monadic monotheism; social ethic; accountability; impending judgment carried out in the last days of life on earth, culminating in the reward of the righteous, paradise, and the damnation of unbelievers and idolaters.
  - Also in Mecca, as long as his wife Khadija lived, he was the husband of one wife.

In Medina

- He became part of the majority.
- He built a state religion, later to become an empire, and a succession of dynasties.
- He became a political leader, a legislator, a warrior, and a military general.
- He waged wars against his opponents.
- He became a conqueror.
- He addressed his diatribes against Jews and Christians: "From those too, who call themselves Christians, we did take a covenant, but they forgot a good part of the message that we have sent them, so we estranged them, with enmity and hatred between the one and the other, to the Day of Judgment. And soon will Allah show them what it is they have done!" (Q.5:14).

For Christians, Jesus is the reference for living, thinking, doing, behaving, and relating to God and others. He is not ultimately so for Muslims. Such a role is ascribed to the prophet Muhammad. There lies the biggest hurdle. But there are other issues that can facilitate our work. Islam can be seen as follows:
- A brotherhood with whom to share the magnificent and comforting knowledge of the heavenly Father figure that Jesus revealed.
- A religion of peace to which one can introduce the Prince of Peace, Jesus.
- A spiritual path that would greatly benefit from being exposed to the transforming indwelling of the Holy Spirit that reveals Christ.

- A religion that commemorates sacrifice which, according to Scripture, finds its ultimate significance in the atonement and cosmic reconciliation that Christ accomplishes.
- A theocracy that according to Jesus Christ will only be a reality after the Second Coming. A Second Coming that corresponds to the establishment of God's universal kingdom and the Advent of the King of kings and Lord of lords.
- A salvation conceived without Christ's Sacrifice as the Lamb of God that takes away the sin of the world.
- A concept of sin that does not contain the death sentence and the curse that the Scripture says Christ bore in order for the blessing of Abraham to be available to all human beings.
- A righteousness understood apart from the perfect character of Christ and that needs a righteousness that does not come through works.
- A conception of Christ that is not the seal of the prophet nor the specific connotation that the Bible attaches to expressions such as the Word of God, the perfect example of humanity, God the Son who became flesh and dwelt among us.
- A law that does not point to Christ, whom the Bible designates as the end of the law.
- A state religion, a dynasty of rulers, a succession of empires, and a world civilization that have not fulfilled what Judeo-Christian Scriptures call the kingdom of God that Christ embodies.

All world religions are in need either of the whole chain of biblical truth, correction of concepts foreign to God's character, and/or the restoration and fulfillment of legitimate edifices of their beliefs. Adventists understand themselves as God's end-time response to the need of the world before the Second Coming. They are uniquely positioned to share a complete chain of truth and to accompany people of other faiths on their pilgrimage toward complete reformation and to the fulfillment of God's purpose for all peoples.

For Muslims, the journey to the restoration of their Makkan roots and, beyond that, toward fulfillment in Christ is promising. This journey includes respect and honoring the dignity of every person, regardless of their response to what the followers of Christ hold dear to them. Adventists are uniquely positioned to be companions of the pilgrimage of faith in which sincere Muslims are engaged. The biblical metanarrative they have wholeheartedly embraced, the biblical prophetic insights, their emphasis on holistic healing, care for creation, and hope in the Second Coming to heal all the wounds of human existence and reality are a gift God places before the world that is coming to an end.

Conclusion: An Adventist Response

The story of the origins and the end introduces the observers of Islam into a different world of thought. A pre-historic covenant before God fashioned human bodies contains some mythical overtones that are irreconcilable to biblical anthropology and theology. The story of the prostration of the angels before Adam and Satan's refusal to do so strangely resembles the introduction of Jesus to His world and God's request of the angels to worship Him. The differences are irreconcilable. The trajectories they trace are two different stories of salvation.

Muslim eschatology, though using several themes similar to the ones found in the Bible, contains beliefs that erode the very foundations of Christianity. To postulate that Jesus is coming again, will die, and be buried annuls the new covenant and the Christian faith, founded on the resurrection of Christ, the Conqueror of Death. Paradoxically, the biblical Jesus is missing in Islam. His dignity is diminished, His prerogatives usurped and attributed to others. With reference to protology, He is creator (John 1:3). And with reference to eschatology, He is the Coming One (Rev 1:7).

The biblical record informs us of the controversy between Christ and Satan. Part of the Muslim tradition acknowledges that Jesus is going to defeat the antichrist. But the story is mixed with legends from a different logic and from other discourses and trajectories. From a biblical perspective, the great controversy is about the righteousness of God. There is no one righteous but God. God came to us through Jesus to make us righteous.

The most prized value Muslims seek is righteousness. However, in the biblical worldview, righteousness is embodied in God's nature and is inseparable from God. Only the indwelling Holy Spirit of God can produce the fruit of righteousness. Rites and rituals do not confer it. Jesus is our righteousness. For the followers of Jesus, their righteousness is bound to surpass that of the Scribes and the Pharisees. The goal of the plan of salvation is to confer righteousness to God's people.

The antidote to the terror of the last days is the truth of this righteousness, received by faith. the righteousness of Christ imputed to those who put their trust in Him. The One who knew no sin became sin so that we might become the righteousness of God in Him (2 Cor 5:21).

CHAPTER 18

ISRAEL AND THE CHURCH: CONTINUITY AND DISCONTINUITY—I

Richard Davidson

The relationship between Israel and the Church is central to understanding the larger relationship between the Old Testament and the New Testament. It is crucial to identifying the true people of God in Scripture. This has been the focus of vigorous debate among theologians since the inception of the Christian church.[1] Within Seventh-day Adventist discus-

---

[1] Major views include: 1) Replacement Theology (also called supersessionism), that the promises/predictions made to national Israel were conditional upon faithfulness to the covenant and, as a result of their disloyalty by rejecting the Messiah, no longer apply and are superseded by a spiritual, universal fulfillment to the church (see esp. Ronald E. Diprose, *Israel and the Church: The Origins and Effects of Replacement Theology* [Waynesboro, GA: Authentic Media, 2004]); 2) Covenant Theology, that Israel and the Church belong to the one covenant of grace and one people of God—Israel in the Old Testament and the Church (composed of both Jews and Gentiles) in the New Testament (identified by the covenant signs of circumcision and baptism respectively), on which see esp. Richard L. Pratt, Jr., "To the Jew First: A Reformed Perspective," *To the Jew First: The Case for Jewish Evangelism in Scripture and History*, ed. Darrell L. Bock and Mitch Glaser (Grand Rapids, MI: Kregel, 2008), 168–188; 3) Dispensational Theology, maintaining two distinct salvation plans for humanity with the church age that began at Pentecost, ending with a pre-tribulation rapture of Christians to heaven and the promises/predictions made to national Israel being literally fulfilled after a seven-year tribulation period that follows this rapture and as a result of which the Jewish people will be converted and accept Jesus at the second advent (see Dale S. DeWitt, *Dispensational Theology in America During the Twentieth Century: Theological Development and Cultural Context* [Grand Rapids, MI: Grace Bible College, 2002], 53–76, 293–327); and 4) Two-covenant Theology, that Jews and Christians are favorably related to God by two distinct, divinely sanctioned, covenants—Christianity's covenant for Gentiles through Jesus Christ and Judaism's covenant for Jews through Torah (see, e.g., Clark M. Williamson, *A Guest in the House of Israel: Post-Holocaust Church Theology* [Louisville, KY: Westminster/John

sions, some voices have emphasized continuity, whereas others have focused on discontinuity. In this study, I suggest that Seventh-day Adventists, with their unique understanding of the eschatological remnant and other biblical doctrines, are able to set forth a comprehensive view which takes seriously the elements of both continuity and discontinuity found in Scripture.[2]

Definitions of Israel

As we will observe throughout this study, the term "Israel" can refer to a number of entities in biblical and post-biblical times. There is need to carefully define how the term Israel is used to distinguish the various entities described by this term in our discussion.[3]

Biblical-historical Israel

This term refers to the historical people, physical descendants of the patriarch Jacob/Israel or those who joined this group through marriage or spiritual adoption from other nations.

National (or theocratic) Israel

The term "national" (or "theocratic") Israel refers to the "political entity" of Israel "with its theocratic claim" that existed from the time of the Exodus from Egypt up to A.D. 70 and destruction of Jerusalem, particularly as represented by its theocratic leaders.[4]

Knox, 1993]). Other views combine various aspects of these four major approaches. Further, see Walter C. Kaiser, Jr., *The Promise-Plan of God: A Biblical Theology of the Old and New Testaments* (Grand Rapids, MI: Zondervan, 2008), 29–31. I discuss and critique these various views more fully in the longer version of this study, "Israel and the Church," presented at the Biblical Research Committee Meeting, Spring 2012.

[2] Basic elements of this position (with slightly different nomenclature) may be found in Jacques B. Doukhan, *The Mystery of Israel* (Hagerstown, MD: Review and Herald, 2004); *idem*, *Israel and the Church: Two Voices for the Same God* (Peabody, MA: Hendrickson, 2002); the essays in Richard Elofer, ed., *Comfort, Comfort My People: Towards a Growing Adventist-Jewish Friendship* (Berrien Springs, MI: Department of World Mission, 2009); Clinton Wahlen, "Are the Jews Today Responsible for the Death of Christ?" *Interpreting Scripture: Bible Questions and Answers*, ed. Gerhard Pfandl (Hagerstown, MD: Biblical Research Institute, 2010), 297–300; and *idem*, "Will All Jews Be Saved?" in ibid., 351–354.

[3] In defining this terminology, I am indebted to (but do not follow precisely) the description of the "multiplicity of faces of 'Israel'" as presented by Doukhan, *Mystery of Israel*, 109–112 (citation 109).

[4] Ellen White often denotes this usage by the expression "Israel as a nation" or the "Jewish nation."

Jewish Israel

This group "consists of the community of Jews who survived the exile of Babylon and settled around Eastern and Western Europe (probably Ashkenazic Jews), as well as those who fled Palestine after the fall of Jerusalem and settled around the Mediterranean (probably the Sephardic Jews)."[5] A sub-category within Jewish Israel may be called Political Israel. This term refers to the modern State of Israel, created in 1948 after the Holocaust. It belongs within the same cultural and historical context as Jewish Israel and, like Jewish Israel, incorporates peoples from various cultural, ethnic, and geographical horizons.[6]

Christian Israel

This term refers to the "faithful remnant" of biblical-historical Israel, who have accepted Jesus as the Messiah. It is comprised of those who are "descendant by birth of the early Jewish Christians, but also, and more important, by conversions through the intense evangelistic and political activities of Christians throughout the world."[7]

Spiritual Israel

This term refers to the "faithful remnant," the true followers of God throughout both Old Testament and New Testament times (it is not a designation reserved only for the Church which replaced national Israel, as some have used the term).[8]

Eschatological Israel

This is the end-time movement of God's faithful followers described in Revelation as "the remnant of her [the woman's] seed, who keep the commandments of God and have the testimony of Jesus Christ" (Rev 12:17).[9]

Apocalyptic (or Heavenly) Israel

This Israel is "the only one that counts—the 'heavenly Israel' in the

---

[5] Ibid., 110.

[6] Ibid.

[7] Doukhan, *Mystery of Israel*, 111. "Christian Israel" is another name for "the Way" (Acts 9:2; 19:9, 23; 24:14, 22; cf. 18:25–26; 22:4), the "sect of the Nazarenes" (Acts 24:5), the "Church of God" (1 Cor 15:9; 1 Thess 2:14), or simply "the Church" (*ekklēsia*, over 100 times in the New Testament).

[8] This is in harmony with Ellen White's usage in *Patriarchs and Kings,* 713 and elsewhere.

[9] See Doukhan, *Mystery*, 87–107, for a depiction of this eschatological Israel, the Seventh-day Adventist Church, which is "the only religious movement that ultimately brought the Messiah and the Torah together" (87).

New Jerusalem."[10] This group is the "all Israel" of Rom 11:26, comprised of both Jews and Gentiles, all humans who will be saved, as One People of God.

Thesis and Methodology of this Study

A well-rounded presentation of the relationship between Israel and the Church must examine both the elements of continuity and discontinuity that emerge from the biblical portrayal.[11] The biblical basis for the distinction between Israel and the Church is found in the Old Testament, and this will be the starting point for our discussion. In the Old Testament, we will examine the question of who constitutes biblical and spiritual Israel, and also look at references (in LXX) to the Old Testament *ekklēsia* ("church"). We will sketch the original divine plan for Israel's mission to the world (as presented in the classical prophets) and the Old Testament theology of the remnant. We will also explore the apocalyptic revelation of what would actually happen to national Israel (according to divine foreknowledge expressed in Daniel 9).

In the New Testament, the biblical argument stressing continuity between Israel and the Church (although not ignoring discontinuity) is presented most directly and clearly by Paul in Romans 9–11, while the aspects of discontinuity (without ignoring continuity) are set forth most forcefully in Jesus' statements to the Jewish leaders who had rejected him (recorded in Matt 21:43 and 23:39). We will examine these passages and, in the process, deal briefly with various other New Testament texts that support either continuity or discontinuity.

In the New Testament discussion, we begin with the epistles, not only because Romans 9–11 contains the most comprehensive and focused treatment of the subject, but also because Romans 9–11, and most of the related passages in the Epistles, were probably written before the Gospels and Acts. After looking at relevant passages in the New Testament epistles and then in the Gospels/Acts, we will look briefly at the book of Revelation. There, we encounter a climactic synthesis of the biblical material on

---

[10] Ibid., 115.

[11] The need for seeing both continuity and discontinuity has been recognized by a number of recent scholarly studies. See, e.g., Marten H. Woudstra, "Israel and the Church: A Case for Continuity," *Continuity and Discontinuity: Perspectives on the Relationship Between the Old and New Testaments; Essays in Honor of S. Lewis Johnson, Jr.*, ed. John S. Feinberg (Westchester, IL: Crossway, 1988), 237; and Walter Riggans, "Towards an Evangelical Doctrine of the Church: The Church and Israel," *Churchman* 103/2 (1989): 132. Within Adventism, see esp. Gunnar Pedersen, "Continuity and Discontinuity between the Church and Israel," *Comfort, Comfort My People: Towards a Growing Adventist-Jewish Friendship*, ed. Richard Elofer (Berrien Springs, MI: Department of World Mission, Andrews University, 2009), 11–25.

the relationship between Israel and the church. Along with surveying the biblical evidence, we will also occasionally critique various views on this subject that have been proposed in the history of scholarship.

Israel and the Church in the Old Testament: Continuity and Discontinuity

The Name "Israel" and Israel's Fundamentally Spiritual Nature

Foundational to any discussion of Israel and the Church is an understanding of the term "Israel" in the Old Testament, both in its historical and philological dimensions. From a historical perspective, recent scholarship has examined the breadth of usage of the designation "Israel" within the Old Testament, revealing how the term has been understood to refer to various entities down to the close of the Hebrew canon.[12]

From a philological perspective, it has often been concluded that no satisfactory etymological derivation of the term "Israel" is available.[13] However, the biblical text clearly connects the meaning of "Israel" to the root *srh* "to contend, struggle, wrestle": "And He [the Angel] said, 'Your name shall no longer be called Jacob, but Israel; for you have struggled [*srh*] with God and with men, and have prevailed'" (Gen 32:28). The name "Israel" from its very inception is used in the context of the spiritual character of the one who bore the name. Thus "people of Israel" are ultimately those who, like their "father" Jacob/Israel, have undergone a spiritual transformation—a spiritual people. Israel's spiritual relationship with God is foundational to all other relations (see, e.g., Exod 4:22–23; 19:3–6; 29:43–46; Deut 10:12, 16; 30:6).[14]

Israel as an Inclusive People

The term "Israel" can be used for the national entity known by this name. But who constituted this national entity? To answer this question we must understand the ancient Near Eastern concept of "ethnicity." Although a people-group, such as Israel or her national neighbors, traced their biological roots to a single ancestor, ethnicity included more than the direct physical descendants of a common ancestor. A person was considered fully part of a people-group if he/she identified with and chose to accept the God

---

[12] See Philip R. Davies, *In Search of 'Ancient Israel'* (Sheffield: Sheffield Academic Press, 1992), 52; and esp. Ganoune Diop, "The Name 'Israel' and Related Expressions in the Books of Amos and Hosea" (Ph.D. diss., Andrews University, 1995), 17–21.

[13] See summary of discussion and hypotheses in Diop, "Israel," 15–17.

[14] See also Alva J. McClain, *The Greatness of the Kingdom: An Inductive Study of the Kingdom of God* (Winona Lake, IN: BMH Books, 1959), 66–68.

(and accompanying prevailing culture and religion) of that nation.[15]

Old Testament Israel was composed of direct physical descendants of Jacob *plus* many others from various nations who accepted Israel's God Yahweh, and chose to become part of the covenant community.[16] Both those who were of direct physical descent from Jacob and Gentiles who joined God's covenant people were all called "Israel;" none were to be considered second-class citizens of the Israelite nation.

In the Old Testament prophetic portrayals of Israel's eschatological future, a dominant feature is the prediction of an influx of Gentiles to be accepted as part of the Israelite nation.[17] The classical prophets make clear that those Gentiles who accept the religion of Yahweh are to be regarded as native Israelites, with all the privileges pertaining to it (Isa 56:1–8; Ezek 47:22–23). There were not two plans for two different groups of God-fearing people in the Old Testament; all were called to join the one community of God, biblical-historical Israel.

The Divine Plan for Israel: What Might Have Been (Classical Prophecy)

Within the Old Testament, there are two different genres or types of predictive prophecy: apocalyptic (the visions of Daniel) and classical or general prophecy (including the predictive kingdom prophecies regarding Israel found outside of Daniel). Classical and apocalyptic prophecy each involve specific hermeneutical rules of interpretation, which arise out of an examination of the biblical evidence. The classical prophets present two different options: God's plan for blessing Israel if they heed the prophetic call to remain faithful to His covenant, but also the certainty of punitive judgment and the reception of the covenant curses if Israel persists in covenant unfaithfulness. A brief summary of God's original promise-plan for Israel may be helpful at this point in the discussion.[18]

---

[15] See Randall W. Younker, "The Emergence of the Ammonites: Sociocultural Transformation on the Transjordan Plateau during the Late Bronze/Iron Age Transition," (Ph.D. diss., University of Arizona, 1997).

[16] Note the following examples: the multitude of the Egyptians at the time of the Exodus (Exod 12:38); Zipporah the Midian/Cushite (Exod 2:16, 21; Num 12:1); Rahab the Canaanite and her family (Josh 2:1; 5:22–25); Ruth the Moabite (Ruth 1:16–17); Uriah the Hittite (2 Sam 11); and the many Persians who joined Israel (Esther 9:27).

[17] See esp. Isaiah 2:2–3; 45:14, 20; 49:6–22; 55:5; 56:7–8; 60:1–11; 66:18–20; Jeremiah 3:17; 16:19; Zephaniah 3:9; Haggai 2:7; Zechariah 2:11; 8:20–23; cf. the discussion of these passages in the next section of this study.

[18] The following description of the original divine plan for Israel is condensed from my articles, "Biblical Principles for Interpreting Old Testament Classical Prophecy," *Prophetic Principles: Crucial Exegetical, Theological, Historical and Practical Insights*, ed. Ron du Preez (Lansing, MI:

Throughout the Old Testament, God's plan was for Israel to reach out to those peoples and nations around them, inviting them to become part of God's covenant people. But the Old Testament prophets (most notably the gospel prophet Isaiah) provide the most intensified vision of God's sweeping mission program for a repentant and faithful Israel after the Babylonian exile. According to this programmatic vision, as the people of Israel are gathered back to the Promised Land, God pardons and cleanses them from their sins, gives them a new heart, puts His Spirit within them, and causes them to walk in His statutes (Ezek 36:24-28; cf. Isa 40:1-2; Jer 31:31-34). As Israel loyally serves God and receives the concomitant covenant blessings, all the nations see her righteousness and glory and call her blessed (Isa 62:1-2; 61:9; Mal 3:12); Jerusalem becomes a praise and glory before all nations (Jer 33:9). From exalted Zion goes forth the Law (Isa 2:2-3 = Micah 4:1-2); God's people become His witnesses (Isa 43:10; 44:8), a light to the nations (42:1, 6; 49:6; 51:4), giving a universal offer of salvation (45:22) and warning of judgment (Jonah; various oracles against the nations).

The response: Nations come to the light (Isa 60:3). They run to Jerusalem (Isa 66:18-20; cf. 2:2; 45:20; 49:6-22; 55:5; 56:8) to seek the Lord (Zech 8:20-23) and join themselves to Him (Isa 56:7-8; Zech 2:11). Nation after nation, admitting the falsity of their ancestral religion (Jer 16:19), "come over to" Israel, acknowledging that the Lord is the only true God (Isa 45:14). The nations go up to the house of the Lord—which is called "a house of prayer for all peoples" (Isa 56:7)—to seek instruction in His ways and to serve Him "shoulder to shoulder" (Isa 2:3 = Micah 4:2; Zeph 3:9). Eventually "all nations" are gathered to Jerusalem and call it "the throne of the Lord" (Jer 3:17). Those aliens from other nations who "join themselves to the Lord," i.e. give their allegiance to Yahweh and hold fast to His covenant with Israel, are considered to be fully part of the covenant community of Israel (Isa 56:1-8; Ezek 47:22-23). As nations accept the Lord and His Messiah, Israel extends its borders (Amos 9:12), until its dominion embraces the world (Isa 27:6; Zech 9:10).[19]

The Fulfillment of the Divine Plan for Old Testament Israel

One of the most pressing questions regarding the Old Testament

---

Michigan Conference of Seventh-day Adventists, 2007), 23-27; and "Interpreting Old Testament Prophecy," *Understanding Scripture: An Adventist Approach*, ed. George W. Reid (Silver Spring, MD: Biblical Research Institute, 2005), 193-195.

[19] See Ellen G. White, *Christ's Object Lessons* (Washington, DC: Review and Herald, 1941), 290: "As the numbers of Israel increased they were to enlarge their borders until their kingdom should embrace the world."

promises made to Israel concerns the fulfillment (or non-fulfillment) of the numerous Old Testament classical prophecies predicting the glorious eschatological, geopolitical future of Israel. From our vantage point, more than two millennia after the Old Testament era, it becomes apparent that many prophecies concerning the future of Israel as a nation have not come about as predicted in the Old Testament. Have these prophecies concerning Israel failed? Will they never be fulfilled? Or are they still part of the divine plan for the future? If they are yet to be fulfilled, what is the nature of this eschatological fulfillment?

Very different answers have been given to these questions. According to dispensationalists, the divine predictions to the patriarchs concerning the geopolitical aspects of Israel's history, as well as the spiritual blessings, are seen to be unconditional, based upon irrevocable divine promises (Gen 12:1–7; 17:8; 26:3–5; cf. 2 Sam 7:12–17; Psa 89:34–37; etc.). Although the Jewish people temporarily forfeited the kingdom promises because of their initial rejection of Christ, dispensationalists understand the Bible to predict that in the last days they will be gathered together as a geopolitical entity and restored to their land again (Lev 26:40–45; Deut 30:1–10), and a repentant Jewish State of Israel will eventually receive the literal fulfillment of all the Old Testament kingdom prophecies.

According to replacement theologians, on the other hand, the promises/predictions made regarding Israel as a nation were conditional upon their faithfulness to the covenant. Since the Jewish nation proved disloyal to the covenant in their rejection of the Messiah, they have permanently forfeited their right to the Old Testament kingdom promises. These promises will only be fulfilled, if at all, to the Church—the "New Israel," which has replaced what they term as "ethnic" (biological, Jewish) Israel.

Replacement theologians are correct in recognizing that the geopolitical prophecies made by the Old Testament classical prophets are couched within the framework of covenant relationship, in which God's people are always free to remain faithful to the covenant and reap the covenant blessings, or persist in unfaithfulness and receive the covenant curses. In this respect, the kingdom prophecies of the classical prophets may be seen as conditional in nature. At the same time, dispensationalists have rightly pointed to forceful Old Testament divine promises made to the patriarchs and to David that appear to be unconditional, even (and especially) concerning geopolitical aspects of Israel's future. How can both of these positions, affirming conditionality and unconditionality of the geopolitical promises to Israel, be reconciled?

An important key is found in understanding several crucial features of biblical covenants, as described in the Old Testament. First, on the most basic level, all the divine covenants of Scripture are part of one unconditional promise of God to work out salvation for the human race, stated first in Gen 3:15, and elaborated in each succeeding development of this one unified covenant (see, e.g., the promises of Gen 12, later incorporated into the Abrahamic covenant of Gen 15 and 17).[20] Thus the coming of the Messiah to fulfill God's redemptive covenant promise is unconditional, totally independent of human choice. However, the actualization of the divine promise in the lives of humans is conditional upon the response of each individual in accepting the Messiah's gift of salvation.

A second feature of Old Testament covenants, particularly the Abrahamic and Davidic covenants, parallels ancient Near Eastern royal covenants of grant,[21] where a king grants land (or position) to one of his subjects and his descendants in perpetuity in recognition of the servant's loyalty. So God promised to Abraham and his descendants a grant of land in perpetuity, based upon the covenant loyalty of Abraham (Gen 12:7; 15:7; 17:8; Gen 26:3-5; etc.). To David, God gave the additional irrevocable promise, under oath, of a never-ending kingdom (2 Sam 7:12-16; Ps 89:34-37). These geopolitical features of the covenant clearly go beyond spiritual blessings.

A third feature of biblical covenants also parallels the ancient Near Eastern covenants of grant, where only the grantee's descendants who remain loyal to the crown actually share in the perpetual grant. Generation after generation of descendants might forfeit their right to the royal grant, but eventually that which was granted will be restored to loyal descendants. So in Scripture, God bequeaths, in perpetuity, the land of promise to Abraham and his line of descendants, and the royal throne and kingdom of Israel to David and his sons. Though generations may pass in which the divine grant, with its geopolitical features, has been forfeited, yet in the future all that was promised under the divine grant will be restored to Abraham's descendants who are loyal to the "everlasting covenant" made to him (Gen 17:7, 13, 19).

---

[20] For Seventh-day Adventist studies of the covenant and its unity throughout the Two Testaments, see esp. Hans K. LaRondelle, *Our Creator Redeemer: An Introduction to Biblical Covenant Theology* (Berrien Springs, MI: Andrews University Press, 2005); Skip MacCarty, *In Granite or Ingrained? What the Old and New Covenants Reveal About the Gospel, the Law, and the Sabbath* (Berrien Springs, MI: Andrews University Press, 2007); cf. Gerhard Hasel, *Covenant in Blood* (Mountain View, CA: Pacific Press, 1982), revised and updated by Michael Hasel, as *The Promise: God's Everlasting Covenant* (Nampa, ID: Pacific Press, 2002). For evangelical scholars beyond Adventist circles, see esp. Thomas Edward McComiskey, *The Covenants of Promise: A Theology of the Old Testament Covenants* (Grand Rapids, MI: Baker, 1985); and O. Palmer Robertson, *The Christ of the Covenants* (Phillipsburg, NJ: Presbyterian and Reformed Publishing, 1980).

[21] See Moshe Weinfeld, "The Covenants of Grant in the Old Testament and the Ancient Near East," *AOS* 90 (1976): 184-203.

The last, and I believe most crucial, feature of the Old Testament covenants, concerns who comprises the covenant people who are to receive the kingdom promises made to Abraham. We have already seen that Old Testament Israel was composed of direct physical descendants of Jacob plus a multitude of others from various nations who accepted Israel's God Yahweh, and chose to become part of the covenant community. They were all called "Israel;" none were to be considered second-class citizens in the geopolitical reality of the Israelite nation. Within the nation of Israel could be found the faithful remnant who were the actual carrier of the covenant promises.

The "Two Israels:" The Historical Nation and the Faithful Covenant-keeping Remnant

Within the nation of Israel, there was always a "spiritual" (i.e. faithful) remnant. They not only took the name of "Israelite," but also gave evidence of true covenant loyalty to the God of Israel (e.g., Isa 10:22–23; Jer 23:3; Joel 2:32; Micah 2:12; Zeph 3:3; Mal 3:16–18). In his penetrating studies of the theology of the remnant in Scripture, Gerhard Hasel shows how, throughout the history of Old Testament Israel, there were three types of remnant in Israel:[22]

> The first is simply a *historical remnant* made up of survivors of a catastrophe. The second consists of the *faithful* remnant, distinguished from the former group by their genuine spirituality and true faith relationship with God; this remnant is the carrier of all divine election promises. The third is most appropriately designated the *eschatological* remnant, consisting of those of the faithful remnant who go through the cleansing judgments and apocalyptic woes of the end time and emerge victoriously after the Day of Yahweh as the recipients of the everlasting kingdom."[23]

Hasel identifies the "faithful remnant" as the "carrier of all divine election promises." The faithful remnant of Israel was the true "spiritual" Israel, carriers of the covenant promises, ones who could rightfully in-

---

[22] Gerhard F. Hasel, "Remnant," *ISBE* 4:130–134, here 130; see also idem, *The Remnant: The History and Theology of the Remnant Idea From Genesis to Isaiah* (Berrien Springs, MI: Andrews University Press, 1972); idem, "Remnant," *IDBSup*, 735–736; cf. Kenneth Mulzac, "The Remnant Motif in the Context of Judgment and Salvation in the Book of Jeremiah" (Ph.D. diss., Andrews University, 1995); and Tarsee Li, "The Remnant in the Old Testament," *Toward a Theology of the Remnant: An Adventist Ecclesiological Perspective*, ed. Ángel Manuel Rodríguez (Silver Spring, MD: Biblical Research Institute, 2009), 23–41.

[23] Hasel, "Remnant," 4:130.

herit the blessings of the covenant of grant made to Abraham. The faithful remnant sometimes were "invisible" (such as the seven thousand faithful followers of Yahweh during the time of Israel's apostasy under King Ahab, 1 Kings 19:18), but usually were a clearly identified faithful community (such as the faithful remnant who returned from the Babylonian exile under the leadership of Ezra (Zech 2:7/Hebrew text 2:11; Haggai 1:2, 14; 2:2; Ezra 1:4; 9:8, 13–15). The prophets also predicted the existence of a future eschatological and faithful remnant community (e.g., Joel 2:32 [Heb. 3:5]; Zech 8:6, 11–12; 13:8–9). With the coming of Christ in the "last days" (Heb 1:1–2), this motif of the eschatological/faithful remnant becomes the key to Paul's understanding of the relationship between Israel and the church (esp. Rom 9–11), pointing to elements of continuity and discontinuity.

We may state that the Old Testament presents the concept of "two Israels" running throughout much of Old Testament history. The first is the historical, national, geopolitical entity of Israel, and the second is the faithful remnant within Israel.

The Old Testament "Church" (Ekklēsia)

In the LXX, the word *ekklēsia* is used about 80 times in the canonical books of the Old Testament (another 22 times in the Apocrypha). It consistently translates the Hebrew word *qahal* ("[summons to or act of] assembly"). Although it can have a breadth of meaning, the word *qahal* often refers to the people of Israel, in an intimate covenant relationship with Yahweh. In Deuteronomy it "means above all the congregation gathered to conclude the covenant at Sinai (Deut. 9:10; 10:4). It is qualified by being linked to the name of Yahweh (cf. especially Deut. 23:2ff.). The word stands here for the people which Yahweh has summoned...."[24] The word *qahal* (and its Greek translation *ekklēsia*) "had also a religious element alongside that of a special, solemn assembly."[25] This word is aptly suited to describe the faithful remnant of Israel who would be gathered to Christ as the eschatological covenant community of faith.

The Divine Foreknowledge and Apocalyptic Prophecy

Whereas classical prophecy presented "what might have been" if Israel as a nation had been faithful to the covenant, the apocalyptic prophecies of Daniel indicate "what will be." The classical prophetic scenario was conditional upon the response of the nation; apocalyptic prophecy is

---

[24] Lothar Coenen, "Church," *NIDNTT*, 1:293.

[25] Ibid.

unconditional, as it describes what God foreknew would actually happen. Apocalyptic prophecy reveals that God has absolute foreknowledge and is not taken by surprise. He knows, in detail what will actually happen, what the human choices will be, and that His ideal plan for Israel (what *might have been*) would not come to pass the way He originally planned. The apocalyptic prophecies of Daniel were written (from the vantage point of God's foreknowledge) to show what *would be*.[26]

Whereas the original divine plan for Israel was that Jerusalem become "the mighty metropolis of the earth" and last forever, the apocalyptic prophecy of Daniel 9 revealed Jerusalem's destruction and desolation after the coming of the Messiah. This is not the place to examine the prophecy of Daniel 9 in detail,[27] except to note what Daniel 9 does *not* say. Many have spoken of the seventy-weeks prophecy as a "time of probation" for Israel, in order to give the Jewish people a chance to accept the Messiah. But the language of "probation" implies conditionality, and does not fit into the schema of deterministic, unconditional, apocalyptic prophecy. Daniel does not describe "probationary time" for the Jewish people, but as Ellen White aptly puts it, time "specially pertaining to the Jews" or "the period especially allotted to the Jews."[28] Furthermore, while Daniel 9 predicts the culmination and termination of the sacrificial system, the destruction of Jerusalem, and even implies the end of the theocracy, the prophecy says nothing about the rejection of the Jewish people.

According to Daniel 9, even though the city and temple of Jerusalem will be destroyed, and the promises of a glorious earthly future for the kingdom of Israel with it, Daniel does not suggest that these kingdom promises will never be fulfilled. While the geopolitical aspects of the kingdom are not part of Daniel's description of God's people after the destruc-

---

[26] See my discussion of the hermeneutics of apocalyptic prophecy, "Biblical Principles for Interpreting Apocalyptic Prophecy," *Prophetic Principles: Crucial Exegetical, Theological, Historical and Practical Insights*, ed. Ron du Preez (Lansing, MI: Michigan Conference of Seventh-day Adventists, 2007), 43–73. Some ask: What would happen if the leaders of the covenant people had chosen differently and how would Daniel have been fulfilled, for example, in its prediction of the destruction of Jerusalem (Dan 9)? The answer is simple: If God, in His foreknowledge, foresaw that the leaders of the geo-political entity of Israel would have accepted the Messiah, and the geo-political nation of Israel would have enlarged their borders to encompass the world, then Daniel would not need to have been written!
Others question whether God can have absolute foreknowledge of the future without interfering with human freedom. But divine foreknowledge is not incompatible with human freedom. On this issue, see esp. William Lane Craig, *The Only Wise God: The Compatibility of Divine Foreknowledge and Human Freedom* (Grand Rapids, MI.: Baker, 1987).

[27] See Jacques Doukhan, "The Seventy Weeks of Daniel 9: An Exegetical Study," *AUSS* 17/1 (1979): 1–22.

[28] Ellen G. White, *The Great Controversy* (Washington, DC: Review and Herald, 1888) 326–327.

tion of Jerusalem until the eschaton, one can easily conclude from Daniel 7:18, 27, that the Son of Man is returning with the "everlasting kingdom" (v. 27) so that "the saints shall receive the kingdom, and possess the kingdom forever, even forever and ever" (v. 18). We will see, later in our study, how Jesus allowed for the classical prophetic scenario of Israel's future to be a possibility. But toward the end of His ministry, He explicitly focused attention on the prophecies of Daniel referring to the destruction and desolation of Jerusalem and drew the implications for the future of Israel.

Israel and the Church in Romans 9-11

Romans 9-11: Structure and Argument

Recent discussion in Pauline theology has demonstrated the centrality in Paul's thought of the issue of God's faithfulness to the covenant made to Abraham and his descendants.[29] As part of this overarching theme, Romans 9-11—once considered a relatively insignificant interruption in Paul's epistle dealing with peripheral issues—is now widely recognized as constituting the culmination of the argument of the first eight chapters of the book, "the climax of the theme of the letter."[30] Far from involving "sharp turns, twisted logic,"[31] or employing argumentation that is "neither cohesive nor consistent,"[32] Rom 9-11 is a carefully-crafted argument, following a clear flow of thought, while at the same time set forth in a concentric (chiastic) pattern. Romans 9-11 constitutes the major biblical passage where the future of Israel in the plan of God is addressed directly, thoroughly, and with sustained argument.

---

[29] Whether or not one agrees with all the particulars of the "New Perspective on Paul," no longer can it be ignored or downplayed that Paul's writings place great emphasis upon God's faithfulness to his covenant, His "plan-through-Israel-for-the-world" (N.T. Wright, *Justification: God's Plan and Paul's Vision* [Downers Grove, IL: InterVarsity, 2009], 94). See ibid., for elaboration of this theme, and demonstration of how Romans 9-11 are the culmination of the first eight chapters of the letter.

[30] Christian Beker, "Romans 9-11 in the Context of the Early Church," *Princeton Seminary Bulletin* 11 (1990): 44. Cf. Andrew H. Wakefield, "Romans 9-11: The Sovereignty of God and the Status of Israel," *Review and Expositor* 100 (2003): 65: "Once typically relegated to the status of mere appendix to Paul's great exposition of justification by faith in chapters 1-8, chapters 9-11 are now seen by most commentators as the climax of that argument, and indeed of the book as a whole." See Wright, *Justification*, 240-248, where Wright saves Romans 9-11 for the climatic argument of his book.

[31] James W. Aageson, "Written Also for Our Sake: Paul's Use of Scripture in the Four Major Epistles, with a Study of 1 Corinthians 10," *Hearing the Old Testament in the New Testament*, ed. Stanley E. Porter (Grand Rapids, MI: Eerdmans, 2006), 158.

[32] Beker, "Romans 9-11," 48.

I have worked out elsewhere a detailed chart presenting the (verse-by-verse) structural and logical flow of Paul's argument, as I understand it,[33] and here present only main headings in the chiastic macrostructure of these chapters.

Chart 1

Israel and the Church: The Chiastic Structure Romans 9–11

Introduction: Paul's Anguish Concerning Israel (9:1–3a).
A. Irrevocable Promises: God's promises regarding Israel have not failed or been annulled (9:4–6).
  B. The True Israel (in the past): Not all of Israel, the [natural] seed of Abraham and Isaac, are [true] Israel [the people of God], and the true people of God include both Jews and Gentiles (9:6b–26).
    C. The Remnant: Only a remnant of [literal, historical] Israel will be saved, because the nation as a whole has sought righteousness by works of the law, rather than righteousness by faith in Christ (the goal of the law), the only way both Jew and Greek can find salvation (9:27–10:21).
      D. Non-rejection of Israel: God has not rejected His people Israel (11:1–2).
    C". The Remnant: Just as there was a remnant in Old Testament times, there is now (in Paul's time) a faithful remnant of Israel according to the election of grace (11:2b–10).
  B". The True Israel (in the future): Israel's stumbling is not final, but has occurred in order to provoke them to jealousy through the inclusion of the Gentiles, so that (if they do not persist in unbelief) they may eventually be saved, and in this way all [true] Israel [the people of God, both Jews and Gentiles] will be saved (11:11–28).
A". Irrevocable Promises: The gifts and the calling of God are irrevocable, because of God's promises to the patriarchs (11:29–32).
Conclusion: Doxology (11:34–35).

Romans 9–11: Elements of Continuity

In Rom 9–11, at least eight lines of evidence point to a basic continuity between Israel and the Church.[34]

---

[33] See Davidson, "Israel and the Church," 18–21.

[34] For more complete discussion of this continuity, see Davidson, "Israel and the Church," 22–35;

Continuity in the Promises to Israel

Paul's basic thesis in this central section of his epistle is straight forward: God is faithful in His promises to "His people" Israel. This thesis is repeated for emphasis in the outer members of his chiastic structure (Members A and A´; 9:6a and 11:29): Accentuating his main point even more, Paul restates this idea *twice* more at the very center—the apex—of his chiastic argument (Member D; 11:1, 2b). It is hard to imagine how Paul could have driven home his point more emphatically. This repeated ringing affirmation—that God has been faithful to His promises to Israel; that He has not rejected His people Israel—cannot be overemphasized. The Old Testament promises made to them are still in place and are available to them through the Messiah.

Continuity in the Two-Fold Definition of Israel

Foundational to Paul's remnant theology is his two-fold definition of Israel.[35] In members B and B" of Paul's chiastic structure (9:6–26 and 11:11–27), Paul uses the term Israel in two different senses. Roy Schroeder rightly points out that "in the first use, the word 'Israel' refers to people with blood line. In the second use, the word 'Israel' is a technical term for the people of God."[36]

Citing several Old Testament passages (Gen 21:12 in 9:7; Gen 18:10, 14 in 9:9; Gen 25:23 in 9:12; and Mal 1:2–3 in 9:13), Paul demonstrates (in member B of the chiastic structure) that already according to Old Testament understanding it was ultimately not bloodline that determined who were the children of God, but the ones who were the "children of the Promise" (9:8). Not all of Abraham's biological seed were "Israel," but only those of the line of promise: the descendants of Isaac, and later by God's election of Jacob over the firstborn son Esau. The children of promise came through the line of Jacob.

After an extended discussion defending God's freedom to elect whomsoever He chose (9:14–23), based on His foreknowledge (8:28–30), Paul tacitly expands his definition of the people of God ("Israel"), by indicating that God had called not only Jews but Gentiles (9:24). Paul implies here

---

cf. the concise description of this continuity, dealing with most of the points delineated below, in Ellen White, *Acts of the Apostles*, 374–382.

[35] Leslie N. Pollard, "The Remnant in Pauline Thought," *Toward a Theology of the Remnant: An Adventist Ecclesiological Perspective*, ed. Ángel Manuel Rodríguez (Silver Spring, MD: Biblical Research Institute, 2009), 79: "Paul's understanding of Israel in 9:6–13 is crucial to his argument for the existence of a faithful remnant."

[36] Roy P. Schroeder, "The Relationship between Israel and the Church," *Concordia Journal* 24/3 (1998): 254.

what he will make explicit later, that the "called/elected," both Jews and Gentiles, are part of "Israel," the true people of God (the more restrictive definition of Israel in 9:6).

As we have seen in our Old Testament discussion above, this is not a new concept. In this section of his argumentation, as elsewhere in Rom 9–11, every major point he makes is buttressed by citations from the Old Testament. In fact, over 30% of the content of Rom 9–11 is comprised of Old Testament citations and allusions.[37] The Old Testament is clear that both those who were of direct physical descent from Jacob and those Gentiles who joined God's covenant people were part of the people of "Israel;" none were to be considered second-class citizens in the geopolitical reality of the Israelite nation. And within the nation of Israel, there was always the faithful (or "spiritual") remnant of those who not only took the name of "Israelite" but also gave evidence of their true covenant loyalty to the God of Israel.

A dominant feature in Old Testament prophetic portrayals of Israel's eschatological future is the prediction of an influx of the Gentiles to be accepted as part of biblical-historical Israel. The prophets make clear that those Gentiles who accept the religion of Yahweh are to be regarded as native Israelites, with full privilege. There were not two plans for two different groups of God-fearing people in the Old Testament; all were called to join the singular community of God, "biblical Israel." The influx of Gentiles into Israel during Paul's time is not surprising—it is a fulfillment of Old Testament prophecy.[38]

Member B of Paul's chiastic argument is repeated and reinforced in parallel member B´, Romans 11:11–27. The same "programmatic distinction of two 'Israels'"[39] which marked the beginning of his discussion in Romans 9–11 (9:6) is now re-introduced at the climax of his argumentation in this section. Throughout this section, Paul has been describing how the natural branches of the olive tree (i.e. members of biblical-historical Israel who did not believe in Jesus) have been broken off and branches of the wild olive tree (i.e. believing Gentiles) have been grafted in (11:17, 20), and how, if they do not persist in unbelief, some of the natural (i.e. Jewish) branches can be grafted back in (11:23). In fact, through Paul's ministry, this re-grafting of the natural branches was already happening (11:13–14). Despite the partial hardening within biblical-historical Israel, Paul envisages a steady flow of Jewish people being grafted back

---

[37] Wakefield, "Romans 9–11," 77.

[38] See Eckhard J. Schnabel, "Israel, the People of God, and the Nations," *JETS* 45/1 (2002): 35–57.

[39] N. T. Wright, *The Climax of the Covenant* (Minneapolis, MA: Fortress, 1992), 250.

into the olive tree as they believe in Jesus, and likewise a steady flow of Gentiles (the "wild branches") being grafted in (11:25).

In 11:26, which scholars widely regard as "the climax of the letter,"[40] Paul gives his conclusion of the whole matter: "so [*houtōs*, 'in this way' (not 'then'[41]), i.e. in the way of bringing in the fullness of the Gentiles and the fullness of those of natural Israel who do not persist in unbelief] "all Israel [the true Israel of God, the faithful remnant including both Jews and Gentiles who were grafted in] will be saved."

With regard to the phrase "until the fullness of the Gentiles has come in," Woudstra points out that "the biblical use of the word 'until' does not always mean a later reversal of a given situation (see Ps 110:1; 1 Chron 28:20; Isa 6:9–13). In other words, the apostle's emphasis is not upon some later point in time when there will be a reversal in the hardening in part of the Jews. Rather, the emphasis is upon the word 'so' or 'thus,' 'in this way.' All Israel will be saved in the way of the bringing in of the fullness of the Gentiles."[42]

N.T. Wright insightfully summarizes the meaning of this verse:

> God's method of saving 'all Israel' is to harden ethnic Israel (cp. 9.14 ff.), i.e. not to judge her at once, so as to create a period of time during which the gentile mission could be undertaken, *during the course of which* it remains God's will that the present 'remnant' of believing Jews might be enlarged by the process of 'jealousy', and consequently faith, described above. This whole process is God's way of saving his whole people: that is the meaning of *kai houtōs pas Israēl sōthēsetai*."[43]

---

[40] Beker, "Romans 9–11," 45.

[41] See Wright, *Climax*, 249: "Despite repeated assertions to the contrary, the meaning of ou[twj is not 'then' but 'thus', 'in this manner.'"

[42] Woudstra, "Israel and the Church," 236. Cf. Wright, *Climax*, 249–250 for similar argumentation: "Paul's meaning is not a temporal sequence—first the Gentiles, *then* the Jews. Rather, it is the interpretation of a particular process *as* the salvation of 'all Israel'" (italics his).

[43] Wright, *Climax*, 250. For a survey of the whole gamut of interpretations of this key verse, see William Chi-Chau Fung, "Israel's Salvation: The Meaning of 'All Israel' in Romans 11:26" (doctoral diss., Southern Baptist Theological Seminary, 2004), 9–34. Other scholars who maintain the position argued above, and articulated by Wright, include, e.g., John Calvin, who wrote: "I extend the word *Israel* to include all the people of God, in this sense, 'When the Gentiles have come in, the Jews will at the same time return from their defection to the obedience of faith. The salvation of the whole Israel of God, which must be drawn from both, will thus be completed, and yet in such a way that the Jews, as the firstborn in the family of God, may obtain the first place." John Calvin, *The Epistles of Paul the Apostle to the Romans and to the Thessalonians* (Grand Rapids, MI: Eerdmans, 1961), 255. See also O. Palmer Robertson, *The Israel of God: Yesterday, Today, and Tomorrow* (Phillipsburg, NJ: P & R Publishing, 2000), 187: "'all Israel' consists not of

Clinton Wahlen concurs: "The salvation of 'all Israel' refers to both Jews and Gentiles, which was already a part of prophetic expectations."[44] Israel, the true people of God, consists of both believing Jews and Gentiles. This true "Israel" is identified as the faithful remnant (of Jews and Gentiles) within biblical-historical Israel, not a replacement of the Jewish people by the Christian Church, or a group separate from the Christian church.

Continuity in the Theology of the Remnant

At its core, Romans 9–11 is a theology of the remnant. While remnant terminology is used elsewhere by Paul and other New Testament writers, "it is in Rom 9–11 that we find the most theologically developed use of remnant terminology in the New Testament."[45] In the chiastic structuring of these chapters, parallel members C and C´ (Rom 9:27–10:21 and 11:2b–10) both highlight Paul's remnant theology, and this remnant theology is influential throughout the greater portion of Romans 9–11.

In developing his remnant theology in Romans 9–11, Paul builds upon the Old Testament distinction between the two definitions of Israel we have discussed above—biblical-historical Israel and the faithful/spiritual Israel within the nation who are the true people of God. Furthermore, "Paul uses Old Testament passages to expand the breadth and scope of God's faithful remnant."[46] Paul's argument unfolds with seven main points:

1) The Old Testament Scripture predicted that in the last days only a remnant (*hypoleimma*) of Israel would be saved (Isa 10:22–23; cited in Rom 9:27–28),[47] only a "seed" would be left (Isa 1:9; cited in Rom 9:29),[48]

---

all elect Jews, but of all the elect of God, whether of Jewish or Gentile origin" (see argumentation, 186–192). Cf. Doukhan, *Mystery*, 33–34, 68–71. Herman Ridderbos, *Paul: An Outline of His Theology* (Grand Rapids, MI: Eerdmans, 1975), 358–359; Schnabel, 55–56; Woudstra, 235–237; and most recently Daniel B. Ortiz, La Salvación de "Todo Israel": Estudio Histórico, Exegético y Teológico de Romanos 11:26" (Ph.D. dissertation, River Plate Adventist University, Argentina, 2008).

[44] Wahlen, "All Jews," 354.

[45] Pollard, "Remnant in Pauline Thought," 77.

[46] Ibid., 78. Emphasis his.

[47] The Hebrew of Isaiah 10:22 (*she'ar yashub*) literally translates as "a remnant shall return/repent," but the LXX translates *yashub* as "shall be saved" (*sōthēsetai*). In the salvific context of the whole chapter, this translation well captures the implied meaning of the Hebrew.

[48] Pollard, "Remnant in Pauline Thought," 82, rightly points out that "'Seed' in 9:29 is synonymous with 'remnant' in 9:27" and shows how these two Old Testament citations and Paul's usage of them highlight both the judgment and salvation/hope/assurance aspects of the remnant theme: "His use of remnant language, therefore, presupposes that there has been a judgment, a division in Israel precipitated by the Christ event. . . . Paul connects assurance to his remnant understanding—hope remains for Israel" (ibid.).

and this remnant would include those outside the blood line of Israel (Deut 32:21; Isa 65:1; cited in Rom 10:19-20).

2) In Old Testament times there was a faithful remnant of biblical-historical Israel (1 Kgs 19, cited in Rom 11:2-4), who were considered the true people of God.

3) Likewise, in Paul's day there is a faithful remnant (*leimma*)—in fulfillment of Old Testament prophecy and in parallel with the Old Testament history of Israel in the time of Elijah.[49]

4) Changing metaphors, Paul represents the true people of God, the true Israel, as a cultivated olive tree; and the faithful remnant are its branches (Rom 11:16-17).

5) Some of the branches (unbelieving Jews) are broken off of the olive tree and wild branches (believing Gentiles) are grafted in (Rom 11:17-22), expanding the faithful remnant of Israel (Rom 9:24; 10:10-13; outside Rom 9-11, see Rom 3:29-30; Gal 3:28-29).

6) By grafting in wild branches (believing Gentiles), some of the natural branches that have been broken off will be provoked to jealousy (alluding to Deut 32:21, cited in Rom 10:19), and if they do not persist in unbelief they will be grafted back into the olive tree (Rom 11:23-25), thus further expanding the faithful remnant.

7) In this way (*houtōs*), "all Israel"—the faithful, apocalyptic remnant of Israel, comprised of all of the people of God of all ages, both Jews and Gentiles—will be saved (Rom 11:26).

Paul considered the faithful remnant of his day part of biblical-historical Israel, not a separate group. This is an essential point in his overall argument, showing that God has not rejected Israel.[50] This faithful remnant

---

[49] Scholars have recognized that Paul's ministry unfolds in parallel to that of Elijah. See, e.g., Johannes Munck, *Christ and Israel: An Interpretation of Romans 9-11* (Philadelphia, PA: Fortress, 1967), 13: "Just as Elijah returned from his stay among the Gentiles in order to settle matters between Baal and Yahweh... so Paul is now on his way from the Gentiles so that stubborn Israel may be shown the obedience of faith as it is to be found among Gentile believers."

[50] Charles Horne, "The Meaning of the Phrase 'And Thus All Israel Will Be Saved' (Romans 11:26)," *JETS* 21 (1978): 330: "the salvation of a small remnant from the total mass is ample proof that God's true people have not been, are not now, nor will be cast off. Such is a thought is utterly incompatible with God's electing love (11:5-6)."

was composed of both Jews and Gentiles.[51] The faithful remnant, which Paul elsewhere calls the church (see the section on Ephesians below), is the extension of biblical-historical Israel. The church does not replace biblical-historical Israel, nor does it involve a separate salvation plan from that of Israel. According to Paul, it constitutes the faithful eschatological remnant within Israel. This faithful remnant is not comprised of isolated individuals, but constitutes a remnant covenant community, as we often find in the Old Testament.

It might be asked whether this insistence upon describing the church as the faithful remnant of biblical-historical Israel, and not a separate group apart from Israel, is actually making "a distinction without a difference," since, in either case, the church is comprised of both Jews and Gentiles. For Paul, it was absolutely imperative to make such a distinction, because the faithfulness of God to His promises is at stake. If the church is not comprised of the remnant of biblical-historical Israel, but a separate group, then God has broken His promise never to forsake His people, Israel. This is a distinction *with a difference*, because the integrity of God's word is at stake. Paul repeatedly underscores this "distinction with a difference" throughout Romans 9–11, and elsewhere in his epistles, a distinction that will ultimately be manifested by the ingrafting of natural (Jewish) branches at the end of time (see point 8 below).

The faithful remnant of Israel that comprises the church is not destined to remain a small number. Within Paul's thought, the remnant is "an expansive and inclusive concept.... The remnant will be consummated into one eschatological community."[52] It "will become the totality. It is thus a productive number, not an unchangeable minority."[53] It will swell into "all Israel," as mentioned at the climax of his argument (Rom 11:26). Leslie Pollard summarizes Paul's remnant theology: "In Paul, we find the explicit doctrine of a faithful remnant consisting of believing Jews joined by believing Gentiles. They granted the covenant titles of national Israel, and placed squarely in the stream of God's soteriological activity."[54]

Continuity in the One People of God

Throughout the discussion of Romans 9–11, Paul never describes two separate groups comprising the people of God, consistently point-

---

[51] Dan G. Johnson, "The Structure and Meaning of Romans 11," *CBQ* 46 (1984): 103.

[52] Pollard, "Remnant in Pauline Thought," 81, 84.

[53] Schrenk, "*Leimma*," *TDNT*, 4:212.

[54] Pollard, "Remnant in Pauline Thought," 84.

ing to one true Israel, one faithful remnant. The Gentiles who believe in Christ do not form a *new* People of God. They become part of the one already-existing People of God (Rom 9:24–26, citing Hosea 1:10 and 2:23, showing the applicability of these passages also to the Gentiles whom God has called).[55] This continuity between Israel and the Church becomes most vividly apparent in the analogy of the olive tree. There is only *one* cultivated olive tree—representing "Israel the community of salvation."[56] Gentiles who believe in Jesus are grafted into this one true olive tree (Rom 11:17).

This is not to suggest that unbelieving Jews are still part of the olive tree. No, Paul clearly does not support the concept that unbelieving Jews remain God's people. It is correct that only those branches that are connected to the olive tree are God's people—whether they be Jews or Gentiles. But at the same time, even the "lopped-off branches" are special to Paul (and to God). His desire is that the inclusion of the engrafted Gentiles, many of his Jewish brothers will become jealous and will, by faith in Jesus, become grafted back into the one true Olive Tree.

The consequences of recognizing that there is only one cultivated olive tree are far-reaching in understanding the relationship between Israel and the Church. First, this leaves no room for the dispensationalist dictum, "a dispensationalist keeps Israel and the Church distinct."[57] Dispensationalism, along with two-covenant theology, implies "two peoples of God. But Rom 11:16–25 will permit only *one* people of God, not two!"[58]

The continuity of the People of God, the existence of only one cultivated olive tree, leaves no room for a theology of replacement. Gentile believers are grafted into the cultivated olive tree—the continuation and extension of biblical-historical Israel. The Church is not a replacement for Israel, not a New Israel, but an extension and continuation of true Israel. Anders Nygren makes this point forcefully with regard to Paul's olive tree analogy:

---

[55] George S. Worgul, "Romans 9–11 and Ecclesiology," *BTB* 7/2 (1977): 100, 103: "Paul extends the 'Beloved' beyond the remnant of Israel to now include the Gentiles who, in his perspective, are part of the People of God. Paul interprets Hosea and the 'remnant text' (Is 10:22f) as realized eschatology, i.e. the Gentiles—now within the People of God—are the realization of the prophetic message. The mixed Christian community containing both Jew and Gentile, can bear the technical title *Laos tou Theou*. . . . It is significant to note that Paul never refers to the Christian community as the new People of God *Kainos Laos tou Theou*. . . . It is only in the second century to the third century that the Christian community is called the *Kainos Laos tou Theou* (new People of God)."

[56] Otfried Hofius, "'All Israel Will Be Saved': Divine Salvation and Israel's Deliverance in Romans 9–11," *Princeton Seminary Bulletin* 11 (1990): 33.

[57] Charles Ryrie, *Dispensationalism Today* (Chicago, IL: Moody, 1965), 44, 46.

[58] Horne, "Romans 11:26," 330.

We might have expected a different illustration, that God had the unfruitful tree cut down, and in its place planted a new one by the hand of Christ. But that is not what Paul means. The tree remains; it is a holy and noble tree. . . . Israel is the tree; Israel is God's people. Into this people are introduced and ingrafted the Gentiles who come to faith in Christ and are saved. Salvation consists in the very fact that they are thus ingrafted. It is not their faith that sustains the people of God, but the people of God that sustains them. According to Paul, the Christian church has its roots in the Old Testament, in God's choice of the fathers. . . . Christians are not a new race; they are rather the continuation, the legitimate continuation, of God's Old Testament people.[59]

Finally, it is vital that the Christian church today continue to humbly recognize that its existence cannot be viewed independent of Israel. Over centuries of Christian history, the dominant position was "*the Church against Israel*," but Paul argues that one should view the relationship as "*the Church within Israel*."[60] Dan Johnson levels a strong critique against those who have, knowingly or unknowingly, ruptured the continuity between Israel and the church by regarding the Church as a New Israel: "whoever they may be, they have violated the clear claims of Paul's exposition [in Rom 11]. In Paul's view any church which exists independently of Israel ceases therein to be the church as a part of God's salvation plan and becomes simply another religious society."[61]

Continuity in the One Way of Salvation

According to Paul's argument in Romans 9–11, as in all his epistles, there is only one way of salvation—not by works of the law, but by faith in Jesus Christ (Rom 9:30–33; 10:3–12). This truth forms the bedrock of Paul's argument in Romans 9–11. The Jews who seek a righteousness of law are engaging in a futile search (9:31). All who form part of the true olive tree (Israel, the faithful remnant), Jew or Gentile, are saved by faith in Jesus Christ (10:9–10). Paul could not be clearer: "For there is no distinction between Jew and Greek, for the same Lord over all is rich to all

---

[59] Anders Nygren, *Commentary on Romans* (Philadephia, PA: Fortress, 1949), 399–400.

[60] Paul M. Van Buren, "The Church and Israel: Romans 9–11," *Princeton Seminary Bulletin* 11 (1990): 7 (emphasis his). I disagree with Van Buren's call to move away from Paul to a new position, "*the Church with and for Israel*," which is essentially the two-covenant theology in which the Jewish people is Israel and the Church is a "gathering of Gentiles" (8) supportive of Israel, but "the way of *Torah* is God's way for them, not for us" (16).

[61] Johnson, "Romans 11," 100.

who call upon Him. For whoever calls upon the name of the Lord shall be saved" (10:12–13). In Paul's program of salvation, he consistently maintains "a universal gospel based on justification by faith."[62] There are not two separate paths to salvation, as the two-covenant theologians claim.

Paul's position also stands in contrast to many replacement theologians and dispensationalists who make a dichotomy between law and grace, maintaining that in the New Testament grace replaces Old Testament law. From the time of Marcion, to the theology of Martin Luther[63] and Rudolf Bultmann,[64] to recent charges from former Seventh-day Adventists,[65] one can trace throughout church history a radical opposition between law and grace. In contrast to these views, Paul sets forth a doctrine of salvation that combines law and grace, and demonstrates this from the Old Testament.

Paul's understanding of a single plan of salvation for both Jew and Gentile also makes problematic the interpretation of Romans 9–11 by dispensationalists and other interpreters who see Romans 11:25–26 fulfilled by an end-time rebirth of the entire Jewish nation. For some this involved a miraculous conversion of "all Israel" to Christ; for others they are saved apart from Christ.[66] But whatever the view, it presupposes that salvation, in the end-time, is ultimately based upon "ancestral privilege."[67] This interpretation is opposed to the tenor of Paul's argument throughout Romans 9–11 and the entire epistle: salvation comes by faith in Jesus Christ, and not by ancestral privilege.[68]

---

[62] Ibid., 102.

[63] Martin Luther's law/grace dichotomy is summed up in his statement: "The Law and the Gospel are two doctrines that are absolutely contrary. The Law is the Word of perdition, the Word of wrath, the Word of sadness, the Word of pain, the voice of the Judge, while the Gospel is the Word of salvation, the Word of grace, the Word of comfort, the Word of joy" (Ewald M. Plass, ed. *What Luther Says: An Anthology* [St. Louis, MO: Concordia, 1959], 2:732–733).

[64] See, e.g., Rudolf K. Bultmann, *Jesus and the Word* (New York: Scribner, 1958), 31–33.

[65] See, e.g., regular presentations in *Proclamation!* magazine, published by Life Assurance Ministries, Glendale, AZ, edited by Dale Ratzlaff, former Seventh-day Adventist minister.

[66] See, e.g., Krister Stendahl, *Paul among Jews and Gentiles* (Philadelphia, PA: Fortress, 1976), 4.

[67] Wright, *Climax*, 246, 248: "Paul makes it abundantly clear that there is no covenant membership, and consequently no salvation, for those who simply rest on their ancestral privilege. . . . Paul clearly sees the salvation of Jews in the future as dependent on their coming to Christian faith."

[68] For further critique of the dispensationalist theology as in effect denying the Gospel, see John Gerstner, *Wrongly Dividing the Word of Truth: A Critique of Dispensationalism* (Brentwood, TN: Wolgemuth & Hyatt, 1991), 149–208.

Continuity in Christocentric Focus

The continuity of salvation that Paul presents in Romans 9–11 is centered in Jesus Christ. In 9:32–33, Christ is alluded to as the decisive orientation-point distinguishing Israel as a whole from the faithful remnant in Israel; He is that "Stumbling Stone" over which Israel stumbled. Citing Isa 28:16 in the LXX, Paul points to Christ as the Object of saving faith: "Whosoever believes on Him [Christ, the Stumbling Stone][69] will not be put to shame." In Romans 10:4 Christ is presented as the "goal" (*telos*) of the Torah (10:4).[70] Romans 10:9–10 presents faith in Jesus Christ as the only legitimate way of salvation, for both Jew and Gentile, and v. 11 returns to Isaiah 28:16 to round out the argument. Paul's climax again highlights the christocentric nature of salvation, as he cites Isaiah 59:20–21, a Messianic passage of the coming Deliverer, to buttress his conclusion that "in this way all Israel will be saved" (11:26). All Israel, the faithful people of God through all the ages, will be saved by the same Deliverer, Jesus Christ.

Martin Down pinpoints this basic continuity in the relationship between Israel and the Church: "The continuity consists in the Person of Jesus Christ."[71] Paul's thoroughgoing christocentricism in Romans 9–11 does not allow for a two-covenant theology with two separate ways of salvation, Torah for Jews, and Jesus Christ for Gentiles.

Continuity of the Covenants

In his introduction to Romans 9–11, Paul identifies the Israelites as those to whom belong "the covenants" (9:4). All of the Old Testament covenants (Edenic, Noahic, Abrahamic, Sinaitic, Davidic, and the New Covenant) are part of one everlasting covenant of grace. Paul clearly understood this, as he cites language from the New Covenant promise of Jeremiah 31:33 ("This is my covenant with them") in Romans 11:27, and applies this covenant to "all Israel," comprised of both Jew and Gentile

---

[69] The words "on Him" (Greek *ep' autō*) are not found in the Hebrew text, but the immediate context of this passage (and of Isaiah 8:14 which Paul combines with this one) is messianic/eschatological (the whole "Volume of Immanuel," Isaiah 7–12, which is ultimately Messianic, and Isaiah 28:21–22 are clearly eschatological/Messianic), and thus the Greek translation is appropriate for context.

[70] See Roberto Badenas, *Christ: the End of the Law: Rom 10.4 in Pauline Perspective* (Sheffield: JSOT, 1985).

[71] Martin Down, *The New Jerusalem: Israel, the Church and the Nation* (Cape Town, South Africa: Vineyard International, 2008), 36. Cf. Pedersen, "Continuity and Discontinuity," 18: "With the arrival of the long-promised Messiah, the new and final chapter has now opened in the Israelite storyline. Paul's understanding of the Messiah as the goal and climax of the preceding Israelite story seems to be the hinge on which his definition of the present remnant of Israel turns."

(11:26). The single, unified, everlasting covenant of Scripture joins Israel and the Church into one covenant community, saved by and faithful to the Lord of the covenant, Jesus Christ.

Continuity in Eschatology

Finally, Romans 9–11 affirms a continuity between Israel and the Church in the eschatological perspective that it presents. These chapters must be seen against the eschatological substructure that forms the warp and woof of all New Testament theology.[72] According to New Testament eschatology, the Old Testament, classical, kingdom prophecies have one eschatological (last-day) fulfillment with three stages: 1) inaugurated eschatology, the basic fulfillment of the Old Testament eschatological hopes, climaxing in the earthly life and work of Jesus the Representative Israelite at His first advent; 2) appropriated eschatology, the derived spiritual aspects of fulfillment in Christian Israel (the church) as the Body of Christ in the time between Christ's first and Second Coming; and 3) consummated eschatology, the aspect of final universal fulfillment through apocalyptic Israel (all the redeemed, including both Jews and Gentiles), ushering in the age to come at the second advent of Christ and beyond.

Here we note that in Romans 9–11 Paul affirms all three stages of this eschatological substructure (and elaborates on each in much more detail elsewhere throughout his epistles). First, he depicts inaugurated eschatology: the crucial pivot of salvation history has arrived with the coming of the Messiah, the One who is the embodiment/goal of Old Testament Torah (10:4), but also a "Stumbling Stone" (9:33) who calls for a decision of faith acceptance (10:9–13). Second, Paul highlights appropriated eschatology: the present is a time for the continuation and expansion of biblical-historical Israel through a faithful remnant (the *ekklēsia*, the Church), comprised of Jews and engrafted Gentiles, who place their faith in Jesus (11:5–25). Finally, he alludes to the future time of consummated eschatology, when "all Israel [the true people of God of all ages, Jew and Gentile] will be saved" (11:26). At every stage of this eschatological outworking of God's plan, biblical-historical Israel and the Church are united.

Throughout the time of appropriated eschatology, Paul expresses hope that "some" (11:14), even "the fullness" (11:12) of the natural

---

[72] For elaboration and biblical substantiation of the eschatological substructure of New Testament theology from a Seventh-day Adventist perspective, see, e.g., Richard M. Davidson, "Interpreting Old Testament Prophecy," *Understanding Scripture: An Adventist Approach*, ed. George W. Reid (Silver Spring, MD: Biblical Research Institute, 2005), 183–204; *idem*, "Sanctuary Typology," *Symposium on Revelation–Book I*, ed. Frank B. Holbrook (Silver Spring, MD: Biblical Research Institute, 1992), 99–111.

branches that were lopped off may be re-grafted into "their own olive tree" once more (11:24). He sees this re-acceptance of the natural branches as nothing short of "life from the dead" (11:15).[73]

---

[73] Ellen White writes in similar language of the experience of Jews in these last days who accept the Messiah, and calls for a special work for the Jewish people, and a special work on the part of Jewish believers, in the eschatological setting of last days, saying that there will be many who aid in preparing the way for the Lord's second advent (see esp. *Evangelism*, 577–579).

CHAPTER 19

Israel and the Church: Continuity and Discontinuity—II

Richard Davidson

In this second part of our study on Israel and the church, we will examine a number of passages from the New Testament Epistles that address the elements of continuity, and others that point to elements of discontinuity. This will help us to establish proper boundaries for our analysis and conclusions. However, the bulk of the discussion will be on the relationship between Israel and the church as depicted in the Gospels and Acts. We will close our discussion with an exploration of Revelation's contributions to our topic. This apocalyptic dimension is important for the mission of the church and its connection to Israel.

Other New Testament Epistle Passages Supporting the Continuity Between Israel and the Church

Galatians 3:28–29; 6:16

In Galatians 3:8, Paul cites Genesis 22:18, and in the following verses succinctly sets forth the flow of this Old Testament passage: Abraham's seed refers first to Isaac (Gen 22:16), is broadened to Abraham's many descendants (v. 17a), and then is narrowed to the singular representative Seed, the Messiah (vv. 17 b–18; cf. Gal 3:16). Building upon "the Gospel" in this passage (see Gal 3:8a), Paul insists that those who are "Christ's" are "Abraham's seed" and are "heirs according to the promise" (v. 29). Thus Paul affirms the continuity between the Old Testament seed of Abraham (Israel) and the Christian church. The church is "spiritual Israel," the continuation of the "spiritual Israel" (i.e. faithful followers of God) in Old Testament times.[1]

In his concluding benediction to the church at Galatia, Paul writes: "Peace and mercy to all who follow this rule, even [*kai*] to the Israel of God" (NIV). The phrase "Israel of God" is found nowhere else in the New Testament or in Judaism.[2] To what group does this expression refer—to the believers in Christ or to the nation of Israel? In this verse does Paul speak of one group of people (the Christians in Galatia to whom he is addressing the letter) or does he extend his benediction also to another group (the nation of Israel)? The issue in Galatians 6:16 boils down to the proper translation of the conjunction *kai* in this context: "and," or "even/also" (the appositional sense).

In light of both the immediate and the overall context of the letter, it is best to render the conjunction *kai* in Galatians 6:16 as "even" rather than "and."[3] Concomitantly, it is best to take the phrase "Israel of God" as applying to *all* of the Christian believers together, not to the nation of Israel or just Jewish-Christians. So concludes Richard Longenecker: "All of the views that take 'the Israel of God' to refer to Jews and not Gentiles, while supportable by reference to Paul's wider usage (or non-use) of terms and expressions, fail to take seriously enough the context of the Galatian letter itself."[4] Thus in this passage, as in Romans 9–11, we find continuity between Israel and the believers in Christ (both Jews and Gentiles), who actually comprise the faithful Israel of God.

---

[1] See further discussion in Richard M. Davidson, "The New Testament Use of the Old Testament," *JATS* 5.1 (1994): 30–31.

[2] Hans Dieter Betz, *Galatians* (Philadelphia, PA: Fortress, 1979), 322.

[3] So the NIV, RSV, Phillips translation, etc. See my discussion in Davidson, "Israel and the Church," 36–37. Cf. J. Barton Payne, *Encyclopedia of Biblical Prophecy* (Grand Rapids, MI: Baker, 1973), 100, n. 183, rightly "[t]aking the *kai*, as '*even* upon the Israel of God.' To render it *and*, as if a distinct group of Hebrew-Christians were contemplated, would oppose the thrust of the epistle as a whole. That distinction has now come to an end within God's people."

[4] Richard N. Longenecker, *Galatians* (Dallas, TX: Word, 1990), 298. This interpretation is in harmony with the usage of the conjunction used in the Jewish benediction *Shemoneh Esre* (the Eighteen-petition prayer), to which Paul probably alludes in his mention of "Peace and mercy..." at the beginning of his benediction. The term "peace" is often used in the Pauline benedictions, but never "mercy." He uses these two terms in the same order as in the Jewish blessing. For discussion, see Betz, *Galatians*, 321; Longenecker, *Galatians*, 298; Ridderbos, *Galatians*, 227; Ray, 106. In the Jewish benediction, a six-fold blessing was pronounced "upon us and upon all Israel, your people." Ray (108) notes that "the blessing does not envision two separate groups but rather extends the blessing to the larger group of which the first group is a part ('upon us and upon all of Israel')." Likewise, Paul is giving his version of this blessing upon the followers of Christ to whom pertain the blessings of Israel, even to the [true] Israel of God.

Ephesian 1:3–11; 2:11–22; 3:1–9

In Ephesians Paul makes clear that Gentile Christians and Jewish Christians are fellow citizens in "God's household." The integration of Gentiles into the "household of God" is not an afterthought, but a revelation in Paul's day of the divine "mystery [*mystērion*] of His will" (Eph 1:9; cf. 3:3; Col 1:26; Rom 11:26) planned "before the creation of the world" (Eph 1:4; cf. vv. 5, 11; 3:9). Through the cross, Christ has "made both [Jew and Gentile] one, and has broken down the middle wall of division" (Eph 2:14). In Jesus Christ, the Gentiles, who were once "aliens from the commonwealth of Israel and strangers from the covenants of promise" (Eph 2:12) have become "fellow citizens with God's people and members of God's household, built upon the foundation of the apostles and prophets, with Christ Jesus himself as the chief cornerstone (Eph 2:19–20).

The "mystery" [*mystērion*] mentioned by Paul in Ephesians is the same mystery referred to in Romans 11:26: "This mystery is that through the gospel the Gentiles are heirs together with Israel, members together of one body, and sharers together in the promise in Christ Jesus" (Eph 3:6 NIV). Three times the apostle stresses the concept of "together"—using three different Greek words with the prefix *syn-* (meaning "together"): *synklēronoma*, *syssōma*, and *symmetocha*. Hans LaRondelle draws the implication for the relationship between Israel and the church:

> No theological system is justified, therefore, in rebuilding the dividing wall between Israel and the Church. The reception of Gentiles into Israel's household has been compared with the reception of the prodigal son into his father's house, in Jesus' parable (Luke 15:11–32). The father embraced the lost son when he returned in shame, while the elder son begrudged the father's generosity. So must the largely gentile Church in Paul's time realize that Gentiles have entered into the house of Israel as their Father's house and are entitled to partake fully of Israel's covenants as fellow citizens and co-heirs (cf. Romans 8:17). The sonship of Gentiles is an adoption into an already existing household.[5]

This perspective of Paul leaves no room for the position of classic dispensationalism, in which there are two plans of God, one for Gentiles and one for Jews. "The Church as the united worship of God by Jews and Gentiles in one body, is not a temporary solution for an emergency situation

---

[5] LaRondelle, *Israel of God*, 112–113.

caused by the rejection of Christ by the nation of Israel. The uniting of two previously separated branches of the human race in Christ is *the* mystery, the substance and essence of God's eternal plan."[6]

Hebrews 8:7–13; 10:15–18

The author of Hebrews makes the longest Old Testament citation anywhere in the New Testament, twice quoting the new covenant promise of Jeremiah 31:31–34 (Heb 8:8–12; 10:16–17). This Old Testament citation clearly refers to biblical-historical Israel ("Behold, the days are coming, says the Lord, when I will make a new covenant *with the house of Israel and with the house of Judah*"), but the author of Hebrews insists that the fulfillment of this new covenant promise has come to individual Jews and Gentiles in the Church: "God's new covenant with Israel *has found* its true fulfillment in Christ's enthronement at the right hand of God as the better High Priest for Israel. . . . [Hebrews 8] proclaims the gospel message that the promised 'new covenant' has been ratified by the atoning sacrifice of Christ and is now powerfully effective in the risen Christ (see Hebrews 4:14–16; 5:5, 6, 10; 6:19–20; 7:11–27; 8:1–2; 9:14, 24; 12:24; 13:20)."[7] There are not "two new covenants," as some dispensational writers claim, nor a new covenant applicable only to a future repentant "ethnic" Israel, as others suggest. There is but one, valid, new covenant, the fulfillment of Jeremiah 31, ratified by Christ's sacrifice, and now applicable to both Jews and Gentiles who believe in Jesus.[8] Such fulfillment may be seen to "refute dispensationalism's basic premise that God's dealings with Israel remain separate from his dealings with the church."[9] It affirms the basic continuity between Israel and the church as presented by Paul in Romans 9–11, Galatians 6:16 and Ephesians.

1 Peter 1:2–3; 2:4–9; 5:1–4

Peter addresses his first epistle to "the pilgrims [or 'exiles,' *parapidēmos*] of the Dispersion [*diaspora*]," using language found in Judaism for the Jewish people of the "Diaspora" (areas outside of Palestine), but here Peter is clearly addressing the Christian church, including both Jews and Gentiles.[10] Peter's language of "the people of God," (2:10;

---

[6] Ibid., 113.

[7] Ibid., 116.

[8] For discussion, with exact citations from dispensationalist writers, see ibid., 114–121.

[9] Daniel P. Fuller, *Gospel and Law: Contrast or Continuum? The Hermeneutics of Dispensationalism and Covenant Theology* (Grand Rapids, MI: Eerdmans, 1980), 165.

[10] See D.A. Carson, Douglas J. Moo, and Leon Morris, *An Introduction to the New Testament* (Grand

citing Hos 1:9-10; 2:23), as well as other Old Testament language used for biblical-historical Israel—"royal priesthood, a holy nation, His own special people," 2:5, 9, citing Exodus 19:5-6—points unmistakably to a continuity between Israel and the Church. Peter calls the believers "the flock of God," alluding both to Ezekiel's prediction of the restored faithful remnant of Israel as the eschatological flock ruled by the Messianic Shepherd (Ezek 34), and to Jesus' conscious fulfillment of this prophecy (Luke 12:32; John 10:16). The church is that eschatological faithful remnant of Israel, the "spiritual house" of God (2:5), the continuation of the one People of God (2:10).[11]

Elements of Discontinuity between Israel and the Church in the New Testament Epistles

Although the major emphasis of Pauline theology is upon the continuity between the faithful remnant of Israel and the church, one must not overlook elements of discontinuity in his writing as well.

Romans 9-11

In Romans 9-11, there is a discontinuity between the unbelieving Jews (the severed branches of the olive tree) and the faithful remnant of Israel (the covenant community of the olive tree, i.e. the church). Every element of continuity in Romans 9-11, described above, implies a discontinuity as well, between those Israelites "according to the flesh" who do not accept Christ and the faithful remnant of Israel who do accept Him. Acceptance of the Messiah becomes the great eschatological divide in Israel. The Israelites "according to the flesh" who do not accept Christ cannot claim to be part of the faithful remnant; they cannot inherit the covenant promises while they remain in unbelief; they cannot claim status as the people of God. However, Paul does not rule out the possibility that these severed branches (unbelieving Jews) can be grafted back onto the olive tree if they do not persist in unbelief. In fact, his passion is that "by any means" he may "provoke to jealousy those who are my flesh and save some of them" (Rom 11:14). Paul longs for the discontinuity to be overcome, as severed branches are grafted back onto the one true olive tree.

Rapids, MI: Zondervan, 1992), 425; Donald Guthrie, *New Testament Introduction* (Downers Grove, IL: InterVarsity, 1990), 784-786.

[11] For a summary of Old Testament covenant promises being seen by New Testament writers as fulfilled in the Church, in addition to those I have mentioned, see esp. LaRondelle, *Israel of God*, 98-123.

Other Passages in the New Testament Epistles

A major aspect of discontinuity is between the Old Testament ceremonial system, in force for biblical-historical Israel before Christ's death, and its annulment for the New Testament church, as that typical system met its Antitype in Christ's death (Col 2:14–17; Eph 2:15). For the New Testament church (the faithful remnant of Israel), physical circumcision is no longer the sign of belonging to the covenant people (although inward/spiritual circumcision is still imperative); baptism, incumbent upon both Jewish and Christian believers, is the equivalent New Testament sign of the People of God (Rom 2:25–29; 6:1–5; Gal 5:1–15; Eph 2:11–13; Col 2:11–13). Gentiles who accepted Jesus as Messiah were no longer required to be circumcised or to keep the Old Testament ceremonial law (Acts 15).[12]

Another discontinuity is found in the fact that while Old Testament Israel looked forward to the coming of the Messiah, the New Testament church (the faithful remnant of Israel) has accepted the Messiah's coming as historical reality. For the church, the inauguration of the kingdom in Jesus has already occurred, although the consummation of the kingdom is still future and believers are living in the "tension" between the "already" and the "not yet."

Even though it was God's plan for the various nations of the Gentiles to join with Israel in the worship of God in Old Testament times, such incorporating of believing Gentiles with the people of God was limited. In New Testament times, however, God unveils the "mystery" discussed above: "that through the gospel the Gentiles are heirs together with Israel, members together of one body, and sharers together in the promise in Christ Jesus" (Eph 3:6 NIV). The church brings into existence the oneness between Jews and Gentiles designed by God from the foundation of the world. The faithful remnant of biblical-historical Israel is expanded into a worldwide movement of "spiritual Israel," the true seed of Abraham (Gal 3:29).

The New Testament church continues to be described in terms of the People of God (see discussion above) and the marriage metaphor, the Bride of Christ (Eph 1:22; 3:10, 21; 5:23–32), as the Old Testament Israel was Yahweh's bride (Isa 54:5; 62:4–5; Jer 2:2–3; Ezek 16; Hos 2; etc.). New metaphors are also applied to the New Testament church: the church as a body (Rom 12:3–8; 1 Cor 12:12–26; Eph 1:22–23; 4:1–16) with Christ as the Head (Eph 1:22; 4:15; Col 1:18); and the church (both corporately

---

[12] For discussion, see Richard M. Davidson, "Which Torah Laws Should Gentile Christians Obey? The Relationship Between Leviticus 17 18 and Acts 15" (paper presented at the Evangelical Theological Society 59th Annual Meeting, San Diego, CA, 15 November 2007).

and individually) as a temple of the Holy Spirit (Eph 2:21–22; 1 Cor 3:16–17; 6:19; 2 Cor 6:16, 19). Recognizing the New Testament church to be in fundamental continuity with the faithful remnant of biblical-historical Israel does not diminish the precious regard with which Paul and the other New Testament writers speak of God's New Testament church.

Israel and the Church in the Gospels and the Book of Acts

Israel and the Church in the Gospels: Continuity

Old Testament Classical Prophecy and Jesus' Ministry

As we have seen in the Old Testament section of this study, the kingdom promises to Israel began to be fulfilled, especially upon Israel's return from the Babylonian exile. These promises were to climax in the first advent of the Messiah in "the last days" (Heb 1:2). When the Messiah, Israel's ultimate King and Representative Israelite, came to earth, He brought about a basic fulfillment of all these kingdom promises in Himself (Matt 12:28; 2 Cor 1:20). Through His life, death and resurrection, He inaugurated the "rule" or "reign" of God on earth (which He called "the kingdom of heaven/God").[13] The term "kingdom of heaven" is used 31 times in the New Testament, all in the Gospel of Matthew. The term "kingdom of God" is found five times in Matthew, 13 times in Mark, 32 times in Luke, and twice in John.

At Christ's first advent, He shared the spiritual principles of the "kingdom of heaven." The people of Israel, in general, "heard Him gladly" (Mark 12:37), and although many misunderstood His immediate mission to be that of a political deliverer of Israel from Roman occupation, they widely hailed Him as the Messiah (Matt 21:1–11). On the day of His resurrection, the disciples traveling to Emmaus stated that Jesus "was a Prophet mighty in deed and word before God and *all the people*" (Luke 24:19). The Gospel writers constantly describe the popularity of Jesus among the Jews, so much so that the Jewish leaders were afraid to act against Jesus.[14]

During His earthly ministry of three and one-half years, Jesus also reached out to the Gentiles in harmony with the Old Testament kingdom prophecies, signaling the spiritual nature of His kingdom that would break down the partition between Jews and Gentiles. He mingled freely with the Samaritans (John 4), rewarded the faith of the centurion at Capernaum (Matt 8), healed the daughter of the Canaanite woman in Phoenicia (Matt

---

[13] See esp. the discussion in the classic work by George Eldon Ladd, *The Gospel of the Kingdom: Scriptural Studies in the Kingdom of God* (Grand Rapids, MI: Eerdmans, 1959).

[14] See, e.g., Matthew 21:26, 46; Mark 11:18, 32.

15), and welcomed the visit of the Greeks (John 12).

According to the gospel accounts, Jesus, the Messianic Representative of Israel, may, in a sense, be regarded as the ultimate Faithful Remnant of Israel, as He recapitulated in His life the experience of ancient Israel, succeeding where historical Israel failed. The story of Jesus is "Israel's story played out in a single life. . . . *the history of Israel in miniature.*"[15] For example, the first five chapters of Matthew describe Jesus as the Representative of Israel experiencing a New Exodus: coming out of Egypt after a death decree (Matt 2:15), and going through His antitypical Red Sea experience in His baptism (Matt 3; cf. 1 Cor 10:1-2). This is followed by His wilderness experience of 40 days, paralleling the 40 years of ancient Israel in the wilderness. During this time Jesus indicates His own awareness of His role as the Remnant of Israel in the New Exodus by consistently meeting the devil's temptations with quotations from Deuteronomy 6-8 (where ancient Israel's temptations in the wilderness are summarized). Jesus appears on the Mount as a new Moses, with His twelve disciples representing the tribes of Israel, and repeats the Law as Moses did at the end of the wilderness sojourn. Matthew and the other Synoptic Gospels also depict the death and resurrection of Jesus as a New Exodus.[16]

Jesus' Church (ekklēsia): The Remnant of Israel

Jesus instituted His church (*ekklēsia*) in harmony with the Old Testament (LXX *ekklēsia* standing for Hebrew *qahal* "congregation"), to describe those within Israel who are in covenant relationship with Yahweh. The term *ekklēsia* , as used in the Gospel of Matthew, describes the faithful remnant within Israel, identified as those accepting the Messiah promised in Old Testament times (Matt 16:18; 18:17).[17] This remnant is not an exclusive one, as in Qumran, but, as demonstrated by John the Baptist, is open to all who demonstrated the "fruit" of true repentance (Matt 3:8). According to Matthew, "the church is an expanded Israel. It is a continuation of the true remnant of Israel to which Gentile believers have been added."[18]

---

[15] N. T. Wright, *The New Testament and the People of God* (Minneapolis, MA: Fortress, 1992), 402.

[16] Note, e.g., how, at the Transfiguration, the first Moses speaks to the New Moses about His *exodus* which He was to accomplish at Jerusalem (Luke 9:31). Jesus' death is His ultimate Red Sea experience. After His resurrection, He remains in the wilderness of this earth 40 days (like Israel's 40 years in the wilderness) and then as the New Joshua enters heavenly Canaan as the pioneer and perfecter of our faith. See George Balentine, "Death of Christ as a New Exodus," *RE* 59 (1962): 27-41; and *idem*, "The Concept of the New Exodus in the Gospels" (Th.D. diss., Southern Baptist Theological Seminary, 1961).

[17] See Gerhard Hasel, "Remnant," 4:134: "Though the noun 'remnant' is absent from the Gospels, the concept has a prominent place."

[18] Daniel Steffen, "The Future of Israel within the Matthean Church" (paper presented at the an-

Jesus and the Restoration of Israel

Through the faithful remnant, the church, it was Jesus' intention to restore Israel, in harmony with the many Old Testament promises of Israel's restoration after judgment. The "gathering" of the Twelve to Himself "represented at least symbolically, a 'regathering of the twelve tribes of Israel.'"[19] According to all three Synoptic Gospels, this faithful remnant was sent on a mission to "gather the lost sheep of the house of Israel" (Matt 10:6; cf. Mark 6:6-13; Luke 9:1-6), and "in the Matthean version of the sending discourse, the focus gradually shifts toward a more universal concern, which finds further development in the great commission (Matt 28:19-20; cf. 24:14)."[20] The Gospels use language of "building and planting" to speak of this remnant (Matt 15:13), and the imagery of the Shepherd and His sheep, evoking similar Old Testament language.[21] The reference in John 10:16 to "other sheep . . . not of this fold" highlights the expansive aspect of the remnant.

It appears that part of Jesus' intention for the restoration of Israel included the desire that the Old Testament kingdom prophecies also be fulfilled in their *geopolitical* features by theocratic Israel as they accepted the Messiah and extended the Messianic kingdom throughout the world. Although, as with the remnant concept of the Old Testament, this was not to be accomplished by force. In describing His mission strategy, Jesus utilizes language both from the classical prophets and from the apocalyptic book of Daniel (but not from those prophecies of Daniel that predict the destruction of Jerusalem).[22]

Throughout most of His ministry, until just before His death, Jesus seems to have operated on the premise of the potential fulfillment of the Old Testament classical kingdom prophecies through the nation of Israel. Daniel Steffan examines some of these possible references to the fulfillment of Old Testament kingdom prophecies.[23] Jesus promises that the "meek will inherit the earth" (Matt 5:5), in fulfillment of the promise in

---

nual ETS Meeting, Nov 16, 2000), 4.

[19] Clinton Wahlen, "The Remnant in the Gospels," *Toward a Theology of the Remnant,* ed. Ángel M. Rodríguez (Silver Spring, MD: Biblical Research Institute, 2009), 68. See ibid., pp. 61-76, for more complete treatment of the remnant motif in the Gospels.

[20] Ibid., 69.

[21] See ibid., 74-75 for discussion. New Testament passages using the shepherd-sheep imagery include Matthew 10:6; 15:24; 26:31; Luke 12:32; John 10:16.

[22] See Reimar Vetne, "The Influence and Use of Daniel in the Synoptic Gospels" (Ph.D. diss., Andrews University, 2011), passim.

[23] Steffen, "The Future of Israel," 1-21.

Psalm 37:11 (cf. Deut 4:1; 16:20; Isa 57:13; 60:21). He describes what many scholars have seen as the "Messianic Banquet" (Matt 8:5–13), in which Gentiles from east and west will join with Jews "and sit down with Abraham, Isaac, and Jacob in the kingdom of heaven" (Matt 8:11–12). This expectation of the restoration of Israel is prominent not only in the Gospel of Matthew but also Luke.[24]

Ellen White perceptively writes: "Had Israel as a nation preserved her allegiance to Heaven, Jerusalem would have stood forever, the elect of God."[25] In connection with Jesus' weeping over Jerusalem at the time of His triumphal entry (Luke 19:41–44), White elaborates on the glorious divine intention for the nation of Israel:

> If Jerusalem had known what it was her privilege to know, and had heeded the light which Heaven had sent her, she might have stood forth in the pride of prosperity, the queen of kingdoms, free in the strength of her God-given power. There would have been no armed soldiers standing at her gates, no Roman banners waving from her walls. The glorious destiny that might have blessed Jerusalem had she accepted her Redeemer rose before the Son of God. He saw that she might through Him have been healed of her grievous malady, liberated from bondage, and established as the mighty metropolis of the earth. From her walls the dove of peace would have gone forth to all nations. She would have been the world's diadem of glory.[26]

Even at the time of His triumphant entry, there was still opportunity for Israel's theocratic leaders, to respond in repentance and acceptance of the Messiah:

> When the fast westering sun should pass from sight in the heavens, Jerusalem's day of grace would be ended. While the procession was halting on the brow of Olivet, it was not yet too late for

---

[24] See esp. Jacob Jervell, *Luke and the People of God* (Minneapolis, MN: Augsburg, 1972), esp. 41–112. Joseph B. Tyson, *Luke, Judaism, and the Scholars: Critical Approaches to Luke-Acts* (Columbia, SC: University of South Carolina Press, 1999), 94, summarizes Jervell's "fundamental axiom, namely that the church that Luke describes is the 'restored Israel,' composed of repentant Jews and those Gentiles who had previously been associated with them." Cf. Richard Bauckham, "The Restoration of Israel in Luke-Acts," *Restoration: Old Testament, Jewish, and Christian Perspectives*, ed. James M. Scott (Leiden: Brill, 2001), 435–487.

[25] Ellen G. White, *The Great Controversy Controversy* (Washington, DC: Review and Herald, 1888), 18.

[26] Ellen G. White, *Desire of Ages* (Mountain View, CA: Pacific Press, 1898), 576.

Jerusalem to repent. The angel of mercy was then folding her wings to step down from the golden throne to give place to justice and swift-coming judgment. But Christ's great heart of love still pleaded for Jerusalem, that had scorned His mercies, despised His warnings, and was about to imbrue her hands in His blood. If Jerusalem would but repent, it was not yet too late. While the last rays of the setting sun were lingering on temple, tower, and pinnacle, would not some good angel lead her to the Saviour's love, and avert her doom? . . . . If Jerusalem will hear the call, if she will receive the Saviour who is entering her gates, she may yet be saved.[27]

But the theocratic leaders did not repent, and the "great discontinuity" descended upon national Israel as a theocratic, geopolitical entity.

National Israel and the Church in Gospels and Acts: Discontinuity

The Geopolitical, Theocratic Discontinuity

Although the people of Israel, in general, were favorable to Jesus, many of the religio-political leaders opposed him. Jesus gave them opportunity after opportunity to accept Him, patiently answered their questions, provided evidence upon evidence of His messiahship. But instead of responding in repentance and acceptance of Jesus as Messiah, the hearts of these religio-political leaders became more and more hardened, more and more determined to destroy Him. Finally, the day of decision on the part of Israel's leadership arrived.

In fulfillment of the Passover typology, on the tenth day of Nisan, when the Paschal lamb was set aside for slaughter (Exod 12:3), Jesus, by his triumphal entry on the ninth day and his cleansing of the temple on the tenth day of Nisan, precipitated his being set apart on the tenth day for sacrifice as the Sanhedrin met and decided to find a way to trap Him and then condemn Him to death (Mark 11:1–18; cf. Luke 19:47).[28] This set the stage for Jesus' parable that has widely been interpreted as announcing the rejection of the Jewish people and their replacement by the Gentile church.

Matthew 21:43

After the decision by the official body of Jewish leaders to formally

---

[27] Ibid., 578.

[28] For support of this chronology of the last week of Jesus' life, see, e.g., *AdvBibComm*, 5:233. Cf. *Desire of Ages*, 593. Jesus marks this rejection by Israel's leaders in the enacted parable of the withered fig tree (Matt 21:18–19).

condemn Him, Jesus directly addressed "the chief priests and elders" (Matt 21:23, 45) with His parable of wicked vinedressers/tenants (Matt 21:33–40). The parable climaxes with Jesus' words recorded in v. 43: "Therefore I say to you, the kingdom of God will be taken from you and given to a nation bearing the fruits of it." David Turner rightly notes that "Christian exegesis has often viewed 21:43 as predicting the demise of Israel as the people of God and its replacement by the predominantly gentile church."[29] Is this interpretation correct? Several considerations provide evidence to help us decide.

First, it is vital to the interpretation of this parable to understand that it is specifically addressed to the "chief priests and elders" (v. 23). Matthew reiterates in v. 42, "Jesus said to them [the chief priests and elders] . . . ." And in v. 45, Matthew explicitly records: "Now when the chief priests and Pharisees heard His parables, they perceived that He was speaking of them."[30] Second, in recording the parable and the historical circumstances of its telling, Matthew carefully distinguishes between the Jewish leaders who rejected Jesus (to whom the parable is addressed) and "the multitudes" of the general Jewish populace who supported Jesus (v. 46). The Jewish leaders were not able to "lay hands on Him" because "they feared the multitudes, because they [the multitudes] took Him for a prophet" (v. 46).

Third, the vineyard represents Israel, just as in Isaiah 5 (the Old Testament passage after which Jesus was probably modeling his parable).[31] The tenants of the vineyard stand for Israel's theocratic leaders. "The identification of the recalcitrant tenants with the current religious leaders is clear."[32] Jesus describes how the tenants or vinedressers mistreated the servants sent to receive the fruit from the vineyard. When the landowner finally sent his own son, they killed him. He then asks the Jewish leaders what the owner of the vineyard will do to the tenants, and they unwittingly condemn themselves as they answer: "He will destroy those wicked men miserably, and lease his vineyard to other vinedressers who will render to him the fruits in their seasons" (v. 41). Then Jesus cites Psalm 118:22–23, regarding the stone which the builders rejected becoming the chief cornerstone of the building (v. 42), again alluding to the

---

[29] David L. Turner, *Matthew* (Grand Rapids, MI: Baker, 2008), 517.

[30] On the Markan version of these events, culminating in the parable of the wicked tenants, see Clinton Wahlen, "The Temple in Mark and Contested Authority," *Biblical Interpretation* 15 (2007): 248–267.

[31] See esp. Isaiah 5:7: "For the vineyard of the Lord of hosts is the house of Israel." The parable in Isaiah 5 reached its historical fulfillment in the exile of Israel and Judah.

[32] Turner, *Matthew*, 517.

Jewish leaders as the builders who rejected Him, the Chief Cornerstone.[33]

Fourth, one must note contrasts between the "Song of the Vineyard" in Isaiah 5 and Jesus' parable. Isaiah 5 makes no mention of the tenants or vinedressers. In Isaiah 5, the vineyard itself is destroyed (vv. 5–6, which was fulfilled historically at the time of the Exile, in fulfillment of the covenant curses of Deut 28), while in Jesus' parable the tenants are destroyed (according to the Jewish leaders' interpretation) or the vineyard is taken away from them (Jesus' interpretation) and the vineyard is given over to others. The vineyard—Israel—is not destroyed.

Finally, the term *ethnos* in this passage must be seen in its larger canonical as well as immediate context. In the Old Testament, the LXX uses the noun *ethnos* about 1000 times (mostly in the plural *ethnē* for the "nations" besides Israel). In the vast majority of references, the term translates the Hebrew word *goy* "nation, people," and refers to the non-Israelite nations, while the Greek word *laos* translates the Hebrew term *'am* "people, nation, tribe," and refers to the people of Israel (although in over 130 references *ethnos* translates the Hebrew *'am*).[34] In the New Testament, the term *ethnos* occurs 162 times, and "no longer has as matter of course the meaning which overwhelmingly predominates in the Old Testament."[35] It can refer to the Jewish people (at least 14 times; e.g., Luke 7:5; 23:2; John 11:48–52; 18:35; Acts 10:22) as well as to the Gentiles.

In Matthew, the term *ethnos* occurs 15 times, and all eight occurrences before 21:43 are in the plural referring to the "Gentiles." If *ethnos* in this verse were referring to the Gentiles, one would expect it to appear in the plural. After this verse, all but one of the remaining occurrences in Matthew are in the plural, referring universally to "all nations." In Matthew 24:7, one finds the only other place in the Gospel where *ethnos* occurs in the singular, and here we find a clue to its meaning in Matt 21:43: "nation [*ethnos*] shall rise against nation [*ethnos*], and kingdom [*basileia*] against kingdom [*basileia*]." By distinguishing between *ethnos* with *basileia* (the latter term clearly referring to the geo-political aspects of a kingdom), Matthew seems to imply that *ethnos* does not refer to the political aspects, but rather carries its fundamental meaning of a "group of people." Only the immediate context can indicate which group of people is being referred to by the term.

Daniel Harrington issues the strong counsel concerning the impor-

---

[33] John Nolland, *The Gospel of Matthew: A Commentary on the Greek Text* (Grand Rapids, MI: Eerdmans, 2005), 877–878, provides evidence from the text and Qumran parallels for the "in-any-case evident reference of the builders to Jewish religious leaders" (878).

[34] Hans Bietenhard, "People," *NIDNTT*, 2:790–791.

[35] Ibid., 793.

tance of the immediate context here: "since this text is so important in Jewish-Christian dialogue, it should be read carefully with an eye to the context of Matt 21:41, 43. The context—a dispute with Israel's leaders—should control the interpretation of *ethnos* and supersessionist claims should be avoided."[36] In light of the context, Harrington is on the right track when he states that "it seems unwise to take *ethnos* in 21:43 ('the kingdom of God will be . . . given to a nation bearing fruit') as a reference to the Gentile Church or even the Church understood as a 'third race' besides Jews and Gentiles. It should be understood in its most basic sense as a 'group of people,' in this case the leaders of the Jewish Christian community."[37]

One could assert that "all these lines of evidence indicate that the parable concerns the *leadership* of Israel. Matthew contends that the tenant farmers, not the vineyard, must be replaced."[38] Who are the "other tenant farmers" (v. 41)? Harrington appropriately suggests, "These are presumably the leaders of the Jewish-Christian community. They are not the same as 'all Israel' (which is the vineyard). There is no reason here to assume that the 'others' are Gentiles and that the handing over of leadership involves the rejection of Israel."[39]

This is not to say those of the common people of Israel who were misled by the leadership to reject Jesus have no blame. But the leadership is more blameworthy, in that they led astray many of the common people. The leadership is ultimately to blame as they officially reject Jesus in the Sanhedrin, and thus divorce the nation from the geopolitical theocracy.

Jesus does announce a discontinuity in this parable, but it is not a discontinuity between Israel and the Church, as commonly claimed by replacement theologians. Rather, it is the discontinuity between the theocratic Jewish leadership who rejected Jesus, and the leadership of the faithful remnant of Israel, the Jewish-Christian leaders consisting of Christ's disciples. The vineyard remains constant, as does the olive tree in

---

[36] Ibid., 304–305.

[37] Ibid., 304.

[38] Daniel J. Harrington, *The Gospel of Matthew* (Collegevile, MN: Liturgical, 1991), 304.

[39] Ibid., 302. Turner concurs with this caution: "Many scholars take 21:43 as teaching that a new 'nation,' the church, has replaced the nation of Israel in God's plan. But this is dubious if the kingdom is taken from the leaders, not from Israel. . . . According to 21:45, the Jewish leaders realize that Jesus is talking about them, not Israel as a whole. It is thus a mistake to view 21:43 as indicating the replacement of Israel by the gentile church" (Turner, *Matthew*, 517). Cf. Ellen White, *Acts of the Apostles* (Mountain view, CA: Pacific Press, 1911), 16, who identifies the "other husbandmen" as Christ's disciples. In a wider sense, Ellen White elsewhere identifies the "other husbandmen" with God's "covenant-keeping people" (Ellen W. White, *Patriarchs and Prophets* (Mountain View, CA: Pacific Press, 1958) 714).

Romans 9–11. God has not rejected His people Israel. He has handed over the "kingdom of God" to the "nation" (*ethnos*, or "group of people") bearing fruit, i.e. the faithful remnant within Israel, the Jewish Christian community. "This community should be viewed as the eschatological remnant of Israel . . . . This Jewish remnant becomes the nucleus of the nascent church."[40]

Ellen White recognizes that the vinedressers in this parable refer to the Jewish leadership, when she writes:

> In the parable of the vineyard it was the husbandmen whom Christ pronounced guilty. It was they who had refused to return to their lord the fruit of his ground. In the Jewish nation it was the priests and teachers who, by misleading the people, had robbed God of the service which He claimed. It was they who turned the nation away from Christ. . . . For the rejection of Christ, with the results that followed, they were responsible. A nation's sin and a nation's ruin were due to the religious leaders.[41]

Even in the midst of the discontinuity involving the theocratic leadership, Jesus does not totally close the door for Jewish leaders to accept Him as Messiah individually. He concludes His remarks with the pronouncement (v. 44): "And whoever falls on this stone [the Chief Cornerstone, Himself] will be broken [in repentance], but on whomever it falls, it will grind him to powder [eternal destruction]." The book of Acts informs us that in the time of the early Church "a great many of the priests were obedient to the faith" (Acts 6:7).

Ellen White also points out how the parable contains a lesson for the Christian church, lest Christians smugly think they could not turn away from the kingdom of God like the Jewish nation through their leaders:

> In our day are not the same influences at work? Of the husbandmen of the Lord's vineyard are not many following in the steps of the Jewish leaders? Are not religious teachers turning men away from the plain requirements of the word of God? Instead of educating them in obedience to God's law, are they not educating them in transgression? From many of the pulpits of the churches the people are taught that the law of God is not bind-

---

[40] Turner, *Matthew*, 519.
[41] Ellen G. White, *Christ's Object Lessons* (Washington, DC: Review and Herald, 1941), 304–305 (cf. the larger context, 293–295).

ing upon them."[42]

Again she writes: "The great sin of the Jews was their rejection of Christ; the great sin of the Christian world would be their rejection of the law of God, the foundation of His government in heaven and earth."[43]

Matthew 23:37–38

Following the parable of the vinedressers, Jesus tells another parable (of the wedding feast 22:1–14), and answers more questions from the Jewish leaders seeking to entangle and condemn Him (22:23–46; see Matt 22:15). After Jesus effectively silences His accusers with profound, unanswerable replies to their trick questions, He then speaks "to the multitudes and to His disciples" (Matt 23:1), and pronounces woes upon the scribes and Pharisees (Matt 23:13–36). This constitutes, in effect, the covenant curses upon the leaders who have rejected their covenant Lord. He speaks no longer as a gentle entreator, but as a judge with rebuke and condemnation.[44] The Jewish theocratic leaders had made their decision against Christ their King, and by doing so were divorcing themselves and the nation from God. Then comes the anguishing cry of a "separation struggle"[45] wrung from the heart of Jesus as He laments over His beloved city:

> O Jerusalem, Jerusalem, the one who kills the prophets and stones those who are sent to her! How often I wanted to gather your children together, as a hen gathers her chicks under her wings, but you were not willing! See! You're house is left to you desolate. For I say to you, you shall see Me no more till you say, "Blessed is He who comes in the name of the Lord" (Matt 23:37–38).

These verses preserve the last recorded public words of Jesus to Isra-

---

[42] Ibid, 305. See her extended discussion in pp. 296–306. Interestingly, she concludes her application of the parable to the Christian church, with a quotation from Romans 11:17–21, where Paul warns the Gentiles not to boast of being grafted into the olive tree, lest they themselves be cut off in unbelief.

[43] White, *The Great Controversy*, 22. Here is a special place for Adventist mission, to uphold both the Messiah and the Torah, Christ and the Law. Here also is a place to recognize the viability of the suggestion of Doukhan, *Israel and the Church*, 90–94, that the Jewish people, in upholding the law through the centuries of Christian spurning of the law, have been a witness to the perpetuity of the Law. Ellen White writes that "among the Jews are some who, like Saul of Tarsus, are mighty in the Scriptures, and these will proclaim with wonderful power the immutability of the law of God. The God of Israel will bring this to pass in our day" (White, *Acts of the Apostles*, 381).

[44] White, *Desire of Ages*, 619.

[45] Ibid., 620.

el as a theocratic entity. Here Jesus announces to Jerusalem, "Your house is left unto you desolate." There are several suggestions as to what "your house" refers: "to Jerusalem, since the lament is first addressed to her, . . . to Israel [as a national entity], . . . or to the temple in whose precincts Jesus was preaching (21:23; 24) and whose destruction was about to be predicted (24:2)."[46] We could say that "there seems to be no need to choose only one of these options; all three are closely allied and rise and fall together."[47] But as Jesus had recently referred to "My house" when He cleansed the temple (Matt 21:13), it is likely that the temple is particularly in view. Instead of calling the temple "My house" (as in the citation from Isa 56:7 in Matt 21:13), Jesus now calls it "your house." Ellen White gives this penetrating interpretation:

> But Israel as a nation had divorced herself from God. The natural branches of the olive tree were broken off. Looking for the last time upon the interior of the temple, Jesus said with mournful pathos, "Behold, your house is left unto you desolate. For I say unto you, Ye shall not see Me henceforth, till ye shall say, Blessed is He that cometh in the name of the Lord." Hitherto He had called the temple His Father's house; but now, as the Son of God should pass out from those walls, God's presence would be withdrawn forever from the temple built to His glory. Henceforth its ceremonies would be meaningless, its services a mockery.[48]

The Apocalyptic Description of Jerusalem's Fate: Matthew 24 and Daniel 9

One cannot emphasize enough that it is in the exact context where the Jewish leaders have made the decision which, in effect, divorces the nation of Israel from God, why, as a result, Jesus, for the first time in His ministry, refers to the prediction of the destruction of Jerusalem as portrayed in Daniel 9. When the Jewish leaders rejected Jesus and forfeited the theocratic leadership, the divine plan set forth in the classical prophets for the eternal status of Jerusalem as "the mighty metropolis of the earth" gave way to the apocalyptic portrait of Jerusalem's destruction and

---

[46] D. A. Carson, "Matthew," *The Expositor's Bible Commentary*, ed. F. E. Gaebelein (Grand Rapids, MI: Zondervan, 1992), 8:487.

[47] Ibid.

[48] White, *Desire of Ages*, 620.

desolation.[49] Classical prophecy had presented "what might have been" if Israel as a nation had been faithful to the covenant; apocalyptic prophecy indicates "what will be" according to the foreknowledge of God. The classical prophetic scenario was conditional upon the response of the nation; apocalyptic prophecy is unconditional, because it describes what God foreknew would actually happen.

In His Olivet Discourse (Matt 24), Jesus predicts the destruction of Jerusalem, referring explicitly to the prophecy of Daniel 9:27 (Matt 24:15). I have dealt in detail with Matthew 24 elsewhere, and shown other parallels to Daniel's prophecies of Jerusalem's destruction in Luke's Gospel, as well as the apocalyptic pattern of the entire discourse.[50] Here I emphasize the shift from the classical prophetic perspective (with its conditionality) to apocalyptic (with its "deterministic" certainty).

As we have noted above in the Old Testament discussion, while Daniel 9 predicts the destruction of Jerusalem, and implies the end of the theocracy, the prophecy says nothing about the rejection of the Jewish people. This point is emphasized as God speaks to Daniel of "your people" (Israel, cf. v. 7) repeatedly in Daniel 9 (vv. 15–16, 19, 24), and continues to use this designation, even when describing events after the time of Christ in the latter days (Dan 10:14; 12:1bis). Daniel's people—Israel—are still in existence in the latter days and still considered God's people *but in need of accepting the Messiah.*

Even though, according to Daniel 9 (and Jesus' interpretation in Matt 24), the city and temple of Jerusalem will be destroyed, and thus the promises of a glorious future for the kingdom of Israel are seemingly dashed, Jesus does not end His Olivet Discourse without hope for the kingdom promises ever to be fulfilled. Matthew 24:29–31 describes the Second Advent of Christ, returning as the Son of Man (referred to in Dan 7), "with power and great glory." One can easily fill in the blanks from Daniel 7:18, 27, and conclude that the Son of Man is returning with the "everlasting kingdom" (v. 27) so that "the saints shall receive the kingdom, and possess the kingdom forever, even forever and ever" (v. 18). This is clarified further in the statement Jesus will make to the those on His right hand

---

[49] See Davidson, "Interpreting Old Testament Prophecy," 183–204 for the biblical basis for the distinction between classical and apocalyptic prophecy. Note that dispensationalists also generally recognize that Jesus "offered" the kingdom to the nation of Israel, but that it was rejected (see, e.g., McClain, *Greatness of the Kingdom*, 304–320), but the distinction is not clearly made between classical and apocalyptic prophecy, with their separate scenarios for the future of Israel.

[50] Richard M. Davidson, "'This Generation Shall Not Pass' (Matt 24:34): Failed or Fulfilled Prophecy?" *The Cosmic Battle for Planet Earth: Essays in Honor of Norman R. Gulley*, ed. Ronald A. G. du Preez and Jiří Moskala (Berrien Springs, MI: Old Testament Department, Seventh-day Adventist Theological Seminary, Andrews University, 2003), 307–319.

from "all the nations" gathered to Him: "Then the King will say to those on His right hand, 'Come, you blessed of My Father, inherit the kingdom prepared for you from the foundation of the world'" (Matt 25:34). This universal, glorious, fulfillment of the Old Testament kingdom promises will be further expanded upon in the book of Revelation (see below).

Matthew 27:25

One more passage widely employed to posit a radical discontinuity between Israel and the Church is Matthew 27:25. In Pilate's Judgment hall, after Pilate had washed his hands of the innocent blood of Jesus, "all the people answered and said, 'His blood be on us and on our children.'" This statement is often taken as proof that the people of Israel as a whole had rejected Christ, and thus deserved to be cursed. This passage has fomented anti-Semitism as Christians have hurled accusations of "Christ-killers" and the like against the Jewish people down through Christian history.

A look at the context of this statement puts a different light on the matter. According to v. 20, "the chief priests and elders persuaded the crowd that they should ask for Barabbas and destroy Jesus." It was the Jewish leadership that fomented the crowd against Jesus.[51] Furthermore, the crowd was actually a "mob,"[52] comprised largely of the "hardened rabble" of Jerusalem.[53] They were an "ignorant mob,"[54] stirred up by the Jewish leadership. Ellen White provides the additional insight that joining the mob were actually demons in human form.[55] Such a group hardly represented the overall populace of Jerusalem, let alone the multitudes throughout the land of Israel who regarded Jesus as the Messiah, or at least, as a true Prophet (see discussion above). The statement of this "mob" certainly does not imply that the entire Jewish people had rejected Christ. It was only a small minority of the entire Jewish world population, comprised largely of an ignorant, hardened rabble, who were following the promptings of the Jewish leadership.[56]

---

[51] White, *Desire of Ages*, 732, 736, 746.

[52] Ellen White repeatedly calls this crowd "the mob" (ibid., 703, 723, 731, 732, 733, 734, 736, 738, etc.).

[53] Ibid., 703 speaks of "the clamor of the mob, many of them the rabble of Jerusalem;" 746 calls the mob the "hardened rabble."

[54] Ibid., 746.

[55] Ibid., 733.

[56] The Gospel of John also indicates that the general populace was not responsible for Jesus' death. Ekkehardt Mueller summarizes: "John makes it clear that the common people were not involved in the plot to kill Jesus and had nothing to do with his crucifixion," (Ekkehardt Mueller,

Nonetheless, these words, although instigated by Jewish leaders, had been spoken by people from the Jewish nation, in the courtroom of Pilate, and represented a legal statement of Jewish representatives. In this sense, the people of Israel had made their choice. The legal setting implies that Israel's status as the theocratic nation of the Lord had been formally forfeited. A significant number of the people as well as the leaders who urged them on, had rejected Christ. But this does not imply that Israel as a people had been rejected by God. This verse is the equivalent of the Pauline statement that natural branches had been lopped off of the olive tree. As long as they persisted in unbelief, these Jewish people who had uttered these words would not receive the covenant blessings, but the covenant curses. Ellen White points to the serious nature and consequences of this legal pronouncement by the people.[57] There is clear discontinuity here, between the unfaithful in Israel and the faithful remnant of Israel. But nowhere is implied that because the unfaithful in Israel had rejected Jesus, God had rejected the Jewish people as a whole.[58]

About the same time as these words were spoken, the Gospel of John records the words of the chief priests to Pilate (John 19:15): "We have no king but Caesar." This rejection of a divine King meant the official withdrawal from theocracy by the Jewish leaders.[59] When Christ hung upon the Cross, Israel ceased to be a theocratic nation in the eyes of God. Ellen White puts it thus: "When Christ should hang upon the cross of Calvary, Israel's day as a nation favored and blessed of God would be ended."[60]

The Book of Acts, A.D. 34, and the Stoning of Stephen

The book of Acts makes clear Israel's withdrawal from the theocracy at the time of Jesus' crucifixion did not mean the rejection of the Jewish people. The nucleus of the Christian church (the olive tree of Rom 9–11) was the Jewish Twelve and the many other Jews who accepted Jesus before His ascension. After His ascension, multitudes of Jews accepted the Messiah and became part of the faithful remnant of Israel (i.e. the church).

"The Jews and the Messianic Community in Johannine Literature," *DavarLogos* 4/2 [2005]: 175). Mueller shows that in John's Gospel the term "Jews" is used sometimes to describe the Jewish leaders and sometimes to describe the Jewish people as a whole (ibid., 149–180).

[57] See esp. White, *Desire of Ages*, 738–739.

[58] Also note carefully the words of Ellen White in *Acts of the Apostles*, 375–76 which balance and help interpret her other statements: "Even though Israel had rejected His Son, God did not reject them.... Notwithstanding Israel's failure as a nation, there remained among them a goodly remnant of such as should be saved...."

[59] White, *Desire of Ages*, 737–738.

[60] White, *The Great Controversy*, 20.

On the day of Pentecost ten days after His ascension, thousands of Jews were converted in a single day (Acts 2:41), and the steadily growing New Testament covenant community, in continuity with the one in the Old Testament, was comprised primarily of Jews, to whom were added another multitude of Gentiles in response to the preaching of the followers of the Way (Acts 2:47; 4:4; 5:14; 6:1, 7; 9:31; 13:43; 14;1; 17:4, 12; 18:10; 19:23, 26; 21:20). Acts 21:20 refers to "many thousands of believers . . .among the Jews." Jacques Doukhan points out how the Greek term for "thousands" here is *murias*, which literally means "ten thousand," and in the plural denotes at least 20,000 Jewish Christians in Jerusalem (out of a total population in the city of perhaps 80,000).[61]

In A.D. 34, when the Sanhedrin condemned Stephen to death and persecuted Christ's followers (Acts 7), the Jewish nation "sealed its rejection of the gospel" and, with it, the theocracy.[62] This was the climax of theocratic Israel's rejection of the Messiah described by many New Testament passages.[63]

The language of Stephen's speech is in the form of a covenant lawsuit. He plays the part of the Old Testament prophets representing Yahweh, as the prosecuting attorney bringing indictments against the leaders of Israel for breach of covenant.[64] The lawsuit is directed against the Sanhedrin, Israel's theocratic leaders, not against the people of Israel as a whole. And as with the Old Testament covenant lawsuits against the leadership of Israel (e.g., Micah 6; Hos 4; Isa 3), the resultant judgment led to the end of national Israel (in A.D. 70). A faithful remnant of Israel was preserved, and continued to be the nucleus of the People of God. Such continuity seems to be underscored by reference in the speech to the "church [*ekklēsia*] in the wilderness" (Acts 7:38).

Jacob Jervell well summarizes Luke's understanding of the relationship between Israel and the Church as presented in Acts as well as his Gospel:

---

[61] Nahman Avigad, "Jerusalem: The Second Temple Period," *The New Encyclopedia of Archaeological Excavations in the Holy Land*, ed. Ephraim Stern (Jerusalem: Israel Exploration Society, 1993), 2: 721. See also the discussion in Doukhan, *Israel and the Church*, 28–32, of the whole picture of phenomenal church growth among the Jews in the early church. Cf., Richard Bauckham, "James and the Jerusalem Community," *Jewish Believers in Jesus: The Early Centuries*, ed. Oskar Skarsaune and Reidar Hvalvik (Peabody, MA: Hendrickson, 2007), 55–95.

[62] White, *The Great Controversy* 328.

[63] For the various steps in the Jewish leaders' rejection of Christ, often through the Sanhedrin, see esp. the following: Matthew 23:32–39; 26:3–5, 14–16, 57–68; Mark 14:1–2, 10–11, 53–65; Luke 22:2–6, 66–71; John 11:47–57.

[64] See William Shea, "The Prophecy of Daniel 9:24–27," *The Seventy Weeks, Leviticus, and the Nature of Prophecy*, ed. Frank B. Holbrook (Washington, DC: Biblical Research Institute, 1986), 80–83; and Wilson Paroschi, "The Prophetic Significance of Stephen," *JATS* 9/1–2 (1998): 343–361.

Luke's own view is that the Twelve are enthroned as the new leaders of Israel—there is but one!—while the old leaders are rejected because they rejected God's Messiah, Jesus.... Luke never had any conception of the church as the new or true Israel. Luke is rather concerned to show that when the gospel was preached, the one people of God, Israel, was split in two. The result is that those Jews who do not accept the gospel are purged from Israel; the history of the people of God, of the one and only Israel, continues among those obedient Jews who believe in Jesus. The promises given to Israel are being fulfilled among the Jewish Christians. The initial mission to Jews was not a failure according to Luke, but a success; thousands upon thousands of Jews were converted. And these Jews bring the gospel to the Gentiles, thus fulfilling God's promises to Israel that Gentiles would join with them at the end of time.[65]

New Testament Eschatology in Light of the Theocratic Discontinuity

We have already outlined the New Testament eschatological groundplan, with its three stages of inaugurated, appropriated, and consummated eschatology. Here we add that the *mode* of fulfillment in each of these aspects of fulfillment is differentiated according to the physical and/or spiritual presence of Christ the King with regard to His kingdom. First, in Christ's earthly ministry, when as the Representative Israelite He was physically present, the fulfillment was literal and local, centered in Him. So, for example, the "gathering" prophecies (Deut 30, Ezek 36–37, etc.) received an initial fulfillment as He literally gathered the twelve disciples and many other Jewish followers to Himself (Matt 5:1; John 10:14–16; 11:52; Matt 12:30, Matt 23:37).

Second, during the time of the Church, when Christ is only spiritually present (that is, through His Spirit), and geopolitical aspects of the Old Testament promises are delayed by the suspension of the Old Testament theocracy, the fulfillment is spiritual and universal. The Old Testament "gathering prophecies" are fulfilled as Christian Israel is spiritually (not physically) and universally gathered by faith to Christ (Matt 18:20; Heb 12:22; Rev 14:6–12). The geopolitical language related to Israel takes on a spiritual, universal, and/or heavenly meaning. For example, Mt. Zion is used spiritually for the universal church (Rom 9:33; 1 Pet 2:6), which now is the "royal priesthood and holy nation" (1 Pet 2:9; cf. Exod 19:6), or refers to the heavenly city of Jerusalem, to which the earthly believ-

---

[65] Jervell, *Luke and the People of God*, 16–15.

ers are spiritually (by faith, but not physically) gathered (Gal 4:26; Heb 12:22–24).

Finally, at the time of the second advent of Christ when He physically returns and literally reunites the people of God to Himself the fulfillment is gloriously literal and universal. With regard to the Old Testament "gathering prophecies," at the second advent, Christ literally and gloriously gathers all His people to Himself (Matt 24:31; 2 Thess 2:1; Luke 13:28–29; Rev 21–22). Especially in the book of Revelation, the various Old Testament depictions of the end-time scenario find glorious literal, universal, fulfillment centered in Christ the Conquering King and His people, the apocalyptic Israel.

The Climactic Synthesis: The Book of Revelation

The book of Revelation confirms this eschatological ground-plan of the New Testament, as it presents in its sweep of salvation history (past, present and future) all three phases of the one eschatological fulfillment of Old Testament kingdom promises. Jesus Himself (inaugurated eschatology) is presented in terms borrowed from the language of Israel's theocracy and cult: the Lamb (27 times), the "Lion of the tribe of Judah" (5:5), "the Root [and the Offspring] of David" (5:5; 22:16), the high priest (1:13–16), the "Beginning and the End" (22:14; cf. Isa 41:4).

During the time of the Church (appropriated eschatology), John frequently describes the covenant people of God in the time of the Church in language relating to Israel. For example, the believers in Christ are called "priests/kings" (1:6; 5:10; cf. Exod 19:5–6). Those who worship at the temple in the "holy city" (11:1–2), are equated with the saints (13:5–7), both undergoing the same period of persecution (42 months). Continuity between Israel and the Church is also indicated in Revelation 12 by use of the term "woman," who had on her head "a garland of twelve stars" (v. 1), to describe both the Jewish covenant community at the time of Christ's birth (vv. 4, 13), and the experience of the persecuted church in later centuries (vv. 14–16). At the same time, the counterfeit people of God, those who claim to be part of the faithful remnant, "spiritual Israel," but do not really follow Him, are depicted in Israel terminology as "those who say they are Jews and are not," who are really "of the synagogue of Satan" (Rev 2:9; 3:9).

Toward the end of the period of the Church, John predicts a last-day movement of God's covenant-keeping people, "the remnant of her [the woman's] seed, who keep the commandments of God and have the testimony of Jesus Christ" (Rev 12:17). This group transcends the categories of both Christian and Jewish Israel as it upholds both the validity of Torah and the Messiahship of Jesus. This "eschatological" Israel, also referred to as the 144,000, is called to give a special end-time message of the Three Angels to prepare the world for the Second Coming of Christ (Rev 14).[66] This group, also described as "the saints" (Rev 13:10; 14:12), stand through the final time of trouble (cf. Dan 12:1), and are shielded from the seven last plagues.[67]

The book of Revelation focuses particularly up the third (consummated) phase of eschatology, upon the final, universal-literal fulfillment of the Old Testament end-time prophecies at the Second Coming of Christ, during the millennium, and in the New Earth. John describes the post-millennial battle against the forces of evil in the language of Ezekiel 38–39.[68] "Gog and Magog"—now referring to all of the enemies of God throughout the ages—are repulsed in their attack against God's holy city and His people, and consumed in the lake of fire (Rev 20:8–9). The New Jerusalem, eternal home of the saints in the earth made new, is largely depicted in the language of Isaiah 54 and Ezekiel 40–48, and is fulfilled as "God will wipe every tear from their eyes" (Rev 21:4). The seed of Abraham will inherit the Promised Land, which already in the Old Testament was expanded to include the entire earth. The meek finally "inherit the earth" (Ps 37:11; cf. Matt 5:5)!

The book of Revelation makes clear that this end-time fulfillment of the covenant promises made to Old Testament Israel is not experienced by the Jewish people as a separate group, but by all the people of God, including both Jews and Gentiles—"apocalyptic Israel." This becomes especially apparent as all the promises made to the churches in Revelation 1–3 return in Revelation 20–22 as consummated realities in the New Jerusalem. The divine promise to the church at Ephesus, "I will grant to eat of the tree of life, which is in the paradise of God" (Rev 2:7)—an allusion to Ezekiel's vision of the eschatological temple (Ezek 47)—is fulfilled in the New Jerusalem (Rev 22:1–2). Again, Revelation's descriptions of the redeemed saints utilize imagery from both Israel and the church, showing them to be one united People of God: all sing "the Song of Moses…and the song of the Lamb" (Rev 15:3); all enter into the same city, whose gates have the "names of the twelve tribes of the sons of Israel" (Rev 21:12),

---

[66] See Richard P. Lehmann, "The Remnant in the Book of Revelation," *Toward a Theology of the Remnant*, ed. Ángel M. Rodríguez (Silver Spring, MD: Biblical Research Institute, 2009), 108–112, for a description of this eschatological Israel, the Seventh-day Adventist Church, which is "the only religious movement that ultimately brought the Messiah and the Torah together" (87).

[67] See Hans K. LaRondelle, "The Remnant and the Three Angels' Messages," *Handbook of Seventh-day Adventist Theology*, ed. Raoul Dederen (Hagerstown, MD: Review and Herald, 2000), 870–871.

[68] For a full discussion, see Jiří Moskala, "Toward the Fulfillment of the Gog and Magog Prophecy of Ezekiel 38–39," *JATS* 18/2 (2007): 243–273.

while its foundations contain "the twelve names of the twelve apostles of the Lamb" (Rev 21:14).

Summary and Implications

The key to understanding the relationship between Israel and the Church in Scripture is found in the concept of the remnant. The biblical perspective on this question centers on what may be termed the Christocentric covenant-faithful remnant. In the Old Testament, within biblical-historical Israel was found a faithful remnant (spiritual Israel), comprised both of biological Jews and Gentiles who had accepted Yahweh and joined the covenant community. In New Testament times, within biblical-historical Israel, Jesus established a faithful remnant community, the church (*ekklēsia*), comprised of a nucleus of Jews, initially led by the Twelve, to whom have been added through the centuries both Jews and Gentiles who have accepted Jesus as the Messiah and have joined the covenant community (Christian Israel). Those who through the centuries remained true to God's word, the church "in the wilderness" (Rev 12:6, 14), constitute the faithful remnant (spiritual Israel), the continuation and extension of biblical-historical Israel. In the last days, the book of Revelation predicts the existence of an eschatological remnant of the woman's offspring, who will "keep the commandments of God and have the testimony of Jesus Christ" (Rev 12:17). This eschatological Israel will proclaim the Three Angels' Message, preparing the world for Christ's Second Coming. At the Second Coming, the faithful remnant (spiritual Israel) of all ages will finally be gathered together, some through resurrection and others through translation. This apocalyptic Israel will inherit all the covenant promises made to biblical-historical Israel, including (after the millennium in heaven) the land (the New Earth) and the everlasting kingdom.

It was God's intention (according to the classical prophecies) that national-theocratic Israel extend her borders to embrace the world, and that Jerusalem never be destroyed, but become the metropolis of the earth and the missionary center for proclaiming the gospel to the Gentiles. But with the divorce of national Israel from the theocracy, brought about by the legal decision of its leaders in rejecting Jesus, the geopolitical features of the Old Testament covenant promises could not be literally fulfilled in the flow of earth's history before Christ's second advent. As predicted in Daniel 9, the city of Jerusalem was destroyed (70 A.D.). Thus the major point of discontinuity between biblical-historical Israel and the Church is the end of the geopolitical theocracy, the "Jewish nation."[69]

---

[69] Ellen White often uses this term "Jewish nation" (or "Jews as a nation") when indicating the

But this did not mean the end of the remnant of biblical-historical Israel as God's people. Throughout the period of the Christian era, the spiritual blessings of the covenant have been enjoyed by God's covenant people (spiritual Israel), the faithful remnant of biblical-historical Israel comprised of both Jews and Gentiles. The universal church, or Christian Israel, as the body of Christ, receives the fulfillment of all the kingdom promises (Gal 3:29), but it is only a spiritual fulfillment. The geopolitical language takes on a spiritual, universal, and/or heavenly meaning. Nevertheless, the "geopolitical"[70] features of the covenant promises are not permanently annulled. And they are not fulfilled by Jewish Israel in the restoration of a Jewish state at the end of time. Rather, at the second advent of the Messiah, apocalyptic Israel, comprised of all the faithful people of God (spiritual Israel) throughout all ages, including both Jews and Gentiles, will be resurrected to experience the ultimate, universal, glorious, literal fulfillment of *all* the Old Testament geopolitical covenant promises! Note Ellen White's amazing statement:

> That which God purposed to do for the world through Israel, the chosen nation, He will finally accomplish through His church on earth today. He has 'let out His vineyard unto other husbandmen,'

---

end of the geopolitical theocratic entity of Israel (e.g., *Acts of the Apostles*, 379; *Christ's Object Lessons*, 295, 305; *The Great Controversy*, 35; *Patriarchs and Kings*, 711, 713), but she does not imply in these statements that God had rejected the Jewish people. In the one chapter of her written corpus where Ellen White most directly and extensively focuses on this issue of whether or not God rejected Israel (*Acts of the Apostles*, 374–382), she makes this point very plain. Here is a sample of her comments: "The Jews were God's chosen people, through whom He had purposed to bless the entire race.... Even though Israel rejected His Son, God did not reject them. ... Notwithstanding Israel's failure as a nation, there remained among them a goodly remnant of such as such as should be saved.... When the early Christian church was founded, it was composed of these faithful Jews who recognized Jesus of Nazareth as the one for whose advent they had been longing.... Paul likens the remnant in Israel to a noble olive tree, some of whose branches have been broken off. He compares the Gentiles to branches from a wild olive tree, grafted into the parent stock.... Through unbelief and the rejection of Heaven's purpose for her, Israel as a nation had lost her connection with God. But the branches that had been separated from the parent stock God was able to reunite with the true stock of Israel—the remnant who had remained true to the God of their fathers.... 'And so all Israel shall be saved.' ... Thus Paul shows that God is abundantly able to transform the hearts of Jew and Gentile alike, and to grant to every believer in Christ the blessings promised to Israel.... In the closing proclamation of the gospel... God expects His messengers to take particular interest in the Jewish people whom they find in all parts of the earth."

[70] I use the term "geopolitical" for the apocalyptic fulfillment but, by this term, I do not mean the literal fulfillment of the Old Testament prophecies in a renewed religio-political State of Israel on earth before the Second Coming of Christ, as dispensationalists claim. Rather, I refer to the territorial and kingdom aspects of the Old Testament covenant promises, which will ultimately be fulfilled in a literal, universal manner in the New Earth with God's eternal kingdom centered in the New Jerusalem, as described in Revelation 20–22.

even to His covenant-keeping people, who faithfully 'render Him the fruits in their seasons.' Never has the Lord been without true representatives on this earth who have made His interests their own. These witnesses for God are numbered among the spiritual Israel, and to them will be fulfilled *all the covenant promises* made by Jehovah to His ancient people.[71]

In heaven during the millennium, "all Israel" (Rom 11:26), God's covenant people of all ages, will reign with Christ in the New Jerusalem. After the millennium, this "apocalyptic Israel" will finally receive their eternal inheritance in the Earth Made New (Rev 20–22). While the cultural-specific aspects of the Old Testament geopolitical covenant promises will be universalized, a final literal fulfillment is nonetheless certain.

Now, as in the time of Paul, many of the "natural branches" (unbelieving Jews) are broken off of the one true Olive Tree, and believing Gentiles are being grafted in. But Paul states his hope that this grafting in of Gentiles may make the natural branches jealous, so that "some" (Rom 11:14), even "the fullness" (Rom 11:12) of them may not continue in unbelief but accept Jesus the Messiah and be re-grafted "into their own olive tree" (Rom 11:24). As in the days of Paul, the faithful remnant of prophecy now has the privilege of extending this offer of "re-grafting" to our Jewish brothers and sisters who have not yet accepted the Messiah. And thus "all Israel"—God's true people, both Jews and Gentiles of all ages—will be saved! To Him be all the glory!

---

[71] Ellen G. White, *Patriarchs and Kings,* 713–714, emphasis mine.

CHAPTER 20

WORLD RELIGIONS AND SALVATION: AN ADVENTIST VIEW

Ángel Manuel Rodríguez

Every ecclesiology faces the important and unavoidable question of the fate of the non-evangelized—persons found in different world religions who have never heard about Jesus, much less His redemptive work on behalf of the human race.[1] The topic is particularly important today, when the church is dynamically involved in its mission to world religions. This is also a topic of lively discussion among theologians and missiologists from different Christian traditions. In this study, I will review the different approaches to the question of Christian soteriology in the context of world religions and the exclusivism presupposed in biblical soteriology by the phrase *solus Christus* ("only through Christ"). I will also examine evidence that appears to point to a soteriological openness based on the Trinitarian will to save. Finally, I will highlight some aspects of a pneumatological approach that may help us in developing a biblical view of the topic compatible with Adventist theology. My ultimate objective is not to provide a solution, but to stimulate more reflection on the subject of the salvation of the non-evangelized. Our discussion will deal with several important theological topics such as soteriology, pneumatology, theodicy, and a Trinitarian mission.

---

[1] We should recognize that even in the Christian world there are many who hardly have any significant knowledge of the gospel of salvation through Christ. They belong to the unreached and are also objects of the mission of the church. For an introduction to this phenomenon, see K. Rajendran, "Unreached People," *DMT*, 415–419.

Solus Christus, Salvation, and World Religions

The mission of the church presupposes a particular understanding of God and a specific soteriology. In the fulfillment of the mission, there is an interaction between the Godhead and those who have accepted Christ as Savior and Lord that must be explored and analyzed to better understand its very nature. The soteriological activity of the Godhead surfaces with particular force in regards to the salvation of the non-evangelized.

Suggested Answers

From very early in its history, the Christian church dealt with the question of the fate of those who died without the knowledge of Jesus. At the risk of oversimplifying, I suggest that the prevailing view during the first millennium of the Christian era was that there was no salvation outside the church (*Extra Ecclesiam, nulla salus*, "Outside the Church, no salvation").[2] This way of thinking began to change with the discovery of the new world and the realization that its inhabitants had never heard of Christianity. Since then, the question has been debated, and is still being debated, in the setting of global modes of communication and transportation. World religions are now partners in dialogue and cannot be ignored. The basic question is that of the identity of the Christian church, particularly the identity of the Adventist Church, based on some very specific biblical claims.

The debate over the question of salvation for those who have not heard the gospel has produced different and contradictory answers. The suggestions offered are usually organized around three well-known models. They are commonly referred to as inclusivism, pluralism, and exclusivism.[3] *Inclusivism* generally argues that Christ is the normative way of salvation, but that salvation is also possible through other religions. A Muslim or a Hindu can be saved through Christ. These are "anonymous Christians."[4] *Pluralism* teaches that all religions are equally valid and that

---

[2] For a careful study on the history of this concept, see Francis A. Sullivan, *Salvation Outside the Church? Tracing the History of the Catholic Response* (Mahwah, NJ: Paulist Press, 1992). This view was the official position of the Catholic Church up to the Second Vatican Council; see Joseph H. Wong, "Anonymous Christians: Karl Rahner's Pneuma-Christocentrism and an East-West Dialogue," *TS* 55 (1994): 611.

[3] This was done by Alan Race, *Christians and Religious Pluralism* (Maryknoll, NY: Orbis Books, 1982). For a brief, but useful, introduction to the three models, consult Gavin D'Acosta, "Other Faiths and Christianity," *Blackwell Encyclopedia of Modern Christian Thought*, ed. Alister E. McAlister (Malden, MA: Blackwell Publishers, 1993), 411–416, and Carl E. Braaten, "Hearing the Other: The Promise and the Problem of Pluralism," *CTM* 24.5 (1997): 394–400.

[4] The phrase was introduced in the discussion by the Catholic theologian, Karl Rahner, "Anony-

there are many saviors and Jesus is simply one of them. *Exclusivism* maintains that Jesus is the only Savior—it affirms *solus Christus*—and that in order to be saved one should confess Him and put his or her faith in Him. These categories have been useful in the discussion, but they have been seriously criticized to the point of near obsolescence.[5]

Inclusivism is considered to be impracticable, because each religion has its own particular goal. World religions do not have a common ultimate destination, e.g., to be with God. Further, all world religions are basically exclusivists. They claim that one can only enjoy the goals of a particular religion by adopting it. The adherents of each religion consider it as the one and only true religion.[6] Although *pluralism* claims that there are many goals offered by world religions, it ultimately establishes its own universal, abstract religious goal (e.g., the common experience of salvation or liberation).[7] Perhaps what seems to be emerging from this confusion is the view that salvation takes different shapes under divine providence.[8] According to this theory, salvation expresses itself in three different forms. The first is in its absence; some people will be lost. Second, it can be imperfectly fulfilled through a non-Christian religion—

---

mous Christians," *Investigations*, vol. 6, 390–398. "Anonymous Christians" designates individuals in world religions who have implicit faith in Jesus. This faith is expressed in that particular context through fidelity and dedication to the duties or responsibilities that humans confront in their daily life. Thus the person is responding to God's grace and implicitly accepting the mystery of Christ. He also argues that Christianity is the absolute religion and that it is for all by divine design. Non-Christian religions can lead to salvation until the followers are confronted by the message of the Christian church. For a useful summary and discussion of Rahner's views, see Wong, "Anonymous Christians," 612–615. For a more detailed description of the theological and philosophical foundations of the concept and the influence of Thomas Aquinas accompanied by a critique of it, see George R. Summer, *The First and the Last: The Claim of Jesus Christ and the Claims of Other Religious Traditions* (Grand Rapids, MI: Eerdmans, 2004), 76–88.

[5] See Joseph DeNoia, "The Universality of Salvation and the Diversity of Religious Aims," *World Mission*, Winter (1981–1982): 2–15; and T. C. Casiño, "Revelation," *DMT*, 342.

[6] For a discussion of those issues, see Gerald R. McDermont, *God's Rivals: Why Has God Allowed Different Religions?* (Downers Grove, IL: IVP Academic, 2007), 23.

[7] Ibid.

[8] I should mention that others are attempting to introduce new terminology in the discussion. For instance, Peter Schineller, "Christ and Church," *TS* 37 (1976): 50, suggested *ecclesiocentric*, *Christocentric*, and *theocentric*. Terrance L. Tiessen, *Reassessing Salvation in Christ and World Religions: Who Can Be Saved?* (Downers Grove, IL: InterVarsity, 2004), 32–47. He uses *ecclesiocentrism* (only those who hear the gospel can be saved); *agnosticism* (not sure that God has means of saving those who do not hear the gospel); *accessibilism* (Jesus is the exclusive means of salvation and salvation is accessible to those who do not know the gospel, but not through their religion); *religious instrumentalism* (Jesus is unique, but salvation is possible though non-Christian religions); and *relativism* (there is not one religion that has final truth; salvation is possible through any religion). It remains to be seen whether this new terminology will be accepted by the scholarly community. See also Casiño, "Revelation," 342–343.

experiencing the limited goals of that religion. Third, it can be perfectly experienced in an eternal communion with the Trinitarian God of the Christians.[9]

It is obvious that Christians are still struggling with a proper understanding of Christian soteriology in the context of world religions. Most of the answers are incompatible with the witness of Scripture, while others introduce the question of theodicy into the discussion. How could a just and loving God condemn people to eternal perdition because they were born in non-Christian countries? How could they be justly condemned for a lack of knowledge that they could not avoid? We certainly need to look at the issue in a way that is compatible with the message of salvation found in the Bible. I will also examine what Ellen G. White has to say on this topic.

Biblical Evidence for Exclusivism

It is extremely difficult to ignore the radical nature of biblical religion and its claim to uniqueness. The biblical evidence is overwhelming in support of this view. In the Old Testament, it is only through Abraham that the nations of the earth will be blessed (Gen 12:1-3).[10] It was God's intention to universalize the revelation entrusted to Israel and to fill the earth with the glory of the Lord. The coming of the Messiah universalizes this revelation and the element of uniqueness becomes even more specific. For instance, Jesus said: "Now this is eternal life: that they may know you, the only true God, and Jesus Christ, whom you have sent" (John 17:3). Peter reaffirmed this conviction: "Salvation is found in no one else" (Acts 4:12). In fact, the gospel commission requires that the knowledge of salvation through Christ be proclaimed to every person (Matt 28:18-20; cf. Rev 14:6-12). We are also informed that salvation requires faith in Jesus (Rom 1:16; 10:9; Acts 16:30-34). The saving death of Jesus and the exclusive claim that salvation is only through Him—*solus Christus*—lay at the very foundation of the mission of the church.

I will suggest that the uniqueness of the Christian faith is grounded in two important biblical teachings. The first one is the universality of sin. The problem humanity faces is a common one, and therefore it cannot be circumscribed to a particular culture. Paul, referring to Jews and Gentiles, concludes: "There is no difference, for all have sinned and fall short of the glory of God" (Rom 3:22b-23). The human condition transcends culture,

---

[9] See S. Mark Heim, *The Depth of the Richness: A Trinitarian Theology of Religious Ends* (Grand Rapids, MI: Eerdmans, 2000). For a brief evaluation of this view, see McDemont, *God's Rivals*, 24-26.

[10] All Bible texts are quoted from the NIV.

geography, and religion, whether people are aware of it or not. There is a natural enmity toward God in the human heart, and death and sin reign over it (5:10, 14; 6:11). Consequently "the whole world is held accountable to God" (3:19) and is under condemnation (5:18).

The problem we face is not only universal; it is also cosmic. What is taking place on the planet is part of a cosmic conflict between good and evil; between God and evil powers. Every human being, every social structure, and every religion is involved, one way or another, in this conflict. Evil powers do not only aim at gaining the loyalty of human beings and corrupting their spiritual and moral lives, but they also seek to distort the gracious and loving image or character of the biblical God in the eyes of humans. It is impossible for human beings to prevail over these evil forces alone. This grim picture of the human condition is not God's last word for us.

The second teaching important for our purpose is the universal nature of the remedy for sin and evil in the world.[11] Through His death on the cross, the Son of God permanently defeated in the cosmic conflict all evil powers, making it possible for humans to obtain through Him freedom from them (Col 2:15). This benefit of the death of the Redeemer is "for all" (2 Cor 5:14–15). His sacrificial death on the cross is the only means of reconciliation with God. God reconciled the world through the death of Christ and not in any other person (5:19). He "gave Himself as a ransom for all" (1 Tim 2:5). John adds that Jesus "was the true light that gives light to every man" (1:9). Because of His reconciling work Jesus is "Lord of all" (Acts 10:36). The mission of the church is born out of the recognition that the human predicament is universal and that the grace of God through Christ is also universal. Jesus said to His disciples, "All authority in heaven and on earth has been given to me. Therefore go and make disciples of all nations" (Matt 28:18–19a). The mission is global because every human being is in need of salvation. But it is grounded on the fact that the Father granted "all authority in heaven and on earth" only to Jesus. No one can compete with Him.

Access to Salvation

Based on this evidence, it would be impossible to speak about the salvation of those who have not heard the gospel of salvation through Christ's sacrificial death. But before we reach final conclusions, we should take into consideration some other biblical materials. First, the Bible speaks about individuals outside the corporate body of God's people who

---

[11] On this topic, see Gerald O'Collins, *Jesus Our Redeemer: A Christian Approach to Salvation* (New York: Oxford University Press, 2007), 219–224.

were also servants of God. Job was not an Israelite, and yet the Lord identified him as His servant (1:1). This was also the case with Melchizedek, a Canaanite who was a true servant of the Lord (Gen 14:17–24). How did the Lord reach these people with His message of salvation? The Bible is not clear about this, but it does imply that God was active outside the line of servants He had chosen through Abraham.

Second, the mission of the church was and will always be God's mission. This understanding of mission, which seems to be common among missiologists,[12] needs to be emphasized. Mission did not originate with the church, but with God; it has always remained His. It is always *missio Dei*.[13] Before there was a human being, the Godhead formulated a rescue plan for the human race in which each member of the Godhead was to be involved. The Father initiated it by sending His Son as our Savior (John 3:16). Every aspect of the earthly ministry of Jesus was a fulfillment of God's saving mission for the human race. At the close of His ministry, Jesus said to the Father that He had completed "the work you gave me to do" on earth (John 17:3). This aspect of the divine mission was concluded, but other aspects would follow it in which the Father, Jesus, and the Holy Spirit were to continue to be involved in mission. The Spirit was always personally involved in the divine mission, speaking to the prophets and preserving the divine revelation. Jesus was filled by the Spirit of the Lord in fulfilling His mission (e.g., Isa 11:1–5: Matt 3:16–17).

The Spirit empowered the church to accomplish its mission (Acts 1:8). The deep connection between the church and the Spirit indicates that, although the church came into existence for mission, the mission was God's. The Spirit fulfilled it through the church. In the presence of believers, the Spirit, in agreement with the divine design, uses them to accomplish the mission. But what would God do in the absence of Christian believers? I propose that the Spirit continues to be responsible for the realization of the mission. When the visible expression of the people of God is not accessible in a region of the world, for any reason, God's saving mission to the world is not deactivated. We have to take into consideration the divine will to save as witnessed in the Bible. God still "wants all men to be saved and to come to a knowledge of the truth" (1 Tim 2:4). But how does this happen?

---

[12] See for instance, David J. Bosch, *Witnesses to the World: The Christian Mission in Theological Perspective* (Atlanta, GA: John Knox, 1980), 239–248.

[13] We cautiously use this phrase because it is used in some theological circles to exclude the involvement of the church in mission. This view tends to be common in the field of ecumenism. Our understanding of it is explained in the text. There is a significant amount of literature on this topic. See L. Pachuau, "Missio Dei," *DMT*, 232–234.

Special and General Revelation: Cognitive Ground for Salvation

Until now our main emphasis has been on the knowledge of God and on a soteriology revealed to us through the special revelation God gave His people through God's prophets, His Son, and the apostles. The Spirit has preserved that revelation for us in the Scriptures. There, God has revealed the divine plan for the salvation of the human race in an unparalleled way. Outside of Scripture, no one will ever find such a clear and penetrating exposition of the divine intention manifested to us through the Son of God. Since that is the case, one has to conclude that knowledge is indispensable in the process of salvation. Through the special revelation now preserved in Scripture, God has abundantly provided for us from the depths of His wisdom. But not everyone on the planet has had access to that body of revelation.

If the mission of the church is God's mission, and if in the absence of believers the Spirit continues to fulfill the divine mission, I suggest that knowledge of God is also available to those who have no access to God's special revelation. We should keep in mind that, first, creation reveals something about its Creator. The wisdom of God is found in the natural world because every aspect of it was originally a divine thought. Even after the fall, nature continues to reveal, imperfectly, the wisdom and power of God.[14] Paul seems to argue that such a level of knowledge is only enough to condemn humans (Rom 1:19–25), but the question is whether it is also enough to *lead* them to salvation. The psalmist wrote, "The heavens declare the glory of God; the skies proclaim the works of his hands. Day after day they put forth speech; night after night they display knowledge ... Their voice goes out into all the earth, their words to the ends of the world" (19:1–2, 4). Nature reveals to every human being something about God. The perception of that revelation is possible because humans seem to have a natural religious awareness implanted by God in the human heart at creation. Ellen G. White commented, "The Gentiles are to be judged according to the light that is given to them, according to the

---

[14] Ellen G. White comments: "All created things, in their original perfection, were an expression of the thought of God. To Adam and Eve nature was teeming with divine wisdom. But by transgression man was cut off from learning of God through direct communion and, to a great degree, through His works. The earth, marred and defiled by sin, reflects but dimly the Creator's glory. It is true that His object lessons are not obliterated. Upon every page of the great volume of His created works may still be traced His handwriting. Nature still speaks of her Creator. Yet these revelations are partial and imperfect. And in our fallen state, with weakened powers and restricted vision, we are incapable of interpreting aright. We need the fuller revelation of Himself that God has given in His written word" (*Education* [Mountain View, CA: Pacific Press, 1903], 16–17). Because of evil, nature cannot provide a clear picture of God. That fuller revelation is found in the Bible.

impressions they had received of their Creator in nature."[15]

Our second point is closely related to the previous one. The human capacity to reason makes it possible for God to impart knowledge to humans who have no access to His special revelation. In such cases, reason operates not only on the basis of what is seen in nature, but also through divine providences. The operations of nature are under the control of the Lord. Paul says that "in him [Jesus] all things hold together" (Col 1:17). It is God "who causes his sun to rise on the evil and the good, and sends rain on the righteous and the unrighteous" (Matt 5:45). Paul adds that God "gives all men life and breath and everything else . . . . God did this so that men would seek him and perhaps reach out for him and find him, though he is not far from each one of us" (Acts 17:25c, 27). Ellen G. White adds, that the Gentiles

> Have reasoning powers, and can distinguish God in his created works. God speaks to all men through his providence in nature. He makes known to all that he is the living God. The Gentiles could reason that the things that are made could not have fallen into the exact order, and worked out a designed purpose, without a God who has originated all. They could reason from cause to effect, that it must be that there was a first cause, an intelligent agent, that could be no other than the eternal God. The light of God in nature is shining continually into the darkness of heathenism, but many who see this light do not glorify the Lord as God.[16]

This clearly suggests that God can use general revelation to lead the individual to glorify Him.

Third, there is also a moral consciousness in humans that God can use to reach them in the absence of the special revelation preserved in Scripture for us. This is related to the fact that humans were created in God's image (Gen 1:26–27). The fall has not totally obliterated the divine image in human nature. Perhaps this could be called ethical or moral intuitionism. Occasionally humans are able to directly apprehend the moral within a particular situation.[17] We do seem to have a sense of duty that pushes us to aim at what we think is right, although by ourselves we are unable to practice the good. This awareness is usually called the conscience. Jesus

---

[15] "The Gospel of Both Jews and Gentiles," *Signs of the Times*, August 12, 1889.

[16] Ibid.

[17] On ethical intuitionism, see Walter Sinnott-Armstrong, "Intuitionism," *Encyclopedia of Ethics*, ed. Lawrence C. Becker and Charlotte B. Becker (New York: Routledge, 2001), 2:879–882.

seems to have been referring to this when He said, "If you, then, though you are evil, know how to give good gifts to your children, how much more will your Father in heaven give good gifts to those who ask him" (Matt 7:11). Paul also referred to this aspect of human nature: "When the Gentiles, who do not have the law, do by nature things required by the law, they are a law for themselves, even though they do not have the law, since they show that the requirements of the law are written on their hearts, their consciences also bearing witness, and their thoughts now accusing, now even defending them" (Rom 2:14-15).

Fourth, there are also what could be called particular revelations,[18] occasionally given to the Gentiles, that differ from what we call special and general revelations. We find some examples of this phenomenon in the Bible, and Ellen G. White addresses it. For instance, in a dream, God reprimanded Abimelech, king of Gerar, for taking the wife of Abraham, and instructed him about what to do (Gen 20:1-3). He also spoke to Pharaoh in a dream that Joseph later interpreted (41:25-28). God gave revelations to Balaam (Num 22:9; 23:11; 24:2-4) and spoke to Pharaoh Neco (2 Chr 35:20-22). We could also mention the dream of Nebuchadnezzar in Daniel 2:1 and the experience of Cornelius, a Gentile who feared God but who did not have a Christian to teach him. The Lord directly spoke to him in a vision and guided him to Peter (Acts 10:1-10).

What I am suggesting is that God has not left Himself without witnesses among nations living in deep spiritual darkness. The incidents listed above were isolated cases, but they establish the possibility that God may have spoken throughout history in similar ways to many other persons in different places and outside His covenant community. Ellen White supports this line of argument:

> Outside of the Jewish nation there were men who foretold the appearance of a divine instructor. These men were seeking for truth, and to them the Spirit of Inspiration was imparted. One after another, like the stars in the darkened heavens, such teachers had arisen. Their words of prophecy had kindled hope in the hearts of thousands of the Gentile world.[19]

---

[18] Tiessen, *Who Can Be Saved?*, 113-120, prefers to use the word "specific" to distinguish it from "general" and "special" revelations. I have chosen "particular" in order to emphasis its uniqueness.

[19] Ellen G. White, *Desire of Ages* (Mountain View, CA: Pacific Press, 1898), 33. She also wrote, "Even among the heathen there were men though whom Christ was working to uplift the people from their sin and degradation. But these men were despised and hated. Many of them suffered a violent death" (ibid., 35).

She is clearly describing what I have called "particular revelations" given under the inspiration of the Holy Spirit.

God has revealed Himself in different ways to humans outside His covenant community—to which He entrusted the privileges and responsibilities of His special revelation. Here a word of caution is necessary. We should make a distinction between knowledge and salvation. Although knowledge is needed in order to be saved, knowledge by itself does not save sinners. We have been told that,

> Our standing before God depends, not upon the amount of light we have received, but upon the use we make of what we have. Thus even the heathen who choose the right as far as they can distinguish it, are in more favorable condition than are those who have had great light, and profess to serve God, but who disregard the light, and by their daily life contradict their profession.[20]

General revelation, particular revelation, and even special revelation are not enough for the salvation of a soul. Whenever we use the phrase "saving knowledge" we should define what we mean by it, because this knowledge in and by itself is not salvific. Humans need something else.

Pneumatology and Mission: The Illumination of the Spirit

At this point in our study we need to introduce another important element, perhaps the most important one—the Holy Spirit in the human heart; the *illumination* of the Spirit. Without the Spirit, the human mind will misunderstand God's special revelation, the general revelation in nature, and the particular revelations received by some individuals. We are back to the affirmation made earlier that the mission of the church is God's mission, and that in the absence of believers the Spirit Himself fulfills it. I will suggest that Jesus, through the mysterious work of the Spirit, continues to be "the true light that gives light to every man" (John 1:9). Since the Spirit "blows wherever it pleases" (John 3:6), it could be suggested that among people living out of contact with the people of God there have been individuals who, when touched by the Spirit, sincerely yearn for something better (cf. James 1:17). In this specific case Ellen G. White is very precise when she says,

> Among all nations, kindreds, and tongues, He [God] sees men and women who are praying for light and knowledge. Their souls are

---

[20] Ibid., 239.

unsatisfied.... They are honest in heart and desire to learn a better way [**specific revelation**]. Although in the depths of heathenism [**non-evangelized**], with no knowledge of the written law of God nor of His Son Jesus [**no special revelation**], they have revealed in manifold ways the working of a divine power on mind and character [**transformed through the Spirit**].[21]

This statement makes a number of important points. First, these are sincere and honest people who are dissatisfied with what they have and long for something better, for a better way. Second, they are praying for more light, "groping as blind men." She is probably referring to this same experience when she says, "the uneducated heathen learns his lessons through nature and through his own necessities, and, dissatisfied with darkness, he is reaching out for light, searching for God in the First Great Cause."[22] And then she adds, "God speaks to the heathen."[23] Third, they do not have the benefit of special revelation, but the Spirit has been transforming their mind and character. They are being guided by the Spirit. Elsewhere, Ellen White indicates that "the Holy Spirit has implanted the grace of Christ in the heart of the savage."[24] She attributes this to Jesus, as the light that enlightens every human being. White seems to suggest that, through the Spirit, Christ is abiding in their hearts.[25] Common grace is also available to non-Christians, and if they positively respond to it they will be transformed. They can experience the saving power of God in mind and character. Their knowledge of God may be extremely limited, but God has used it, and through the power of the Spirit they have been transformed.

Such understanding of the work of the Spirit in the heart of non-Christians needs some more clarification in order to avoid misunderstandings. First, the work of divine grace through the Spirit does not legitimize any particular world religion. It does not lead down the path of religious pluralism or inclusivism. In fact, what I described basically rejects the soteriological significance of both. In biblical theology, grace and salvation are

---

[21] Ellen G. White, *Prophets and Kings* (Mountain View, CA: Pacific Press, 1917), 376. The comments in boldface placed within brackets are mine.

[22] Ellen G. White, *The Upward Look* (Washington, DC: Review and Herald, 1982), 278. She goes on to add: "Many of the pagan philosophers had a knowledge of God that was pure; but degeneracy, the worship of created things, began to obscure this knowledge. The handiwork of God in the natural world—the sun, the moon, the stars—were worshiped" (ibid.).

[23] Ibid.

[24] Ellen G. White, *Christ's Object Lessons* (Washington, DC: Review and Herald, 1900), 386.

[25] Ibid.

not mediated through a sacramental function of human instruments or institutions, but through the ministry of Christ in the heavenly sanctuary and the work of the Spirit in the human heart. In that reconciling work, God does not recognize national, religious, or ethnic distinctions. "His love is so broad, so deep, so full, that it penetrates anywhere."[26] Of course, in His work the Spirit could use fragments of truth that may be present in any religion, but He is not bound by such elements and much less by the religions themselves. God has other ways of reaching them without having to go through their system of religious beliefs or their religious institutions. It may sound too strong, but I am willing to say that God reaches the non-evangelized and any human being in spite of the religious system within which they find themselves.

The second clarification that I would like to make has to do with the impact that our conclusions may have on the mission of the church. It would be easy to conclude that since God Himself is in charge of the mission and since He is reaching in different ways those who have not heard the gospel, the mission of the church is irrelevant. This conclusion places the mission of the church in tension and conflict with the mission of God by suggesting that one of the two is unnecessary. It ignores the fact that the mission of the church is always God's mission, or in other words, is the most efficient way by which God fulfills His mission to the world. When the church engages in mission, it is doing so in obedience to the Risen Lord, and not as an optional activity. The church is the church to the extent to which it is involved in mission. Finally, God's sovereignty is limitless, and consequently He can use any other means He may consider necessary to reach those who live in spiritual darkness without neutralizing any other method. This work of God among the un-evangelized, about which the church may know very little or nothing, prepares the world for the church to fulfill its global mission (*a preparatio evangelica*).

Thirdly, we should not conclude that since among non-Christians, we have a group who has experienced reconciliation independent of the mission of the remnant, that there is no need for an end-time remnant people of God. Some may ask, should not such persons be considered God's remnant people in those religions?[27] Such a conclusion would ignore that we are not legitimizing world religions. The biblical concept of the end-time remnant legitimizes the existence of the larger group, from which it was

---

[26] White, *Prophets and Kings*, 370.

[27] For an evaluation of the idea that there is a remnant of God's people in every world religion, see Frank M. Hasel, "The Remnant in Contemporary Adventist theology," *Toward a Theology of the Remnant: An Adventist Ecclesiological Perspective*, ed. Ángel M. Rodríguez (Silver Spring, MD: Biblical Research Institute, 2009), 166–170.

preserved. What I have described in this paper is not different from what Adventists have traditionally stated concerning the different Christian denominations and churches. We believe that there is a significant number of God's people in Babylon. They are sincere believers who, in spite of their denominational membership, have a close fellowship with the Lord and are open to the Scriptures. They need to hear the present truth proclaimed by the end-time remnant people of God in preparation for the return of our Lord. It is through the mission of the remnant that they come out of Babylon and become part of the visible people of God.[28]

We could then conclude that, in the case of those who have never heard the gospel, there are those who have surrendered their lives to the work of the Spirit in their hearts and who, when confronted with the message of the end-time remnant, will embrace it. They need the fuller revelation of God found in the Scripture in order to better understand the loving character of God, the magnificent revelation of it in Jesus Christ, and to be ready to confront the end-time deceptions of the enemy. Their present knowledge is not enough for them to be able to unmask the nature of that deception. Therefore, the mission of God's end-time remnant to the world is simply indispensable and compatible with the work of the Spirit among the world religions.

Conclusion

When dealing with the topic of the salvation of the non-evangelized, we should begin with the question of whose mission it is. I have suggested that the mission of reconciling humans to God originated in God and that it was, is, and will continue to be God's mission (*missio Dei*). Those who accept the divine offer of salvation are incorporated by God in the fulfillment of His saving mission. We explicitly see this in the election of Israel, and later in the constitution of the church as the covenant people of God, to whom He entrusted His self-revelation. This special revelation clarified for humans the seriousness of their condition and the divine plan for their reconciliation with God. The covenant community was the beneficiary of this reconciling action and became God's instrument in proclaiming it to the rest of the human race.

We have raised the question of the ultimate fate of those who, for a variety of reasons, did not hear the message of salvation through Christ. We have suggested that, in such non-ideal conditions, the Holy Spirit continues to fulfill the Trinitarian mission of salvation based on the divine

---

[28] For a fuller treatment of this topic, see Ángel M. Rodríguez, "Concluding Essay: God's End-Time Remnant and the Christian Church," *Toward a Theology of the Remnant*, 201–226.

will to save the human race. Humans are all sinners and in need of salvation. Through the work of the Spirit in the human heart and mind, the non-evangelized could receive by different means—including particular revelations—a limited knowledge of God that the Spirit can use to lead them and to offer to them something better than what they have. As those who are sincere listen to the silent and powerful witness of the Spirit in their lives, and as they surrender their hearts to His loving influence, they can become beneficiaries of Christ's saving grace. This will result in the transformation of their minds and characters. They have been reconciled to God through Christ.

Such individuals form part of the invisible dimension of the church of Christ, to which the people of God, who are still in Babylon, also belong. Both groups need to hear the message that God's visible end-time remnant proclaim. This will help them understand aspects of God's saving plan that will contribute to delivering them from the Satanic deceptions of the last days and that will bring together the fullness of the visible eschatological remnant from every nation, people, and tongue. This remnant will be grounded in the Scripture, God's special revelation, and will be fully surrendered to Jesus as Savior and Lord. It is to this end that the Godhead is involved in mission and that we have been incorporated into it. Soteriology and pneumatology should always be kept together in the *missio Dei*.

CHAPTER 21

Adventist Mission Today: A Personal Reflection

William G. Johnsson

Seventh-day Adventists have always been a missionary people. Before we even had a name, mission flowed in our veins. Mission was our raison d'etre. Mission impelled us to go to "every nation, kindred, tongue, and people" (Rev 14:6). Mission catapulted us from a disappointed body of North American believers to a world church connected together with presence in more than 200 nations. To ask about Adventist mission today, therefore, might seem superfluous. Mission is what Adventists do—what we have always done. Adventists and mission are inseparable, joined at the hip. Or are they?

Much has changed since the good ship Adventist launched some 160 years ago. The world changed. The "mission field" changed. Attitudes towards mission changed. Adventists changed.

In particular, the Christian message itself finds itself placed in a posture radically different from that of the 18th century, when the modern era of missions was inaugurated, or the 19th century when the Adventist mission began. Today, Christianity is but one voice amid many competing world faiths. Islam, Hinduism, Buddhism, Sikhism, among others, are not only resurgent, but aggressive in seeking and winning followers. Often, Christianity is set back on its heels, forced to play defense.

It is against such a background that this paper takes up the issue of Adventist mission. I offer an intentional (and in places painful), personal reflection; not an attempt to research the work of others and weigh their findings. I will proceed in three stages: first, the changed and changing face of Adventist mission; second, a discussion of whether the traditional motto, "the gospel to all the world in this generation," can still be taken seriously; and last, suggestions on changes that need to take place in Adventist mission.

The Changed and Changing Face of Adventist Mission

During our senior year at Avondale College, Noelene and I received a call to serve in India. This was remarkable on at least three counts: we had not yet graduated, we had not applied for overseas service, and we were not engaged—let alone married. The terms of the call and the duties we were to fill presupposed that we would be partners in the mission: I as dean of boys and a Bible teacher, Noelene as matron of the younger boys, at Vincent Hill School, a boarding academy at Mussoorie in northern India.

As extraordinary as was the placing of the call by the leaders of our work in Southern Asia, we did not need an extended period of deliberation to give our answer. The motto of the college, "For a greater vision of world needs," was emblazoned on the wall of the chapel and the school badge. We imbibed it over and over as we learned of the heroes of Adventist mission. After earnest prayer, we responded as did the young prophet Isaiah who saw the Lord in the Temple and heard the call in his bones: "Whom shall I send? And who will go for us?" We said along with him: "Here am I. Send me" (Isa 6:8).

Noelene and I graduated from Avondale in November, married in December, and three weeks later we sailed for India. We arrived in India with stars in our eyes. Although India had long been termed "the Gibraltar of heathenism," we would succeed where a long line of equally dedicated missionaries before us had failed. After several months of learning Hindi in a language school and three years at Vincent Hill School, we felt the urge to work more directly for the people of India and asked to be assigned to the field for evangelistic-pastoral work. The "brethren" heeded our request. But to our pleasant surprise, our new post was to be Spicer Memorial College to teach in the School of Theology. Spicer would be our home for the next 12 years.

Life at Spicer was comfortable and happy. There were about a dozen overseas families on the faculty, so we had a pleasant social life. We lived in sprawling bungalows on a pretty campus, with servants to care for the garden and help with food preparation, cleaning, and baby care. The Indian staff, by contrast, were assigned to much smaller dwellings. Although we shopped together in the same market and ate the same foods, our salaries were multiples of theirs. We usually gathered after church for a combined meal in the driveway of a fellow missionary's home. Under big, spreading shade trees, we ate well and spent the afternoon gossiping or sharing the latest news from the States. Every Christmas, we would get in our vehicles and drive off to the Poona Yacht Club, where we feasted together. This too was restricted to missionaries.

I recount this history with a sense of shame, wondering how Noelene and I, with so many stars in our eyes, could have been so unchristian in our attitudes and behavior. In sharing this sad account, I can think of only one aspect that casts a positive light. During our second furlough, we were off campus for nearly three years as I studied for the Ph.D. degree at Vanderbilt University. During this extended time away we had opportunity to reflect on what we had left behind at Spicer and resolved that when we returned we would make some changes. We would no longer attend "Whites only" social gatherings on Sabbath or at Christmas. Others also had begun moving in the same direction. Within months "Whites only" gatherings at Spicer were no more.

As I recall those Spicer years, a hymn we often sang comes to mind. Written in 1819 by Reginald Heber, it encapsulated the thinking of that era of mission:

> From Greenland's icy mountains, from India's coral strand;
> Where Africa's sunny fountains roll down their golden sand:
> From many an ancient river, from many a palmy plain,
> They call us to deliver their land from error's chain.
>
> What though the spicy breezes blow soft o'er Ceylon's isle;
> Though every prospect pleases, and only man is vile?
> In vain, with lavish kindness, the gifts of God are strewn;
> The heathen in his blindness bows down to wood and stone
>
> Shall we, whose souls are lighted from wisdom from on high,
> Shall we to those benighted the lamp of life deny?
> Salvation! O salvation! The joyful sound proclaim,
> Till earth's remotest nation has learned Messiah's Name.
>
> Waft, waft, ye winds, His story, and you, ye waters, roll,
> Till, like a sea of glory, it spreads from pole to pole:
> Till for His ransomed people the Lamb for sinners slain,
> Redeemer, King, Creator, in bliss returns again.

Today, the hymn is jarring. Its tone is condescending, breathing an air of superiority light-years removed from the mission Jesus left us: "For even the Son of Man did not come to be served but to serve" (Mark 10:45).[1]

---

[1] Biblical quotes are from NIV.

The apostle Paul, missionary par excellence to the Gentiles, wrote about the blindness of those who refused to embrace the glorious light of the gospel (2 Cor 4:3-4). He called for the people of his day to turn from their worship of dumb idols to the God who made heaven and earth (1 Cor 8:4-6; Acts 14:14-17). But his approach, exemplified by the speech on Mars Hill, was a call to something better—to rise higher rather than a denigration of the worship of the day. Considering the scope and number of Paul's letters, we find surprisingly little space given to refuting idol worship.

In the portrayal above of mission as it was, I have highlighted shortcomings. A fair accounting should also include the other side of the story: the unselfishness, the sacrifice, the devotion, the bravery, the love of the people, even if couched in a patronizing context. Mission and missionaries led to profound, positive change for individuals and for societies. Schools, hospitals, orphanages, and clinics were established. And thousands of gravestones—many of them unmarked, except by the Lord of the mission—bear mute testimony to the heroic aspect of the age of mission.

Thus, as we review Adventist mission as it was, we find reason to both rejoice and repent. The colonial thinking of the times, marked by condescension and paternalism, shaped attitudes, perspectives, and conduct.

Changed Context

Today, we notice several areas where Adventist mission finds itself in changed, and sometimes radically changed, conditions:

1. A changed attitude to Christian mission. Once widely appreciated, the term "missionary" has become a suspect designation. For many in the mission field it conjures the age of imperialism. Even in the West, many Christians, Adventists included, react with ambivalence to missions and missionary.

2. Negative attitudes on the part of governments. With the rise of national independence and the casting off the imperial yoke, nations have become negative, even hostile, toward Christian mission. They view it as the vestigial remains of what was, a denigration of longstanding beliefs and the culture of a nation. We are paying a price. In the past, all too often, the message of Christ was blended with the message of western culture, with neither missionary nor convert understanding or making any distinction between the two.

3. Resurgent world religions. Fifty years ago, students of history predicted the demise of religion in the face of science and technology. However, the reverse has occurred. A revival of interest in religion—all religions—has taken place. Hinduism, Buddhism, and Islam have been injected with new life in newly emergent or newly wealthy nations and spread across the globe, multiplying in Europe and the USA. In Europe, in particular, fears are raised against the day when Muslims in some countries will constitute a majority.

4. The academic study of religion and religions. An educated person today is expected to have a working knowledge of world religions. Religious study has become part of standard academic curriculum. As world religions are studied comparatively, the approach considered appropriate sets aside questions of truth values and avoids comparing the best features of one's religion with the worst of another's. The conclusion prevails that all religions, Christianity included, embody both good and bad elements, and that none has the standing to claim superiority over others. Each person is to choose according to his or her preferences.[2]

5. The collapse of Christendom. Much more than liberal optimism went up in smoke in the Great War (1914–18). Then, so-called Christian nations slaughtered one another on a massive scale. Whatever moral superiority Christendom may have sought to claim prior to the carnage was utterly discredited by the conflict's end. The Second World War did not restore the myth of "Christendom:" The horrors of the Holocaust were perpetrated in the land of the Protestant Reformation, while the United States—arguably the most "Christian" nation—resorted to atomic weapons. These developments inevitably weakened the arguments for, and appeal of, Christian mission. Adventist mission has shared in this loss of moral authority.

6. The reversal of mission. Today, Adventist mission finds itself (along with other Christian institutions) confronted by an extraordinary reversal. Mission now flows both ways: Muslims, Buddhists, and Hindus build their mosques and temples in the West and engage in propagating their religion. And most troubling to us is when people, especially the youth, raised in a Christian environment embrace one of these religions. Adventists have not been immune to this trend.

7. A loss of nerve. Despite the shining successes of Adventist mission, the task never seemed more daunting. Our message has spread far and wide. But against the backdrop of Planet Earth's 6.9 billion inhabitants, our gains are scarcely a drop in the proverbial bucket. More troubling is our impact on Islam, Buddhism, and Hinduism—nearly 3 billion people—has been slight. How can the task ever be accomplished? We Adventists have been at it for more than 160 years and barely made a dent. Will the work ever be finished? Can it?

---

[2] These courses customarily are based on evolutionary understanding, with religion evolving from totemism to polytheism and then monotheism.

8. A lack of love for mission. For me, perhaps the most distressing aspect of the prevailing Adventist mission is the attitude many of us hold toward those from other religions. 9/11 threw America off kilter and large numbers of Adventist have been affected. Too many of the saints distrust Muslims or anyone who matches their stereotype.

With some 1.5 billion followers, Islam is the second-largest religion in the world. Are we to suggest that Muslims are not included in the Adventist mission? Where is the love that flows from heaven—first, when "God so loved the world that He gave His only Son;" then, as that love constrains us, we go forth in response to the command of the Master: "As the Father sent me, I am sending you" (John 20:21)?

With this sobering background, we are ready to examine what the mission means today.

Mission: What is Our Task Today?

We must allow the Scriptures to guide our understanding of mission. The instruction in God's Word takes priority over all other prevailing arguments and strategies. I contend that the Bible lays down a four-fold foundation for our task:

1. The mission is God's mission. God commands; we are to obey. God takes the initiative. Success is in His hands, not ours. We are not to be anxious or yield to hubris or frustration. "My word shall not return unto me void," He promises (Isa 55:11). We are to go forth confident that He, Lord of time and space, is working in all things to accomplish the divine purpose. Questions of possibility or impossibility do not arise with God. Nothing is impossible if we allow Him to be Lord of the work.

2. Salvation is only through the Son, Jesus Christ. "There is no other name under heaven given to men by which we must be saved" (Acts 4:12). "He who has the Son has life; he who does not have the Son does not have life" (1 John 5:12). Jesus is unique, in both person and work. He is the Way, the Truth and the Life; no one comes to the Father except through Him (John 14:6). Two vital considerations flow from this fact. First, all religions, whatever wisdom and noble ideas they may embody, fall short because they do not set forth Jesus as the Way to God. In and of themselves they cannot open the door to salvation.

Does this mean that only those who have heard the gospel and accepted Jesus as Savior and Lord can be saved? Not at all. Such a view fails to take account of abounding grace: "Where sin abounded, grace superabounded" (Rom 5:20, my translation). To consign so many to hopelessness, because they were denied the opportunity to hear the name of Jesus, overlooks the force of Paul's line of argument in Romans 5:12–21.

Sin abounds throughout the world, but so does grace, and even more so. From the very first inroads of sin on our planet, grace abounded. "I will put enmity between you and the woman, and between your seed and her seed," God declared (Gen 3:15). That divine enmity is the work of grace, working to turn people everywhere toward God and set them free.[3]

God is free. He worked outside the covenant community to bring men and women to Himself, transforming them into His followers—Melchizedek (Gen 14:18-20); Jethro (Exod 18:1-27); Job (Job 1:1-2), Naaman (2 Kings 5:1); the Magi (Matt 2:1-12); and so on. He worked with the Gentiles, energizing their conscience so that they obeyed His law even without being aware of it (Rom 2:14-16). God is working everywhere! Although the church is His agency for the salvation of humankind, grace knows no bounds of time or place.

3. The end of time will witness a huge ingathering. "After this I looked and there before me was a great multitude that no one could count, from every nation, tribe, people and language, standing before the throne and in front of the Lamb. They were wearing white robes and were holding palm branches in their hands" (Rev 7:9). They are described as having "come out of the great tribulation; they have washed their robes and made them white in the blood of the Lamb" (v. 14).

The universality of this throng makes clear that they all do not derive from "Christian" lands. With Christianity today constituting only about one-third of the world's population, it seems the "great multitude" will comprise many people *originally* located among the world's religions.

4. The Seventh-day Adventist Church is to play a major role. In the final developments before the eschaton, we are to be a creative remnant, highlighting the character of God and calling all peoples of the world to put God first. God uses a variety of people and movements, but He calls our church to be His voice to proclaim His commandments and the faith of Jesus.

How our church will become the catalyst that unites God's true followers in all the world and in all religions, is not clear to us at this time. However, our God thinks big and so should we. God's plan of salvation, now thousands of years along in its course, will not end with a whimper. Adventists, called and commissioned with a divine mandate, should be humbled—not proud. We should feel the need for divine power to represent the Master aright and to discharge our responsibility to His glory: "We are therefore Christ's ambassadors, as though God were making his appeal through us. We implore you [all people] on Christ's behalf: Be rec-

---

[3] See Ángel Manuel Rodríguez, "World Religions and Salvation: An Adventist View," in this volume for more on this topic.

onciled to God" (2 Cor 5:20). We are God's partners, His servants through whom people come to believe. One plants, another waters; but only God can make the seed grow (1 Cor 3:5–7).

Our mission today is what it has been since the inception of the Seventh-day Adventist Church: to tell all people about Jesus the Savior and warn them that the hour of judgment has come and Jesus will soon return. Against the backdrop of the world scene— resurgent world religions, secularism, materialism and Christian apathy—we seek to discharge our mandate through a variety of approaches. We adapt the method, but not the message. The mission remains the same because it goes back to the Risen Lord Himself, who commanded: "All authority in heaven and on earth has been given to me. Therefore go and make disciples of all nations, baptizing them in the name of the Father and of the Son and of the Holy Spirit, and teaching them to obey everything I have commanded you. And surely I am with you always, to the very end of the age" (Matt 28:18–20).

This command contains four imperatives: go, make disciples, baptize, instruct. Among these, the original text makes clear that the primary command is to make disciples. The other three are subsidiary and attendant. Thus, the divine commission is: *Make disciples* in all nations by *going, baptizing,* and *instructing.* It is not our place to modify the command. We are not to question or doubt its ultimate success. We are to be ambassadors, agents of salvation, planters and waterers in the gospel garden where God alone makes the seed grow.

If our essential mission today remains the same, what has changed or should change, especially vis-à-vis the world religions?

Mission Today: Changes

For most of our existence we have directed our efforts toward Christians rather than Muslims, Hindus, and Buddhists. Work among the latter has been slow and difficult, with meager results. Given the enormity and difficulty of the task, it would be tempting to either fall into a defeatist stance that virtually writes off this section of the mission or to postpone hope for significant change to the last events before the Second Coming, when God will step in to finish the work.

Such a stance, however, would be a dereliction of duty. The same argument could be extended to the total mission, and it would signal disobedience. The Lord has never given us the option of choosing among mission fields: our mandate is to the whole world, to every nation, kindred, tongue, and people. We are not to choose the easy fields and neglect the difficult; we are to plant in all soils, not knowing beforehand what will prosper (Eccl 11:6).

The changes in Adventist mission today, with particular reference to the world religions, should take place in at least four areas—intentionality, theology, engagement, and attitudes.

1. Intentionality. Breaking years of patterns will require a high degree of intentionality. Followers of the world religions will not be drawn to Christ and the church through the conventional methods of outreach. They must be reached through approaches tailored to their background. The policy, "Roadmap for Mission," calls the leadership of the world church to such intentionality.[4] It makes clear that our task is not to affirm people in their own religion—to make Hindus better Hindus, Muslims better Muslims, Buddhists better Buddhists, and so on. Our task is to lead them to Jesus, Savior of the world. It calls for modified approaches, employing the writings of other religions to build bridges and contextualization, defined as "the intentional and discriminating attempt to communicate the gospel in a culturally meaningful way."[5]

Further, the "Roadmap" advocates helping people develop expertise in the writings of other religions, along with literature and programs to train clergy and lay members in reaching adherents of world religions. It calls for strategic planning and the allocation of human and financial resources to fulfill the needs of the mission.

2. Theology. Adventists have yet to come to grips with the intellectual and theological challenges posed by world religions. They have extensive writings, with scholars and revered teachers of intellectual breadth and spiritual insight. A major task of Adventist mission today is to come to a position, vis-à-vis these religions, with their scriptures and leading figures.[6] For instance, how should Adventists regard Islam as a religion? What about Muhammad and the Qu'ran? Are we to take seriously Muhammad's claim to have received messages from Allah?

Parallel questions can be raised for Buddhism, Hinduism, Sikhism, and Judaism. We need to develop a theological understanding of these religions, treating each one separately because of the vast differences among them. Only as we engage in such an endeavor can Adventist mission take seriously the challenge of world religions. The undertaking of such an endeavor presupposes that world religions contain positive elements that make their study worthwhile. This evaluation is the founda-

---

[4] See Appendix: "Roadmap for Mission."

[5] Appendix: "Roadmap," p. 458.

[6] Stefan Hoeschele, "The Emerging Adventist Theology of Religious Discourse: Participants, Positions, Particularities," in Bruce L. Bauer (ed.), *A Man of Passionate Reflection* (Berrien Springs, MI: Andrews University Press, 2011), 355–376, calls for the development of an Adventist theology of religions.

tion for the "Roadmap for Missions:" "The genuine quest for God in world religions provides a pathway for the proclamation of the gospel."[7]

Not all Adventists agree that world religions embody a "genuine quest for God." Some put them in categories of ignorance, superstition, or even Satanic deceptions. However, we should point out that wherever and whenever humans are found, we encounter religion. Religious expression, as varied as humanity and culture, may seem quaint or even repulsive, but it contains a central core. As *homo religiosus*, each one of us hungers for God. Augustine captured our desire for God well: "Thou hast made us for Thyself, and our hearts are restless until they find rest in thee." In terms of biblical theology, *homo religiosus* derives from our origin in God. We were made in God's image. Although that image has been marred by the Fall, it has not been obliterated. Our first parents found their highest joy in worshiping the Creator. Ever since, their offspring seek the same sort of fulfillment.

In this regard, Paul's speech on Mars Hill is instructive, both for what he does *not* say and for what he argues. Referring to the altar marked to The Unknown God [Agnostos Theos], he does *not* call their worship ignorant or superstitious, let alone satanic. Rather he notes that the Athenians are "very religious"—a compliment rather than a rebuke (Acts 17:22–23).

Paul's presentation then takes a significant turn. He states that "The Unknown God" of their altar is the very One he has come to proclaim. This is the God who created heaven and earth, who orders and guides the world, and in whom "we live and move and have our being" (v. 28). It is a bold step of logic: The good news centered in Jesus is the *realization*, the *fulfillment* of the Athenians' attempt to satisfy their God-hunger. The implications for Adventist mission to the world religions are profound.

3. Engagement. Mission to followers of the world religions involves three overlapping stages. The most basic stage is interaction and co-operation. This corresponds to what is often termed "friendship evangelism," where we become acquainted with Muslims, Hindus, or Buddhists and learn to appreciate them as fellow human beings. The second stage is conversation. Here, we spend time listening to one another, seeking to learn and understand, correcting misinformation and removing stereotypes. At this point, we do not attempt to prove that our beliefs are correct and theirs false. It is the opening of the door, laying out respective beliefs on the table. For this stage to be fruitful, we must be open and candid, sharing ourselves, becoming vulnerable.

The third stage is Christian witness. As the opportunity presents itself, and the Holy Spirit guides, we sense the *kairos*, the decisive moment

---

[7] Appendix: "Roadmap," p. 455

to share what Jesus means to us. It is only at this stage, which may take weeks or months to reach, that potential relationship-destroying teachings, such as the deity of Jesus, should be broached.

4. Attitudes. Adventist mission is comprehensive in its scope. It includes proclaiming, making disciples, baptizing, and inviting converts into the *ecclesia*—the end-time community of believers in Jesus who worship God the Creator and Redeemer. There is a tendency among some Adventists to distrust people of other religions. If they live in a country where Christians are in the minority, centuries of effort just to survive in their faith have erected barriers and have limited communication. Adventists in these circumstances are content simply to be left alone, without disturbing the status quo.

For Adventists in so-called Christian lands, negative attitudes take a different turn. Here the influx of Muslims, Hindus, and Buddhists, often with large families, disquiets them. They see the familiar patterns of their culture disturbed and threatened. In the United States, the events of 9/11 have engendered widespread suspicion and prejudice among some Adventists toward Muslims. Such negative attitudes have two consequences, both harmful to mission. First, because of distrust and suspicious, they avoid contact rather than share Jesus. Second, they do not welcome them into the *koinonia*, the fellowship that should be at the heart of the congregation. This not only affects attitudes toward mission to the world religions overseas, but to mission within our own borders. Under the impact of liberalized immigration laws, the mission field has come home. Our neighbors, the mail carrier, the checkout clerk in the supermarket, our doctor, our dentist, our taxi driver are Muslims, Sikhs, Hindus, Buddhists. God has brought them to us. They are *here*! What sort of missionaries will we be to them?

There are no easy answers in this situation. Attitudes don't change suddenly. A continuing process of education from all agencies of the church—pulpit, classroom, media—will have to take up the challenge. The greatest need of all is a heart of love: a heart that, touched and changed by the Holy Spirit, has risen above fear, suspicion, and prejudice; a heart that burns with passion to see Muslims, Jews, Sikhs, Hindus, and Buddhists brought to saving faith in Jesus and to be part of His remnant people.

Conclusion

This is the task and challenge of Adventist mission today. It has never seemed as daunting, never so impossible. It is the impossible dream. But Adventists have been dreamers from the outset. We dream big. We think big. And God loves that word, *impossible*. "With men this is impossible, but with God all things are possible" (Matt 19:26).

APPENDIX

Roadmap for Mission[1]

Rationale—God's mission for this world motivates and informs our mission. For this reason, mission is the lifeblood of the Seventh-day Adventist Church. Mission is woven into our identity; mission defines who we are and why we exist. Early in our movement, we took the Great Commission (Matt 28:18-20) as our divine mandate motivated by the vision of the everlasting gospel reaching every nation, tribe, language, and people (Rev 14:6-12). The genuine quest for God in world religions provides a pathway for the proclamation of the gospel.

Under the blessing of the Lord, our Church has grown, reaching to Earth's farthest bounds. When we began, our mission placed us among people who had traditions of Christianity. Today, however, mission takes us to populations that are rooted in other world religions. Furthermore, in some areas of the world, conversion to Christianity is frowned upon or even runs the risk of threatening one's person and life. The history of Christianity indicates that this has practically always been the case.

At the same time, the spirit of the age encourages acceptance of all world religions as valid expressions of the human spirit and discourages efforts to persuade people to turn from one religion to another. Some Christian theologians even argue that the task of missions is to affirm people in their own religion—to make Hindus better Hindus, Muslims better Muslims, Buddhists better Buddhists, and so on.

Among Seventh-day Adventists, one finds a variety of initiatives and methodologies toward people of different religions and cultures. While the concern for mission is commendable, the proliferation of approaches makes it all the more imperative for the organized Church to articulate simply and clearly the nature of our mission—what it is and how we go

---

[1] Document voted during the 2009 General Conference Annual Council and published in the *General Conference Working Policy 2011-2012* (Hagerstown, MD: Review and Herald, 2011), A20 (pp. 43-49).

about it—firmly grounded in the authority of the Scriptures.

We must find our roadmap for mission in the specific instructions and acts of Jesus and the apostles as recorded in the Scriptures. In His sovereignty, the Lord takes initiatives to reveal Himself to men and women through a variety of means. For instance, in the Old Testament, we read of people outside the circle of the chosen people who were followers of God—Melchizedek (Gen 14:18-20), Jethro (Exod 18:1-27), Naaman (2 Kgs 5:1). Likewise, the New Testament tells of the Magi (Matt 2:1-12), of Gentiles who were "God-fearers" (Acts 13:43, 50; 16:14; 17:4, 17), and of others who obeyed God's law through following their conscience (Rom 2:14-16). Such examples, however, do not provide a template for Seventh-day Adventist mission; they simply provide laudable examples of the Lord's working.

The Mission—Seventh-day Adventist mission is centered in God's loving gift of His Son to be the Savior of the world. We are to share this good news with all people, telling them that "Salvation is found in no one else, for there is no other name under heaven given to men by which we must be saved" (Acts 4:12), and that "whoever believes in Him shall not perish but have eternal life" (John 3:16).

At its core, mission is bearing witness through word and life and in the power of the Holy Spirit. As the Lord commanded Israel of old, "You are my witnesses, . . . and my servant whom I have chosen" (Isa 43:10), so the Risen Lord commands us, "You will receive power when the Holy Spirit comes on you; and you will be my witnesses in Jerusalem, and in all Judea and Samaria, and to the ends of the earth" (Acts 1:8).

Seventh-day Adventist mission is comprehensive in its scope. It involves proclaiming the good news to the whole world (Matt 24:14), making disciples of all nations by going, baptizing, and teaching them (Matt 28:18-20), and inviting them into the *ecclesia*—the end-time community of believers in Jesus who worship God the Creator and Redeemer (Rev 12:17; 14:6, 7).

This community, the Church, is the body of Christ (1 Cor 12, Eph 1:21, 22; 4:4-6). In this fellowship where Jesus is confessed as Savior and Lord, and where the Scriptures provide the foundation for instruction, members experience the transforming power of the new life in Christ. They love one another (John 13:31, 32); they are united, despite differences of race, culture, gender, or social standing (Eph 2:12-14; Gal 3:28); and they grow in grace (2 Peter 3:18). They, in turn, go out to make disciples of other people, and they carry forward Jesus' ministry of compassion, help, and healing to the world (Matt 10:7, 8).

Although other Christians also preach the gospel, Seventh-day Adventists understand our special calling as proclaiming the good news of salvation and obedience to God's commandments. This proclamation takes place during the time of God's judgment and in the expectation of the soon return of Jesus, bringing to an end the cosmic conflict (Rev 14:6, 7; 20:9-10).

Seventh-day Adventist mission, therefore, involves a process of proclamation that builds up a community of believers "who keep the commandments of God and have the faith of Jesus" (Rev 14:12). They live lives of service to others and eagerly await the second coming of the Lord.

Fulfilling the Mission—Our mission remains unchanged wherever we find ourselves in the world. How we fulfill it—how we go about it—however, takes a variety of forms depending on differences in culture and conditions in society. Fulfilling the mission where non-Christian religions prevail often entails significant modifications in approaching the task. We encounter cultural differences, other writings that are deemed sacred, and sometimes restrictions in religious freedom.

1. The Example of the Apostles—The conditions Seventh-day Adventists face in sharing the message of Jesus to people of other religions largely parallel those that the apostles encountered. How they went about the mission is instructive for us today.

The first Christians faced a world of many deities. It was also a dangerous world, as the Caesars in Rome increasingly demanded not only respect, but worship as divine. Yet they risked everything they had, even their lives, which many lost, in an unbreakable commitment to their Savior.

In this environment, the apostles always uplifted Jesus Christ as mankind's only hope. They did not shrink from proclaiming who He was and what He had done. They announced forgiveness and new life through Him alone, and they called people everywhere to repentance in view of judgment to come and the return of Jesus (Acts 2:38; 8:4; 1 Cor 2:2). And they proclaimed that only one person could rightly be adored as Lord—Jesus Christ: "For even if there are so-called gods, whether in heaven or on earth (as indeed there are many 'gods' and many 'lords'), yet for us there is but one God, the Father . . . and there is but one Lord, Jesus Christ, . . ." (1 Cor 8:5, 6).

Although they modified their approach in keeping with the audience, they never deviated from proclaiming the uniqueness of Jesus as the hope of the world. They never suggested that they had come to help their hearers find a deeper spiritual experience within their own religions; on the contrary, they challenged them to turn to the salvation provided in Christ. Thus, the Apostle Paul in Athens began his discourse on Mars Hill by referring to the gods the people were worshipping, but led them to the message of Jesus and His resurrection (Acts 17:22-31).

2. Writings of Other Religions—Paul made references to non-biblical

writings in his speech in Athens and his letters (Acts 17:38; 1 Cor 15:33; Titus 1:12), but he gave priority to the Scriptures (the Old Testament) in his proclamation and instruction to the new Christian communities (Acts 13:13-47; 2 Tim 3:16, 17; 4:2).

In Seventh-day Adventist witness, the writings of other religions can be useful in building bridges by pointing to elements of truth that find their fullest and richest significance in the Bible. These writings should be used in a deliberate attempt to introduce people to the Bible as the inspired Word of God and to help them transfer their allegiance to the Scriptures as the source of faith and practice. However, the nurture and spiritual growth of new believers must be accomplished on the basis of the Bible and its exclusive authority (see *Statements, Guidelines, and Other Documents*, June 2005 edition, "Guidelines for Engaging in Global Mission").

3. Contextualization—Jesus, as our model, was the perfect example of love in His relationships with others. As we imitate Him in our mission, we should open our hearts in honest and loving fellowship. The Apostle Paul described how he adapted his approach to his audience: "Though I am free and belong to no man, I make myself a slave to everyone, to win as many as possible. To the Jews I became like a Jew, to win the Jews. To those under the law I became like one under the law (though I myself am not under the law), so as to win those under the law. To those not having the law I became like one not having the law (though I am not free from God's law but am under Christ's law), so as to win those not having the law. To the weak I became weak, to win the weak. I have become all things to all men so that by all possible means I might save some" (1 Cor 9:19-22). The apostles did not make it difficult for people to accept the gospel and join the fellowship of the Christian community, but they did not shrink from declaring the full purpose of God for them (cf. Acts 15:19; 20:20-24).

From Paul's example arises contextualization—the intentional and discriminating attempt to communicate the gospel in a culturally meaningful way. For Seventh-day Adventist mission, contextualization must be faithful to the Scriptures, guided by the Spirit, and relevant to the host culture, remembering that all cultures are judged by the gospel.

As the Church seeks to adapt its approach to mission in a very diverse world, the danger of syncretism—the blending of religious truth and error—is a constant challenge. Contextualization should be done within a specific cultural location, close to where the people live; it is a process that should involve church leaders, theologians, missiologists, local people, and ministers.

4. Openness and Identity—Paul sought to be open and honest in his

presentation of the gospel: "We have renounced secret and shameful ways; we do not use deception, nor do we distort the word of God. On the contrary, by setting forth the truth plainly we commend ourselves to every man's conscience in the sight of God" (2 Cor 4:2). Likewise, we are to carry out our mission, and identify ourselves as Seventh-day Adventists, in a manner that avoids creating formidable barriers.

In seeking to find connections with people from other religions, the theme of cosmic conflict, which is found in various expressions, may be a useful starting point. Other areas that can prove helpful are prophecy, modesty and simplicity, and healthful living.

5. Transitional Groups—In some situations, Seventh-day Adventist mission may include the formation of transitional groups (usually termed Special Affinity Groups) that lead the people from a non-Christian religion into the Seventh-day Adventist Church. In forming such groups, a clear plan that emphasizes the end result should be followed. These groups should be established and nurtured only with the endorsement and collaboration of church administration. Although some situations may require an extended period of time to complete the transition, leaders of these groups should make every effort to lead the people into membership in the Seventh-day Adventist Church within a deliberate time plan (see also B 10 28 and B 10 30).

Any ministry or group that is formed with the intention of representing the Seventh-day Adventist Church in any part of the world will endeavor to promote both the theological and organizational unity of the Church. Although the theological dimension may be given the chief emphasis in the initial stages of the group, the leader of the group should intentionally lead its members to a sense of Seventh-day Adventist identity and an awareness of Church organization, with growing participation in the lifestyle, practices, and mission of the Church.

6. Baptism and Church Membership—Candidates for baptism shall confess Jesus Christ as Savior and Lord (Rom 10:9), accept the message and mission of the Seventh-day Adventist Church as summarized in the Fundamental Beliefs, and understand that they are joining a worldwide fellowship that is loyal to God and awaits the second coming of Jesus.

7. Opportunities and Needs—Today, because of immigration and other factors, followers of world religions are found throughout the world. In this new context, leaders in all the world divisions should develop specific plans to bring the Seventh-day Adventist message to these peoples.

For the fulfillment of the mission globally, the Church needs to help people develop expertise in the writings of other religions, along with literature and programs to train clergy and lay members in reaching adherents of these religions. The Global Mission Study Centers should play a major, but not exclusive, role in these endeavors.

Worldwide, our pastors and members need to be educated to accept new believers from world religions. This will require the developing of competence among leaders, local elders, pastors, missionaries, and front-line workers.

In the allocation of human and financial resources, the needs of the mission to people of other world religions should be included as part of strategic planning.

8. Where Freedom is Restricted—Our mission takes us at times to societies where religious freedom is severely restricted. These areas of the world are not to be abandoned; rather, new methods of fulfilling the mission are to be attempted. These include the "tentmaker" approach, which is when individuals use their occupation to support themselves financially, usually in a challenging mission area for the purpose of Christian outreach. Another approach is to simply encourage those from such countries who have become Seventh-day Adventists in another society to return to their home countries as ambassadors for Christ. And even where a human presence is not possible, the witness through radio, television, or the Internet may, like the altars left behind by Abraham on his wanderings (Gen 12:7), be used by the Spirit to lead men and women to accept the Advent message.

Conclusion—The mission to reach followers of world religions poses substantial challenges. However, the mission itself remains unchanged because it is God's mission. Through whatever approach we follow, its end result is to lead men and women into membership with those who confess Jesus Christ as Savior and Lord, who embrace the Fundamental Beliefs of the Seventh-day Adventist Church, demonstrating the transforming power of the Holy Spirit, and looking forward to the soon coming of Christ. They shall identify themselves with the worldwide Seventh-day Adventist Church in doctrine, life values, hope, and mission.

God, the Lord of the mission, is free and sovereign. He can and does intervene to reveal Himself in various ways, drawing people to Himself and awakening them to His majesty and sovereignty. But to His Church He has entrusted His mission (2 Cor 5:18-21). It is a comprehensive mission, but it is a single mission. He has not established parallel or multiple tracks for us to follow, which is to say, we should all be committed to the same beliefs and be organized and work in harmony with the world Church.

Selected Scripture Index

OLD TESTAMENT

Genesis
1:1	362
1:2	303
1–11	66
1:26–27	436
2:7	303
3:15	449
4:26b	65
5:24	2, 66
9:21	2
9:26	4
11:9	4
12:1–3	4, 63, 432
12:3	66, 106
12:7	383
13:14–15	5
14:17–24	67
15:13–16	76
18:10–14	389
18:19	68
20:1–3	437
25:2	10
26:3–5	383
26:5	67
32:28	379
41:25–28	437
45:5–8	69
50:19–21	69

Exodus
6:7	8
12:3	411
18:1	75
18:11–12	10
19:4–6	63
19:5	8
19:5–6	6, 68, 405
19:6	6, 141
19:10–11	245
22:21	9
23:6–10	9
32	8
32:11–12	112
33:19	65
34:5	65
34:10	8
34:11–16	57
35:4-40:38	50

Leviticus
19:18	9

Numbers
6:24–26	72
11:29	9
15:38–40	57
16:41	9
22:5	10
22:9	437
24:17–19	76

Deuteronomy
6:4–5	293
6:4–9	64
25:4	326
26:5–9	293
28:10	6
30:11–14	330
31:16	57
32:21	393

Joshua
2:9–14	75
24:31	11

Judges
2:16	11

1 Samuel
Sam 12:8	69

1 Kings
13:1–5	12
17:9–24	69

2 Kings
8:7–15	69
17:5–11	14
25:12	14

2 Chronicles
2:11–12	71
20:20	343, 359
35:20–22	437

Ezra
3–7	74
6:21	16
7:11–28	70

Nehemiah
2:1–10	70
8:2–8	325
8:8	340

Esther
4:12–14	71
8:15–17	71
8:17	16

Job
1:1, 9	75
2:3	75
12:13	274
26:10	50
42:10–11, 16	75

Psalms
33:11	274
40:6–8	50
57:9	72
67:1–7	72
67:2	65
68:11	72
68:31	72
72:11	72
75:9	151
76:12	72
82:8	72
86:9	72
87:4–6	72
89:34–37	383
92:12	49
96:2–9	72
104:30	304

105:1–2	72	61:3	49	Joel	
105:26	69	61:9–11	73	2:28–32	306
117:1–2	72	62:2	73	2:32	74
118:22–23	412	62:4–5	406	3:1–3	76
119:33	343	66:2	343		
119:63	331	66:19	65, 69, 73	Amos	
126:2–3	72	66:23	69, 73	2:11–12	14
137:5	15			5:21	13
145:4–5	64	Jeremiah		9:6	50
145:11–12	72	11:16–17	49	9:7	76
		21:4–5	12	9:11–12	328
Proverbs		25:8–14	108		
1:25	274	27:22	108	Micah	
4:18	337	29:10–14	15	4:1–2	71
8:14	274	31:4, 28	50	4:2	74
8:27–31	50	31:31–34	404	6:6–8	50
14:12	324	34:18–20	5	6:8	66
15:22	337	51:9	109		
24:6	337			Zephaniah	
29:18	359	Ezekiel		2:11	73
		20:12	75	3:9	73
Ecclesiastes		28:11–19	252	3:10	73
11:6	450	36:25–28	306	3:17	74
		44:23–24	340		
Isaiah				Zechariah	
1:12–17	13	Daniel		2:11	13, 74
1:19–20	14	1:2	109	4:1–10	136
2:3	74	1:3	116	8:23	71
2:3–4	71	1:4	116		
5:4	14	1:8	115	Malachi	
5:7	49	3:26	125	1:2–3	389
6:8	444	4:2, 25	125	1:11	74, 183
8:20	262, 323, 337	4:27	113	2:7	139, 340
10:22–23	392	5:1, 21	125	3:1	139
11:9	355	5:11	115	4:5–6	78
14:12–15	252	5:23	109	4:5	145
19:23–25	77	6:25–27	76		
19:24–25	13	6:25–28	74	NEW TESTAMENT	
28:16	398	7:1–29	109		
38:19	64	7:13–14	109	Matthew	
39:1–8	73	12:2	110	4:8–10	83
42:1–9	67	12:10	111	5:14	86
48:13	50	7:1–14	105	5:45	436
49:1–7	67	7:18, 27	387	7:11	437
50:4–9	67	8:11–12	118	9:14–15	57
52:13–53:12	67	8:14	221	9:33	84
53:11	111	9:24–27	110	12:29	161
55:11	448	9:25	110	12:46–50	21
56:1–8	380	9:27	418	13:36–43	87
59:19	74	10:13, 20–21	118	13:44–45	87
59:20–21	398	12:3	112	15:3, 6	324
60:1–3	86			16:18	20, 50
60:3	74	Hosea		16:19	156
60:6–7	74	1:9–10	405	18:15–17	339
61:1–3	67	11:1–2	14	18:17	20

Selected Scripture Index

18:21	164	8:12	84, 86	17:30–31	90		
19:26	453	9:5	84, 86	20:17, 28	311		
20:1–16	88	10:1–18	21	20:27	274		
21:1–11	407	10:16	79	20:28	23		
21:13	417	13:14	215	21:20	421		
21:33–46	49	14:16–17	303	22:16	181		
21:43	411	14:26	304	28:13–15	35		
23:37–38	416	15:1–8	21, 49				
24:9–12, 24	155	15:4–5	247	Romans			
24:14	101, 230	16:8	304	1:20–23	324		
24:29–31	418	16:13	304, 331	2:14–15	437		
25:34	419	17:3	432, 434	3:2	326		
27:25	419	17:6	246	5:12–21	448		
28:18–19a	433	17:18	254	5:20	448		
28:18–20	36, 432, 450	17:20–21	246	8:14–15	306		
28:19	101	17:21	231, 247	8:29	274		
28:19–20	112	19:15	420	9–11	24, 387, 390		
28:20	20	20:21	448	10:9	301		
		20:23	156	10:12–13	397		
Mark		20:30–31	331	11:11–27	390		
1:15	82	21:15–17	21	11:17–24	49		
1:17	85			11:26	391		
3:14	85	Acts		12:3–8	406		
4:30	87	1:3, 8	88	12:4–5	46		
10:45	83, 445	1:13–14	308	12:4–8	331		
11:1–18	411	1:22	307	12:6–8	318		
12:1–12	49	1:26	309	13:11–14	53		
16:16	181	2:7–11	306	16:16	35		
		2:16	306	19:1–2, 4	435		
Luke		2:42	331				
1:3–4	330	4:12	432, 448	1 Corinthians			
1:79	246	5:11	22	1:2	24		
10:7	326	6:1–6	309	1:14–16	92		
12:32	21	6:7	415	2:11, 14	342		
13:28–29	423	6:8	311	3:6–9	49		
14:33–35	86	7:38	22	3:9b–17	50		
20:9–19	49	8:30–31	341	8:4–6	446		
22:25–26	320	9:1–30	311	9:1–14	36		
24:19	407	9:31	22	9:9, 19–23	93		
24:27	340	10:44–47	88	10:1–5	285		
24:44	325	11:28	35	10:1-22	46		
24:45	340	13:1–2	313	10:16–17	46		
24:49	88	14:14–17	446	10:17	46		
		14:23	92, 308	10:32	24		
John		15:11	317	11:2	297, 338		
1:1a, 3a	362	15:14	78	11:16	25		
1:5–10	35	15:22	22	11:18	20, 24		
1:9	86, 438	15:25	317	11:29	46		
1:14	256	16:4	35	12:3	306		
3:6	438	16:6	317	12:6–8	318		
3:16	434	16:30–34	432	12:12–27	46–47		
3:28–30	57	17:11	331	12:18	47		
4:1–42	355	17:22–23	452	12:25–26	47		
6:45	342	17:24–29	57	12:28–30	318		
7:17	343	17:25c, 27	436	14:36	34		

15:1–3	95	**Philippians**		6:4–6	164
15:9	24	1:1	26	7:1–3	75
16:9	139	4:15, 21–22	26	7:11–17	75
16:16	38			8:7–13	404
		Colossians		10:15–18	404
2 Corinthians		1:17	436	10:26	164
2:17	341	1:18	29, 406	10:35–39	96
3:14–16	95	2:8	324	12:3	96
3:14–18	342	2:14–17	406	12:23	30
3:18	256	2:15	433	13:17	38
4:3–4	446	2:18–19	48		
5:14–15	433	4:3	139	**James**	
5:20	450	4:10	92	1:1	97
6:14–7:1	51	4:16	35	2:2	30
6:16	25			2:7	97
10:3–6	53			5:14	30
11:1–3	57	**1 Thessalonians**			
12:15	81	1:1	26	**1 Peter**	
11:1–4	57	2:14	25	1:1	30, 97
		5:8	53	1:2–3	404
		5:12	38	2:4–5	30
Galatians		5:21	339	2:4–8	51
1:1, 15–16	90			2:4–9	404
1:6–9	94	**2 Thessalonians**		2:9	30, 78
1:8–9	338	1:4	25	2:8	155
3:13	6	2:1	423	2:9	98, 141, 330
3:28–29	401	2:3–12	155	2:17	31
6:10	25			3:15	97
6:16	401	**1 Timothy**		4:14–16	97
		1:3	297, 338	5:1–4	404
Ephesians		2:4	434	5:9	31
1:3–11	403	2:5	433	5:13	31
1:4–5, 7, 11	274	3:15	26		
1:14	306	6:3	297	**2 Peter**	
1:20–23	27	6:20	324	1:19–21	342
1:22–23	406			1:20–21	306
2:11–22	403	**2 Timothy**		3:11	250
2:11–30	27	1:10	245		
2:15	406	1:13	338	**1 John**	
2:19–22	51	2:17–18	26	1:9	155
2:21–22	407	2:30–21	26	2:1	138
3:1–9	403	3:1–9	26	4:1	155, 339
3:6	79, 406	3:15–16	342	5:12	448
3:6–12	78	3:15–17	306		
3:10	256	4:14–15	26	**2 John**	
3:14–15	57			1:1	31
4:1–16	47	**Titus**		1:13	31
4:3–13	331	1:5, 7	311	7	98
4:4–6	28, 249	1:5–9	26	7–11	338
4:11	318	2:14	26		
4:15–16	291	3:10	299	**3 John**	
5:21–33	58			1:6, 9–10	31
5:23–32	406	**Hebrews**		5–8	99
5:31	28	3:12	96		
5:32	245	4:12	133, 306		
6:10–20	54	4:13–16	155		

Selected Scripture Index

Jude		
14–15		66
Revelation		
1:3		330
1:4, 5		134
1:4–8		147
1:5		141
1:5–6, 17–19		99
1:6		330
1:10		135
1:11		138
1:19		138
1:20		32, 139
2:6		146
2:12		133
2:14		76
2:14–15		146
2:24		32
3:9, 19		148
3:11–18		149
4:2		135
4:5		134
4:11		150
6:9		140
7:3		32
7:9		449
7:9–17		32
8:2–3		139
9:17–18		137
9:20–21		151
10:7		130
10:11		143
11:8		148
11:13		152
11:15		139
12:7–12		252
12:10		32
12:17		32, 132, 140, 285, 423
13:1–10		148
14:1–5		32
14:1–12		148
14:4		57
14:6		143, 443
14:6, 8–9		139
14:6–12		36, 101, 145, 219, 230, 362, 432
14:8–11		155
14:17–20		152
17:2		151
17:3		135
17:6		140
18:1–2		139
18:4		32, 150, 152
19:2, 5		32
19:13		133
20:8–9		424
20:11–15		101
21:3		32
21:6		104
21:9		32
21:10		135
22:3, 6		32, 131
22:9		140
22:17		32, 135
22:18–20		132

Subject Index

144,000, 148
1888 General Conference session, 228, 235

Abraham, 4, 6, 10, 62, 67–68, 364, 383, 432
  a missionary, 67
  figure and functions of, 364
  the nations will be blessed, 432
  to be a blessing to others, 67
  to teach his children, 68
Adam and Eve, 65
Adventist ecclesiology, 55, 59, 209, 222
Adventist education, 78
Adventist-Evangelical Ecclesiology, 227
Adventists, 219, 233, 449
  end-time remnant, 219, 233
  should be humbled, 449
Aesop's fable, 47
Agabus, 35
Akkadian prophecies, 123
all Israel, 391
almsgiving, 174
Alpha and Omega, 147
altars, 67
Ambrose of Milan, 179, 184
  mystagogical preaching, 184
Anabaptists, 208, 211, 213, 265
Anabaptist theology, 208
Ananias, 312
anatomy, 116
angels, 118, 139
  agents of God, 139
  may stand for human beings, 139
  mediate revelation, 139
  stand for the leaders of the churches, 139
Anthony of the Desert, 175
antichrist, 221
Antipas, 140

anti-Semitism, 419
antitype, 406
apocalyptic prophecies, 16, 267, 385
Apocrypha, 325
Apollos, 50
apostasy, 3, 11, 13, 17, 34, 37, 58, 98, 146–147, 155
  among Christians, 37
  among God's people, 11
  as-adultery, 58
  predicted in the New Testament, 155
  supported by deceptive signs, 147
  worship of the dragon, 147
apostles, 22, 36, 308, 310, 326
  primary group of leaders, 308
  servants or ministers, 310
  unique, singular position, 326
apostolic church, 233
  delegated authority, 233
  ecclesiastical authority, 233
  holding of general councils, 233
  recognition of autonomy, 233
  relationship to other congregations, 233
  representative government, 233
apostolic succession, 169, 330
  resist corrective ideas, 170
  the succession of teaching, 170
Aquinas, 263
Aramaic, 122
Aristotelian metaphysics, 269
ascension, 137, 270
ascetic ethic, 176
ascetic movement, 176
ascetic rigor, 178
Asia Minor, 99
astrology, 116

Athanasius, 175, 178
atonement, 9, 236, 278, 362
  for sins, 9
  redemption from sin, 362
  restoration of God's cosmic sovereignty, 362
atoning work of Christ, 57
Augustine, 161, 170, 182, 187, 263
  binding, 188
  church cannot be deceived, 161
  Church cannot err, 187
  view of church tradition, 187
authority, 162, 171, 213, 232, 320, 324, 336
  dependent on loyalty to God's Word, 232
  earned, 171
  General Conference in session, 336
  in the church, 320
  of ecclesiastical tradition, 324
  official, 171
  of the church, 213
  within the Church, 162

Babylon, 32, 37, 106, 114, 116, 123, 140, 149–150, 221, 224, 233, 441
  of Revelation, 224
  persecutes, 32
  the great city, 37
  the great harlot, 32
  will be judged, 32
Babylonian mythology, 123
Babylonian Talmud, 16
Balaam, 10, 75, 146, 437
  non-Israelite prophet, 10
  pronounced messianic prophecies, 75
  to curse Israel, 10
baptism, 28, 88, 162, 180–182, 214, 406

after the New Testament, 181
an objective holiness, 181
at the beginning of life, 181
by immersion, 181
by the Spirit, 88
for the forgiveness of past sins, 181
infant, 182, 214
means of insuring salvation, 181
put off, 181
Barnabas, 35
believers, 52–53
Belshazzar, 109, 117, 126
Bereans, 331
Bible, 106, 162, 234, 276, 292, 324, 332
  basis of church unity, 332
  blueprint, 106
  only creed, 292
  unerring guide to truth, 324
biblical covenants, 382
biblical standards, 251
biblical theology, 64
bishops, 26, 166–167, 169–170, 175–176, 320
  above presbyters and deacons, 171
  forgive sins, 166
  head of church hierarchy, 171
  in communion with, 166
  patrons of salvation, 175
  precedence over presbyters, 169
  the high priests, 171
  wield the keys of the kingdom, 176
blessings, 7
Boaz, 11
book of life, 101
Buddhism, 363, 366

Calvin, 202, 281
  baptism, 204
  church as "Body of Christ", 202
  ecclesiastical structure, 202
  efficacy of the sacraments, 204
  ministry of the church, 202
  ordination of ministers, 203
  pastors govern the church, 203
  pastors received "the power of the keys", 203
  representative model, 203
  sacraments as tokens, or signs, 204
  spiritualized the great controversy, 281
  the Lord's Supper, 205

Canaan, 9
Canaanite religion, 11
canon of the New Testament, 36
canonization of the Old Testament, 325
casting of lots, 309
catacombs, 172
Celsus, 162
Christ, 47, 58, 265, 267, 269, 272, 278–279, 282, 291, 304
  advocate, 278
  a historical, living person in heaven, 272
  a Man of sorrows, 278
  anointed, 304
  ascended, 270–271, 278
  as revealed in Scripture, 265
  atonement, 99
  baptized by the Spirit, 304
  blood, 167
  center of all love and light, 280
  center of belief and practice, 291
  center of God's system of reality, 282
  conceived of the Holy Spirit, 304
  empowered, 304
  great center of creation, 282
  in human form, 278
  in humiliation, 278
  in the heavenly sanctuary, 267
  in place of sinners, 282
  mediator, 282
  resurrected, 278
  the bride price, 58
  the "head", 47
  to come again, 101, 278
Christian apologists, 161
Christian church, 262
  adapted its teachings, 262
  replaced hermeneutical presuppositions, 262

Christians, 97, 141
  a chosen people, 97
  Jew and Gentile, 97
  proclaim Christ, 141
church, 22, 38, 48, 50, 52, 56, 202, 323, 325, 395
  adopt the models and metaphor of its time, 60
  agency of salvation, 213
  and culture, 23s1
  and predestination, 202
  and sola Scriptura, 323
  and the Canon, 326
  and the synagogue, 308
  as a flock, 23
  as a household, 26
  as army, 52–53
  as building/Temple, 50
  as family and bride, 56
  as plant/field/vineyard/vine, 48
  as the means of salvation, 202
  body of Christ, 28, 34
  built on the apostles and prophets, 318
  called to proclaim God's message, 143
  care for the whole person, 87
  chief purpose, 192
  colonial imagery, 60
  community of believers, 247
  conduit of grace, 156
  consists of "brothers", 26
  consists of the "elect", 30
  continuation of the "spiritual Israel", 396, 401
  constitutes faithful eschatological remnant, 394
  defined as the bishop, 166
  democracy, 60
  discipline, 339
  diversity of gifts, 47
  does not replace biblical-historical Israel, 394
  episcopal government, 33
  exerts authority, 34
  faithful remnant of Israel, 405
  fullness of, 34
  gathering of people, 195
  global, 19
  God's household, 28
  governance, 215–216

Subject Index

government, 33, 37
hierarchical structure, 33, 162, 167
holy and blameless, 28
holy temple, 27
house of Israel, 30
image of the temple, 25
imperial expansion, 60
infallible in doctrinal declarations, 156
interpret the Scriptures, 343
is subject to Christ, 28
justified by God's grace, 195
local and universal, 19
local entity, 32, 38
membership, 34
new humanity, 28, 248
no salvation outside, 202
of God, 25
one universal, 25
organized around its bishop, 192
people of God, 30
pragmatic perspective, 233
purchased, 23
reflected feudal models, 60
repository of the oracles of God, 327
spiritual community of Christ, 270
spiritual house, 30
take effective control of salvation, 162, 167
three marks, 195
universal, 32
Church Manual, 226, 232, 335, 339
church order, 26, 162
church orders, 187
church policies, 339
circumcision, 316
  in Egypt, 6
  no longer a sign, 406
  not a universal law, 89
  sign of the covenant, 6
Clement of Alexandria, 177
Clement of Rome, 158
Comforter, 305–306
common grace, 439
communion, 280–281
  as participation, 280
  with God, 281, 284
compassion, 173
compromise, 122
Conference of Churches, 216

confession, 163, 166, 301
confessors, 165, 172
congregationalism, 33, 38, 216
consensus, 295, 316, 329, 347
consensus fidelium, 249, 317
Constantine I, 163
Constantinian shift, 60
consummated eschatology, 399
consummation, 104
contextualization, 90, 123
conversion, 126, 152, 182
Cornelius, 437
cosmic conflict, 53, 84, 127, 433
  between good and evil, 433
  light and darkness, 84
Council of Jamnia, 325
Council of Jerusalem, 35, 315, 328–329
covenant, 4
  between God and Israel, 111
  between Yahweh and Israel, 9, 111
  conditional, 8
  curses, 416
  Jews and Gentiles, 30
  of salvation, 283
  promises, 315
  with Abraham, 5
covenants of grant, 383
creation, 1, 435
creation story, 362
creed, 287, 296, 298
cross-cultural conflicts, 121
cross-cultural context, 119
cultural symbols, 123
Cyprian, 164, 170, 174, 184
  and Christian ministry, 170
  exclusive forgiveness, 184
  gave his money to the church, 174
  the bishop is minister of the church, 170
Cyril, 178
Cyrus, 76

Daniel, 15, 119, 325
  a man of deep convictions, 115
  as a missionary, 70
  helped Nebuchadnezzar, 70
  message of judgment, 126
  restoration of the temple, 110

successful witness, 119
worldview, 108
Darius, 117, 127
Darius the Mede, 76
darkness, 97
David, 11–12, 383
day of atonement, 222
day of judgment, 371
deacons, 26, 89, 309
Decalogue, 9
Decian persecution, 164
defilement, 121
denominationalism, 209
denominations, 224, 227, 264, 281
Diaspora, 107, 404
didaskalia, 290
diet, 115
disappointment, 222–223, 267
disciple, 85
  implies learning, 85
disciples, 85–86
discipleship, 85
discontinuity, 405
dispensationalism, 382, 395, 403
divine providences, 436
divine warrior, 54
divine will, 434
doctrinal purity, 338
doctrine, 293
doctrine/teaching, 290
  beliefs of the Christian faith, 290
  connected to preaching, 290
  essential data of the faith, 290
doxology, 147
dreams and visions, 118
dualism, 98

Ebed Yahweh, 67
ecclesiological challenges, 234
ecclesiological models, 229
  cristocentric, 229
  functional, 229
  of church organization, 229
ecclesiological principles, 156
ecumenical movement, 240
ecumenism, 240
education, 300
Egypt, 7, 9, 48, 67
Egypt and Assyria, 77
  called the people of God, 72, 77

worship together, 77
ekklēsia, 19
  a gathering of people, 19
  groups of believers, 31
  in Acts, 22
  in Antioch, 22
  local church, 22
  those who believe in Jesus, 19
  three different groups, 24
elders, 22, 26, 35–36, 89, 308
election, 17, 64, 441
  inseparable from mission, 64
  of Israel, 441
  of one people, 17
Elijah, 69, 137, 145
Elisha, 69
Ellen G. White, 345
  a crucial role, 345
  as a genuine, non-canonical prophetess, 345
  confirming biblical truth, 347
  counseled many church leaders, 353
  ecclesiological contribution, 345
  encouraged Bible study, 348
  Great Controversy motif, 347
  help contemporary believers to persevere, 358
  in the formation and organization, 350
  missiological thinking, 354
  motivate church leaders, 356
  reproving error, 347
embodied souls, 270
empathy, 122
end-time prophecies, 113
end-time remnant, 239
Enlil, 123
Enoch, 2–3, 66
Enuma Elish, 124
epistemology, 265
equality, 9
eschatological expectation, 58
eschatology, 422
  appropriated, 422
  consummated, 422
  inaugurated, 422
Esther, 16, 70–71
ethics, 361, 363
  foundation for biblical, 363

love owed to everyone, 363
sanctity of every human life, 363
the foundation of, 364
Ethiopian eunuch, 341
ethnicity, 379
ethnos, 413, 415
  faithful remnant within Israel, 415
  group of people, 413
  leaders of the Jewish Christian community, 414
  referring to the "Gentiles", 413
  referring universally to "all nations", 413
Eucharist, 165–166, 183, 186, 199
  as a sacrifice, 183
  guarantee of salvation, 165
  mystagogical understanding, 183
  the reception of salvation, 186
evangelism, 75
evangelization, 103
evil, 15
exclusivism, 429, 431
exile, 14, 106
extispicy, 116
Ezra, 70

faith, 10, 53, 63, 214, 272, 283, 306, 316, 320, 398
  and salvation, 194
  in Christ, 96
  in God in exile, 114
  in Jesus, 94, 395
  in Jesus Christ, 398
  in one God, 9
  in the face of death, 177
  in the sovereignty of God, 119
  in Yahweh, 10
  of Jesus, 101
  of the missionaries, 96
faithfulness, 141, 165
faithful remnant, 74, 79
false prophet, 147
false teachers, 26, 98
family, 57, 78
fellowship, 2
festivals, 13
figs, 14
final judgment, 101,

103–104, 151, 160
Flood, 3, 65
food, 121
food laws, 89
foreknowledge, 385
forgiveness, 17, 102, 155–156, 165, 176
  comes through the church, 166
  received from bishops and priests, 167
fragmentation, 243

Gabriel, 119
General Conference, 229
Gentiles, 7
  among God's people, 13
  being grafted in, 391
  outpouring of the Spirit, 88
  to join with Israel, 406
Gideon, 11
gift of prophecy, 35, 223
gift of tongues, 88
glorification, 96
gnostics, 157
God, 2, 4, 7–8, 50, 56, 61, 63–64, 69, 75–77, 82, 109, 112–114, 118, 130, 138, 173, 365, 389, 440
  a builder, 50
  a Savior, 365
  as Creator, 50
  center of existence, 2
  concern for the oppressed, 113
  Creator and giver of life, 64
  disciplines, 56
  dwelling, 8–9
  Father of Israel, 56
  grace, 4
  has access to the whole of reality, 365
  has a mission, 63
  immutable, 173
  intervenes in human history, 114
  is holy, 75
  is sovereign over all, 82, 108
  loves, 56
  most glorious missionary, 77
  not rejected Israel, 389
  of Heaven, 109, 112
  possesses intrinsic immor-

Subject Index

tality, 365
promises to Israel, 389
protects, 56
reaches the non-evangelized, 440
Redeemer of Israel, 7
sovereignty, 4
the Father, 130
to speak through dreams and visions, 118
transcendent, 173
travel companion, 8
walking with, 2
will send missionaries, 69
worked outside of Israel, 75
worked with other nations, 76
God's freedom to elect, 389
God's angels, 138
God's end-time remnant, 145
God's faithfulness, 14, 387
God's judgment, 69
against Babylon, 109
ultimate purpose, 69
God's last message, 153
God's mission, 101, 133, 144,
begins at Creation, 63
divine enterprise, 153
inclusive of all nations, 78
in the context of the great controversy, 139
the proclamation of His message, 134
Trinity is involved, 153
God's people, 2, 71, 75, 152
are still in Babylon, 152
to be a light to the world, 71
to be an objective lesson, 75
ultimate destiny, 2
God's plan, 14, 381
God's true worshipers, 73
Gog and Magog, 424
gospel, 91, 149
fulfillment of prophecy, 95
harvest, 94
misunderstood or misconstrued, 94
power of God for salvation, 94–95
grace, 117, 155, 211, 274, 354–355, 433
becomes effective, 355
of God through Christ, 433
universally accessible to all, 354

gratitude, 174
great controversy, 278, 280, 283, 347
Ellen White's unifying principle, 348
the gospel message, 278
the history of God's love, 278
great disappointment, 191
greed, 10
Greek philosophy, 284
guilt, 181

Handbook of Seventh-day Adventist Theology, 239
Hanif, 367
hardening, 390
heavenly sanctuary, 223, 253, 267, 271–272, 284, 440
heresy, 146, 297
hermeneutical paradigm, 265
hermeneutical presuppositions, 269–270
hermeneutical principles, 268, 276, 341
hermeneutics of Adventist pioneers, 269
Hinduism, 365
historicist method, 267
holiness, 176, 178, 186
Holocaust, 447
holy, 184
Eucharist, 184
Mary, 184
saints, 184
Holy Life, 115
holy living, 179
Holy Spirit, 11, 20, 22, 88, 186, 212, 217, 271, 279, 295
addresses believers, 135
a fulfillment of God's promises, 306
and the Church, 303
came to the disciples, 306
Christ's representative, 304
forms a new community, 320
given to all members, 318
illumines the minds, 306, 438
inspired the Word of God, 306
introduced to us, 303

involved in mission, 434
promise of, 306
sent out by Father and Son, 134
speaks through the Scriptures, 306
Spirit of prophecy, 135
symbol of seven spirits, 134
testifies about Jesus, 304
used judges and prophets, 304
used kings, 304
utters a final invitation, 135
works outside the church, 305
works with the church, 317
honesty, 9, 117
hope, 2, 6, 9, 16–17, 58, 78, 108–109, 132, 148, 221, 253, 277, 286, 399, 418
for the kingdom promises, 418
in Christ, 253
in the Second Coming, 221
of restoration, 108
hospitality, 102
Huldrych Zwingli, 200, 205
Eucharist was a *memorial*, 206
sacraments as signs, 205
vestiges of Catholic sacramentalism, 206

idolatry, 146
Ignatius of Antioch, 168, 172
immortality, 223, 233
inaugurated eschatology, 399
incarnation, 86, 245
incense, 164
inclusivism, 430
individualism, 33, 38, 244
indulgences, 155
infallibility of the church, 156
inquisition, 297
interdependence, 47
investigative judgment, 150
invisible church, 200, 210
Irenaeus, 156, 169, 187
Church guarantees a correct reading of Scripture, 158
contributes to establish the rule of faith, 157
Islam, 366

Subject Index

a different world of thought, 374
antichrists, 370
conflict between God and Satan, 368
cosmic signs, 369
death of the Messiah at the end of time, 370
divine sovereignty in terms of power, 366
eschatology, 369
forewarned Adam, 368
God created Adam, 368
Gog and Magog, 371
Mahdi and the Messiah, 370
natural religion of all human beings, 366
no need for atonement, 369
pre-historic covenant, 366
protology, 366
Israel, 6, 9, 11, 48, 62, 68, 106, 245, 375–376, 379–380, 384, 387, 392–393, 407, 416, 420
and the Church, 375, 387
and the Church in the Gospels, 407
an inclusive people, 379
an influx of Gentiles, 380
apocalyptic, 377
as a theocratic entity, 417
a "spiritual" (i.e., faithful) remnant, 384
believing Jews and Gentiles, 392
biblical-historical, 376
ceased to be a theocratic nation, 420
continuity and discontinuity, 376
descended into apostasy, 11
eschatological, 377
God has not rejected Israel, 393
Jewish, 377
multitude of others, 384
national, 376
of faith, 245
physical descendants of Jacob, 384
spiritual, 377
spiritual character of, 379
the faithful remnant, 392
to be a blessing, 106
to be committed to a holy life, 68
was peculiar, 9
Israel of God, 402

Jacob, 68
Jeremiah, 15
Jerusalem, 12, 36
Jesus, 20–21
    and the restoration of Israel, 409
    as apostle and high priest, 96
    as a true Prophet, 419
    as divine-human Son, 96
    as Savior, 88
    as the Messiah, 419
    as Witness, 132
    chosen and precious cornerstone, 51
    criterion to God's will and character, 365
    earthly ministry of, 407
    established a faithful remnant, 425
    expectation of the restoration of Israel, 410
    faithful until death, 132
    faithful witness, 141, 147
    firstborn of the dead, 141
    from incarnation to glorification, 27
    gathering a special people, 21
    good shepherd, 21
    head of His church, 27
    high priestly ministry, 100
    instituted His church, 408
    is Brother, 56
    loves us, 147
    Messianic representative of Israel, 408
    reached out to the Gentiles, 407
    redeemed us, 147
    revealed the Father, 132
    Savior, 450
    sent out His disciples, 85
    son of David, 83
    Suffering Servant, 83
    "tabernacled" among us, 86
    the center, 246
    the Way to God, 448
    to threaten Satan's kingdom, 84
    ultimate Faithful Remnant of Israel, 408
    utterly unique, 448
    will come again, 147
    witness par excellence, 140
Jethro, 10, 75, 449
Jewish leaders, 411, 417
Jews, 15–16
Jezebel, 146
Job, 75, 434, 449
John Calvin, 200
John Chrysostom, 178, 185
John in Ephesus, 158
John Paul II, 188
John the Baptist, 84
John Wesley, 264
Jonah, 69
Joseph, 15, 69
joy, 74
Judaism, 183
judges, 11
judgment, 6, 14, 87, 103, 109, 146, 450
    favorable, 110
    of God, 14
    unfavorable, 110
justice, 12
justification by faith, 200, 239, 264, 397
Justin Martyr, 156, 181, 183

Keturah, 10
kingdom of God, 82, 84
    allegiance to Jesus, 83
    realized aspect, 83
    remains future, 83
    universalized, 84
kingdom of heaven, 407
knowledge, 435, 438
    is indispensable, 435
    itself does not save, 438
    needed in order to be saved, 438

lamb, 147–148, 152
lament Psalms, 13
lampstands, 143
landmarks, 275, 338
law, 136
lawgiver, 8
laying on of hands, 217, 314
leaders, 217
letters to the Churches, 236
libellus, 165
liberal/critical scholars, 341
liberal revisionists, 236

Subject Index

lifestyle, 162, 177, 359
little horn, 118
Lord's Supper, 214
  a memorial of what Christ accomplished, 215
  a sense of fellowship, 215
love, 9, 102, 291, 319
loyalty, 151
Luther, 194, 263
  the genuine church, 194
  to reform the church, 263
  true church of God, 194
  turned to Scripture, 263
  two Christendoms, 194
Lutheran Reformation, 193
Lutheran World Federation, 241
Luther's theology, 196
  all true Christians share a common priesthood, 196
  baptism was the initiative of God, 198
  rejected transubstantiation, 198
  sacramental theology, 197
  sacraments were still necessary for salvation, 198
  saw a need for ordained ministry, 196

magicians and astrologers, 116
mammon, 173
Marcion, 157, 174, 177, 397
Marduk, 124, 126
mark of the beast, 100, 152
Mars Hill, 446, 452
martyr cults, 173
martyrdom, 141
martyrs, 172
  as mediators before God, 172
  associated with the apostles Peter and Paul, 172
  became Christian heroes, 172
  immediately go to heaven after death, 171
  stories, 172
Mary, 184
master metaphor, 59
mathematics, 116
Matthias, 307

mediation of Christ, 9, 179, 272
medicine, 116
medieval ecclesiology, 192
Melchizedek, 7, 75, 434, 449
Melito of Sardis, 157
mercy, 101, 111
Mesopotamia, 16
message, 95, 275
  Christ's incarnation and ministry, 274
  church should proclaim, 130
  commandments of God, 274
  faith of Jesus, 274
  from the true God, 122
  God's grace, 274
  God's judgment hour, 274
  harmonious system, 275
  many truths, 275
  of salvation, 95
  plan of salvation, 274
  recipient is the world, 273
  system of truth, 277
  the fear of the Lord, 274
  worship of God the Creator, 274
Messiah, 5, 9, 367, 383, 386, 399, 401, 407, 415, 421, 432
  a future hope, 110
  as a warrior, 110
  cut off, 110
  in the context of wars, 110
  the Anointed One, 110
  the great eschatological divide in Israel, 405
  will save the world, 111
  work of, 110
metanarratives, 283
metaphor, 42–44, 47, 56–58
  bride/wife of Christ, 57
  christological focus, 58
  family of God, 57
  is "irreducible", 42
  meaning of, 42
  of God as a father, 56
  sub-metaphors, 47
  tenor, 43–44
  vehicle, 43–44
  working definition, 43
metaphors, 41, 232, 318, 406
metaphysics, 265
Methodist, 216
Michael, 110, 118
Middle Ages, 162–163, 166,

189, 263
millennium, 160, 427
ministry in the church, 216
  under the guidance of the Spirit, 314
missio Dei, 105, 107, 117, 127, 441
mission, 22, 36, 65
  accepting God's ultimate goal, 77
  activity of God himself, 108
  Among World Religions, 361
  and Abraham, 66
  as a privilege, 63
  as Witness, 88
  before Abraham, 65
  commission and a blessing, 313
  conditions, 446
  conversion of Gentiles, 89
  engages all people, 78
  Entrusted to Israel, 68
  in Acts, 88
  in Oneness, 257
  in the Book of Revelation, 129
  in the Old Testament, 61
  in the Prophets, 72
  in the Psalms, 71
  inward focus, 64
  is comprehensive, 453
  is egalitarian, 102
  is God's mission, 448
  is holistic, 102
  is incarnational, 101
  is strategic and systematic, 103
  It is always missio Dei, 434
  leads to worship, 79
  of the Church, 139
  not a human performance, 63
  of the Old Testament people, 64
  of the remnant, 285
  outward focus, 64
  raison d'etre, 443
  Strategy, 91
  the most important image of, 86
  theocentric, 63
  through a godly lifestyle, 97
  to the Cosmos, 256
  to the world religions, 451

to the World, 255
victorious in the end, 103
universal in scope, 65
missionaries, 98
mission theology, 64
monarchy, 12
monks, 176
   authority, 176
   considerable earned authority, 178
   live the most righteous of lifestyles, 176
   most serious Christians, 176
Montanus, 168
Moses, 9–10, 68, 137
Muhammad, 371
   a military general, 372
   a succession of dynasties, 372
   became a political leader, 372
   built a state religion, 372
   initiated a religious movement, 372
Muslims, 364–365, 448

Naaman, 69, 449
nations, 71
   accountable to God, 76
   heard about the God of Israel, 71
   judged by God, 76
   who are saved, 101
Nebuchadnezzar, 14, 108–109, 113, 116, 121, 124–125, 437
Nehemiah, 70
neoplatonic ontology, 269
new covenant, 404
new light, 337
Noah, 2, 66
norma normata, 296
notae ecclesiae, 195

offshoot movements, 234
olive tree, 24, 390, 393, 395
ontology, 265
open-door Adventists, 221
ordained priesthood, 192
ordinance, 213, 215
ordination, 170
organizational structure, 229
   Asiatic Division Mission, 230
   European Division Conference, 230
   five levels, 230
   North American Division Conference, 230
Origen, 158
   establishes church tradition, 160
   forgiveness was not cheap, 162
   hermeneutics of biblical interpretation, 158
   interprets Scripture from a Platonic perspective, 160
   truth is defined by tradition, 159
overseer, 311

paenitentia, 163
paganism, 186
parables of the Kingdom, 87
particular revelations, 437
patronage, 174
Paul, 23–24, 27, 35, 53, 55
   already in heaven, 171
   and his co-workers, 54
   and Mission, 90
   apostle and missionary, 36
   a single plan of salvation, 397
   combines law and grace, 397
   established churches, 94
   His conversion, 311
   missionary, 446
   mixing metaphors, 59
   ordained leaders, 92
   remnant theology, 392
   uses temple imagery, 51
   uses the term Israel, 389
   willingness to sacrifice, 90
penance, 162–163, 166
Pentecost, 22, 88, 306, 395, 421
people of God, 3, 13, 30, 404
   a community of faith, 3
   an olive tree, 49
   nation of Israel, 13
   outside of Israel, 13
   worshiped Him, 3
persecution, 89, 98, 102, 118, 134, 163, 172
Peter Lombard, 166
Pharaoh, 437
Philip, 311, 341

philosophical hermeneutics, 285
pluralism, 430
politics, 12
Polycarp of Smyrna, 158, 172
polytheism, 9
Pontifex Maximus, 177
Pope Leo X, 155
Porphyry, 182
prayer, 55, 111, 115, 186, 275, 343
   for the remnant of Judah, 111
   for understanding, 343
   in the life of a missionary, 115
predestination, 201
presbyters, 167
present truth, 222
presuppositions, 42, 342
priests, 52, 169, 185
priesthood, 183
priesthood of all believers, 200, 209–210, 330
priesthood of Christians, 142
Priscilla and Maximilla, 168
progressive revelation, 337
promise, 4
   and fulfillment, 84
   of the land, 5
   of the Seed, 6
   of the Son, 6
prophecy, 4, 10, 35, 136
prophetic authority, 138
prophetic gift, 348
prophetic interpretation, 222
prophetic word, 74
prophets, 12, 119, 167
   in the *Didache*, 167
   rebuking the people, 12
   spoke against false religious systems, 78, 142
   symbolic actions, 120
   using local cultural processes, 119
Protestant Reformation, 191, 265

Radical Reformation, 206
   church of God was in heaven, 207
   local congregations, 208
   ministry, 208
   religious liberty, 207
   return to biblical Christianity, 206

Subject Index

the church on earth, 207
Rahab, 76
rebellion, 17
re-creation, 64
redemption, 8, 150
Reformation, 192
regeneration, 181
relics, 179
remnant, 11, 17, 107, 140, 264
  being-in-hope, 286
  be vigilant, 249
  challenge ecclesiological status quo, 268
  comprised both of biological Jews and Gentiles, 425
  correct understanding of prophecy, 277
  covenant-faithful, 425
  elected for mission, 75
  emerging, visible, biblical, 269
  end-time remnant, 32
  eschatological, 384
  eschatological Israel, 423
  faithful, 384
  have the spirit of prophecy, 142
  historical, 384
  in a strange land, 14
  interconnected system of truth, 277
  in the gospels, 20
  its message and mission, 269
  not exclusive, 408
  of God, 211
  of Israel would be saved, 392
  of Judah, 50
  of Revelation 12:17, 37
  of the woman's seed, 100
  preaching all biblical truths, 355
  reemerged from Scripture and history, 285
  spiritual and visible community, 272
  spirituality of, 285
  turn to Scripture, 268
  two Israels, 385
  worldwide movement, 406
repentance, 12, 14, 113, 151, 155, 162, 410

replacement theologians, 382
restoration of Israel, 111
resurrection, 88, 90, 137, 151, 278, 407
reverence, 180, 187
revival, 266, 446
Righteousness by faith, 228

Sabbatarian Adventists, 223
  defined their doctrinal system, 227
  develop an overseas mission, 226
  did not accept any formal creed, 225
  end-time "remnant", 224
  General Conference, 223
  little flock, 224
  local churches, 223
  more Christ-centered emphasis, 227
  organizational developments, 223
  organize themselves as the Seventh-day Adventist Church, 225
  representative form of church organization, 224
  revised their organizational structure, 227
  State conferences, 223
Sabbath, 191
Sacerdotalism, 180
sacrament of baptism, 195
sacramental theology, 192, 208
sacraments, 176
  foundation of the Christian church, 270
  in the early church, 180
  limited to seven, 193
  necessary for salvation, 193
  the material element God needs, 271
sacrifice, 164, 183
sacrifice of praise, 183
sacrifice typology, 183
sacrificial system, 9
saints, 179
salvation, 6, 17, 98, 139, 147–148, 341, 156, 365
  be experienced, 102
  by grace through faith, 234

  in the form of merit, 167
  into the hands of the bishops, 180
  of all the nations, 112
  of the non-evangelized, 430, 441
  ours by faith, 244
  outside the church, 430
  requires faith in Jesus, 432
  still available, 150
  through the church, 166
salvation history, 49, 83
sanctification, 179
sanctity of the church, 52
sanctuary, 220
Sanhedrin, 308, 414, 421
science, 116
Scripture, 136, 156–157, 159, 175, 195, 212, 222
  at the center of the church, 341
  corporate element in the study, 331
  emerging from tradition, 263
  final norm of truth, 323
  tradition and truth, 187
  ultimate court of appeal, 323
Second Advent, 221, 246, 418
  anticipated in hope, 246
  of Christ, 418
Second Coming, 57, 145, 147–148, 220, 223–224, 267, 356, 362, 424
self-preservation, 244
Servant of the Lord, 67
seven churches, 143
seven plagues, 149
seven seals, 146
Seventh-day Adventists Answer Questions on Doctrine, 235
Seventh-day Adventists Believe..., 239
seven trumpets, 146, 151
seventy weeks, 386
sexual immorality, 146
shut door, 221, 356
Sikhism, 443
simony, 167
Sinai, 8–9
Sinai covenant, 8
sola fide et gratia, 200

sola scriptura, 296
sola Scriptura, 200
sola, tota, and *prima Scriptura*, 285
soli Deo Gloria, 200
solo Christo, 200
Solomon, 12
Song of the Vineyard, 413
Son of God, 245
Son of Man, 109, 387
  celestial figure, 109
  returning with the "everlasting kingdom", 387
soteriology, 162, 176, 192
sovereignty of God, 200
Spirit of God, 66, 84
spiritual conflict, 118
spiritual gifts, 27, 35, 318, 332
spirituality, 115
Statement of Fundamental Beliefs, 287
  accepted as authoritative, 334
  a derived authority, 293, 334
  a rule that is ruled, 334
  a Spirit-directed consensus, 334
  authority of, 293
  church's current consensus on biblical truth, 333
  consistent with scriptural sufficiency, 293
  discriminatory or judging aspect of, 298
  faithful expression of biblical truth, 298
  formal set of doctrines, 290
  grounded in the Bible, 292
  is not a creed, 287
  juridical role, 298
  not a substitute for the Bible, 289
  positive role of, 287
  represents "present truth", 294
  role in promoting unity, 299
  rooted in history, 293
  system of beliefs, 290
  to distinguish between truth and error, 298
  understood as a set of *didaskalia*, 291
Stephen, 311, 421

strategy, 114
subjectivism, 342
Sub-metaphors, 51
suffering, 97, 136, 141, 282
symbolism, 99, 137
synagogue, 30
syncretism, 29
synthesis, 263
Systematic Benevolence, 350

tabernacle, 9, 50
teaching, 340
temple, 12, 16, 51, 71, 111–112
Tertullian, 162–164, 177
theocracy, 9, 12, 386
theocratic leaders, 410, 412
theodicy, 432
Theodoret, 178
theology, 105
theophany, 245
three angels' messages, 148, 362
tithe, 75
tithing, 36
tradition, 187
  a hermeneutical guide, 266
  and Scripture, 264
  as a source of theology, 266
  as the teaching and practice of a church, 294
  as Truth, 156
  emergence of Christian, 261
  recognized source of biblical hermeneutics, 265
  the safeguard of truth, 188
  went wrong, 187
traditionalists, 237
tradition-as-truth, 161
transubstantiation, 184
Trinity, 282
truth, 79, 141, 250
  Adventist perspective, 291
  aim at building a community, 290
  as found in Scripture, 306
  defines the community's identity, 332
  in its fullness, 103
  of the gospel, 94, 103
  personified, 98
  secured in the Church, 158

Trypho, 156
two-covenant theology, 395
two witnesses, 135, 137
typology, 169, 183, 411
  of the priesthood, 169
  the Paschal lamb, 411
  way of expressing the Christian ministry, 169

Union Conferences, 229, 352
Union Missions, 229, 352
unity, 243
  in Lifestyle, 250
  in Message, 249
  in Mission, 253
  in Worldview, 252
universalism, 101
universal sacrifice, 183

vices, 101
victory, 103
virtue, 179
visible church, 193, 210, 212

William Miller, 220
wisdom, 86, 117
wise men, 121
witnesses, 7, 140
Women, 72
Word of God, 133
work of Christ, 52
world religions, 361, 363, 373, 447
  accounts of creation, 365
  and Salvation, 429
  end of the world, 365
  extensive writings, 451
  partners in dialogue, 430
worldview, 253
worship, 12–13, 17, 74, 150, 186
  formalistic, 13
  outward ritual, 13

Yahweh, 9

Zephaniah, 73
Zion, 124
Zippora, 10